MAGILL INDEX
TO
MASTERPLOTS

MAGILL INDEX
TO
MASTERPLOTS

Cumulative Indexes

1963–1993

SALEM PRESS

Pasadena, California   Englewood Cliffs, New Jersey

Library of Congress Cataloging-in-Publication Data
Magill index to masterplots, 1963-1993.
    p. cm.
    ISBN 0-89356-599-7
    1. Literature—Stories, plots, etc.—Indexes. 2.
Authors—Biography—Indexes. I. Magill, Frank
Northen, 1907-   . II Title: Index to masterplots, 1963-
1993. III Title: Magill index to masterplots.
Z6511.M252   1993
[PN44]   93-18633
016.809–dc20   CIP

PUBLISHER'S NOTE

This index to the Masterplots publications combines and collates the indexes from the multivolume reference sets in this family of publications about books, plays, poems, and stories. The twelve-volume Revised Edition combines the contents of all editions published prior to 1976 and replaces those earlier editions. The Revised Category Editions (American, British, and European Fiction) compile in individual three-volume sets the appropriate titles selected from the twelve-volume Masterplots. Cyclopedia of World Authors and Cyclopedia of Literary Characters provide author biographies and character descriptions for the works included in the twelve-volume Revised Edition, completing the first generation of the Masterplots family.

The second generation of Masterplots publications have been published under the series name Masterplots II. They include African American Literature Series, American Fiction Series, British and Commonwealth Fiction Series, Drama Series, Juvenile and Young Adult Biography Series, Juvenile and Young Adult Fiction Series, Nonfiction Series, Poetry Series, Short Story Series, and World Fiction Series, adding Masterplots treatment for many additional works of literature. In the Masterplots tradition, Cyclopedia of World Authors II and Cyclopedia of Literary Characters II supplement the Masterplots II titles by providing author biographies and character descriptions for many of the works included in the ten series.

Hence, the current index offers, in one location, a guide to discussions of books, plays, stories, poems, authors, and characters appearing in the sixty volumes of the Masterplots publications. Entries are followed by a code indicating the series in which the discussion appears, which in turn is followed by the page or pages locating the discussion:

CLC	Cyclopedia of Literary Characters
CLCII	Cyclopedia of Literary Characters II
CWA	Cyclopedia of World Authors
CWAII	Cyclopedia of World Authors II
MP	Masterplots, Revised Edition
MP:AF	Masterplots, Revised Category Edition: American Fiction Series
MP:BF	Masterplots, Revised Category Edition: British Fiction Series
MP:EF	Masterplots, Revised Category Edition: European Fiction Series
MPII:AF	Masterplots II: American Fiction Series
MPII:AfAm	Masterplots II: African American Literature Series
MPII:BCF	Masterplots II: British and Commonwealth Fiction Series
MPII:D	Masterplots II: Drama Series
MPII:JYABio	Masterplots II: Juvenile and Young Adult Biography Series
MPII:JYAFic	Masterplots II: Juvenile and Young Adult Fiction Series
MPII:NF	Masterplots II: Nonfiction Series
MPII:P	Masterplots II: Poetry Series
MPII:SS	Masterplots II: Short Story Series
MPII:WP	Masterplots II: World Fiction Series

Alphabetization is by word rather than letter, and transposed elements are disregarded; hence, "Jacob, Max," precedes *Jacob and the Angel*." Hyphenated compounds are treated as two separate words if the two elements could stand independently (as in "fifty-five") but are treated as one word if one of the elements could not stand alone (as in "non-being"). Numerals are alphabetized as though they were spelled out ("*1919*" under "nineteen-nineteen"), as are common abbreviations: "Mr." as "mister"; "Mrs." as "mistress"; "St." as "saint"; "Dr." as "doctor." The *Mc* particle in names such as McPherson is alphabetized as though it were spelled *Mac*.

There are two prominent exceptions to the alpha-by-word rule: First, surnames composed of more than one element are alphabetized as though one word; hence, "Le Carré, John" is preceded by "*Leatherstocking Tales*." Second, series of enumerated titles by the same author (such as the plays *Henry IV, Part I*, *Henry IV, Part II*, and *Henry V*, all by William Shakespeare) appear in numerical order rather than alphabetical order, for the sake of logical consistency.

Titles of books, plays, stories, essays, and poems are followed, in parentheses, by the author's surname; in an index of this size and scope, the editors found that further identification, by means of a first initial or a first name, was sometimes necessary to avoid confusion with another author.

Code System

CLC   *Cyclopedia of Literary Characters.* 2 vols. Salem Press, Englewood Cliffs, N.J. 1963.

CWA   *Cyclopedia of World Authors.* 3 vols. Salem Press, Englewood Cliffs, N.J. 1974.

MP   *Masterplots, Revised Edition.* 12 vols. Salem Press, Englewood Cliffs, N.J. 1976.

MP:AF   *Masterplots, Revised Category Edition: American Fiction Series.* 3 vols. Salem Press, Englewood Cliffs, N.J. 1985.

MP:BF   *Masterplots, Revised Category Edition: British Fiction Series.* 3 vols. Salem Press, Englewood Cliffs, N.J. 1985.

MP:EF   *Masterplots, Revised Category Edition: European Fiction Series.* 3 vols. Salem Press, Englewood Cliffs, N.J. 1985.

MPII:AF   *Masterplots II: American Fiction Series.* 4 vols. Salem Press, Englewood Cliffs, N.J. 1986.

MPII:SS   *Masterplots II: Short Story Series.* 6 vols. Salem Press, Pasadena, Calif. 1986.

MPII:BCF   *Masterplots II: British and Commonwealth Fiction Series.* 4 vols. Salem Press, Pasadena, Calif. 1987.

MPII:WF   *Masterplots II: World Fiction Series.* 4 vols. Salem Press, Pasadena, Calif. 1987.

MPII:NF   *Masterplots II: Nonfiction Series.* 4 vols. Salem Press, Pasadena, Calif. 1989.

CWAII   *Cyclopedia of World Authors II.* 4 vols. Salem Press, Pasadena, Calif. 1989.

CLCII   *Cyclopedia of Literary Characters II.* 4 vols. Salem Press, Pasadena, Calif. 1990.

MPII:D   *Masterplots II: Drama Series.* 4 vols. Salem Press, Pasadena, Calif. 1990.

MPII:JYAFic   *Masterplots II: Juvenile and Young Adult Fiction Series.* 4 vols. Salem Press, Pasadena, Calif. 1991.

MPII:P   *Masterplots II: Poetry Series.* 6 vols. Salem Press, Pasadena, Calif. 1992.

MPII:JYABio   *Masterplots II: Juvenile and Young Adult Biography Series.* 4 vols. Salem Press, Pasadena, Calif. 1993.

MPII:AfAm   *Masterplots II: African American Literature Series.* 3 vols. Salem Press, Pasadena, Calif. 1994.

TITLE INDEX

A

"A" (Zukofsky) MPII:P I-1

"A & P" (Updike) MPII:SS I-1

A ciascuno il suo. *See* Man's Blessing, A

À combien l'amour revient aux vieillards. *See* Splendors and Miseries of Courtesans, The

A maçã no escuro. *See* Apple in the Dark, The

"A menor mulher do mundo." *See* "Smallest Woman in the World, The"

"A terceira margem do rio." *See* "Third Bank of the River, The"

Aaron's Rod (Lawrence) CLCII I-1; MPII:BCF I-1

Abbé Constantin, The (Halévy) CLC I-1; MP I-1; MP:EF I-1

Abbess of Crewe, The (Spark) CLCII I-1; MPII:BCF I-6

ABC of Reading (Pound) MPII:NF I-1

Abe Lincoln Grows Up (Sandburg) MPII:JYABio I-1

Abe Lincoln in Illinois (Sherwood) CLC I-1; MP I-4

Abel Sánchez (Unamuno) CLCII I-3; MPII:WF I-1

Abendland. *See* Occident, The

Abendlied. *See* Evening Song

Abendmahl. *See* Evening Meal

"Abenteuer der Sylvester Nacht, Die." *See* "New Year's Eve Adventure, A"

About David (Pfeffer) MPII:JYAFic I-1

". . . about the cool water." *See* When We with Sappho

Abraham and Isaac (Unknown) CLC I-2; MP I-8

Abraham Lincoln (Daugherty, J.) MPII:JYABio I-5

Abraham Lincoln (Sandburg) MP I-11

Absalom, Absalom! (Faulkner) CLC I-3; MP I-14; MP:AF I-1

Absalom and Achitophel (Dryden) CLC I-4; MP I-19

Absentee, The (Edgeworth) CLC I-5; MP I-21; MP:BF I-1

"Absolution" (Fitzgerald) MPII:SS I-5

Absurd Person Singular (Ayckbourn) CLCII I-4; MPII:D I-1

Abyss, The (Yourcenar) CLCII I-5; MPII:WF I-6

Acceptance World, The. *See* Dance to the Music of Time, A

Accident, The (Wiesel) CLCII I-7; MPII:WF I-12

Accidental Death of an Anarchist (Fo) CLCII I-8; MPII:D I-6

"Ace in the Hole" (Updike) MPII:SS I-9

Acharnians, The (Aristophanes) CLC I-6; MP I-26

Achterhuis, Het. *See* Diary of a Young Girl, The.

Acolyte, The (Astley) CLCII I-9; MPII:BCF I-12

Acoso, El. *See* Manhunt

Acquainted with Grief (Gadda) CLCII I-10; MPII:WF I-16

Across (Handke) CLCII I-11; MPII:WF I-20

Across Five Aprils (Hunt, I.) MPII:JYAFic I-4

Across the River and into the Trees (Hemingway) CLCII I-11; MPII:AF I-1

Act One (Hart, M.) MPII:JYABio I-9

Actor in Exile (Malone) MPII:JYABio I-12

Ada or Ardor (Nabokov) CLCII I-12; MPII:AF I-6

Adam Bede (Eliot, G.) CLC I-7; MP I-29; MP:BF I-7

Adam of the Road (Gray, E.) MPII:JYAFic I-7

Adding Machine, The (Rice, Elmer) CLCII I-14; MPII:D I-11

Addresses (Lincoln) MP I-32

Admirable Crichton, The (Barrie) CLC I-9; MP I-35

"Admiral and the Nuns, The" (Tuohy) MPII:SS I-12

"Admirer, The" (Singer) MPII:SS I-16

Adolf Hitler (Dolan) MPII:JYABio I-16

Adolphe (Constant) CLC I-10; MP I-39; MP:EF I-5

Adonais (Shelley, P.) MPII:P I-6

"Adulterous Woman, The" (Camus) MPII:SS I-19

Adulthood Rites. *See* Xenogenesis Trilogy, The.

"Adventure of the Dancing Men, The" (Doyle) MPII:SS I-23
"Adventure of the German Student" (Irving, W.) MPII:SS I-27
"Adventure of the Speckled Band, The" (Doyle) MPII:SS I-31
Adventures of Augie March, The (Bellow) MP I-43; MP:AF I-7
Adventures of Gil Blas of Santillane. See Gil Blas
Adventures of Hajji Baba of Ispahan, The. See Hajji Baba of Ispahan
Adventures of Huckleberry Finn (Twain) CLC I-495; MP V-2755; MP:AF I-11; MPII:JYAFic I-10
Adventures of Pinocchio, The (Collodi) MPII:JYAFic I-13
Adventures of Roderick Random, The. See Roderick Random
Adventures of Sherlock Holmes, The (Doyle) MPII:JYAFic I-16
Adventures of Simplicissimus, The. See Simplicissimus the Vagabond
Adventures of Tom Sawyer, The (Twain) CLC II-1145; MP XI-6604; MP:AF I-17
Adventures of Tom Sawyer, The (Twain) MPII:JYAFic I-19
"Advice to a Prophet" (Wilbur) MPII:P I-10
"Advice to King Lear" (Cassity) MPII:P I-13
"Aeneas at Washington" (Tate, A.) MPII:P I-16
Aeneid, The (Vergil) CLC I-11; MP I-46
Aerodrome, The (Warner) CLCII I-16; MPII:BCF I-16
"Aeroplanes at Brescia, The" (Davenport) MPII:SS I-34
Aesop's Fables (Aesop) MP I-51; MP:EF I-10
Aesthetic (Croce) MP I-53
Af Borgslaegtens Historie. See Guest the One-Eyed
Affair, The (Snow) MP I-56; MP:BF I-11. See also Strangers and Brothers
"Affliction" (IV) (Herbert, G.) MPII:P I-19
African Heroes (Mitchison) MPII:JYABio I-20
Afrocentricity (Asante) MPII:AfAm I-1
"After Apple-Picking" (Frost) MPII:P I-23

After Babel (Steiner) MPII:NF I-7
After Many a Summer Dies the Swan (Huxley) CLCII I-17; MPII:BCF I-22
"After Saturday Nite Comes Sunday" (Sanchez, S.) MPII:SS I-38
"After Someone's Death" (Tranströmer) MPII:P I-26
After Strange Gods (Eliot, T. S.) MP I-60
After the Banquet (Mishima) CLCII I-19; MPII:WF I-24
"After the Fair" (Thomas) MPII:SS I-43
After the Fall (Miller, A.) CLCII I-20; MPII:D I-17
After the First Death (Cormier) MPII:JYAFic I-22
"After the Storm" (Hemingway) MPII:SS I-46
"After the Surprising Conversions" (Lowell, R.) MPII:P I-29
After Virtue (MacIntyre) MPII:NF I-12
Afternoon Men (Powell) CLCII I-21; MPII:BCF I-27
Afternoon of a Faun, The (Mallarmé) MPII:P I-32
Against Interpretation and Other Essays (Sontag) MPII:NF I-19
Against the Fall of Night (Clarke, Arthur) MPII:JYAFic I-25
Against the Grain (Huysmans) CLC I-13; MP I-62; MP:EF I-13
"Age, The" (Mandelstam, O.) MPII:P I-36
Âge de raison, L'. See Roads to Freedom, The
Age of Innocence, The (Wharton) CLC I-14; MP I-65; MP:AF I-23
Age of Reason, The (Paine) MP I-70
Age of Reason, The (Sartre). See Roads to Freedom, The
Age of Wonders, The (Appelfeld) CLCII I-22; MPII:WF I-29
Agents and Patients (Powell) CLCII I-23; MPII:BCF I-32
Agneau, L'. See Lamb, The
Agnes Grey (Brontë, A.) CLC I-15; MP I-73; MP:BF I-16
Agony and the Ecstasy, The (Stone, I.) CLCII I-24; MPII:AF I-12
Aguila y la serpiente, El. See Eagle and the Serpent, The

Ah Q cheng-chuan. *See* True Story of Ah Q, The

Ahasverus död. *See* Tobias trilogy, The

"Ahogado más hermoso del mundo." *See* "Handsomest Drowned Man in the World, The"

Aiglon, L' (Rostand) CLC I-590; MP VI-3222

"Ajanta" (Rukeyser) MPII:P I-39

Ajax (Sophocles) CLC I-16; MP I-77

Akatsuki no tera. *See* Sea of Fertility, The

Aké (Soyinka) MPII:JYABio I-24; MPII:NF I-24

Al filo del agua (Yáñez) CLC I-17; MP I-81

Albany Cycle, The (Kennedy, W.) MPII:AF I-18

"Albatross, The" (Hill, S.) MPII:SS I-49

Alcestis (Euripides) CLC I-18; MP I-84

Alchemist, The (Jonson) CLC I-19; MP I-88

Aleck Maury, Sportsman (Gordon) CLC I-20; MP I-93; MP:AF I-28

"Aleph, The" (Borges) MPII:SS I-52

Alexanderplatz, Berlin. *See* Berlin Alexanderplatz

Alexandria Quartet, The (Durrell) MP I-96; MP:BF I-20

Alice Adams (Tarkington) CLC I-21; MP I-104; MP:AF I-32

Alice Hamilton (Grant) MPII:JYABio I-28

Alice's Adventures in Wonderland (Carroll) CLC I-22; MP I-107; MP:BF I-30; MPII:JYAFic I-28

"Alien Corn, The" (Maugham) MPII:SS I-56

"Alienista, O." *See* "Psychiatrist, The"

"All Bread" (Atwood) MPII:P I-44

All-Bright Court (Porter, C.) MPII:AfAm I-5

All Creatures Great and Small (Herriot) MPII:JYABio I-31; MPII:NF I-29

All Fall Down (Herlihy) MP I-112; MP:AF I-35

All Fools (Chapman) CLC I-24; MP I-114

All for Love (Dryden) CLC I-24; MP I-117

All God's Children Need Traveling Shoes (Angelou) MPII:AfAm I-11; MPII:NF I-34

All God's Chillun Got Wings (O'Neill) CLCII I-26; MPII:D I-22

All Green Shall Perish (Mallea) CLCII I-26; MPII:AF I-25

All Hallows' Eve (Williams, Charles) MP I-122; MP:BF I-36

All Men Are Brothers (Shih Nai-an) CLC I-26; MP I-125; MP:EF I-17

All Men Are Enemies (Aldington) CLCII I-28; MPII:BCF I-37

"All My Pretty Ones" (Sexton) MPII:P I-47

All My Sons (Miller, A.) CLCII I-29; MPII:D I-27

All Our Yesterdays (Ginzburg) CLCII I-31; MPII:WF I-34

All Quiet on the Western Front (Remarque) CLC I-27; MP I-130; MP:EF I-23; MPII:JYAFic I-32

All That Fall (Beckett) CLCII I-32; MPII:D I-33

All the King's Men (Warren) CLC I-28; MP I-133; MP:AF I-38

All the Strange Hours (Eiseley) MPII:JYABio I-35

"All the Years of Her Life" (Callaghan) MPII:SS I-60

All Things Bright and Beautiful (Herriot) MPII:JYABio I-39

All Things Wise and Wonderful (Herriot) MPII:JYABio I-43

"All You Zombies—" (Heinlein) MPII:SS I-63

Allegory of Love, The (Lewis, C. S.) MP I-138

"Allegro, L'" (Milton) MPII:P I-50

All's Well That Ends Well (Shakespeare) CLC I-29; MP I-143

Almanac for Moderns, An (Peattie) MP I-146

Almayer's Folly (Conrad) CLC I-30; MP I-149; MP:BF I-40

"Almos' a Man." *See* "Man Who Was Almost a Man, The"

"Alpine Idyll, An" (Hemingway) MPII:SS I-66

"Altar of the Dead, The" (James, H.) MPII:SS I-70

"Altarwise by Owl-Light" (Thomas, D.) MPII:P I-53

Alturas de Macchu Picchu. *See* Heights of Macchu Picchu, The

Always the Young Strangers (Sandburg) MPII:JYABio I-47

"Alyosha the Pot" (Tolstoy) MPII:SS I-74

Amadeus (Shaffer, P.) CLCII I-33; MPII:D I-37

Amadís de Gaul (Lobeira) CLC I-31; MP I-152; MP:EF I-26

Amant, L'. See Lover, The

"Amazing Grace in the Back Country" (Warren) MPII:P I-56

"Ambassador Diaries of Jean de Bosschère and Edgar Poe, The" (Dubie) MPII:P I-59

Ambassadors, The (James, H.) CLC I-32; MP I-156; MP:AF I-44

Ambiguous Adventure (Kane) CLCII I-34; MPII:WF I-39

"Ambitious Guest, The" (Hawthorne) MPII:SS I-78

Ambrosio. See Monk, The

Amelia (Fielding) CLC I-33; MP I-161; MP:BF I-44

America (Blake) MPII:P I-62

America Hurrah (van Itallie) CLCII I-36; MPII:D I-44

America Is in the Heart (Bulosan) MPII:JYABio I-51

"America! America!" (Schwartz) MPII:SS I-81

American, The (James, H.) CLC I-34; MP I-166; MP:AF I-49

American Buffalo (Mamet) CLCII I-37; MPII:D I-49

American Childhood, An (Dillard) MPII:JYABio I-55; MPII:NF I-39

American Commonwealth, The (Bryce) MP I-169

American Doctor's Odyssey, An (Heiser) MPII:JYABio I-59

American Dream, An (Mailer) CLCII I-38; MPII:AF I-29

American Dream, The (Albee) CLCII I-39; MPII:D I-55

American Evasion of Philosophy, The (West, C.) MPII:AfAm I-18

American Fugitive in Europe, The. See Autobiographical Writings of William Wells Brown, The.

American Hunger (Wright, R.) MPII:AfAm I-142

American Indian Women (Gridley) MPII:JYABio I-63

American Notebooks, The (Hawthorne) MP I-172

American Painter in Paris (Wilson, Ellen) MPII:JYABio I-67

American Scene, The (James) MPII:NF I-44

American Tragedy, An (Dreiser) CLC I-35; MP I-175; MP:AF I-53

America's Coming-of-Age (Brooks, V.) MP I-179

America's Ethan Allen (Holbrook) MPII:JYABio I-71

America's Mark Twain (McNeer) MPII:JYABio I-75

America's Own Mark Twain (Eaton) MPII:JYABio I-79

America's Robert E. Lee (Commager) MPII:JYABio I-83

Amerika (Kafka) CLCII I-40; MPII:WF I-45

Amigo Manso, El. See Our Friend Manso

"Among School Children" (Yeats) MPII:P I-65

Among the Believers (Naipaul) MPII:NF I-50

"Among the Dangs" (Elliott) MPII:SS I-85

Among Women Only (Pavese) CLCII I-41; MPII:WF I-50

Amores (Ovid) MP I-183

Amorosa Fiammetta, L' (Boccaccio) CLC I-591; MP VI-3240; MP:EF II-746

Amortajada, La. See Shrouded Woman, The

Amos Fortune, Free Man (Yates) MPII:JYABio I-86

Amphitryon (Plautus) CLC I-37; MP I-185

Amphitryon 38 (Giraudoux) CLC I-37; MP I-189

An die Parzen. See To the Fates

Anabasis (Perse) MP I-192

Anabasis, The (Xenophon) MP I-196

Anamnesis (Voegelin) MPII:NF I-56

Anancy's Score (Salkey) MPII:AfAm I-24

Anatomy Lesson, The (Roth, P.) CLCII I-42. See also Zuckerman Bound

Anatomy of Criticism (Frye) MPII:NF I-61

Anatomy of Melancholy, The (Burton, R.) MP I-200

Anchor's Aweigh (Latham) MPII:JYABio I-90

"And Death Shall Have No Dominion" (Thomas, D.) MPII:P I-68

. . . And Now Miguel (Krumgold) MPII:JYAFic I-35

And Quiet Flows the Don (Sholokhov) CLC I-38; MP I-202; MP:EF I-31

". . . and the earth did not part" (Rivera) MPII:SS I-89

And Tomorrow the Stars (Hill, K.) MPII:JYABio I-94

Andersen's Fairy Tales (Andersen) MP:EF I-34; MP I-205

Andorra (Frisch) CLCII I-43; MPII:D I-60

"Andrea del Sarto" (Browning, R.) MPII:P I-71

Andrew Carnegie (Judson) MPII:JYABio I-98

Andrew Jackson (Coit) MPII:JYABio I-102

Andria (Terence) CLC I-38; MP I-212

Andromache (Euripides) CLC I-40; MP I-216

Andromache (Racine) CLC I-41; MP I-219

Andromeda Strain, The (Crichton) CLCII I-44; MPII:AF I-34

"Angel" (Merrill, James) MPII:P I-75

Angel Dust Blues (Strasser) MPII:JYAFic I-38

Ángel Guerra (Pérez Galdós) CLC I-42; MP I-223; MP:EF I-43

"Angel Levine" (Malamud) MPII:SS I-92

"Angel of the Bridge, The" (Cheever, J.) MPII:SS I-95

Ángel Pavement (Priestley) CLCII I-45; MPII:BCF I-43

Angela Davis (Davis, A.) MPII:AfAm I-30

"Angels, The" (Rilke) MPII:P I-79

Angels Fall (Wilson, L.) CLCII I-47; MPII:D I-66

"Angle of Geese" (Momaday) MPII:P I-82

Angle of Repose (Stegner) CLCII I-48; MPII:AF I-38

Anglo-Saxon Attitudes (Wilson, Angus) CLCII I-49; MPII:BCF I-48

Angry Abolitionist (Archer) MPII:JYABio I-106

Angst des Tormanns beim Elfmeter, Die. See Goalie's Anxiety at the Penalty Kick, The

Anguilla, L'. See Eel, The

Animal Farm (Orwell) CLCII I-51; MPII:BCF I-53; MPII:JYAFic I-41

"Animula" (Eliot, T. S.) MPII:P I-85

Ann the Word (Campion, N.) MPII:JYABio I-110

Anna (Almedingen) MPII:JYAFic I-45

Anna and the King of Siam (Landon) MPII:JYABio I-114

Anna Christie (O'Neill) CLC I-43; MP I-226

Anna Karénina (Tolstoy) CLC I-44; MP I-229; MP:EF I-47

Anna of the Five Towns (Bennett, A.) CLC I-46; MP I-233; MP:BF I-50

"Annabel Lee" (Poe) MPII:P I-88

Annals of Tacitus, The (Tacitus) MP I-236

Annals of the Parish (Galt) CLC I-47; MP I-240; MP:BF I-54

Annals of the Roman People (Livy) MP I-243

Anne of Green Gables (Montgomery) MPII:JYAFic I-49

Anne of the Thousand Days (Anderson, Maxwell) CLCII I-52; MPII:D I-71

Annie John (Kincaid) MPII:AfAm I-35

Annie Oakley and the World of Her Time (Alderman) MPII:JYABio I-118

Anniversaries (Johnson, U.) CLCII I-53; MPII:WF I-55

Annonce faite à Marie, L'. See Tidings Brought to Mary, The

Another Country (Baldwin) CLCII I-55; MPII:AF I-43; MPII:AfAm I-41

Another Life (Trifonov) CLCII I-57; MPII:WF I-60

Ansichten eines Clowns. See Clown, The

Anthony Adverse (Allen, H.) CLC I-47; MP I-246; MP:AF I-58

Anthony Burns (Hamilton) MPII:JYABio I-121

Anti-Memoirs (Malraux) MPII:NF I-68

Antigone (Anouilh) CLCII I-58; MPII:D I-77

Antigone (Sophocles) CLC I-48; MP I-250

Antiquary, The (Scott, Sir W.) CLC I-49; MP I-254; MP:BF I-58

Antony and Cleopatra (Shakespeare) CLC I-50; MP I-258

Anxiety of Influence, The (Bloom, H.) MPII:NF I-75

Anya (Schaeffer, S.) MPII:JYAFic I-53

"Anyone lived in a pretty how town" (Cummings) MPII:P I-91

Apache Warrior (Cooke, D.) MPII:JYABio I-125

Apalache (Metcalf) MPII:NF I-79

Apes of God, The (Lewis, W.) CLCII I-59; MPII:BCF I-58

Apocalypse (Lawrence) MPII:NF I-85

"Apocalypse at Solentiname" (Cortázar) MPII:SS I-99

Apollo. See Apollo and Marsyas

"Apollo and Marsyas" (Herbert, Z.) MPII:P I-94

Apologia pro Vita Sua (Newman, J.) MP I-263

Apology for the Life of Colley Cibber, Comedian, An (Cibber) MP I-266

Apostle, The (Asch) CLC I-53; MP I-269; MP:AF I-62

Appalachee Red (Andrews) MPII:AfAm I-47

Apple in the Dark, The (Lispector) CLCII I-62; MPII:AF I-48

Apple of the Eye, The (Wescott) CLC I-54; MP I-273; MP:AF I-66

Appointment in Samarra (O'Hara, J.) CLC I-55; MP I-276; MP:AF I-70

Apprenticeship of Duddy Kravitz, The (Richler) CLCII I-63; MPII:BCF I-63

Après-midi d'un faune, L'. See Afternoon of a Faun, The

"April Witch, The" (Bradbury) MPII:SS I-103

"Aptekarsha." See "Chemist's Wife, The"

Arabian Nights' Entertainments, The (Unknown) CLC I-55; MP I-281; MP:EF I-52

"Araby" (Joyce) MPII:SS I-106

Arbitration, The (Menander) CLC I-56; MP I-288

Árbol de la ciencia, El. See Tree of Knowledge, The

Arcadia (Sidney) CLC I-57; MP I-293; MP:BF I-62

"Archaic Torso of Apollo" (Rilke) MPII:P I-98

Archaïscher Torso Apollos. See Archaic Torso of Apollo

Archer in the Marrow (Viereck) MPII:P I-101

Archimedes and the Door of Science (Bendick) MPII:JYABio I-129

Architect and the Emperor of Assyria, The (Arrabal) CLCII I-65; MPII:D I-82

Architecte et l'Empereur d'Assyrie, L'. See Architect and the Emperor of Assyria, The

Arco y la lira, El. See Bow and the Lyre, The

Are You in the House Alone? (Peck, Richard) MPII:JYAFic I-57

Are You There, God? It's Me, Margaret (Blume) MPII:JYAFic I-61

Areopagitica (Milton) MP I-299

Argenis (Barclay) CLC I-59; MP I-302; MP:BF I-69

Ariel (Maurois) MPII:JYABio I-133

"Ariel" (Plath) MPII:P I-106

"Ark of Bones" (Dumas) MPII:SS I-110

"Arkhierey." See "Bishop, The"

Arkhipelag GULag, 1918-1956. See Gulag Archipelago, 1918-1956, The

Arme Heinrich, Der (Hartmann von Aue) CLC I-60; MP I-307

Armed with Courage (McNeer and Ward) MPII:JYABio I-137

Armies of the Night, The (Mailer) CLCII I-65; MPII:AF I-51

Arms and the Man (Shaw, G.) CLCII I-67; MPII:D I-88

Arne (Björnson) CLC I-61; MP I-310; MP:EF I-61

Around the World in Eighty Days (Verne) CLCII I-68; MPII:JYAFic I-65; MPII:WF I-66

"Arrest of Oscar Wilde at the Cadogan Hotel, The" (Betjeman) MPII:P I-109

Arrivants, The. See Poetry of Edward Kamau Brathwaite, The.

Arrow of God (Achebe) CLCII I-69; MPII:BCF I-67

Arrowsmith (Lewis, S.) CLC I-61; MP I-313; MP:AF I-75

Ars amatoria (Ovid) MP I-317

Ars Poetica (Horace) MP I-319

Art and Illusion (Gombrich) MPII:NF I-90

"Art of Living, The" (Gardner) MPII:SS I-114

"Art of Poetry, The" (Tomlinson) MPII:P I-112

"Art of Poetry, The" (Verlaine) MPII:P I-115

"Art poétique. *See* Art of Poetry, The" (Verlaine)

Artamène (Scudéry) CLC I-63; MP I-322; MP:EF I-64

Artamonov Business, The (Gorky) CLC I-64; MP I-326; MP:EF I-68

"Artificial Nigger, The" (O'Connor, Flannery) MPII:SS I-118

"Artist of the Beautiful, The" (Hawthorne) MPII:SS I-122

Arturo's Island (Morante) CLCII I-70; MPII:WF I-71

As a Man Grows Older (Svevo) CLCII I-71; MPII:WF I-75

As for Me and My House (Ross) CLCII I-72; MPII:BCF I-72

As I Lay Dying (Faulkner) CLC I-64; MP I-330; MP:AF I-80

As the Crow Flies (Clarke, Austin) CLCII I-74; MPII:D I-94

"As the Dead Prey Upon Us" (Olson) MPII:P I-119

As You Like It (Shakespeare) CLC I-66; MP I-334

"Ash, The" (Heyen) MPII:P I-123

Ash Wednesday (Eliot, T. S.) MP I-339

"Ashes" (Levine) MPII:P I-126

Ashes (Żeromski) CLC I-67; MP I-341; MP:EF I-73

Ashes and Diamonds (Andrzejewski) CLCII I-75; MPII:WF I-80

Asiatics, The (Prokosch) CLCII I-76; MPII:AF I-56

Asmodeus. *See* Diable Boiteux, Le

"Aspern Papers, The" (James, H.) CLCII I-77; MPII:SS I-125

Assault on Mount Helicon (Barnard) MPII:NF I-97

Assistant, The (Malamud) CLCII I-78; MPII:AF I-61

Astillero, El. *See* Shipyard, The

"Astrologer's Day, An" (Narayan) MPII:SS I-129

Astrophil and Stella (Sidney) MPII:P I-129

Asya (Turgenev) CLCII I-80; MPII:WF I-85

At Hsieh T'iao's High Mansion in Hsuän-chou. *See* Farewell to Li Yun in the Xie Tiao Pavilion, A

At Lady Molly's. *See* Dance to the Music of Time, A, *and* Dance to the Music of Time: Second Movement, A

"At Melville's Tomb" (Crane, H.) MPII:P I-135

At Play in the Fields of the Lord (Matthiessen) CLCII I-81; MPII:AF I-65

At Swim-Two-Birds (O'Brien, F.) CLCII I-82; MPII:BCF I-77

At the Back of the North Wind (MacDonald) MPII:JYAFic I-69

"At the Ball Game" (Williams, W.) MPII:P I-138

"At the Bay" (Mansfield) MPII:SS I-132

At the Bottom of the River (Kincaid) MPII:AfAm I-52

"At the Bottom of the River" (Kincaid) MPII:SS I-135

At the Sign of the Reine Pédauque (France) CLC I-68; MP I-345; MP:EF I-77

Atala (Chateaubriand) CLC I-69; MP I-349; MP:EF I-81

Atalanta in Calydon (Swinburne) CLC I-69; MP I-353

Atem, Der. *See* Gathering Evidence

"Au lecteur." *See* To the Reader

"Aubade" (Empson) MPII:P I-141

Aucassin and Nicolette (Unknown) CLC I-70; MP I-356; MP:EF I-85

Audubon (Warren) MPII:P I-145

Aufstieg und Fall der Stadt Mahagonny. *See* Rise and Fall of the City of Mahagonny

Augenspiel, Das. *See* Play of The Eyes, The

"Auguries of Innocence" (Blake) MPII:P I-150

"August Moon" (Warren) MPII:P I-153

August 1914 (Solzhenitsyn) CLCII I-84; MPII:WF I-90

Aunt Dan and Lemon (Shawn) CLCII I-86; MPII:D I-99

Aunt Julia and the Scriptwriter (Vargas Llosa) CLCII I-87; MPII:AF I-71

Aunt's Story, The (White) CLCII I-88; MPII:BCF I-81

Aura (Fuentes) CLCII I-90; MPII:AF I-76

"Auroras of Autumn, The" (Stevens, W.) MPII:P I-156

Aus Meinem Leben und Deken. *See* Out of My Life and Thought.

"Auspice of Jewels" (Riding) MPII:P I-159

Australia Felix. *See* Fortunes of Richard Mahony, The

"Auto Wreck" (Shapiro) MPII:P I-162

Autobiographical Novel, An (Rexroth) MPII:NF I-104

Autobiographical Writings of William Wells Brown, The (Brown, W.) MPII:AfAm I-58

Autobiographies. *See* Autobiography of William Butler Yeats, The

Autobiographies of Chester Himes, The (Himes) MPII:AfAm I-65

Autobiography (Chesterton) MPII:NF I-109

Autobiography, An (Trollope) MP I-359

Autobiography of Alice B. Toklas, The (Stein) MPII:JYABio I-141

Autobiography of an Ex-Coloured Man, The (Johnson, J.) CLCII I-92; MPII:AF I-81; MPII:AfAm I-72

Autobiography of Benjamin Franklin, The (Franklin) MP I-362; MPII:JYABio I-145

Autobiography of Benjamin Robert Haydon, The (Haydon) MP I-365

Autobiography of Benvenuto Cellini, The (Cellini) MP I-368

Autobiography of Leigh Hunt, The (Hunt, L.) MP I-373

Autobiography of LeRoi Jones/Amiri Baraka, The (Baraka) MPII:JYABio I-148

Autobiography of Lincoln Steffens, The (Steffens) MPII:JYABio I-152; MPII:NF I-115

Autobiography of Malcolm X, The (Malcolm X) MPII:AfAm I-78; MPII:JYABio I-156; MPII:NF I-121

Autobiography of Mark Twain, The (Twain) MPII:JYABio I-160

Autobiography of Miss Jane Pittman, The (Gaines) CLCII I-93; MPII:AF I-87; MPII:AfAm I-84; MPII:JYAFic I-73

Autobiography of W. E. B. Du Bois, The (Du Bois, W. E. B.) MPII:AfAm I-90; MPII:JYABio I-164

Autobiography of William Butler Yeats, The (Yeats) MP I-376

Autobiography of William Carlos Williams, The (Williams) MPII:NF I-127

Autocrat of the Breakfast-Table, The (Holmes) MP I-379

Auto-da-Fé (Canetti) CLCII I-91; MPII:WF I-95

"Autopista del sur, La." *See* "Southern Thruway, The"

Autopsia, E. *See* Autopsy, The

"Autopsy, The" (Eltis) MPII:P I-166

"Autumn Begins in Martins Ferry, Ohio" (Wright, James) MPII:P I-169

"Autumn Day" (Rilke) MPII:P I-172

"Autumn Leaves" (Prévert) MPII:P I-175

Autumn of the Patriarch, The (García Márquez) CLCII I-95; MPII:AF I-92

"Autumn Song" (Verlaine) MPII:P I-178

Avalovara (Lins) CLCII I-97; MPII:AF I-97

Aventure ambiguë, L'. *See* Ambiguous Adventure

"Avenue Bearing the Initial of Christ into the New World, The" (Kinnell) MPII:P I-181

Avgust chetyrnadtsatogo. *See* August 1914

Awake and Sing! (Odets) CLCII I-98; MPII:D I-104

Awakening of Spring, The (Wedekind) CLC I-71; MP I-383

Awakenings (Sacks) MPII:NF I-132

Awkward Age, The (James, H.) MP I-387; MP:AF I-85

Axe, The (Undset) CLC I-71; MP I-391; MP:EF I-88

Axel's Castle (Wilson) MP I-395

Azur, L'. *See* Azure, The

"Azure, The" (Mallarmé) MPII:P I-185

B

Baal (Brecht) MP I-397

"Babas del Diablo, Las." *See* "Blow-Up"

Babbitt (Lewis, S.) CLC I-72; MP I-400;
MP:AF I-90

Babel-17 (Delany, S.) CLCII I-99; MPII:AF
I-102; MPII:AfAm I-96; MPII:JYAFic
I-76

"Babii Yar" (Yevtushenko) MPII:P I-188

Babiy Yar. *See* Babii Yar

"Babylon Revisited" (Fitzgerald) MPII:SS
I-140

Bacchae, The (Euripides) CLC I-74; MP I-405

Bachelors, The (Spark) MP I-409; MP:BF
I-75

Back to Methuselah (Shaw) CLC I-75; MP
I-412

Backwater. *See* Pilgrimage

"Bad Characters" (Stafford, J.) MPII:SS
I-144

Badenheim, 'ir nofesh. *See* Badenheim 1939

Badenheim 1939 (Appelfeld) CLCII I-101;
MPII:WF I-101

"Badger" (Clare) MPII:P I-191

Baga (Pinget) CLCII I-102; MPII:WF I-107

Bahía de silencio, La. *See* Bay of Silence, A

Bailey's Café (Naylor) MPII:AfAm I-102

Bajan Trilogy, The. *See* Poetry of Edward
Kamau Brathwaite, The.

"Balakirev's Dream" (Tranströmer) MPII:P
I-194

Balakirevs Drom. *See* Balakirev's Dream

Balboa (Syme) MPII:JYABio I-168

Balcon, Le. *See* Balcony, The

Balcony, The (Genet) CLCII I-103; MPII:D
I-109

Bald Soprano, The (Ionesco) CLCII I-105;
MPII:D I-116

Balkan trilogy, The (Manning, O.) CLCII
I-106; MPII:BCF I-86

Ballad of Benny Perhaps, The (Brinsmead)
MPII:JYAFic I-80

Ballad of Peckham Rye, The (Spark) CLCII
I-108; MPII:BCF I-91

Ballad of Reading Gaol, The (Wilde)
MPII:P I-198

"Ballad of the Sad Café, The" (McCullers)
CLCII I-109; MPII:SS I-147

Ballet Shoes (Streatfeild) MPII:JYAFic I-83

Balthazar (Balzac). *See* Quest of the
Absolute, The

Balthazar (Durrell). *See* Alexandria Quartet,
The

Bambi (Salten) CLC I-78; MP I-415;
MP:EF I-92; MPII:JYAFic I-87

"Bambino, The" (Sinclair) MPII:SS I-151

Banana Bottom (McKay) CLCII I-110;
MPII:AF I-106; MPII:AfAm I-108

Bang the Drum Slowly (Harris, M.) CLCII
I-112; MPII:AF I-111; MPII:JYAFic I-92

Bangüê. *See* Plantation Boy

Banjo (McKay) CLCII I-113; MPII:AF
I-116

"Banquet, The" (Herbert, G.) MPII:P I-202

Banya. *See* Bathhouse, The

Barabbas (Lagerkvist) CLC I-78; MP I-419;
MP:EF I-96

"Barbados" (Marshall) MPII:SS I-154

Barbara Jordan (Jordan, B. *and* Hearon)
MPII:JYABio I-172

Barbarian in the Garden (Herbert) MPII:NF
I-138

Barbarzyca w ogrodzie. *See* Barbarian in
the Garden

Barber of Seville, The (Beaumarchais) CLC
I-79; MP I-423

Barchester Towers (Trollope) CLC I-80;
MP I-426; MP:BF I-79

Barefoot in the Head (Aldiss) CLCII I-114;
MPII:BCF I-98

Barefoot in the Park (Simon, N.) CLCII
I-115; MPII:D I-122

Bark Tree, The (Queneau) CLCII I-116;
MPII:WF I-111

"Barn Burning" (Faulkner) MPII:SS I-158

Bàrnabo delle montagne. *See* Bàrnabo of
the Mountains

Bàrnabo of the Mountains (Buzzati) CLCII
I-177; MPII:WF I-116

Barnaby Rudge (Dickens) CLC I-81; MP
I-431; MP:BF I-85

Barometer Rising (MacLennan) CLCII
I-118; MPII:BCF I-103

Baron in the Trees, The (Calvino) CLCII
I-119; MPII:WF I-121

Baron Münchausen's Narrative (Raspe)
CLC I-84; MP I-435; MP:EF I-101

Barone rampante, Il. *See* Baron in the Trees,
The

Barracks, The (McGahern) CLCII I-121;
MPII:BCF I-108

Barrage contre la Pacifique, Un. *See* Sea
Wall, The

Barrio Boy (Galarza) MPII:JYABio I-176

Barren Ground (Glasgow) CLC I-84; MP
I-438; MP:AF I-96

Barry Lyndon (Thackeray) CLC I-85; MP
I-443; MP:BF I-91

Barsetshire series. *See* Barchester Towers;
Doctor Thorne; Framley Parsonage; Last
Chronicle of Barset; Small House at
Allington, The; *and* Warden, The

Bartholomew Fair (Jonson) CLC I-86; MP
I-446

"Bartleby the Scrivener" (Melville)
MPII:SS I-162

"Basement Room, The" (Greene) MPII:SS
I-166

Basic Training of Pavlo Hummel, The
(Rabe, D.) CLCII I-122; MPII:D I-127

Bass Saxophone, The (Škvoreck) CLCII
I-123; MPII:WF I-126

Bassaxofon. *See* Bass Saxophone, The

Bašta, pepeo. *See* Garden, Ashes

Bataille de Pharsale, La. *See* Battle of
Pharsalus, The

Bateau ivre, Le. *See* Drunken Boat, The

Bathazar. *See* Alexandria Quartet, The

Bathhouse, The (Mayakovsky) CLCII
I-124; MPII:D I-133

Batouala (Maran) CLC I-88; MP I-451;
MP:EF I-105

"Batter my heart, three-person'd God"
(Donne) MPII:P I-205

Battle of Pharsalus, The (Simon, C.) CLCII
I-125; MPII:WF I-131

"Bau, Der." *See* "Burrow, The"

"Bavarian Gentians" (Lawrence, D. H.)
MPII:P I-208

Bay of Silence, The (Mallea) CLC I-89; MP
I-454; MP:AF I-101

Beach of Falesá, The (Stevenson) CLC
I-89; MP I-456; MP:BF I-95

Beachmasters (Astley) CLCII I-126;
MPII:BCF I-114

"Beacons, The" (Baudelaire) MPII:P I-211

Bear, The (Faulkner) MPII:JYAFic I-96

Bear's Heart (Supree) MPII:JYABio I-180

"Bearded Oaks" (Warren) MPII:P I-215

"Beast in the Jungle, The" (James, H.)
MPII:SS I-169

Beat to Quarters. *See* Captain Horatio
Hornblower *and* Horatio Hornblower
series, The

Beauchamp's Career (Meredith, G.) CLC
I-90; MP I-460; MP:BF I-99

Beautiful and Damned, The (Fitzgerald, F.
S.) CLCII I-127; MPII:AF I-122

Beauty and Sadness (Kawabata) CLCII
I-128; MPII:WF I-136

Beautyful Ones Are Not Yet Born, The
(Armah) CLCII I-129; MPII:BCF I-118

Beaux' Stratagem, The (Farquhar) CLC
I-91; MP I-464

Beaver Coat, The (Hauptmann) CLC I-92;
MP I-469

"Because I could not stop for Death"
(Dickinson, E.) MPII:P I-219

Becket (Anouilh) CLCII I-130; MPII:D I-139

"Beckoning Fair One, The" (Onions)
MPII:SS I-173

Bedbug, The (Mayakovsky) CLCII I-132;
MPII:D I-146

"Beet Queen, The" (Erdrich) MPII:SS I-177

Beethoven, Master Musician (Goss)
MPII:JYABio I-183

Beetlecreek (Demby) CLCII I-133;
MPII:AF I-126; MPII:AfAm I-114

Beggar in Jerusalem, A (Wiesel) CLCII
I-135; MPII:WF I-141

"Beggar My Neighbor" (Jacobson) MPII:SS
I-181

Beggar on Horseback (Connelly) CLCII
I-136; MPII:D I-153

Beggar Queen, The. *See* Westmark trilogy,
The

Beggars' Bush, The (Fletcher *and*
Massinger) CLC I-92; MP I-472

Beggar's Opera, The (Gay) CLC I-94; MP
I-476

"Beggarwoman of Locarno, The" (Kleist)
MPII:SS I-184

Beginnings (Reed, G.) MPII:JYABio I-187

Beginnings of Architecture, The. *See* Eternal Present, The

Beginnings of Art, The. *See* Eternal Present, The

Behave Yourself, Bethany Brant (Beatty, P.) MPII:JYAFic I-100

Beichte eines Toren, Die. *See* Confession of a Fool, The

"Beim Bau der chinesischen Mauer." *See* "Great Wall of China, The"

Bel-Ami (Maupassant) CLC I-95; MP I-481; MP:EF I-108

Bel Ria (Burnford) MPII:JYAFic I-103

Belaia noch. *See* White Night

Bell, The (Murdoch) MP I-485; MP:BF I-104

Bell for Adano, A (Hersey) CLC I-96; MP I-488; MP:AF I-104; MPII:JYAFic I-106

Bell Jar, The (Plath) CLCII I-137; MPII:AF I-131

"Belle Dame sans Merci, La" (Keats) MPII:P I-222

Bellefleur (Oates) CLCII I-138; MPII:AF I-136

"Bells for John Whiteside's Daughter" (Ransom) MPII:P I-225

Beloved (Morrison) MPII:AfAm I-119; MPII:JYAFic I-109

"Belye nochi." *See* "White Nights"

Ben Hur (Wallace) CLC I-96; MP I-491; MP:AF I-107

Bend in the River, A (Naipaul, V. S.) CLCII I-139; MPII:BCF I-124

Bend Sinister (Nabokov) CLCII I-141; MPII:AF I-142

"Benediction" (Baudelaire) MPII:P I-228

Benefactors (Frayn) CLCII I-142; MPII:D I-158

Ben-Gurion (St. John) MPII:JYABio I-191

"Benito Cereno" (Melville) CLC I-97; MP I-495; MP:AF I-111; MPII:SS I-188

Benito Juárez (Wepman) MPII:JYABio I-195

Benjamin Banneker (Lewis, C.) MPII:JYABio I-199

Benjamin Franklin (Fleming) MPII:JYABio I-203

Benjamin Franklin (Meltzer) MPII:JYABio I-207

Benjamin West and His Cat Grimalkin (Henry) MPII:JYABio I-211

Beowulf (Unknown) CLC I-98; MP I-500

Bérénice (Racine) CLC I-99; MP I-504

"Bericht für eine Akademie, Ein." *See* "Report to an Academy, A"

Berlin Alexanderplatz (Döblin) CLCII I-143; MPII:WF I-146

Beso de la mujer araña, El. *See* Kiss of the Spider Woman

Bespokoynaya yunost. *See* Story of a Life, The

Bessonnitsa. Gomer. Tugie parusa. *See* Insomia. Homer. Taut Sails

Besuch der alten Dame, Der. *See* Visit, The

"Bet, The" (Chekhov) MPII:SS I-192

Beton. *See* Concrete

Betrayal (Pinter) CLCII I-145; MPII:D I-163

Betrayed by Rita Hayworth (Puig) CLCII I-146; MPII:AF I-146

Betrothed, The (Manzoni) CLC I-100; MP I-507; MP:EF I-113

Betsey Brown (Shange) MPII:AfAm I-125; MPII:JYAFic I-112

Better Class of Person, A (Osborne) MPII:NF I-144

Between the Acts (Woolf) CLC I-101; MP I-512; MP:BF I-108

Beulah Quintet, The (Settle) MPII:AF I-151

Bevis of Hampton (Unknown) CLC I-101; MP I-516

Beyond Dark Hills (Stuart) MPII:NF I-150

Beyond Good and Evil (Nietzsche) MP I-520

"Beyond the Alps" (Lowell, R.) MPII:P I-231

Beyond the Bedroom Wall (Woiwode) CLCII I-147; MPII:AF I-161

"Beyond the Glass Mountain" (Stegner) MPII:SS I-196

"Bezhin Meadow" (Turgenev) MPII:SS I-200

Bible in Spain, The (Borrow) MP I-528

"Biblioteca de Babel, La." *See* "Library of Babel, The"

Biedermann und die Brandstifter. *See* Firebugs, The

"Big Blonde" (Parker) MPII:SS I-203
Big Knife, The (Odets) CLCII I-150;
  MPII:D I-169
Big Sea, The (Hughes, L.) MPII:AfAm
  I-131; MPII:JYABio I-215; MPII:NF
  I-156
Big Sky, The (Guthrie) CLC I-102; MP
  I-531; MP:AF I-116
Big Sleep, The (Chandler) CLCII I-151;
  MPII:AF I-166
Big Tiger and Christian (Mühlenweg)
  MPII:JYAFic I-116
"Big Two-Hearted River" (Hemingway)
  MPII:SS I-206
Biglow Papers, The (Lowell, J.) MP I-535
Bijoux, Les. See Jewels, The
Bilgewater (Gardam) MPII:JYAFic I-119
Bill Peet (Peet) MPII:JYABio I-219
Billard um halbzehn. See Billiards at
  Half-Past Nine
Billiards at Half-Past Nine (Böll) CLCII
  I-153; MPII:WF I-152
Billy Budd, Foretopman (Melville) CLC
  I-104; MP I-538; MP:AF I-121
Billy Phelan's Greatest Game (Kennedy,
  W.) CLCII I-154. See also Albany
  Cycle, The
Biloxi Blues (Simon, N.) CLCII I-155;
  MPII:D I-175
Bilvav yamim. See In the Heart of the Seas
Biodlares död, En. See Death of a
  Beekeeper, The
Biographia Literaria (Coleridge) MP I-544
Bioi parallloi. See Ten Famous Lives
"Birches" (Frost) MPII:P I-234
Bird at My Window (Guy) MPII:AfAm
  I-136
Birds, The (Aristophanes) CLC I-105; MP
  I-547
Birds Fall Down, The (West, R.) CLCII
  I-157; MPII:BCF I-129
Birthday King, The (Fielding) CLCII I-158;
  MPII:BCF I-134
Birthday Party, The (Pinter) CLCII I-159;
  MPII:D I-180
"Birthmark, The" (Hawthorne) MPII:SS
  I-210
"Bishop, The" (Chekhov) MPII:SS I-214

"Bishop Orders His Tomb at Saint Praxed's
  Church, The" (Browning, R.) MPII:P
  I-237
Bismarck (Taylor, A.) MPII:JYABio I-222
"Bit of a Smash in Madras, A"
  (Maclaren-Ross) MPII:SS I-218
"Bitter Honeymoon" (Moravia) MPII:SS
  I-222
"Blacáman the Good, Vendor of Miracles"
  (García Márquez) MPII:SS I-227
Black American Leaders (Young, M.)
  MPII:JYABio I-226
"Black Angel, The" (Coulette) MPII:P I-240
Black Arrow, The (Stevenson) CLC I-106;
  MP I-552; MP:BF I-113
Black Beauty (Sewell, A.) MPII:JYAFic
  I-122
Black Boy (Wright, R.) MPII:AfAm I-142;
  MPII:JYABio I-229; MPII:NF I-162
"Black Cat, The" (Poe) MPII:SS I-231
Black Cauldron, The. See Prydain
  chronicles, The
Black Elk Speaks (Black Elk)
  MPII:JYABio I-233
Black Hermit, The (Ngugi) CLCII I-160;
  MPII:D I-185
"Black Hills Survival Gathering, 1980"
  (Hogan) MPII:P I-243
Black Ice (Cary, L.) MPII:AfAm I-149
Black Lamb and Grey Falcon (West, R.)
  MP I-556
Black Like Me (Griffin) MPII:JYABio I-237
Black Men (Madhubuti) MPII:AfAm I-155
Black Mischief (Waugh) CLCII I-161;
  MPII:BCF I-139
"Black Prince, The" (Grau) MPII:SS I-235
Black Prince, The (Murdoch) CLCII I-162;
  MPII:BCF I-145
Black Robe (Moore) CLCII I-163;
  MPII:BCF I-150
Black Stallion, The (Farley) MPII:JYAFic
  I-125
Black Swan, The (Mann) MP I-559; MP:EF
  I-119
"Black Tambourine" (Crane, H.) MPII:P
  I-246
Black Thunder (Bontemps) CLCII I-164;
  MPII:AF I-171; MPII:AfAm I-161
"Black Tickets" (Phillips, J.) MPII:SS I-239

Black Valley (Wast) CLC I-107; MP I-562; MP:AF I-127

"Black Woman" (Senghor) MPII:P I-249

"Blackberry Eating" (Kinnell) MPII:P I-253

Blackberry Winter (Mead, M.) MPII:JYABio I-240

"Blackberry Winter" (Warren) MPII:SS I-242

"Blackcurrant River" (Rimbaud) MPII:P I-256

Blacker the Berry, The (Thurman) CLCII I-166; MPII:AF I-175; MPII:AfAm I-167

Blacks, The (Genet) CLCII I-167; MPII:D I-190

"Blank Page, The" (Dinesen) MPII:SS I-246

Blasting and Bombardiering (Lewis, W.) MPII:NF I-168

Blaubart. See Bluebeard

Blé en herbe, Le. See Ripening Seed, The

Bleak House (Dickens) CLC I-107; MP I-566; MP:BF I-118

Blendung, Die. See Auto-da-Fé

Bless the Beasts and Children (Swarthout) MPII:JYAFic I-128

"Blessed Damozel, The" (Rossetti, D.) MPII:P I-260

Blindfold Games (Ross) MPII:NF I-172

"Bliss" (Mansfield) MPII:SS I-250

Blithe Spirit (Coward) CLCII I-169; MPII:D I-195

Blithedale Romance, The (Hawthorne) CLC I-110; MP I-571; MP:AF I-131

"Blizzard, The" (Pushkin) MPII:SS I-254

Blood Brother (Arnold, E.) MPII:JYAFic I-132

"Blood-Burning Moon" (Toomer) MPII:SS I-258

Blood Knot, The (Fugard) CLCII I-169; MPII:D I-200

Blood of the Lamb, The (De Vries) CLCII I 170; MPII:AF I-181

Blood Wedding (García Lorca) CLC I-112; MP I-574

Bloodsmoor Romance, A (Oates) CLCII I-171; MPII:AF I-186

Bloody Poetry (Brenton) CLCII I-172; MPII:D I-207

Blooming (Toth) MPII:NF I-178

Blossoming World, The (Bates) MPII:NF IV-1628

Blot in the 'Scutcheon, A (Browning, R.) CLC I-112; MP I-578

"Blow-Up" (Cortázar) MPII:SS I-262

Blowfish Live in the Sea (Fox) MPII:JYAFic I-135

Blue Bird, The (Maeterlinck) CLCII I-173; MPII:D I-213

Blue Boy (Giono) CLCII I-175; MPII:WF I-158

Blue Fin (Thiele) MPII:JYAFic I-138

Blue Highways (Heat-Moon) MPII:NF I-184

"Blue Hotel, The" (Crane, S.) MPII:SS I-266

"Blue Meridian" (Toomer) MPII:AfAm I-173

Blue Mountains of China, The (Wiebe) CLCII I-176; MPII:BCF I-154

Blue Remembered Hills (Sutcliff) MPII:JYABio I-244

Blue Room, The (Simenon) CLCII I-177; MPII:WF I-164

Bluebeard (Frisch) CLCII I-178; MPII:WF I-169

Blues for Mister Charlie (Baldwin) CLCII I-179; MPII:AfAm I-182; MPII:D I-219

Bluest Eye, The (Morrison) CLCII I-180; MPII:AF I-191; MPII:AfAm I-188; MPII:JYAFic I-141

Bo Jackson (Devaney) MPII:JYABio I-248

"Boarding House, The" (Joyce) MPII:SS I-270

Boarding-House, The (Trevor) CLCII I-182; MPII:BCF I-158

"Bobok" (Dostoevski) MPII:SS I-273

"Bobo's Metamorphosis" (Miłosz) MPII:P I-263

Bodalsia telenok s dubom. See Oak and the Calf, The

"Body of Summer" (Eltis) MPII:P I-267

Boesman and Lena (Fugard) CLCII I-183; MPII:D I-225

Bogmail (McGinley) CLCII I-184; MPII:BCF I-163

Bohemians of the Latin Quarter, The (Murger) CLC I-113; MP I-581; MP:EF I-122

Bolívar, the Liberator (Syme) MPII:JYABio I-252

Bondman, The (Massinger) CLC I-113; MP I-585

Bonds of Interest, The (Benavente) CLC I-115; MP I-589

Bone People, The (Hulme) CLCII I-185; MPII:BCF I-168

Bonecrack (Francis) CLCII I-186; MPII:BCF I-172

Bonnes, Les. *See* Maids, The

"Bontche Shveig." *See* "Bontsha the Silent"

"Bontsha the Silent" (Peretz) MPII:SS I-277

Book of Bebb, The (Buechner) CLCII I-187; MPII:AF I-196

Book of Ephraim, The. *See* Changing Light at Sandover, The

Book of Laughter and Forgetting, The (Kundera) CLCII I-190; MPII:WF I-174

Book of Lights, The (Potok) CLCII I-192; MPII:AF I-202

Book of Songs (Heine) MP I-593

Book of the Courtier, The (Castiglione) MP I-596

Book of the Thousand and One Nights, The. *See* Arabian Nights' Entertainment, The

Book of Thel, The (Blake) MPII:P I-270

Book of Three, The. *See* Prydain chronicles, The

Books Do Furnish a Room. *See* Dance to the Music of Time, A

Books of the Small Souls, The. *See* Small Souls

Boquitas pintadas. *See* Heartbreak Tango

Borderline (Hospital) CLCII I-193; MPII:BCF I-177

Boris Godunov (Pushkin) CLC I-115; MP I-599

Born in Captivity (Wain) CLCII I-194; MPII:BCF I-181

Borough: A Poem in Twenty-Four Letters, The (Crabbe) MP I-602

Borrowers, The (Norton, M.) MPII:JYAFic I-145

Borstal Boy (Behan) MPII:NF I-190

Bosnian Chronicle (Andrić) CLCII I-195; MPII:WF I-182

Bostonians, The (James, H.) MP I-605; MP:AF I-135

Boswell's London Journal: 1762-1763 (Boswell) MP I-608

Botchan (Natsume) CLCII I-196; MPII:WF I-188

"Bottle Imp, The" (Stevenson) MPII:SS I-281

"Bottle of Milk for Mother, A" (Algren) MPII:SS I-285

Bouc émissaire, Le. *See* Scapegoat, The

"Boule de Suif" (Maupassant) MPII:SS I-289

Bound for Glory (Guthrie) MPII:JYABio I-256

Bourgeois Gentleman, The (Molière) CLC I-116; MP II-611

Bouts de bois de Dieu, Les. *See* God's Bits of Wood

Bouvard and Pécuchet (Flaubert) CLC I-117; MP II-615; MP:EF I-127

Bow and the Lyre, The (Paz) MPII:NF I-196

Bowen's Court (Bowen, E.) MPII:NF I-201

"Bowmen of Shu, The" (Davenport) MPII:SS I-293

Box of Delights, The (Masefield) MPII:JYAFic I-148

"Boxcar of Chrysanthemums" (Enchi) MPII:SS I-297

Boy (Dahl) MPII:JYABio I-260

Boys in the Band, The (Crowley) CLCII I-197; MPII:D I-230

Boys of Summer, The (Kahn) MPII:NF I-206

Bracknels, The (Reid) CLC I-119; MP II-619; MP:BF I-124

Braggart Soldier, The (Plautus) CLC I-119; MP II-623

"Brahma" (Emerson) MPII:P I-273

Brand (Ibsen) CLC I-120; MP II-627

Brave New World (Huxley, A.) CLC I-121; MP II-631; MP:BF I-128; MPII:JYAFic I-151

Bread and Honey. *See* Walk a Mile and Get Nowhere

"Bread and Wine" (Hölderlin) MPII:P I-276

Bread and Wine (Silone) CLC I-122; MP II-636; MP:EF I-131

Bread Givers (Yezierska) CLCII I-198; MPII:AF I-207

Break of Noon (Claudel) CLCII I-199; MPII:D I-237

Breakthrough to the Big League (Robinson, J., *and* Duckett) MPII:JYABio I-264

Breakthroughs in Science (Asimov) MPII:JYABio I-267

Brian Piccolo (Morris, J.) MPII:JYABio I-271

Bridal Canopy, The (Agnon) CLCII I-200; MPII:WF I-194

"Bride Comes to Yellow Sky, The" (Crane, S.) MPII:SS I-300

Bride of Lammermoor (Scott, Sir W.) CLC I-122; MP II-640; MP:BF I-134

Brideshead Revisited (Waugh) CLC I-123; MP II-645; MP:BF I-139

Bridge, The (Crane, H.) MP II-649; MPII:P I-280

"Bridge of Dreams, The" (Tanizaki) MPII:SS I-304

Bridge of San Luis Rey, The (Wilder, T.) CLC I-124; MP II-651; MP:AF I-139

Bridge on the Drina, The (Andri) MP II-656; MP:EF I-136

Bridge to Terabithia (Paterson) MPII:JYAFic I-155

Bridge to the Sun (Terasaki) MPII:JYABio I-274

Brief an Lord Liszt. *See* Letter to Lord Liszt

"Brief Journey West, The" (Nemerov) MPII:P I-285

Brief Life, A (Onetti) CLCII I-201; MPII:AF I-212

Brief Lives (Aubrey) MP II-659

"Brief Pause in the Organ Recital" (Tranströmer) MPII:P I-288

Briefe an Felice. *See* Letters to Felice

Briefe über Cézanne. *See* Letters on Cézanne

"Brigadier and the Golf Widow, The" (Cheever, J.) MPII:SS I-308

Bright Shadow (Thomas, D.) MPII:AfAm I-194

Brighter Sun, A (Selvon) CLCII I-203; MPII:AfAm I-200; MPII:BCF I-185

Brighton Beach Memoirs (Simon, N.) CLCII I-205; MPII:D I-243

Brighton Rock (Greene) CLCII I-206; MPII:BCF I-191

Britannicus (Racine) CLC I-125; MP II-662

Broad and Alien Is the World (Alegría) CLC I-126; MP II-666; MP:AF I-144

Brod und Wein. *See* Bread and Wine

"Broken Boat" (Tu Fu) MPII:P I-292

"Broken Home, The" (Merrill, James) MPII:P I-295

Broken Jug, The (Kleist) CLC I-127; MP II-671

"Broken Tower, The" (Crane, H.) MPII:P I-298

Brontës and Their World, The (Bentley) MPII:JYABio I-278

Bronze Bow, The (Speare) MPII:JYAFic I-158

Bronze Horseman, The (Pushkin) MP II-674

Brosok na yug. *See* Story of a Life, The

Brother Ass (Barrios) MP II-677; MP:AF I-149

Brothers, The (Terence) CLC I-127; MP II-681

Brothers and Keepers (Wideman) MPII:AfAm I-206; MPII:NF I-212

Brothers Ashkenazi, The (Singer) CLC I-128; MP II-684; MP:EF I-140

Brothers Karamazov, The (Dostoevski) CLC I-129; MP II-688; MP:EF I-144

Brown Decades, The (Mumford) MP II-693

Brown Girl, Brownstones (Marshall) MPII:AfAm I-212

Browning Version, The (Rattigan) CLCII I-207; MPII:D I-250

Bruno's Dream (Murdoch) CLCII I-208; MPII:BCF I-196

Brushwood Boy, The (Kipling) CLC I-130; MP II-696; MP:BF I-143

Brut, The (Layamon) CLC I-131; MP II-699

Buchanan Dying (Updike) CLCII I-209; MPII:D I-255

Büchse der Pandora, Die. *See* Pandora's Box

"Buckdancer's Choice" (Dickey) MPII:P I-301

Buddenbrooks (Mann) CLC I-133; MP II-702; MP:EF I-150

Buddha in der Glorie. *See* Buddha in Glory

"Buddha in Glory" (Rilke) MPII:P I-304

Buenas conciencias, Las. *See* Good Conscience, The

"Building, The" (Larkin) MPII:P I-307

Bull from the Sea, The (Renault) CLCII II-831; MPII:BCF II-920

Bullet Park (Cheever, J.) CLCII I-210; MPII:AF I-216

Bullivant and the Lambs (Compton-Burnett) MP:BF I-147

Bulwark, The (Dreiser) CLC I-135; MP II-707; MP:AF I-154

Bumblebee Flies Anyway, The (Cormier) MPII:JYAFic I-162

Burger's Daughter (Gordimer) CLCII I-212; MPII:BCF I-201

Buried Alive. *See* House of the Dead, The

Buried Child (Shepard) CLCII I-213; MPII:D I-260

"Buried Life, The" (Arnold, M.) MPII:P I-310

Burmese Days (Orwell) CLCII I-214; MPII:BCF I-206

Burn, The (Aksyonov) CLCII I-215; MPII:WF I-200

"Burning a Book" (Stafford, W.) MPII:P I-313

"Burning Babe, The" (Southwell) MPII:P I-316

Burning Brand, The (Pavese) MPII:NF I-218

"Burning the Tomato Worms" (Forché) MPII:P I-319

Burning Water (Bowering) CLCII I-217; MPII:BCF I-211

Burnt-Out Case, A (Greene, G.) MP II-711; MP:BF I-150

Burr (Vidal) CLCII I-219; MPII:AF I-221

"Burrow, The" (Kafka) MPII:SS I-312

Bus Stop (Inge) CLCII I-221; MPII:D I-267

Bushk hiwa. *See* Secret History of the Lord of Musashi, The

Bussy d'Ambois (Chapman) CLC I-136; MP II-714

"But at the Stroke of Midnight" (Warner) MPII:SS I-316

"But so as by Fire" (Oppen) MPII:P I-322

Butley (Gray, S.) CLCII I-222; MPII:D I-273

Butt, Der. *See* Flounder, The

"Butterfly" (Sachs) MPII:P I-325

Buyer's Market, A. *See* Dance to the Music of Time, A

By Love Possessed (Cozzens) CLCII I-223; MPII:AF I-226

"Bypassing Rue Descartes" (Miłosz) MPII:P I-328

"Byzantium" (Yeats) MPII:P I-331

C

Cab at the Door, A (Pritchett) MPII:NF I-223

Cabala, The (Wilder, T.) CLC I-136; MP II-719; MP:AF I-159

Caballo de los sueños. *See* Dream Horse

Cabin, The (Blasco Ibáñez) CLC I-137; MP II-722; MP:EF I-156

Caddie Woodlawn (Brink, C.) MPII:JYAFic I-166

Cadmus (Unknown) CLC I-138; MP II-725; MP:EF I-160

Caesar and Cleopatra (Shaw) CLC I-138; MP II-728

Caesar or Nothing (Baroja) CLC I-139; MP II-731; MP:EF I-163

Caesars, The (Massie, A.) MPII:JYABio I-281

Cahier d'un retour au pays natal. *See* Return to My Native Land

Cain (Byron) CLC I-140; MP II-734

Caine Mutiny, The (Wouk) CLCII I-224; MPII:AF I-231

Cakes and Ale (Maugham) CLC I-140; MP II-737; MP:BF I-154

Caleb Williams (Godwin) CLC I-141; MP II-740; MP:BF I-158

Caliban's Filibuster (West, P.) CLCII I-225; MPII:BCF I-215

"California Swimming Pool" (Olds) MPII:P I-334

Caligula (Camus) CLCII I-226; MPII:D I-278

Call, The (Hersey) CLCII I-227; MPII:AF I-237

Call It Courage (Sperry) MPII:JYAFic I-170

Call It Sleep (Roth) MP II-744; MP:AF I-162

Call Me Charley (Jackson, J.) MPII:JYAFic I-173

Call of the Wild, The (London) CLC I-142; MP II-748; MP:AF I-167; MPII:JYAFic I-178

"Camberwell Beauty, The" (Pritchett) MPII:SS I-320

Cambio de piel. *See* Change of Skin, A

Cambridge (Phillips, C.) MPII:AfAm I-219

Camera Lucida (Barthes) MPII:NF I-227

Camera Obscura. *See* Laughter in the Dark

Camille (Dumas, *fils*) CLC I-142; MP II-751

Campaspe (Lyly) CLC I-143; MP II-754

Campion Towers (Beatty *and* Beatty) MPII:JYAFic I-182

"Canary for One, A" (Hemingway) MPII:SS I-323

Cancer Journals, The (Lorde) MPII:AfAm I-225

Cancer Ward (Solzhenitsyn) CLCII I-228; MPII:WF I-205

Candida (Shaw) CLC I-143; MP II-757

Candide (Voltaire) CLC I-144; MP II-759; MP:EF I-167; MPII:JYAFic I-185

Candle for St. Jude, A (Godden) MPII:JYAFic I-188

Candle in the Wind, The. *See* Once and Future King, The

Cane (Toomer) MPII:AfAm I-232

Cannery Row (Steinbeck) CLCII I-231; MPII:AF I-242

Cannibal, The (Hawkes) MP II-763; MP:AF I-171

"Canonization, The" (Donne) MPII:P I-337

Cantatrice chauve, La. *See* Bald Soprano, The

Canterbury Tales, The (Chaucer) CLC I-146; MP II-769

Canticle for Leibowitz, A (Miller, W.) CLCII I-233; MPII:AF I-247

"Canto 49" (Pound) MPII:P I-343

"Canto 1" (Pound) MPII:P I-340

"Canto 74" (Pound) MPII:P I-347

Cantos (Pound) MP II-776

"Cap for Steve, A" (Callaghan) MPII:SS I-326

Capricornia (Herbert, X.) CLCII I-234; MPII:BCF I-220

Captain Blackman (Williams, John) CLCII I-236; MPII:AF I-252; MPII:AfAm I-238

Captain Cook (Syme) MPII:JYABio I-285

Captain Digby Grand. *See* Digby Grand

Captain Horatio Hornblower (Forester) CLC I-148; MP II-779; MP:BF I-163. *See also* Horatio Hornblower series

Captain John Ericsson (Burnett, C.) MPII:JYABio I-289

Captain Singleton (Defoe) CLC I-149; MP II-783; MP:BF I-168

Captain with the Whiskers, The (Kiely) CLCII I-237; MPII:BCF I-225

Captain's Daughter, The (Pushkin) CLC I-150; MP II-792; MP:EF I-172

Captains Courageous (Kipling) CLC I-150; MP II-787; MP:BF I-173; MPII:JYAFic I-191

Captive Mind, The (Miłosz) MPII:NF I-232

Captives, The (Plautus) CLC I-151; MP II-797

"Careful" (Carver) MPII:SS I-330

Caretaker, The (Pinter) MP II-800

Carl Sandburg, Yes (Rogers) MPII:JYABio I-293

Carmen (Mérimée) CLC I-152; MP II-803; MP:EF I-178

Carmina (Catullus) MP II-806

Carrie's War (Bawden) MPII:JYAFic I-194

Carry on, Mr. Bowditch (Latham) MPII:JYABio I-296

Carta de creencia. See Letter of Testimony

Cartier Sails the St. Lawrence (Averill) MPII:JYABio I-299

Carved Lions, The (Molesworth) MPII:JYAFic I-198

Carvers' George (Means) MPII:JYABio I-303

Casa in collina, La. See House on the Hill, The

Casa verde, La. See Green House, The

Casamiento, El. See Marriage, The

Casanova's Chinese Restaurant. See Dance to the Music of Time, A, and Dance to the Music of Time: Second Movement, A

Case of Sergeant Grischa, The (Zweig) CLC I-152; MP II-809; MP:EF I-181

"Cask of Amontillado, The" (Poe) MPII:SS I-334

Cass Timberlane (Lewis, S.) CLC I-153; MP II-813; MP:AF I-178

Cassandra (Wolf) CLCII I-239; MPII:WF I-210

Caste (Robertson) CLC I-154; MP II-816

Castello dei destini incrociati, Il. See Castle of Crossed Destinies, The

Castle, The (Kafka) CLC I-154; MP II-820; MP:EF I-185

Castle of Crossed Destinies, The (Calvino) CLCII I-240; MPII:WF I-216

Castle of Fratta, The (Nievo) CLC I-155; MP II-823; MP:EF I-189

Castle of Llyr, The. See Prydain chronicles, The

Castle of Otranto, The (Walpole, Horace) CLC I-156; MP II-829; MP:BF I-178

Castle Rackrent (Edgeworth) CLC I-157; MP II-834; MP:BF I-183

Castle to Castle (Céline) CLCII I-241; MPII:WF I-221

Casuals of the Sea (McFee) CLC I-158; MP II-839; MP:BF I-189

"Casualty" (Heaney) MPII:P I-351

Cat, The (Colette) CLCII I-243; MPII:WF I-229

Cat and Mouse (Grass) MP II-842; MP:EF I-195

Cat Ate My Gymsuit, The (Danziger) MPII:JYAFic I-202

Cat on a Hot Tin Roof (Williams, T.) MP II-845

Cat Who Went to Heaven, The (Coatsworth) MPII:JYAFic I-206

"Catbird Seat, The" (Thurber) MPII:SS I-337

"Catch, The" (e) MPII:SS I-340

Catch-22 (Heller) MP II-848; MP:AF I-181

Catcher in the Rye, The (Salinger) CLCII I-244; MPII:AF I-259; MPII:JYAFic I-209

Catherine Carmier (Gaines) MPII:AfAm I-243

Cathleen ni Houlihan (Yeats) CLCII I-245; MPII:D I-284

Catiline (Jonson) CLC I-159; MP II-852

"Cats" (Baudelaire) MPII:P I-354

Cat's Cradle (Vonnegut) CLCII I-246; MPII:AF I-264

Caucasian Chalk Circle, The (Brecht) CLCII I-247; MPII:D I-288

Caught (Green, Henry) CLCII I-248; MPII:BCF I-230

Cavalier, The. See Woodstock

Cavaliere inesistente, Il. See Non-existent Knight, The

"Cavalleria Rusticana" (Verga) CLC I-160; MP II-855; MP:EF I-198

Caves du Vatican, Les. *See* Lafcadio's Adventures
Cawdor (Jeffers) CLC I-161; MP II-858
Cecilia (Burney) CLC I-162; MP II-861; MP:BF I-193
"Celebrated Jumping Frog of Calaveras County, The" (Twain) MPII:SS I-344
"Celestial Omnibus, The" (Forster) MPII:SS I-348
Celestina (Rojas) CLC I-163; MP II-865; MP:EF I-201
"Cemetery by the Sea, The" (Valéry) MPII:P I-357
Cenci, The (Artaud) CLCII I-249; MPII:D I-293
Cenci, The (Shelley, P.) CLC I-164; MP II-869
Centaur, The (Updike) CLCII I-250; MPII:AF I-269
Century of the Wind. *See* Memory of Fire
Ceremonies in Dark Old Men (Elder) MPII:AfAm I-249
Ceremony (Silko) MPII:JYAFic I-213
Ceremony in Lone Tree (Morris, Wright) MP II-872; MP:AF I-186
Ceremony of Innocence, The (Ribman) CLCII I-252; MPII:D I-299
Ceremony of Innocence, The (Highwater). *See* Ghost Horse cycle, The
César Birotteau (Balzac) CLC I-165; MP II-876; MP:EF I-206
César Chávez (Levy) MPII:JYABio I-307
Cesarz. *See* Emperor, The
Cette voix. *See* That Voice
Chain of Chance, The (Lem) CLCII I-253; MPII:WF I-234
"Chain of Love, A" (Price) MPII:SS I-351
Chain of Voices, A (Brink, A.) CLCII I-254; MPII:BCF I-235
Chainbearer, The (Cooper, J. F.) CLC I-166; MP II-880; MP:AF I-191
Chairs, The (Ionesco) CLCII I-255; MPII:D I-305
Chaises, Les. *See* Chairs, The
Chambre bleue, La. *See* Blue Room, The
Chambre claire, La. *See* Camera Lucida
Champion (Mead, C.) MPII:JYABio I-311
Chaneysville Incident, The (Bradley, D.) CLCII I-256; MPII:AF I-274; MPII:AfAm I-254

Change of Heart, A (Butor) CLCII I-257; MPII:WF I-239
Change of Skin, A (Fuentes) CLCII I-259; MPII:AF I-279
"Change" (Woiwode) MPII:SS I-355
Changeling, The (Middleton *and* Rowley) CLC I-167; MP II-885
Changing Light at Sandover, The (Merrill, James) MPII:P I-360
Changing Places (Lodge) CLCII I-260; MPII:BCF I-241
Changing Room, The (Storey) CLCII I-261; MPII:D I-312
"Channel Firing" (Hardy) MPII:P I-365
Chanson d'automne. *See* Autumn Song
Chanson du Mal-Aimé, La. *See* Song of the Poorly Loved, The
Chant of Jimmie Blacksmith, The (Keneally) CLCII I-262; MPII:BCF I-247
Chanticleer of Wilderness Road (Le Sueur) MPII:JYABio I-315
Chaplin, the Movies, and Charlie (Jacobs, D.) MPII:JYABio I-319
"Charles" (Jackson, S.) MPII:SS I-359
Charles Darwin (Gregor) MPII:JYABio I-323
Charles Darwin and the Origin of Species (Karp) MPII:JYABio I-326
Charles Darwin's Diary of the Voyage of H.M.S. *Beagle* (Darwin) MPII:JYABio I-330
Charles Demailly (Goncourt *and* Goncourt) CLC I-168; MP I-888; MP:EF I-210
Charles Dickens (Johnson, Edgar) MPII:JYABio I-336
Charles Dickens (Priestley) MPII:JYABio I-333
Charles O'Malley (Lever) CLC I-169; MP II-892; MP:BF I-198
Charley Starts from Scratch (Jackson) MPII:JYAFic I-173
Charlie and the Chocolate Factory (Dahl) MPII:JYAFic I-216
Charlotte's Web (White, E. B.) MPII:JYAFic I-220
Charmed Life (Jones, Diana) MPII:JYAFic I-224
Charterhouse of Parma, The (Stendhal) CLC I-169; MP II-895; MP:EF I-214

Chassidische Schriften. *See* Hasidic Scriptures

Chast' rechi. *See* Part of Speech, A

Chaste Maid in Cheapside, A (Middleton) CLC I-171; MP II-900

Chats, Les. *See* Cats

Chatte, La. *See* Cat, The

"Cheap in August" (Greene) MPII:SS I-361

Cheaper by the Dozen (Gilbreth *and* Carey, E.) MPII:JYABio I-340

Cheer the Lonesome Traveler (Lacy) MPII:JYABio I-344

"Chef-d'œuvre inconnu, Le." *See* "Unknown Masterpiece, The"

"Chelovek v futlyare." *See* "Man in a Case, The"

Chemins de la liberté, Les. *See* Roads to Freedom, The

Chemist Who Lost His Head, The (Grey) MPII:JYABio I-348

"Chemist's Wife, The" (Chekhov) MPII:SS I-364

Chercheuses de poux, Les. *See* Seekers of Lice, The

Chéri (Colette) CLC I-172; CLCII I-264; MP II-905; MP:EF I-219; MPII:WF I-243

Cherokee (Echenoz) CLCII I-265; MPII:WF I-248

Cherokee Chief (Clark, E.) MPII:JYABio I-352

Cherry Orchard, The (Chekhov) CLC I-173; MP II-908

Cheval sans tête, Le. *See* Horse Without a Head, The

Chevalier de Maison Rouge, The. *See* Chevalier of the Maison Rouge, The

Chevalier of the Maison Rouge, The (Dumas, *père*) CLC I-174; MP II-912; MP:EF I-223

Chevengur (Platonov) CLCII I-266; MPII:WF I-252

Cheyenne Autumn (Sandoz) CLCII I-267; MPII:AF I-285

Chiave a stella, La. *See* Monkey's Wrench, The

"Chicago" (Sandburg) MPII:P I-368

Chicago Poems (Sandburg) MP II-918

"Chickamauga" (Bierce) MPII:SS I-368

Chicken Soup with Barley (Wesker) CLCII I-269; MPII:D I-317

Chickencoop Chinaman, The (Chin) CLCII I-270; MPII:D I-323

Chiendent, Le. *See* Bark Tree, The

Chijin no ai. *See* Naomi

Child of the Owl (Yep) MPII:JYAFic I-227

Child Story. *See* Slow Homecoming

Childe Byron (Linney) CLCII I-271; MPII:D I-329

Childe Harold's Pilgrimage (Byron) MP II-921

"Childe Roland to the Dark Tower Came" (Browning, R.) MPII:P I-371

Childermass, The. *See* Human Age, The

Childhood and Schooldays. *See* Story of a Life, The

Childhood, Boyhood, Youth (Tolstoy) MP II-924; MP:EF I-229

"Childhood of Luvers, The" (Pasternak) MPII:SS I-372

Childhood's End (Clarke, Arthur C.) CLCII I-272; MPII:AF I-290; MPII:JYAFic I-230

Children of a Lesser God (Medoff) CLCII I-274; MPII:D I-335

Children of Crisis (Coles) MPII:NF I-237

Children of Dune. *See* Dune series, The

Children of God (Fisher) CLC I-175; MP II-927; MP:AF I-196

Children of Green Knowe, The. *See* Green Knowe books, The

Children of Heracles, The (Euripides) CLC I-176; MP II-930

Children of Kaywana. *See* Kaywana trilogy, The

Children of the Games. *See* Holy Terrors, The

Children of the Ghetto (Zangwill) CLC I-177; MP II-933; MP:BF I-202

Children of Violence (Lessing, D.) CLCII I-275; MPII:BCF I-252

"Children on Their Birthdays" (Capote) MPII:SS I-376

"Children's Campaign, The" (Lagerkvist) MPII:SS I-380

Children's Hour, The (Hellman) CLCII I-279; MPII:D I-341

"Child's Drawings, A" (Shalamov) MPII:SS I-384

Child's Reminiscence, A. *See* Out of the Cradle Endlessly Rocking

Childtimes (Greenfield *and* Little, L.) MPII:JYABio I-356

Chimmoku. *See* Silence

"Chimney Sweeper, The" (Blake) MPII:P I-374

Chimneys of Green Knowe, The. *See* Green Knowe books, The

China Men (Kingston) MPII:NF I-244

Chinaberry Tree, The (Fauset) MPII:AfAm I-259

Chinese des Schmerzes, Der. *See* Across

Chinese Wall, The (Frisch) CLCII I-280; MPII:D I-347

Chinesische Mauer, Die. *See* Chinese Wall, The

Chips with Everything (Wesker) MP II-937

Chita (Hearn) CLC I-178; MP II-940; MP:AF I-200

Chocolate Soldier, A (Colter) MPII:AfAm I-265

Chocolate War, The (Cormier) MPII:JYAFic I-233

Choice of Weapons, A (Parks) MPII:JYABio I-359

Chosen, The (Potok) CLCII I-281; MPII:AF I-295; MPII:JYAFic I-237

Chosen Place, the Timeless People, The (Marshall) MPII:AfAm I-271

Chouans, The (Balzac) CLC I-178; MP II-943; MP:EF I-232

Chrissie (Evert Lloyd) MPII:JYABio I-362

Christ Recrucified. *See* Greek Passion, The

Christ Stopped at Eboli (Levi, C.) CLCII I-283; MPII:WF I-257

"Christabel" (Coleridge) MPII:P I-377

Christmas Carol, A (Dickens) CLC I-179; MP II-947; MP:BF I-207

"Christmas Morning" (O'Connor, Frank) MPII:SS I-388

Christopher Columbus, Mariner (Morison) MPII:JYABio I-365

Chronicle of a Death Foretold (García Márquez) CLCII I-284; MPII:AF I-300

Chronicle of the Conquest of Granada, A (Irving, W.) MP II-950

Chronicle of the Fortunes of Richard Mahony, The. *See* Fortunes of Richard Mahony, The

Chronicles of Froissart (Froissart) MP II-953

Chronicles of Narnia, The (Lewis, C. S.) MPII:JYAFic I-240

Chronique (Perse) MP II-956

"Chrysanthemums, The" (Steinbeck) MPII:SS I-392

Chto k chemu. *See* What It's All About

"Church Going" (Larkin) MPII:P I-380

Ciascuno a suo modo. *See* Each in His Own Way

Cicero's Orations (Cicero) MP II-959

Cid, The (Corneille) CLC I-180; MP II-961

Cien años de soledad. *See* One Hundred Years of Solitude

Cimetière marin, Le. *See* Cemetery by the Sea, The

Cinkos, A. *See* Loser, The

Cinna (Corneille) CLC I-180; MP II-966

"Cinnamon Shops" (Schulz) MPII:SS I-396

Cinq-Mars (Vigny) CLC I-181; MP II-969; MP:EF I-236

Cinquième Fils, Le. *See* Fifth Son, The

Circle, The (Maugham) CLCII I-286; MPII:D I-353

Circle of Chalk, The (Unknown) CLC I-182; MP II-973

"Circular Ruins, The" (Borges) MPII:SS I-399

"Circus Animals' Desertion, The" (Yeats) MPII:P I-383

Circus Is Coming, The (Streatfeild) MPII:JYAFic I-245

"Cistern, The" (Seferis) MPII:P I-386

Citadel, The (Cronin) CLCII I-287; MPII:BCF I-262

Cities of Salt (Munif) CLCII I-287. *See also* Mudun al-milh

Citizen of New Salem (Horgan) MPII:JYABio I-369

Città e la casa, La. *See* City and the House, The

Città invisibili, Le. *See* Invisible Cities

City (Simak) MPII:JYAFic I-248

City and the House, The (Ginzburg) CLCII I-289; MPII:WF I-262

City and the Pillar, The (Vidal) CLCII I-291; MPII:AF I-306

City and the Stars, The. *See* Against the Fall of Night

City Builder, The (Konrád) CLCII I-292; MPII:WF I-267

"City in the Sea, The" (Poe) MPII:P I-389

Ciudad y los perros, La. *See* Time of the Hero, The

CIVIL warS, the (Wilson, R.) CLCII I-293; MPII:D I-358

Clair de lune. *See* Moonlight

Clara Barton (Boylston) MPII:JYABio I-373

Clarel (Melville) MPII:P I-392

Clarence Darrow (Faber) MPII:JYABio I-377

Clarence Darrow for the Defense (Stone, I.) MPII:JYABio I-381

Clarissa (Richardson, S.) CLC I-183; MP II-976; MP:BF I-211

Claudius the God and His Wife Messalina (Graves) CLC I-184; MP II-981; MP:BF I-216

"Clay" (Joyce) MPII:SS I-403

Clayhanger Trilogy, The (Bennett, A.) CLC I-185; MP II-984; MP:BF I-220

Clea. *See* Alexandria Quartet, The

"Clean, Well-Lighted Place, A" (Hemingway) MPII:SS I-406

Clear Horizon. *See* Pilgrimage

Clear Light of Day (Desai) CLCII I-294; MPII:BCF I-267

"Clear Night" (Paz) MPII:P I-397

Cleopatra (Leighton) MPII:JYABio I-385

Cleopatra's Children (Desmond) MPII:JYABio I-389

Cligés (Chrétien de Troyes) CLC I-187; MP II-989

Clinging to the Wreckage (Mortimer) MPII:NF I-249

Cloak of Light, A (Morris) MPII:NF IV-1696

Clockwork Orange, A (Burgess) CLCII I-295; MPII:BCF I-271; MPII:JYAFic I-251

Cloister and the Hearth, The (Reade) CLC I-188; MP II-993; MP:BF I-225

Closed Garden, The (Green, J.) CLC I-189; MP II-998; MP:EF I-240

Closely Watched Trains (Hrabal) CLCII I-296; MPII:WF I-272

Closing of the American Mind, The (Bloom, A.) MPII:NF I-255

Clotel (Brown, W.) MPII:AfAm I-277

"Cloud, Castle, Lake" (Nabokov) MPII:SS I-409

Cloud Forest, The (Matthiessen) MP II-1003

Cloud Howe. *See* Scots Quair, A

Cloud Nine (Churchill) CLCII I-297; MPII:D I-365

Clouds, The (Aristophanes) CLC I-189; MP II-1006

Cloven Viscount, The (Calvino) CLCII I-299; MPII:WF I-277

Clown, The (Böll) CLCII I-300; MPII:WF I-281

Cochise (Wyatt, E.) MPII:JYABio I-393

Cock-a-Doodle Dandy (O'Casey) CLCII I-301; MPII:D I-370

Cocktail Party, The (Eliot, T. S.) CLC I-190; MP II-1010

Coffin for Dimitrios, A (Ambler) CLCII I-303; MPII:BCF I-276

Cognizione del dolore, La. *See* Acquainted with Grief

Coin in Nine Hands, A (Yourcenar) CLCII I-304; MPII:WF I-286

Cold Comfort Farm (Gibbons) MP II-1016; MP:BF I-230

Cold Storage (Ribman) CLCII I-306; MPII:D I-377

Cold Wind Blowing, A. *See* Mantlemass series, The

"Collar, The" (Herbert, G.) MPII:P I-401

Collected Letters of D. H. Lawrence, The (Lawrence, D. H.) MP II-1019

Collected Poems (de la Mare) MP II-1022

Collected Poems, 1934-1952 (Thomas) MP II-1025

Collector, The (Fowles) CLCII I-307; MPII:BCF I-281

"Collector of Treasures, The" (Head) MPII:SS I-413

Collegians, The (Griffin) CLC I-191; MP II-1028; MP:BF I-234

Colomba (Mérimée) CLC I-192; MP II-1031; MP:EF I-245

Colonel Jacque. *See* History of Colonel Jacque, The

"Color of Darkness" (Purdy) MP II-1034; MP:AF I-203; MPII:SS I-418

Color Purple, The (Walker, A.) CLCII I-308; MPII:AF I-311; MPII:AfAm I-284; MPII:JYAFic I-255

"Colossus, The" (Plath) MPII:P I-404

Colours in the Dark (Reaney) CLCII I-309; MPII:D I-382

Columbus Sails (Hodges) MPII:JYABio I-397

Come Alive at 505 (Brancato) MPII:JYAFic I-258

Come Back, Little Sheba (Inge) CLCII I-310; MPII:D I-387

Come Sing, Jimmy Jo (Paterson) MPII:JYAFic I-261

Comedians, The (Greene) CLCII I-311; MPII:BCF I-288

Comedy of Calisto and Melibea," "The. See Celestina

Comedy of Errors, The (Shakespeare) CLC I-192; MP II-1037

"Comendadora, La." See "Nun, The"

Comforters, The (Spark) CLCII I-312; MPII:BCF I-293

"Coming, Aphrodite" (Cather) MPII:SS I-422

Coming into the Country (McPhee) MPII:NF I-260

Coming of Age in Mississippi (Moody) MPII:JYABio I-401

Coming Up Down Home (Brown, Cecil) MPII:AfAm I-290

Coming Up for Air (Orwell) CLCII I-314; MPII:BCF I-297

Comment aiment les filles. See Splendors and Miseries of Courtesans, The

Comment c'est. See How It Is

Commentaries (Caesar) MP II-1040

Common Reader, The. See Literary Essays of Virginia Woolf, The

Como en la guerra. See He Who Searches

Compagnie. See Company

Compagnons de la fortune, Les. See Companions of Fortune

Companions of Fortune (Guillot) MPII:JYAFic I-264

Company (Beckett) CLCII I-314; MPII:BCF I-303; MPII:WF I-291

"Company, The" (Creeley) MPII:P I-407

Company of Women, The (Gordon) CLCII I-316; MPII:AF I-315

Complaint, The (Young, E.) MP II-1042

Compleat Angler, The (Walton) MP II-1044

"Composed upon Westminster Bridge, September 3, 1802" (Wordsworth) MPII:P I-410

Compromise, The (Dovlatov) CLCII I-317; MPII:WF I-295

Comrades (Strindberg) CLC I-194; MP II-1047

Comte de Monte-Cristo, Le. See Count of Monte Cristo, The

Comus (Milton) CLC I-194; MP II-1051

"Concerning Exaggeration, or How, Properly, to Heap Up" (Olson) MPII:P I-414

Concerning Illustrious Men (Suetonius) MP II-1054

"Concerning Necessity" (Carruth) MPII:P I-417

Concluding (Green, Henry) CLCII I-318; MPII:BCF I-307

Conclusioni provvisorie. See Provisional Conclusions

Conclusive Evidence. See Speak, Memory

Concord Rebel (Derleth) MPII:JYABio I-405

Concrete (Bernhard) CLCII I-319; MPII:WF I-300

Condition, Elevation, Emigration, and Destiny of the Colored People of the United States Politically Considered, The (Delany, M.) MPII:AfAm I-296

Confederacy of Dunces, A (Toole) CLCII I-320; MPII:AF I-319

Confederate General from Big Sur, A (Brautigan) CLCII I-321; MPII:AF I-325

Confederates (Keneally) CLCII I-322; MPII:BCF I-312

Confession of a Fool, The (Strindberg) CLCII I-324; MPII:WF I-304

Confessions (Augustine) MP II-1057

Confessions (Rousseau) MP II-1060

Confessions of a Mask (Mishima) CLCII I-325; MPII:WF I-310

Confessions of an English Opium Eater (De Quincey) MP II-1063

Confessions of Felix Krull, Confidence Man (Mann) CLC I-195; MP II-1067; MP:EF I-249

Confessions of Nat Turner, The (Styron) CLCII I-326; MPII:AF I-330

Confessions of Zeno (Svevo) CLCII I-328; MPII:WF I-315

Confidence Man, The (Melville) CLC I-196; MP II-1071; MP:AF I-207

Confidential Clerk, The (Eliot, T. S.) MP II-1074

Confieso que he vivido. See Memoirs

Conformist, The (Moravia) CLCII I-329; MPII:WF I-319

Conformista, Il. See Conformist, The

"Conforti." See "Consolation"

Coningsby (Disraeli) CLC I-196; MP II-1077; MP:BF I-238

Conjectures of a Guilty Bystander (Merton) MPII:NF I-265

Conjure-Man Dies, The (Fisher, R.) MPII:AfAm I-302

Conjure Woman, The (Chesnutt) CLC I-197; MP II-1080; MP:AF I-211; MPII:AfAm I-308

Connecticut Yankee in King Arthur's Court, A (Twain) CLC I-198; MP II-1083; MP:AF I-215

Connection, The (Gelber) CLCII I-330; MPII:D I-391

"Connoisseur of Chaos" (Stevens, W.) MPII:P I-420

Conquered, The (Mitchison) MPII:JYAFic I-267

Conqueror and Hero (Krensky) MPII:JYABio I-409

Conquistador (MacLeish) MP II-1088

Conrad's War (Davies, A.) MPII:JYAFic I-270

Conscience of the Rich, The (Snow) MP II-1091; MP:BF I-242. See also Strangers and Brothers

Conscious Lovers, The (Steele, R.) CLC I-198; MP II-1094

Conservationist, The (Gordimer) CLCII I-331; MPII:BCF I-318

Considerations on the Principal Events of the French Revolution (Staël) MP II-1100

"Consolation" (Verga) MPII:SS I-425

Consolations of Philosophy, The (Boethius) MP II-1104

Conspiracy of Knaves (Brown, D.) MPII:JYAFic I-274

Constance (Clapp) MPII:JYAFic I-278

Consuelo (Sand) CLC I-199; MP II-1106; MP:EF I-253

"Contemplations" (Bradstreet) MPII:P II-423

Contender, The (Lipsyte) MPII:JYAFic I-281

Contending Forces (Hopkins, P.) MPII:AfAm I-313

Content of Our Character, The (Steele, S.) MPII:AfAm I-319

Contesto, Il. See Equal Danger

"Continuous" (Harrison) MPII:P II-427

Contractor, The (Storey) CLCII I-333; MPII:D I-397

"Convalescence" (Cunningham) MPII:P II-430

"Convergence of the Twain, The" (Hardy) MPII:P II-433

Conversation About Dante (Mandelstam, O.) MPII:NF I-270

Conversation in the Cathedral (Vargas Llosa) CLCII I-334; MPII:AF I-335

"Conversation with Leonardo, A" (Ciardi) MPII:P II-436

Conversations of Goethe with Eckermann and Soret (Eckermann) MP II-1109

Conversazione in Sicilia. See In Sicily

"Conversion of the Jews, The" (Roth) MPII:SS I-429

"Cool Web, The" (Graves) MPII:P II-440

Coonardoo (Prichard) CLCII I-335; MPII:BCF I-322

Copley (Ripley) MPII:JYABio I-412

Copperhead, The (Frederic) CLC I-200; MP II-1113; MP:AF I-220

"Corinna's Going A-Maying" (Herrick) MPII:P II-443

Coriolanus (Shakespeare) CLC I-201; MP II-1116

Corn Is Green, The (Williams, E.) CLCII I-336; MPII:D I-402

Cornerstone, The (Oldenbourg) MP II-1121; MP:EF I-257

"Corona" (Celan) MPII:P II-446

Coronation (Donoso) CLCII I-337;
   MPII:AF I-340
Coronel no tiene quien le escriba, El. *See*
   No One Writes to the Colonel
Correction (Bernhard) CLCII I-338;
   MPII:WF I-323
Corregidora (Jones, G.) CLCII I-339;
   MPII:AF I-346; MPII:AfAm I-324
Correspondances. *See* Correspondences
"Correspondence" (Coulette) MPII:P II-449
"Correspondences" (Baudelaire) MPII:P
   II-452
Corridors of Power. *See* Strangers and
   Brothers
Corsican Brothers, The (Dumas, *père*) CLC
   I-202; MP II-1124; MP:EF I-260
"Corsons Inlet" (Ammons) MPII:P II-455
Coscienza di Zeno, La. *See* Confessions of
   Zeno
Cosmos (Gombrowicz) CLCII I-340;
   MPII:WF I-328
Cossacks, The (Tolstoy) CLC I-203; MP
   II-1128; MP:EF I-264
Count Frontenac and New France Under
   Louis XIV (Parkman) MP II-1133
Count Julian (Goytisolo) CLCII III-974;
   MPII:WF III-958
Count of Monte-Cristo, The (Dumas, *père*)
   CLC I-204; MP II-1136;; MPII:JYAFic
   I-284
"Count's Wife, The" (Buzzati) MPII:SS
   I-448
Counterfeiters, The (Gide) CLC I-206; MP
   II-1140; MP:EF I-274
Counterfeiters, The (Kenner) MPII:NF I-275
"Counterparts" (Joyce) MPII:SS I-433
Counterpoints (Needham) MPII:NF I-281
Countess de Charny (Dumas, *père*) CLC
   I-207; MP II-1146; MP:EF I-281
Country Doctor, The (Balzac) CLC I-209;
   MP II-1152; MP:EF I-285
Country Doctor, A (Jewett) CLC I-208; MP
   II-1149; MP:AF I-224
"Country Doctor, A" (Kafka) MPII:SS I-437
Country Girls, The. *See* Country Girls
   Trilogy, The
Country Girls Trilogy, The (O'Brien, E.)
   CLCII I-341; MPII:BCF I-327

Country House, The (Galsworthy) CLC
   I-210; MP II-1155; MP:BF I-246
"Country Husband, The" (Cheever, J.)
   MPII:SS I-440
"Country Love Story, A" (Stafford)
   MPII:SS I-444
Country of the Pointed Firs, The (Jewett)
   CLC I-211; MP II-1158; MP:AF I-227
Country Place (Petry) MPII:AfAm I-330
"Country Stars" (Meredith, W.) MPII:P
   II-458
"Country Walk, A" (Kinsella) MPII:P II-4
Country Wife, The (Wycherley) CLC I-21
   MP II-1162
Coup, The (Updike) CLCII I-342; MPII:A
   I-351
Coup de dés jamais n'abolira le hasard, Un
   See Dice-Throw, A
Coup de Grâce (Yourcenar) CLCII I-344;
   MPII:WF I-332
Couples (Updike) CLCII I-345; MPII:AF
   I-356
Cours de linguistique générale. *See* Course
   in General Linguistics
Course in General Linguistics (Saussure)
   MPII:NF I-288
Court of the Stone Children, The (Cameron
   MPII:JYAFic I-289
Courtesan, The (Aretino) CLC I-212; MP
   II-1168
Courtship of Miles Standish, The
   (Longfellow) CLC I-213; MP II-1172
Cousin Bazilio (Eça de Queiróz) CLCII
   I-348; MPII:WF I-337
Cousin Bette (Balzac) CLC I-213; MP
   II-1175; MP:EF I-289
Cousin Pons (Balzac) CLC I-215; MP
   II-1180; MP:EF I-294
Cowards, The (Škvorecк) CLCII I-349;
   MPII:WF I-341
Coxcomb, The (Beaumont *and* Fletcher)
   CLC I-218; MP II-1185
"Cœur simple, Un." *See* "Simple Heart, A"
Crack-Up, The (Fitzgerald) MPII:NF I-293
Cradle Song, The (Martínez Sierra) CLC
   I-218; MP II-1188
Cranford (Gaskell) CLC I-219; MP II-1191;
   MP:BF I-250
Crazy Horse (Garst) MPII:JYABio I-416

"Crazy Jane Talks with the Bishop" (Yeats) MPII:P II-464

"Crazy Sunday" (Fitzgerald) MPII:SS I-452

Cream of the Jest, The (Cabell) CLC I-220; MP II-1194; MP:AF I-231

"Cricket, The" (Tuckerman) MPII:P II-467

Cricket in Times Square, The (Selden) MPII:JYAFic I-292

Crime and Punishment (Dostoevski) CLC I-221; MP II-1197; MP:EF I-299

Crime of Sylvestre Bonnard, The (France) CLC I-222; MP II-1202; MP:EF I-304

Crimes of the Heart (Henley) CLCII I-350; MPII:D I-407

Crisis, The (Churchill, W.) CLC I-223; MP II-1207; MP:AF I-235

Crisis, The (Paine) MP II-1211

Cristo si è fermato a Eboli. See Christ Stopped at Eboli

Critic, The (Sheridan) CLC I-224; MP II-1214

Critical Essays of William Hazlitt, The (Hazlitt) MP II-1217

"Critical Introduction to The Best of S. J. Perelman by Sidney Namlerep, A" (Perelman) MPII:SS I-456

Critical Path (Fuller, R. B.) MPII:NF I-299

"Critique de la Vie Quotidienne" (Barthelme, D.) MPII:SS I-459

Critique of Pure Reason (Kant) MP II-1220

Crock of Gold, The (Stephens) CLC I-224; MP III-1223; MP:BF I-254

Crome Yellow (Huxley, A.) CLC I-225; MP III-1226; MP:BF I-258

Crónica de una muerte anunciada. See Chronicle of a Death Foretold

Cross Creek (Rawlings) MPII:JYABio I-419

"Cross Ties" (Kennedy, X. J.) MPII:P II-470

"Crossing Brooklyn Ferry" (Whitman) MPII:P II-473

"Crossing into Poland" (Babel) MPII:SS II-463

Crotchet Castle (Peacock) CLC I-226; MP III-1229; MP:BF I-261

Crowds and Power (Canetti) MPII:NF I-304

Crucible, The (Miller, A.) CLCII I-351; MPII:D I-414

"Cruel and Barbarous Treatment" (McCarthy) MPII:SS II-467

"Cruise of The Breadwinner, The" (Bates) MPII:SS II-471

Cruise of the Cachalot, The (Bullen) CLC I-227; MP III-1232; MP:BF I-265

Cruising Speed (Buckley) MPII:NF I-310

Crusaders for Freedom (Commager) MPII:JYABio I-423

"Crusoe in England" (Bishop, E.) MPII:P II-476

Crusoe's Daughter (Gardam) CLCII I-352; MPII:BCF I-333

Cry, the Beloved Country (Paton) CLC I-227; MP III-1235; MP:EF I-310

Crying of Lot 49, The (Pynchon) CLCII I-354; MPII:AF I-361

Crystal World, The (Ballard) CLCII I-355; MPII:BCF I-339

Cudjo's Cave (Trowbridge) CLC I-228; MP III-1238; MP:AF I-239

Cultural Literacy (Hirsch) MPII:NF I-316

Culture and Anarchy (Arnold, M.) MP III-1242

Culture and Value (Wittgenstein) MPII:NF I-321

Cupid and Psyche (Unknown) CLC I-229; MP III-1245; MP:EF I-314

"Curriculum Vitae" (Menashe) MPII:P II-479

Curse of the Starving Class (Shepard) CLCII I-356; MPII:D I-420

Custer's Last Stand (Reynolds) MPII:JYABio I-427

Custom House, The (King, F.) CLCII I-357; MPII:BCF I-344

Custom of the Country, The (Wharton) CLC I-229; MP III-1249; MP:AF I-244

Cuttlefish, The (Witkiewicz) CLCII I-359; MPII:D I-425

Cyclone, The. See Strong Wind

Cyclops, The (Euripides) CLC I-230; MP III-1252

Cymbeline (Shakespeare) CLC I-231; MP III-1255

Cypresses Believe in God, The (Gironella) MP III-1259; MP:EF I-319

Cyrano de Bergerac (Rostand) CLC I-233; MP III-1262

Cyropaedia (Xenophon) MP III-1267; MP:EF I-322

D

Da (Leonard) CLCII I-360; MPII:D II-431

"Da" i "net." *See* "Yes" and "No"

"Daddy" (Plath) MPII:P II-482

Daddy Was a Number Runner (Meriwether) MPII:AfAm I-335

"Daddy Wolf" (Purdy) MPII:SS II-474

Dados eternos, Los. *See* Eternal Dice, The

Dagbok för Selma Lagerlöf. *See* Diary of Selma Lagerlöf, The

Dahomean, The (Yerby) MPII:AfAm I-341

Daisy Miller (James, H.) CLC I-234; MP III-1270; MP:AF I-248

Daiyon kampyki. *See* Inter Ice Age 4

Dalyokie gody. *See* Story of a Life, The

"Dama s sobachkoi." *See* "Lady with the Dog"

Damaged Souls (Bradford, G.) MP III-1273

Damals war es Friedrich. *See* Friedrich

Damballah. *See* Homewood trilogy, The

"Damballah" (Wideman) MPII:SS II-476

Dame Care (Sudermann) CLC I-234; MP III-1275; MP:EF I-326

"Damma s sobachkoi." *See* Lady with the Dog, The

Damnation of Theron Ware, The (Frederic) CLC I-235; MP III-1279; MP:AF I-251

Damned, The. *See* Wretched of the Earth, The

Damnés de la terre, Les. *See* Wretched of the Earth, The

Dämonen, Die. *See* Demons, The

Damskii master. *See* Ladies' Hairdresser

Dance in the Sun, A (Jacobson) CLCII I-361; MPII:BCF I-350

Dance of Death, The (Strindberg) CLC I-236; MP III-1283

Dance of the Forests, A (Soyinka) CLCII I-362; MPII:D II-437

Dance to the Music of Time, A (Powell) MP III-1288; MP:BF I-269

Dance to the Music of Time: Second Movement, A (Powell) MP III-1293

Dance to the Piper (De Mille) MPII:JYABio I-431

Dandelion Wine (Bradbury) MPII:JYAFic I-295

Dangerous Acquaintances (Laclos) CLC I-236; MP III-1299; MP:EF I-330

Dangerous Connections. *See* Dangerous Acquaintances

"Dangers de l'inconduite, Les." *See* "Gobseck"

Dangling Man (Bellow) CLCII I-363; MPII:AF I-366

Daniel Boone (Brown, J.) MPII:JYABio I-439

Daniel Boone (Daugherty, J.) MPII:JYABio I-435

Daniel Deronda (Eliot, G.) CLC I-237; MP III-1304; MP:BF I-278

Daniel Martin (Fowles) CLCII I-364; MPII:BCF I-354

Dans le labyrinthe. *See* In the Labyrinth

Danse Macabre (King, S.) MPII:NF I-327

Dante (Eliot, T. S.) MP III-1308

"Dante and the Lobster" (Beckett) MPII:SS II-480

Daphnis and Chloë (Longus) CLC I-239; MP III-1310; MP:EF I-335

Dar. *See* Gift, The

"Daring Young Man on the Flying Trapeze, The" (Saroyan) MPII:SS II-484

Dark Behind the Curtain, The (Cross) MPII:JYAFic I-298

Dark Child, The (Laye) CLCII I-366; MPII:WF I-345

"Dark City, The" (Aiken) MPII:SS II-488

Dark Is Rising sequence, The (Cooper, S.) MPII:JYAFic I-302

Dark Journey, The (Green, J.) CLC I-240; MP III-1313; MP:EF I-338

Dark Laughter (Anderson, S.) CLC I-241; MP III-1317; MP:AF I-255

Darkness at Noon (Koestler) CLC I-242; MP III-1321; MP:EF I-342

Darkness Visible (Golding) CLCII I-367; MPII:BCF I-360

"Darling, The" (Chekhov) MPII:SS I-492

Daughter of Earth (Smedley) CLCII I-368; MPII:AF I-373

Daughter of Han, A (Pruitt) MPII:JYABio I-443

Daughters (Marshall) MPII:AfAm I-345

"Daughters of the Late Colonel, The" (Mansfield) MPII:SS II-495

David. *See* I Am David

David Copperfield (Dickens) CLC I-242; MP III-1324; MP:BF I-283; MPII:JYAFic I-307

David Harum (Westcott) CLC I-247; MP III-1331; MP:AF I-260

Davita's Harp (Potok) MPII:JYAFic I-311

Dawn. *See* Xenogenesis Trilogy, The.

"Dawn of Remembered Spring" (Stuart) MPII:SS II-499

Dawni mistrzowie. *See* Old Masters

Dawn's Left Hand. *See* Pilgrimage

Day in the Death of Joe Egg, A (Nichols) CLCII I-370; MPII:D II-443

"Day Lady Died, The" (O'Hara, F.) MPII:P II-485

Day Lincoln Was Shot, The (Bishop, J.) MPII:JYABio I-447

Day No Pigs Would Die, A (Peck, Robert) MPII:JYAFic I-315

Day of Pleasure, A (Singer) MPII:JYABio I-451

Day of the Scorpion, The. *See* Raj Quartet, The

"Day Stalin Died, The" (Lessing, D.) MPII:SS II-502

"Day the Flowers Came, The" (Madden) MPII:SS II-507

Days of Hope. *See* Man's Hope

Days of the Turbins (Bulgakov) CLCII I-371; MPII:D II-449

De abajo, Los. *See* Underdogs, The

"De Daumier-Smith's Blue Period" (Salinger) MPII:SS II-546

De dónde son los cantantes. *See* From Cuba with a Song

De la grammatologie. *See* Of Grammatology

De Profundis (Wilde) MP III-1334

De quelques formes primitives de classification. *See* Primitive Classification

De Rerum Natura (Lucretius) MP III-1337

"Dead, The" (Joyce) CLCII I-372; MPII:SS II-510

Dead Class, The (Kantor, T.) CLCII I-373; MPII:D II-456

Dead Fires (Lins do Rêgo) CLC I-247; MP III-1339

"Dead Gallop" (Neruda) MPII:P II-488

Dead Man Leading (Pritchett) CLCII I-374; MPII:BCF I-364

Dead Souls (Gogol) CLC I-248; MP III-1342; MP:EF I-345

Dead Yesterdays. *See* All Our Yesterdays

Deadlock. *See* Pilgrimage

Deaf Child Listened, A (Neimark) MPII:JYABio I-455

"Deal in Wheat, A" (Norris) MPII:SS II-516

Dean's December, The (Bellow) CLCII I-375; MPII:AF I-378

Dear Brutus (Barrie) CLC I-249; MP III-1345

"Dear John, Dear Coltrane" (Harper, M.) MPII:P II-491

Dear Mr. Henshaw (Cleary) MPII:JYAFic I-318

Dear Shadows (Wain) MPII:NF I-331

"Death and the Child" (Crane, S.) MPII:SS II-520

Death and the King's Horseman (Soyinka) CLCII I-377; MPII:D II-463

Death and the Lover. *See* Narcissus and Goldmund

"Death be not proud" (Donne) MPII:P II-495

Death Be Not Proud (Gunther) MPII:JYABio I-459

Death Comes for the Archbishop (Cather) CLC I-251; MP III-1349; MP:AF I-264

"Death Fugue" (Celan) MPII:P II-498

"Death in Midsummer" (Mishima) MPII:SS II-524

Death in the Afternoon (Hemingway) MPII:NF I-337

"Death in the Dawn" (Soyinka) MPII:P II-501

Death in the Family, A (Agee, James) MP III-1354; MP:AF I-269; MPII:JYAFic I-321

"Death in the Woods" (Anderson) MPII:SS II-528

"Death in Venice" (Mann) CLC I-253; MP III-1357; MP:EF I-349; MPII:SS II-532

Death of a Beekeeper, The (Gustafsson) CLCII I-378; MPII:WF I-349

Death of a Hero (Aldington) CLC I-254; MP III-1362; MP:BF I-291

"Death of a Huntsman" (Bates) MPII:SS
II-535

Death of a Salesman (Miller, A.) CLC
I-255; MP III-1365

"Death of a Traveling Salesman" (Welty)
MPII:SS II-539

Death of Ahasuerus, The. *See* Tobias
trilogy, The

Death of Artemio Cruz, The (Fuentes) MP
III-1369; MP:AF I-273

Death of Grass, The (Christopher)
MPII:JYAFic I-324

"Death of Ivan Ilyich, The" (Tolstoy) CLC
I-256; MP III-1373; MP:EF I-354;
MPII:SS II-542

Death of Synge and Other Passages from an
Old Diary, The. *See* Autobiography of
William Butler Yeats, The

Death of the Fox (Garrett) CLCII I-379;
MPII:AF I-384

Death of the Gods, The (Merezhkowsky)
CLC I-256; MP III-1377; MP:EF I-359

Death of the Heart, The (Bowen, E.) CLC
I-257; MP III-1381; MP:BF I-295;
MPII:JYAFic I-327

Death of Virgil, The (Broch) CLC I-257;
MP III-1385; MP:EF I-363

Death on the Installment Plan (Céline)
CLCII I-380; MPII:WF I-353

Death Ship, The (Traven) MP III-1388;
MP:AF I-278

"Death's Blue-Eyed Girl" (Pastan) MPII:P
II-505

Death's Duell (Donne) MP III-1391

Deathwatch (Genet) CLCII I-382; MPII:D
II-471

Deathwatch (White, R.) MPII:JYAFic I-330

Debit and Credit (Freytag) CLC I-258; MP
III-1393; MP:EF I-367

Deborah Sampson (Felton) MPII:JYABio
I-463

Debut, The (Brookner) CLCII I-383;
MPII:BCF I-370

Decadence. *See* Artamonov Business, The

Decameron, The (Boccaccio) MP III-1397;
MP:EF I-371

Decay of the Angel, The. *See* Sea of
Fertility, The

Decline and Fall (Waugh) CLC I-259; MP
III-1404; MP:BF I-299

Deephaven (Jewett) CLC I-260; MP
III-1409; MP:AF I-282

"Deer Dance/For Your Return" (Silko)
MPII:P II-508

Deerslayer, The (Cooper, J. F.) CLC I-260;
MP III-1413; MP:AF I-286. *See also*
Leatherstocking Tales, The

Defence of Guenevere and Other Poems,
The (Morris, William) MP III-1417

Defence of Poesie (Sidney) MP III-1420

Defence of Poetry, A (Shelley, P.) MP
III-1423

"Defender of the Faith" (Roth) MPII:SS
II-550

Defenestration of Prague (Howe, S.) MPII:P
II-511

Defense, The (Nabokov) CLCII I-384;
MPII:WF I-359

Defense of the Constitutions of Government
of the United States of America, A
(Adams, J.) MP III-1426

"Definition of Love, The" (Marvell) MPII:P
II-516

Deirdre (Stephens) CLC I-262; MP
III-1428; MP:BF I-305

Deirdre of the Sorrows (Synge) CLC I-263;
MP III-1432

"Dejection" (Coleridge) MPII:P II-519

Delicate Balance, A (Albee) CLCII I-385;
MPII:D II-475

"Delicate Prey, The" (Bowles, P.) MPII:SS
II-553

"Delight in Disorder" (Herrick) MPII:P
II-522

Delphine (Staël) CLC I-263; MP III-1436;
MP:EF I-380

"Delta Autumn" (Faulkner) MPII:SS II-557

Delta Wedding (Welty) CLC I-264; MP
III-1439; MP:AF I-290

"Deluge at Norderney, The" (Dinesen)
MPII:SS II-561

Dem (Kelley, W.) MPII:AfAm I-351

Demian (Hesse) CLCII I-386; MPII:JYAFic
I-333; MPII:WF I-364

Democracy (Didion) CLCII I-387; MPII:AF
I-389

Democracy in America (Tocqueville) MP
III-1443
Democratic Vistas (Whitman) MP III-1446
Demon, The (Lermontov) MP III-1449
"Demon Lover, The" (Bowen, E.) MPII:SS
II-565
Demons, The (Doderer) CLCII I-389;
MPII:WF I-369
Den som inte hoppas. See He Who Does
Not Hope
Denier du rêve. See Coin in Nine Hands, A
Deptford Trilogy, The (Davies, R.) CLCII
I-390; MPII:BCF I-375
Deputy, The (Hochhuth) CLCII I-393;
MPII:D II-481
Dernier des Justes, Le. See Last of the Just, The
Dernière Incarnation de Vautrin, La. See
Splendors and Miseries of Courtesans, The
"Descent, The" (Williams, W.) MPII:P
II-525
Descent into Hell (Williams, Charles) MP
III-1452; MP:BF I-310
"Descent into the Maelström, A" (Poe)
MPII:SS II-568
Descent of Man, and Selection in Relation
to Sex (Darwin) MP III-1455
"Desdichado, El" (Nerval) MPII:P II-528
Desert Exile (Uchida) MPII:JYABio I-467
Desert Solitaire (Abbey) MPII:NF I-342
"Deserted Village, The" (Goldsmith)
MPII:P II-531
Deserto dei Tartari, Il. See Tartar Steppe,
The
Desierta de piedra. See Stone Desert
Design for Living (Coward) CLCII I-394;
MPII:D II-486
Desire Under the Elms (O'Neill) CLC
I-265; MP III-1458
"Désirée's Baby" (Chopin) MPII:SS II-572
Dessa Rose (Williams, S.) MPII:AfAm
I-357
Destiny Bay (Byrne) CLC I-266; MP
III-1463; MP:BF I-314
Det heliga landet. See Tobias trilogy, The
Detained (Ngugi) MPII:NF I-348
"Detective Story" (Auden) MPII:P II-535
"Detskie kartinki." See "Child's Drawings, A"
"Detstvo Lyuvers." See "Childhood of
Luvers, The"

Deuxième Sexe, Le. See Second Sex, The
"Devil and Daniel Webster, The" (Benét)
MPII:SS II-575
"Devil and Tom Walker, The" (Irving, W.)
MPII:SS II-579
Devil in a Blue Dress (Mosley) MPII:AfAm
I-362
Devil upon Two Sticks. See Diable boiteux,
Le
Devils, The (Dostoevski). See Possessed,
The
Devils, The (Whiting) CLCII I-395; MPII:D
II-492
Devil's Elixir, The (Hoffman) CLC I-267;
MP III-1467; MP:EF I-384
Devotion (Strauss) CLCII I-396; MPII:WF
I-376
Devotion of the Cross, The (Calderón de la
Barca) CLC I-267; MP III-1471
"Devouring Time, blunt thou the lion's
paws," See Sonnet 19
Dharma Bums, The (Kerouac) CLCII I-397;
MPII:AF I-394
"Di Grasso" (Babel) MPII:SS II-600
Diable boiteux, Le (Lesage) CLC I-268; MP
III-1474; MP:EF I-388
Diaczego Klaysycy. See Why the Classics
Dialogic Imagination, The (Bakhtin)
MPII:NF I-355
Dialogue des héros de roman
(Boileau-Despréaux) MP III-1479
Dialogues of Plato, The (Plato) MP III-1482
"Diamond as Big as the Ritz, The"
(Fitzgerald) MPII:SS II-582
"Diamond Lens, The" (O'Brien, F.)
MPII:SS II-587
Diana of the Crossways (Meredith, G.) CLC
I-269; MP III-1486; MP:BF I-318
Diaries of Kafka: 1910-1923, The (Kafka)
MP III-1491
Diaries of Paul Klee, The (Klee) MPII:NF
I-361
Diario de la guerra del cerdo. See Diary of
the War of the Pig
Diary (Evelyn) MP III-1494
Diary (Gombrowicz) MPII:NF I-367
Diary (Pepys) MP III-1497
Diary and Letters of Mme. D'Arblay, The
(Burney) MP III-1499

Diary of a Country Priest, The (Bernanos) CLC I-270; MP III-1503; MP:EF I-394

Diary of a Mad Old Man (Tanizaki) CLCII I-398; MPII:WF I-381

"Diary of a Madman, The" (Gogol) MPII:SS II-591

Diary of a Writer (Dostoevski) MP III-1506

Diary of a Young Girl, The (Frank) MPII:JYABio I-471

Diary of Anaïs Nin, The (Nin) MPII:NF I-373

Diary of Henry Crabb Robinson, The (Robinson, H.) MP III-1509

Diary of Selma Lagerlöf, The (Lagerlöf) MPII:NF I-380

Diary of the War of the Pig (Bioy Casares) CLCII I-399; MPII:AF I-400

Diary of Virginia Woolf, The (Woolf) MPII:NF I-386

"Dice-Throw, A" (Mallarmé) MPII:P II-538

Dicey's Song (Voigt) MPII:JYAFic I-337

"Dichter, Der." See "Poet, The"

"Difference, The" (Glasgow) MPII:SS II-595

Different Drummer, A (Kelley, W.) CLCII I-400; MPII:AF I-404; MPII:AfAm I-368

Digby Grand (Whyte-Melville) CLC I-270; MP III-1512; MP:BF I-324

"Digging" (Heaney) MPII:P II-542

Dimanche de la vie, Le. See Sunday of Life, The

Dimitri Roudine. See Rudin

Dimple Hill. See Pilgrimage

Dining Room, The (Gurney) CLCII I-402; MPII:D II-497

Dinner at the Homesick Restaurant (Tyler) CLCII I-403; MPII:AF I-409

Dinner Party, The (Mauriac, C.) MP III-1516; MP:EF I-398

"Directive" (Frost) MPII:P II-545

"Dirge" (Fearing) MPII:P II-549

Dirty Linen (Stoppard) CLCII I-404; MPII:D II-502

"Disabled Debauchee, The" (Wilmot) MPII:P II-552

Disappearance, The (Guy) MPII:JYAFic I-341

Disappearing Acts (McMillan) MPII:AfAm I-373

Disciple, The (Bourget) CLC I-271; MP III-1519; MP:EF I-402

Disclosing the Past (Leakey) MPII:JYABio I-475

Discourse on the Origin of Inequality (Rousseau) MP III-1522

Discourses (Aretino) MP III-1524

Discoverer of the Unseen World (Payne, A.) MPII:JYABio I-479

"Disent les imbéciles." See "Fools Say"

Disinherited Mind, The (Heller) MPII:NF I-393

"Disorder and Early Sorrow" (Mann) MPII:SS II-604

Dispatches (Herr) MPII:NF I-398

"Displaced Person, The" (O'Connor, Flannery) MPII:SS II-607

Dispossessed, The (Le Guin) CLCII I-405; MPII:AF I-413

Disprezzo, Il. See Ghost at Noon, A

"Distant Episode, A" (Bowles, P.) MPII:SS II-610

"Distant Footsteps, The" (Vallejo) MPII:P II-555

Distant Relations (Fuentes) CLCII I-406; MPII:AF I-418

"District Doctor, The" (Turgenev) MPII:SS II-614

Divan, The (Hfiz) MP III-1527

"Divers Doth Use" (Wyatt, T.) MPII:P II-558

Divine Comedy, The (Dante Alighieri) CLC I-272; MP III-1529

Divine Fire, The (Sinclair, M.) CLC I-275; MP III-1534; MP:BF I-329

Divine Love and Wisdom (Swedenborg) MP III-1537

Diviners, The (Laurence) CLCII I-407; MPII:BCF I-383

"Diving into the Wreck" (Rich) MPII:P II-561

Division of the Spoils, A. See Raj Quartet, The

"Diwan Trilogy" (Ekelöf) MPII:P II-564

Dwn över Fursten av Emgión. See Diwan Trilogy

Dni Turbinykh. See Day of the Turbins

"Do Not Go Gentle into That Good Night" (Thomas, D.) MPII:P II-569

"Dockery and Son" (Larkin) MPII:P II-572

Dr. Beaumont and the Man with the Hole in His Stomach (Epstein *and* Epstein) MPII:JYABio I-482

Doctor Copernicus (Banville) CLCII II-409; MPII:BCF I-388

Dr. Elizabeth (Clapp) MPII:JYABio I-485

Doctor Faustus (Mann) CLC I-276; MP III-1539; MP:EF I-406

Doctor Faustus (Marlowe) CLC I-278; MP III-1543

"Dr. Heidegger's Experiment" (Hawthorne) MPII:SS II-617

Doctor in Spite of Himself, The (Molière) CLC I-279; MP III-1546

Dr. Jekyll and Mr. Hyde (Stevenson) CLC I-280; MP III-1550; MP:BF I-333

Dr. Johnson and His World (Brown, I.) MPII:JYABio I-489

Doctor Pascal (Zola) CLC I-280; MP III-1553; MP:EF I-411

Dr. Schweitzer of Lambaréné (Cousins) MPII:JYABio I-493

Doctor Thorne (Trollope) CLC I-281; MP III-1558; MP:BF I-337

Doctor Tom Dooley, My Story (Dooley) MPII:JYABio II-497

Doctor Zhivago (Pasternak) MP III-1561; MP:EF I-417

"Doctor's Son, The" (O'Hara, J.) MPII:SS II-621

Dodsworth (Lewis, S.) CLC I-283; MP III-1565; MP:AF I-294

"Dog" (Ferlinghetti) MPII:P II-575

Dog Beneath the Skin, The (Auden *and* Isherwood) CLCII II-410; MPII:D II-507

Dog Soldiers (Stone, R.) CLCII II-411; MPII:AF I-423

Dog Years (Grass) CLCII II-412; MPII:WF I-386

Doidinho. *See* Plantation Boy

"Doktor Murkes gesammeltes Schweigen." *See* "Murke's Collected Silences"

Dolina Issy. *See* Issa Valley, The

Dollmaker, The (Arnow) CLCII II-414; MPII:AF I-428

Doll's House, A (Ibsen) CLC I-284; MP III-1570

Dom na naberezhnoi. *See* House on the Embankment, The

Dombey and Son (Dickens) CLC I-286; MP III-1574; MP:BF I-341

Dominique (Fromentin) CLC I-288; MP III-1579; MP:EF I-422

"Domino" (Merrill, James) MPII:P II-579

Don Carlos (Schiller) CLC I-289; MP III-1582

Don Flows Home to the Sea, The (Sholokhov) CLC I-290; MP III-1585; MP:EF I-426

Don Goyo (Aguilera Malta) CLCII II-416; MPII:AF I-434

Don Juan (Byron) CLC I-291; MP III-1590

Don Juan (Molière) CLC I-293; MP III-1595

Don Juan Tenorio (Zorrilla) CLC I-294; MP III-1599

Don Quixote de la Mancha (Cervantes) CLC I-294; MP III-1603; MP:EF I-431

Don Segundo Sombra (Güiraldes) CLC I-296; MP III-1609; MP:AF I-299

Doña Bárbara (Gallegos) CLC I-296; MP III-1614; MP:AF I-304

Dona Flor and Her Two Husbands (Amado) CLCII II-416; MPII:AF I-439

Doña Perfecta (Pérez Galdós) CLC I-298; MP III-1618; MP:EF I-438

"Donagh, The" (Carleton) MPII:SS II-624

Donne di Messina, Le. *See* Women of Messina

Don't Ride the Bus on Monday (Meriwether) MPII:JYABio II-500

Doomed City, The. *See* City in the Sea, The

Door in the Wall, The (de Angeli) MPII:JYAFic I-344

Dopisy Olze. *See* Letters to Olga

Dôra, Doralina (Queiroz) CLCII II-418; MPII:AF I-445

"Dordogne" (Ekelöf) MPII:P II-582

"Dos Elenas, Las." *See* "Two Elenas, The"

Dostoevsky (Berdyaev) MP III-1621

Dotazník, aneb modlitba za jedno msto a přítele. *See* Questionnaire, The

Double, The (Dostoevski) CLCII II-419; MPII:WF I-390

Double-Dealer, The (Congreve) CLC I-298; MP III-1624

Double Helix, The (Watson) MPII:JYABio
II-503; MPII:NF I-404
Double Life of Pocahontas, The (Fritz)
MPII:JYABio II-507
Dove (Graham, R.) MPII:JYABio II-510
"Dove, That Stayed Outside" (Rilke)
MPII:P II-585
"Dover Beach" (Arnold, M.) MPII:P II-588
Down and Out in Paris and London
(Orwell) MPII:NF I-409
Down from the Hill (Sillitoe) CLCII II-420;
MPII:BCF I-393
Down There (Huysmans) CLC I-300; MP
III-1627; MP:EF I-441
Downfall, The (Zola) CLC I-300; MP
III-1629; MP:EF I-444
Dracula (Stoker) CLC I-301; MP III-1633;
MP:BF I-347
"Draft of Shadows, A" (Paz) MPII:P II-592
Dragon Can't Dance, The (Lovelace) CLCII
II-421; MPII:AfAm I-379; MPII:BCF I-398
Dragon Seed (Buck) CLC I-302; MP
III-1638; MP:AF I-309
Dragon's Teeth. See Cousin Bazilio
Dragonsong (McCaffrey) MPII:JYAFic I-347
Dragonwings (Yep) MPII:JYAFic I-350
Dram-shop, The. See Drink
Dramatic Lyrics. See Dramatic Monologues
and Lyrics of Browning
Dramatic Monologues and Lyrics of
Browning (Browning, R.) MP III-1641
Dramatic Romances and Lyrics. See
Dramatic Monologues and Lyrics of
Browning
Dramatis Personae (Browning, R.) MP
III-1644
Dramatis Personae (Yeats). See
Autobiography of William Butler Yeats,
The
"Dream Horse" (Neruda) MPII:P II-596
Dream Journey, A (Hanley) CLCII II-423;
MPII:BCF I-403
"Dream of a Ridiculous Man, The"
(Dostoevski) MPII:SS II-628
Dream of the Golden Mountains, The
(Cowley) MPII:NF I-414
Dream of the Red Chamber (Tsao Hsüeh-
ch'in) CLC I-302; MP III-1648;
MP:EF I-448

Dream on Monkey Mountain (Walcott)
CLCII II-424; MPII:AfAm I-385;
MPII:D II-513
Dream Play, A (Strindberg) CLCII II-425;
MPII:D II-518
Dream Songs, The (Berryman) MPII:P
II-600
Dream-Time, The (Treece) MPII:JYAFic
I-354
"Dream Variations" (Hughes, L.) MPII:P
II-605
Dreambook for Our Time, A (Konwicki)
CLCII II-426; MPII:WF I-395
Dreamers and Doers (Richards, N.)
MPII:JYABio II-513
"Dreamers in a Dead Language" (Paley)
MPII:SS II-632
Dreams into Deeds (Peavy and Smith, U.)
MPII:JYABio II-517
Dreamsnake (McIntyre) MPII:JYAFic I-357
Dreigroschenoper, Die. See Threepenny
Opera, The
Drink (Zola) CLC I-306; MP III-1653;
MP:EF I-454
Drinking Gourd, The (Monjo) MPII:JYAFic
I-360
"Drive in the Country, A" (Greene)
MPII:SS II-636
Drömspel, Ett. See Dream Play, A
"Drover's Wife, The" (Lawson) MPII:SS
II-639
Drowned and the Saved, The (Levi)
MPII:NF I-420
Drugaya zhizn'. See Another Life
Drugie Berega. See Speak, Memory
Drums (Boyd) CLC I-307; MP III-1656;
MP:AF I-313
Drums Along the Mohawk (Edmonds) CLC
I-307; MP III-1659; MP:AF I-317
Drums Under the Window. See Mirror in
My House
"Drunkard, The" (O'Connor, Frank)
MPII:SS II-643
"Drunken Boat, The" (Rimbaud) MPII:P
II-608
"Dry September" (Faulkner) MPII:SS II-646
Duce, Il (Lyttle) MPII:JYABio II-521
Duchess of Malfi, The (Webster) CLC
I-308; MP III-1664

"Duel, The" (Chekhov) CLCII II-428;
    MPII:SS II-650
"Duel" (Matheson) MPII:SS II-653
Duino Elegies (Rilke) MP III-1669
Duke (Gutman) MPII:JYABio II-525
"Dulce et Decorum Est" (Owen) MPII:P
    II-611
Dumb Waiter, The (Pinter) CLCII II-429;
    MPII:D II-524
D'un château l'autre. See Castle to Castle
Dunciad, The (Pope) MP III-1672
Dune. See Dune series, The
Dune Messiah. See Dune series, The
Dune series, The (Herbert, F.) CLCII
    II-430; MPII:AF I-451; MPII:JYAFic
    I-363
"Dunwich Horror, The" (Lovecraft)
    MPII:SS II-657
Durango Street (Bonham) MPII:JYAFic
    I-368

"Dushechka." See "Darling, The"
Dust Tracks on a Road (Hurston)
    MPII:AfAm I-390; MPII:JYABio II-529
Dusty Answer (Lehmann) CLCII II-433;
    MPII:BCF I-408
Dutchman (Baraka) CLCII II-434;
    MPII:AfAm I-394; MPII:D II-529
"Dvadtsat'shest' i odna." See "Twenty-six
    Men and a Girl"
Dvärgen. See Dwarf, The
Dvenadtsat'. See Twelve, The
Dvoynik. See Double, The
Dwarf, The (Lagerkvist) CLCII II-435;
    MPII:WF I-399
Dying. See I heard a Fly buzz—when I
    died—
Dynasts, The (Hardy) CLC I-310; MP
    III-1675
Dziennik. See Diary

E

Each in His Own Way (Pirandello) CLCII
II-436; MPII:D II-534

Eagle and the Serpent, The (Guzmán) MP
III-1679; MP:AF I-322

Eagle of the Ninth, The (Sutcliff)
MPII:JYAFic I-371

Early Diary of Anaïs Nin, The. *See* Diary of
Anaïs Nin, The

Earth (Zola) CLC I-311; MP III-1682;
MP:EF I-458

Earthly Paradise, The (Morris, William) MP
III-1687

Earthly Powers (Burgess) CLCII II-437;
MPII:BCF I-413

"Earthquake in Chile, The" (Kleist)
MPII:SS II-661

Earthsea series, The (Le Guin)
MPII:JYAFic I-375

East of Eden (Steinbeck) CLC I-313; MP
III-1689; MP:AF I-326

"Easter Morning" (Ammons) MPII:P II-614

"Easter 1916" (Yeats) MPII:P II-617

Eastward Ho! (Chapman, Jonson, *and*
Marston) CLC I-313; MP III-1693

Eating People Is Wrong (Bradbury, M.)
CLCII II-439; MPII:BCF I-418

"Eating Poetry" (Strand) MPII:P II-620

Ebereschenhof, Die. *See* Rowan Farm

Ebony and Ivory (Powys, L.) MP III-1697;
MP:BF I-352

Ebony Tower, The (Fowles) CLCII II-440;
MPII:BCF I-422

Ecclesiazusae, The (Aristophanes) CLC
I-314; MP III-1699

Echoing Grove, The (Lehmann) CLCII
II-442; MPII:BCF I-427

Eclogues (Vergil) MP III-1702

Écrits (Lacan) MPII:NF I-425

Écriture et la différence, L'. *See* Writing and
Difference

"Ecstasy, The" (Donne) MPII:P II-623

Ecstasy of Rita Joe, The (Ryga) CLCII
II-443; MPII:D II-540

Eden End (Priestley) CLCII II-444; MPII:D
II-546

Edge of the Cloud, The. *See* Flambards
trilogy, The

Edge of the Storm, The (Yáñez) MP:AF
I-331

"Edge" (Plath) MPII:P II-626

Edible Woman, The (Atwood) CLCII
II-445; MPII:BCF I-432

Edmund Campion (Waugh) MP III-1705

Educated Cat, The. *See* Life and Opinions
of Kater Murr, The

Education of Henry Adams, The (Adams,
H.) MP III-1708; MPII:JYABio II-533

Education of Little Tree, The (Carter)
MPII:JYABio II-537

"Edward and God" (Kundera) MPII:SS
II-664

Edward the Second (Marlowe) CLC I-315;
MP III-1711

"Eel, The" (Montale) MPII:P II-629

Effi Briest (Fontane) CLC I-317; MP
III-1716; MP:EF I-464

Efter en döda. *See* After Someone's Death

"Egg, The" (Anderson) MPII:SS II-668

Egmont (Goethe) CLC I-317; MP III-1719

Egoist, The (Meredith, G.) CLC I-318; MP
III-1723; MP:BF I-355

Eichmann in Jerusalem (Arendt) MPII:NF
I-431

"Eight Views of Tokyo" (Dazai) MPII:SS
II-672

1876 (Vidal) CLCII II-446; MPII:AF I-457

Eighth Day, The (Wilder, T.) CLCII II-447;
MPII:AF I-462

"Eighty-Yard Run, The" (Shaw) MPII:SS
II-677

Einstein (Clark, R.) MPII:JYABio II-541

Einstein on the Beach (Wilson, R., *and*
Glass) CLCII II-449; MPII:D II-551

El Señor Presidente (Asturias) MP III-1726

Elder Statesman, The (Eliot, T. S.) MP
III-1728

Eldest Son, The. *See* Mantlemass series, The

Eleanor and Franklin (Lash) MPII:JYABio
II-545

Elective Affinities (Goethe) CLC I-319; MP
III-1731; MP:EF I-468

Electra (Euripides) CLC I-320; MP III-1735

Electric Kool-Aid Acid Test, The (Wolfe)
MPII:NF II-437

Elegia di Madonna Fiametta. *See* L'Amorosa Fiammetta

Elegia dla N. N. *See* Elegy for N. N.

Elegies of Propertius, The (Propertius) MP III-1739

Elegy 18. *See* On His Mistress

"Elegy for N. N." (Miłosz) MPII:P I-632

"Elegy of Fortinbras" (Herbert, Z.) MPII:P II-635

Elegy of Madonna Fiametta. *See* L'Amorosa Fiammetta

"Elegy to the Memory of an Unfortunate Lady" (Pope) MPII:P II-638

Elegy Written in a Country Churchyard (Gray) MPII:P II-641

Elementary Forms of the Religious Life, The (Durkheim) MPII:NF II-443

Elizabeth and Essex (Strachey) MPII:JYABio II-549

Elizabeth the Great (Jenkins) MPII:JYABio II-553

"Ellen West" (Bidart) MPII:P II-644

"Elm" (Plath) MPII:P II-648

Elmer Gantry (Lewis, S.) MP III-1742; MP:AF I-335

Èloges and Other Poems (Perse) MP III-1746

Eloise. *See* New Héloïse, The

Elsewhere, Perhaps (Oz) CLCII II-450; MPII:WF I-403

Embers (Beckett) CLCII II-451; MPII:D II-557

Embezzler, The (Auchincloss) CLCII II-452; MPII:AF II-467

Emigrants, The (Bojer) CLC I-321; MP III-1749; MP:EF I-473

Emigrants of Ahadarra, The (Carleton) CLC I-322; MP III-1752; MP:BF I-359

Emil and the Detectives (Kästner) MPII:JYAFic I-383

Emil und die Detektive. *See* Emil and the Detectives

Émile (Rousseau) CLC I-322; MP III-1755; MP:EF I-476

Emilia Galotti (Lessing, G.) CLC I-323; MP III-1758

Emily Dickinson (Longsworth) MPII:JYABio II-557

Eminent Victorians (Strachey) MP III-1760

Emma (Austen) CLC I-324; MP III-1763; MP:BF I-363

Emmeline and Her Daughters (Noble) MPII:JYABio II-561

Emperor, The (Kapuciski) MPII:NF II-449

Emperor Jones, The (O'Neill) CLC I-325; MP III-1769

"Emperor of Ice-Cream, The" (Stevens, W.) MPII:P II-651

Emperor's Winding Sheet, The (Walsh) MPII:JYAFic I-387

Empire of the Sun (Ballard) CLCII II-453; MPII:BCF I-437

Emploi du temps, L'. *See* Passing Time

Empress of All Russia (Noble) MPII:JYABio II-564

"Empress's Ring, The" (Hale) MPII:SS II-680

En que satisface un recelo con la retórica del llanto. *See* This afternoon, my love

En värld är varje människa. *See* Everyone Is a World

"Enchanted Doll, The" (Gallico) MPII:SS II-683

"End, The" (Beckett) MPII:SS II-686

End of Bad Roads, The. *See* Splendors and Miseries of Courtesans, The

End of the Affair, The (Greene) CLCII II-454; MPII:BCF I-442

End of the Battle, The. *See* Sword of Honour

"End of the Game" (Cortázar) MPII:SS II-689

End of the Road, The (Barth) MP III-1772; MP:AF I-339

"End of the Seers' Convention" (Fearing) MPII:P II-654

End of the World News, The (Burgess) CLCII II-455; MPII:BCF I-447

End to Torment (H. D.) MPII:NF II-454

End Zone (DeLillo) CLCII II-457; MPII:AF II-472

"Ende einer Welt, Das." *See* "World Ends, A"

Endgame (Beckett) CLCII II-458; MPII:D II-563

Endless Steppe, The (Hautzig) MPII:JYABio II-568

"Enduring Chill, The" (O'Connor, Flannery) MPII:SS II-692

Endymion (Keats) MPII:P II-657
Endymion (Lyly) CLC I-325; MP III-1774
Enemies (Singer) CLCII II-458; MPII:AF
II-476; MPII:WF I-409
"Enemies, The" (Thomas) MPII:SS II-695
Enemy at Green Knowe, An. *See* Green
Knowe books, The
Enemy of the People, An (Ibsen) CLC
I-326; MP III-1777
"Enfant malade, L'." *See* "Sick Child, The"
Enfant noir, L'. *See* Dark Child, The
"Engagement in Santo Domingo, The"
(Kleist) MPII:SS II-698
Engel, Die. *See* Angels, The
Engineer of Human Souls, The (Škvoreck)
CLCII II-460; MPII:WF I-414
England Under the Stuarts (Trevelyan) MP
III-1781
English Notebooks, The (Hawthorne) MP
III-1784
English Teacher, The. *See* Grateful to Life
and Death
Ennead, The (Mark) MPII:JYAFic I-391
Enoch Arden (Tennyson) CLC I-328; MP
III-1787
"Enoch Soames" (Beerbohm) MPII:SS
II-702
"Enormous Radio, The" (Cheever, J.)
MPII:SS II-706
Enormous Room, The (Cummings) CLC
I-328; MP III-1789; MP:AF I-342
Enquiry Concerning Human Understanding,
An (Hume) MP III-1793
Enrico IV. *See* Henry IV
Entertainer, The (Osborne) CLCII II-461;
MPII:D II-569
Entertaining Mr. Sloane (Orton) CLCII
II-462; MPII:D II-574
Entrada a la madera. *See* Entrance into Wood
"Entrance into Wood" (Neruda) MPII:P
II-661
"Entropy" (Pynchon) MPII:SS II-709
"Envoy of Mr. Cogito, The" (Herbert, Z.)
MPII:P II-664
Envy (Olesha) CLCII II-463; MPII:WF
I-421
"Envy" (Ozick) MPII:SS II-712
"Eolian Harp, The" (Coleridge) MPII:P
II-667

Epic of Gilgamesh, The (Unknown) CLC
I-329; MP III-1796
Epigrams of Martial (Martial) MP III-1800
Epigrams of Meleager, The (Meleager) MP
III-1802
Epilogue. *See* Country Girls Trilogy, The
Epilogue: The Prague Orgy. *See* Prague
Orgy, The, *and* Zuckerman Bound
Epinicia (Pindar) MP III-1805
Epipsychidion (Shelley, P.) MPII:P II-670
"Epistle Containing the Strange Medical
Experience of Karshish, the Arab
Physician, An" (Browning, R.) MPII:P
II-674
Epistle to Dr. Arbuthnot (Pope) MPII:P II-677
Epistle II. To a Lady (Pope) MPII:P II-680
Epistles of Horace, The (Horace) MP
III-1808
Epitaph of a Small Winner (Machado de
Assís) CLC I-330; MP:AF I-346; MP
III-1811
Epithalamion (Spenser) MPII:P II-684
Equal Danger (Sciascia) CLCII II-464;
MPII:WF I-425
Equations of Love, The (Wilson, E.) CLCII
II-465; MPII:BCF I-452
"Equilibrists, The" (Ransom) MPII:P II-687
Equus (Shaffer, P.) CLCII II-466; MPII:D
II-579
Erasers, The (Robbe-Grillet) CLCII II-467;
MPII:WF I-430
"Erdbeben in Chili." *See* "Earthquake in
Chile, The"
Erde und Feuer. *See* Silesian Tetralogy, The
Erec and Enide (Chrétien de Troyes) CLC
I-331; MP III-1816
Erewhon (Butler) CLC I-331; MP III-1822;
MP:BF I-370
Erinnerungen, Träume, Gedanken von C. G.
Jung. *See* Memories, Dreams, Reflections
"Eros Turannos" (Robinson, E.) MPII:P
II-691
Erste Polka, Die. *See* Silesian Tetralogy, The
Erwählte, Der. *See* Holy Sinner, The
"Erzähler, Der." *See* Storyteller, The
Eskimos, Chicanos, Indians. *See* Children of
Crisis
Esmond in India (Jhabvala) CLCII II-468;
MPII:BCF I-456

Espoir, L'. *See* Man's Hope

Essais (Montaigne) MP III-1825

Essay Concerning Human Understanding,
An (Locke, J.) MP III-1828

Essay of Dramatic Poesy, An (Dryden) MP
III-1831

Essay on Criticism (Pope) MP III-1834

Essay on Man (Pope) MP IV-1837

Essay Towards a New Theory of Vision, An
(Berkeley) MP IV-1840

Essays (Bacon) MP IV-1842

Essays: First and Second Series (Emerson)
MP IV-1845

Essays of a Biologist (Huxley, J.) MP
IV-1848

Essays of Amiri Baraka, The (Baraka)
MPII:AfAm I-400

Essays of Max Beerbohm, The (Beerbohm)
MP IV-1866

Essays of G. K. Chesterton, The (Chesterton)
MP IV-1859

Essays of Elia and Last Essays of Elia (Lamb)
MP IV-1857

Essays of Ralph Ellison, The (Ellison)
MPII:AfAm I-406

Essays of Aldous Huxley, The (Huxley, A.)
MP IV-1851

Essays of C. L. R. James, The (James)
MPII:AfAm I-412

Essays of Edgar Allan Poe, The (Poe) MP
IV-1854

Essays of Ishmael Reed, The (Reed)
MPII:AfAm I-418

Essays of Henry David Thoreau, The
(Thoreau) MP IV-1863

Este domingo. *See* This Sunday

Este, que ves, engaño colorido. *See* This
painted lie you see

"Esther" (Toomer) MPII:SS II-716

Esther Waters (Moore, G.) CLC I-332; MP
IV-1870; MP:BF I-374

Estrangement. *See* Autobiography of
William Butler Yeats, The

"Eternal Dice, The" (Vallejo) MPII:P II-694

Eternal Present, The (Giedion) MPII:NF II-460

"Ethan Brand" (Hawthorne) MPII:SS II-720

Ethan Frome (Wharton) CLC I-333; MP
IV-1873; MP:AF I-351

Ethics (Bonhoeffer) MPII:NF II-466

Ethics (Spinoza) MP IV-1876

Ethik. *See* Ethics (Bonhoeffer)

Eubie Blake (Rose) MPII:JYABio II-572

Eugene Aram (Bulwer-Lytton) CLC I-334;
MP IV-1879; MP:BF I-378

Eugene Onegin (Pushkin) CLC I-334; MP
IV-1883

Eugénie Grandet (Balzac) CLC I-335; MP
IV-1886; MP:EF I-480

Eunuch, The (Terence) CLC I-336; MP
IV-1891

Euphues and His England (Lyly) CLC
I-338; MP IV-1894; MP:BF I-382

Euphues, the Anatomy of Wit (Lyly) CLC
I-338; MP IV-1898; MP:BF I-387

Eva Perón (Fraser *and* Navarro) MPII:JYABio
II-576

Eva Trout (Bowen, E.) CLCII II-470;
MPII:BCF I-461

Evan Harrington (Meredith, G.) CLC I-339;
MP IV-1902; MP:BF I-391

Eva's Man (Jones, G.) CLCII II-471;
MPII:AF II-481; MPII:AfAm I-424

Evangeline (Longfellow) CLC I-340; MP
IV-1906

"Evangelio según Marco, El." *See* "Gospel
According to Mark, The"

Eve of St. Agnes, The (Keats) CLC I-340;
MP IV-1909

Evelina (Burney) CLC I-341; MP IV-1913;
MP:BF I-395

"Eveline" (Joyce) MPII:SS II-724

"Evening Meal" (Rilke) MPII:P II-697

"Evening Performance, An" (Garrett)
MPII:SS II-727

"Evening Song" (Trakl) MPII:P II-700

Everlasting Man, The (Chesterton)
MPII:NF II-471

Every Man in His Humour (Jonson) CLC
I-343; MP IV-1918

Every Man out of His Humour (Jonson)
CLC I-344; MP IV-1924

"Everyday Use" (Walker) MPII:SS II-731

Everyman (Unknown) CLC I-345; MP
IV-1928

"Everyone Is a World" (Ekelöf) MPII:P
II-703

"Everything That Rises Must Converge"
(O'Connor, Flannery) MPII:SS II-735

"Ewigen Melodien" (Heyen) MPII:P II-706
Excellent Women (Pym) CLCII II-473;
   MPII:BCF I-466
Except the Lord. See Second Trilogy
"Exeat" (Smith, S.) MPII:P II-709
"Execration upon Vulcan, An" (Jonson)
   MPII:P II-712
Executioner's Song, The (Mailer) CLCII
   II-474; MPII:AF II-486
Exemplary Novels (Cervantes Saavedra)
   MP IV-1933; MP:EF II-485
Exeter Blitz, The (Rees) MPII:JYAFic I-394
Exile and the Kingdom (Camus) MP
   IV-1936; MP:EF II-489
Exiles (Arlen) MPII:NF II-476
Exiles (Joyce) CLC I-345; MP IV-1939
Exile's Return (Cowley) MPII:NF II-481
Exit the King (Ionesco) CLCII II-475;
   MPII:D II-585

Exodus (Uris) CLCII II-475; MPII:AF
   II-491
Expedition of Humphry Clinker, The. See
   Humphry Clinker
"Expérience de la vie d'usine." See Factory
   Journal
"Experiment in Misery, An" (Crane, S.)
   MPII:SS II-739
Explico algunas cosas. See Few Things
   Explained, A
Explosion in a Cathedral (Carpentier)
   CLCII II-477; MPII:AF II-496
Eye of the Storm, The (White) CLCII
   II-478; MPII:BCF I-472
Eyeless in Gaza (Huxley) CLCII II-480;
   MPII:BCF I-478
"Eyes of Night-Time" (Rukeyser) MPII:P
   II-715
Ezra (Kops) CLCII II-481; MPII:D II-590

F

F. Scott Fitzgerald (Greenfeld) MPII:JYABio II-580

Fable, A (Faulkner) CLC I-346; MP IV-1942; MP:AF I-354

Fable for Critics, A (Lowell, J.) MP IV-1948; MPII:P II-718

Fables (La Fontaine) MP IV-1951

Faces and Masks. See Memory of Fire

Faces in My Time. See To Keep the Ball Rolling

"Faces of Blood Kindred, The" (Goyen) MPII:SS II-743

"Facing the Snow" (Tu Fu) MPII:P II-721

Fackel im Ohr, Die. See Torch in My Ear, The

Factory Journal (Weil) MPII:NF II-487

Facts, The (Roth) MPII:NF II-492

Faerie Queene, The (Spenser) CLC I-347; MP IV-1953

Fahrenheit 451 (Bradbury, R.) CLCII II-482; MPII:AF II-501; MPII:JYAFic I-397

Fair, The (Arreola) CLCII II-483; MPII:AF II-505

Fair Maid of Perth, The (Scott, Sir W.) CLC I-351; MP IV-1958; MP:BF I-400

Fairly Honourable Defeat, A (Murdoch) CLCII II-485; MPII:BCF I-483

Faith and the Good Thing (Johnson, C.) CLCII II-487; MPII:AF II-510; MPII:AfAm I-430

"Faith in a Tree" (Paley) MPII:SS II-747

Faith, Sex, Mystery (Gilman) MPII:NF II-497

Faithful Shepherdess, The (Fletcher) CLC I-352; MP IV-1962

Falcon and the Dove, The (Duggan) MPII:JYABio II-583

Falconer (Cheever, J.) CLCII II-488; MPII:AF II-515

"Falešn autostop." See "Hitchhiking Game, The"

Fall, The (Camus) MP IV-1965; MP:EF II-493

"Fall of the House of Usher, The" (Poe) CLC I-353; MP IV-1968; MP:AF I-360; MPII:SS II-751

Fallen Angels (Myers) MPII:JYAFic I-401

"Falling" (Dickey) MPII:P II-724

Familia lejana, Una. See Distant Relations

Familiar Essays of William Hazlitt, The (Hazlitt) MP IV-1974

Family (Cooper, J. C.) MPII:AfAm I-436

"Family Affair, A" (Maupassant) MPII:SS II-755

Family at Gilje, The (Lie) CLC I-354; MP IV-1977; MP:EF II-497

Family Conspiracy, The (Phipson) MPII:JYAFic I-404

Family Failing, A (Arundel) MPII:JYAFic I-408

Family Happiness (Tolstoy) CLCII II-489; MPII:WF I-435

Family of Pascual Duarte, The (Cela) MP IV-1980; MP:EF II-501

Family Reunion, The (Eliot, T. S.) CLC I-355; MP IV-1983

Family Robinson Crusoe, The. See Swiss Family Robinson, The

Family Voices (Pinter) CLCII II-490; MPII:D II-595

Famous All Over Town (Santiago) MPII:JYAFic I-412

Famous American Negroes (Hughes, L.) MPII:JYABio II-587

Famous American Women (Stoddard) MPII:JYABio II-591

Famous Mexican Americans (Morey, J., and Dunn) MPII:JYABio II-595

Famous Puerto Ricans (Newlon) MPII:JYABio II-599

"Fancy Woman, The" (Taylor) MPII:SS II-759

Fanny Kemble's America (Scott, J.) MPII:JYABio II-603

Far Away and Long Ago (Hudson) MP IV-1986

Far from the Madding Crowd (Hardy) CLC I-356; MP IV-1990; MP:BF I-405

Far Journey of Oudin, The. See Guyana Quartet, The

Far Tortuga (Matthiessen) CLCII II-491; MPII:AF II-521

Far Voyager (Latham) MPII:JYABio II-607

Farewell from Nowhere (Maximov) CLCII II-492; MPII:WF I-440

Farewell, My Lovely (Chandler) CLCII II-493; MPII:AF II-527

Farewell Party, The (Kundera) CLCII II-494; MPII:WF I-446

"Farewell, thou art too dear for my possessing," *See* Sonnet 87

Farewell to Arms, A (Hemingway) CLC I-357; MP IV-1995; MP:AF I-366

"Farewell to Li Yun in the Xie Tiao Pavilion, A" (Li Po) MPII:P II-727

Farewell to Manzanar (Houston *and* Houston) MPII:JYABio II-611

"Farewell Without a Guitar" (Stevens, W.) MPII:P II-731

Farthest Shore, The. *See* Earthsca series, The

Fat Girl, The (Sachs) MPII:JYAFic I-415

"Fat of the Land, The" (Yezierska) MPII:SS II-763

Fate of the Earth, The (Schell) MPII:NF II-502

Father, The (Strindberg) CLC I-358; MP IV-2000

"Father and Son" (Kunitz) MPII:P II-734

Father Goriot (Balzac) CLC I-359; MP IV-2007; MP:EF II-505

"Father of My Country, The" (Wakoski) MPII:P II-737

Fathers, The (Tate) MP IV-2012; MP:AF I-371

Fathers and Sons (Turgenev) CLC I-361; MP IV-2015; MP:EF II-510

"Father's Daughters, The" (Spark) MPII:SS II-767

Fathers of Industries (Fanning) MPII:JYABio II-615

Faust (Goethe) CLC I-362; MP IV-2020

FDR Story, The (Peare) MPII:JYABio II-619

"Fear and Trembling" (Warren) MPII:P II-740

Federalist, The (Hamilton, Madison, *and* Jay) MP IV-2025

Felisa Rincón de Gautier (Gruber) MPII:JYABio II-623

Felita (Mohr) MPII:JYAFic I-418

Felix Holt, the Radical (Eliot, G.) CLC I-364; MP IV-2029; MP:BF I-410

Felix Mendelssohn (Kupferberg) MPII:JYABio II-627

"Felix Randal" (Hopkins, G.) MPII:P II-743

"Fellow Diners" (Rítsos) MPII:P II-746

Fellowship of the Ring, The (Tolkien) MP IV-2033; MP:BF I-414. *See also* Lord of the Rings, The

Female Friends (Weldon) CLCII II-495; MPII:BCF I-488

Female Man, The (Russ) CLCII II-496; MPII:AF II-532

Feminine Mystique, The (Friedan) MPII:NF II-507

"Femme adultère, La." *See* "Adulterous Woman, The"

Femme noire. *See* Black Woman

Fences (Wilson, August) CLCII II-498; MPII:AfAm I-442; MPII:D II-600

"Fenêtres, Les. *See* Windows" (Apollinaire)

"Fenêtres, Les. *See* Windows, The" (Mallarmé)

Fenian Cycle. *See* Finn Cycle, The

Ferdydurke (Gombrowicz) CLCII II-499; MPII:WF II-451

Feria, La. *See* Fair, The

Fermo e Lucia. *See* Betrothed, The

"Fern Hill" (Thomas, D.) MPII:P II-749

Fêtes galantes (Verlaine) MP IV-2038. *See also* Moonlight

Feuilles mortes, Les. *See* Autumn Leaves

"Few Things Explained, A" (Neruda) MPII:P II-752

Fiasco (Lem) CLCII II-500; MPII:WF II-456

Ficciones (Borges) MP IV-2040; MP:AF I-375

"Ficelle, La." *See* "Piece of String, The"

Fiddler's House, The (Colum) CLCII II-501; MPII:D II-605

"Field of Mustard, The" (Coppard) MPII:SS II-771

Field of Vision, The (Morris, Wright) MP IV-2042; MP:AF I-378

"Field Work" (Heaney) MPII:P II-755

Fields, The (Richter, C.) CLC I-366; MP IV-2046; MP:AF I-382

Fiesta en noviembre. *See* Fiesta in November

Fiesta in November (Mallea) MP IV-2050; MP:AF I-386

Fifth Business. *See* Deptford Trilogy, The

Fifth Chinese Daughter (Wong) MPII:JYABio II-631

Fifth Queen Crowned, The. *See* Fifth Queen, The

Fifth Queen, The (Ford, F.) MP IV-2055; MP:BF I-420

Fifth Son, The (Wiesel) CLCII II-502; MPII:WF II-461

Fifties, The (Wilson) MPII:NF IV-1500

"Fight" (García Lorca) MPII:P II-758

"Fight, The" (Thomas) MPII:SS II-774

Fighting Ground, The (Wortis) MPII:JYAFic I-421

"Figure in the Carpet, The" (James, H.) MPII:SS II-777

File No. 113 (Gaboriau) CLC I-366; MP IV-2058; MP:EF II-515

Filo del agua, Al. *See* Edge of the Storm, The

Filostrato, Il (Boccaccio) MP IV-2062

Fin de Chéri, La. *See* Last of Chéri, The

Fin de partie. *See* Endgame

"Fin, La." *See* "End, The"

"Final del juego." *See* "End of the Game"

Final Mist, The (Bombal) CLCII II-503; MPII:AF II-537

Final Payments (Gordon) CLCII II-504; MPII:AF II-542

Financial Expert, The (Narayan) CLCII II-505; MPII:BCF II-493

Financier, The (Dreiser) CLC I-367; MP IV-2067; MP:AF I-391

Find Debbie. *See* Siblings, The

Fine White Dust, A (Rylant) MPII:JYAFic I-424

Finn Cycle, The (Unknown) CLC I-369; MP IV-2071; MP:BF I-424

Finnegans Wake (Joyce) CLC I-370; MP IV-2076; MP:BF I-430

"Fir Trees" (Apollinaire) MPII:P II-761

Fire-Dwellers, The (Laurence) CLCII II-506; MPII:BCF II-509

Fire from Heaven (Renault) CLCII II-508; MPII:BCF II-498

Fire Next Time, The (Baldwin) MPII:AfAm I-448; MPII:NF II-512

"Fire on the Hills" (Jeffers) MPII:P II-765

Fire on the Mountain (Desai) CLCII II-509; MPII:BCF II-504

Fire Raisers, The. *See* Firebugs, The

Firebugs, The (Frisch) CLCII II-510; MPII:D II-610

Fireflies (Naipaul, S.) CLCII II-511; MPII:BCF II-514

First Circle, The (Solzhenitsyn) CLCII II-512; MPII:WF II-465

"First Communions" (Rimbaud) MPII:P II-768

"First Dream" (Cruz, S.) MPII:P II-772

First in Their Hearts (Fleming) MPII:JYABio II-635

First Love (Turgenev) CLCII II-516; MPII:JYAFic I-427; MPII:WF II-470

First Mondays. *See* Monday Conversations

First Polka, The. *See* Silesian Tetralogy, The

"Firstborn" (Woiwode) CLCII II-517; MPII:SS II-781

"Fish, The" (Moore, M.) MPII:P II-775

Fisher King, The (Powell) CLCII II-518; MPII:BCF II-520

Fisher Maiden, The (Björnson) CLC I-371; MP IV-2079; MP:EF II-519

Fiskadoro (Johnson, Denis) MPII:JYAFic II-431

Five Children and It (Nesbit) MPII:JYAFic II-435

"Five-Forty-Eight, The" (Cheever, J.) MPII:SS II-785

"Five-Twenty" (White) MPII:SS II-788

Five Women Who Loved Love (Ibara Saikaku) CLC I-372; MP IV-2082; MP:EF II-522

Fixer, The (Malamud) CLCII II-519; MPII:AF II-548

Flagellants, The (Polite) MPII:AfAm I-455

Flambards in Summer. *See* Flambards trilogy, The

Flambards trilogy, The (Peyton) MPII:JYAFic II-438

Flanders Road, The (Simon, C.) CLCII II-520; MPII:WF II-475

Flaubert's Parrot (Barnes, J.) CLCII II-521; MPII:BCF II-526

Flaws in the Glass (White) MPII:NF II-517

"Flea, The." *See* "Lefty"

"Fleeing" (Sachs) MPII:P II-778
Fliehendes Pferd, Ein. *See* Runaway Horse
Flies, The (Azuela) MP IV-2085; MP:AF I-395
Flies, The (Sartre) MP IV-2089
"Flight" (Steinbeck) MPII:SS II-792
Flight of Swans, A. *See* Mantlemass series, The
Flight to Canada (Reed, I.) CLCII II-522; MPII:AF II-551; MPII:AfAm I-460
Flint's Island (Wibberley) MPII:JYAFic II-443
Floating Opera, The (Barth) CLCII II-524; MPII:AF II-557
Flood Warning (Berna) MPII:JYAFic II-447
Florence Nightingale (Nolan) MPII:JYABio II-639
Florence Nightingale, 1820-1910 (Woodham-Smith) MPII:JYABio II-643
Flounder, The (Grass) CLCII II-525; MPII:WF II-481
"Flowering Judas" (Porter) MPII:SS II-795
Flowering Peach, The (Odets) CLCII II-527; MPII:D II-616
Flowers of Evil (Baudelaire) MP IV-2092
Flush (Woolf) MPII:JYABio II-647
"Fly, The" (Holub) MPII:P II-780
"Fly, The" (Mansfield) MPII:SS II-799
Flying Colours. *See* Horatio Hornblower series, The
"Flying Home" (Ellison) MPII:SS II-803
Fogo morto (Lins do Rêgo) MP:AF I-400
Folded Leaf, The (Maxwell) MPII:JYAFic II-451
Folie et déraison. *See* Madness and Civilization
Folks, The (Suckow) MP IV-2094; MP:AF I-404
Folkways (Sumner) MP IV-2097
Foma Gordeyev (Gorky) CLC I-373; MP IV-2100; MP:EF II-526
Fontamara (Silone) MP IV-2104; MP:EF II-530
Fool for Love (Shepard) CLCII II-529; MPII:D II-622
Fool of Quality, The (Brooke, H.) CLC I-374; MP IV-2107; MP:BF I-434
Fool's Errand, A (Tourgée) MP IV-2110; MP:AF I-408

"Fools Say" (Sarraute) CLCII II-530; MPII:WF II-486
Footsteps (Garfield) MPII:JYAFic II-454
For colored girls who have considered suicide/ when the rainbow is enuf (Shange) CLCII II-531; MPII:AfAm I-467; MPII:D II-627
"For a Freshman Reader" (Justice) MPII:P II-783
"For a Sister" (Rich) MPII:P II-786
"For Esmé—with Love and Squalor" (Salinger) MPII:SS II-809
"For Plants" (Snyder) MPII:P II-789
"For the Hillmother" (Montague) MPII:P II-792
"For the Marriage of Faustus and Helen" (Crane, H.) MPII:P II-795
"For the Union Dead" (Lowell, R.) MPII:P II-798
For Whom the Bell Tolls (Hemingway) CLC I-374; MP IV-2114; MP:AF I-413
Forbidden Forest, The (Eliade) CLCII II-532; MPII:WF II-491
Force de l'âge, La. *See* Prime of Life, The
"Force That Through the Green Fuse Drives the Flower, The" (Thomas, D.) MPII:P II-801
Forerunner, The. *See* Romance of Leonardo da Vinci, The
Forêt interdite, La. *See* Forbidden Forest, The
Forever (Blume) MPII:JYAFic II-457
"Forge, The" (Heaney) MPII:P II-804
Fork River Space Project, The (Morris) CLCII II-534; MPII:AF II-561
"Form of Women, A" (Creeley) MPII:P II-807
Formes élémentaires de la vie religieuse, Les. *See* Elementary Forms of the Religious Life, The
Forsyte Saga, The (Galsworthy) CLC I-376; MP IV-2119; MP:BF I-438
Forten the Sailmaker (Douty) MPII:JYABio II-651
Forties, The (Wilson) MPII:NF IV-1500
Fortitude (Walpole, Hugh) CLC I-377; MP IV-2124; MP:BF I-443
Fortress, The (Walpole, Hugh) CLC I-378; MP IV-2128; MP:BF I-447

Fortunata and Jacinta (Pérez Galdós) CLC
I-379; MP IV-2132; MP:EF II-534

Fortunate Man, A (Berger) MPII:NF II-521

Fortunate Mistress, The. *See* Roxana

Fortunes and Misfortunes of the Famous
Moll Flanders. *See* Moll Flanders

Fortunes of Nigel, The (Scott, W.) CLC
I-380; MP IV-2137; MP:BF I-452

Fortunes of Richard Mahony, The
(Richardson, H.) CLC I-382; MP
IV-2142; MP:BF I-458

Forty Days of Musa Dagh, The (Werfel)
CLC I-382; MP IV-2145; MP:EF II-539

Foundation and Empire. *See* Foundation
trilogy, The

Foundation Pit, The (Platonov) CLCII
II-534; MPII:WF II-497

Foundation trilogy, The (Asimov) CLCII
II-536; MPII:AF II-565; MPII:JYAFic
II-460

Foundation. *See* Foundation trilogy, The

Fountain Overflows, The (West, R.) CLCII
II-540; MPII:BCF II-532

Four-Gated City, The. *See* Children of
Violence

Four-Minute Mile, The (Bannister)
MPII:JYABio II-655

Four Quartets (Eliot, T. S.) MP IV-2148

Four Women in a Violent Time (Crawford)
MPII:JYABio II-659

Four Years. *See* Autobiography of William
Butler Yeats, The

Fourth Form Friendship, A (Brazil)
MPII:JYAFic II-464

Fox, The (Lawrence) CLCII II-541;
MPII:BCF II-538

Fra Lippo Lippi (Browning, R.) MPII:P II-810

Frågar du mig var jag finns. *See* If You Ask
Me

Fragmented Life of Don Jacobo Lerner, The
(Goldemberg) CLCII II-542; MPII:AF
II-572

Framley Parsonage (Trollope) CLC I-383;
MP IV-2151; MP:BF I-462

Franchiser, The (Elkin) CLCII II-543;
MPII:AF II-576

Francis Drake (Syme) MPII:JYABio II-662

Frank Lloyd Wright (Twombly)
MPII:JYABio II-666

Frankenstein (Shelley, M.) CLC I-385; MP
IV-2154; MP:BF I-466

Frankenstein Unbound (Aldiss) CLCII
II-544; MPII:BCF II-542

Franklin Delano Roosevelt (Johnson, G.)
MPII:JYABio II-670

Franny and Zooey (Salinger) MP IV-2157;
MP:AF I-418

Fraternity (Galsworthy) CLC I-386; MP
IV-2159; MP:BF I-470

Free at Last (Bontemps) MPII:JYABio
II-674

Free Fall (Golding) MP IV-2163; MP:BF
I-475

Free to Be Muhammad Ali (Lipsyte)
MPII:JYABio II-678

"Free Union" (Breton) MPII:P II-813

Freedom of the City, The (Friel) CLCII
II-545; MPII:D II-633

Freedom or Death (Kazantzakis) MP
IV-2166; MP:EF II-543

Freedom Road (Fast) MPII:JYAFic II-467

French Lieutenant's Woman, The (Fowles)
CLCII II-546; MPII:BCF II-549

French Revolution, The (Carlyle) MP
IV-2169

French Without Tears (Rattigan) CLCII
II-547; MPII:D II-639

"Freshest Boy, The" (Fitzgerald) MPII:SS
II-813

Friar Bacon and Friar Bungay (Greene, R.)
CLC I-386; MP IV-2172

Friday (Tournier) CLCII II-548; MPII:WF
II-502

Friedrich (Richter, H.) MPII:JYAFic II-470

Friend (Yolen) MPII:JYABio II-682

"Friend of Kafka, A" (Singer) MPII:SS
II-817

Friendly Persuasion, The (West, J.)
MPII:JYAFic II-474

Friends, The (Guy) MPII:JYAFic II-478

Friends and Heroes. *See* Balkan trilogy, The

Frithiof's Saga (Tegnér) CLC I-387; MP
IV-2175

Frogs, The (Aristophanes) CLC I-388; MP
IV-2178

From "A." *See* "A"

From Bauhaus to Our House (Wolfe)
MPII:NF II-527

From Berlin to Jerusalem (Scholem) MPII:NF II-534

From Cuba with a Song (Sarduy) CLCII II-550; MPII:AF II-581

From Here to Eternity (Jones, J.) CLCII II-551; MPII:AF II-586

"From the Beam" (Celan) MPII:P II-816

From the Eagle's Wing (Swift, H.) MPII:JYABio II-686

From the Mixed-up Files of Mrs. Basil E. Frankweiler (Konigsburg) MPII:JYAFic II-481

From the Rising of the Sun (Miłosz) MPII:P II-819

From the Terrace (O'Hara, J.) CLCII II-552; MPII:AF II-591

Frontier in American History, The (Turner) MP IV-2182

Frontiers of Dance (Terry, W.) MPII:JYABio II-690

"Frost at Midnight" (Coleridge) MPII:P II-824

Fruit of the Tree, The (Wharton) CLC I-389; MP IV-2185; MP:AF I-421

Fruits of the Earth (Grove) CLCII II-554; MPII:BCF II-553

Full Moon (Wodehouse) CLCII II-555; MPII:BCF II-557

Funeral, The (Steele, R.) CLC I-390; MP IV-2188

Funeral Games (Renault) CLCII II-557; MPII:BCF II-561

"Funeral Oration for a Mouse" (Dugan) MPII:P II-827

"Funes, the Memorious" (Borges) MPII:SS II-820

Funnyhouse of a Negro (Kennedy, A.) CLCII II-558; MPII:AfAm I-474; MPII:D II-645

Fürsorgliche Belagerung. See Safety Net, The

"Fury of Aerial Bombardment, The" (Eberhart) MPII:P II-830

Ften rjin nikki. See Diary of a Mad Old Man

Futile Life of Pito Pérez, The (Romero) CLCII II-559; MPII:AF II-597

G

G. (Berger, J.) CLCII II-560; MPII:BCF
II-567

Gabriela, Clove and Cinnamon (Amado)
MP IV-2192; MP:AF I-425

Gabriela, cravo e canela. *See* Gabriela,
Clove and Cinnamon

Gacela de la muerte oscura. *See* Gacela of
the Dark Death

Gacela del amor imprevisto. *See* Gacela of
Unforeseen Love

"Gacela of the Dark Death" (García Lorca)
MPII:P II-833

"Gacela of Unforeseen Love"
(García Lorca) MPII:P II-836

Galileo (Brecht) CLCII II-562; MPII:D
II-650

Galope muerto. *See* Dead Gallop

Gambler, The (Dostoevski) CLC I-390; MP
IV-2195; MP:EF II-547

"Gambling" (Baudelaire) MPII:P II-839

Games Were Coming, The (Anthony)
CLCII II-563; MPII:BCF II-572

"Gamlet Shchigrovskogo uezda." *See*
"Hamlet of the Shchigrovsky District"

Gammage Cup, The (Kendall)
MPII:JYAFic II-485

Gandhi (Eaton) MPII:JYABio II-694

"Garden" (H. D.) MPII:P II-842

"Garden, The" (Marvell) MPII:P II-845

Garden, The (Strong) CLC I-392; MP
IV-2200; MP:BF I-479

Garden, Ashes (Kiš) CLCII II-564;
MPII:WF II-507

Garden of Earthly Delights, The (Clarke,
M.) CLCII II-565; MPII:D II-654

"Garden of Forking Paths, The" (Borges)
MPII:SS II-824

Garden of the Finzi-Continis, The (Bassani)
CLCII II-566; MPII:WF II-511

Garden Party, The (Havel) CLCII II-567;
MPII:D II-660

"Gardener, The" (Kipling) MPII:SS II-828

Gardener's Dog, The (Vega) CLC I-392;
MP IV-2203

Gargantua and Pantagruel (Rabelais) CLC
I-393; MP IV-2208; MP:EF II-553

Gargoyles (Bernhard) CLCII II-568;
MPII:WF II-516

Garibaldi (Syme) MPII:JYABio II-698

Garram the Hunter (Best) MPII:JYAFic
II-488

Gates of the Forest, The (Wiesel) CLCII
II-570; MPII:WF II-520

Gather Together in My Name (Angelou)
MPII:JYABio II-702

Gathering Evidence (Bernhard) MPII:NF
II-539

Gathering of Days, A (Blos) MPII:JYAFic
II-491

Gathering of Old Men, A (Gaines)
MPII:AfAm I-480; MPII:JYAFic II-494

Gaucho, The (Hernández) CLC I-394; MP
IV-2213

Gaudier-Brzeska (Pound) MPII:NF II-544

Gaudy Night (Sayers) CLCII II-571;
MPII:BCF II-577

Gay-Neck (Mukerji) MPII:JYAFic II-498

Gazapo (Sainz) CLCII II-572; MPII:AF
II-602

Gdzie wschodzi sloce i kedy zapada. *See*
From the Rising of the Sun

Gemini (Giovanni) MPII:AfAm I-486;
MPII:NF II-549

Gemini (Tournier) CLCII II-573; MPII:WF
II-524

General Introduction to Psychoanalysis, A
(Freud) MP IV-2218

"General William Booth Enters into
Heaven" (Lindsay) MPII:P II-848

Generous Man, A (Price) CLCII II-574;
MPII:AF II-607

Genesis. *See* Memory of Fire

"Genius," The (Dreiser) CLC I-395; MP
IV-2221; MP:AF I-428

Gentle Ben (Morey, W.) MPII:JYAFic
II-501

Gentleman Dancing Master, The
(Wycherley) CLC I-396; MP IV-2226

"Gentleman from Cracow, The" (Singer)
MPII:SS II-831

"Gentleman from San Francisco, The"
(Bunin) MPII:SS II-835

Gentleman Usher, The (Chapman) CLC
I-396; MP IV-2230
Gentlemen in England (Wilson, A. N.)
CLCII II-575; MPII:BCF II-582
Geoffrey Chaucer of England (Chute)
MPII:JYABio II-705
Geography of a Horse Dreamer (Shepard)
CLCII II-577; MPII:D II-666
George Bernard Shaw (Coolidge, O.)
MPII:JYABio II-709
George Passant. See Strangers and Brothers
George Washington (Cunliffe)
MPII:JYABio II-717
George Washington Carver (Holt)
MPII:JYABio II-721
George Washington, Leader of the People
(Judson) MPII:JYABio II-713
"Georgia Dusk" (Toomer) MPII:P II-851
Georgia O'Keeffe (Gherman) MPII:JYABio
II-729
Georgia O'Keeffe (O'Keeffe)
MPII:JYABio II-725
Georgia Scenes (Longstreet) MP IV-2233;
MP:AF I-433
Georgics (Vergil) MP IV-2236
Gerettete Zunge, Die. See Tongue Set Free,
The
Germinal (Zola) CLC I-397; MP IV-2238;
MP:EF II-558
Germinie Lacerteux (Goncourt and
Goncourt) CLC I-398; MP IV-2242;
MP:EF II-563
Geronimo: The Man, His Time, His Place
(Debo) MPII:JYABio II-741
Geronimo: His Own Story (Geronimo)
MPII:JYABio II-733
Geronimo: The Last Apache War Chief
(Wyatt, E.) MPII:JYABio II-737
Geronimo's Story of His Life. See
Geronimo: His Own Story.
"Gerontion" (Eliot, T. S.) MPII:P II-854
Gertrude Stein (Greenfeld) MPII:JYABio
II-745
Geschichten Jaakobs, Die. See Joseph and
His Brothers
Getting Out (Norman) CLCII II-577;
MPII:D II-672
Gettysburg (Singmaster) MP IV-2246;
MP:AF I-436

Gewicht der Welt, Das. See Weight of the
World, The
"Ghost and Flesh, Water and Dirt" (Goyen)
MPII:SS II-839
Ghost at Noon, A (Moravia) CLCII II-578;
MPII:WF II-529
Ghost Horse cycle, The (Highwater)
MPII:JYAFic II-504
Ghost of Thomas Kempe, The (Lively)
MPII:JYAFic II-508
Ghost Sonata, The (Strindberg) CLCII
II-579; MPII:D II-678
Ghost Writer, The (Roth, P.) CLCII II-580.
See also Zuckerman Bound
Ghosts (Ibsen) CLC I-399; MP IV-2250
Giant Steps (Abdul-Jabbar and Knobler)
MPII:JYABio II-749
Giants in the Earth (Rölvaag) CLC I-400;
MP IV-2255; MP:AF I-440
Giants of Jazz (Terkel) MPII:JYABio II-753
Giardino dei Finzi-Contini, Il. See Garden
of the Finzi-Continis, The
Gift, The (Nabokov) CLCII II-581;
MPII:WF II-534
"Gift, The" (Steinbeck) MPII:SS II-843. See
also Red Pony, The
Gift of Good Land, The (Berry) MPII:NF
II-555
"Gift of the Magi, The" (O. Henry)
MPII:SS II-847
Gigi (Colette) CLCII II-582; MPII:WF
II-539
Gil Blas (Lesage) CLC I-401; MP IV-2260;
MP:EF II-567
Gil Blas of Santillane. See Gil Blas
Gilded Age, The (Twain and Warner) CLC
I-402; MP IV-2263; MP:AF I-445
Giles Goat-Boy (Barth) CLCII II-584;
MPII:AF II-613
"Gimpel the Fool" (Singer) MPII:SS II-850
Ginger Man, The (Donleavy) CLCII II-585;
MPII:AF II-618; MPII:BCF II-586
Ginger Pye (Estes) MPII:JYAFic II-512
"Giornata d'uno scrutatore, La." See
"Watcher, The"
Giovanni's Room (Baldwin) CLCII II-586;
MPII:AF II-623; MPII:AfAm I-492
Girl Called Boy, A (Hurmence)
MPII:JYAFic II-516

Girl from Yamhill, A (Cleary) MPII:JYABio
    II-757
Girl Green as Elderflower, The (Stow)
    CLCII II-587; MPII:BCF II-590
Girl in White Armor, The (Paine)
    MPII:JYABio II-761
Girl in Winter, A (Larkin) CLCII II-589;
    MPII:BCF II-597
Girl on the Outside, The (Walter)
    MPII:JYAFic II-519
Girl, 20 (Amis) CLCII II-590; MPII:BCF
    II-602
Girl with a Pen (Kyle) MPII:JYABio II-765
Girls in Their Married Bliss. See Country
    Girls Trilogy, The
"Girls in Their Summer Dresses, The"
    (Shaw) MPII:SS II-853
"Giui de Mopassan." See "Guy de
    Maupassant"
Give Us Each Day (Dunbar-Nelson)
    MPII:AfAm I-498
Giver, The (Hall, L.) MPII:JYAFic II-523
"Gladius Dei" (Mann) MPII:SS II-857
Glance Away, A (Wideman) CLCII II-591;
    MPII:AF II-628
Glasperlenspiel, Das. See Glass Bead Game,
    The
Glass Bead Game, The (Hesse) CLCII
    II-592; MPII:WF II-543
Glass Key, The (Hammett) CLC I-403; MP
    IV-2267; MP:AF I-449
Glass Menagerie, The (Williams, T.) CLC
    I-403; MP IV-2270
Glass of Blessings, A (Pym) CLCII II-594;
    MPII:BCF II-607
"Gleaner, The" (Bates) MPII:SS II-860
Glengarry Glen Ross (Mamet) CLCII
    II-595; MPII:D II-684
Gli sposi promesi. See Betrothed, The
"Glimpse into Another Country" (Morris)
    MPII:SS II-863
Gos pana. See His Master's Voice
Go Ask Alice (Anonymous) MPII:JYAFic
    II-526
Go-Between, The (Hartley) CLCII II-597;
    MPII:BCF II-612
Go Down, Moses (Faulkner) MP IV-2272;
    MP:AF I-453

"Go from me. Yet I feel that I shall stand"
    See Sonnet 6
Go Tell It on the Mountain (Baldwin) MP
    IV-2276; MP:AF I-458
Go Tell It on the Mountain (Baldwin)
    MPII:AfAm I-505
Go Tell It on the Mountain (Baldwin)
    MPII:JYAFic II-529
Go Up for Glory (Russell) MPII:JYABio
    II-768
Goalie's Anxiety at the Penalty Kick, The
    (Handke) CLCII II-598; MPII:WF II-549
Goat Song (Werfel) CLC I-404; MP
    IV-2279
"Goats and Monkeys" (Walcott) MPII:P
    III-857
"Goblin Market" (Rossetti, C.) MPII:P
    III-860
"Gobseck" (Balzac) MPII:SS II-867
God Beneath the Sea, The (Garfield and
    Blishen) MPII:JYAFic II-533
God Bless the Child (Hunter, K.)
    MPII:AfAm I-511
God Bless You, Mr. Rosewater (Vonnegut)
    CLCII II-599; MPII:AF II-634
God on the Rocks (Gardam) CLCII II-600;
    MPII:BCF II-617
Gödel, Escher, Bach (Hofstadter) MPII:NF
    II-561
Gods Are Athirst, The (France) CLC I-405;
    MP IV-2282; MP:EF II-571
God's Bits of Wood (Sembène) CLCII
    II-601; MPII:WF II-553
"God's Grandeur" (Hopkins, G.) MPII:P
    III-864
God's Little Acre (Caldwell) CLCII II-603;
    MPII:AF II-639
Gogo no eik. See Sailor Who Fell from
    Grace with the Sea, The
"Gogol's Wife" (Landolfi) MPII:SS II-871
"Going Home" (Trevor) MPII:SS II-876
Going on Sixteen (Cavanna) MPII:JYAFic
    II-537
"Going to Meet the Man" (Baldwin)
    MPII:SS II-880
"Gold Bug, The" (Poe) CLC I-406; MP
    IV-2286; MP:AF I-462; MPII:SS II-889
"Gold Coast" (McPherson) MPII:SS II-885

Gold-Rimmed Eyeglasses, The (Bassani) CLCII II-604; MPII:WF II-557

Golden Apples, The (Welty) MP IV-2289; MP:AF I-465

Golden Ass of Lucius Apuleius, The (Apuleius) CLC I-406; MP IV-2292; MP:EF II-575

Golden Bough, The (Frazer) MP IV-2296

Golden Bowl, The (James, H.) CLC I-407; MP IV-2299; MP:AF I-469

Golden Boy (Odets) CLC I-409; MP IV-2304

"Golden Honeymoon, The" (Lardner) MPII:SS II-893

Golden Notebook, The (Lessing, D.) CLCII II-605; MPII:BCF II-621

Golden Serpent, The (Alegría) CLCII II-607; MPII:AF II-645

"Golden Verses" (Nerval) MPII:P III-867

Goldengrove (Walsh) MPII:JYAFic II-540

"Golfers" (Layton) MPII:P III-870

"Goloeditsa." See "Icicle, The"

Gommes, Les. See Erasers, The

Goncourt Journals, The (Goncourt and Goncourt) MP IV-2307

Gondoliers, The (Gilbert) CLC I-409; MP IV-2310

Gone with the Wind (Mitchell, M.) CLC I-410; MP IV-2313; MP:AF I-474

"Gonzaga Manuscripts, The" (Bellow) MPII:SS II-896

Good Apprentice, The (Murdoch) CLCII II-608; MPII:BCF II-627

Good Companions, The (Priestley) CLC I-410; MP IV-2316; MP:BF I-483

Good Conscience, The (Fuentes) CLCII II-610; MPII:AF II-650

"Good Country People" (O'Connor, Flannery) MPII:SS II-900

Good Earth, The (Buck) CLC I-411; MP IV-2319; MP:AF I-478

"Good Man Is Hard to Find, A" (O'Connor, Flannery) MPII:SS II-903

Good Master, The (Seredy) MPII:JYAFic II-544

Good Morning, Midnight (Rhys) CLCII II-612; MPII:BCF II-632

Good Night, Prof, Dear (Townsend) MPII:JYAFic II-553

Good Night, Sweet Prince (Fowler) MPII:JYABio II-772

Good Person of Setzuan, The. See Good Woman of Setzuan, The

Good Soldier, The (Ford) CLCII II-613; MPII:BCF II-637

Good Soldier, The (Hašek) MP IV-2324; MP:EF II-580

Good Terrorist, The (Lessing, D.) CLCII II-614; MPII:BCF II-643

Good Woman of Setzuan, The (Brecht) CLCII II-615; MPII:D II-689

Goodbye Look, The (Macdonald) CLCII II-616; MPII:AF II-655

Goodbye, Mr. Chips (Hilton) CLC I-412; MP IV-2328; MP:BF I-487

"Goodbye, My Brother" (Cheever, J.) MPII:SS II-907

Good-bye, My Lady (Street) MPII:JYAFic II-550

Good-bye to All That (Graves) MPII:NF II-567

Goodbye to the Purple Sage (Benedict) MPII:JYAFic II-547

"Good-Morrow, The" (Donne) MPII:P III-873

Goodnight! (Tertz) CLCII II-617

"Goose Fish, The" (Nemerov) MPII:P III-876

"Gooseberries" (Chekhov) MPII:SS II-911

Gorboduc (Norton, T., and Sackville) CLC I-412; MP IV-2332

Gormenghast trilogy, The (Peake) CLCII II-618; MPII:BCF II-648

Gormenghast. See Gormenghast trilogy, The

"Gospel According to Mark, The" (Borges) MPII:SS II-915

"Gospel Singers" (Hughes, L.) MPII:SS II-918

"Gospodin iz San Frantsisko." See "Gentleman from San Francisco, The"

Gospodjica. See Woman from Sarajevo, The

Gossip from the Forest (Keneally) CLCII II-621; MPII:BCF II-655

Governess, The (Fielding, S.) MPII:JYAFic II-557

Grammar of Motives. A (Burke) MPII:NF II-573

"Grammarian's Funeral, A" (Browning, R.) MPII:P III-879

Grand Hotel (Baum) CLC I-414; MP IV-2335; MP:EF II-585

Grand Voyage, Le. *See* Long Voyage, The

Grande Alerte, La. *See* Flood Warning

Grandissimes, The (Cable) CLC I-414; MP IV-2338; MP:AF I-483

Grandma Moses (Oneal) MPII:JYABio II-780

Grandma Moses, Painter (Biracree) MPII:JYABio II-776

Grandmothers, The (Wescott) CLC I-416; MP IV-2341; MP:AF I-487

Grania (Gregory) CLCII II-622; MPII:D II-696

Grapes of Wrath, The (Steinbeck) CLC I-417; MP IV-2344; MP:AF I-491

"Graphomaniacs" (Sinyavsky) MPII:SS II-922

Grateful to Life and Death (Narayan) CLCII II-623; MPII:BCF II-660

Gravity and Grace (Weil) MPII:NF II-578

Gravity's Rainbow (Pynchon) CLCII II-624; MPII:AF II-661

"Greasy Lake" (Boyle, T.) MPII:SS III-925

Great American Negroes. *See* Great Black Americans.

Great American Novel, The (Roth, P.) CLCII II-626; MPII:AF II-666

Great Artists of America (Freedgood) MPII:JYABio II-784

Great Black Americans (Richardson, B., *and* Fahey) MPII:JYABio II-787

Great Dune trilogy, The. *See* Dune trilogy, The

Great Expectations (Dickens) CLC I-418; MP IV-2349; MP:BF I-491

Great Fortune, The. *See* Balkan trilogy, The

Great Galeoto, The (Echegaray) CLC I-420; MP IV-2355

Great Gatsby, The (Fitzgerald, F.) CLC I-421; MP IV-2358; MP:AF I-496

Great God Brown, The (O'Neill) CLCII II-628; MPII:D II-701

"Great Good Place, The" (James, H.) MPII:SS III-929

Great Hunger, The (Kavanagh) MPII:P III-882

Great Meadow, The (Roberts, E.) CLC I-422; MP IV-2363; MP:AF I-501

"Great Mountains, The." *See* Red Pony, The

Great Plains, The (Webb, W.) MP IV-2367

Great Ponds, The (Amadi) CLCII II-629; MPII:BCF II-665

Great River (Horgan) MPII:NF II-584

Great Testament, The (Villon) MP IV-2370

Great Valley, The (Johnston) CLC I-423; MP IV-2372; MP:AF I-505

"Great Wall of China, The" (Kafka) MPII:SS III-932

Great White Hope, The (Sackler) CLCII II-630; MPII:D II-706

"Greek Interpreter, The" (Doyle) MPII:SS III-936

Greek Passion, The (Kazantzakis) MP IV-2375; MP:EF II-589

Green Bay Tree, The (Bromfield) CLC I-424; MP IV-2378; MP:AF II-509

Green Card (Akalaitis) CLCII II-631; MPII:D II-711

Green Dolphin County. *See* Green Dolphin Street

Green Dolphin Street (Goudge) MPII:JYAFic II-561

"Green enravishment of human life" (Cruz, S.) MPII:P III-885

Green Fool, The (Kavanagh) MPII:NF II-589

Green Grow the Lilacs (Riggs) CLC I-425; MP IV-2382

Green Hills of Africa (Hemingway) MPII:NF II-595

Green House, The (Vargas Llosa) CLCII II-632; MPII:AF II-672

Green Huntsman, The. *See* Lucien Leuwen

Green Knowe books, The (Boston) MPII:JYAFic II-565

Green Man, The (Amis) CLCII II-633; MPII:BCF II-670

Green Mansions (Hudson) CLC I-425; MP IV-2386; MP:BF I-497; MPII:JYAFic II-570

Green Mountain Boys, The (Thompson, D.) CLC I-426; MP IV-2389; MP:AF II-514

Green Pastures, The (Connelly) CLCII II-634; MPII:D II-717

"Green Tea" (Le Fanu) MPII:SS III-940

Greene's Groatsworth of Wit Bought with a Million of Repentance (Greene, R.) MP IV-2394

"Greenleaf" (O'Connor, Flannery) MPII:SS III-944

Greenwitch. See Dark Is Rising sequence, The

Grendel (Gardner) CLCII II-637; MPII:AF II-677

Grettir the Outlaw. See Grettir the Strong

Grettir the Strong (Unknown) CLC I-427; MP IV-2396; MP:EF II-593

Grey Granite. See Scots Quair, A

Grey King, The. See Dark Is Rising sequence, The

"Greyhound People" (Adams, A.) MPII:SS III-948

Grief Observed, A (Lewis, C. S.) MPII:NF II-601

Grifel'naia oda. See Slate Ode, The

Gringa, La (Sánchez, F.) CLC I-429; MP IV-2401

Grobnica za Borisa Davidovia. See Tomb for Boris Davidovich, A

"Grodek" (Trakl) MPII:P III-888

Grosser-Tiger und Kompass-Berg. See Big Tiger and Christian

"Groundhog, The" (Eberhart) MPII:P III-891

Group, The (McCarthy, M.) CLCII II-638; MPII:AF II-682

Group Portrait with Lady (Böll) CLCII II-641; MPII:WF II-562

Growing Up (Baker, R.) MPII:JYABio II-791; MPII:NF II-606

Growing Up Female in America (Merriam) MPII:JYABio II-794

Growing Up Puerto Rican (Cooper, P.) MPII:JYABio II-798

Growth of the Soil (Hamsun) CLC I-429; MP IV-2404; MP:EF II-599

Grüne Heinrich, Der (Keller) CLC I-430; MP IV-2408; MP:EF II-603

Gruppenbild mit Dame. See Group Portrait with Lady

Guard of Honor (Cozzens) CLC I-431; MP IV-2412; MP:AF II-520

Guardian of the Word, The (Laye) CLCII II-643; MPII:WF II-567

Gucio zaczarowany. See Bobo's Metamorphosis

Guerra del fin del mundo, La. See War of the End of the World, The

Guerrillas (Naipaul, V. S.) CLCII II-644; MPII:BCF II-675

"Guest, The" (Camus) MPII:SS III-952

Guest for the Night, A (Agnon) CLCII II-645; MPII:WF I-194

Guest the One-Eyed (Gunnarsson) CLC I-432; MP IV-2416; MP:EF II-607

"Guests of the Nation" (O'Connor, Frank) MPII:SS III-956

Guide, The (Narayan) MP IV-2418; MP:EF II-610

Guide to Kulchur (Pound) MPII:NF II-611

Gulag Archipelago, 1918-1956, The (Solzhenitsyn) MPII:NF II-617

Gulliver's Travels (Swift) CLC I-432; MP IV-2421; MP:BF I-501; MPII:JYAFic II-574

Gull's Hornbook, The (Dekker) MP IV-2426

"Gun Shop, The" (Updike) MPII:SS III-959

Guns of Bull Run, The (Altsheler) MPII:JYAFic II-577

Gunslinger (Dorn) MPII:P III-894

"Gusev" (Chekhov) MPII:SS III-962

Gute Mensch von Sezuan, Der. See Good Woman of Setzuan, The

Gutenberg Galaxy, The (McLuhan) MPII:NF II-624

"Guy de Maupassant" (Babel) MPII:SS III-966

Guy Mannering (Scott, Sir W.) CLC I-433; MP IV-2429; MP:BF I-507

Guy of Warwick (Unknown) CLC I-434; MP IV-2433

Guyana Quartet, The (Harris, W.) CLCII II-646; MPII:AfAm I-517; MPII:BCF II-679

Guzmán de Alfarache (Alemán) CLC I-435; MP IV-2437; MP:EF II-613

H

Habana para un infante difunto, La. *See*
Infante's Inferno
Habit of Being, The (O'Connor) MPII:NF
II-630
Hadji Murad (Tolstoy) CLCII II-649;
MPII:WF II-571
Hadrian's Memoirs (Yourcenar) MP
V-2443; MP:EF II-620
Hagar's Daughter. *See* Magazine Novels of
Pauline Hopkins, The.
"Haircut" (Lardner) MPII:SS III-970
Hairy Ape, The (O'Neill) CLCII II-651;
MPII:D II-723
Hajji Baba of Ispahan (Morier) CLC I-436;
MP V-2446; MP:BF I-511
Hakhnasat kala. *See* Bridal Canopy, The
Hakluyt's Voyages (Hakluyt) MP V-2450
Half-Back, The (Barbour) MPII:JYAFic
II-580
Halfback Tough (Dygard) MPII:JYAFic
II-584
Ham Funeral, The (White) CLCII II-652;
MPII:D II-727
"Ha-mitpahat." *See* "Kerchief, The"
Hamlet, The (Faulkner) CLC I-436; MP
V-2454; MP:AF II-525
Hamlet of Stepney Green, The (Kops)
CLCII II-653; MPII:D II-732
"Hamlet of the Shchigrovsky District"
(Turgenev) MPII:SS III-973
Hamlet, Prince of Denmark (Shakespeare)
CLC I-437; MP V-2457
Hampshire Days (Hudson) MP V-2462
Handful of Dust, A (Waugh) CLC I-440;
MP V-2464; MP:BF I-516
Handley Cross (Surtees) CLC I-440; MP
V-2467; MP:BF I-520
Handmaid's Tale, The (Atwood) CLCII
II-654; MPII:BCF II-690
Hands Around. *See* Ronde, La
"Handsomest Drowned Man in the World,
The" (García Márquez) MPII:SS III-977
Handy Andy (Lover) CLC I-441; MP
V-2470; MP:BF I-524
Hangman's House (Byrne) CLC I-442; MP
V-2473; MP:BF I-528
Hans Brinker (Dodge) MPII:JYAFic II-588

Hans Christian Andersen (Godden)
MPII:JYABio II-802
"Hap" (Hardy) MPII:P III-899
Hapgood (Stoppard) CLCII II-656; MPII:D
II-737
"Happy August the Tenth" (Williams, T.)
MPII:SS III-981
"Happy Autumn Fields, The" (Bowen, E.)
MPII:SS III-985
Happy Days (Beckett) CLCII II-657;
MPII:D II-742
Happy Endings Are All Alike (Scoppettone)
MPII:JYAFic II-591
Hard Times (Dickens) CLC I-443; MP
V-2477; MP:BF I-532
Hardy Boys series, The (Dixon)
MPII:JYAFic II-595
Harland's Half Acre (Malouf) CLCII
II-658; MPII:BCF II-695
"Harlem" (Hughes, L.) MPII:P III-902
Harmonium (Stevens, W.) MP V-2480
"Harmony" (Lardner) MPII:SS III-989
Harp of a Thousand Strings (Davis, H. L.)
CLC I-445; MP V-2484; MP:AF II-529
Harp-Weaver and Other Poems, The
(Millay) MP V-2489
Harpoon of the Hunter (Markoosie)
MPII:JYAFic II-599
Harriet Said (Bainbridge) CLCII II-658;
MPII:BCF II-700
Harriet the Spy (Fitzhugh) MPII:JYAFic
II-602
Harriet Tubman (Petry) MPII:JYABio
II-806
Harrow and Harvest. *See* Mantlemass series,
The
Harrowing of Hubertus, The. *See* Kaywana
trilogy, The
Haru no yuki. *See* Sea of Fertility, The
"Hasidic Scriptures" (Sachs) MPII:P III-905
Hasty Heart, The (Patrick) CLCII II-660;
MPII:D II-747
Haunted Palace, The (Winwar)
MPII:JYABio II-810
Haunting of Safekeep, The (Bunting)
MPII:JYAFic II-605
Haute Surveillance. *See* Deathwatch

52

Havelok the Dane (Unknown) CLC I-445; MP V-2492

Hawaii (Michener) CLCII II-661; MPII:AF II-688

Hawkmistress! (Bradley, M.) MPII:JYAFic II-608

Hazard of New Fortunes, A (Howells) CLC I-446; MP V-2495; MP:AF II-535

He Heard America Sing (Purdy) MPII:JYABio II-814

"He Who Does Not Hope" (Ekelöf) MPII:P III-908

He Who Searches (Valenzuela) CLCII II-663; MPII:AF II-696

Headbirths (Grass) CLCII II-665; MPII:WF II-578

"Headless Hawk, The" (Capote) MPII:SS III-993

Headlong Hall (Peacock) CLC I-447; MP V-2498; MP:BF I-536

Healers, The (Armah) CLCII II-666; MPII:BCF II-705

Hearing Secret Harmonies. See Dance to the Music of Time, A

"Heart, The" (Trakl) MPII:P III-911

Heart Is a Lonely Hunter, The (McCullers) CLC I-447; MP V-2501; MP:AF II-539

Heart of a Dog, The (Bulgakov) CLCII II-667; MPII:WF II-583

Heart of a Woman, The (Angelou) MPII:JYABio II-818

"Heart of Autumn" (Warren) MPII:P III-914

Heart of Aztlán (Anaya) MPII:JYAFic II-612

Heart of Darkness (Conrad) CLC I-448; MP V-2505; MP:BF I-539

Heart of Midlothian, The (Scott, Sir W.) CLC I-449; MP V-2510; MP:BF I-544

Heart of the Matter, The (Greene, G.) CLC I-450; MP V-2515; MP:BF I-550

Heartbreak House (Shaw, G.) CLC I-451; CLCII II-669; MP V-2520; MPII:D II-752

Heartbreak Tango (Puig) CLCII II-670; MPII:AF II-701

"Heart's Needle" (Snodgrass) MPII:P III-917

Heat and Dust (Jhabvala) CLCII II-671; MPII:BCF II-710

Heat of the Day, The (Bowen, E.) CLC I-453; MP V-2523; MP:BF I-555

Heaven's My Destination (Wilder, T.) CLC I-453; MP V-2528; MP:AF II-543

"Heavy Bear Who Goes with Me, The" (Schwartz) MPII:P III-921

Hebräische Melodien. See Hebrew Melodies

"Hebrew Melodies" (Heine) MPII:P III-924

Hedda Gabler (Ibsen) CLC I-454; MP V-2532

Heidi (Spyri) MPII:JYAFic II-616

Heidi Chronicles, The (Wasserstein) CLCII II-673; MPII:D II-758

Heidis Lehr und Wanderjahre. See Heidi

Heights of Macchu Picchu, The (Neruda) MPII:P III-928

Heimkehr. See Homecoming

Heimkehr der Fronttruppen. See November 1918

Heimskringla (Snorri Sturluson) CLC I-456; MP V-2537; MP:EF II-623

Helen (Euripides) CLC I-458; MP V-2544

Helen Keller (Bigland) MPII:JYABio II-822

"Helian" (Trakl) MPII:P III-932

Heliga Landet, Det. See Tobias trilogy, The

Helter-Skelter (Moyes) MPII:JYAFic II-619

Hemsöborna. See Natives of Hemsö, The

"Henceforth, from the Mind" (Bogan) MPII:P III-935

Henderson the Rain King (Bellow) MP V-2547; MP:AF II-547

Henry David Thoreau (Krutch) MPII:JYABio II-826

Henry Esmond (Thackeray) CLC I-459; MP V-2550; MP:BF I-560

Henry the Eighth (Shakespeare) CLC I-460; MP V-2555

Henry the Fifth (Shakespeare) CLC I-462; MP V-2558

Henry IV (Pirandello) CLCII II-674; MPII:D II-764

Henry the Fourth, Part One (Shakespeare) CLC I-464; MP V-2562

Henry the Fourth, Part Two (Shakespeare) CLC I-464; MP V-2567

Henry the Fourth, Parts One and Two (Shakespeare) CLC I-464

Henry the Sixth, Part One (Shakespeare) CLC I-466; MP V-2572

Henry the Sixth, Part Three (Shakespeare)
CLC I-466; MP V-2580
Henry the Sixth, Part Two (Shakespeare)
CLC I-466; MP V-2576
Henry the Sixth, Parts One, Two, and Three
(Shakespeare) CLC I-466
"Her First Ball" (Mansfield) MPII:SS III-997
Her Privates, We (Manning, F.) CLCII
II-675; MPII:BCF II-717
"Her Table Spread" (Bowen, E.) MPII:SS
III-1000
"Herakleitos" (Davenport) MPII:SS III-1003
Herakles Mad (Euripides) CLC I-468; MP
V-2584
Herbert Hoover Story, The (Peare)
MPII:JYABio II-830
Herbsttag. See Autumn Day
Hercules and His Twelve Labors
(Unknown) CLC I-470; MP V-2587;
MP:EF II-631
Hereward the Wake (Kingsley, C.) CLC
I-470; MP V-2591; MP:BF I-566
Heritage and Its History, A
(Compton-Burnett) MP V-2594; MP:BF
I-570
Herland (Gilman) CLCII II-676; MPII:AF
II-706
Hermano asno, El. See Brother Ass
Hero Ain't Nothin' but a Sandwich, A
(Childress) MPII:AfAm II-523;
MPII:JYAFic II-623
Hero and Leander (Marlowe) MPII:P III-938
Hero and the Crown, The (McKinley)
MPII:JYAFic II-626
Hero of Our Time, A (Lermontov) CLC
I-471; MP V-2597; MP:EF II-636
Hero with a Thousand Faces, The
(Campbell, J.) MPII:NF II-636
"Herodias" (Flaubert) MPII:SS III-1007
Heroes and History (Sutcliff) MPII:JYABio
II-834
"Heroes in the Dark House, The" (Kiely)
MPII:SS III-1011
"Heroes of Childhood, The" (McGrath)
MPII:P III-942
Heroes of Mexico (Rosenblum)
MPII:JYABio II-838
Heroes of the American Revolution (Davis,
B.) MPII:JYABio II-842

Heroes of the American West (Pappas)
MPII:JYABio II-846
Heroides (Ovid) MP V-2601
Herries chronicle, The. See Fortress, Judith
Paris, Rogue Herries, and Vanessa
Herself Surprised (Cary, J.) CLC I-472; MP
V-2603; MP:BF I-574
Herz, Das. See Heart, The
Herzog (Bellow) CLCII II-677; MPII:AF
II-712
Hesperides (Herrick) MP V-2606
Hiding Place. See Homewood trilogy, The
"Higgler, The" (Coppard) MPII:SS III-1014
High Cotton (Pinckney) MPII:AfAm II-529
High King, The. See Prydain chronicles, The
High Wind in Jamaica, A. See Innocent
Voyage, The
High Wind Rising, A (Singmaster) CLC
I-472; MP V-2609; MP:AF II-551
"High Windows" (Larkin) MPII:P III-945
Hijo de hombre. See Son of Man
Hill of Dreams, The (Machen) CLC I-473;
MP V-2613; MP:BF I-578
Hillingdon Hall (Surtees) CLC I-474; MP
V-2616; MP:BF I-582
"Hills Like White Elephants" (Hemingway)
MPII:SS III-1018
Hiob. See Job
Hippolytus (Euripides) CLC I-474; MP
V-2620
Hiroshima (Hersey) MPII:NF II-641
His Master's Voice (Lem) CLCII II-678;
MPII:WF II-588
His Own Where (Jordan, J.) MPII:AfAm
II-535; MPII:JYAFic II-629
"His Son, in His Arms, in Light, Aloft"
(Brodkey) MPII:SS III-1022
Historia Calamitatum (Abélard) MP V-2624
History (Morante) CLCII II-679; MPII:WF
II-593
History and Remarkable Life of the Truly
Honourable Colonel Jacque, The. See
History of Colonel Jacque, The
History Man, The (Bradbury, M.) CLCII
II-680; MPII:BCF II-721
History of a Scoundrel, The. See Bel-Ami
History of Amelia, The. See Amelia
History of Colonel Jacque, The (Defoe)
CLC I-475; MP V-2627; MP:BF I-586

History of England, The (Macaulay) MP V-2631

History of Frederick II of Prussia (Carlyle) MP V-2634

History of Henry Esmond, Esq., The. *See* Henry Esmond

History of King Richard III (More, Sir T.) MP V-2637

History of Mr. Polly, The (Wells) CLC I-476; MP V-2640; MP:BF I-590

History of New York, by Diedrich Knickerbocker, A (Irving, W.) MP V-2643

History of Pendennis, The. *See* Pendennis

History of Rasselas, The. *See* Rasselas

History of Sandford and Merton, The. *See* Sandford and Merton

History of the Adventures of Joseph Andrews, The. *See* Joseph Andrews

History of the Conquest of Mexico (Prescott) MP V-2646

History of the Decline and Fall of the Roman Empire, The (Gibbon) MP V-2649

History of the Peloponnesian War (Thucydides) MP V-2652

History of the Persian Wars, The (Herodotus) MP V-2655

History of the Rebellion and Civil Wars in England (Hyde) MP V-2658

History of the Reign of King Henry VII (Bacon) MP V-2660

History of Tom Jones, a Foundling, The. *See* Tom Jones

"Hitchhiking Game, The" (Kundera) MPII:SS III-1026

Hitty, Her First Hundred Years (Field) MPII:JYAFic II-631

Hive, The (Cela) MP V-2663; MP:EF II-641

Hizakurige (Jippensha Ikku) CLC I-478; MP V-2667; MP:EF II-646

H.M.S. Pinafore (Gilbert) CLC I-478; MP V-2669

Ho teleutaios peirasmos. *See* Last Temptation of Christ, The

Hobbit, The (Tolkien) CLCII II-681; MPII:BCF II-727; MPII:JYAFic II-635

"Hodel" (Aleichem) MPII:SS III-1029

Hojarasca, La. *See* Leaf Storm

Hj no umi. *See* Sea of Fertility, The

"Hollow Men, The" (Eliot, T. S.) MPII:P III-948

Holy Ghosts (Linney) CLCII II-683; MPII:D II-769

Holy Land, The. *See* Tobias trilogy, The

Holy Place (Fuentes) CLCII II-684; MPII:AF II-717

Holy Sinner, The (Mann) CLCII II-685; MPII:WF II-599

Holy State and the Profane State, The (Fuller) MP V-2672

Holy Terrors, The (Cocteau) CLC I-479; MP V-2675; MP:EF II-648

Holzfällen (Bernhard) MPII:WF II-603. *See also* Woodcutters

Homage to Catalonia (Orwell) MPII:NF II-645

Homage to Mistress Bradstreet (Berryman) MP V-2678

Homage to Sextus Propertius (Pound) MPII:P III-951

Homba. *See* Sea of Fertility, The

Hombres de maíz. *See* Men of Maize

"Home" (Phillips, J.) MPII:SS III-1033

Home (Rybczynski) MPII:NF II-651

Home Before Dark (Bridgers) MPII:JYAFic II-638

Home Before Dark (Cheever, S.) MPII:JYABio II-850

Home Before Morning (Van Devanter) MPII:JYABio II-854

Home-maker, The (Fisher) CLCII II-686; MPII:AF II-728

Home to Harlem (McKay) CLCII II-687; MPII:AF II-722; MPII:AfAm II-540

Home to the Wilderness (Carrighar) MPII:JYABio II-857

"Homecoming" (Celan) MPII:P III-956

Homecoming, The (Pinter) CLCII II-688; MPII:D II-774

"Homecoming" (Walcott) MPII:P III-959

Homecomings. *See* Strangers and Brothers

Homesick (Fritz) MPII:JYABio II-861

"Homesickness" (Tsvetayeva) MPII:P III-962

Homewood trilogy, The (Wideman) CLCII II-689; MPII:AF II-732; MPII:AfAm II-546

Homme qui regardait passer les trains, L'. *See* Man Who Watched the Trains Go By, The

Homme révolté, L'. *See* Rebel, The

Homo Faber (Frisch) CLCII II-692; MPII:WF II-608

Honest Whore, Part One, The (Dekker *and* Middleton) CLC I-479; MP V-2680

Honest Whore, Part Two, The (Dekker) CLC I-479; MP V-2684

Honey in the Horn (Davis, H. L.) CLC I-480; MP V-2688; MP:AF II-555

Honeycomb. *See* Pilgrimage

Honorary Consul, The (Greene) CLCII II-693; MPII:BCF II-732

Honourable Schoolboy, The (le Carré) CLCII II-694; MPII:BCF II-737

Hoops (Myers) MPII:JYAFic II-641

Hoosier Schoolmaster, The (Eggleston) CLC I-481; MP V-2691; MP:AF II-559

Hope Abandoned (Mandelstam, N.) MPII:NF II-656

Hope Against Hope (Mandelstam, N.) MPII:NF II-662

Hopscotch (Cortázar) CLCII II-695; MPII:AF II-739

Horace (Corneille) CLC I-482; MP V-2695

Horacker (Raabe) CLCII II-697; MPII:WF II-612

Horatio Hornblower series, The (Forester) MPII:JYAFic II-644. *See also* Captain Horatio Hornblower

Horloger d'Everton, L'. *See* Watchmaker of Everton, The

Horse and His Boy, The. *See* Chronicles of Narnia, The

"Horse and Two Goats, A" (Narayan) MPII:SS III-1037

"Horse Dealer's Daughter, The" (Lawrence) MPII:SS III-1041

Horse Without a Head, The (Berna) MPII:JYAFic II-649

Horseman on the Roof, The (Giono) CLCII II-699; MPII:WF II-618

"Horses, The" (Hughes, Ted) MPII:P III-965

Horse's Mouth, The (Cary, J.) CLC I-482; MP V-2699; MP:BF I-593

"Horseshoe Finder, The" (Mandelstam, O.) MPII:P III-968

Horseshoe Robinson (Kennedy, J. P.) CLC I-483; MP V-2702; MP:AF II-563

Hostage, The (Behan) CLCII II-700; MPII:D II-778

Hot l Baltimore, The (Wilson, L.) CLCII II-701; MPII:D II-783

"Hôte, L'." *See* "Guest, The"

Hotel du Lac (Brookner) CLCII II-702; MPII:BCF II-743

Hotel New Hampshire, The (Irving, J.) CLCII II-703; MPII:AF II-743

House at Pooh Corner, The (Milne) MPII:JYAFic IV-1637

House Behind the Cedars, The (Chesnutt) CLCII II-705; MPII:AF II-748; MPII:AfAm II-552

House by the Churchyard, The (Le Fanu) CLC I-484; MP V-2705; MP:BF II-597

House by the Medlar Tree, The (Verga) CLC I-485; MP V-2709; MP:EF II-652

House for Mr. Biswas, A (Naipaul, V. S.) CLCII II-706; MPII:BCF II-748

House in Norham Gardens, The (Lively) MPII:JYAFic II-653

House in Paris, The (Bowen, E.) CLC I-486; MP V-2714; MP:BF II-602

"House in the Heart, The" (Nye) MPII:P III-971

"House in Turk Street, The" (Hammett) MPII:SS III-1045

House Made of Dawn (Momaday) CLCII II-707; MPII:AF II-754; MPII:JYAFic II-657

House of All Nations (Stead) CLCII II-708; MPII:BCF II-753

House of Atreus, The (Aeschylus) CLC I-486; MP V-2719

House of Blue Leaves, The (Guare) CLCII II-710; MPII:D II-789

House of Gentlefolk, A (Turgenev) CLC I-487; MP V-2724; MP:EF II-657

House of Mirth, The (Wharton) CLC I-489; MP V-2729; MP:AF II-567

House of Sixty Fathers, The (De Jong) MPII:JYAFic II-661

House of Stairs (Sleator) MPII:JYAFic II-665

House of the Dead, The (Dostoevski) CLCII II-711; MPII:WF II-623

House of the Seven Gables, The
(Hawthorne) CLC I-491; MP V-2734;
MP:AF II-572
House of the Sleeping Beauties, The
(Kawabata) CLCII II-712; MPII:WF
II-629
House on the Embankment, The (Trifonov)
CLCII II-713; MPII:WF II-633
House on the Hill, The (Pavese) CLCII
II-715; MPII:WF II-639
"House with the Grape-vine, The" (Bates)
MPII:SS III-1049
House with the Green Shutters, The
(Douglas, G.) CLC I-492; MP V-2739;
MP:BF II-608
"Housebreaker of Shady Hill, The"
(Cheever, J.) MPII:SS III-1052
Householder, The (Jhabvala) CLCII II-716;
MPII:BCF II-758
"How Claeys Died" (Sansom) MPII:SS
III-1056
"How do I love thee? Let me count the
ways." See Sonnet 43
How Do I Love Thee? (Waite)
MPII:JYABio II-865
How Far Can You Go? See Souls and
Bodies
How Green Was My Valley (Llewellyn)
CLC I-493; MP V-2742; MP:BF II-612
"How I contemplated the world from the
Detroit House of Correction and began
my life over again" (Oates) MPII:SS
III-1060
"How I Finally Lost My Heart" (Lessing,
D.) MPII:SS III-1064
How It Is (Beckett) CLCII II-717; MPII:WF
II-644
"How It Was Done in Odessa" (Babel)
MPII:SS III-1067
"How Mr. Rabbit Was Too Sharp for Mr.
Fox." See "Wonderful Tar-Baby Story,
The"
"How Much Land Does a Man Need?"
(Tolstoy) MPII:SS III-1070
How Much Love Costs Old Men. See
Splendors and Miseries of Courtesans,
The
"How the Devil Came Down Division
Street" (Algren) MPII:SS III-1073

Howards End (Forster) CLC I-493; MP
V-2745; MP:BF II-616
"Howl" (Ginsberg) MPII:P III-974
Hsüan-chou hsieh-t'iao-lou chien-pei
chiao-shu shu-yün. See Farewell to Li
Yun in the Xie Tiao Pavilion, A
Huasipungo (Icaza) CLC I-494; MP
V-2750. See also Villagers, The
Hubertus. See Kaywana trilogy, The
Huckleberry Finn. See Adventures of
Huckleberry Finn, The
Hudibras (Butler) CLC I-497; MP V-2760
Hugh Selwyn Mauberly (Pound) MPII:P
III-978
Hugh Wynne, Free Quaker (Mitchell, S.)
CLC I-497; MP V-2763; MP:AF II-577
Hugo and Josephine (Gripe) MPII:JYAFic
II-668
Hugo och Josefin. See Hugo and Josephine
Huis clos. See No Exit
"Human Abstract, The" (Blake) MPII:P
III-982
Human Age, The (Lewis, W.) CLCII
II-718; MPII:BCF II-764
Human Comedy, The (Saroyan) CLC I-498;
MP V-2766; MP:AF II-581
Humboldt's Gift (Bellow) CLCII II-721;
MPII:AF II-759
Humphry Clinker (Smollett) CLC I-499;
MP V-2769; MP:BF II-621
Hunchback of Notre Dame, The (Hugo, V.)
CLC I-500; MP V-2774; MP:EF II-663
Hundejahre. See Dog Years
Hundred Million Francs, A. See Horse
Without a Head, The
Hundred Penny Box, The (Mathis)
MPII:JYAFic II-672
Hunger (Hamsun) CLC I-502; MP V-2780;
MP:EF II-670
"Hunger Artist, A" (Kafka) MPII:SS
III-1077
Hunger of Memory (Rodríguez)
MPII:JYABio II-869; MPII:NF II-668
"Hunter Gracchus, The" (Kafka) MPII:SS
III-1081
"Hunting Season" (Greenberg) MPII:SS
III-1085
Huon de Bordeaux (Unknown) CLC I-502;
MP V-2784; MP:EF II-674

I

I Always Wanted to Be Somebody (Gibson)
MPII:JYABio II-873

"I Am" (Clare) MPII:P III-1002

I Am a Cat (Natsume) CLCII II-724;
MPII:WF II-648

I Am a Stranger on the Earth (Dobrin)
MPII:JYABio II-877

I Am David (Holm) MPII:JYAFic II-676

I Am the Cheese (Cormier) MPII:JYAFic
II-679

"I cannot live with You—" (Dickinson, E.)
MPII:P III-1005

I, Charlotte Forten, Black and Free
(Longsworth) MPII:JYABio II-881

I, Claudius (Graves) CLC I-507; MP
V-2803; MP:BF II-632

I de dage. See Giants in the Earth

I det fria. See Out in the Open

"I Don't Have to Show You No Stinking
Badges!" (Valdez) CLCII II-726;
MPII:D II-799

"I felt a Funeral in my Brain" (Dickinson,
E.) MPII:P III-1008

I for One . . . (Sargeson) CLCII II-726;
MPII:BCF II-772

I Get on the Bus (McKnight) MPII:AfAm
II-563

"I have a terrible fear of being an animal"
(Vallejo) MPII:P III-1011

"I Have Forgotten the Word I Wanted to
Say" (Mandelstam, O.) MPII:P III-1014

"I heard a Fly buzz—when I died—"
(Dickinson, E.) MPII:P III-1017

I Heard the Owl Call My Name (Craven)
MPII:JYAFic II-682

I, Juan de Pareja (Borton de Treviño)
MPII:JYAFic II-685

I Knock at the Door. See Mirror in My
House

"I Know a Man" (Creeley) MPII:P III-1020

I Know Why the Caged Bird Sings
(Angelou) MPII:AfAm II-569;
MPII:JYABio II-885; MPII:NF II-673

"I like to see it lap the Miles—" (Dickinson,
E.) MPII:P III-1024

I Like It Here (Amis) CLCII II-728;
MPII:BCF II-777

"I Look Out for Ed Wolfe" (Elkin) MPII:SS
III-1088

"I married" (Niedecker) MPII:P III-1027

I Mary (Randall, R.) MPII:JYABio II-889

I Never Promised You a Rose Garden
(Green, Hannah) CLCII II-728; MPII:AF
II-769; MPII:JYAFic II-688

I Remember St. Petersburg. See My St.
Petersburg.

"I sing of Olaf glad and big" (Cummings)
MPII:P III-1030

"I Sing the Body Electric" (Whitman)
MPII:P III-1033

I Speak for Thaddeus Stevens (Singmaster)
MP V-2806

"I Stand Here Ironing" (Olsen) MPII:SS
III-1091

"I taste a liquor never brewed—"
(Dickinson, E.) MPII:P III-1037

"I Thought once how Theocritus had sung"
See Sonnet 1

"I Wandered Lonely As a Cloud"
(Wordsworth) MPII:P III-1040

"I Want to Know Why" (Anderson)
MPII:SS III-1095

I Wear the Morning Star. See Ghost Horse
cycle, The

"I Will Fight No More Forever" (Beal)
MPII:JYABio II-893

I Will Marry When I Want (Ngugi and
Ngugi) CLCII II-729; MPII:D II-804

I Wonder as I Wander (Hughes, L.)
MPII:AfAm I-131; MPII:JYABio II-897

Ia slovo pozabyl, chto ia khotel skazat. See I
Have Forgotten the Word I Wanted to
Say

"Iber a Hitl." See "On Account of a Hat"

"Ice" (Ai) MPII:P III-1043

Ice (Kavan) CLCII II-730; MPII:BCF II-782

Ice Age, The (Drabble) CLCII II-731;
MPII:BCF II-787

"Ice House, The" (Gordon) MPII:SS
III-1099

"Ice Wagon Going Down the Street, The"
(Gallant) MPII:SS III-1103

Iceland Fisherman, An (Loti) CLC I-508;
MP V-2810; MP:EF II-678

59

Iceman Cometh, The (O'Neill) CLCII II-732; MPII:D II-809

"Icicle, The" (Sinyavsky) MPII:SS III-1106

"Idea of Order at Key West, The" (Stevens, W.) MPII:P III-1046

Ides of March, The (Wilder, T.) CLC I-509; MP V-2814; MP:AF II-584

Idiot, The (Dostoevski) CLC I-510; MP V-2817; MP:EF II-682

"Idiots First" (Malamud) MPII:SS III-1109

"Idle Days on the Yann" (Dunsany) MPII:SS III-1112

Idler, The (Johnson, S.) MP V-2822

Idylls of the King, The (Tennyson) CLC I-511; MP V-2825

If Beale Street Could Talk (Baldwin) CLCII II-733; MPII:AF II-774

If He Hollers Let Him Go (Himes) CLCII II-734; MPII:AF II-778; MPII:AfAm II-575

"If I leave all for thee, wilt thou exchange" See Sonnet 35

If I Love You, Am I Trapped Forever? (Kerr) MPII:JYAFic II-691

If Not Now, When? (Levi, P.) CLCII II-735; MPII:WF II-653

If on a Winter's Night a Traveler (Calvino) CLCII II-736; MPII:WF II-659

If This Is a Man (Levi) MPII:NF II-678

"If thou must love me, let it be for nought" See Sonnet 14

If Winter Comes (Hutchinson) CLC I-513; MP V-2831; MP:BF II-636

"If You Ask Me" (Ekelöf) MPII:P III-1049

If You Could See What I Hear (Sullivan and Gill) MPII:JYABio II-901

Ignatius His Conclave (Donne) MP V-2834

Iliad, The (Homer) CLC I-513; MP V-2837

Iliad, The (Weil) MPII:NF II-684

Iliade, L'. See Iliad, The

I'll Get There (Donovan) MPII:JYAFic II-695

Ill-Made Knight, The. See Once and Future King, The

Ill Seen Ill Said (Beckett) CLCII II-738; MPII:WF II-664

Illness as Metaphor (Sontag) MPII:NF II-689

Illywhacker (Carey, P.) CLCII II-739; MPII:BCF II-794

"I'm a Fool" (Anderson) MPII:SS III-1116

I'm Not Stiller (Frisch) CLCII II-740; MPII:WF II-669

Im Westen nichts Neues. See All Quiet on the Western Front

Images and Shadows (Origo) MPII:NF II-694

Imaginary Conversations (Landor) MP V-2842

Imaginary Life, An (Malouf) CLCII II-742; MPII:BCF II-799

"Imagination Dead Imagine" (Beckett) MPII:SS III-1119

"Imagined Scenes" (Beattie) MPII:SS III-1122

Imago. See Xenogenesis Trilogy, The.

Imitation of Christ, The (Thomas à Kempis) MP V-2845

Immense Journey, The (Eiseley) MPII:NF II-699

Immoralist, The (Gide) CLCII II-743; MPII:WF II-673

Immoraliste, L'. See Immoralist, The

"Impalpabilities, The" (Tomlinson) MPII:P III-1052

"Imperial Adam" (Hope, A. D.) MPII:P III-1055

Importance of Being Earnest, The (Wilde) CLC I-517; MP V-2847

"Impulse" (Aiken, C.) MPII:SS III-1126

"In a Dark Time" (Roethke) MPII:P III-1058

In a Free State (Naipaul, V. S.) CLCII II-744; MPII:BCF II-804

"In Another Country" (Hemingway) MPII:SS III-1130

"In California" (Simpson) MPII:P III-1061

In Chancery. See Forsyte Saga, The

In Cold Blood (Capote) MPII:NF II-704

"In Cold Hell, in Thicket" (Olson) MPII:P III-1064

In der blauen Ferne. See In the Blue Distance

In der Flucht. See Fleeing

"In der Strafkolonie." See "In the Penal Colony"

"In Dreams Begin Responsibilities" (Schwartz) MPII:SS III-1134

In Dubious Battle (Steinbeck) CLC I-518; MP V-2850; MP:AF II-588

"In Greenwich There Are Many Gravelled Walks" (Calisher) MPII:SS III-1137

In Joy Still Felt (Asimov) MPII:NF II-709

In Kindling Flame (Atkinson) MPII:JYABio II-905

In Memoriam (Tennyson) MP V-2853

"In Memory of Sigmund Freud" (Auden) MPII:P III-1068

"In Memory of W. B. Yeats" (Auden) MPII:P III-1071

In Memory Yet Green (Asimov) MPII:NF II-714

In My Father's Court (Singer) MPII:NF II-719

In Parenthesis (Jones, David) MPII:P III-1074

In Patagonia (Chatwin) MPII:NF II-725

In Praise of Shadows (Tanizaki) MPII:NF II-731

"In Santa Maria del Popolo" (Gunn) MPII:P III-1079

In Sicily (Vittorini) CLCII II-745; MPII:WF II-681

"In Tenebris" (Hardy) MPII:P III-1082

In That Dawn. See Story of a Life, The

In the American Grain (Williams, W.) MP V-2856

In the Beginning (Potok) CLCII II-746; MPII:AF II-782

"In the Blue Distance" (Sachs) MPII:P III-1086

"In the Cage" (James, H.) MPII:SS III-1141

In the Castle of My Skin (Lamming) CLCII II-747; MPII:AfAm II-581; MPII:BCF II-809

"In the Evening" (Akhmatova) MPII:P III-1090

"In the Garden of the North American Martyrs" (Wolff) MPII:SS III-1146

"In the Heart of the Heart of the Country" (Gass) MPII:SS III-1150

In the Heart of the Seas (Agnon) CLCII II-749; MPII:WF I-194

In the Labyrinth (Robbe-Grillet) CLCII II-750; MPII:WF II-686

"In the Naked Bed, in Plato's Cave" (Schwartz) MPII:P III-1093

"In the Penal Colony" (Kafka) MPII:SS III-1154

"In the Ruins of an Ancient Temple" (Rítsos) MPII:P III-1096

In the Shadow of Man (Goodall) MPII:JYABio II-909

In the Shadow of the Glen (Synge) CLCII II-750; MPII:D II-815

"In the Thirtieth Year" (Cunningham) MPII:P III-1099

In the Time of Greenbloom (Fielding) CLCII II-751; MPII:BCF II-814

"In the Waiting Room" (Bishop, E.) MPII:P III-1102

"In the White Night" (Beattie) MPII:SS III-1158

In the Wilderness (Undset) CLC I-519; MP V-2861; MP:EF II-687

In the Wine Time (Bullins) CLCII II-753; MPII:AfAm II-587; MPII:D II-820

In the Wine Time (Bullins)

"In the Winter of My Thirty-Eighth Year" (Merwin) MPII:P III-1105

In the Year of the Boar and Jackie Robinson (Lord, B.) MPII:JYAFic II-699

In Vain. See I cannot live with You—

In Watermelon Sugar (Brautigan) CLCII II-754; MPII:AF II-787

Inadmissible Evidence (Osborne) CLCII II-755; MPII:D II-826

Inazuma-byshi (Sant Kyden) CLC I-520; MP V-2864; MP:EF II-691

Ince Memed. See Memed, My Hawk

Incident at Vichy (Miller, A.) CLCII II-756; MPII:D II-831

Incidents in the Life of a Slave Girl (Jacobs, H.) MPII:AfAm II-592

Incognito (Dumitriu) MP V-2868; MP:EF II-696

Increased Difficulty of Concentration, The (Havel) CLCII II-757; MPII:D II-835

Incredible Journey, The (Burnford) MPII:JYAFic II-703

Independent People (Laxness) CLC I-521; MP V-2872; MP:EF II-701

"Indian Burying Ground, The" (Freneau) MPII:P III-1108

"Indian Camp" (Hemingway) MPII:SS III-1162

Indian Captive (Lenski) MPII:JYABio II-913

Indian Chiefs (Freedman) MPII:JYABio II-916

Indian in the Cupboard, The (Banks) MPII:JYAFic II-706

Indian Summer (Howells) CLC I-522; MP V-2877; MP:AF II-591

Indian Summer (Stifter) CLCII II-757; MPII:WF II-691

"Indian Uprising, The" (Barthelme, D.) MPII:SS III-1165

Indiana (Sand) CLC I-523; MP V-2880; MP:EF II-707

Indians (Kopit) CLCII II-759; MPII:D II-840

Indifferenti, Gli. *See* Time of Indifference, The

"Indissoluble Matrimony" (West, R.) MPII:SS III-1169

In'ei raisan. *See* In Praise of Shadows

Inês de Castro (Ferreira) CLC I-524; MP V-2883

"Infant Prodigy, The" (Mann) MPII:SS III-1173

Infante's Inferno (Cabrera Infante) CLCII II-760; MPII:AF II-792

Infants of the Spring (Powell). *See* To Keep the Ball Rolling

Infants of the Spring (Thurman) MPII:AfAm II-597

Infernal Machine, The (Cocteau) CLCII II-761; MPII:D II-846

Inferno (Strindberg) CLCII II-762; MPII:WF II-697

Informer, The (O'Flaherty) CLC I-524; MP V-2886; MP:BF II-640

Ingoldsby Legends, The (Ingoldsby) MP V-2891

Inhabitants, The (Morris) MPII:NF II-736

Inheritors, The (Golding) MP V-2894; MP:BF II-645

Inimitable Jeeves, The (Wodehouse) CLCII II-763; MPII:BCF II-820

Inishfallen, Fare Thee Well. *See* Mirror in My House

Injury and Insult. *See* Insulted and the Injured, The

"Innen und Aussen." *See* "Within and Without"

"Innocence" (O'Faoláin) MPII:SS III-1176

Innocent Voyage, The (Hughes, R.) CLC I-525; MP V-2897; MP:BF II-649

Innocent Wayfaring, The (Chute) MPII:JYAFic II-709

Innommable, L'. *See* Trilogy, The, *and* Unnamable, The

Inquiry Concerning Political Justice, An (Godwin) MP V-2901

Inquisitoire, L'. *See* Inquisitory, The

Inquisitory, The (Pinget) CLCII II-764; MPII:WF II-701

"Insomnia. Homer. Taut Sails." (Mandelstam, O.) MPII:P III-1111

Inspector Calls, An (Priestley) CLCII II-765; MPII:D II-852

Inspector General, The (Gogol) CLC I-526; MP V-2904

"Instructions for John Howell" (Cortázar) MPII:SS III-1180

Insular Possession, An (Mo) CLCII II-766; MPII:BCF II-825

Insulted and the Injured, The (Dostoevski) CLCII II-767; MPII:WF II-706

Intellectual Follies, The (Abel) MPII:NF II-742

Intensive Care (Frame) CLCII II-769; MPII:BCF II-831

Inter Ice Age 4 (Abe) CLCII II-770; MPII:WF II-711

"Interest in Life, An" (Paley) MPII:SS III-1184

Interesting Narrative of the Life of Olaudah Equiano, or Gustavus Vassa, the African, The (Equiano) MPII:AfAm II-603

Interim. *See* Pilgrimage

"Interlopers, The" (Saki) MPII:SS III-1187

Interpretation of Cultures, The (Geertz) MPII:NF II-747

Interpretation of Dreams, The (Freud) MP V-2908

Interpreters, The (Soyinka) CLCII II-770; MPII:BCF II-836

Interrupted Life, An (Hillesum) MPII:NF II-751

Interstellar Pig (Sleator) MPII:JYAFic II-712

Intruder, The (Townsend) MPII:JYAFic II-715

Intruder in the Dust (Faulkner) CLC I-527; MP V-2911; MP:AF II-595

Invention of Morel, The (Bioy Casares) CLCII II-772; MPII:AF II-798

Investigation, The (Lem) CLCII II-773; MPII:WF II-717

Invincible, The (Lem) CLCII II-774; MPII:WF II-722

Invincible Louisa (Meigs) MPII:JYABio II-920

Invisible Cities (Calvino) CLCII II-774; MPII:WF II-727

"Invisible Man, The" (Chesterton) MPII:SS III-1191

Invisible Man (Ellison) MP V-2915; MP:AF II-599; MPII:AfAm II-607; MPII:JYAFic II-719

Invisible Man, The (Wells) CLC I-528; MP V-2918; MP:BF II-653

Invitation au Voyage, L'. See Invitation to the Voyage, The

Invitation to a Beheading (Nabokov) CLCII II-775; MPII:WF II-732

"Invitation to the Voyage, The" (Baudelaire) MPII:P III-1114

Iola Leroy (Harper, F.) MPII:AfAm II-614

Iolanthe (Gilbert) CLC I-528; MP V-2922

Ion (Euripides) CLC I-529; MP V-2925

Iphigenia in Aulis (Euripides) CLC I-530; MP V-2928

Iphigenia in Tauris (Euripides) CLC I-532; MP V-2931

"Irish Airman Foresees His Death, An" (Yeats) MPII:P III-1117

Irish Melodies (Moore, T.) MP V-2935

Iron Earth, Copper Sky (Kemal) CLCII IV-1718; MPII:WF IV-1754

Iron in the Soul. See Roads to Freedom, The

Iron Lily, The. See Mantlemass series, The

Ironweed (Kennedy, W.) CLCII II-776. See also Albany Cycle, The

"Irrepressibly bronze, beautiful & mine" (Shange) MPII:P III-1120

Is That You, Miss Blue? (Kerr) MPII:JYAFic II-723

Isaac Newton (Tannenbaum and Stillman) MPII:JYABio II-923

Ishi, Last of His Tribe (Kroeber) MPII:JYABio II-926

Island of Crimea, The (Aksyonov) CLCII II-778; MPII:WF II-737

Island of the Blue Dolphins (O'Dell) MPII:JYAFic II-726

Islands in the Stream (Hemingway) CLCII II-780; MPII:AF II-803

"Islas nuevas, Las." See "New Islands"

Isola di Arturo, L'. See Arturo's Island

Israel Potter (Melville) CLC I-533; MP V-2938; MP:AF II-603

"Israfel" (Poe) MPII:P III-1123

Issa Valley, The (Miłosz) CLCII II-781; MPII:WF II-743

"Istoriia moei golubiatni." See "Story of My Dovecot, The"

It Is Better than It Was (Calderón de la Barca) CLC I-534; MP V-2942

It Is Worse than It Was (Calderón de la Barca) CLC I-534; MP V-2945

"It May Never Happen" (Pritchett) MPII:SS III-1194

"It weeps in my heart" (Verlaine) MPII:P III-1126

Italian, The (Radcliffe) CLC I-535; MP V-2948; MP:BF II-657

Itching Parrot, The (Fernández de Lizardi) CLC I-536; MP V-2955; MP:AF II-607

It's an Aardvark-Eat-Turtle World (Danziger) MPII:JYAFic II-730

It's Like This, Cat (Neville) MPII:JYAFic II-734

Ivanhoe (Scott, Sir W.) CLC I-536; MP V-2959; MP:BF II-665

Ivona, Princess of Burgundia (Gombrowicz) CLCII II-782; MPII:D II-857

Ivory Swing, The (Hospital) CLCII II-784; MPII:BCF II-843

"Ivy Day in the Committee Room" (Joyce) MPII:SS III-1197

"Ivy Gripped the Steps" (Bowen, E.) MPII:SS III-1201

Iwona, ksiniczka Burgunda. See Ivona, Princess of Burgundia

J

Jack of Newberry (Deloney) CLC I-538; MP V-2964; MP:BF II-671

Jack Sheppard (Ainsworth) CLC I-538; MP V-2969; MP:BF II-676

"Jackals and Arabs" (Kafka) MPII:SS III-1205

Jackie Robinson (Allen, M.) MPII:JYABio II-929

"Jacklighting" (Beattie) MPII:SS III-1208

Jacob Have I Loved (Paterson) MPII:JYAFic II-737

Jacob's Room (Woolf) CLCII II-785; MPII:BCF II-848

Jacques le fataliste et son maître. See Jacques the Fatalist and His Master

Jacques the Fatalist and His Master (Diderot) CLCII II-785; MPII:WF II-748

"Jäger Gracchus, Der." See "Hunter Gracchus, The"

Jahrestage. See Anniversaries

Jailbird (Vonnegut) CLCII II-786; MPII:AF II-809

Jake's Thing (Amis) CLCII II-787; MPII:BCF II-852

Jalna (de la Roche) CLC I-539; MP V-2973; MP:AF II-611

Jalousie, La. See Jealousy

James Edward Oglethorpe (Blackburn) MPII:JYABio II-933

James Weldon Johnson (Felton) MPII:JYABio II-937

Jamie (Bennett, Jack) MPII:JYAFic II-741

Jane Addams (Meigs) MPII:JYABio II-941

Jane Addams of Hull House (Wise) MPII:JYABio II-945

Jane Eyre (Brontë, C.) CLC I-540; MP V-2976; MP:BF II-681; MPII:JYAFic II-745

"Japanese Quince, The" (Galsworthy) MPII:SS III-1211

Jar of Dreams, A (Uchida) MPII:JYAFic II-749

"Jardín de senderos que se bifurcan, El." See "Garden of Forking Paths, The"

Jason and the Golden Fleece (Unknown) CLC I-542; MP V-2981; MP:EF II-710

Java Head (Hergesheimer) CLC I-543; MP V-2985; MP:AF II-615

Jawaharlal Nehru (Lengyel) MPII:JYABio II-948

Jazz (Morrison) MPII:AfAm II-619

Jazz Country (Hentoff) MPII:JYAFic II-752

J. B. (MacLeish) CLCII II-788; MPII:D III-861

Jealousy (Robbe-Grillet) CLCII II-790; MPII:WF II-755

Jean le bleu. See Blue Boy

"Jean-ah Poquelin" (Cable) MPII:SS III-1214

Jean-Christophe (Rolland) CLC I-543; MP V-2988; MP:EF II-714

Jefferson and Hamilton (Bowers) MP V-2993

Jennie (Martin) MPII:JYABio II-952

Jennie Gerhardt (Dreiser) CLC I-544; MP V-2996; MP:AF II-619

Jerusalem Delivered (Tasso) CLC I-545; MP V-3000

Jesse Owens (Baker, W.) MPII:JYABio II-956

Jeu, Le. See Gambling

Jeu Süss. See Power

Jew of Malta, The (Marlowe) CLC I-546; MP V-3004

"Jewbird, The" (Malamud) MPII:SS III-1218

Jewel in the Crown, The. See Raj Quartet, The

"Jewels, The" (Baudelaire) MPII:P III-1129

Jewess of Toledo, The (Grillparzer) CLC I-547; MP V-3008

"Jewish Cemetery at Newport, The" (Longfellow) MPII:P III-1132

Jill (Larkin) CLCII II-790; MPII:BCF II-857

"Jim Baker's Bluejay Yarn" (Twain) MPII:SS III-1222

Joan of Arc (Churchill) MPII:JYABio II-960

Joanna Godden (Kaye-Smith) CLC I-548; MP V-3012; MP:BF II-687

Job (Roth, J.) CLCII II-792; MPII:WF II-760

Joe Louis (Jakoubek) MPII:JYABio II-963

Joe Turner's Come and Gone (Wilson, August) CLCII II-793; MPII:AfAm II-625; MPII:D III-866

Johann Sebastian Bach (Reingold)
MPII:JYABio II-967
John Brown (Graham, L.) MPII:JYABio
II-970
John Brown's Body (Benét) CLC I-549;
MP V-3016
John Bull's Other Island (Shaw, G.) CLC
II-794; MPII:D III-871
John-Christopher. See Jean-Christophe
John Diamond. See Footsteps
John Dryden (Eliot, T. S.) MP V-3020
John Halifax, Gentleman (Mulock) CLC
I-550; MP V-3023; MP:BF II-691
John Inglesant (Shorthouse) CLC I-551; MP
V-3026; MP:BF II-695
"John Napper Sailing Through the
Universe" (Gardner) MPII:SS III-1226
John Paul Jones, Fighting Sailor (Sperry)
MPII:JYABio II-973
Johnny Tremain (Forbes) MPII:JYAFic II-756
Joke, The (Kundera) CLCII II-795; MPII:WF
II-766
"Jolly Corner, The" (James, H.) MPII:SS
III-1230
Jonah's Gourd Vine (Hurston) MPII:AfAm
II-631
Jonathan Wild (Fielding) CLC I-551; MP
V-3030; MP:BF II-699
"Jordan's End" (Glasgow) MPII:SS III-1234
"Jorinda and Jorindel" (Gallant) MPII:SS
III-1237
Jorrocks' Jaunts and Jollities (Surtees) CLC
I-552; MP V-3033; MP:BF II-703
Joseph and His Brothers (Mann) CLCII
II-797; MPII:WF II-772
Joseph Andrews (Fielding) CLC I-552; MP
V-3036; MP:BF II-707
Joseph Balsamo. See Memoirs of a
Physician
Joseph, der Ernährer. See Joseph and His
Brothers
Joseph in Egypt. See Joseph and His
Brothers
Joseph the Provider. See Joseph and His
Brothers
Joseph und seine Brüder. See Joseph and
His Brothers
Joseph Vance (De Morgan) CLC I-554; MP
V-3041; MP:BF II-713

"Josephine the Singer" (Kafka) MPII:SS
III-1241
Jour, Le. See Accident, The
Journal of a Solitude (Sarton) MPII:NF
II-756
Journal of a Tour to the Hebrides (Boswell)
MP V-3044
Journal of the Fictive Life (Nemerov)
MPII:NF II-762
Journal of the Plague Year, A (Defoe) MP
V-3047; MP:BF II-717
Journal of Thoreau, The (Thoreau) MP
V-3050
Journal to Eliza (Sterne) MP V-3053
Journal to Stella (Swift) MP V-3056
Journals, 1939-1983 (Spender) MPII:NF
II-767
Journals of André Gide, The (Gide) MP
VI-3059
Journals of Charlotte Forten Grimké, The
(Grimké) MPII:AfAm II-636
Journals of Denton Welch, The (Welch)
MPII:NF II-773
Journals of Dorothy Wordsworth
(Wordsworth, D.) MP VI-3062
Journals of Lewis and Clark, The (Lewis,
M. and Clark, William) MP VI-3065
Journey Back, The (Reiss) MPII:JYABio
II-977
Journey into Fear (Ambler) CLCII II-799;
MPII:BCF II-862
"Journey of the Magi" (Eliot, T. S.) MPII:P
III-1135
Journey to Armenia (Mandelstam, O.)
MPII:NF II-779
Journey to the Center of the Earth (Verne)
CLCII II-800; MPII:WF II-781
Journey to the End of the Night (Céline)
CLC I-555; MP VI-3068; MP:EF II-720
Journey to the Sky (Highwater) CLCII
II-801; MPII:AF II-814
Journey to the West, The. See Monkey
Journey to Topaz and Journey Home
(Uchida) MPII:JYAFic II-759
Journey Toward Freedom (Bernard)
MPII:JYABio II-981
Journeyman Years. See Wilhelm Meister's
Travels

Journey's End (Sherriff) CLC I-556; MP VI-3071

Jovial Crew, A (Brome) CLC I-556; MP VI-3075

Joy of Man's Desiring (Giono) CLCII II-802; MPII:WF II-786

Joy of the Worm (Sargeson) CLCII II-803; MPII:BCF II-866

Juan sin tierra. See Juan the Landless

Juan the Landless (Goytisolo) CLCII III-974; MPII:WF III-958

Jubiabá (Amado) CLCII II-804; MPII:AF II-819

Jubilee (Walker, M.) CLCII II-806; MPII:AF II-825; MPII:AfAm II-642

Jude the Obscure (Hardy) CLC I-557; MP VI-3079; MP:BF II-721

Judgment Day. See Studs Lonigan

Judith Hearne. See Lonely Passion of Judith Hearne, The

Judith Paris (Walpole, Hugh) CLC I-558; MP VI-3084; MP:BF II-726

Jules Verne (Jules-Verne) MPII:JYABio II-985

Jules Verne: The Man Who Invented the Future (Born) MPII:JYABio II-989

"Julia and the Bazooka" (Kavan) MPII:SS III-1245

Julie of the Wolves (George, J.) MPII:JYAFic II-764

Julius Caesar (Shakespeare) CLC I-559; MP VI-3089

July's People (Gordimer) CLCII II-807; MPII:BCF II-872

Jumpers (Stoppard) CLCII II-808; MPII:D III-877

Junge Joseph, Der. See Joseph and His Brothers

Jungle, The (Sinclair, U.) CLC I-560; MP VI-3094; MP:AF II-623

Jungle Book, The (Kipling) MPII:JYAFic II-767

Jungle Books, The (Kipling) CLC I-561; MP VI-3097; MP:BF II-731

"Junk" (Wilbur) MPII:P III-1138

Juno and the Paycock (O'Casey) CLC I-562; MP VI-3100

Jurgen (Cabell) CLC I-563; MP VI-3105; MP:AF II-626

Just Above My Head (Baldwin) CLCII II-809; MPII:AF II-830; MPII:AfAm II-648

Justice (Galsworthy) CLC I-564; MP VI-3108

Justine. See Alexandria Quartet, The

K

"K, The" (Olson) MPII:P III-1141
"Kaddish" (Ginsberg) MPII:P III-1144
"Kak eto delalos v Odesse." *See* "How It Was Done in Odessa"
"Kaleidoscope" (Verlaine) MPII:P III-1147
Kalevala, The (Lönnrot) CLC I-565; MP VI-3111
Kalkwerk, Das. *See* Lime Works, The
Kälte, Die. *See* Gathering Evidence
Kamen no kokuhaku. *See* Confessions of a Mask
Kamera obskura. *See* Laughter in the Dark
"Kamienny wiat." *See* "World of Stone, The"
Kamongo (Smith, H.) MP VI-3115; MP:AF II-630
Kangaroo (Aleshkovsky) CLCII II-811; MPII:WF II-790
Kangaroo (Lawrence) CLCII II-812; MPII:BCF II-877
Kanthapura (Rao) CLCII II-813; MPII:BCF II-882
Kapital, Das (Marx) MP VI-3117
Karl and Rosa. *See* November 1918
Karl Marx Play, The (Owens) CLCII II-815; MPII:D III-883
Kaspar (Handke) CLCII II-816; MPII:D III-890
Katar. *See* Chain of Chance, The
Kate Fennigate (Tarkington) CLC I-565; MP VI-3120; MP:AF II-632
Käthe Kollwitz (Klein, M. *and* Klein, A.) MPII:JYABio II-993
Katia (Almedingen) MPII:JYABio III-997
Kaukasische Kreidekreis, Der. *See* Caucasian Chalk Circle, The
Kaywana Blood. *See* Kaywana trilogy, The
Kaywana trilogy, The (Mittelholzer) CLCII II-817; MPII:BCF II-887
"Keela, the Outcast Indian Maiden" (Welty) MPII:SS III-1248
Keep the Aspidistra Flying (Orwell) CLCII II-820; MPII:BCF II-894
Keep Tightly Closed in a Cool Dry Place (Terry, M.) CLCII II-821; MPII:D III-895
Keepers of the House, The (Grau) CLCII II-822; MPII:AF II-835

Kein Ort. *See* No Place on Earth
Keller, Der. *See* Gathering Evidence
Kenguru. *See* Kangaroo (Aleshkovsky)
Kenilworth (Scott, Sir W.) CLC I-566; MP VI-3123; MP:BF II-735
"Kepi, The" (Colette) MPII:SS III-1252
Kepler (Banville) CLCII II-823; MPII:BCF II-899
"Kerchief, The" (Agnon) MPII:SS III-1255
Kestrel, The. *See* Westmark trilogy, The
Keys of Mantlemass, The. *See* Mantlemass series, The
Keys of the Kingdom, The (Cronin) CLCII II-824; MPII:BCF II-904
Khadzi-Murat. *See* Hadji Murad
"Khozyain i rabotnik." *See* "Master and Man"
Ki-Yu. *See* Panther
Kidnapped (Stevenson) CLC I-568; MP VI-3127; MP:BF II-739; MPII:JYAFic II-771
Kidnapping of Christina Lattimore, The (Nixon) MPII:JYAFic II-774
"Kikuguruma." *See* "Boxcar of Chrysanthemums"
Killdeer, The (Reaney) CLCII II-825; MPII:D III-900
Killer, The (Ionesco) CLCII II-827; MPII:D III-905
Killer-of-Death (Baker, B.) MPII:JYAFic II-777
"Killers, The" (Hemingway) MPII:SS III-1259
Killing Ground, The (Settle) CLCII II-827. *See also* Beulah Quintet, The
Kim (Kipling) CLC I-568; MP VI-3130; MP:BF II-743; MPII:JYAFic II-781
Kind, Ein. *See* Gathering Evidence
Kind of Alaska, A (Pinter) CLCII II-829; MPII:D III-910
Kindergarten (Rushforth) CLCII II-829; MPII:BCF II-909
Kindergeschichte. *See* Slow Homecoming
Kindheitsmuster. *See* Patterns of Childhood
Kindly Ones, The. *See* Dance to the Music of Time, A, *and* Dance to the Music of Time: Second Movement, A

Kindred (Butler, O.) MPII:AfAm II-654

King and No King, A (Beaumont *and* Fletcher) CLC I-569; MP VI-3133

King Horn (Unknown) MP VI-3137

King Jesus (Graves) CLCII II-830; MPII:BCF II-915

King John (Bale) CLC I-569; MP VI-3140

King John (Shakespeare) CLC I-570; MP VI-3144

King Lear (Shakespeare) CLC I-572; MP VI-3148

King Matt the First (Korczak) MPII:JYAFic II-784

King Must Die, The (Renault) CLCII II-831; MPII:BCF II-920

"King of Harlem, The (García" Lorca) MPII:P III-1150

King of the Golden River, The (Ruskin) CLC I-574; MP VI-3153; MP:BF II-747; MPII:JYAFic II-788

King of the Mountains, The (About) CLC I-575; MP VI-3156; MP:EF II-724

King of the Wind (Henry) MPII:JYAFic II-791

King Paradox (Baroja) CLC I-575; MP VI-3159; MP:EF II-728

"King Solomon" (Rosenfeld) MPII:SS III-1262

King Solomon's Mines (Haggard) CLC I-576; MP VI-3163; MP:BF II-751; MPII:JYAFic II-796

King, the Greatest Alcalde, The (Vega) CLC I-577; MP VI-3168

Kingdom of God, The (Martínez Sierra) CLC I-578; MP VI-3173

Kingdom of This World, The (Carpentier) CLCII II-834; MPII:AF II-840

"Kingfishers, The" (Olson) MPII:P III-1153

Kings in Exile (Daudet) CLC I-578; MP VI-3176; MP:EF II-733

"King's Indian, The" (Gardner) CLCII II-835; MPII:SS III-1265

King's Row (Bellamann) CLC I-579; MP VI-3179; MP:AF II-636

Kinkakuji. *See* Temple of the Golden Pavilion, The

Kipps (Wells) CLC I-580; MP VI-3182; MP:BF II-757

"Kiss, The" (Chekhov) MPII:SS III-1270

Kiss of the Spider Woman (Puig) CLCII II-837; MPII:AF II-845

Kit Carson (Garst) MPII:JYABio III-1001

Kitchen, The (Wesker) CLCII II-837; MPII:D III-915

"Kittens" (Peters) MPII:P III-1157

"Kleine Herr Friedemann, Der." *See* "Little Herr Friedemann"

"Kleist in Thun" (Walser) MPII:SS III-1273

Klingsor's Last Summer (Hesse) CLCII II-839; MPII:WF II-797

Klingsors letzter Sommer. *See* Klingsor's Last Summer

Klop. *See* Bedbug, The

Knekht, Der. *See* Slave, The

Kniga skitany. *See* Story of a Life, The

Knight of the Burning Pestle, The (Beaumont *and* Fletcher) CLC I-581; MP VI-3185

Knights, The (Aristophanes) CLC I-582; MP VI-3189

Know Nothing (Settle) CLCII II-839. *See also* Beulah Quintet, The

Knowledge of Language (Chomsky) MPII:NF II-786

Kojinteki na taiken. *See* Personal Matter, A

Kompleks polski. *See* Polish Complex, The

Kompromiss. *See* Compromise, The

Kon-Tiki (Heyerdahl) MPII:JYABio III-1005

Konerne ved vandposten. *See* Women at the Pump, The

Kopfgeburten. *See* Headbirths

Korrektur. *See* Correction

Kort paus i orgelkonserten. *See* Brief Pause in the Organ Recital

Kshoku ichidai otoko. *See* Life of an Amorous Man, The

Kosmos. *See* Cosmos

Kost Kosti. *See* One Bone to Another

Kotlovan. *See* Foundation Pit, The

Krapp's Last Tape (Beckett) CLCII II-841; MPII:D III-920

Kreutzer Sonata, The (Tolstoy) CLC I-583; MP VI-3192; MP:EF II-736

Kristin Lavransdatter (Undset) CLC I-584; MP VI-3195; MP:EF II-740

Król Marciu Pierwszy. *See* King Matt the First

"Kryzhovnik." *See* "Gooseberries"

"Kubla Khan" (Coleridge) MPII:P III-1160

Kuchibue o fuku toki. *See* When I Whistle

"Kugelmass Episode, The" (Allen, W.) MPII:SS III-1276

"Kunstwerk im Zeitalter seiner technischen Reproduzierbarkeit, Das." *See* Work of Art in the Age of Mechanical Reproduction, The

Kuntsnmakher fun Lublin, Der. *See* Magician of Lublin, The

Kurka Wodna. *See* Water Hen, The

"Kurtser Fraytik, Der." *See* "Short Friday"

Kurze Brief zum langen Abschied, Der. *See* Short Letter, Long Farewell

Kusamakura. *See* Three-Cornered World, The

Kutonet veha-Pasim. *See* Tzili

Kwaku (Heath) MPII:AfAm II-659

L

Labyrinth of Solitude, The (Paz) MP
VI-3200
"Lace" (Boland) MPII:P III-1164
Lad (Terhune) MPII:JYAFic II-799
Ladies' Hairdresser (Grekova) CLCII
II-841; MPII:WF II-802
Ladies of Seneca Falls, The (Gurko)
MPII:JYABio III-1009
Lady Chatterley's Lover (Lawrence) CLCII
II-842; MPII:BCF II-927
Lady for Ransom, The (Duggan) MP
VI-3203; MP:BF II-761
Lady From the Sea, The (Ibsen) CLC I-586;
MP VI-3206
"Lady in Kicking Horse Reservoir, The"
(Hugo, R.) MPII:P III-1167
Lady into Fox (Garnett) CLC I-587; MP
VI-3210; MP:BF II-765
"Lady Lazarus" (Plath) MPII:P III-1170
"Lady Macbeth of the Mtsensk District"
(Leskov) CLCII II-844; MPII:SS
III-1280
"Lady of Shalott, The" (Tennyson) MPII:P
III-1174
Lady of the Lake, The (Scott, Sir W.) CLC
I-588; MP VI-3213
"Lady or the Tiger?, The" (Stockton)
MPII:SS III-1284
Lady Queen Anne (Hodges) MPII:JYABio
III-1013
Lady Sings the Blues (Holiday)
MPII:AfAm II-664; MPII:JYABio
III-1017
Lady Windermere's Fan (Wilde) CLC
I-588; MP VI-3216
"Lady with the Dog, The" (Chekhov)
CLCII II-846; MPII:SS III-1288
Lady's Not for Burning, The (Fry) CLC
I-589; MP VI-3219
Lafcadio's Adventures (Gide) CLCII
II-847; MPII:WF II-806
"Lagoon, The" (Conrad) MPII:SS III-1292
Lais, Le (Villon) MP VI-3226
Lais of Marie de France, The (Marie de
France) MP VI-3230
"Lake Isle of Innisfree, The" (Yeats)
MPII:P III-1178

Lalla Rookh (Moore, T.) CLC I-590; MP
VI-3237
Lamb, The (Mauriac) CLCII II-848;
MPII:WF II-811
"Lamb to the Slaughter" (Dahl) MPII:SS
III-1295
Lament for Ignacio Sánchez Mejías
(García Lorca) MPII:P III-1181
"Lamia" (Keats) MPII:P III-1185
Lanark (Gray, A.) CLCII II-850; MPII:BCF
II-934
Land I Lost, The (Huynh) MPII:JYABio
III-1021
Land of Ulro, The (Miłosz) MPII:NF II-792
"Landarzt, Ein." See "Country Doctor, A"
Landlocked. See Children of Violence
"Landscape with Two Graves and an
Assyrian Dog" (García Lorca) MPII:P
III-1188
Langsame Heimkehr. See Slow
Homecoming
Langston Hughes (Meltzer) MPII:JYABio
III-1025
Language of Goldfish, The (Oneal)
MPII:JYAFic II-802
Language, Thought, and Reality (Whorf)
MPII:NF II-798
Lantern Bearer, The (Wood) MPII:JYABio
III-1029
Lantern Bearers, The (Sutcliff)
MPII:JYAFic II-806
Lao Ts'an youji. See Travels of Lao Ts'an,
The
"Lapis Lazuli" (Yeats) MPII:P III-1191
Largo Desolato (Havel) CLCII II-851;
MPII:D III-926
Lark and the Laurel, The. See Mantlemass
series, The
Lassie Come-Home (Knight, Eric)
MPII:JYAFic II-810
Last Algonquin, The (Kazimiroff)
MPII:JYABio III-1033
Last and First Men (Stapledon) MPII:BCF
II-939
Last Athenian, The (Rydberg) CLC I-592;
MP VI-3243; MP:EF II-750
Last Battle, The. See Chronicles of Narnia, The

Last Chronicle of Barset, The (Trollope) CLC I-592; MP VI-3246; MP:BF II-768

"Last Class, The" (Daudet) MPII:SS III-1298

Last Days of Pompeii, The (Bulwer-Lytton) CLC I-594; MP VI-3249; MP:BF II-772

Last Elizabethan, The (Fecher) MPII:JYABio III-1037

Last Gentleman, The (Percy) CLCII II-853; MPII:AF II-850

Last Incarnation of Vautrin, The. *See* Splendors and Miseries of Courtesans, The

Last Meeting of the Knights of the White Magnolia, The (Jones, P.) CLCII II-854; MPII:D III-932

"Last Mohican, The" (Malamud) MPII:SS III-1302

Last of Chéri, The (Colette) CLCII I-264; MPII:WF I-243

Last of Summer, The (O'Brien) CLC I-595; MP VI-3253; MP:BF II-776

Last of the Barons, The (Bulwer-Lytton) CLC I-595; MP VI-3257; MP:BF II-780

Last of the Just, The (Schwarz-Bart) CLCII II-856; MPII:WF II-816

Last of the Mohicans, The (Cooper, J. F.) CLC I-596; MP VI-3261; MP:AF II-639. *See also* Leatherstocking Tales, The

Last of the Red-Hot Lovers (Simon, N.) CLCII II-857; MPII:D III-938

Last of the Vikings, The (Bojer) CLC I-597; MP VI-3266; MP:EF II-754

Last of the Wine, The (Renault) MP VI-3271; MP:BF II-784

Last Picture Show, The (McMurtry) CLCII II-858; MPII:AF II-854; MPII:JYAFic II-814

"Last Poem" (Berrigan) MPII:P III-1195

Last Post, The. *See* Parade's End

Last Puritan, The (Santayana) CLC I-598; MP VI-3274; MP:AF II-645

Last Temptation of Christ, The (Kazantzakis) CLCII II-859; MPII:WF II-820

"Last Things" (Meredith, W.) MPII:P III-1198

Last Things (Snow). *See* Strangers and Brothers

Last Tycoon, The (Fitzgerald, F.) CLC I-599; MP VI-3277; MP:AF II-649

Late George Apley, The (Marquand) CLC I-599; MP VI-3280; MP:AF II-653

Late Mattia Pascal, The (Pirandello) CLC I-600; MP VI-3285; MP:EF II-759

Laughing Boy (La Farge) CLCII II-860; MPII:AF II-860

Laughter (Bergson) MP VI-3289

Laughter in the Dark (Nabokov) CLCII II-861; MPII:WF II-825

Laundromat, The. *See* Third and Oak: The Laundromat

"Laura" (Saki) MPII:SS III-1305

Lavengro (Borrow) CLC I-601; MP VI-3292; MP:BF II-787

Lawd Today (Wright) CLCII II-862; MPII:AF II-864; MPII:AfAm II-670

Lawrence of Arabia (MacLean) MPII:JYABio III-1040

Lay of Igor's Campaign, The (Unknown) MP VI-3296

Lay of the Last Minstrel, The (Scott, W.) CLC I-603; MP VI-3299

Lazarillo de Tormes (Unknown) CLC I-604; MP VI-3302; MP:EF II-763

Lazarus Laughed (O'Neill) CLCII II-863; MPII:D III-944

Leader by Destiny (Eaton) MPII:JYABio III-1044

Leader of the Lower School, The (Brazil) MPII:JYAFic II-817

"Leader of the People, The." *See* Red Pony, The

Leaf Storm (García Márquez) CLCII II-864; MPII:AF II-868

Lean Lands, The (Yáñez) CLCII II-865; MPII:AF II-873

"Leaning Tower, The" (Porter) MPII:SS III-1309

Lear (Bond) CLCII II-866; MPII:D III-949

"Learning a Dead Language" (Merwin) MPII:P III-1201

Learning Tree, The (Parks) MPII:AfAm II-676

Leatherstocking Tales, The (Cooper, J. F.) MPII:JYAFic II-821. *See also* Deerslayer, The; Last of the Mohicans, The; Pathfinder, The; Pioneers, The; *and* Prairie, The

Leave It to Psmith (Wodehouse) CLCII
II-868; MPII:BCF II-944
"Leaves" (Updike) MPII:SS III-1313
Leaves of Grass (Whitman) MP VI-3307
"Leaving the Yellow House" (Bellow)
MPII:SS III-1317
Leben des Galilei. See Galileo
Lebensansichten des Katers Murr. See Life
and Opinions of Kater Murr, The
Leçon, La. See Lesson, The
"Leda and the Swan" (Yeats) MPII:P
III-1204
"Ledi Makbet Mtsenskogo uyez da." See
"Lady Macbeth of the Mtsensk District"
Lee and Grant at Appomattox (Kantor, M.)
MPII:JYABio III-1048
Lee of Virginia (Freeman) MPII:JYABio
III-1052
Left Hand of Darkness, The (Le Guin)
CLCII II-869; MPII:AF II-878
Left-Handed Woman, The (Handke) CLCII
II-870; MPII:WF II-830
"Lefty" (Leskov) MPII:SS III-1320
"Legal Aid" (O'Connor, Frank) MPII:SS
III-1325
"Legend" (Crane, H.) MPII:P III-1207
Legend Days. See Ghost Horse cycle, The
Legend of Good Women, The (Chaucer)
CLC I-605; MP VI-3311
"Legend of St. Julian, Hospitaler, The"
(Flaubert) MPII:SS III-1328
"Legend of Sleepy Hollow, The" (Irving,
W.) CLC I-606; MP VI-3314; MP:AF
II-659; MPII:SS III-1331
Legend of the Moor's Legacy (Irving, W.)
CLC I-607; MP VI-3317; MP:AF II-663
Legend of Tyl Ulenspiegel, The (Coster)
CLC I-607; MP VI-3321; MP:EF II-768
Legs (Kennedy, W.) CLCII II-871. See also
Albany Cycle, The
Lehre der Sainte-Victoire, Die. See Slow
Homecoming
Leif Eriksson (Shippen) MPII:JYABio
III-1056
Leif the Unlucky (Haugaard) MPII:JYAFic
II-826
"Lemon, A" (Neruda) MPII:P III-1210
"Lemon Trees, The" (Montale) MPII:P
III-1213

"Lenore" (Poe) MPII:P III-1216
"Lenz" (Büchner) CLCII II-872; MPII:SS
III-1335
Leonard Bernstein (Ewen) MPII:JYABio
III-1059
Leonardo da Vinci (Noble) MPII:JYABio
III-1066
Leonardo da Vinci: The Universal Genius
(Williams, Jay) MPII:JYABio III-1063
Leopard, The (Bødker) MPII:JYAFic II-830
Leopard, The (Tomasi di Lampedusa) MP
VI-3324; MP:EF II-772
Leoparden. See Leopard, The
Leopards and Lilies (Duggan) MP VI-3327;
MP:BF II-792
Less than Angels (Pym) CLCII II-873;
MPII:BCF II-949
Less Than One (Brodsky) MPII:NF II-802
Lesson, The (Ionesco) CLCII II-875;
MPII:D III-954
"Lesson, The" (Simic) MPII:P III-1219
Lesson Before Dying, A (Gaines)
MPII:AfAm II-682
Lesson from Aloes, A (Fugard) CLCII
II-875; MPII:D III-959
Lesson of Mont-Sainte-Victoire, The. See
Slow Homecoming
"Lesson of the Master, The" (James, H.)
MPII:SS III-1339
Let Me Breathe Thunder (Attaway)
MPII:AfAm II-688
"Let me not to the marriage of true minds."
See Sonnet 116
Let the Circle Be Unbroken (Taylor, M.)
MPII:AfAm II-694
Let the Dead Bury Their Dead (Kenan)
MPII:AfAm II-699
Let Us Now Praise Famous Men (Agee,
James) MP VI-3330
"Letter from a Distant Land" (Booth)
MPII:P III-1222
"Letter of Testimony" (Paz) MPII:P III-1225
"Letter to Elizabeth Mayer. See New Year
Letter" (Auden)
"Letter to Lord Byron" (Auden) MPII:P
III-1228
Letter to Lord Liszt (Walser) CLCII II-876;
MPII:WF II-836

Letters and Papers from Prison
(Bonhoeffer) MPII:NF II-807
Letters from an American Farmer
(Crèvecœur) MP VI-3333
Letters from the Underworld (Dostoevski)
CLC I-608; MP VI-3336; MP:EF II-776
Letters of Charles Lamb, The (Lamb) MP
VI-3341
Letters of D. H. Lawrence, The. See
Collected Letters of D. H. Lawrence, The
Letters of Emily Dickinson, The
(Dickinson) MP VI-3344
Letters of F. Scott Fitzgerald, The
(Fitzgerald, F.) MP VI-3347
Letters of John Keats, The (Keats) MP
VI-3350
Letters of Madame de Sévigné, The
(Sévigné) MP VI-3353
Letters of Pliny the Younger, The (Pliny)
MP VI-3355
Letters of Robert Frost, The (Frost) MP
VI-3358
Letters of Thomas Gray, The (Gray) MP
VI-3361
Letters of Thomas Wolfe, The (Wolfe) MP
VI-3364
Letters of Walpole, The (Walpole, Horace)
MP VI-3368
Letters of William Cowper, The (Cowper)
MP VI-3371
Letters on Cézanne (Rilke) MPII:NF II-812
Letters to Felice (Kafka) MPII:NF II-819
Letters to His Son (Chesterfield) MP
VI-3374
Letters to Olga (Havel) MPII:NF II-825
Letting Go (Roth, P.) CLCII II-878;
MPII:AF II-883
Leviathan (Hobbes) MP VI-3376
"Leviathan" (Merwin) MPII:P III-1232
"Levsha." See "Lefty"
"Leyenda de la Tatuana." See "Tatuana's
Tale"
Liber Amoris (Hazlitt) CLC I-609; MP
VI-3379
Liberal Imagination, The (Trilling)
MPII:NF II-830
Liberators of Latin America (Young and
Young) MPII:JYABio III-1070

"Library of Babel, The" (Borges) MPII:SS
III-1342
Libro de Manuel. See Manual for Manuel, A
Lie Down in Darkness (Styron) MP
VI-3382; MP:AF II-667
Lie of the Mind, A (Shepard) CLCII II-879;
MPII:D III-964
Lieh-kuo chih (Fêng) MP VI-3385; MP:EF
II-782
Life, A (Leonard) CLCII II-880; MPII:D
III-970
Life, Adventures, and Piracies of the
Famous Captain Singleton, The. See
Captain Singleton
Life and Adventures of Martin Chuzzlewit,
The. See Martin Chuzzlewit
Life and Death of Cardinal Wolsey, The
(Cavendish) MP VI-3389
Life and Death of Mary Wollstonecraft, The
(Tomalin) MPII:JYABio III-1074
Life and Death of Mr. Badman, The
(Bunyan) CLC I-610; MP VI-3392;
MP:BF II-796
Life and Extraordinary Adventures of
Private Ivan Chonkin, The (Voinovich)
CLCII II-881; MPII:WF II-841
Life and Opinions of Kater Murr, The
(Hoffmann) CLCII II-883; MPII:WF
II-849
Life and Opinions of Tristram Shandy,
Gentleman, The. See Tristram Shandy
Life and Strange Surprising Adventures of
Robinson Crusoe, The. See Robinson
Crusoe
Life and Strange Surprizing Adventures of
Robinson Crusoe, of York, Mariner, The.
See Robinson Crusoe
Life & Times of Michael K (Coetzee)
CLCII II-884; MPII:BCF II-954
Life Before Man (Atwood) CLCII II-885;
MPII:BCF II-959
Life in London (Egan) CLC I-610; MP
VI-3394; MP:BF II-799
Life is a Dream (Calderón de la Barca) CLC
I-611; MP VI-3398
Life Is Elsewhere (Kundera) CLCII II-886;
MPII:WF II-855
Life of an Amorous Man, The (Ihara)
CLCII II-888; MPII:WF II-860

Life of Cardinal Wolsey and Metrical Versions from the Original Autograph Manuscript. *See* Life and Death of Cardinal Wolsey, The

Life of Dr. Robert Sanderson, The. *See* Lives

Life of John Donne, The. *See* Lives

Life of Man, The (Andreyev) CLCII II-889; MPII:D III-975

Life of Mr. George Herbert, The. *See* Lives

Life of Mr. Jonathan Wild the Great, The. *See* Jonathan Wild

Life of Mr. Richard Hooker, The. *See* Lives

Life of Nelson (Southey) MP VI-3403

Life of Richard Savage (Johnson, S.) MP VI-3406

Life of Samuel Johnson, LL.D., The (Boswell) MP VI-3409

Life of Sir Henry Wotton, The. *See* Lives

Life of Winston Churchill, The (Wibberley) MPII:JYABio III-1078

Life on the Mississippi (Twain) MP VI-3412

Life Sketches (Hersey) MPII:JYABio III-1081

"Life-Story" (Barth) MPII:SS III-1348

Life with Father (Day, C.) CLC I-612; MP VI-3415; MP:AF II-670

"Lifeguard" (Updike) MPII:SS III-1345

"Ligeia" (Poe) CLC I-613; MP VI-3418; MP:AF II-674; MPII:SS III-1352

Light (Figes) CLCII II-890; MPII:BCF II-965

Light and the Dark, The. *See* Strangers and Brothers

Light in August (Faulkner) CLC I-613; MP VI-3423; MP:AF II-679

Light in the Dark, A (Meltzer) MPII:JYABio III-1085

Light in the Forest, The (Richter, C.) MPII:JYAFic II-834

"Lightning" (Barthelme, D.) MPII:SS III-1355

"Like as the waves make towards the pibbled shore," *See* Sonnet 60

Like One of the Family (Childress) MPII:AfAm II-706

"Like the Night" (Carpentier) MPII:SS III-1359

Liliom (Molnár) CLC I-615; MP VI-3428

"Lilla fälttåget, Det." *See* "Children's Campaign, The"

Lime Twig, The (Hawkes) MP VI-3431; MP:AF II-684

Lime Works, The (Bernhard) CLCII II-891; MPII:WF II-866

Limoni, I. *See* Lemon Trees, The

Lincoln (Freedman) MPII:JYABio III-1089

Lincoln (Vidal) CLCII II-892; MPII:AF II-887

Linden Hills (Naylor) MPII:AfAm II-712

"Lines: Composed a Few Miles Above Tintern Abbey" (Wordsworth) MPII:P III-1235

"Lines: When the Lamp Is Shattered" (Shelley, P.) MPII:P III-1238

Link, The (Strindberg) CLC I-615; MP VI-3434

Linkshändige Frau, Die. *See* Left-Handed Woman, The

Lion and the Jewel, The (Soyinka) CLCII III-893; MPII:D III-981

Lion Country. *See* Book of Bebb, The

Lion of Flanders, The (Conscience) CLC I-616; MP VI-3438; MP:EF II-787

Lion, the Witch, and the Wardrobe, The. *See* Chronicles of Narnia, The

"Lions, Harts, Leaping Does" (Powers) MPII:SS III-1363

"Lispeth" (Kipling) MPII:SS III-1367

Listen America (Stoutenburg *and* Baker, L.) MPII:JYABio III-1093

Listen for the Fig Tree (Mathis) MPII:JYAFic II-838

"Listeners, The (de la" Mare) MPII:P III-1241

"Listening to the Music of Arsenio Rodriguez Is Moving Closer to Knowledge" (Cruz, V.) MPII:P III-1244

Literary Essays of Virginia Woolf, The (Woolf) MP VI-3442

Little Big Man (Berger, T.) CLCII III-893; MPII:AF II-891; MPII:JYAFic II-842

Little Boy in Search of God, A (Singer) MPII:NF II-835

Little by Little (Little, J.) MPII:JYABio III-1097

"Little Car, The" (Apollinaire) MPII:P III-1247

Little Clay Cart, The (Shudraka) CLC
I-617; MP VI-3444
"Little Cloud, A" (Joyce) MPII:SS III-1371
Little Dorrit (Dickens) CLC I-617; MP
VI-3448; MP:BF II-803
Little Duke, The (Yonge) MPII:JYAFic
II-845
Little Foxes, The (Hellman) CLC I-620; MP
VI-3451
Little Girls, The (Bowen, E.) CLCII III-895;
MPII:BCF II-971
"Little Herr Friedemann" (Mann) MPII:SS
III-1375
Little Hotel, The (Stead) CLCII III-896;
MPII:BCF II-975
Little House in the Big Woods (Wilder, L.)
MPII:JYAFic II-848
Little House on the Prairie (Wilder, L.)
MPII:JYAFic II-851
Little Katia. See Katia.
Little Lord Fauntleroy (Burnett, F.)
MPII:JYAFic II-854
Little Men (Alcott) MPII:JYAFic II-857
Little Minister, The (Barrie) CLC I-621; MP
VI-3454; MP:BF II-807
Little Prince, The (Saint-Exupéry)
MPII:JYAFic II-861
Little Princess, A (Burnett, F.)
MPII:JYAFic III-864
Little Scholar Learning to Talk, The. See
Rollo series, The
Little Town on the Prairie (Wilder, L.)
MPII:JYAFic II-868
Little Wilson and Big God (Burgess)
MPII:NF II-841
Little Women (Alcott) CLC I-622; MP
VI-3458; MP:AF II-687; MPII:JYAFic
III-871
Littlepage Manuscripts, The. See Chain-
bearer, The; Redskins, The; and Satanstoe
"Live Acts" (Bernstein) MPII:P III-1251
Lives (Walton) MP VI-3461
Lives and Times of Peter Cooper, The
(Gurko) MPII:JYABio III-1101
Lives of a Cell, The (Thomas, L.) MPII:NF
II-846
Lives of Girls and Women (Munro) CLCII
III-898; MPII:BCF II-980
Lives of Pearl Buck, The (Block)
MPII:JYABio III-1105
Lives of the Caesars (Suetonius) MP
VI-3464
Lives of the Kings of Norway, The. See
Heimskringla
Lives of the Poets (Johnson, S.) MP VI-3468
Living (Green, Henry) CLCII III-899;
MPII:BCF II-984
Living Principle, The (Leavis) MPII:NF
II-850
"Living Relic, A" (Turgenev) MPII:SS
III-1379
Living up the Street (Soto) MPII:JYABio
III-1109
"Livingstone's Companions" (Gordimer)
MPII:SS III-1383
Livre du rire et de l'oubli, Le. See Book of
Laughter and Forgetting, The
Liza of Lambeth (Maugham) CLC I-622;
MP VI-3471; MP:BF II-812
Lizard's Tail, The (Valenzuela) CLCII
III-900; MPII:AF II-896
Llanto por Ignacio Sánchez Mejías. See
Lament for Ignacio Sánchez Mejías
Lo-t'o Hsiang-tzu. See Rickshaw
Local Anaesthetic (Grass) CLCII III-902;
MPII:WF II-872
"Lodging for the Night, A" (Stevenson)
MPII:SS III-1387
Loitering with Intent (Spark) CLCII III-903;
MPII:BCF III-989
Lolita (Nabokov) CLCII III-904; MPII:AF
II-901
"London" (Blake) MPII:P III-1254
London (Johnson, S.) MPII:P III-1257
Lone Journey (Eaton) MPII:JYABio
III-1112
"Loneliness of the Long-Distance Runner,
The" (Sillitoe) MPII:SS IV-1391
Lonely Crowd, The (Riesman) MPII:NF
II-856
Lonely Girl, The. See Country Girls
Trilogy, The
Lonely Londoners, The (Selvon) CLCII
III-905; MPII:AfAm II-718; MPII:BCF
III-993
Lonely Passion of Judith Hearne, The (Moore)
CLCII III-907; MPII:BCF III-998

Long Ago When I Was Young (Nesbit) MPII:JYABio III-1116

Long and Happy Life, A (Price) MP VI-3474; MP:AF II-691

Long Day's Journey into Night (O'Neill) CLCII III-908; MPII:D III-986

Long Dream, The (Wright, R.) CLCII III-909; MPII:AF II-906; MPII:AfAm II-724

Long Goodbye, The (Chandler) CLCII III-910; MPII:AF II-911

Long Journey, The (Jensen) CLC I-623; MP VI-3477; MP:EF II-791

Long Loneliness, The (Day) MPII:NF II-861

Long Night, The (Lytle) CLC I-624; MP VI-3483; MP:AF II-694

Long Voyage, The (Semprun) CLCII III-911; MPII:WF II-878

Long Way Around, The. *See* Slow Homecoming

Long Way Up, A (Valens) MPII:JYABio III-1120

Longest Journey, The (Forster) CLC I-625; MP VI-3487; MP:BF II-816

Look at Me (Brookner) CLCII III-912; MPII:BCF III-1003

Look Back in Anger (Osborne) MP VI-3490

Look Homeward, Angel (Wolfe) CLC I-625; MP VI-3494; MP:AF II-698; MPII:JYAFic III-875

Looking Backward (Bellamy) CLC I-626; MP VI-3497; MP:AF II-702

"Looking for Mr. Green" (Bellow) MPII:SS IV-1395

Lookout Cartridge (McElroy) CLCII III-914; MPII:AF II-916

Loom, The (Kelly, R.) MPII:P III-1261

"Loons, The" (Laurence) MPII:SS IV-1399

Loot (Orton) CLCII III-915; MPII:D III-992

Lord God Made Them All, The (Herriot) MPII:JYABio III-1124

Lord Jim (Conrad) CLC I-627; MP VI-3500; MP:BF II-820

Lord of the Flies (Golding) MP VI-3505; MP:BF II-825; MPII:JYAFic III-879

Lord of the Rings, The (Tolkien) MPII:JYAFic III-883. *See* Fellowship of the Ring, The; Return of the King, The; *and* Two Towers, The

Lorna Doone (Blackmore) CLC I-628; MP VI-3508; MP:BF II-829

Loser, The (Konrád) CLCII III-915; MPII:WF II-884

Losing Battles (Welty) CLCII III-917; MPII:AF II-922

"Lost baby poem, the" (Clifton) MPII:P III-1266

Lost Flying Boat, The (Sillitoe) CLCII III-918; MPII:BCF III-1008

Lost Honor of Katharina Blum, The (Böll) CLCII III-919; MPII:WF II-890

Lost Horizon (Hilton) CLC I-629; MP VI-3512; MP:BF II-833

Lost Illusions (Balzac) CLC I-630; MP VI-3518; MP:EF II-798

Lost in America (Singer) MPII:NF II-835

"Lost in the Funhouse" (Barth) MPII:SS IV-1403

Lost Lady, A (Cather) CLC I-631; MP VI-3521; MP:AF II-706

"Lost Pilot, The" (Tate, J.) MPII:P III-1269

Lost Steps, The (Carpentier) CLCII III-921; MPII:AF II-927

Lost Weekend, The (Jackson, C.) CLC I-632; MP VI-3524; MP:AF II-710

"Lotos-Eaters, The" (Tennyson) MPII:P III-1272

"Lottery, The" (Jackson, S.) MPII:SS IV-1406

Lou Gehrig (Graham, F.) MPII:JYABio III-1128

Louis Lambert (Balzac) CLCII III-922; MPII:WF II-896

Louis Pasteur (Wood, L.) MPII:JYABio III-1131

"Love Among the Ruins" (Browning, R.) MPII:P III-1280

Love and Salt Water (Wilson, E.) CLCII III-923; MPII:BCF III-1013

"Love Calls Us to the Things of This World" (Wilbur) MPII:P III-1283

"Love Decoy, The" (Perelman) MPII:SS IV-1409

Love Feast. *See* Book of Bebb, The

Love for Love (Congreve) CLC I-633; MP VI-3527

Love for Lydia (Bates) CLCII III-924; MPII:BCF III-1017

Love in a Wood (Wycherley) CLC I-634;
  MP VI-3530
Love in the Ruins (Percy) CLCII III-925;
  MPII:AF III-933
"Love is not all" (Millay) MPII:P III-1286
Love Letters of J. Timothy Owen, The
  (Greene, C.) MPII:JYAFic III-887
Love Medicine (Erdrich) CLCII III-927;
  MPII:AF III-938; MPII:JYAFic III-890
Love, or a Season, A (Stolz) MPII:JYAFic
  III-894
"Love Poem" (Nims) MPII:P III-1289
"Love Song of J. Alfred Prufrock, The"
  (Eliot, T. S.) MPII:P III-1292
"Love" (III) (Herbert, G.) MPII:P III-1276
Loved and the Lost, The (Callaghan) CLCII
  III-928; MPII:BCF III-1022
Loved One, The (Waugh) CLCII III-929;
  MPII:BCF III-1027
Lover, The (Duras) CLCII III-931;
  MPII:WF II-901
"Lover sheweth how he is forsaken of such
  as he sometime enjoyed, The." See They
  Flee from Me
Love's Labour's Lost (Shakespeare) CLC
  I-634; MP VI-3534
Loving (Green, H.) CLC I-636; MP
  VI-3537; MP:BF II-839
Lower Depths, The (Gorky) CLC I-636; MP
  VI-3540
Loyalties (Galsworthy) CLC I-638; MP
  VI-3544
Lu Ann Hampton Laverty Oberlander
  (Jones, P.) CLCII III-932; MPII:D
  III-997
Lubimow. See Makepeace Experiment, The
Lucien Leuwen (Stendhal) CLC I-639; MP
  VI-3547; MP:EF II-802
Lucinda Brayford (Boyd) CLCII III-933;
  MPII:BCF III-1033
Luck of Barry Lyndon, The. See Barry
  Lyndon

Luck of Ginger Coffey, The (Moore) CLCII
  III-935; MPII:BCF III-1039
"Luck of Roaring Camp, The" (Harte)
  MPII:SS IV-1412
Luck of Roaring Camp and Other Sketches,
  The (Harte) MP VI-3551; MP:AF II-713
Lucky Jim (Amis) MP VI-3554; MP:BF
  II-843
Lucy (Kincaid) MPII:AfAm II-730
Lucy Gayheart (Cather) CLCII III-936;
  MPII:AF III-943
Ludell and Willie (Wilkinson)
  MPII:JYAFic III-898
"Luke Havergal" (Robinson, E.) MPII:P
  IV-1295
"Lullaby" (Auden) MPII:P IV-1298
"Lullaby" (Silko) MPII:SS IV-1416
"Luna di miele, sole di fiele." See "Bitter
  Honeymoon"
Luna e i falò, La. See Moon and the
  Bonfires, The
"Lune de pluie, La." See "Rainy Moon, The"
"Lupa, La." See "She-Wolf, The"
Lusiads, The (Camoëns) CLC I-639; MP
  VI-3557
Luther (Osborne) CLCII III-937; MPII:D
  III-1002
"Lycidas" (Milton) MPII:P IV-1301
Lydie Breeze (Guare) CLCII III-938;
  MPII:D III-1007
Lyric Poetry of George Gordon, Lord
  Byron, The, MP VI-3562
Lyric Poetry of James Russell Lowell, The,
  MP VI-3565
Lyric Poetry of John Milton, The, MP
  VI-3569
Lyric Poetry of Edmund Spenser, The, MP
  VI-3573
Lysistrata (Aristophanes) CLC I-640; MP
  VI-3578
"Lyubka the Cossack" (Babel) MPII:SS
  IV-1420

M

Ma Rainey's Black Bottom (Wilson,
August) CLCII III-939; MPII:AfAm
II-736; MPII:D III-1012
Mabinogion, The (Unknown) CLC I-641;
MP VI-3582; MP:BF II-847
Mac Flecknoe (Dryden) MPII:P IV-1305
Macbeth (Shakespeare) CLC I-642; MP
VI-3589
Machine infernale, La. See Infernal
Machine, The
McTeague (Norris) CLC I-644; MP
VI-3594; MP:AF II-717
Macunaíma (Andrade) CLCII III-940;
MPII:AF III-948
Madame Bovary (Flaubert) CLC I-645; MP
VI-3599; MP:EF II-806
Madame Curie (Curie) MPII:JYABio III-1135
Madame Sarah (Skinner) MPII:JYABio
III-1139
"Madame Tellier's Establishment"
(Maupassant) MPII:SS IV-1424
"Madame Zilensky and the King of
Finland" (McCullers) MPII:SS IV-1427
Mademoiselle de Maupin (Gautier) CLC
I-647; MP VI-3604; MP:EF II-812
Madman and the Nun, The (Witkiewicz)
CLCII III-941; MPII:D III-1017
Madman's Defense, A. See Confession of a
Fool, The
Madman's Manifesto, A. See Confession of
a Fool, The
Madmen and Specialists (Soyinka) CLCII
III-942; MPII:D III-1023
Madmen of History (Hook) MPII:JYABio
III-1143
Madness and Civilization (Foucault)
MPII:NF II-866
Madras House, The (Granville-Barker) CLC
I-648; MP VI-3607
Madwoman in the Attic, The (Gilbert and
Gubar) MPII:NF II-872
Madwoman of Chaillot, The (Giraudoux)
CLC I-649; MP VI-3611
Magazine Novels of Pauline Hopkins, The
(Hopkins, P.) MPII:AfAm II-742
Maggie (Crane, S.) CLC I-649; MP
VI-3614; MP:AF II-722

Magic (Johnson, Earvin, and Levin)
MPII:JYABio III-1146
"Magic Barrel, The" (Malamud) MPII:SS
IV-1431
Magic Mountain, The (Mann) CLC I-650;
MP VI-3618; MP:EF II-816
Magic Skin, The. See Wild Ass's Skin, The
Magic Stone, The (Farmer) MPII:JYAFic
III-901
Magician of Lublin, The (Singer) CLCII
III-944; MPII:AF III-954; MPII:WF
III-905
Magician's Nephew, The. See Chronicles of
Narnia, The
Magister Ludi. See Glass Bead Game, The
Magnalia Christi Americana (Mather) MP
VI-3623
Magnificent Obsession, The (Douglas, L.)
CLC I-652; MP VI-3626; MP:AF II-726
"Magus, A" (Ciardi) MPII:P IV-1308
Magus, The (Fowles) CLCII III-945;
MPII:BCF III-1044
Mahabharata, The (Unknown) CLC I-652;
MP VI-3629
Maid of Honour, The (Massinger) CLC
I-653; MP VI-3634
Maids, The (Genet) CLCII III-946; MPII:D
III-1031
Maid's Tragedy, The (Beaumont and
Fletcher) CLC I-654; MP VI-3638
Maim'd Debauchee, The. See Disabled
Debauchee, The
Main Currents in American Thought
(Parrington) MP VI-3642
Main Street (Lewis, S.) CLC I-655; MP
VI-3645; MP:AF II-730
Main-Travelled Roads (Garland) MP
VI-3650; MP:AF II-735
"Maison Tellier, La." See "Madame
Tellier's Establishment"
Maître de la parole, Le. See Guardian of the
Word, The
Major Barbara (Shaw) CLC I-656; MP
VI-3652
Make a Joyful Noise unto the Lord!
(Jackson, J.) MPII:JYABio III-1150

Make Way for Sam Houston (Fritz) MPII:JYABio III-1153

Makepeace Experiment, The (Sinyavsky) CLCII III-947; MPII:WF III-909

Making It (Podhoretz) MPII:NF II-878

Making of Americans, The (Stein) CLCII III-948; MPII:AF III-958

Making of Mind, The (Luria) MPII:NF II-884

Makioka Sisters, The (Tanizaki) CLCII III-950; MPII:WF III-915

Ma'kom a'her. See Elsewhere, Perhaps

Mal vu mal dit. See Ill Seen Ill Said

Maa apokalipsa. See Minor Apocalypse, A

Malcolm (Purdy) MP VI-3655; MP:AF II-737

Malcontent, The (Marston) CLC I-657; MP VI-3658

Malign Fiesta. See Human Age, The

Malone Dies (Beckett) CLCII III-951. See also Trilogy, The

Malone meurt. See Malone Dies and Trilogy, The

Maltese Falcon, The (Hammett) CLC I-658; MP VI-3661; MP:AF II-740

Mama (McMillan) MPII:AfAm II-748

Mama Day (Naylor) MPII:AfAm II-753

Man Against the Sky, The (Robinson, E.) MP VI-3664

Man and Superman (Shaw) CLC I-658; MP VI-3667

Man Could Stand Up, A. See Parade's End

Man Died, The (Soyinka) MPII:NF III-889

Man for All Seasons, A (Bolt) CLCII III-952; MPII:D III-1037

Man fun Notseres, Der. See Nazarene, The

"Man in a Case, The" (Chekhov) MPII:SS IV-1434

Man in the Holocene (Frisch) CLCII III-954; MPII:WF III-920

"Man-Moth, The" (Bishop, E.) MPII:P IV-1312

Man of Feeling, The (Mackenzie) CLC I-660; MP VII-3669; MP:BF II-855

Man of Mode, The (Etherege) CLC I-660; MP VII-3672

Man of Molokai (Roos) MPII:JYABio III-1156

Man of Property, The. See Forsyte Saga, The

Man-Shy (Davison) MPII:JYAFic III-907

"Man That Corrupted Hadleyburg, The" (Twain) MPII:SS IV-1437

Man Who Built a City, The (Weir) MPII:JYABio III-1160

Man Who Came to Dinner, The (Kaufman and Hart) CLCII III-954; MPII:D III-1043

Man Who Cried I Am, The (Williams, John) CLCII III-956; MPII:AF III-962; MPII:AfAm II-759

"Man Who Invented Sin, The" (O'Faoláin) MPII:SS IV-1440

Man Who Killed the Deer, The (Waters) CLCII III-957; MPII:AF III-966

Man Who Loved Children, The (Stead) CLCII III-958; MPII:BCF III-1050

"Man Who Was Almost a Man, The" (Wright) MPII:SS IV-1444

Man Who Was Thursday, The (Chesterton) CLC I-661; MP VII-3676; MP:BF II-859

Man Who Watched the Trains Go By, The (Simenon) CLCII III-959; MPII:WF III-925

"Man Who Would Be King, The" (Kipling) CLCII III-960; MPII:SS IV-1447

Man with a Bull-Tongue Plow (Stuart) MP VII-3680

"Man with the Blue Guitar, The" (Stevens, W.) MPII:P IV-1315

Man with the Golden Arm, The (Algren) CLCII III-961; MPII:AF III-971

Man Without a Country, The (Hale) CLC I-662; MP VII-3683; MP:AF II-744

Man Without a Face, The (Holland) MPII:JYAFic III-904

Man Without Qualities, The (Musil) CLCII III-962; MPII:WF III-930

"Manatsu no Shi." See "Death in Midsummer"

Manchild in the Promised Land (Brown, Claude) MPII:AfAm II-765; MPII:JYABio III-1164

Mandelbaum Gate, The (Spark) CLCII III-964; MPII:BCF III-1057

Man'en san'nen no futtoboru. See Silent Cry, The

Manette Salomon (Goncourt and Goncourt) CLC I-662; MP VII-3686; MP:EF II-821

Manfred (Byron) CLC I-663; MP VII-3690

Manhattan. *See* Manhattan, 1975

"Manhattan, 1975" (Rakosi) MPII:P
IV-1319

Manhattan Transfer (Dos Passos) CLC
I-663; MP VII-3693; MP:AF II-748

Manhunt (Carpentier) CLCII III-965;
MPII:AF III-977

Mann Moses und die monotheistiche
Religion, Der. *See* Moses and
Monotheism

Mann ohne Eigenschaften, Der. *See* Man
Without Qualities, The

Manon Lescaut (Prévost) CLC I-664; MP
VII-3696; MP:EF II-826

Man's Blessing, A (Sciascia) CLCII
III-966; MPII:WF III-939

Man's Fate (Malraux) CLC I-665; MP
VII-3700; MP:EF II-830

Man's Hope (Malraux) CLCII III-967;
MPII:WF III-945

Man's Search for Meaning (Frankl)
MPII:NF III-896

Manservant and Maidservant. *See* Bullivant
and the Lambs

Mansfield Park (Austen) CLC I-666; MP
VII-3704; MP:BF II-864

Mansion, The (Faulkner) MP VII-3707;
MP:AF II-752

Manticore, The. *See* Deptford Trilogy, The

Mantlemass series, The (Willard)
MPII:JYAFic III-911

Manual for Manuel, A (Cortázar) CLCII
III-969; MPII:AF III-981

"Many Are Disappointed" (Pritchett)
MPII:SS IV-1455

"Map, The" (Bishop, E.) MPII:P IV-1322

"Map of Montana in Italy, A" (Hugo, R.)
MPII:P IV-1326

Marat/Sade (Weiss) CLCII III-971; MPII:D
III-1049

Marble Faun, The (Hawthorne) CLC I-667;
MP VII-3710; MP:AF II-756

Marbot (Hildesheimer) CLCII III-973;
MPII:WF III-952

Marc Chagall (Greenfeld) MPII:JYABio
III-1167

Marc Chagall (Kagan) MPII:JYABio
III-1170

Marching On (Boyd) CLC I-668; MP
VII-3714; MP:AF II-761

Mardi, and a Voyage Thither (Melville)
CLC I-669; MP VII-3717; MP:AF II-765

Margaret Mead (Rice, Edward)
MPII:JYABio III-1174

Margin of Hope, A (Howe) MPII:NF III-901

Margot Fonteyn (Fonteyn) MPII:JYABio
III-1177

Maria Chapdelaine (Hémon) CLC I-669;
MP VII-3721; MP:AF II-769;
MPII:JYAFic III-917

Maria Magdalena (Hebbel) CLC I-670; MP
VII-3725

Mariage d'amour, Un. *See* Thérèse Raquin

Marian Anderson (Newman, S.)
MPII:JYABio III-1180

"Mariana" (Tennyson) MPII:P IV-1330

Marianne (Marivaux) CLC I-671; MP
VII-3728; MP:EF II-834

Marie Antoinette. *See* Chevalier de Maison
Rouge, The

Marilyn (Mailer) MPII:NF III-907

"Mario and the Magician" (Mann) MPII:SS
IV-1458

Marius the Epicurean (Pater) CLC I-671;
MP VII-3732; MP:BF II-868

"Mark on the Wall, The" (Woolf) MPII:SS
IV-1462

Mark Twain (Meltzer) MPII:JYABio
III-1184

Marked by Fire (Thomas, J.) MPII:AfAm
II-771; MPII:JYAFic III-920

Market Harborough (Whyte-Melville) CLC
I-672; MP VII-3736; MP:BF II-873

Marks of Identity (Goytisolo) CLCII
III-974; MPII:WF III-958

Marmion (Scott, Sir W.) CLC I-672; MP
VII-3739

"Marquise of O——, The" (Kleist) CLCII
III-976; MPII:SS IV-1466

Marquise von O——, Die. *See* "Marquise
of O——, The"

"Marriage" (Corso) MPII:P IV-1334

Marriage, The (Gombrowicz) CLCII
III-977; MPII:D III-1054

"Marriage" (Moore, M.) MPII:P IV-1338

Marriage à la Mode (Dryden) CLC I-673;
MP VII-3742

Marriage of Figaro, The (Beaumarchais) CLC I-674; MP VII-3745

Marse Chan (Page) CLC I-674; MP VII-3748; MP:AF II-773

Martha Quest. *See* Children of Violence

Martian Chronicles, The (Bradbury, R.) CLCII III-979; MPII:AF III-986

Martin Chuzzlewit (Dickens) CLC I-675; MP VII-3751; MP:BF II-877

Martín de Porres, Hero (Bishop, C.) MPII:JYABio III-1188

Maru (Head) CLCII III-980; MPII:BCF III-1062

Mary (Mebane) MPII:JYABio III-1192

Mary (Nabokov) CLCII III-981; MPII:WF III-965

Mary Barton (Gaskell) MP VII-3756; MP:BF II-883

Mary Olivier (Sinclair) CLCII III-982; MPII:BCF III-1067

Mary Poppins series, The (Travers) MPII:JYAFic III-923

Mashenka. *See* Mary

Mask of Anarchy, The (Shelley, P.) MPII:P IV-1341

Mask of Dimitrios, The. *See* Coffin for Dimitrios, A

Masks (Enchi) CLCII III-983; MPII:WF III-970

"Masks" (Sanchez, S.) MPII:P IV-1345

Masot Binyamin haacharon miTudelah. *See* Travels of the Last Benjamin of Tudela

"Masque of the Red Death, The" (Poe) MPII:SS IV-1471

Massacre at Fall Creek, The (West, J.) MPII:JYAFic III-928

Masse und Macht. *See* Crowds and Power

"Master and Man" (Tolstoy) MPII:SS IV-1475

Master and Margarita, The (Bulgakov) CLCII III-984; MPII:WF III-976

Master Builder, The (Ibsen) CLC I-679; MP VII-3759

"MASTER HAROLD" . . . and the boys (Fugard) CLCII III-986; MPII:D III-1059

Master i Margarita. *See* Master and Margarita, The

Master of Ballantrae, The (Stevenson) CLC I-680; MP VII-3764; MP:BF II-887

Master of Go, The (Kawabata) CLCII III-986; MPII:WF III-983

Master of the Mill, The (Grove) CLCII III-987; MPII:BCF III-1072

Master Simon's Garden (Meigs) MPII:JYAFic III-931

Master Skylark (Bennett, John) MPII:JYAFic III-935

Masters, The (Snow) MP VII-3768; MP:BF II-892. *See also* Strangers and Brothers

Mastro-don Gesualdo (Berga) CLC I-681; MP VII-3771; MP:EF II-838

Matchlock Gun, The (Edmonds) MPII:JYAFic III-938

Matchmaker, The (Wilder, T.) CLCII III-988; MPII:D III-1065

"Matrenin dvor." *See* "Matryona's House"

"Matryona's House" (Solzhenitsyn) MPII:SS IV-1480

Matter and Memory (Bergson) MP VII-3776

Matthew Henson (Gilman, M.) MPII:JYABio III-1195

Mtwe. *See* Cuttlefish, The

Maud Martha (Brooks, G.) MPII:JYAFic III-942; MPII:AfAm II-777

Mauerspringer, Der. *See* Wall Jumper, The

Maurice (Forster) CLCII III-989; MPII:BCF III-1076

Max Havelaar (Multatuli) CLC I-682; MP VII-3778; MP:EF II-844

Maxims, The (La Rochefoucauld) MP VII-3782

Maximus Poems, The (Olson) MPII:P IV-1348

"May Day" (Fitzgerald) MPII:SS IV-1485

May Wine, The. *See* I taste a liquor never brewed—

Mayn Tatn's Bes-din Shtub. *See* In My Father's Court

Mayor of Casterbridge, The (Hardy) CLC I-683; MP VII-3784; MP:BF II-896

Mayor of Zalamea, The (Calderón de la Barca) CLC I-684; MP VII-3788

M. C. Higgins, the Great (Hamilton) MPII:AfAm II-783; MPII:JYAFic III-946

Me, Me, Me, Me, Me (Kerr) MPII:JYABio III-1199

Measure for Measure (Shakespeare) CLC I-685; MP VII-3793

Measure of Time, A (Guy) MPII:AfAm II-788

Medea (Euripides) CLC I-686; MP VII-3798

Meditación, Una. *See* Meditation, A

Meditation, A (Benet) CLCII III-990; MPII:WF III-988

Meditations (Aurelius) MP VII-3802

Meek Heritage (Sillanpää) CLC I-687; MP VII-3804; MP:EF II-849

Meeting at Telgte, The (Grass) CLCII III-991; MPII:WF III-994

"Meeting the British" (Muldoon) MPII:P IV-1353

Meijin. *See* Master of Go, The

Mellstock Quire, The. *See* Under the Greenwood Tree

Melmoth the Wanderer (Maturin) CLC I-689; MP VII-3809; MP:BF II-901

Member of the Wedding, The (McCullers) CLC I-690; CLCII III-992; MP VII-3815; MP:AF II-776; MPII:D III-1071; MPII:JYAFic III-950

Memed, My Hawk (Kemal) CLCII III-993; MPII:WF III-999

Memento Mori (Spark) MP VII-3820; MP:BF II-908

Memnon. *See* Zadig

"Mémoire. *See* Memory" (Rimbaud)

Mémoires. *See* Autobiography of Benjamin Franklin, The

Mémoires de la vie privée de Benjamin Franklin. *See* Autobiography of Benjamin Franklin, The.

Memoirs (Casanova de Seingalt) MP VII-3823

Memoirs (Neruda) MPII:NF III-912

Memoirs of a Cavalier, The (Defoe) CLC I-691; MP VII-3826; MP:BF II-912

Memoirs of a Dutiful Daughter (de Beauvoir) MPII:NF III-917

Memoirs of a Fox-Hunting Man (Sassoon) CLC I-691; MP VII-3830; MP:BF II-916

Memoirs of a Midget (de la Mare) CLC I-692; MP VII-3833; MP:BF II-920

Memoirs of a Physician (Dumas, *père*) CLC I-692; MP VII-3836; MP:EF II-854

Memoirs of an Infantry Officer (Sassoon) CLC I-693; MP VII-3842; MP:BF II-924

Memoirs of Hadrian. *See* Hadrian's Memoirs

Memoirs of the Forties (Maclaren-Ross) MPII:NF III-923

Mémoirs d'une jeune fille rangée. *See* Memoirs of a Dutiful Daughter

Memorandum, The (Havel) CLCII III-995; MPII:D III-1077

Memoria del fuego. *See* Memory of Fire

"Memorial for the City" (Auden) MPII:P IV-1356

Memórias pósthumas de Bráz Cubas. *See* Epitaph of a Small Winner

Memories, Dreams, Reflections (Jung) MPII:NF III-928

Memories of a Catholic Girlhood (McCarthy) MPII:NF III-933

"Memory" (Rimbaud) MPII:P IV-1359

"Memory" (Rossetti, C.) MPII:P IV-1363

Memory of Fire (Galeano) MPII:NF III-937

Men and Women (Browning, R.) MP VII-3846. *See also* Dramatic Monologues and Lyrics of Browning

Men at Arms. *See* Sword of Honour

Men of Ideas (Loeper) MPII:JYABio III-1203

Men of Maize (Asturias) CLCII III-996; MPII:AF III-991

Men of Mathematics (Bell) MPII:JYABio III-1207

Menaechmi, The (Plautus) CLC I-694; MP VII-3849

Mendiant de Jérusalem, Le. *See* Beggar in Jerusalem, A

"Mending Wall" (Frost) MPII:P IV-1366

Menindo engenho. *See* Plantation Boy

Menino de engenho. *See* Plantation Boy

Mensch erscheint im Holozän, Der. *See* Man in the Holocene

"Mental Traveller, The" (Blake) MPII:P IV-1369

Menteur, Le (Corneille) CLC I-695; MP VII-3852

Menuhah nekhonah. *See* Perfect Peace, A

Merchant of Venice, The (Shakespeare) CLC I-695; MP VII-3855

Meridian (Walker, A.) CLCII III-997; MPII:AF III-997; MPII:AfAm II-794

Meriggiare pallido e assorto. *See* Wall, The

Merry Adventures of Robin Hood, The (Pyle) MPII:JYAFic III-954

Merry-Go-Round in the Sea, The (Stow) CLCII III-998; MPII:BCF III-1081

Merry Wives of Windsor, The (Shakespeare) CLC I-697; MP VII-3860

Message in the Bottle, The (Percy) MPII:NF III-944

Messenger, The (Wright, C.) MPII:AfAm II-800

Messengers of Day. See To Keep the Ball Rolling

Messer Marco Polo (Byrne) CLC I-698; MP VII-3863; MP:BF II-928

Mestiere di vivere, Il. See Burning Brand, The

Metafizyka dwugowego ciclcia. See Metaphysics of a Two-Headed Calf

"Metamorphoses" (Cheever, J.) MPII:SS IV-1489

Metamorphoses, The (Ovid) MP VII-3866

"Metamorphosis" (Glück) MPII:P IV-1372

"Metamorphosis, The" (Kafka) CLCII III-999; MPII:SS IV-1493

Metaphysics of a Two-Headed Calf (Witkiewicz) CLCII III-1000; MPII:D III-1082

"Metel" (Pushkin). See "Blizzard, The"

"Metel" (Tolstoy). See "Snow-Storm, The"

Météores, Les. See Gemini

Micah Clarke (Doyle) CLC II-699; MP VII-3869; MP:BF II-931

Michael (Wordsworth) MPII:P IV-1375

Michael and His Lost Angel (Jones, Henry) CLC II-699; MP VII-3873

Michelangelo (Ripley) MPII:JYABio III-1210

Mickelsson's Ghosts (Gardner) CLCII III-1001; MPII:AF III-1002

Microbe Hunters (De Kruif) MPII:JYABio III-1214

Mid-Channel (Pinero) CLC II-700; MP VII-3877

Middle Age of Mrs. Eliot, The (Wilson, Angus) CLCII III-1004; MPII:BCF III-1086

Middle Ground, The (Drabble) CLCII III-1005; MPII:BCF III-1091

Middle Moffat, The. See Moffats series, The

Middle of the Journey, The (Trilling) CLCII III-1006; MPII:AF III-1007

Middle Parts of Fortune, The. See Her Privates, We

"Middle Passage" (Hayden) MPII:P IV-1379

Middle Passage (Johnson, C.) MPII:AfAm II-805

Middle Passage, The (Naipaul) MPII:NF III-950

Middlemarch (Eliot, G.) CLC II-700; MP VII-3879; MP:BF II-935

Midnight Folk, The (Masefield) MPII:JYAFic III-958

Midnight Oil (Pritchett) MPII:NF III-955

Midnight's Children (Rushdie) CLCII III-1007; MPII:BCF III-1097

"Midsummer Night Madness" (O'Faoláin) MPII:SS IV-1497

Midsummer Night's Dream, A (Shakespeare) CLC II-703; MP VII-3885

Mighty and Their Fall, The (Compton-Burnett) MP VII-3890; MP:BF II-942

Mighty Hard Road (Terzian and Cramer) MPII:JYABio III-1218

Migrants, Sharecroppers, Mountaineers. See Children of Crisis

Miguel Street (Naipaul, V. S.) CLCII III-1008; MPII:BCF III-1102

Mikado, The (Gilbert) CLC II-704; MP VII-3893

Mikha'el sheli. See My Michael

Mikrographia. See Miniature

Military Philosophers, The. See Dance to the Music of Time, A

Mill on the Floss, The (Eliot, G.) CLC II-705; MP VII-3896; MP:BF II-945

Mill on the Po, The (Bacchelli) CLC II-707; MP VII-3901; MP:EF II-861

Milton (Blake) MPII:P IV-1383

"Milton by Firelight" (Snyder) MPII:P IV-1387

Mimesis (Auerbach) MPII:NF III-960

Mimic Men, The (Naipaul, V. S.) CLCII III-1010; MPII:BCF III-1106

"Mind Is an Enchanting Thing, The" (Moore, M.) MPII:P IV-1391

Mind of Primitive Man, The (Boas) MP VII-3906

Minds, Brains, and Science (Searle) MPII:NF III-965

"Miniature" (Rítsos) MPII:P IV-1394

"Minister's Black Veil, The" (Hawthorne) MPII:SS IV-1501

Ministry of Fear, The (Greene, G.) CLC II-708; MP VII-3909; MP:BF II-951

"Miniver Cheevy" (Robinson, E.) MPII:P IV-1398

Minna von Barnhelm (Lessing, G.) CLC II-709; MP VII-3912

Minnipins, The. See Gammage Cup, The

Minor Apocalypse, A (Konwicki) CLCII III-1011; MPII:WF III-1006

Minty Alley (James, C. L. R.) CLCII III-1012; MPII:AfAm II-811; MPII:BCF III-1109

Mirabell. See Changing Light at Sandover, The

Miracle of the Rose (Genet) CLCII III-1013; MPII:WF III-1011

Miracle Worker, The (Gibson) CLCII III-1015; MPII:D III-1089

Miracles on Maple Hill (Sorensen) MPII:JYAFic III-962

Mirror for Witches, A (Forbes) CLC II-710; MP VII-3917; MP:AF II-782

Mirror in My House (O'Casey) MPII:NF III-971

Misanthrope, The (Molière) CLC II-711; MP VII-3921

Miscellanies (Cowley) MP VII-3926

Mischling, Second Degree (Koehn) MPII:JYABio III-1222

Miser, The (Molière) CLC II-712; MP VII-3928

Misérables, Les (Hugo, V.) CLC II-713; MP VII-3931; MP:EF II-866

Mismo Tiempo, El. See Same Time

"Miss Brill" (Mansfield) MPII:SS IV-1505

Miss Julie (Strindberg) CLC II-715; MP VII-3936

Miss Lonelyhearts (West, N.) CLC II-716; MP VII-3941; MP:AF II-787

"Miss Ogilvy Finds Herself" (Hall) MPII:SS IV-1509

Miss Peabody's Inheritance (Jolley) CLCII III-1016; MPII:BCF III-1116

Miss Ravenel's Conversion from Secession to Loyalty (De Forest) CLC II-717; MP VII-3945; MP:AF II-792

"Miss Tempy's Watchers" (Jewett) MPII:SS IV-1513

Missolonghi Manuscript, The (Prokosch) CLCII III-1018; MPII:AF III-1012

Mr. Bass's Planetoid. See Mushroom Planet series, The

Mr. Bell Invents the Telephone (Shippen) MPII:JYABio III-1226

Mr. Beluncle (Pritchett) CLCII III-1018; MPII:BCF III-1121

Mr. Britling Sees It Through (Wells) CLC II-717; MP VII-3949; MP:BF II-955

Mr. Bullivant and His Lambs (Compton-Burnett) MP VII-3952

"Mr. Edwards and the Spider" (Lowell, R.) MPII:P IV-1401

Mr. Facey Romford's Hounds (Surtees) CLC II-718; MP VII-3954; MP:BF II-959

Mr. Justice Holmes (Judson) MPII:JYABio III-1230

Mr. Midshipman Easy (Marryat) CLC II-719; MP VII-3960; MP:BF II-966; MPII:JYAFic III-965

Mr. Palomar (Calvino) CLCII III-1020; MPII:WF III-1015

Mister Roberts (Heggen) CLC II-720; MP VII-3964; MP:AF II-796

Mr. Sammler's Planet (Bellow) CLCII III-1020; MPII:AF III-1017

Mr. Sampath. See Printer of Malgudi, The

Mr. Sponge's Sporting Tour (Surtees) CLC II-721; MP VII-3967; MP:BF II-970

Mr. Stone and the Knights Companion (Naipaul, V. S.) CLCII III-1022; MPII:BCF III-1126

Mr. Weston's Good Wine (Powys, T.) CLC II-721; MP VII-3970; MP:BF II-974

Mrs. Bridge (Connell) CLCII III-1023; MPII:AF III-1022

Mrs. Caliban (Ingalls) CLCII III-1024; MPII:BCF III-1131

Mrs. Dalloway (Woolf) CLC II-722; MP VII-3973; MP:BF II-978

Mrs. Dane's Defence (Jones, Henry) CLC II-724; MP VII-3978

"Mrs. Fortescue" (Lessing, D.) MPII:SS IV-1515

Mrs. Frisby and the Rats of NIMH (O'Brien, R.) MPII:JYAFic III-968

Mistress of the Inn, The (Goldoni) CLC II-724; MP VII-3982

Mrs. Stevens Hears the Mermaids Singing (Sarton) CLCII III-1025; MPII:AF III-1028

Mrs. Warren's Profession (Shaw, G.) CLCII III-1026; MPII:D III-1095

Mit Allen Gedanken. See With All My Thoughts

Mithridate (Racine) CLC II-725; MP VII-3987

Miyamoto Musashi. See Musashi.

"Mnogo li cheloveku zemli nuzhno?" See "How Much Land Does a Man Need?"

Mobile (Butor) CLCII III-1027; MPII:WF III-1021

Moby Dick (Melville) CLC II-725; MP VII-3992; MP:AF II-800

Mock Astrologer, The (Calderón de la Barca) CLC II-728; MP VII-3998

Model Childhood, A. See Patterns of Childhood

Modern Chivalry (Brackenridge) CLC II-728; MP VII-4001; MP:AF II-806

Modern Comedy, A (Galsworthy) CLC II-729; MP VII-4005; MP:BF II-983

Modern Instance, A (Howells) CLC II-730; MP VII-4010; MP:AF II-811

Modern Midas, A (Jókai) CLC II-731; MP VII-4015; MP:EF II-872

Modification, La. See Change of Heart, A

Moe Berg (Kaufman, Fitzgerald, and Sewell, T.) MPII:JYABio III-1233

Moetsukita chizu. See Ruined Map, The

Moffats series, The (Estes) MPII:JYAFic III-971

"Moglie con le ali, La." See "Count's Wife, The"

"Moglie di Gogol, La." See "Gogol's Wife"

"Moi pervyi gus." See "My First Goose"

Moll Flanders (Defoe) CLC II-732; MP VII-4020; MP:BF II-988

Molloy (Beckett) CLCII III-1028. See also Trilogy, The

Mom, the Wolf Man, and Me (Klein, N.) MPII:JYAFic III-975

Moment of True Feeling, A (Handke) CLCII III-1029; MPII:WF III-1026

Monarch and Conspirators (Southworth) MPII:JYABio III-1237

Monday Conversations (Sainte-Beuve) MP VII-4025

Monk, The (Lewis, Matthew) CLC II-733; MP VII-4027; MP:BF II-993

"Monkey, The" (Dinesen) MPII:SS IV-1519

Monkey (Wu Ch'eng-en) CLC II-733; MP VII-4030; MP:EF II-878

Monkey Grip (Garner, H.) CLCII III-1030; MPII:BCF III-1137

Monkey's Wrench, The (Levi, P.) CLCII III-1032; MPII:WF III-1031

Monsieur Beaucaire (Tarkington) CLC II-735; MP VII-4034; MP:AF II-816

Monsieur D'Olive (Chapman) CLC II-736; MP VII-4037

Monsieur Lecoq (Gaboriau) CLC II-736; MP VII-4040; MP:EF II-883

"Monster, The" (Crane, S.) MPII:SS IV-1523

Monstre Gai. See Human Age, The

Mont Blanc (Shelley, P.) MPII:P IV-1405

Mont-Oriol (Maupassant) CLC II-737; MP VII-4045; MP:EF II-889

Mont-Saint-Michel and Chartres (Adams, H.) MP VII-4049

Montgomery's Children (Perry) MPII:AfAm II-817

Month in the Country, A (Turgenev) CLC II-738; MP VII-4052

Month of Sundays, A (Updike) CLCII III-1033; MPII:AF III-1032

"Moon and Madness" (Singer) MPII:SS IV-1528

Moon and Sixpence, The (Maugham) CLC II-739; MP VII-4056; MP:BF II-997

Moon and the Bonfires, The (Pavese) CLCII III-1034; MPII:WF III-1036

"Moon Deluxe" (Barthelme, F.) MPII:SS IV-1532

Moon for the Misbegotten, A (O'Neill) CLCII III-1035; MPII:D III-1100

Moon Is a Harsh Mistress, The (Heinlein) CLCII III-1036; MPII:AF III-1037

Moon Story, The. *See* Bracknels, The

"Moonlight" (Verlaine) MPII:P IV-1408

"Moonlit Night" (Tu Fu) MPII:P IV-1412

Moonrise, Moonset (Konwicki) CLCII III-1037; MPII:WF III-1041

Moonstone, The (Collins, Wilke) CLC II-740; MP VII-4059; MP:BF II-1001

"Moose, The" (Bishop) MPII:P IV-1415

More Than Human (Sturgeon) MPII:JYAFic III-978

Morning, Noon, and Night (Cozzens) CLCII III-1037; MPII:AF III-1042

Morning Watch, The (Agee, James) CLCII III-1039; MPII:AF III-1050

Mornings in Mexico (Lawrence) MPII:NF III-976

"Morro Rock" (Hongo) MPII:P IV-1418

Mort à crédit. *See* Death on the Installment Plan

Morte accidentale di un anarchico. *See* Accidental Death of an Anarchist

Morte d'Arthur, Le (Malory) CLC II-742; MP VII-4063; MP:BF II-1006

Morte d'Urban (Powers) CLCII III-1040; MPII:AF III-1055

Morte dans l'âme, La. *See* Roads to Freedom, The

Moscas, Los. *See* Flies, The

Moses and Monotheism (Freud) MPII:NF III-982

Moses, Man of the Mountain (Hurston) CLCII III-1041; MPII:AF III-1061; MPII:AfAm II-823

Mosquitoes (Faulkner) CLCII III-1042; MPII:AF III-1066

"Most Dangerous Game, The" (Connell, R.) MPII:SS IV-1535

"Most of It, The" (Frost) MPII:P IV-1421

"Mote in the Middle Distance, H*nry J*m*s, The" (Beerbohm) MPII:SS IV-1538

"Mother, The" (Brooks, G.) MPII:P IV-1424

Mother, The (Deledda) CLC II-744; MP VII-4068; MP:EF II-894

Mother (Gorky) CLC II-744; MP VII-4072; MP:EF II-899

Mother and Son (Compton-Burnett) MP VII-4076; MP:BF II-1012

Mother and Two Daughters, A (Godwin) CLCII III-1043; MPII:AF III-1072

Mother Courage and Her Children (Brecht) CLCII III-1046; MPII:D III-1105

Mother Hubberd's Tale (Spenser) MP VII-4078

Mother Ireland (O'Brien) MPII:NF III-987

Mother Jones (Atkinson) MPII:JYABio III-1241

Mother Night (Vonnegut) CLCII III-1047; MPII:AF III-1078

Motion of Light in Water, The (Delany, S.) MPII:AfAm II-829

Mots, Les. *See* Words, The

Mots et les choses, Les. *See* Order of Things, The

Moucha. *See* Fly, The

Mouchette (Bernanos) CLCII III-1048; MPII:WF III-1045

Mound Builders, The (Wilson, L.) CLCII III-1049; MPII:D III-1110

Mount Rushmore Story, The (St. George) MPII:JYABio III-1244

Mountain and the Valley, The (Buckler) CLCII III-1051; MPII:BCF III-1143

"Mountain Tavern, The" (O'Flaherty) MPII:SS IV-1541

Mountolive. *See* Alexandria Quartet, The

Mourning Becomes Electra (O'Neill) CLC II-745; MP VII-4081

Mouse and His Child, The (Hoban) MPII:JYAFic III-982

Mousetrap, The (Christie) CLCII III-1052; MPII:D III-1116

Moveable Feast, A (Hemingway) MP VII-4087; MPII:JYABio III-1248

Moved Outers, The (Means) MPII:JYAFic III-986

Moves Make the Man, The (Brooks, B.) MPII:JYAFic III-989

Moviegoer, The (Percy) CLCII III-1053; MPII:AF III-1083

"Mower, Against Gardens, The" (Marvell) MPII:P IV-1427

Mozart (Komroff) MPII:JYABio III-1252

"Ms. Found in a Bottle" (Poe) MPII:SS IV-1451

Much Ado About Nothing (Shakespeare) CLC II-746; MP VII-4090

Mudun al-milh (Munf) MPII:WF III-1049. *See also* Cities of Salt

Muerta de Artemio Cruz, La. *See* Death of Artemio Cruz, The

Mulata (Asturias) CLCII III-1054; MPII:AF III-1087

Mumbet (Felton) MPII:JYABio III-1256

Mumbo Jumbo (Reed, I.) CLCII III-1055; MPII:AF III-1094; MPII:AfAm II-835

Mundo es ancho y ajena, El. *See* Broad and Alien Is the World

"Mur, Le." *See* "Wall, The"

Murder in the Cathedral (Eliot, T. S.) CLC II-748; MP VII-4094

Murder of Roger Ackroyd, The (Christie) CLCII III-1056; MPII:BCF III-1148

Murderer, The (Heath) CLCII III-1057; MPII:BCF III-1153

"Murders in the Rue Morgue, The" (Poe) MPII:SS IV-1544

"Murke's Collected Silences" (Böll) MPII:SS IV-1548

Murphy (Beckett) CLCII III-1059; MPII:BCF III-1157

Musashi (Yoshikawa) MPII:JYABio III-1260

"Musée des Beaux Arts" (Auden) MPII:P IV-1430

Mushroom Planet series, The (Cameron) MPII:JYAFic III-993

Musical Honors (Barne) MPII:JYAFic III-996

Mutineers, The (Armstrong, R.) MPII:JYAFic III-999

Mutiny on the Bounty (Nordhoff *and* Hall, J.) CLC II-749; MP VII-4099; MP:AF II-819; MPII:JYAFic III-1003

Mutter Courage und ihre Kinder. *See* Mother Courage and Her Children

"Muzhik Marey." *See* "Peasant Marey, The"

My. *See* We

My Amputations (Major) MPII:AfAm II-842

My Ántonia (Cather) CLC II-749; MP VII-4103; MP:AF II-823; MPII:JYAFic III-1007

My Brilliant Career (Franklin) CLCII III-1060; MPII:BCF III-1161

My Brother Sam Is Dead (Collier, James *and* Collier, C.) MPII:JYAFic III-1010

My Cousin Rachel (du Maurier) MPII:JYAFic III-1013

My Dinner with André (Shawn *and* Gregory) CLCII III-1061; MPII:D III-1121

"My Father in the Night Commanding No" (Simpson) MPII:P IV-1433

"My father moved through dooms of love" (Cummings) MPII:P IV-1436

"My First Goose" (Babel) MPII:SS IV-1552

My First Summer in the Sierra (Muir) MPII:JYABio III-1264

My Friend Flicka (O'Hara, J.) MPII:JYAFic III-1016

My Heart and My Flesh (Roberts) CLCII III-1062; MPII:AF III-1100

"My Kinsman, Major Molineux" (Hawthorne) MPII:SS IV-1556

"My Last Afternoon with Uncle Devereux Winslow" (Lowell, R.) MPII:P IV-1439

"My Last Duchess" (Browning, R.) MPII:P IV-1443

My Life and Hard Times (Thurber) MP VII-4108

"My Life had stood—a Loaded Gun—" (Dickinson, E.) MPII:P IV-1446

My Life in the Bush of Ghosts (Tutuola) CLCII III-1063; MPII:BCF III-1167

My Life of Absurdity. *See* Autobiographies of Chester Himes, The.

My Life with Martin Luther King, Jr. (King, C.) MPII:AfAm II-848

My Lord, What a Morning (Anderson, Marian) MPII:JYABio III-1268

"My Man Bovanne" (Bambara) MPII:SS IV-1560

My Michael (Oz) CLCII III-1065; MPII:WF III-1054

"My mistress' eyes are nothing like the sun." *See* Sonnet 130

"My Mother Would Be a Falconress" (Duncan) MPII:P IV-1449

My Name Is Asher Lev (Potok) CLCII III-1067; MPII:AF III-1105

"My Oedipus Complex" (O'Connor, Frank) MPII:SS IV-1564

"My Papa's Waltz" (Roethke) MPII:P
IV-1453
My St. Petersburg (Almedingen)
MPII:JYABio III-1272
My Several Worlds (Buck) MPII:JYABio
III-1276
My Shadow Ran Fast (Sands)
MPII:JYABio III-1280
"My Side of the Matter" (Capote) MPII:SS
IV-1567
"My Sweetest Lesbia" (Campion, T.)
MPII:P IV-1456
"My Warszawa" (Oates) MPII:SS IV-1571
"Myris: Alexandria, 340 A.D." (Cavafy)
MPII:P IV-1459
Myris: Alexandria tou 340 M.X. See Myris:
Alexandria, 340 A.D.
Myshlenie i rech. See Thought and
Language
Mysterier. See Mysteries
Mysteries (Hamsun) CLCII III-1068;
MPII:WF III-1059

Mysteries of Paris, The (Sue) CLC II-752;
MP VII-4111; MP:EF II-904
Mysteries of Udolpho, The (Radcliffe) CLC
II-753; MP VII-4115; MP:BF II-1015
Mysterious Island, The (Verne) CLC II-754;
MP VII-4121; MP:EF II-909
"Mysterious Kôr" (Bowen, E.) MPII:SS
IV-1575
"Mysterious Stranger, The" (Twain) CLCII
III-1069; MPII:SS IV-1578
Mystery for Mr. Bass, A. See Mushroom
Planet series, The
Mystery of Edwin Drood, The (Dickens)
CLC II-755; MP VII-4125; MP:BF
II-1022
Mystery of the Charity of Charles Péguy,
The (Hill, G.) MPII:P IV-1462
Myth of Sisyphus, The (Camus) MP
VII-4128
Mythistorema (Seferis) MPII:P IV-1467
Mythistorima. See Mythistorema

N

Na doske malinovoi, chervonnoi. *See* On a
Board of Raspberry and Pure Gold
Na smert' druga. *See* To a Friend
Na trabach ï na cytrze. *See* With Trumpets
and Zithers
"Nabeg." *See* "Raid, The"
Nachalo nevedomogo veka. *See* Story of a
Life, The
Nachdenken über Christa T. *See* Quest for
Christa T., The
Nachsommer, Der. *See* Indian Summer
"Nairobi" (Oates) MPII:SS IV-1582
Nakanune. *See* On the Eve
Naked and the Dead, The (Mailer) CLCII
III-1070; MPII:AF III-1110
Naked Lunch (Burroughs, W.) CLCII
III-1071; MPII:AF III-1114
Naked to Mine Enemies (Ferguson)
MPII:JYABio III-1284
Naked Year, The (Pilnyak) CLC II-755; MP
VII-4131; MP:EF II-913
Name of the Rose, The (Eco) CLCII
III-1072; MPII:WF III-1065
Names, The (Momaday) MPII:NF III-991
Nana (Zola) CLC II-756; MP VII-4135;
MP:EF II-918
Nancy Drew series, The (Keene)
MPII:JYAFic III-1019
Nansen (Hall, A.) MPII:JYABio III-1288
Naomi (Tanizaki) CLCII III-1074;
MPII:WF III-1070
Napoleon (Chandler) MPII:JYABio III-1292
Napoleon (Komroff) MPII:JYABio III-1296
Napoleon of Notting Hill, The (Chesterton)
CLC II-757; MP VII-4140; MP:BF
II-1026
Napoleon Symphony (Burgess) CLCII
III-1075; MPII:BCF III-1171
Narcissa Whitman (Eaton) MPII:JYABio
III-1300
Narcissus and Goldmund (Hesse) CLCII
III-1077; MPII:WF III-1074
Narrative of Arthur Gordon Pym, The (Poe)
CLC II-758; MP VII-4143; MP:AF
II-828
Narrative of the Life of David Crockett, A
(Crockett) MP VII-4146

Narrative of the Life of Frederick Douglass
(Douglass) MPII:AfAm II-854;
MPII:JYABio III-1304
Narrative of the Lord's Wonderful Dealings
with John Marrant, a Black, A (Marrant)
MPII:AfAm II-859
Narrative of the Uncommon Sufferings, and
Surprizing Deliverance of Briton
Hammon, a Negro Man, A (Hammon)
MPII:AfAm II-864
Narrative of William Wells Brown, A
Fugitive Slave. *See* Autobiographical
Writings of William Wells Brown, The.
"Narrow Fellow in the Grass, A"
(Dickinson, E.) MPII:P IV-1472
Narrows, The (Petry) MPII:AfAm II-869
Narziss und Goldmund. *See* Narcissus and
Goldmund
Nashedshii podkovu. *See* Horseshoe Finder,
The
"Nasty Story, A" (Dostoevski) MPII:SS
IV-1586
Nathan the Wise (Lessing, G.) CLC II-759;
MP VII-4149
"National Honeymoon" (Horgan) MPII:SS
IV-1590
"National Velvet" (Bagnold) MPII:JYAFic
III-1023
"Native of Winby, A" (Jewett) MPII:SS
IV-1594
Native Realm (Miłosz) MPII:NF III-997
Native Son (Wright) CLC II-760; MP
VII-4152; MP:AF II-832; MPII:AfAm
II-875; MPII:JYAFic III-1027
Natives of Hemsö, The (Strindberg) CLCII
III-1077; MPII:WF III-1079
Natives of My Person (Lamming) CLCII
III-1078; MPII:AfAm II-881; MPII:BCF
III-1176
Natural, The (Malamud) CLCII III-1080;
MPII:AF III-1119
Natural Symbols (Douglas) MPII:NF
III-1003
Nausea (Sartre) CLC II-761; MP VII-4157;
MP:EF II-924
"Navajo Blanket, A" (Swenson) MPII:P
IV-1475

Nazarene, The (Asch) CLC II-761; CLCII
  III-1081; MP VII-4161; MP:AF II-837;
  MPII:WF III-1085
"Necklace, The" (Maupassant) MPII:SS
  IV-1597
Nectar in a Sieve (Markandaya) CLCII
  III-1082; MPII:BCF III-1182
Needle's Eye, The (Drabble) CLCII
  III-1083; MPII:BCF III-1188
Negotiations of Thomas Woolsey, the Great
  Cardinall of England, The. See Life and
  Death of Cardinal Wolsey, The
Nègres, Les. See Blacks, The
"Negro Speaks of Rivers, The" (Hughes, L.)
  MPII:P IV-1478
Neige était sale, La. See Snow Was Black,
  The
"Neighbor Rosicky" (Cather) MPII:SS
  IV-1602
Neighbor to the World (Block)
  MPII:JYABio III-1308
"Neighbors" (Oliver) MPII:SS IV-1605
"Neither Out Far nor In Deep" (Frost)
  MPII:P IV-1481
Nemureru bijo. See House of the Sleeping
  Beauties, The
Neshome Ekspeditsyes. See Shosha
Nesnesitelná lehkost bytí. See Unbearable
  Lightness of Being, The
Nest of Simple Folk, A (O'Faoláin) CLC
  II-762; MP VII-4165; MP:BF II-1030
Netochka Nezvanova (Dostoevski) CLCII
  III-1084; MPII:WF III-1089
Neuve monstruos, Los. See Nine Monsters,
  The
"Nevada Gas" (Chandler) MPII:SS IV-1608
Never Come Morning (Algren) CLCII
  III-1085; MPII:AF III-1124
New Atlantis (Bacon) MP VII-4168
New Criticism, The (Ransom) MP VII-4171
New Day (Reid) CLCII III-1087;
  MPII:BCF III-1193
New Don Quixote, The. See Tartarin of
  Tarascon
New England Love Story, A (Gaeddert)
  MPII:JYABio III-1312
New-Found-Land (Stoppard) CLCII I-404;
  MPII:D II-502

New Grub Street, The (Gissing) CLC
  II-763; MP VII-4174; MP:BF II-1034
New Héloïse, The (Rousseau) CLC II-764;
  MP VII-4177; MP:EF II-928
"New Islands" (Bombal) MPII:SS IV-1612
New Life, A (Malamud) CLCII III-1088;
  MPII:AF III-1129
New Men, The. See Strangers and Brothers
New Mondays. See Monday Conversations
New Negro, The (Locke, A.) MPII:AfAm
  II-887
New Way to Pay Old Debts, A (Massinger)
  CLC II-765; MP VII-4180
New World Trilogy, A. See Poetry of
  Edward Kamau Brathwaite, The.
"New Year Letter" (Auden) MPII:P IV-1484
"New Year Letter" (Tsvetayeva) MPII:P
  IV-1489
"New Year's Eve Adventure, A"
  (Hoffmann) MPII:SS IV-1616
New York Diary of Ned Rorem, The. See
  Paris and New York Diaries of Ned
  Rorem, The
Newcomes, The (Thackeray) CLC II-766;
  MP VII-4185; MP:BF II-1038
Ngaahika Ndeenda. See I Will Marry When
  I Want
Niagara (Butor) CLCII III-1089; MPII:WF
  III-1093
Nibelungenlied, The (Unknown) CLC
  II-770; MP VII-4190; MP:EF II-932
Nicholas and Alexandra (Massie, R.)
  MPII:JYABio III-1316
Nicholas and the Wool-Pack (Harnett)
  MPII:JYAFic III-1031
Nicholas Nickleby (Dickens) CLC II-771;
  MP VII-4195; MP:BF II-1044
Nick of the Woods (Bird) CLC II-775; MP
  VII-4199; MP:AF II-841
Nickel Mountain (Gardner) CLCII III-1091;
  MPII:AF III-1134
Niels Lyhne (Jacobsen) CLC II-776; MP
  VII-4205; MP:EF II-938
Niezwycióny i inne opowiadania. See
  Invincible, The
Nigger of the "Narcissus," The (Conrad)
  CLC II-776; MP VII-4209; MP:BF
  II-1049
"Night" (Bly) MPII:P IV-1493

Night (O'Brien, E.) CLCII III-1092; MPII:BCF III-1198

Night (Wiesel) MPII:NF III-1008

Night and Day (Stoppard) CLCII III-1093; MPII:D III-1128

Night and Day (Woolf) CLCII III-1094; MPII:BCF III-1203

"Night and Morning" (Clarke, Austin) MPII:P IV-1496

Night Flight (Saint-Exupéry) CLC II-777; MP VII-4212; MP:EF II-942

Night in the Luxembourg, A (Gourmont) CLC II-778; MP VII-4215; MP:EF II-946

'night, Mother (Norman) CLCII III-1095; MPII:D III-1133

Night Must Fall (Williams, E.) CLCII III-1096; MPII:D III-1138

Night of the Iguana, The (Williams, T.) CLCII III-1097; MPII:D III-1143

Night Poem. See Sleepers, The

Night Rider (Warren) MP VII-4218; MP:AF II-848

"Night-Sea Journey" (Barth) MPII:SS IV-1624

Night Swimmers, The (Byars) MPII:JYAFic III-1035

"Nightfall" (Asimov) MPII:SS IV-1620

Nightmare Abbey (Peacock) CLC II-778; MP VII-4221; MP:BF II-1053

Nightwood (Barnes, D.) CLCII III-1099; MPII:AF III-1139

"Nikki-Rosa" (Giovanni) MPII:P IV-1499

Nilda (Mohr) MPII:JYAFic III-1038

Nils Holgerssons underbara resa genom Sverige. See Wonderful Adventures of Nils, The

"Nine Monsters, The" (Vallejo) MPII:P IV-1502

Nine Tailors, The (Sayers) CLCII III-1100; MPII:BCF III-1208

Nineteen Eighty-Four (Orwell) CLC II-779; MP VII-4224; MP:BF II-1057

1959 (Davis, T.) MPII:AfAm II-893

1934 (Moravia) CLCII III-1101; MPII:WF III-1098

Ninety-two in the Shade (McGuane) CLCII III-1102; MPII:AF III-1145

Ningen shikkaku. See No Longer Human

Nino (Angelo) MPII:JYAFic III-1042

Nisei Daughter (Sone) MPII:JYABio III-1320

No Blade of Grass. See Death of Grass, The

No Exit (Sartre) CLCII III-1103; MPII:D III-1148

No Laughing Matter (Wilson, Angus) CLCII III-1104; MPII:BCF III-1213

No Longer at Ease (Achebe) CLCII III-1105; MPII:BCF III-1219

No Longer Human (Dazai) CLCII III-1107; MPII:WF III-1103

No More Parades. See Parade's End

No Name (Collins, Wilkie) CLC II-780; MP VII-4227; MP:BF III-1061

No One Writes to the Colonel (García Márquez) CLCII III-1108; MPII:AF III-1151

No Place on Earth (Wolf) CLCII III-1109; MPII:WF III-1108

No Trifling with Love (Musset) CLC II-781; MP VII-4231

Nobleman's Nest, A. See House of Gentlefolk, A

Noche en claro. See Clear Night

Nocturne (Swinnerton) CLC II-781; MP VII-4235; MP:BF II-1065

"Nocturne" (Tranströmer) MPII:P IV-1505

Nocturne parisien. See Parisian Nocturne

Nocturno de San Ildefonso. See San Ildefonso Nocturne

Noise of Time, The (Mandelstam, O.) MPII:NF III-1013

"Noiseless Patient Spider, A" (Whitman) MPII:P IV-1508

Nome della rosa, Il. See Name of the Rose, The

Non-existent Knight, The (Calvino) CLCII III-1110; MPII:WF III-1113

"Noon Wine" (Porter) MPII:SS IV-1628. See also Pale Horse, Pale Rider

Nord. See North

Nordsee, Die. See North Sea, The

Nordy Bank (Porter, S.) MPII:JYAFic III-1045

Norman Conquests, The (Ayckbourn) CLCII III-1111; MPII:D III-1153

North (Céline) CLCII I-241; MPII:WF I-121

North Sea, The (Heine) MPII:P IV-1511

North to Freedom. See I Am David

Northanger Abbey (Austen) CLC II-782;
MP VII-4238; MP:BF II-1068

Northern Lass, The (Brome) CLC II-783;
MP VII-4243

Northwest Passage (Roberts, K.) MP
VII-4247; MP:AF II-852

"Nose, The" (Gogol) MPII:SS IV-1633

Nostromo (Conrad) CLC II-783; MP
VII-4250; MP:BF II-1074

Not Honour More. See Second Trilogy

Not Without Laughter (Hughes, L.) CLCII
III-1113; MPII:AF III-1155

Notebooks, 1960-1977 (Fugard) MPII:NF
III-1019

Notebooks of Leonardo da Vinci, The
(Vinci) MP VII-4255

Notes for Another Life (Bridgers)
MPII:JYAFic III-1048

Notes from a Bottle Found on the Beach at
Carmel (Connell) MP VII-4258

Notes from the Century Before (Hoagland)
MPII:NF III-1023

Notes from the Underground. See Letters
from the Underworld

Notes of a Native Son (Baldwin)
MPII:AfAm II-899; MPII:NF III-1029

Notes on the State of Virginia (Jefferson)
MP VII-4260

Notes Towards the Definition of Culture
(Eliot) MPII:NF III-1034

Nothing (Green, Henry) CLCII III-1114;
MPII:BCF III-1224

Nothing Happens in Carmincross (Kiely)
CLCII III-1115; MPII:BCF III-1228

Nothing Is Impossible (Aldis)
MPII:JYABio III-1324

Nothing Like the Sun (Burgess) CLCII
III-1116; MPII:BCF III-1233

Notre-Dame des Fleurs. See Our Lady of
the Flowers

Nouvelle Héloïse, La. See New Héloïse, The

Nouvelle Histoire de Mouchette. See
Mouchette

November 1918 (Döblin) CLCII III-1117;
MPII:WF III-1118

Novice, The (Lermontov) MP VII-4263

"Novogodnee. See New Year Letter"
(Tsvetayeva)

Now and Then (Buechner) MPII:NF
III-1041

"Now Sleeps the Crimson Petal"
(Tennyson) MPII:P IV-1515

Nœud de vipères, Le. See Vipers' Tangle

Nuit, La. See Night (Wiesel)

"Nun, The" (Alarcón) MPII:SS IV-1637

Nuns and Soldiers (Murdoch) CLCII
III-1120; MPII:BCF III-1238

"Nun's Mother, The" (Lavin) MPII:SS
IV-1640

"Nutting" (Wordsworth) MPII:P IV-1518

O

O Beulah Land (Settle) CLCII III-1122. *See also* Beulah Quintet, The

O die Schornsteine. *See* O the Chimneys

O, How the Wheel Becomes It! (Powell) CLCII III-1123; MPII:BCF III-1243

O Modlitwie. *See* On Prayer

O Pioneers! (Cather) CLC II-785; MP VII-4265; MP:AF II-856

"O the Chimneys" (Sachs) MPII:P IV-1522

Oak and Ivy (Gayle) MPII:JYABio III-1328

Oak and the Calf, The (Solzhenitsyn) MPII:NF III-1046

Oath, The (Wiesel) CLCII III-1124; MPII:WF III-1125

Obaka san. *See* Wonderful Fool

Oberland. *See* Pilgrimage

"Oblako, ozero, bashnya." *See* "Cloud, Castle, Lake"

Oblomov (Goncharov) CLC II-787; MP VII-4270; MP:EF II-949

Obscene Bird of Night, The (Donoso) CLCII III-1125; MPII:AF III-1160

Obsceno pájaro de la noche, El. *See* Obscene Bird of Night, The

Occasion for Loving (Gordimer) CLCII III-1126; MPII:BCF III-1248

Occhiali d'oro, Gli. *See* Gold-Rimmed Eyeglasses, The

"Occident, The" (Trakl) MPII:P IV-1524

"Occurrence at Owl Creek Bridge, An" (Bierce) MPII:SS IV-1643

October Light (Gardner) CLCII III-1127; MPII:AF III-1165

"Octopus, An" (Moore, M.) MPII:P IV-1527

Octopus, The (Norris) CLCII III-1129; MPII:AF III-1171

Oda al limon. *See* Lemon, A

Oda al olor de la leña. *See* Smell of Cordwood, A

Oda al santísmo sacrament o del Alter. *See* Ode to the Most Holy Eucharist

Odd Couple, The (Simon, N.) CLCII III-1130; MPII:D III-1158

Odd Destiny (Lomask) MPII:JYABio III-1333

Odd Woman, The (Godwin) CLCII III-1131; MPII:AF III-1176

"Ode: Intimations of Immortality" (Wordsworth) MPII:P IV-1531

"Ode, Inscribed to W. H. Channing" (Emerson) MPII:P IV-1535

"Ode on a Grecian Urn" (Keats) MPII:P IV-1538

"Ode on Melancholy" (Keats) MPII:P IV-1541

"Ode to a Nightingale" (Keats) MPII:P IV-1544

Ode to Aphrodite (Sappho) MP VII-4273

"Ode to Evening" (Collins) MPII:P IV-1547

"Ode to Psyche" (Keats) MPII:P IV-1550

"Ode to the Confederate Dead" (Tate, A.) MPII:P IV-1554

"Ode to the Most Holy Eucharist (García Lorca) MPII:P IV-1558

"Ode to the West Wind" (Shelley, P.) MPII:P IV-1562

Odin den Ivana Denisovicha. *See* One Day in the Life of Ivan Denisovich

"Odour of Chrysanthemums" (Lawrence) MPII:SS IV-1648

Odyssey, The (Homer) CLC II-788; MP VII-4275

Oedipus at Colonus (Sophocles) CLC II-792; MP VII-4280

Oedipus Tyrannus (Sophocles) CLC II-793; MP VII-4284

Œuvre au noir, L'. *See* Abyss, The

Of a Fire on the Moon (Mailer) MPII:NF III-1052

Of Courage Undaunted (Daugherty, J.) MPII:JYABio III-1337

Of Grammatology (Derrida) MPII:NF III-1057

Of Human Bondage (Maugham) CLC II-794; MP VII-4288; MP:BF II-1080

Of Mice and Men (Steinbeck) CLC II-795; MP VII-4294; MP:AF II-861

"Of Modern Poetry" (Stevens, W.) MPII:P IV-1565

Of One Blood. *See* Magazine Novels of Pauline Hopkins, The.

Of Plimouth Plantation (Bradford, W.) MP VIII-4297

"Of This Time, Of That Place" (Trilling) MPII:SS IV-1652

Of Time and the River (Wolfe) CLC II-796; MP VIII-4300; MP:AF II-865

Offending the Audience (Handke) CLCII III-1132; MPII:D III-1164

Officers and Gentlemen. *See* Sword of Honour

"Official Position, An" (Maugham) MPII:SS IV-1656

Ogre, The (Tournier) CLCII III-1133; MPII:WF III-1129

Oh, Lizzie! (Faber) MPII:JYABio III-1341

Oh What a Paradise It Seems (Cheever, J.) CLCII III-1134; MPII:AF III-1180

"Oh, Whistle, and I'll Come to You, My Lad" (James, M.) MPII:SS IV-1660

Oiseau bleu, L'. *See* Blue Bird, The

Okhrannaya gramota. *See* Safe-Conduct, A

Oktiabr shestnadtsatogo (Solzhenitsyn) CLCII III-1135; MPII:WF III-1134

Ol' Prophet Nat (Panger) MPII:JYABio III-1345

Old and the Young, The (Pirandello) CLC II-797; MP VIII-4305; MP:EF II-953

Old Bachelor, The (Congreve) CLC II-798; MP VIII-4309

"Old Bird, The" (Powers) MPII:SS IV-1664

Old Blood, The. *See* Kaywana trilogy, The

Old Calabria (Douglas, N.) MP VIII-4313

Old Curiosity Shop, The (Dickens) CLC II-799; MP VIII-4316; MP:BF II-1087

Old Devils, The (Amis) CLCII III-1136; MPII:BCF III-1253

"Old Forest, The" (Taylor) MPII:SS IV-1668

Old Fortunatus (Dekker) CLC II-802; MP VIII-4319

Old Maid, The (Wharton) CLC II-803; MP VIII-4322; MP:AF II-870

Old Man, The (Trifonov) CLCII III-1138; MPII:WF III-1141

Old Man and the Sea, The (Hemingway) CLC II-804; MP VIII-4325; MP:AF II-874

"Old Masters" (Herbert, Z.) MPII:P IV-1568

Old Mortality (Porter, K.) CLC II-804; MP VIII-4330; MP:AF II-879; MPII:SS IV-1672. *See also* Pale Horse, Pale Rider

Old Mortality (Scott, Sir W.) CLC II-805; MP VIII-4334; MP:BF II-1091

"Old Red" (Gordon) MPII:SS IV-1676

Old Regime in Canada, The (Parkman) MP VIII-4338

Old St. Paul's (Ainsworth) CLC II-807; MP VIII-4341; MP:BF II-1096

"Old Vemish" (Targan) MPII:SS IV-1680

Old Wives' Tale, The (Bennett, A.) CLC II-808; MP VIII-4344; MP:BF II-1100

Old Wives' Tale, The (Peele) CLC II-809; MP VIII-4349

"Old Woman Magoun" (Freeman) MPII:SS IV-1684

"Old-World Landowners" (Gogol) MPII:SS IV-1688

Old Yeller (Gipson) MPII:JYAFic III-1051

Oldest Living Graduate, The (Jones, J.) CLCII III-1139; MPII:D III-1169

Oldtown Folks (Stowe) CLC II-810; MP VIII-4353; MP:AF II-883

"Olga Poems" (Levertov) MPII:P IV-1571

Oliver Twist (Dickens) CLC II-812; MP VIII-4358; MP:BF II-1105; MPII:JYAFic III-1054

Ölmez otu. *See* Undying Grass, The

Omensetter's Luck (Gass) CLCII III-1140; MPII:AF III-1184

Omoo (Melville) CLC II-813; MP VIII-4364; MP:AF II-888

"On a Board of Raspberry and Pure Gold" (Mandelstam, O.) MPII:P IV-1575

"On Account of a Hat" (Aleichem) MPII:SS IV-1692

"On First Looking into Chapman's Homer" (Keats) MPII:P IV-1578

On Growth and Form (Thompson) MPII:NF III-1063

On Heroes and Tombs (Sábato) CLCII III-1142; MPII:AF III-1188

On Heroes, Hero-Worship and the Heroic in History (Carlyle) MP VIII-4368

"On His Mistress" (Donne) MPII:P IV-1581

On Human Conduct (Oakeshott) MPII:NF III-1071

On Liberty (Mill) MP VIII-4370

On Moral Fiction (Gardner) MPII:NF III-1077

On My Honor (Bauer) MPII:JYAFic III-1057

On Our Way (Patterson, R., Mebel, *and* Hill, G.) MPII:JYABio III-1348

On Overgrown Paths (Hamsun) MPII:NF III-1082

"On Prayer" (Miłosz) MPII:P IV-1584

On the Banks of Plum Creek (Wilder, L.) MPII:JYAFic III-1060

"On the Death of Dr. Robert Levet" (Johnson, S.) MPII:P IV-1587

On the Eve (Turgenev) CLCII III-1143; MPII:WF III-1146

On the Law of War and Peace (Grotius) MP VIII-4373

"On the Morning of Christ's Nativity" (Milton) MPII:P IV-1590

"On the Move" (Gunn) MPII:P IV-1593

On the Origin of Species (Darwin) MP VIII-4376

On the Road (Kerouac) CLCII III-1145; MPII:AF III-1193

On the Sublime (Unknown) MP VIII-4378

On the Way Home (Wilder, W.) MPII:JYABio III-1352

"On the Wounds of Our Crucified Lord" (Crashaw) MPII:P IV-1596

"Once" (Walker) MPII:P IV-1599

Once and Future King, The (White, T. H.) MP VIII-4381; MP:BF II-1112; MPII:JYAFic III-1063

Once in a Lifetime (Kaufman and Hart) CLCII III-1145; MPII:D III-1174

"One Bone to Another" (Popa) MPII:P IV-1602

One Day, The (Hall) MPII:P IV-1606

One Day in the Life of Ivan Denisovich (Solzhenitsyn) CLCII III-1147; MPII:WF III-1152

One Day of Life (Argueta) CLCII III-1148; MPII:AF III-1198

One-Eyed Cat (Fox) MPII:JYAFic III-1070

One Flew over the Cuckoo's Nest (Kesey) CLCII III-1149; MPII:AF III-1203

One Hundred Years of Solitude (García Márquez) CLCII III-1150; MPII:AF III-1207

"£1,000,000 Bank Note, The" (Twain) MPII:SS IV-1697

One of Ours (Cather) CLCII III-1154; MPII:AF III-1213

"One of the Missing" (Bierce) MPII:SS IV-1701

"One Ordinary Day, with Peanuts" (Jackson) MPII:SS IV-1705

One Way to Heaven (Cullen) CLCII III-1155; MPII:AF III-1217; MPII:JYAFic III-1067

One Writer's Beginnings (Welty) MPII:JYABio III-1355; MPII:NF III-1087

Onion John (Krumgold) MPII:JYAFic III-1073

Only Earth and Sky Last Forever (Benchley) MPII:JYAFic III-1076

Onnamen. See Masks

"Open Boat, The" (Crane, S.) MPII:SS IV-1709

"Open Casket" (McPherson) MPII:P IV-1611

Open Heart. See Book of Bebb, The

"Open House" (Gordimer) MPII:SS IV-1712

"Open House" (Roethke) MPII:P IV-1614

"Open Window, The" (Saki) MPII:SS IV-1716

Operetka. See Operetta

Operetta (Gombrowicz) CLCII III-1156; MPII:D III-1180

Oppenheimer and the Atomic Bomb (Larsen, R.) MPII:JYABio III-1359

Optimist's Daughter, The (Welty) CLCII III-1157; MPII:AF III-1222

Or, L'. See Sutter's Gold

Oration on the Dignity of Man (Pico della Mirandola) MP VIII-4385

Orb of the World, The. See Heimskringla

Ordeal of Civility, The (Cuddihy) MPII:NF III-1092

Ordeal of Gilbert Pinfold, The (Waugh) MP VIII-4387; MP:BF II-1117

Ordeal of Richard Feverel, The (Meredith, G.) CLC II-814; MP VIII-4390; MP:BF II-1121

Order of Things, The (Foucault) MPII:NF III-1098

Ordinary Jack (Cresswell) MPII:JYAFic III-1079

Ordinary People (Guest) MPII:JYAFic III-1082

Oreach nata lalun. See Guest for the Night, A

"Oread" (H. D.) MPII:P IV-1617

Oregon Trail, The (Parkman) MP VIII-4394
Orfeo (Politian) CLC II-814; MP VIII-4398
Orientalism (Said) MPII:NF III-1102
Origins of Totalitarianism, The (Arendt) MPII:NF III-1107
Orlando (Woolf) CLC II-815; MP VIII-4400; MP:BF II-1126
Orlando Furioso (Ariosto) CLC II-816; MP VIII-4404
Orlando Innamorato (Boiardo) CLC II-819; MP VIII-4410
Orley Farm (Trollope) CLC II-821; MP VIII-4415; MP:BF II-1130
Oroonoko (Behn) CLC II-823; MP VIII-4421; MP:BF II-1137
Orphan, The (Otway) CLC II-823; MP VIII-4425
Orphée. See Orpheus
Orpheus (Cocteau) CLCII III-1159; MPII:D III-1185
Orpheus and Eurydice (Unknown) CLC II-824; MP VIII-4428; MP:EF II-957
Ortadirek. See Wind from the Plain, The
Örtlich betäubt. See Local Anaesthetic
Osaka san. See Wonderful Fool
Oste sledované vlaky. See Closely Watched Trains
Ostrov Krym. See Island of Crimea, The
Othello (Shakespeare) CLC II-825; MP VIII-4431
Other Leopards (Williams, D.) CLCII III-1160; MPII:BCF III-1258
Other One, The (Colette) CLC II-826; MP VIII-4436; MP:EF II-961
"Other Paris, The" (Gallant) MPII:SS IV-1719
Other People's Worlds (Trevor) CLCII III-1161; MPII:BCF III-1262
Other Side of the Mountain: Part I, The. See Long Way Up, A.
Other Side of the Mountain: Part II, The (Valens) MPII:JYABio III-1363
"Other Two, The" (Wharton) MPII:SS IV-1723
Other Voices, Other Rooms (Capote) MPII:JYAFic III-1085
Otherwise Engaged (Gray, S.) CLCII III-1161; MPII:D III-1191

Otoño del patriarca, El. See Autumn of the Patriarch, The
Ottepel. See Thaw, The
Où mènent les mauvais chemins. See Splendors and Miseries of Courtesans, The
Our Friend Manso (Pérez Galdós) CLCII III-1163; MPII:WF III-1157
Our House in the Last World (Hijuelos) MPII:JYAFic III-1089
Our Lady of the Flowers (Genet) CLCII III-1164; MPII:WF III-1163
Our Mutual Friend (Dickens) CLC II-827; MP VIII-4440; MP:BF II-1141
Our Nig (Wilson, H.) MPII:AfAm II-905
Our Town (Wilder, T.) CLC II-829; MP VIII-4443
Our Village (Mitford) CLC II-830; MP VIII-4446; MP:BF II-1145
Out from This Place (Hansen) MPII:JYAFic IV-1620
"Out in the Open" (Tranströmer) MPII:P IV-1620
Out of Africa (Dinesen) MPII:JYABio III-1367
Out of My Life and Thought (Schweitzer) MP VIII-4449; MPII:JYABio III-1371
Out of Silence into Sound (Burlingame) MPII:JYABio III-1375
"Out of the Cradle Endlessly Rocking" (Whitman) MPII:P IV-1623
Out of the Silent Planet. See Space Trilogy, The
"Outcasts of Poker Flat, The" (Harte) MPII:SS IV-1727
Outer Dark (McCarthy, C.) CLCII III-1166; MPII:AF III-1227
"Outpost of Progress, An" (Conrad) MPII:SS IV-1732
"Outside the Machine" (Rhys) MPII:SS IV-1737
Outsider, The (Sábato) CLCII III-1167; MPII:AF III-1232
Outsider, The (Wright, R.) CLCII III-1168; MPII:AF III-1238; MPII:AfAm II-911
Outsiders, The (Hinton) MPII:JYAFic III-1093
"Outstation, The" (Maugham) MPII:SS IV-1741

Ováder. *See* Stormy Weather

Over Sea, Under Stone. *See* Dark Is Rising sequence, The

"Overcoat, The" (Gogol) CLC II-830; MP VIII-4452; MP:EF III-965; MPII:SS IV-1745

"Overcoat II, The" (Boyle, T.) MPII:SS IV-1749

Overdrive (Buckley) MPII:NF III-1113

"Ovid in the Third Reich" (Hill, G.) MPII:P IV-1626

Owl in the Cedar Tree (Momaday) MPII:JYAFic III-1097

Owl Service, The (Garner, A.) MPII:JYAFic III-1100

Ox-Bow Incident, The (Clark, Walter) CLC II-831; MP VIII-4457; MP:AF II-892; MPII:JYAFic III-1103

Oxherding Tale (Johnson, C.) MPII:AfAm II-918

Ozhog. *See* Burn, The

"Ozymandias" (Shelley, P.) MPII:P IV-1629

P

Pablo Picasso (Lyttle) MPII:JYABio
III-1379

"Pacing Goose, The" (West, J.) MPII:SS
IV-1753

Pack My Bag (Green) MPII:NF III-1118

Paean, A. *See* Lenore

Pagan Place, A (O'Brien, E.) CLCII
III-1169; MPII:BCF III-1267

Painted Bird, The (Kosinski) CLCII
III-1170; MPII:AF III-1243

Painted Turtle (Major) MPII:AfAm II-924

Painter of Our Time, A (Berger, J.) CLCII
III-1171; MPII:BCF III-1272

Paisaje con dos tumbas y un perro asirio.
See Landscape with Two Graves and an
Assyrian Dog

Palace of the Peacock. *See* Guyana Quartet,
The

Palais des Beaux Arts. *See* Musée des
Beaux Arts

"Palata No. 6." *See* "Ward No. 6"

Pale Fire (Nabokov) MP VIII-4462; MP:AF
II-897

Pale Horse, Pale Rider (Porter, K.) MP
VIII-4465; MP:AF II-901

"Pale Horse, Pale Rider" (Porter, K.)
MPII:SS IV-1756

Palm-Wine Drinkard, The (Tutuola) MP
VIII-4469; MP:EF III-970

Palomar. *See* Mr. Palomar

Pamela (Richardson, S.) CLC II-832; MP
VIII-4472; MP:BF II-1149;
MPII:JYAFic III-1106

Pan (Hamsun) CLCII III-1172; MPII:WF
III-1168

Pandora's Box (Wedekind) CLCII III-1173;
MPII:D III-1197

Panegyricus. *See* Letters of Pliny the
Younger, The

"Pangolin, The" (Moore, M.) MPII:P
IV-1632

Panther (Haig-Brown) MPII:JYAFic
III-1109

"Panther, The" (Rilke) MPII:P IV-1636

Pantomime (Walcott) CLCII III-1174;
MPII:D III-1202

Papa Hemingway (Hotchner) MPII:JYABio
III-1383

Paper Men, The (Golding) CLCII III-1175;
MPII:BCF III-1277

Parade's End (Ford, F.) CLC II-833; MP
VIII-4477; MP:BF II-1155

"Paradise" (O'Brien, E.) MPII:SS IV-1759

Paradise Lost (Milton) CLC II-835; MP
VIII-4482

Paradise Regained (Milton) CLC II-836;
MP VIII-4487

Paradiso (Lezama Lima) CLCII III-1176;
MPII:AF III-1248

Paradox, King. *See* King Paradox

"Paraguay" (Barthelme, D.) MPII:SS
IV-1764

Parallel Lives (Plutarch) MP VIII-4490

Paravents, Les. *See* Screens, The

Pardoner's Tale, The (Wain) CLCII
III-1178; MPII:BCF III-1282

"Pari." *See* "Bet, The"

Paris and New York Diaries of Ned Rorem,
The (Rorem) MPII:NF III-1124

Paris Diary of Ned Rorem, The. *See* Paris
and New York Diaries of Ned Rorem,
The

"Parisian Dream" (Baudelaire) MPII:P
IV-1639

"Parisian Nocturne" (Verlaine) MPII:P
IV-1642

"Parker's Back" (O'Connor, Flannery)
MPII:SS IV-1768

Parliament of Fowls, The (Chaucer) MP
VIII-4493

"Parsley Garden, The" (Saroyan) MPII:SS
IV-1771

"Part of Speech, A" (Brodsky) MPII:P
IV-1646

Partage de Midi. *See* Break of Noon

Party Going (Green, Henry) CLCII
III-1179; MPII:BCF III-1288

"Parure, La." *See* "Necklace, The"

Parzival (Wolfram von Eschenbach) CLC
II-837; MP VIII-4495

Pasado en claro. *See* Draft of Shadows, A

Pasos lejanos, Los. *See* Distant Footsteps,
The

Pasos perdidos, Los. *See* Lost Steps, The
Passage, The (Palmer) CLCII III-1180;
  MPII:BCF III-1293
Passage to India, A (Forster) CLC II-838;
  MP VIII-4500; MP:BF II-1161
"Passage to India" (Whitman) MPII:P
  IV-1650
Passing (Larsen, N.) CLCII III-1182;
  MPII:AF III-1253; MPII:AfAm II-929
Passing Time (Butor) CLCII III-1183;
  MPII:WF III-1173
Passion Flower, The (Benavente) CLC
  II-840; MP VIII-4505
Passion in Rome, A (Callaghan) CLCII
  III-1184; MPII:BCF III-1298
Passion Play (Nichols) CLCII III-1185;
  MPII:D III-1209
"Passionate Shepherd to His Love, The"
  (Marlowe) MPII:P IV-1653
Passions of the Soul, The (Descartes) MP
  VIII-4510
Paston Letters A. D. 1422-1509, The
  (Paston Family) MP VIII-4513
Pastors and Masters (Compton-Burnett) MP
  VIII-4516; MP:BF II-1167
"Pat Shelema." *See* "Whole Loaf, A"
Patagoni (Metcalf) MPII:NF III-1129
Paterson (Williams, W.) MP VIII-4519
Path to Rome, The (Belloc) MP VIII-4521
Path to the Nest of Spiders, The (Calvino)
  CLCII III-1186; MPII:WF III-1178
Pathfinder, The (Cooper, J. F.) CLC II-840;
  MP VIII-4524; MP:AF II-906. *See also*
  Leatherstocking Tales, The
Patience (Gilbert) CLC II-842; MP
  VIII-4528
Patrician, The (Galsworthy) CLC II-842;
  MP VIII-4531; MP:BF II-1171
Patrick Henry (Campion, T.) MPII:JYABio
  III-1387
Patriot, The (Fogazzaro) CLC II-843; MP
  VIII-4534; MP:EF III-973
"Patriotism" (Mishima) MPII:SS IV-1775
Patterns of Childhood (Wolf) CLCII
  III-1187; MPII:WF III-1183
Paul Bunyan (Stevens, J.) CLC II-843; MP
  VIII-4537; MP:AF II-910
Paul Revere and the World He Lived In
  (Forbes) MPII:JYABio III-1391

Paul Robeson (Hamilton) MPII:JYABio
  III-1395
"Paul's Case" (Cather) MPII:SS IV-1779
Pauvre Christ de Bomba, Le. *See* Poor
  Christ of Bomba, The
Payton (Sufrin) MPII:JYABio III-1399
Pea gjengrodde stier. *See* On Overgrown
  Paths
Peabody Sisters of Salem, The (Tharp)
  MPII:JYABio III-1403
Peace, The (Aristophanes) CLC II-844; MP
  VIII-4541
"Peach Stone, The" (Horgan) MPII:SS
  IV-1782
"Pearl, The" (Steinbeck) CLCII III-1188;
  MPII:SS IV-1785
"Pearl of the World, The." *See* Pearl, The
"Peasant Marey, The" (Dostoevski)
  MPII:SS IV-1789
Peasants, The (Reymont) CLC II-845; MP
  VIII-4544; MP:EF III-977
Peder Seier. *See* Peder Victorious
Peder Victorious (Rölvaag) CLC II-847;
  MP VIII-4549; MP:AF II-914
"Pedersen Kid, The" (Gass) MPII:SS
  IV-1793
"Pedestrian Accident, A" (Coover) MPII:SS
  IV-1796
Pedro Páramo (Rulfo) MP VIII-4552;
  MP:AF II-918
Pedro Sánchez (Pereda) CLC II-847; MP
  VIII-4556; MP:EF III-983
Peer Gynt (Ibsen) CLC II-848; MP
  VIII-4559
Peg Woffington (Reade) CLC II-850; MP
  VIII-4562; MP:BF II-1175
Pelican, The (Strindberg) CLCII III-1189;
  MPII:D III-1214
Pelikanen. *See* Pelican, The
Pelle the Conqueror (Nexö) CLC II-851;
  MP VIII-4566; MP:EF III-987
Pélléas and Mélisande (Maeterlinck) CLC
  II-852; MP VIII-4569
Peñas arriba (Pereda) CLC II-852; MP
  VIII-4572; MP:EF III-991
Pendennis (Thackeray) CLC II-853; MP
  VIII-4575; MP:BF II-1179
Penguin Island (France) CLC II-855; MP
  VIII-4579; MP:EF III-994

Penn (Vining) MPII:JYABio III-1407

Penny for a Song, A (Whiting) CLCII III-1190; MPII:D III-1220

Penrod (Tarkington) MPII:JYAFic III-1112

Pensées (Pascal) MP VIII-4584

"Penseroso, Il" (Milton) MPII:P IV-1656

Pentimento (Hellman) MPII:NF III-1135

People Betrayed, A. *See* November 1918

People of Hemsö, The. *See* Natives of Hemsö, The

People of Juvik, The (Duun) CLC II-857; MP VIII-4587; MP:EF III-999

People of the City (Ekwensi) CLCII III-1192; MPII:BCF III-1302

People, Yes, The (Sandburg) MP VIII-4593

Pepita Jiménez (Valera) CLC II-858; MP VIII-4595; MP:EF III-1006

Peppermint Pig, The (Bawden) MPII:JYAFic III-1115

Peregrine Pickle (Smollett) CLC II-859; MP VIII-4599; MP:BF II-1185

"Perekhod cherez Zbruch." *See* "Crossing into Poland"

Perelandra. *See* Space Trilogy, The

"Perfect Day for Bananafish, A" (Salinger) MPII:SS IV-1800

Perfect Peace, A (Oz) CLCII III-1193; MPII:WF III-1190

Perfect Spy, A (le Carré) CLCII III-1194; MPII:BCF III-1306

"Perfume, The" (Donne) MPII:P IV-1659

Pericles, Prince of Tyre (Shakespeare) CLC II-861; MP VIII-4603

Perimenontas tous varvarous. *See* Waiting for the Barbarians

Periodic Table, The (Levi) MPII:NF III-1141

Periquillo, El. *See* Itching Parrot, The

Persecution and Assassination of Jean-Paul Marat as Performed by the Inmates of the Asylum of Charenton Under the Direction of the Marquis de Sade, The. *See* Marat/Sade

Persian Boy, The (Renault) CLCII III-1195; MPII:BCF III-1313

Persian Letters (Montesquieu) MP VIII-4607

Persians, The (Aeschylus) CLC II-862; MP VIII-4609

Personae (Pound) MP VIII-4612

Personal Knowledge (Polanyi) MPII:NF III-1146

Personal Matter, A (e) CLCII III-1197; MPII:WF III-1195

Persuasion (Austen) CLC II-863; MP VIII-4615; MP:BF II-1190

Pervaya lyubov. *See* First Love

Pesanteur et la grâce, La. *See* Gravity and Grace

Pešanik (Kiš) CLCII III-1197; MPII:WF III-1199

Petals of Blood (Ngugi) CLCII III-1198; MPII:BCF III-1320

Peter and Wendy. *See* Peter Pan

Peter Graves (du Bois, W. P.) MPII:JYAFic III-1119

Peter Ibbetson (du Maurier, G.) CLC II-864; MP VIII-4618; MP:BF II-1194

Peter Pan (Barrie) CLC II-865; MP VIII-4622; MPII:JYAFic III-1122

Peter Pan Bag, The (Kingman) MPII:JYAFic III-1126

"Peter Quince at the Clavier" (Stevens, W.) MPII:P IV-1662

Peter Simple (Marryat) CLC II-866; MP VIII-4626; MP:BF II-1199

Peter, the Revolutionary Tsar (Putnam) MPII:JYABio III-1410

Peter Whiffle (Van Vechten) CLC II-867; MP VIII-4629; MP:AF II-923

Peter Zenger (Galt) MPII:JYABio III-1414

Petersburg (Bely) CLCII III-1199; MPII:WF IV-1442

Petit Prince, Le. *See* Little Prince, The

"Petit Soldat." *See* "Two Little Soldiers"

Petite Auto, La. *See* Little Car, The

Petrified Forest, The (Sherwood) CLCII III-1200; MPII:D III-1225

"Petrified Man" (Welty) MPII:SS IV-1804

Phantom Tollbooth, The (Juster) MPII:JYAFic III-1129

Phares, Les. *See* Beacons, The

Pharisienne, La. *See* Woman of the Pharisees, A

Phèdre (Racine) CLC II-867; MP VIII-4632

Phenomenon of Man, The (Teilhard de Chardin) MP VIII-4636

Philadelphia Fire (Wideman) MPII:AfAm
    II-935
Philadelphia, Here I Come! (Friel) CLCII
    III-1202; MPII:D III-1230
Philadelphia Story, The (Barry) CLCII
    III-1203; MPII:D III-1235
Philaster (Beaumont *and* Fletcher) CLC
    II-868; MP VIII-4639
"Philhellene" (Cavafy) MPII:P IV-1665
Philippics, The (Demosthenes) MP
    VIII-4644
Philoctetes (Sophocles) CLC II-870; MP
    VIII-4647
Philosopher or Dog? (Machado de Assis)
    MP VIII-4650; MP:AF II-927
Philosophiae Naturalis Principia
    Mathematica (Newton) MP VIII-4653
Philosophical Explanations (Nozick)
    MPII:NF III-1153
Philosophical Treatises and Moral
    Reflections of Seneca (Seneca) MP
    VIII-4656
Philosophy and the Mirror of Nature
    (Rorty) MPII:NF III-1158
Philosophy of Art (Taine) MP VIII-4659
Phineas Finn (Trollope) CLC II-871; MP
    VIII-4662; MP:BF III-1203
Phineas Redux (Trollope) CLC II-871; MP
    VIII-4666; MP:BF III-1207
Phoenician Women, The (Euripides) CLC
    II-872; MP VIII-4670
"Phonemics" (Spicer) MPII:P IV-1668
Phormio (Terence) CLC II-873; MP
    VIII-4673
Photograph, A (Shange) CLCII III-1204;
    MPII:AfAm II-941 MPII:D III-1241
Physical Basis of Life, The (Huxley, T.) MP
    VIII-4677
Physicists, The (Dürrenmatt) CLCII
    III-1206; MPII:D III-1246
Physiker, Die. *See* Physicists, The
Piano Lesson, The (Wilson, August)
    MPII:AfAm II-947
"Piano" (Lawrence, D. H.) MPII:P IV-1672
Pickwick Papers (Dickens) CLC II-874; MP
    VIII-4680; MP:BF III-1212
Picnic (Inge) CLCII III-1207; MPII:D
    III-1252
"Picture Bride" (Song) MPII:P IV-1675

Picture of Dorian Gray, The (Wilde) CLC
    II-878; MP VIII-4686; MP:BF III-1218
Pictures in the Hallway. *See* Mirror in My
    House
"Piece of Steak, A" (London) MPII:SS
    IV-1807
"Piece of String, The" (Maupassant)
    MPII:SS IV-1810
"Pied Beauty" (Hopkins, G.) MPII:P
    IV-1679
Pierre (Melville) CLC II-879; MP
    VIII-4690; MP:AF II-930
"Pierre Menard, Author of the *Quixote*"
    (Borges) MPII:SS IV-1814
Pierres crieront, Les. *See* Stones Cry Out,
    The.
"Pigeon Feathers" (Updike) MPII:SS
    IV-1817
Pigeon Post (Ransome) MPII:JYAFic
    III-1133
Pigman, The (Zindel) MPII:JYAFic III-1137
"Pike" (Hughes, Ted) MPII:P IV-1682
Piknik na obochine. *See* Roadside Picnic
"Pikovaya dama." *See* "Queen of Spades,
    The"
Pilgrim at Sea. *See* Tobias trilogy, The
Pilgrim at Tinker Creek (Dillard) MPII:NF
    III-1163
Pilgrim Hawk, The (Wescott) MP
    VIII-4693; MP:AF II-934
Pilgrim på havet. *See* Tobias trilogy, The
Pilgrimage (Richardson, D.) CLC II-880;
    MP VIII-4696; MP:BF III-1222
Pilgrimage of Charlemagne, The
    (Unknown) CLC II-881; MP VIII-4700
Pilgrimen. *See* Tobias trilogy, The
Pilgrim's Progress, The (Bunyan) CLC
    II-882; MP VIII-4705; MP:BF III-1227;
    MPII:JYAFic III-1140
Pillars of Society, The (Ibsen) CLC II-883;
    MP VIII-4710
Pilot, The (Cooper, J. F.) CLC II-884; MP
    VIII-4714; MP:AF II-938
Pincher Martin (Golding) CLCII III-1208;
    MPII:BCF III-1325
Pine Barrens, The (McPhee) MPII:NF
    III-1168
Ping-Pong (Adamov) MP VIII-4719

Pioneers, The (Cooper, J. F.) CLC II-886; MP VIII-4722; MP:AF II-944. *See also* Leatherstocking Tales, The

Pioneers in Petticoats. *See* Women Who Led the Way.

Piosenka o Kocu wiata. *See* Song on the End of the World, A

Pippi Langstrump. *See* Pippi Longstocking

Pippi Longstocking (Lindgren) MPII:JYAFic III-1144

Pirates of Penzance, The (Gilbert) CLC II-888; MP VIII-4726

Pit, The (Norris) CLC II-889; MP VIII-4729; MP:AF II-949

"Pit and the Pendulum, The" (Poe) MPII:SS IV-1821

Pitch Dark (Adler) CLCII III-1209; MPII:AF III-1258

"Pity this busy monster,manunkind" (Cummings) MPII:P IV-1685

"Pkhentz" (Sinyavsky) MPII:SS IV-1824

"Place for No Story, The" (Jeffers) MPII:P IV-1688

Places Where I've Done Time (Saroyan) MPII:JYABio III-1418

Plague, The (Camus) CLC II-889; MP VIII-4734; MP:EF III-1010

Plaideurs, Les (Racine) CLC II-891; MP VIII-4740

Plaidoyer d'un fou, Le. *See* Confession of a Fool, The

Plain Dealer, The (Wycherley) CLC II-892; MP VIII-4743

Plains Song, for Female Voices (Morris) CLCII III-1210; MPII:AF III-1262

Planet of Junior Brown, The (Hamilton) MPII:JYAFic III-1148

"Planetarium" (Rich) MPII:P IV-1691

Planetarium, The (Sarraute) CLCII III-1211; MPII:WF III-1203

Plantation Boy (Lins do Rêgo) MP VIII-4748; MP:AF II-954

Platero and I (Jiménez) MP VIII-4752; MP:EF III-1017

Platitudes (Ellis) MPII:AfAm II-952

Play It As It Lays (Didion) CLCII III-1212; MPII:AF III-1266

Play of the Eyes, The (Canetti) MPII:NF IV-1546

Playboy of the Western World, The (Synge) CLC II-893; MP VIII-4755

Playing Beatie Bow (Park) MPII:JYAFic III-1151

Playing for Time (Fénelon) MPII:JYABio III-1421

Plays of Cocteau, The (Cocteau) MP VIII-4758

Pleasant Historie of John Winchcomb, in His Younger Yeares Called Jack of Newberry, The. *See* Jack of Newberry

Plenty (Hare) CLCII III-1213; MPII:D III-1258

Plough and the Stars, The (O'Casey) CLC II-894; MP VIII-4761

Plum Bun (Fauset) CLCII III-1215; MPII:AF III-1271; MPII:AfAm II-958

Plumed Serpent, The (Lawrence, D. H.) CLC II-895; MP VIII-4765; MP:BF III-1232

Plutus (Aristophanes) CLC II-896; MP VIII-4770

Pnin (Nabokov) CLCII III-1216; MPII:AF III-1277

P'o ch'uan. *See* Broken Boat

Pocho (Villarreal) MPII:JYAFic III-1155

Podrostok. *See* Raw Youth, A

"Poem Beginning with a Line by Pindar, A" (Duncan) MPII:P IV-1694

Poem of the Cid (Unknown) CLC II-897; MP VIII-4773

"Poem on His Birthday" (Thomas, D.) MPII:P IV-1697

Poem Without a Hero (Akhmatova) MPII:P IV-1700

Poema bez geroya. *See* Poem Without a Hero

Poems (Tennyson) MP VIII-4777

Poems and Ballads (Swinburne) MP VIII-4780

Poems, Chiefly in the Scottish Dialect (Burns) MP VIII-4783

Poems for a Poem. *See* Altarwise by Owl-Light

Poems of Doctor Zhivago, The (Pasternak) MPII:P IV-1705

"Poet, The" (Hesse) MPII:SS IV-1828

Poetical Works of Edward Taylor, The (Taylor, E.) MP VIII-4786

Poetics, The (Aristotle) MP VIII-4789
"Poetry" (Moore, M.) MPII:P IV-1710
Poetry and Truth from My Own Life (Goethe) MP VIII-4792
Poetry of "A. E." (Russell, G.) MP VIII-4795
Poetry of Ai, The MPII:AfAm II-963
Poetry of Conrad Potter Aiken, The MP VIII-4798
Poetry of Anacreon, The MP VIII-4801
Poetry of Maya Angelou, The MPII:AfAm II-968
Poetry of Guillaume Apollinaire, The MP VIII-4805
Poetry of Matthew Arnold, The MP VIII-4808
Poetry of W. H. Auden, The MP VIII-4811
Poetry of Amiri Baraka, The MPII:AfAm II-974
Poetry of George Barker, The MP VIII-4814
Poetry of Bashō, The MP VIII-4816
Poetry of Thomas Lovell Beddoes, The MP VIII-4819
Poetry of Stephen Vincent Benét, The MP IX-5159
Poetry of John Betjeman, The MP VIII-4822
Poetry of Bion, The MP VIII-4825
Poetry of William Blake, The MP VIII-4827
Poetry of Aleksandr Blok, The MP VIII-4830
Poetry of Edmund Charles Blunden, The MP VIII-4833
Poetry of Philip Booth, The MP VIII-4835
Poetry of Edward Kamau Brathwaite, The MPII:AfAm II-979
Poetry of André Breton, The MP VIII-4802
Poetry of Nicholas Breton, The MP IX-5103
Poetry of Emily Brontë MP IX-4932
Poetry of Rupert Brooke, The MP VIII-4838
Poetry of Gwendolyn Brooks, The MPII:AfAm II-985
Poetry of Sterling Brown, The MPII:AfAm II-991
Poetry of William Cullen Bryant, The MP VIII-4841
Poetry of Thomas Campion, The MP VIII-4844
Poetry of Giusuè Carducci, The MP VIII-4847

Poetry of Thomas Carew, The MP VIII-4850
Poetry of Constantine P. Cavafy, The MP VIII-4854
Poetry of Thomas Chatterton, The MP VIII-4857
Poetry of John Clare, The MP VIII-4863
Poetry of Paul Claudel, The MP VIII-4866
Poetry of Lucille Clifton, The MPII:AfAm II-996
Poetry of Wanda Coleman, The MPII:AfAm II-1000
Poetry of Samuel Taylor Coleridge, The MP VIII-4869
Poetry of William Collins, The MP VIII-4873
Poetry of Tristan Corbière, The MP VIII-4876
Poetry of Jayne Cortez, The MPII:AfAm II-1006
Poetry of William Cowper, The MP VIII-4880
Poetry of Richard Crashaw, The MP VIII-4883
Poetry of Sor Juana Inés de la Cruz, The MP IX-5149
Poetry of Countée Cullen, The MPII:AfAm II-1012
Poetry of E. E. Cummings, The MP VIII-4887
Poetry of Samuel Daniel, The MP VIII-4889
Poetry of James Dickey, The MP VIII-4896
Poetry of Emily Dickinson MP IX-4935
Poetry of Owen Dodson, The MPII:AfAm III-1019
Poetry of John Donne, The MP VIII-4900
Poetry of Rita Dove, The MPII:AfAm III-1024
Poetry of Ernest Christopher Dowson, The MP VIII-4903
Poetry of Michael Drayton, The MP VIII-4906
Poetry of John Dryden, The MP IX-4909
Poetry of Joachim Du Bellay, The MP IX-4914
Poetry of Paul Laurence Dunbar, The MPII:AfAm III-1029
Poetry of Richard Eberhart, The MP IX-4918

Poetry of Josef von Eichendorff, The MP
IX-4922
Poetry of Ralph Waldo Emerson, The MP
IX-4928
Poetry of Sergei Esenin, The MP IX-4938
Poetry of Mari Evans, The MPII:AfAm
III-1036
Poetry of James Elroy Flecker, The MP
IX-4941
Poetry of Philip Freneau, The MP IX-4943
Poetry of Robert Frost, The MP IX-4946
Poetry of George Garrett, The MP IX-4952
Poetry of George Gascoigne, The MP
IX-4955
Poetry of Théophile Gautier, The MP
IX-4961
Poetry of Stefan George, The MP IX-5155
Poetry of Nikki Giovanni, The MPII:AfAm
III-1042
Poetry of Oliver Goldsmith, The MP
IX-4964
Poetry of Robert Graves, The MP IX-4968
Poetry of Thomas Gray, The MP IX-4971
Poetry of Donald Hall, The MP IX-4973
Poetry of Thomas Hardy, The MP IX-4976
Poetry of Michael S. Harper, The
MPII:AfAm III-1047
Poetry of Robert Hayden, The MPII:AfAm
III-1052
Poetry of H. D., The MP IX-4979
Poetry of William Ernest Henley, The MP
IX-4982
Poetry of José María de Heredia, The MP
IX-4984
Poetry of Ralph Hodgson, The MP IX-4986
Poetry of Hugo von Hofmannsthal, The MP
IX-4988
Poetry of Friedrich Hölderlin, The MP
IX-4991
Poetry of Gerard Manley Hopkins, The MP
IX-4994
Poetry of Horace, The MP IX-4997
Poetry of George Moses Horton, The
MPII:AfAm III-1058
Poetry of Langston Hughes, The
MPII:AfAm III-1064
Poetry of Victor Hugo, The MP IX-5000
Poetry of Randell Jarrell, The MP IX-5003

Poetry of Robinson Jeffers, The MP
IX-5006
Poetry of Juan Ramón Jiménez, The MP
IX-5009
Poetry of Samuel Johnson, The MP IX-5011
Poetry of Ben Jonson, The MP IX-5014
Poetry of June Jordan, The MPII:AfAm
III-1069
Poetry of Rudyard Kipling, The MP
IX-5019
Poetry of Etheridge Knight, The
MPII:AfAm III-1074
Poetry of Yusef Komunyakaa, The
MPII:AfAm III-1079
Poetry of Jules Laforgue, The MP IX-5022
Poetry of Alphonse Lamartine, The MP
IX-5025
Poetry of Walter Savage Landor, The MP
IX-5028
Poetry of Sidney Lanier, The MP IX-5032
Poetry of Philip Larkin, The MP IX-5035
Poetry of D. H. Lawrence, The MP IX-5037
Poetry of Giacomo Leopardi, The MP
IX-5040
Poetry of Cecil Day Lewis, The MP IX-5043
Poetry of Vachel Lindsay, The MP IX-5046
Poetry of Audre Lorde, The MPII:AfAm
III-1085
Poetry of Richard Lovelace, The MP
IX-5048
Poetry of Robert Lowell, The MP IX-5121
Poetry of Antonio Machado, The MP
IX-5051
Poetry of Claude McKay, The MPII:AfAm
III-1090
Poetry of Archibald MacLeish, The MP
IX-5054
Poetry of Louis MacNeice, The MP IX-5057
Poetry of Haki R. Madhubuti, The
MPII:AfAm III-1097
Poetry of Stéphane Mallarmé, The MP
IX-5059
Poetry of Clemént Marot, The MP IX-5064
Poetry of Andrew Marvell, The MP IX-5067
Poetry of Vladimir Mayakovsky, The MP
IX-5070
Poetry of Herman Melville, The MP
IX-5073

Poetry of George Meredith, The MP IX-5077

Poetry of Michelangelo, The MP IX-5080

Poetry of Gabriela Mistral, The MP IX-4949

Poetry of Marianne Moore, The MP IX-5062

Poetry of Eduard Mörike, The MP IX-5084

Poetry of Moschus, The MP IX-5087

Poetry of Thylias Moss, The MPII:AfAm III-1102

Poetry of Alfred de Musset, The MP IX-5089

Poetry of Nikolai Nekrasov, The MP IX-5092

Poetry of Pablo Neruda, The MP IX-5095

Poetry of Gérard de Nerval, The MP IX-5098

Poetry of Wilfred Owen, The MP IX-5105

Poetry of Boris Pasternak, The MP IX-5107

Poetry of Octavio Paz, The MP IX-5109

Poetry of Charles-Pierce Péguy, The MP IX-5112

Poetry of Matthew Prior, The MP IX-5115

Poetry of Sir Walter Raleigh, The MP IX-5118

Poetry of Dudley Randall, The MPII:AfAm III-1108

Poetry of Carolyn M. Rodgers, The MPII:AfAm III-1114

Poetry of Theodore Roethke, The MP IX-5126

Poetry of Pierre du Ronsard, The MP IX-5131

Poetry of Christina Rossetti, The MP VIII-4860

Poetry of Dante Gabriel Rossetti, The MP VIII-4893

Poetry of Sonia Sanchez, The MPII:AfAm III-1119

Poetry of Judith Shapiro, The MP IX-5133

Poetry of Sir Philip Sidney, The MP IX-5136

Poetry of Edith Sitwell, The MP IX-4920

Poetry of John Skelton, The MP IX-5141

Poetry of Christopher Smart, The MP IX-5146

Poetry of Stephen Spender, The MP IX-5152

Poetry of Wallace Stevens, The MP IX-5161

Poetry of Sir John Suckling, The MP IX-5164

Poetry of Jonathan Swift, The MP IX-5167

Poetry of Allen Tate, The MP IX-5172

Poetry of Theocritus, The MP IX-5175

Poetry of Francis Thompson, The MP IX-5177

Poetry of Henry David Thoreau, The MP IX-5179

Poetry of Melvin B. Tolson, The MPII:AfAm III-1125

Poetry of Thomas Traherne, The MP IX-5181

Poetry of Paul Valéry, The MP IX-5184

Poetry of Henry Vaughan, The MP IX-5187

Poetry of Alfred Victor de Vigny, The MP IX-5191

Poetry of Derek Walcott, The MPII:AfAm III-1131

Poetry of Alice Walker, The MPII:AfAm III-1137

Poetry of Edmund Waller, The MP IX-5194

Poetry of Robert Penn Warren, The MP IX-5197

Poetry of Phillis Wheatley, The MPII:AfAm III-1142

Poetry of John Greenleaf Whittier, The MP IX-5200

Poetry of Richard Wilbur, The MP IX-5203

Poetry of Oscar Wilde, The MP IX-5206

Poetry of Sherley Anne Williams, The MPII:AfAm III-1148

Poetry of William Carlos Williams, The MP IX-5209

Poetry of George Wither, The MP IX-5212

Poetry of William Wordsworth, The MP IX-5215

Poetry of Jay Wright, The MPII:AfAm III-1154

Poetry of Wyatt and Surrey, The MP IX-5219

Poetry of Elinor Wylie, The MP IX-4925

Poetry of William Butler Yeats, The MP IX-5224

Poetry of Al Young, The MPII:AfAm III-1160

Point Counter Point (Huxley, A.) CLC II-898; MP IX-5227; MP:BF III-1237

Pointed Roofs. *See* Pilgrimage

Points for a Compass Rose (Connell)
MPII:NF III-1173
Pokoušení. *See* Temptation
Police, The (Mroek) CLCII III-1217;
MPII:D III-1264
Policja. *See* Police, The
Polish Complex, The (Konwicki) CLCII
III-1218; MPII:WF III-1207
"Political Poem" (Baraka) MPII:P IV-1713
Pollyanna (Porter, E.) MPII:JYAFic III-1159
Polyeucte (Corneille) CLC II-899; MP
IX-5231
Ponder Heart, The (Welty) MP IX-5234;
MP:AF II-958
Poor Christ of Bomba, The (Beti) CLCII
III-1219; MPII:WF III-1214
Poor Folk. *See* Poor People
Poor People (Dostoevski) CLC II-900; MP
IX-5237; MP:EF III-1020
Poor Richard (Daugherty, J.) MPII:JYABio
III-1425
Poor White (Anderson, S.) CLC II-901; MP
IX-5241; MP:AF II-961
Poorhouse Fair, The (Updike) MP IX-5244;
MP:AF II-965
Popió i diament. *See* Ashes and Diamonds
"Poppies in July" (Plath) MPII:P IV-1716
Porgy (Heyward) CLC II-902; MP IX-5247;
MP:AF II-968
Pornografia (Gombrowicz) CLCII III-1221;
MPII:WF III-1221
Pornographer, The (McGahern) CLCII
III-1222; MPII:BCF III-1330
Portage to San Cristóbal of A. H., The
(Steiner) CLCII III-1223; MPII:BCF
III-1335
Porte étroite, La. *See* Strait Is the Gate
Portes de la forêt, Les. *See* Gates of the
Forest, The
Portnoy's Complaint (Roth, P.) CLCII
III-1224; MPII:AF III-1281
"Portobello Road, The" (Spark) MPII:SS
IV-1831
Portrait d'un inconnu. *See* Portrait of a Man
Unknown
"Portrait of a Lady" (Eliot, T. S.) MPII:P
IV-1719
Portrait of a Lady, The (James, H.) CLC
II-903; MP IX-5250; MP:AF II-971

Portrait of a Man Unknown (Sarraute)
CLCII III-1226; MPII:WF III-1225
Portrait of an Artist (Lisle) MPII:JYABio
III-1429
Portrait of Myself (Bourke-White)
MPII:JYABio III-1432
Portrait of the Artist as a Young Dog
(Thomas) MP IX-5256; MP:BF III-1241
Portrait of the Artist as a Young Man, A
(Joyce) CLC II-904; MP IX-5259;
MP:BF III-1245; MPII:JYAFic III-1162
Possédés, Les. *See* Possessed, The
Possessed, The (Camus) CLCII III-1227;
MPII:D III-1269
Possessed, The (Dostoevski) CLC II-905;
MP IX-5264; MP:EF III-1024
Possessing the Secret of Joy (Walker, A.)
MPII:AfAm III-1166
"Post Office, The" (O'Flaherty) MPII:SS
IV-1835
"Postcard from the Volcano, A" (Stevens,
W.) MPII:P IV-1722
Posthumas Memoirs of Bráz Cubas. *See*
Epitaph of a Small Winner
Postman Always Rings Twice, The (Cain)
MP IX-5270; MP:AF II-978
Pot of Gold, The (Plautus) CLC II-908; MP
IX-5273
Potting Shed, The (Greene) CLCII III-1228;
MPII:D III-1274
Povest o zhizni. *See* Story of a Life, The
Power (Feuchtwanger) CLC II-909; MP
IX-5277; MP:EF III-1030
Power and the Glory, The (Greene, G.) CLC
II-910; MP IX-5280; MP:BF III-1250
Power of Darkness, The (Tolstoy) CLC
II-911; MP IX-5283
"Powerhouse" (Welty) MPII:SS IV-1839
Pragmatism (James, William) MP IX-5287
Prague Orgy, The (Roth, P.) CLCII III-1229
Prairie, The (Cooper, J. F.) CLC II-912; MP
IX-5290; MP:AF II-982. *See also*
Leatherstocking Tales, The
Prairie Years, The. *See* Abraham Lincoln
Praise of Folly, The (Erasmus) MP IX-5294
Praisesong for the Widow (Marshall) CLCII
III-1230; MPII:AF III-1286; MPII:AfAm
III-1172

Pravda (Brenton *and* Hare) CLCII III-1232; MPII:D III-1278

Pray, Love, Remember (Stolz) MPII:JYAFic III-1166

"Prayer for My Daughter, A" (Yeats) MPII:P IV-1726

Precious Bane (Webb, M.) CLC II-913; MP IX-5296; ; MP:BF III-1254

Precocious Autobiography, A (Yevtushenko) MPII:JYABio III-1436

Preface to Shakespeare (Johnson, S.) MP IX-5299

Prejudices (Mencken) MP IX-5302

"Prelude" (Mansfield) MPII:SS IV-1843

Prelude, The (Wordsworth, W.) MP IX-5304

"Preludes" (Eliot, T. S.) MPII:P IV-1729

Prcmières Communions, Les. *See* First Communions

Premios, Los. *See* Winners, The

Presence of the Word, The (Ong) MPII:NF III-1179

Pretendent na prestol. *See* Pretender to the Throne

Pretender to the Throne (Voinovich) CLCII II-881; MPII:WF II-841

Píbh inenra lidskch dušî. *See* Engineer of Human Souls, The

Price, The (Miller, A.) CLCII III-1233; MPII:D III-1283

Pride and Prejudice (Austen) CLC II-914; MP IX-5307; MP:BF III-1258

Priglashenie na kazn'. *See* Invitation to a Beheading

Prime of Life, The (de Beauvoir) MPII:NF III-1184

Prime of Miss Jean Brodie, The (Spark) CLCII III-1235; MPII:BCF III-1340; MPII:JYAFic III-1170

Primero Sueño. *See* First Dream

Primitive Classification (Durkheim *and* Mauss) MPII:NF III-1190

Primo Basîlio, O. *See* Cousin Bazilio

Prince, The (Machiavelli) MP IX-5314

Prince and the Pauper, The (Twain) CLC II-915; MP IX-5317; MP:AF II-986; MPII:JYAFic III-1174

Prince Caspian. *See* Chronicles of Narnia, The

"Prince of Darkness" (Powers) MPII:SS IV-1848

Prince of Homburg, The (Kleist) CLC II-916; MP IX-5321

Princess, The (Tennyson) MP IX-5324

Princess Casamassima, The (James, H.) MP IX-5327; MP:AF II-990

Princess Iwona. *See* Ivona, Princess of Burgundia

Princess of Clèves, The (La Fayette) CLC II-917; MP IX-5330; MP:EF III-1034

Principle of Hope, The (Bloch) MPII:NF III-1196

Principles of Literary Criticism (Richards, I. A.) MP IX-5334

Principles of Political Economy (Mill) MP IX-5337

Printer of Malgudi, The (Narayan) CLCII III-1236; MPII:BCF III-1346

Prinzip Hoffnung, Das. *See* Principle of Hope, The

Prison Notebooks (Gramsci) MPII:NF III-1200

Prisoner for God. *See* Letters and Papers from Prison

Prisoner of Grace. *See* Second Trilogy

Prisoner of Zenda, The (Hope, Anthony) CLC II-917; MP IX-5340; MP:BF III-1266; MPII:JYAFic III-1177

Prisons (Settle) CLCII III-1237. *See also* Beulah Quintet, The

"Private Domain" (McPherson) MPII:SS IV-1852

Private Life of the Master Race, The (Brecht) CLC II-918; MP IX-5344

Private Lives (Coward) CLC II-919; CLCII III-1239; MP IX-5347; MPII:D III-1288

Private Papers of Henry Ryecroft, The (Gissing) CLC II-920; MP IX-5350; MP:BF III-1270

Privileged Ones. *See* Children of Crisis

Privy Seal. *See* Fifth Queen, The

"Pro Femina" (Kizer) MPII:P V-1733

"Problem of Cell 13, The" (Futrelle) MPII:SS IV-1856

Professor, The (Brontë, C.) CLC II-920; MP IX-5353; MP:BF III-1274

Professor's House, The (Cather) CLC II-922; MP IX-5357; MP:AF II-994

Profiles in Courage (Kennedy, J. F.) MPII:JYABio III-1439

Prolog. *See* Prologue

"Prologue" (Yevtushenko) MPII:P V-1738

Prologue to an Autobiography (Naipaul) MPII:NF III-1204

Prometheus Bound (Aeschylus) CLC II-924; MP IX-5361

Prometheus Unbound (Shelley, P.) CLC II-925; MP IX-5365

Promise, The (Potok) CLCII I-281; MPII:AF I-295

"Promise, The (Steinbeck)." *See* Red Pony, The

Promised Land, The (Antin) MPII:JYABio III-1443

Promised Land, The (Pontoppidan) CLC II-926; MP IX-5368; MP:EF III-1038

Proper Marriage, A. *See* Children of Violence

Prophet, The (Gibran) MP IX-5372

Proserpine and Ceres (Unknown) CLC II-926; MP IX-5374; MP:EF III-1042

Proshchanie iz niotkuda. *See* Farewell from Nowhere

Prospero's Cell (Durrell) MPII:NF III-1210

"Prosz pastwa do gazu." *See* "This Way for the Gas, Ladies and Gentlemen"

Protestant Ethic and the Spirit of Capitalism, The (Weber) MPII:NF III-1214

Protestantische Ethik und der Geist des Kapitalismus, Die. *See* Protestant Ethic and the Spirit of Capitalism, The

Proust (Beckett) MPII:NF III-1219

"Provisional Conclusions" (Montale) MPII:P V-1741

Prudence Crandall (Yates) MPII:JYABio III-1447

"Prussian Officer, The" (Lawrence) MPII:SS V-1859

Prydain chronicles, The (Alexander, L.) MPII:JYAFic III-1180

Przestanie Pana Cogito. *See* Envoy of Mr. Cogito, The

"Psalm" (Celan) MPII:P V-1745

"Psalm" (Trakl) MPII:P V-1748

"Psychiatrist, The" (Machado de Assis) MPII:SS V-1862

Psycholog erlebt das Konzentrationslager, Ein. *See* Man's Search for Meaning

Publikumsbeschimpfung. *See* Offending the Audience

"Pulley, The" (Herbert, G.) MPII:P V-1751

"Pupil, The" (James, H.) MPII:SS V-1865

Purlie Victorious (Davis, O.) MPII:AfAm III-1178

"Purloined Letter, The" (Poe) MPII:SS V-1868

Purple Dust (O'Casey) CLC II-927; MP IX-5378

Purple Land, The (Hudson) CLC II-928; MP IX-5382; MP:BF III-1278

"Purpose of Altar Boys, The" (Rios) MPII:P V-1754

Pushcart War, The (Merrill, Jean) MPII:JYAFic III-1185

"Pustoy sluchay." *See* "Trifling Occurrence, A"

Puteshestviye v Armeniyu. *See* Journey to Armenia

Pygmalion (Shaw) CLC II-928; MP IX-5385

Pylon (Faulkner) CLCII III-1239; MPII:AF III-1291

Q

Quaderni del carcere. *See* Prison Notebooks

"Quaker Graveyard in Nantucket, The" (Lowell, R.) MPII:P V-1757

Quality of Hurt, The. *See* Autobiographies of Chester Himes, The.

Quality of Mercy, A (West, P.) CLCII III-1240; MPII:BCF III-1351

"Quality of Sprawl, The" (Murray, L.) MPII:P V-1760

Quality Street (Barrie) CLC II-930; MP IX-5387

"Quando si comprende." *See* "War"

Quare Fellow, The (Behan) CLCII III-1241; MPII:D III-1294

Quartet in Autumn (Pym) CLCII III-1243; MPII:BCF III-1355

Que ma joie demeure. *See* Joy of Man's Desiring

Queen Eleanor, Independent Spirit of the Medieval World (Brooks, P.) MPII:JYABio III-1451

Queen of Air and Darkness, The. *See* Once and Future King, The

"Queen of Spades, The" (Pushkin) CLCII III-1244; MPII:SS V-1872

Queen Victoria (Strachey) MP IX-5390; MPII:JYABio III-1455

Queen's Necklace, The (Dumas, *père*) CLC II-930; MP IX-5394; MP:EF III-1046

Quel beau dimanche. *See* What a Beautiful Sunday!

Quentin Durward (Scott, Sir W.) CLC II-931; MP IX-5398; MP:BF III-1282

Quer pasticciaccio brutto de via Merulana. *See* That Awful Mess on Via Merulana

Quest for Christa T., The (Wolf) CLCII III-1245; MPII:WF III-1230

Quest of the Absolute, The (Balzac) CLCII III-1246; MPII:WF III-1236

Questa sera si recita a soggetto. *See* Tonight We Improvise

"Question and Answer in the Mountain" (Li Po) MPII:P V-1764

Question of Power, A (Head) CLCII III-1247; MPII:BCF III-1360

Question of Upbringing, A. *See* Dance to the Music of Time, A

Questionnaire, The (Gruša) CLCII III-1249; MPII:WF III-1240

Quicksand (Larsen, N.) CLCII III-1250; MPII:AF III-1296; MPII:AfAm III-1183

Quiet American, The (Greene) CLCII III-1252; MPII:BCF III-1364

Quill Pens and Petticoats (Stowell) MPII:JYABio III-1459

Quincas Borba. *See* Philosopher or Dog?

Quo Vadis? (Sienkiewicz) CLC II-933; MP IX-5404; MP:EF III-1050

R

"Rabbi Ben Ezra" (Browning, R.) MPII:P
V-1767

Rabbit Angstrom novels, The (Updike)
MPII:AF III-1300

Rabbit Is Rich (Updike) CLCII III-1253.
See also Rabbit Angstrom novels, The

Rabbit Redux (Updike) CLCII III-1254. *See
also* Rabbit Angstrom novels, The

Rabbit, Run (Updike) CLCII III-1257; MP
IX-5407; MP:AF II-998. *See also* Rabbit
Angstrom novels, The

Rachel Carson (Kudlinski) MPII:JYABio
III-1463

Radcliffe (Storey) CLCII III-1257;
MPII:BCF III-1370

Radiance of the King, The (Laye) CLCII
III-1258; MPII:WF III-1245

Radical Chic and Mau-Mauing the Flak
Catchers (Wolfe) MPII:NF III-1225

Ragged Dick (Alger) MPII:JYAFic III-1188

"Ragman's Daughter, The" (Sillitoe)
MPII:SS V-1876

Ragtime (Doctorow) CLCII III-1259;
MPII:AF III-1310; MPII:JYAFic
III-1191

"Raid, The" (Tolstoy) CLCII III-1261;
MPII:SS V-1880

Railway Train, The. *See* I like to see it lap
the Miles—

"Rain" (Maugham) MPII:SS V-1883

Rainbow, The (Lawrence, D. H.) CLC
II-935; MP IX-5410; MP:BF III-1288

Rainbow Jordan (Childress) MPII:JYAFic
III-1195

Raintree County (Lockridge) CLC II-936;
MP IX-5415; MP:AF II-1001

"Rainy Moon, The" (Colette) MPII:SS
V-1887

Raisin in the Sun, A (Hansberry) CLCII
III-1262; MPII:AfAm III-1189; MPII:D
III-1300

Raj Quartet, The (Scott, P.) CLCII III-1263;
MPII:BCF III-1376

Rakovy korpus. *See* Cancer Ward

Ralph Bunche (Haskins) MPII:JYABio
III-1467

Ralph J. Bunche (Kugelmass)
MPII:JYABio III-1471

Ralph Roister Doister (Udall) CLC II-937;
MP IX-5418

"Ram in the Thicket, The" (Morris)
MPII:SS V-1890

Ramayana, The (Valmiki) CLC II-938; MP
IX-5421

Rambler, The (Johnson, S.) MP IX-5426

Rameau's Nephew (Diderot) CLC II-939;
MP IX-5429; MP:EF III-1054

Ramona series, The (Cleary) MPII:JYAFic
III-1198

"Ransom of Red Chief, The" (O. Henry)
MPII:SS V-1894

Rape of Lucrece, The (Shakespeare) CLC
II-940; MP IX-5432

Rape of the Lock, The (Pope) CLC II-940;
MP IX-5436

Raport z oblonego miasta. *See* Report from
the Besieged City

"Rappaccini's Daughter" (Hawthorne)
MPII:SS V-1897

Rascal (North) MPII:JYABio III-1475

"Rashmon" (Akutagawa) CLCII III-1265;
MPII:SS V-1901

Rasselas (Johnson, S.) CLC II-941; MP
IX-5441; MP:BF III-1293

Rat, The (Grass) CLCII III-1266; MPII:WF
III-1252

Rat Man of Paris (West, P.) CLCII III-1267;
MPII:BCF III-1386

Rates of Exchange (Bradbury, M.) CLCII
III-1268; MPII:BCF III-1390

Rat's Mass, A (Kennedy, A.) CLCII
III-1269; MPII:AfAm III-1194; MPII:D
III-1305

Rättin, Die. *See* Rat, The

"Raven, The" (Poe) MPII:P V-1770

Ravenshoe (Kingsley, H.) CLC II-942; MP
IX-5446; MP:BF III-1298

Ravishing of Lol Stein, The (Duras) CLCII
III-1270; MPII:WF III-1257

Ravissement de Lol V. Stein, Le. *See*
Ravishing of Lol Stein, The

Raw Youth, A (Dostoevski) CLCII
III-1271; MPII:WF III-1262

Rayuela. *See* Hopscotch

"Razgover o Dante." *See* Conversation About Dante

Razor's Edge, The (Maugham) CLCII III-1273; MPII:BCF III-1394

R. E. Lee (Freeman) MP IX-5497

Real Life of Sebastian Knight, The (Nabokov) MP IX-5450; MP:AF III-1005

Real Sherlock Holmes, The (Hoehling) MPII:JYABio III-1478

"Real Thing, The" (James, H.) MPII:SS V-1905

Real Thing, The (Stoppard) CLCII III-1274; MPII:D III-1310

"Reasonable Facsimile, A" (Stafford) MPII:SS V-1908

"Reasons for Attendance" (Larkin) MPII:P V-1774

Rebecca (du Maurier, D.) CLC II-943; MP IX-5452; MP:BF III-1302; MPII:JYAFic III-1202

Rebecca of Sunnybrook Farm (Wiggin) MPII:JYAFic III-1206

Rebel, The (Camus) MPII:NF III-1231

Rebel Angels, The (Davies, R.) CLCII III-1275; MPII:BCF III-1399

Rebel Generation, The (Ammers-Küller) MP IX-5456; MP:EF III-1058

Rebel Generation, The (Farquhar) CLC II-944

Rebellion in the Backlands (Cunha) CLCII III-1276; MPII:AF III-1317

"Recessional" (Kipling) MPII:P V-1777

Recherche de l'absolu, La. *See* Quest of the Absolute, The

Reckless Eyeballing (Reed, I.) MPII:AfAm III-1200

"Recluse, A" (de la Mare) MPII:SS V-1913

Recognitions, The (Gaddis) CLCII III-1277; MPII:AF III-1324

Recruiting Officer, The (Farquhar) CLC II-945; MP IX-5459

Rector of Justin, The (Auchincloss) CLCII III-1279; MPII:AF III-1329

Red and the Black, The (Stendhal) CLC II-947; MP IX-5463; MP:EF III-1062

Red Badge of Courage, The (Crane, S.) CLC II-948; MP IX-5468; MP:AF III-1008; MPII:JYAFic III-1210

Red Fox (Roberts, C.) MPII:JYAFic III-1214

"Red-Headed League, The" (Doyle) MPII:SS V-1922

"Red Leaves" (Faulkner) MPII:SS V-1918

Red Pony, The (Steinbeck) CLCII III-1281; MPII:AF III-1334; MPII:JYAFic III-1217

Red Room, The (Strindberg) CLC II-949; MP IX-5473; MP:EF III-1067

Red Roses for Me (O'Casey) CLCII III-1282; MPII:D III-1315

Red Rover, The (Cooper, J. F.) CLC II-950; MP IX-5477; MP:AF III-1013

"Red Wheelbarrow, The" (Williams, W.) MPII:P V-1780

Redburn (Melville) CLC II-951; MP IX-5481; MP:AF III-1017

Redskins, The (Cooper, J. F.) CLC II-951; MP IX-5484; MP:AF III-1021

Reflections from a Diary Kept in 1909. *See* Autobiography of William Butler Yeats, The

Reflex and Bone Structure (Major) MPII:AfAm III-1206

"Refusal to Mourn the Death, by Fire, of a Child in London, A" (Thomas, D.) MPII:P V-1783

Regard du roi, Le. *See* Radiance of the King, The

Regenta, La (Alas) CLCII III-1284; MPII:WF III-1267

Reggie (Jackson, R.) MPII:JYABio III-1482

Región más transparente, La. *See* Where the Air Is Clear

Reigen. *See* Ronde, La

Reino de este mundo, El. *See* Kingdom of This World, The

Reinvindicación del Conde Don Julián. *See* Count Julian

Reivers, The (Faulkner) MP IX-5489; MP:AF III-1027

Rekview. *See* Requiem

Relapse, The (Vanbrugh) CLC II-952; MP IX-5493

Relations in Public (Goffman) MPII:NF III-1236

Religio Laici (Dryden) MPII:P V-1786

"Relocation" (Mura) MPII:P V-1791

"Rembrandt's Hat" (Malamud) MPII:SS V-1926

"Remedies, Maladies, Reasons" (Van Duyn) MPII:P V-1795

"Remembering Titian's Martyrdom of Saint Lawrence" (Graham, J.) MPII:P V-1798

"Remembrance" (Brontë) MPII:P V-1801

Remembrance of Things Past (Proust) CLC II-953; MP IX-5500; MP:EF III-1072

Remembrance Rock (Sandburg) CLC II-955; MP IX-5505; MP:AF III-1032

Removalists, The (Williamson) CLCII III-1285; MPII:D III-1320

"Remove the Predicate" (Coolidge, C.) MPII:P V-1804

Renaissance, The (Pater) MP IX-5511

Renée Mauperin (Goncourt *and* Goncourt) CLC II-957; MP IX-5514; MP:EF III-1078

"Report from the Besieged City" (Herbert, Z.) MPII:P V-1807

"Report to an Academy, A" (Kafka) MPII:SS V-1929

Representative Men (Emerson) MP IX-5518

Reprieve, The. *See* Roads to Freedom, The

Republic, The (Plato) MP IX-5522

Requiem (Akhmatova) MPII:P V-1810

Requiem for a Nun (Faulkner) MP X-5525; MP:AF III-1040

"Requiem for the Plantagenet Kings" (Hill, G.) MPII:P V-1813

"Resemblance Between a Violin Case and a Coffin, The" (Williams, T.) MPII:SS V-1933

"Resolution and Independence" (Wordsworth) MPII:P V-1816

Responsibilities of the Novelist, The (Norris) MP X-5528

Restless Heart (Anouilh) CLCII III-1286; MPII:D III-1325

Restless Spirit: The Story of Robert Frost, A (Bober) MPII:JYABio III-1489

Restless Spirit: The Life of Edna St. Vincent Millay (Gurko) MPII:JYABio III-1486

Restless Years, The. *See* Story of a Life, The

Resurrection (Tolstoy) CLC II-958; MP X-5531; MP:EF III-1082

Return, The (de la Mare) CLC II-958; MP X-5536; MP:BF III-1307

"Return" (Paz) MPII:P V-1819

"Return, The" (Pound) MPII:P V-1823

"Return of a Private, The" (Garland) MPII:SS V-1937

"Return of Chorb, The" (Nabokov) MPII:SS V-1941

Return of the King, The (Tolkien) MP X-5540; MP:BF III-1311. *See also* Lord of the Rings, The

Return of the Native, The (Hardy) CLC II-959; MP X-5545; MP:BF III-1317

Return of the Soldier, The (West, R.) CLCII III-1288; MPII:BCF III-1404

Return of the Twelves, The (Clarke, P.) MPII:JYAFic III-1220

Return to Auschwitz (Hart, K.) MPII:JYABio III-1493

Return to My Native Land (Césaire) MPII:P V-1827

Return to Región (Benet) CLCII III-1289; MPII:WF III-1272

Reve parisien. *See* Parisian Dream

"Revelation" (O'Connor, Flannery) MPII:SS V-1945

"Revenant, A" (de la Mare) MPII:SS V-1948

Revenge for Love, The (Lewis, W.) CLCII III-1290; MPII:BCF III-1410

Revenge of Bussy d'Ambois, The (Chapman) CLC II-961; MP X-5550

Revenger's Tragedy, The (Tourneur) CLC II-961; MP X-5554

Reveries over Childhood and Youth. *See* Autobiography of William Butler Yeats, The

Revolt of the Angels, The (France) CLC II-963; MP X-5558; MP:EF III-1088

Revolt of the Masses, The (Ortega y Gasset) MP X-5562

Revolving Lights. *See* Pilgrimage

Rey de Harlem, El. *See* King of Harlem, The

Reyerta. *See* Fight

Reynard the Fox (Unknown) CLC II-963; MP X-5565; MP:EF III-1092

Rhadamistus and Zenobia (Crébillon) CLC II-964; MP X-5570

"Rhapsody on a Windy Night" (Eliot, T. S.) MPII:P V-1832

Rhinoceros (Ionesco) MP X-5574

Riceyman Steps (Bennett, A.) CLC II-965; MP X-5577; MP:BF III-1323

"Rich Boy, The" (Fitzgerald) MPII:SS V-1952

Richard the Second (Shakespeare) CLC II-965; MP X-5580

Richard the Third (Shakespeare) CLC II-967; MP X-5585

Rickshaw (Lao She) CLCII III-1291; MPII:WF III-1278

Ride Across Lake Constance, The (Handke) CLCII III-1292; MPII:D III-1330

Riders in the Chariot (White, P.) MP X-5590; MP:BF III-1327

Riders to the Sea (Synge) CLCII III-1294; MPII:D III-1337

Rifles for Watie (Keith) MPII:JYAFic III-1224

Rigadoon (Céline) CLCII I-241; MPII:WF I-221

Right Stuff, The (Wolfe) MPII:NF III-1241

Right to an Answer, The (Burgess) CLCII III-1295; MPII:BCF III-1416

Right You Are—If You Think So (Pirandello) CLC II-970; MP X-5593

Rigodon. See Rigadoon

Rihlah ila al-ghad. See Voyage to Tomorrow

Riket grundlœgges. See Giants in the Earth

Rime of Petrarch, Le (Petrarch) MP X-5597

Rime of the Ancient Mariner, The (Coleridge) MP X-5600

Rimers of Eldritch, The (Wilson, L.) CLCII III-1296; MPII:D IV-1343

Ring and the Book, The (Browning, R.) CLC II-970; MP X-5603

Ring of Endless Light, A (L'Engle) MPII:JYAFic III-1227

Ring Round the Moon (Anouilh) CLC II-972; MP X-5608

"Rip Van Winkle" (Irving, W.) CLC II-972; MP X-5611; MP:AF III-1044; MPII:SS V-1957

Ripening Corn, The. See Ripening Seed, The

Ripening Seed, The (Colette) CLCII III-1297; MPII:WF III-1282

Ripple from the Storm, A. See Children of Violence

Rise and Fall of Adolf Hitler, The (Shirer) MPII:JYABio IV-1497

Rise and Fall of César Birotteau. See César Birotteau

Rise and Fall of the City of Mahagonny (Brecht) CLCII III-1298; MPII:D IV-1350

Rise of American Civilization, The (Beard and Beard) MP X-5614

"Rise of Maud Martha, The" (Brooks, G.) MPII:SS V-1961

Rise of Silas Lapham, The (Howells) CLC II-973; MP X-5618; MP:AF III-1047

Rites of Passage (Golding) CLCII III-1299; MPII:BCF III-1422

Ritt über den Bodensee, Der. See Ride Across Lake Constance, The

"Ritter Gluck" (Hoffmann) MPII:SS V-1964

Rivals, The (Sheridan) CLC II-974; MP X-5624

River at Green Knowe, The. See Green Knowe books, The

River Between, The (Ngugi) CLCII III-1300; MPII:BCF III-1428

"River-Merchant's Wife, The" (Pound) MPII:P V-1835

River of Earth (Still) CLC II-975; MP X-5629; MP:AF III-1054

Rivet in Grandfather's Neck, The (Cabell) CLC II-976; MP X-5632; MP:AF III-1058

Rivière de Cassis, La. See Blackcurrant River

Road, The (Soyinka) CLCII III-1302; MPII:D IV-1356

Road from Home, The (Kherdian) MPII:JYABio IV-1501

"Road Not Taken, The" (Frost) MPII:P V-1838

Road to Agra, The (Sommerfelt) MPII:JYAFic III-1231

Road to Mecca, The (Fugard) CLCII III-1303; MPII:D IV-1362

"Road to the Isles" (West, J.) MPII:SS V-1968

Road to Wigan Pier, The (Orwell) MPII:NF III-1247

Roads to Freedom, The (Sartre) CLCII
III-1303; MPII:WF III-1288
Roadside Picnic (Strugatsky *and*
Strugatsky) CLCII III-1306; MPII:WF
III-1295
Roan Stallion (Jeffers) CLC II-977; MP
X-5636
Rob Roy (Scott, Sir W.) CLC II-977; MP
X-5638; MP:BF III-1331
Robber Bridegroom, The (Welty) CLCII
III-1307; MPII:AF III-1339
Robert Lawson, Illustrator (Jones, Helen)
MPII:JYABio IV-1505
Robin Hood's Adventures (Unknown) CLC
II-978; MP X-5642; MP:BF III-1336
Robinson Crusoe (Defoe) CLC II-979; MP
X-5647; MP:BF III-1341; MPII:JYAFic
III-1235
"Rock and Hawk" (Jeffers) MPII:P V-1842
Rock Cried Out, The (Douglas) CLCII
III-1309; MPII:AF III-1344
"Rocking-Horse Winner, The" (Lawrence)
MPII:SS V-1971
Roderick Hudson (James, H.) MP X-5652;
MP:AF III-1062
Roderick Random (Smollett) CLC II-979;
MP X-5656; MP:BF III-1347
Rodzinnia Europa. *See* Native Realm
Rogue Herries (Walpole, Hugh) CLC
II-981; MP X-5661; MP:BF III-1353
Roi des aulnes, Le. *See* Ogre, The
Roi se meurt, Le. *See* Exit the King
Roll of Thunder, Hear My Cry (Taylor, M.)
MPII:AfAm III-1212; MPII:JYAFic
III-1239
Roller Skates (Sawyer) MPII:JYAFic III-1244
Rollo series, The (Abbott) MPII:JYAFic
III-1248
Roman Actor, The (Massinger) CLC II-982;
MP X-5665
"Roman Fever" (Wharton) MPII:SS V-1974
"Roman Sarcophagi" (Rilke) MPII:P
V-1845
Romance of a Schoolmaster, The (Amicis)
CLC II-983; MP X-5669; MP:EF
III-1097
Romance of Leonardo da Vinci, The
(Merezhkowsky) CLC II-984; MP
X-5672; MP:EF III-1101

Romance of the Forest, The (Radcliffe)
CLC II-984; MP X-5675; MP:BF
III-1358
Romance of the Three Kingdoms (Lo
Kuan-chung) CLC II-985; MP X-5681;
MP:EF III-1105
Romance sonámbulo. *See* Somnambule
Ballad
Romantic Comedians, The (Glasgow) CLC
II-986; MP X-5684; MP:AF III-1067
Romantic Ladies, The (Molière) CLC
II-988; MP X-5689
Romany Rye, The (Borrow) CLC II-988;
MP X-5693; MP:BF III-1365
Rome Haul (Edmonds) CLC II-989; MP
X-5697; MP:AF III-1072
Romeo and Juliet (Shakespeare) CLC
II-990; MP X-5700
Römische Sarkophage. *See* Roman
Sarcophagi
Romola (Eliot, G.) CLC II-992; MP
X-5705; MP:BF III-1369
Romulus der Grosse. *See* Romulus the Great
Romulus the Great (Dürrenmatt) CLCII
III-1310; MPII:D IV-1367
Ronde, La (Schnitzler) CLCII III-1312;
MPII:D IV-1372
Room at the Top (Braine) MP X-5709;
MP:BF III-1373
Room on the Hill, A (St. Omer) CLCII
III-1312; MPII:BCF III-1435
Room with a View, A (Forster) CLC II-994;
MP X-5712; MP:BF III-1376
Roosevelt Family of Sagamore Hill, The
(Hagedorn) MPII:JYABio IV-1509
Roots (Haley) MPII:AfAm III-1218;
MPII:NF III-1251
"Rope" (Porter) MPII:SS V-1978
Rory O'More (Lover) CLC II-995; MP
X-5715; MP:BF III-1380
"Rosa" (Ozick) MPII:SS V-1982
Rose and Crown. *See* Mirror in My House
"Rose for Emily, A" (Faulkner) MPII:SS
V-1986
"Rose in the Heart of New York, A"
(O'Brien, E.) MPII:SS V-1990
Rosencrantz and Guildenstern Are Dead
(Stoppard) CLCII III-1314; MPII:D
IV-1378

Rosmersholm (Ibsen) CLC II-995; MP X-5718

Rosshalde (Hesse) CLCII III-1314; MPII:WF III-1300

"Rothschild's Fiddle" (Chekhov) MPII:SS V-1994

Roughing It (Twain) MP X-5722

"Round by Round" (Aiken, C.) MPII:SS V-1998

Route des Flandres, La. See Flanders Road, The

Rowan Farm (Benary-Isbert) MPII:JYAFic III-1251

Roxana (Defoe) CLC II-996; MP X-5725; MP:BF III-1384

Roy Campanella (Schoor) MPII:JYABio IV-1513

Royal Dirk, The (Beatty and Beatty) MPII:JYAFic III-1255

Royal Hunt of the Sun, The (Shaffer, P.) CLCII III-1316; MPII:D IV-1384

Royal Way, The (Malraux) CLCII III-1317; MPII:WF III-1305

Rubáiyát of Omar Khayyám, The (FitzGerald, E.) MP X-5730

Rubyfruit Jungle (Brown, R.) CLCII III-1318; MPII:AF III-1349

Rudin (Turgenev) CLCII III-1319; MPII:WF III-1310

Rue Descartes. See Bypassing Rue Descartes

Rufus M. See Moffats series, The

"Ruinas circulares, Las." See "Circular Ruins, The"

Ruined Map, The (Abe) CLCII III-1321; MPII:WF III-1315

Rule a Wife and Have a Wife (Fletcher) CLC II-996; MP X-5732

Ruling Class, The (Barnes, P.) CLCII III-1322; MPII:D IV-1390

Runaway Horse (Walser) CLCII III-1323; MPII:WF III-1321

Runaway Horses. See Sea of Fertility, The

Runner Mack (Beckham) CLCII III-1324; MPII:AF III-1353; MPII:AfAm III-1224

R.U.R. (Čapek) CLC II-997; MP X-5736

Ruslan and Lyudmila (Pushkin) MP X-5740; MPII:NF III-1257

Russian Thinkers (Berlin) MPII:NF III-1257

R. v. R. (Van Loon) MPII:JYABio IV-1517

S

S/Z (Barthes) MPII:NF III-1263
Sacred Families (Donoso) CLCII III-1325;
 MPII:AF III-1357
Sacred Fount, The (James, H.) MP X-5743;
 MP:AF III-1076
Sacred Journey, The (Buechner) MPII:NF
 III-1269
Sacred Wood, The (Eliot, T. S.) MP X-5748
"Sad Fate of Mr. Fox, The" (Harris, J. C.)
 MPII:SS V-2002
Sad idzie. *See* Trial Begins, The
"Sadness and Happiness" (Pinsky) MPII:P
 V-1848
Safe-Conduct, A (Pasternak) MPII:NF
 III-1274
Safety Net, The (Böll) CLCII III-1326;
 MPII:WF III-1326
"Sailing to Byzantium" (Yeats) MPII:P
 V-1852
"Sailor Off the *Bremen*" (Shaw) MPII:SS
 V-2005
Sailor on Horseback (Stone, I.)
 MPII:JYABio IV-1521
Sailor Who Fell from Grace with the Sea,
 The (Mishima) CLCII III-1328;
 MPII:WF III-1332
Saint, The (Fogazzaro) CLC II-998; MP
 X-5751; MP:EF III-1109
"Saint Augustine's Pigeon" (Connell, E.)
 MPII:SS V-2008
Saint Jack (Theroux) CLCII III-1329;
 MPII:AF III-1362
Saint Joan (Shaw) CLC II-998; MP X-5755
"Saint Judas" (Wright, James) MPII:P
 V-1855
Saint Manuel Bueno, Martyr (Unamuno)
 CLCII III-1329; MPII:WF III-1338
"Saint Marie" (Erdrich) MPII:SS V-2012
St. Peter's Umbrella (Mikszáth) CLC
 II-999; MP X-5757; MP:EF III-1113
St. Petersburg. *See* Petersburg
St. Ronan's Well (Scott, Sir W.) CLC
 II-1000; MP X-5761; MP:BF III-1389
St. Urbain's Horseman (Richler) CLCII
 III-1330; MPII:BCF III-1440
Sajo and the Beaver People (Grey Owl)
 MPII:JYAFic III-1259

Sakuntala (Kalidasa) CLC II-1001; MP
 X-5765
Salammbô (Flaubert) CLC II-1001; MP
 X-5769; MP:EF III-1118
Salar the Salmon (Williamson) MP X-5773;
 MP:BF III-1394
Sally Hemings (Chase-Riboud) MPII:AfAm
 III-1230
Salt Eaters, The (Bambara) MPII:AfAm
 III-1236
Salut. *See* Toast
"Salutation, The" (Traherne) MPII:P V-1858
Salvador (Didion) MPII:NF III-1280
"Same Time" (Paz) MPII:P V-1861
Samson Agonistes (Milton) CLC II-1002;
 MP X-5776
Samuel Adams (Alderman) MPII:JYABio
 IV-1525
Samurai, The (End) CLCII III-1332;
 MPII:WF III-1345
Samurai's Tale, The (Haugaard)
 MPII:JYAFic III-1263
"San Ildefonso Nocturne" (Paz) MPII:P
 V-1864
San Manuel Bueno, mártir. *See* Saint
 Manuel Bueno, Martyr
"Sanatorium Under the Sign of the
 Hourglass" (Schulz) MPII:SS V-2016
Sanctuary (Faulkner) CLC II-1003; MP
 X-5780; MP:AF III-1082
Sand Mountain (Linney) CLCII III-1333;
 MPII:D IV-1396
Sandcastle, The (Murdoch) CLCII III-1334;
 MPII:BCF III-1444
Sandford and Merton (Day, T.) CLC
 II-1004; MP X-5784; MP:BF III-1398
"Sandman, The" (Hoffmann) MPII:SS
 V-2020
Sandman's Eyes, The (Windsor)
 MPII:JYAFic III-1267
Sanine (Artsybashev) CLC II-1004; MP
 X-5787; MP:EF III-1123
Santiago (Belpré) MPII:JYAFic III-1271
Santiago (Clark, A.) MPII:JYAFic III-1274
Sapins, Les. *See* Fir Trees
Sapphira and the Slave Girl (Cather) CLCII
 III-1335; MPII:AF III-1366

Sappho (Daudet) CLC II-1005; MP X-5790; MP:EF III-1127

Sappho (Grillparzer) CLC II-1006; MP X-5793

Sara Crewe. See Little Princess, A

Saragossa (Pérez Galdós) CLC II-1006; MP X-5796; MP:EF III-1131

Sarah Phillips (Lee, A.) MPII:AfAm III-1241

Sarah, Plain and Tall (MacLachlan) MPII:JYAFic III-1278

Sarrasine (Balzac) CLCII III-1337; MPII:WF III-1351

Sartor Resartus (Carlyle) MP X-5799

Sartoris (Faulkner) MP X-5801; MP:AF III-1086

Sasame-yuki. See Makioka Sisters, The

Satanstoe (Cooper, J. F.) CLC II-1007; MP X-5804; MP:AF III-1090

Satin Slipper, The (Claudel) CLCII III-1338; MPII:D IV-1401

"Satire Against Mankind, A" (Wilmot) MPII:P V-1867

Satires (Boileau-Despréaux) MP X-5809

Satires (Juvenal) MP X-5812

Satires (Lucian) MP X-5814

Satiromastix (Dekker) CLC II-1008; MP X-5817

"Saturday Night" (Farrell) MPII:SS V-2025

Saturday Night and Sunday Morning (Sillitoe) CLCII III-1339; MPII:BCF III-1449

Saturday, the Twelfth of October (Mazer, N.) MPII:JYAFic III-1281

Satyricon, The (Petronius) CLC II-1008, MP X-5820; MP:EF III-1135

Sauvage, La. See Restless Heart

Save Me the Waltz (Fitzgerald, Z.) CLCII III-1340; MPII:AF III-1370

Saved (Bond) CLCII III-1341; MPII:D IV-1406

Saving the Appearances (Barfield) MPII:NF III-1286

Sawbones Memorial (Ross) CLCII III-1342; MPII:BCF III-1455

"Scandal in Bohemia, A" (Doyle) MPII:SS V-2029

"Scandalous Woman, A" (O'Brien, E.) MPII:SS V-2033

"Scapegoat, The" (Dunbar) MPII:SS V-2037

Scapegoat, The (Girard) MPII:NF III-1293

Scapegoat, The (Settle) CLCII III-1343. See also Beulah Quintet, The

Scarecrows, The (Westall) MPII:JYAFic III-1285

Scarlet Letter, The (Hawthorne) CLC II-1009; MP X-5826; MP:AF III-1096

Scarlet Pimpernel, The (Orczy) MPII:JYAFic III-1288

Scenes from American Life (Gurney) CLCII III-1345; MPII:D IV-1411

"Scented Herbage of My Breast" (Whitman) MPII:P V-1870

Scepticism and Animal Faith (Santayana) MP X-5831

"Schakale und Araber." See "Jackals and Arabs"

Schlaflose Tage. See Sleepless Days

Schmetterling. See Butterfly

"Scholar-Gypsy, The" (Arnold, M.) MPII:P V-1873

School for Fools, A (Sokolov) CLCII III-1347; MPII:WF III-1356

School for Husbands, The (Molière) CLC II-1010; MP X-5834

School for Scandal, The (Sheridan) CLC II-1011; MP X-5838

School for Wives, The (Molière) CLC II-1012; MP X-5843

"Schreuderspitze, The" (Helprin) MPII:SS V-2041

"Schubertiana" (Tranströmer) MPII:P V-1877

Schwanenhaus, Das. See Swan Villa, The

Schweizerische Robinson, Der. See Swiss Family Robinson, The

Scientists Behind the Inventors (Burlingame) MPII:JYABio IV-1529

Scientists Who Changed the World (Poole and Poole) MPII:JYABio IV-1533

Scorched-Wood People, The (Wiebe) CLCII III-1348; MPII:BCF III-1460

Scornful Lady, The (Beaumont and Fletcher) CLC II-1012; MP X-5848

Scots Quair, A (Gibbon) CLCII III-1349; MPII:BCF III-1465

Scottish Chiefs, The (Porter, J.) CLC II-1013; MP X-5851; MP:BF III-1402

Scott's Last Expedition (Scott, Captain R.) MP X-5855

Screens, The (Genet) CLCII III-1352; MPII:D IV-1416

Scripts of the Pageant. *See* Changing Light at Sandover, The

Sculpting in Time (Tarkovsky) MPII:NF III-1298

"Sculptor's Funeral, The" (Cather) MPII:SS V-2045

Se non ora, quando? *See* If Not Now, When?

Se questo è un uomo. *See* If This Is a Man

Se una notte d'inverno un viaggiatore. *See* If on a Winter's Night a Traveler

Sea and Earth (Sterling) MPII:JYABio IV-1537

Sea and Sardinia (Lawrence) MPII:NF III-1303

Sea and the Jungle, The (Tomlinson) MP X-5858

Sea of Cortez (Steinbeck *and* Ricketts) MPII:NF III-1309

Sea of Fertility, The (Mishima) CLCII III-1354; MPII:WF III-1361

Sea of Grass, The (Richter, C.) CLC II-1014; MP X-5861; MP:AF III-1102

Sea of Troubles, A. *See* Sea Wall, The

Sea Rovers, The (Marrin) MPII:JYABio IV-1541

Sea Wall, The (Duras) CLCII III-1355; MPII:WF III-1367

Sea Wolf, The (London) CLC II-1015; MP X-5865; MP:AF III-1106

"Seafarer, The" (Pound) MPII:P V-1880

Seafaring Women (De Pauw) MPII:JYABio IV-1545

Seagull, The (Chekhov) CLC II-1015; MP X-5868

Seamarks (Perse) MP X-5874

Séance, The (Nixon) MPII:JYAFic III-1292

Search for America, A (Grove) CLCII III-1356; MPII:BCF III-1472

Search for Signs of Intelligent Life in the Universe, The (Wagner) CLCII III-1357; MPII:D IV-1421

"Searchers, The" (Rivera) MPII:P V-1883

Seascape (Albee) CLCII III-1359; MPII:D IV-1427

Season in Hell, A (Rimbaud) MP X-5876

Season of Adventure (Lamming) CLCII III-1360; MPII:AfAm III-1246; MPII:BCF III-1476

Season of Anomy (Soyinka) CLCII III-1362; MPII:BCF III-1482

Seasons, The (Thomson) MP X-5879

"Seaton's Aunt" (de la Mare) MPII:SS V-2049

Second Coming, The (Percy) CLCII III-1363; MPII:AF III-1376

"Second Coming, The" (Yeats) MPII:P V-1886

Second Common Reader, The. *See* Literary Essays of Virginia Woolf, The

Second Foundation. *See* Foundation trilogy, The

Second Jungle Book, The (Kipling) MPII:JYAFic II-767. *See also* Jungle Books, The

Second Man, The (Behrman) CLCII III-1364; MPII:D IV-1433

Second Mrs. Tanqueray, The (Pinero) CLC II-1017; MP X-5882

Second Sex, The (de Beauvoir) MPII:NF III-1314

Second Shepherd's Play, The (Unknown) CLC II-1017; MP X-5886

Second Trilogy (Cary, J.) CLCII III-1365; MPII:BCF IV-1489

Second Wind (Russell *and* Branch) MPII:JYABio IV-1549

Second World War, The (Churchill, W. S.) MP X-5890

Secret Agent, The (Conrad) CLC II-1018; MP X-5893; MP:BF III-1407

Secret Garden, The (Burnett, F.) MPII:JYAFic III-1295

Secret History of the Lord of Musashi, The (Tanizaki) CLCII III-1367; MPII:WF III-1372

Secret House, The (Bodanis) MPII:NF IV-1319

"Secret Integration, The" (Pynchon) MPII:SS V-2053

Secret Ladder, The. *See* Guyana Quartet, The

"Secret Life of Walter Mitty, The" (Thurber) MPII:SS V-2057

Secret of Gumbo Grove, The (Tate, E.) MPII:JYAFic III-1298

Secret of the Andes (Clark, A.)
MPII:JYAFic III-1301

"Secret Sharer, The" (Conrad) CLCII
III-1368; MPII:SS V-2061

Secret Soldier, The (McGovern)
MPII:JYAFic III-1304

Seduction and Betrayal (Hardwick)
MPII:NF IV-1324

Seduction by Light (Young, A.)
MPII:AfAm III-1252

"See the Moon?" (Barthelme, D.) MPII:SS
V-2064

"Seekers of Lice, The" (Rimbaud) MPII:P
V-1889

Seize the Day (Bellow) CLCII III-1369;
MPII:AF III-1382

Seizure of Power, The (Miłosz) CLCII
III-1370; MPII:WF IV-1377

Sejanus, His Fall (Jonson) CLC II-1019;
MP X-5896

Selected Poems (Ransom) MP X-5899

Self Condemned (Lewis, W.) CLCII
III-1371; MPII:BCF IV-1496

"Self-Portrait in a Convex Mirror"
(Ashbery) MPII:P V-1892

Self-Tormentor, The (Terence) CLC
II-1021; MP X-5902

Sem dnei tvoreniia. See Seven Days of
Creation, The

Sembazuru. See Thousand Cranes

"Semejante a la noche." See "Like the Night"

Semeynoye schast'ye. See Family Happiness

Señas de identidad. See Marks of Identity

Senilità. See As a Man Grows Older

Sennik wspóczesny. See Dreambook for
Our Time, A

Señor de Tacuru, El. See Lizard's Tail, The

Señor Presidente, El (Asturias) MP:AF
III-1110

Sense and Sensibility (Austen) CLC
II-1022; MP X-5905; MP:BF III-1411

Sent for You Yesterday. See Homewood
trilogy, The

Sentiero dei nidi di ragno, Il. See Path to the
Nest of Spiders, The

Sentimental Education, A (Flaubert) CLC
II-1023; MP X-5909; MP:EF III-1141

Sentimental Journey, A (Shklovsky) CLCII
III-1372; MPII:WF IV-1382

Sentimental Journey, A (Sterne) CLC
II-1024; MP X-5914; MP:BF III-1415

Sentimental'noye puteshestviye. See
Sentimental Journey, A

Separate Peace, A (Knowles) CLCII
III-1373; MPII:AF III-1387;
MPII:JYAFic III-1308

"September 1, 1939" (Auden) MPII:P
V-1896

September Light. See Silesian Tetralogy,
The

Septemberlicht. See Silesian Tetralogy, The

Seraph on the Suwanee (Hurston)
MPII:AfAm III-1257

"Serapionsbrüder, Die." See "Story of
Scrapion, The"

Serebryagolub. See Silver Dove, The

Serebryanny golub. See Silver Dove, The

Serious Money (Churchill) CLCII III-1374;
MPII:D IV-1438

Serjeant Musgrave's Dance (Arden) CLCII
III-1375; MPII:D IV-1444

Serment de Kolvillàg, Le. See Oath, The

Serpent and the Rope, The (Rao) CLCII
IV-1377; MPII:BCF IV-1501

Serpiente de oro, La. See Golden Serpent,
The

Sertões, Os. See Rebellion in the Backlands

"Sestina: Altaforte" (Pound) MPII:P V-1899

Set This House on Fire (Styron) MP
X-5919; MP:AF III-1113

Setting Free the Bears (Irving, J.) CLCII
IV-1378; MPII:AF III-1392

Setting Sun, The (Dazai) CLCII IV-1379;
MPII:WF IV-1388

Settlers of the Marsh (Grove) CLCII
IV-1380; MPII:BCF IV-1506

Seven Against Thebes (Aeschylus) CLC
II-1025; MP X-5922

Seven Ages, The (Figes) CLCII IV-1381;
MPII:BCF IV-1510

Seven Days of Creation, The (Maximov)
CLCII IV-1383; MPII:WF IV-1393

Seven Gothic Tales (Dinesen) MP X-5926;
MP:EF III-1147

Seven Kings of England (Trease)
MPII:JYABio IV-1553

Seven Madmen, The (Arlt) CLCII IV-1384;
MPII:AF IV-1397

Seven Pillars of Wisdom (Lawrence, T. E.) MP X-5929

Seven Queens of England, The (Trease) MPII:JYABio IV-1557

Seven Short Plays (Gregory) MP X-5932

Seven Storey Mountain, The (Merton) MPII:NF IV-1330

Seven Types of Ambiguity (Empson) MPII:NF IV-1335

Seven Who Fled, The (Prokosch) CLC II-1026; MP X-5934; MP:AF III-1117

Seven Who Were Hanged, The (Andreyev) CLC II-1027; MP X-5939; MP:EF III-1151

Seventeen (Tarkington) CLC II-1027; MP X-5942; MP:AF III-1122

Seventeenth Summer (Daly) MPII:JYAFic IV-1311

Severed Head, A (Murdoch) CLCII IV-1385; MPII:BCF IV-1516

Sexual Perversity in Chicago (Mamet) CLCII IV-1386; MPII:D IV-1449

Shadow Bride, The (Heath) MPII:AfAm III-1263

Shadow Guests, The (Aiken, J.) MPII:JYAFic IV-1315

Shadow of a Bull (Wojciechowska) MPII:JYAFic IV-1318

Shadow of a Gunman, The (O'Casey) CLCII IV-1387; MPII:D IV-1454

Shadow of Night, The (Chapman) MP X-5945

Shadows on the Rock (Cather) CLC II-1028; MP X-5948; MP:AF III-1126

Shah of Shahs (Kapuciski) MPII:NF IV-1341

Shakespeare of London (Chute) MPII:JYABio IV-1561

Shakespeare's Dog (Rooke) CLCII IV-1388; MPII:BCF IV-1523

"Shall I compare thee to a summer's day?" See Sonnet 18

Shame (Rushdie) CLCII IV-1389; MPII:BCF IV-1528

Shan Chung wen ta. See Question and Answer in the Mountain

Shane (Schaefer, J.) MPII:JYAFic IV-1321

Shank's Mare. See Hizakurige

"Shape of Light, A" (Goyen) MPII:SS V-2068

Shay. See Setting Sun, The

She (Haggard) CLC II-1029; MP X-5952; MP:BF III-1421

She Stoops to Conquer (Goldsmith) CLC II-1030; MP X-5957

"She-Wolf, The" (Verga) MPII:SS V-2076

Sheep Well, The (Vega) CLC II-1031; MP X-5962

Shelburne Essays (More, P.) MP X-5966

Sheltered Life, The (Glasgow) CLC II-1033; MP X-5969; MP:AF III-1130

Sheltering Sky, The (Bowles) CLCII IV-1390; MPII:AF IV-1402

Shepheardes Calendar, The (Spenser) MP X-5972

"Sheriff's Children, The" (Chesnutt) MPII:SS V-2072

Shih Ching, The (Confucius) MP X-5976

"Shiiku." See "Catch, The"

Shikasta (Lessing, D.) CLCII IV-1391; MPII:BCF IV-1533

"Shinel." See "Overcoat, The"

Shining, The (King, S.) CLCII IV-1393; MPII:AF IV-1407; MPII:JYAFic IV-1325

"Ship of Death, The" (Lawrence, D. H.) MPII:P V-1903

Ship of Fools (Porter, K.) MP X-5979; MP:AF III-1134

Ship of the Line. See Horatio Hornblower series, The

Shipyard, The (Onetti) CLCII IV-1394; MPII:AF IV-1411

Shirley (Brontë, C.) CLC II-1034; MP X-5985; MP:BF III-1427

Shkola dlia durakov. See School for Fools, A

"Shoemaker Arnold" (Lovelace) MPII:SS V-2080

Shoemaker's Holiday, The (Dekker) CLC II-1035; MP X-5988

"Short Friday" (Singer) MPII:SS V-2084

"Short Happy Life of Francis Macomber, The" (Hemingway) MPII:SS V-2088

Short Letter, Long Farewell (Handke) CLCII IV-1395; MPII:WF IV-1398

Short Stories of Toni Cade Bambara, The MPII:AfAm III-1349

Short Stories of John Cheever, The MP X-6011; MP:AF III-1141

Short Stories of A. E. Coppard, The MP X-5993; MP:BF III-1431

Short Stories of Henry Dumas, The MPII:AfAm III-1355

Short Stories of E. M. Forster, The MP X-5998; MP:BF III-1434

Short Stories of Ernest Hemingway, The MP X-6002; MP:AF III-1145

Short Stories of O. Henry, The MP X-6021; MP:AF III-1149

Short Stories of John Holman, The MPII:AfAm III-1361

Short Stories of Langston Hughes, The MPII:AfAm III-1366

Short Stories of D. H. Lawrence MP X-5995; MP:BF III-1439

Short Stories of James Alan McPherson, The MPII:AfAm III-1371

Short Stories of Katherine Mansfield, The MP X-6018; MP:BF III-1442

Short Stories of Flannery O'Connor, The MP X-6008; MP:AF III-1152

Short Stories of Saki, The MP X-6027; MP:BF III-1445

Short Stories of Peter Taylor MP X-6024; MP:AF III-1156

Short Stories of John Updike, The MP X-6014; MP:AF III-1160

Short Stories of Eudora Welty, The MP X-6005; MP:AF III-1164

Shosha (Singer) CLCII IV-1396; MPII:AF IV-1417; MPII:WF IV-1404

"Shot, The" (Pushkin) MPII:SS V-2093

"Shower of Gold" (Welty) MPII:SS V-2097

Shropshire Lad, A (Housman) MP X-6030

Shrouded Woman, The (Bombal) CLCII IV-1397; MPII:AF IV-1422

Shum vremeni. See Noise of Time, The

Shuttered Windows (Means) MPII:JYAFic IV-1328

Shuttlecock (Swift) CLCII IV-1398; MPII:BCF IV-1538

Siblings, The (Brown, R.) MPII:JYAFic IV-1331

Sibyl, The (Lagerkvist) CLCII IV-1399; MPII:WF IV-1409

Sibyllan. See Sibyl, The

"Sick Call, A (Callaghan) MPII:SS V-2101

"Sick Child, The" (Colette) MPII:SS V-2104

Sickness unto Death, The (Kierkegaard) MP X-6032

Siddhartha (Hesse) CLCII IV-1400; MPII:JYAFic IV-1334; MPII:WF IV-1414

Siege of Krishnapur, The (Farrell) CLCII IV-1401; MPII:BCF IV-1543

Siege of Rhodes, The (Davenant) CLC II-1036; MP X-6035

Siete locos, Los. See Seven Madmen, The

Sigismund (Gustafsson) CLCII IV-1403; MPII:WF IV-1419

Siglo de las luces, El. See Explosion in a Cathedral

Sign in Sidney Brustein's Window, The (Hansberry) CLCII IV-1404; MPII:AfAm III-1268; MPII:D IV-1458

Sign of Four, The (Doyle) CLC II-1037; MP X-6037; MP:BF III-1449

"Signature of All Things, The" (Rexroth) MPII:P V-1906

Signifying Monkey, The (Gates) MPII:AfAm III-1274

Silas Marner (Eliot, G.) CLC II-1038; MP X-6043; MP:BF III-1455

Silence (End) CLCII IV-1405; MPII:WF IV-1425

Silence over Dunkerque (Tunis) MPII:JYAFic IV-1337

Silences (Olsen) MPII:NF IV-1346

Silent Cry, The (e) CLCII IV-1407; MPII:WF IV-1431

Silent Don, The. See And Quiet Flows the Don and Don Flows Home to the Sea, The

"Silent Snow, Secret Snow" (Aiken, C.) MPII:SS V-2108

Silent Spring (Carson) MPII:NF IV-1351

Silent Woman, The (Jonson) CLC II-1039; MP X-6046

Silesian Tetralogy, The (Bienek) CLCII IV-1408; MPII:WF IV-1436

Silmarillion, The (Tolkien) CLCII IV-1410; MPII:BCF IV-1548

Silver Chair, The. See Chronicles of Narnia, The

Silver Crest, The (Chukovsky) MPII:JYABio IV-1565

"Silver Dish, A" (Bellow) MPII:SS V-2112

Silver Dove, The (Bely) CLCII IV-1413; MPII:WF IV-1442

"Silver Mine, The" (Lagerlöf) MPII:SS V-2116

Silver on the Tree. See Dark Is Rising sequence, The

Silver Tassie, The (O'Casey) CLCII IV-1413; MPII:D IV-1465

Simple Gifts (Greenberg) MPII:JYAFic IV-1341

"Simple Heart, A" (Flaubert) MPII:SS V-2120

Simple Honorable Man, A (Richter, C.) MP X-6050; MP:AF III-1168

Simple Story, A (Agnon) CLCII IV-1415; MPII:WF IV-1448

Simplicissimus the Vagabond (Grimmelshausen) CLC II-1040; MP X-6053; MP:EF III-1155

"Since brass, nor stone, nor earth, nor boundless sea," See Sonnet 65

Singapore Grip, The (Farrell) CLCII IV-1416; MPII:BCF IV-1558

Singer of Tales, The (Lord, A.) MPII:NF IV-1356

Singin' and Swingin' and Gettin' Merry Like Christmas (Angelou) MPII:JYABio IV-1569

Sipur pashut. See Simple Story, A

Sir Charles Grandison (Richardson, S.) CLC II-1041; MP X-6056; MP:BF III-1459

Sir Gawain and the Green Knight (Unknown) CLC II-1042; MP X-6060

Sir John van Olden Barnavelt (Fletcher and Massinger) CLC II-1042; MP X-6063

Sir Roger de Coverley Papers, The (Addison, Budgell, and Steele, R.) CLC II-1044; MP X-6067

"Siren" (Okigbo) MPII:P V-1909

"Siren Limits." See "Siren"

Sirens of Titan, The (Vonnegut) CLCII IV-1418; MPII:AF IV-1427

Sistema periodico, Il. See Periodic Table, The

Sister (Greenfield) MPII:JYAFic IV-1344

Sister Carrie (Dreiser) CLC II-1045; MP X-6070; MP:AF III-1171

Sister Mary Ignatius Explains It All for You (Durang) CLCII IV-1419; MPII:D IV-1471

Sister Philomène (Goncourt and Goncourt) CLC II-1046; MP X-6075; MP:EF III-1159

"Sisters, The" (Joyce) MPII:SS V-2124

Sitting Bull: War Chief of the Sioux (O'Connor, R.) MPII:JYABio IV-1577

Sitting Bull: Champion of the Sioux (Vestal) MPII:JYABio IV-1573

Six Characters in Search of an Author (Pirandello) CLC II-1047; MP X-6079

6,810,000 Litres d'eau par seconde. See Niagara

62: A Model Kit (Cortázar) CLCII IV-1420; MPII:AF IV-1433

Skaters, The (Ashbery) MPII:P V-1912

Skates of Uncle Richard, The (Fenner) MPII:JYAFic IV-1347

Skeleton Man, The (Bennett, Jay) MPII:JYAFic IV-1350

"Sketch for an Aesthetic Project" (Wright, Jay) MPII:P V-1915

Sketchbook, 1946-1949, and Sketchbook, 1966-1971 (Frisch) MPII:NF IV-1361

Skin of Our Teeth, The (Wilder, T.) CLC II-1048; MP X-6084

"Skunk Hour" (Lowell, R.) MPII:P V-1918

"Skverny anekdot." See "Nasty Story, A"

"Sky Is Gray, The" (Gaines) MPII:SS V-2128

"Skylepy cynamanowe." See "Cinnamon Shops"

"Slate Ode, The" (Mandelstam, O.) MPII:P V-1921

Slaughterhouse-Five (Vonnegut) CLCII IV-1421; MPII:AF IV-1438

Slave, The (Singer) CLCII IV-1422; MPII:AF IV-1443; MPII:WF IV-1453

Slave Dancer, The (Fox) MPII:JYAFic IV-1354

Slavery and Social Death (Patterson, O.) MPII:AfAm III-1279

ledztwo. See Investigation, The

Sleep-Chasings. See Sleepers, The

Sleep of Reason, The. See Strangers and Brothers

"Sleepers, The" (Whitman) MPII:P V-1924

Sleepless Days (Becker) CLCII IV-1423; MPII:WF IV-1458

Sleepwalkers, The (Broch) CLC II-1049; MP X-6089; MP:EF III-1164

Sleepy Hollow. *See* Legend of Sleepy Hollow, The

Sleuth (Shaffer, A.) CLCII IV-1424; MPII:D IV-1477

"Slide Area, The" (Lambert) MPII:SS V-2132

Slinger. *See* Gunslinger

Slipknot, The (Plautus) CLC II-1050; MP X-6094

Slouching Towards Bethlehem (Didion) MPII:NF IV-1366

Slow Approach of Thunder. *See* Story of a Life, The

Slow Homecoming (Handke) CLCII IV-1425; MPII:WF IV-1462

Ślub. *See* Marriage, The

Small Changes (Piercy) CLCII IV-1426; MPII:AF IV-1448

"Small, Good Thing, A" (Carver) MPII:SS V-2135

Small House at Allington, The (Trollope) CLC II-1050; MP X-6097; MP:BF III-1463

Small Is Beautiful (Schumacher) MPII:NF IV-1372

Small Room, The (Sarton) CLCII IV-1427; MPII:AF IV-1454

Small Souls (Couperus) CLC II-1052; MP X-6101; MP:EF III-1170

Small World (Lodge) CLCII IV-1429; MPII:BCF IV-1563

"Smallest Woman in the World, The" (Lispector) MPII:SS V-2138

"Smell of Cordwood, A" (Neruda) MPII:P V-1927

"Smell of Death and Flowers, The" (Gordimer) MPII:SS V-2142

"Smert Ivana Ilicha." *See* "Death of Ivan Ilyich, The"

"Smiles of Konarak, The" (Dennison) MPII:SS V-2146

Smiley's People (le Carré) CLCII II-694; MPII:BCF IV-1710

Smoke (Turgenev) CLC II-1053; MP X-6105; MP:EF III-1174

Smoky, the Cowhorse (James, Will) MPII:JYAFic IV-1357

Snail on the Slope, The (Strugatsky *and* Strugatsky) CLCII IV-1430; MPII:WF IV-1469

Snake, The (Dickenson). *See* narrow Fellow in the Grass, A

"Snake" (Lawrence, D. H.) MPII:P V-1930

"Snake Charmer, The" (Shalamov) MPII:SS V-2150

Snake Pit, The (Undset) CLC II-1055; MP X-6109; MP:EF III-1178

"Snapshots of a Daughter-in-Law" (Rich) MPII:P V-1934

"Sniper, The" (O'Flaherty) MPII:SS V-2154

"Sniper, The" (Sillitoe) MPII:SS V-2158

Snooty Baronet (Lewis, W.) CLCII IV-1432; MPII:BCF IV-1567

Snopes trilogy, The. *See* Hamlet, The; Mansion, The; *and* Town, The

Snow-Bound (Whittier) CLC II-1056; MP X-6113

Snow Country (Kawabata) CLCII IV-1433; MPII:WF IV-1475

Snow Leopard, The (Matthiessen) MPII:NF IV-1378

"Snow-Storm, The" (Tolstoy) MPII:SS V-2163

Snow Was Black, The (Simenon) CLCII IV-1434; MPII:WF IV-1481

"Snowstorm, The" (Tsvetayeva) MPII:P V-1938

So Big (Ferber) MP X-6115; MP:AF III-1176

So ran ich aus dem Wort. *See* Thus I Ran Out of the Word

So Red the Rose (Young, S.) CLC II-1056; MP X-6118; MP:AF III-1180

So the Wind Won't Blow It All Away (Brautigan) MPII:JYAFic IV-1360

Sobache serdtse. *See* Heart of a Dog, The

Sobre héroes y tumbas. *See* On Heroes and Tombs

Society and Solitude (Emerson) MP X-6122

Society of Mind, The (Minsky) MPII:NF IV-1383

Sohrab and Rustum (Arnold, M.) CLC II-1057; MP X-6125

Soil, The. *See* Earth

Solaris (Lem) CLCII IV-1435; MPII:WF IV-1486

"Soldier, The" (Brooke) MPII:P V-1941

Soldier Doctor (Judson) MPII:JYABio IV-1581

Soldier's Art, The. *See* Dance to the Music of Time, A

"Soldier's Embrace, A" (Gordimer) MPII:SS V-2166

Soldier's Fortune, The (Otway) CLC II-1057; MP X-6128

"Soldier's Home" (Hemingway) MPII:SS V-2170

Soldiers' Pay (Faulkner) CLCII IV-1437; MPII:AF IV-1459

Soldier's Play, A (Fuller, C.) MPII:AfAm III-1283

Soledad Brother (Jackson, G.) MPII:AfAm III-1288

Solid Mandala, The (White) CLCII IV-1438; MPII:BCF IV-1572

Solo (Morris) MPII:NF IV-1696

Soma tou kaloukariou. *See* Body of Summer

Some Americans (Tomlinson) MPII:NF IV-1388

Some Dissenting Voices (Weinberg *and* Weinberg) MPII:JYABio IV-1585

Some Do Not. *See* Parade's End

"Some glory in their birth, some in their skill," *See* Sonnet 91

"Some Like Them Cold" (Lardner) MPII:SS V-2173

"Some of Us Had Been Threatening Our Friend Colby" (Barthelme, D.) MPII:SS V-2177

Some People (Nicolson) MP X-6132

Some Prefer Nettles (Tanizaki) CLCII IV-1439; MPII:WF IV-1491

Some Soul to Keep (Cooper, J. F.) MPII:AfAm III-1294

Somebody's Angel Child (Moore, C.) MPII:JYABio IV-1589

Something Happened (Heller) CLCII IV-1440; MPII:AF IV-1465

"Something Out There" (Gordimer) MPII:SS V-2182

Something Wicked This Way Comes (Bradbury, R.) CLCII IV-1441; MPII:AF IV-1471

Sometimes a Great Notion (Kesey) CLCII IV-1442; MPII:AF IV-1476

"Somewhere I have never travelled,gladly beyond" (Cummings) MPII:P V-1944

Sommersi e i salvati, I. *See* Drowned and the Saved, The

"Somnambule Ballad" (García Lorca) MPII:P V-1947

Son Avenger, The (Undset) CLC II-1058; MP X-6134; MP:EF III-1182

Son of Man (Roa Bastos) CLCII IV-1444; MPII:AF IV-1481

Son of the Middle Border, A (Garland) MP X-6138

Son of the Revolution (Heng *and* Shapiro) MPII:JYABio IV-1593

"Son smeshnogo cheloveka." *See* "Dream of a Ridiculous Man, The"

Sonezaki Shinjû (Chikamatsu Monzaemon) CLC II-1059; MP XI-6141

"Song: To Celia" (Jonson) MPII:P V-1950

"Song for St. Cecilia's Day, A" (Dryden) MPII:P V-1953

Song of a Goat (Clark) CLCII IV-1444; MPII:D IV-1483

Song of Bernadette, The (Werfel) CLC II-1060; MP XI-6144; MP:EF III-1186

Song of Hiawatha, The (Longfellow) CLC II-1060; MP XI-6147

"Song of Myself" (Whitman) MPII:P V-1957

Song of Roland, The (Unknown) CLC II-1061; MP XI-6150; MP:EF III-1190

Song of Solomon (Morrison) CLCII IV-1445; MPII:AF IV-1485; MPII:AfAm III-1299

Song of Songs, The (Sudermann) CLC II-1063; MP XI-6156; MP:EF III-1197

"Song of the Happy Shepherd, The" (Yeats) MPII:P V-1961

Song of the Lark, The (Cather) CLC II-1064; MP XI-6159; MP:AF III-1184

"Song of the Poorly Loved, The" (Apollinaire) MPII:P V-1965

Song of the World, The (Giono) CLC II-1067; MP XI-6163; MP:EF III-1201

"Song on the End of the World, A" (Miłosz) MPII:P V-1969

Sonim de Geshichte fun a Liebe. *See* Enemies

"Sonnet 1" (Browning, E.) MPII:P V-1972

"Sonnet 6" (Browning, E.) MPII:P V-1975

"Sonnet 7" (Browning, E.) MPII:P V-1978

"Sonnet 14" (Browning, E.) MPII:P V-1981
"Sonnet 35" (Browning, E.) MPII:P V-1984
"Sonnet 43" (Browning, E.) MPII:P V-1987
"Sonnet XXVII" (Neruda) MPII:P V-1990
"Sonnet 18" (Shakespeare) MPII:P V-1993
"Sonnet 19" (Shakespeare) MPII:P V-1996
"Sonnet 30" (Shakespeare) MPII:P V-1999
"Sonnet 60" (Shakespeare) MPII:P V-2002
"Sonnet 65" (Shakespeare) MPII:P V-2005
"Sonnet 73" (Shakespeare) MPII:P V-2008
"Sonnet 76" (Shakespeare) MPII:P V-2011
"Sonnet 87" (Shakespeare) MPII:P V-2014
"Sonnet 91" (Shakespeare) MPII:P V-2017
"Sonnet 94" (Shakespeare) MPII:P V-2020
"Sonnet 106" (Shakespeare) MPII:P V-2023
"Sonnet 116" (Shakespeare) MPII:P V-2026
"Sonnet 129" (Shakespeare) MPII:P V-2029
"Sonnet 130" (Shakespeare) MPII:P V-2032
Sonnets from the Portuguese (Browning, E.)
    MP XI-6168
Sonnets of Shakespeare, The (Shakespeare)
    MP XI-6170
Sonnets to Orpheus (Rilke) MP XI-6175
"Sonny's Blues" (Baldwin) MPII:SS V-2186
Sons and Lovers (Lawrence, D. H.) CLC
    II-1067; MP XI-6177; MP:BF III-1468
Sophie's Choice (Styron) CLCII IV-1446;
    MPII:AF IV-1492
Sordello (Browning, R.) MPII:P V-2035
"Sorrow-Acre" (Dinesen) MPII:SS V-2190
Sorrow Beyond Dreams, A (Handke) CLCII
    IV-1448; MPII:WF IV-1496
Sorrows of Werther, The. See Sorrows of
    Young Werther, The
Sorrows of Young Werther, The (Goethe)
    CLC II-1069; MP XI-6182; MP:EF
    III-1206
Sort of Life, A (Greene) MPII:NF IV-1393
"Sorting, wrapping, packing, stuffing"
    (Schuyler) MPII:P V-2040
Sot-Weed Factor, The (Barth) MP XI-6190;
    MP:AF III-1188
Sotileza (Pereda) CLC II-1070; MP
    XI-6186; MP:EF III-1211
Soul Brothers and Sister Lou, The (Hunter,
    K.) MPII:JYAFic IV-1364
Soul on Ice (Cleaver) MPII:AfAm III-1305;
    MPII:JYABio IV-1597
Soulier de satin, Le. See Satin Slipper, The

Souls and Bodies (Lodge) CLCII IV-1448;
    MPII:BCF IV-1577
Souls of Black Folk, The (Du Bois)
    MPII:AfAm III-1309
Sound and the Fury, The (Faulkner) CLC
    II-1070; MP XI-6194; MP:AF III-1193
"Sound of Silver, The." See "Black Prince,
    The"
Sound of the Mountain, The (Kawabata)
    CLCII IV-1450; MPII:WF IV-1501
Sound of Waves, The (Mishima) MP
    XI-6199; MP:EF III-1215
Sound-Shadows of the New World (Mehta)
    MPII:NF IV-1398
Sounder (Armstrong, W.) MPII:JYAFic
    IV-1367
Sour Sweet (Mo) CLCII IV-1451;
    MPII:BCF IV-1581
Source, The (Michener) CLCII IV-1452;
    MPII:AF IV-1498
Sous le soleil de Satan. See Under the Sun
    of Satan
"South, The" (Borges) MPII:SS V-2194
South Goes North, The. See Children of
    Crisis
South Wind (Douglas, N.) CLC II-1072;
    MP XI-6202; MP:BF III-1473
Southern Adventure. See Story of a Life,
    The
"Southern Thruway, The" (Cortázar)
    MPII:SS V-2198
Southpaw, The (Harris, M.) CLCII
    IV-1455; MPII:AF IV-1505
Sovereignty of Good, The (Murdoch)
    MPII:NF IV-1402
Space, Time, and Architecture (Giedion)
    MPII:NF IV-1408
Space Trilogy, The (Lewis, C. S.) CLCII
    IV-1456; MPII:BCF IV-1588
Spanish Bawd, The. See Celestina
Spanish Friar, The (Dryden) CLC II-1073;
    MP XI-6205
Spanish Gipsy, The (Ford, Middleton, and
    Rowley) CLC II-1074; MP XI-6208
Spanish Rogue, The. See Guzmán de
    Alfarache
Spanish Tragedy, The (Kyd) CLC II-1076;
    MP XI-6211
"Sparrow Hills" (Pasternak) MPII:P V-2043

"Spaziergang, Der." *See* "Walk, The"

Speak, Memory (Nabokov) MPII:NF IV-1414

Specimen Days (Whitman) MP XI-6216

Speculations About Jakob (Johnson, U.) MP XI-6219; MP:EF III-1218

Speeches of Malcolm X, The (Malcolm X) MPII:AfAm III-1320

Speeches of Martin Luther King, Jr., The (King, M.) MPII:AfAm III-1314

Speed-the-Plow (Mamet) CLCII IV-1458; MPII:D IV-1486

Speedboat (Adler) CLCII IV-1459; MPII:AF IV-1511

Spell, The (Broch) CLCII IV-1460; MPII:WF IV-1506

Speranza (Delblanc) CLCII IV-1461; MPII:WF IV-1510

"Spinoza of Market Street, The" (Singer) MPII:SS V-2202

Spire, The (Golding) CLCII IV-1462; MPII:BCF IV-1593

Spirit of St. Louis, The (Lindbergh) MPII:JYABio IV-1600

"Spirit of the Age, The" (Hölderlin) MPII:P V-2046

Spirit of the Laws, The (Montesquieu) MP XI-6222

Splendeurs et misères des courtisanes. *See* Splendors and Miseries of Courtesans, The

Splendors and Miseries of Courtesans, The (Balzac) CLCII IV-1463; MPII:WF IV-1516

"Split Cherry Tree" (Stuart) MPII:SS V-2206

Spoilers, The (Beach) CLC II-1077; MP XI-6225; MP:AF III-1198

Spoils of Poynton, The (James, H.) CLC II-1078; MP XI-6228; MP:AF III-1202

Spoilt City, The. *See* Balkan trilogy, The

Spokoinoi nochi (Sinyavsky) MPII:WF IV-1524. *See also* Goodnight!

Spöksonaten. *See* Ghost Sonata, The

Spook Who Sat by the Door, The (Greenlee) MPII:AfAm III-1326

Spoon River Anthology (Masters) MP XI-6233; MPII:P V-2050

Sport of the Gods, The (Dunbar) CLCII IV-1465; MPII:AF IV-1516; MPII:AfAm III-1332

Sporting Club, The (McGuane) CLCII IV-1466; MPII:AF IV-1521

"Spotted Horses" (Faulkner) MPII:SS V-2210

Sprig of Broom, The. *See* Mantlemass series, The

Sprightly Running (Wain) MPII:NF IV-1421

Spring Floods. *See* Torrents of Spring, The (Turgenev)

"Spring Rain" (Pasternak) MPII:P V-2056

Spring Snow. *See* Sea of Fertility, The

"Spring Victory" (Stuart) MPII:SS V-2214

Spunkwater, Spunkwater! (Wood, J.) MPII:JYABio IV-1603

Spy, The (Cooper, J. F.) CLC II-1079; MP XI-6236; MP:AF III-1208

Spy in the House of Love, A (Nin) CLCII IV-1468; MPII:AF IV-1527

Spy Who Came in from the Cold, The (le Carré) CLCII IV-1469; MPII:BCF IV-1599

Spyglass Tree, The (Murray, A.) MPII:AfAm III-1337

"Sredni Vashtar" (Saki) MPII:SS V-2217

Sta ereipia archaiou naou. *See* In the Ruins of an Ancient Temple

Stand, The (King, S.) CLCII IV-1470; MPII:AF IV-1532

Stanley and the Women (Amis) CLCII IV-1472; MPII:BCF IV-1604

"Stantsionnyi smotritel." *See* "Station-master, The"

"Stanzas from the Grande Chartreuse" (Arnold, M.) MPII:P V-2059

Star of Satan, The. *See* Under the Sun of Satan

Star of Seville, The (Unknown) CLC II-1079; MP XI-6242

Starik. *See* Old Man, The

Staring at the Sun (Barnes, J.) CLCII IV-1472; MPII:BCF IV-1609

"Starosvetskiye pomeshchiki." *See* "Old-World Landowners"

Starry Ticket, A. *See* Ticket to the Stars, A

Stars in My Pocket Like Grains of Sand (Delany, S.) MPII:AfAm III-1343

Start in Life, A. *See* Debut, The

Starting Out in the Thirties (Kazin) MPII:NF IV-1427

State Fair (Stong) CLC II-1080; MP XI-6246; MP:AF III-1215

"Station Island" (Heaney) MPII:P V-2062

"Station-master, The" (Pushkin) MPII:SS V-2220

"Steel Flea, The." *See* "Lefty"

"Steeple-Jack, The" (Moore, M.) MPII:P V-2066

Steffie Can't Come Out to Play (Arrick) MPII:JYAFic IV-1370

Stellvertreter, Der. *See* Deputy, The

Step. *See* Steppe, The

"Steppe, The" (Chekhov) CLCII IV-1474; MPII:SS V-2224

Steppenwolf (Hesse) CLC II-1081; MP XI-6250; MP:EF III-1221

Sterna, E. *See* Cistern, The

"Stick of Green Candy, A" (Bowles, J.) MPII:SS V-2228

Stikhi o neizvestnom soldate. *See* Verses on the Unknown Soldier

"Still, Citizen Sparrow" (Wilbur) MPII:P V-2069

"Still to be Neat" (Jonson) MPII:P V-2072

Stiller. *See* I'm Not Stiller

Stoic, The (Dreiser) CLC II-1081; MP XI-6255; MP:AF III-1219

Stone Angel, The (Laurence) CLCII IV-1475; MPII:BCF IV-1614

"Stone Boy, The" (Berriault) MPII:SS V-2232

Stone Desert (Wast) CLC II-1082; MP XI-6259; MP:AF III-1223

Stones Cry Out, The (Szymusiak) MPII:JYABio IV-1607

Stones of Green Knowe, The. *See* Green Knowe books, The

Stones of Venice, The (Ruskin) MP XI-6262

Stonewall (Fritz) MPII:JYABio IV-1610

Stop-Time (Conroy) MPII:NF IV-1432

Stopfkuchen. *See* Tubby Schaumann

"Stopping by Woods on a Snowy Evening" (Frost) MPII:P V-2075

Storia, La. *See* History

"Storm, The" (Chopin) MPII:SS V-2235

Stormy Weather (Strindberg) CLCII IV-1476; MPII:D IV-1491

"Story by Maupassant, A" (O'Connor, Frank) MPII:SS V-2238

Story Catcher, The (Sandoz) MPII:JYAFic IV-1373

Story-Lives of Great Composers (Bakeless) MPII:JYABio IV-1614

Story of a Bad Boy, The (Aldrich) CLC II-1082; MP XI-6265; MP:AF III-1227; MPII:JYAFic IV-1376

Story of a Country Town, The (Howe) CLC II-1083; MP XI-6268; MP:AF III-1231

Story of a Life, The (Paustovsky) MPII:NF IV-1437

Story of an African Farm, The (Schreiner) CLC II-1084; MP XI-6272; MP:EF III-1227

"Story of an Hour, The" (Chopin) MPII:SS V-2241

Story of Burnt Njal, The (Unknown) CLC II-1085; MP XI-6276; MP:EF III-1231

Story of George Gershwin, The (Ewen) MPII:JYABio IV-1618

Story of Gösta Berling, The (Lagerlöf) CLC II-1087; MP XI-6281; MP:EF III-1236

Story of Manon Lescaut and the Chevalier des Grieux. *See* Manon Lescaut

Story of My Boyhood and Youth, The (Muir) MP XI-6286

"Story of My Dovecot, The" (Babel) MPII:SS V-2244

Story of My Life, The (Keller) MPII:JYABio IV-1622

Story of Phillis Wheatley, The (Graham, S.) MPII:JYABio IV-1626

"Story of Serapion, The" (Hoffmann) MPII:SS V-2248

Story of the Guitar (Kao Tse-ch'eng) CLC II-1088; MP XI-6288

Story of the Trapp Family Singers, The (Trapp) MPII:JYABio IV-1630

Story of the Treasure Seekers, The (Nesbit) MPII:JYAFic IV-1379

Story Teller's Story, A (Anderson, S.) MP XI-6291

Storyteller, The (Benjamin) MPII:NF IV-1447

Storyteller (Silko) MPII:NF IV-1442

Stowaway to the Mushroom Planet. *See* Mushroom Planet series, The

Strait Is the Gate (Gide) CLCII IV-1477; MPII:WF IV-1529

Strange Case of Dr. Jekyll and Mr. Hyde.
See Dr. Jekyll and Mr. Hyde

"Strange Fits of Passion Have I Known"
(Wordsworth) MPII:P V-2078

Strange Interlude (O'Neill) CLC II-1089;
MP XI-6294

"Strange Meeting" (Owen) MPII:P V-2081

"Strange Ride of Morrowbie Jukes, The"
(Kipling) MPII:SS V-2252

Strange Stories from a Chinese Studio (P'u
Sung-ling) MP XI-6299; MP:EF III-1241

Stranger, The (Camus) MP XI-6301;
MP:EF III-1244

Stranger at Green Knowe, A. *See* Green
Knowe books, The

Stranger in a Strange Land (Heinlein)
CLCII IV-1478; MPII:AF IV-1536;
MPII:JYAFic IV-1382

Strangers All Are Gone, The. *See* To Keep
the Ball Rolling

Strangers and Brothers (Snow) CLCII
IV-1480; MPII:BCF IV-1619. *See also*
Affair, The; Conscience of the Rich,
The; Corridors of Power; George
Passant; Homecomings; Last Things;
Light and the Dark, The; Masters, The;
New Men, The; Sleep of Reason, The;
and Time of Hope

Strawberry Girl (Lenski) MPII:JYAFic
IV-1385

Streak of Luck, A (Conot) MPII:JYABio
IV-1633

Streamers (Rabe, D.) CLCII IV-1483;
MPII:D IV-1496

Street, The (Petry) MPII:AfAm III-1375

"Street of Crocodiles, The" (Schulz)
MPII:SS V-2256

Street Rod (Felsen) MPII:JYAFic IV-1388

Street Scene (Rice, Elmer) CLC II-1090;
MP XI-6304

Streetcar Named Desire, A (Williams, T.)
MP XI-6308

Strife (Galsworthy) CLC II-1091; MP
XI-6311

Strike the Father Dead (Wain) CLCII
IV-1484; MPII:BCF IV-1633

"Strong Horse Tea" (Walker) MPII:SS
V-2259

Strong Wind (Asturias) CLCII IV-1485;
MPII:AF IV-1541

Structure of Scientific Revolution, The
(Kuhn) MPII:NF IV-1452

Studies in Classic American Literature
(Lawrence, D. H.) MP XI-6314

Studies on Hysteria (Breuer *and* Freud) MP
XI-6317

Studs Lonigan (Farrell) CLC II-1091; MP
XI-6320; MP:AF III-1235; MPII:JYAFic
IV-1392

Study in Scarlet, A (Doyle) CLC II-1092;
MP XI-6322; MP:BF III-1477

Study of History, A (Toynbee) MP XI-6326

"Stumble Between Two Stars" (Vallejo)
MPII:P V-2084

Stunde der wahren Empfindung, Die. *See*
Moment of True Feeling, A

"Sturgeon, The" (Carver) MPII:P V-2087

Subject Was Roses, The (Gilroy) CLCII
IV-1486; MPII:D IV-1503

Such Is My Beloved (Callaghan) CLCII
IV-1487; MPII:BCF IV-1638

Suddenly Last Summer (Williams, T.)
CLCII IV-1488; MPII:D IV-1508

Suder (Everett) MPII:AfAm III-1381

Sugar Cane Cycle, The. *See* Plantation Boy

"Suicide Club, The" (Stevenson) MPII:SS
V-2262

Suicide's Wife, The (Madden) CLCII
IV-1489; MPII:AF IV-1545

Sula (Morrison) CLCII IV-1490; MPII:AF
IV-1550; MPII:AfAm III-1386;
MPII:JYAFic IV-1396

Summa Theologica (Aquinas) MP XI-6329

Summer and Smoke (Williams, T.) CLCII
IV-1492; MPII:D IV-1514

Summer Birds, The (Farmer) MPII:JYAFic
IV-1399

"Summer Evening" (Boyle, K.) MPII:SS
V-2267

"Summer Night, A" (Auden) MPII:P
V-2090

"Summer Night" (Bowen, E.) MPII:SS
V-2271

"Summer Night" (Harjo) MPII:P V-2093

Summer Night 1933, A. *See* Summer Night,
A

Summer of My German Soldier (Greene, B.) MPII:JYAFic IV-1403

"Summer of the Beautiful White Horse, The" (Saroyan) MPII:SS V-2275

Summer of the Great-Grandmother, The (L'Engle) MPII:JYABio IV-1637

Summer of the Seventeenth Doll (Lawler) CLCII IV-1493; MPII:D IV-1520

Summer of the Swans, The (Byars) MPII:JYAFic IV-1406

"Summer Oracle" (Lorde) MPII:P V-2096

Summing Up, The (Maugham) MP XI-6332

"Sun" (Lawrence) MPII:SS V-2278

Sun Also Rises, The (Hemingway) CLC II-1093; MP XI-6335; MP:AF III-1238

Sun and Steel (Mishima) MPII:NF IV-1457

"Sun Rising, The" (Donne) MPII:P V-2099

Sun Stone (Paz) MPII:P V-2102

Sun Yat-sen (Spencer) MPII:JYABio IV-1641

Suna no onna. See Woman in the Dunes, The

"Sunday Morning" (Stevens, W.) MPII:P V-2106

Sunday of Life, The (Queneau) CLCII IV-1494; MPII:WF IV-1533

Sunken Bell, The (Hauptmann) CLC II-1094; MP XI-6341

Sunlight Dialogues, The (Gardner) CLCII IV-1495; MPII:AF IV-1555

Sunset and Evening Star. See Mirror in My House

Sunset Song. See Scots Quair, A

Sunshine (Klein, N.) MPII:JYAFic IV-1410

"Supermarket in California, A" (Ginsberg) MPII:P V-2109

"Supper at Elsinore, The" (Dinesen) MPII:SS V-2281

Suppliants, The (Aeschylus) CLC II-1094; MP XI-6345

Suppliants, The (Euripides) CLC II-1096; MP XI-6349

Suppositi, I (Ariosto) CLC II-1097; MP XI-6352

"Supremacy of the Hunza, The" (Greenberg) MPII:SS V-2285

"Sur, El." See "South, The"

"Sur" (Le Guin) MPII:SS V-2288

Sure Hands, Strong Heart (Patterson, L.) MPII:JYABio IV-1645

Surfacing (Atwood) CLCII IV-1498; MPII:BCF IV-1643

Surprised by Joy (Lewis, C. S.) MPII:NF IV-1462

Surry of Eagle's-Nest (Cooke, J.) CLC II-1097; MP XI-6355; MP:AF III-1244

Sursis, Le. See Roads to Freedom, The

Sursis pour l'orchestre. See Playing for Time.

Survival in Auschwitz. See If This Is a Man

Survivor, The (Keneally) CLCII IV-1499; MPII:BCF IV-1649

Susan B. Anthony (Noble) MPII:JYABio IV-1649

Susette La Fleschc (Crary) MPII:JYABio IV-1652

Sutter's Gold (Cendrars) CLCII IV-1500; MPII:WF IV-1538

Suttree (McCarthy, C.) CLCII IV-1501; MPII:AF IV-1559

Swallow Barn (Kennedy, J. P.) CLC II-1098; MP XI-6359; MP:AF III-1248

Swamp Angel (Wilson, E.) CLCII IV-1503; MPII:BCF IV-1654

Swallows and Amazons (Ransome) MPII:JYAFic IV-1413

Swan Villa, The (Walser) CLCII IV-1504; MPII:WF IV-1542

Swarm in May, A (Mayne) MPII:JYAFic IV-1417

"Sweat" (Hurston) MPII:SS V-2293

"Sweeney Among the Nightingales" (Eliot, T. S.) MPII:P V-2112

Sweet Bird of Youth (Williams, T.) CLCII IV-1505; MPII:D IV-1524

Sweet Dove Died, The (Pym) CLCII IV-1507; MPII:BCF IV-1659

Sweet-Vendor, The. See Vendor of Sweets, The

Sweet Whispers, Brother Rush (Hamilton) MPII:AfAm III-1392; MPII:JYAFic IV-1421

Swiftly Tilting Planet, A (L'Engle) MPII:JYAFic IV-1424

Swiftwater (Annixter) MPII:JYAFic IV-1427

T

"Tables of the Law, The" (Yeats) MPII:SS
V-2300

"Tables Turned, The" (Wordsworth)
MPII:P V-2117

Tade kuu mushi. *See* Some Prefer Nettles

Tagebuch, 1946-1949, *and* Tagebuch,
1966-1971. *See* Sketchbook, 1946-1949,
and Sketchbook, 1966-1971

Tagebücher von Paul Klee. *See* Diaries of
Paul Klee, The

Taiyō to tetsu. *See* Sun and Steel

Take a Girl Like You (Amis) CLCII
IV-1511; MPII:BCF IV-1671

Takeover, The (Spark) CLCII IV-1513;
MPII:BCF IV-1677

Taking of Miss Janie, The (Bullins)
MPII:AfAm III-1404

Tale of a Tub, A (Swift) MP XI-6366;
MP:BF III-1481

Tale of Beatrix Potter, The (Lane)
MPII:JYABio IV-1656

Tale of Genji, The (Murasaki Shikibu) CLC
II-1100; MP XI-6369; MP:EF III-1252

"Tale of the Squint-eyed Left-handed
Gunsmith from Tula and the Steel Flea,
The." *See* "Lefty"

Tale of Two Cities, A (Dickens) CLC
II-1100; MP XI-6373; MP:BF III-1485

Tales of Arabian Nights, The. *See* Arabian
Nights' Entertainments, The

Tales of Ise (Arihara no Narihira) MP
XI-6378; MP:EF III-1257

Tales of Jacob, The. *See* Joseph and His
Brothers

Tales of Soldiers and Civilians (Bierce) MP
XI-6381; MP:AF III-1252

Tales of Uncle Remus (Harris, J. C.) MP
XI-6384; MP:AF III-1256

Tali' al-shajarah, Ya. *See* Tree Climber, The

Talisman, The (Scott, Sir W.) CLC II-1102;
MP XI-6387; MP:BF III-1490

Talley's Folly (Wilson, L.) CLCII IV-1514;
MPII:D IV-1529

Tamar (Jeffers) CLC II-1103; MP XI-6393

Tamburlaine the Great (Marlowe) CLC
II-1104; MP XI-6396

Taming of the Shrew, The (Shakespeare)
CLC II-1106; MP XI-6401

Tango (Mroek) CLCII IV-1515; MPII:D
IV-1534

Taps for Private Tussie (Stuart) CLC
II-1107; MP XI-6405; MP:AF III-1259

"Taqsm al-layl wa-al-nahr." *See* Mudun
al-milh

"Tar" (Williams, C. K.) MPII:P V-2120

Tar Baby (Morrison) MPII:AfAm III-1407

Taran Wanderer. *See* Prydain chronicles,
The

Taras Bulba (Gogol) CLC II-1108; MP
XI-6408; MP:EF III-1260

Tarka the Otter (Williamson) MP XI-6411;
MP:BF III-1497

Tarr (Lewis, W.) CLC II-1109; MP
XI-6413; MP:BF III-1500

Tartar Steppe, The (Buzzati) CLCII
IV-1516; MPII:WF IV-1548

Tartarin of Tarascon (Daudet) CLC II-1110;
MP XI-6417; MP:EF III-1264

Tartuffe (Molière) CLC II-1111; MP
XI-6421

Tarzan of the Apes (Burroughs, E.)
MPII:JYAFic IV-1433

Task, The (Cowper) MP XI-6425

Taste of Honey, A (Delaney) CLCII
IV-1517; MPII:D IV-1538

"Tatuana's Tale" (Asturias) MPII:SS
V-2305

Tauben, die draussen blieb. *See* Dove, That
Stayed Outside

Tea and Sympathy (Anderson, R.) CLCII
IV-1518; MPII:D IV-1543

Teachings of Don Juan, The (Castaneda)
MPII:NF IV-1468

Teacup Full of Roses (Mathis)
MPII:JYAFic IV-1437

Teahouse of the August Moon, The
(Patrick) CLCII IV-1519; MPII:D
IV-1548

"Tears, Idle Tears" (Tennyson) MPII:P
V-2123

Technical Difficulties (Jordan, J.)
MPII:AfAm III-1412

Technique, La. *See* Technological Society, The

Technological Society, The (Ellul) MPII:NF IV-1473

Tecumseh and the Quest for Indian Leadership (Edmunds) MPII:JYABio IV-1660

Teens (Mack) MPII:JYAFic IV-1440

"Teeth Mother Naked at Last, The" (Bly) MPII:P V-2126

Tehanu. *See* Earthsea series, The

Telegraph, The. *See* Lucien Leuwen

"Tell Me a Riddle" (Olsen) MPII:SS V-2308

Tell Me That You Love Me, Junie Moon (Kellogg) CLCII IV-1520; MPII:AF IV-1568

"Tell-Tale Heart, The" (Poe) MPII:SS V-2312

"Tema del traidor y del héroe." *See* "Theme of the Traitor and the Hero"

Tempest, The (Shakespeare) CLC II-1112; MP XI-6427

Temple, The (Herbert, G.) MP XI-6432

Temple Beau, The (Fielding) CLC II-1113; MP XI-6435

Temple of Dawn, The. *See* Sea of Fertility, The

Temple of the Golden Pavilion, The (Mishima) CLCII IV-1522; MPII:WF IV-1554

Temporary Kings. *See* Dance to the Music of Time, A

Temptation (Havel) CLCII IV-1523; MPII:D IV-1554

Temptation of Saint Anthony, The (Flaubert) CLC II-1114; MP XI-6438; MP:EF III-1268

Ten Brave Men (Daugherty, S.) MPII:JYABio IV-1664

Ten Famous Lives (Plutarch) MPII:JYABio IV-1668

Ten North Frederick (O'Hara, J.) CLCII IV-1524; MPII:AF IV-1573

Ten Tall Texans (Kubiak) MPII:JYABio IV-1672

Tenant of Wildfell Hall, The (Brontë, A.) CLC II-1115; MP XI-6442; MP:BF III-1505

Tenants of Moonbloom, The (Wallant) MP XI-6445; MP:AF III-1263

Tenda dos milagres. *See* Tent of Miracles

"Tender Shoot, The" (Colette) MPII:SS V-2316

Tender Is the Night (Fitzgerald, F.) CLC II-1117; MP XI-6448; MP:AF III-1266

Tendoy (Crowder) MPII:JYABio IV-1676

"Tendron, Le." *See* "Tender Shoot, The"

Tengo un miedo de ser un animal. *See* I have a terrible fear of being an animal

Tennin gosui. *See* Sea of Fertility, The

"Tennis Court Oath, The" (Ashbery) MPII:P V-2130

Tennis Players, The (Gustafsson) CLCII IV-1525; MPII:WF IV-1560

Tennisspelarna. *See* Tennis Players, The

Tent of Miracles (Amado) CLCII IV-1526; MPII:AF IV-1578

Tents of Wickedness, The (De Vries) CLCII IV-1528; MPII:AF IV-1583

"Terence, This Is Stupid Stuff" (Housman) MPII:P VI-2133

Terezín Requiem, The (Bor) MPII:JYAFic IV-1443

Terezínské rekviem. *See* Terezín Requiem, The

Terms of Endearment (McMurtry) CLCII IV-1529; MPII:AF IV-1587

Terra Nostra (Fuentes) CLCII IV-1530; MPII:AF IV-1593

Terras do sem fin. *See* Violent Land, The

Terre des hommes. *See* Wind, Sand, and Stars.

"Territory" (Leavitt) MPII:SS V-2320

Teseide, La (Boccaccio) MP XI-6453

Tess of the D'Urbervilles (Hardy) CLC II-1118; MP XI-6457; MP:BF III-1509

Testament of Experience (Brittain) MPII:NF IV-1479

Testament of Friendship (Brittain) MPII:NF IV-1479

Testimony (Shostakovich) MPII:NF IV-1485

"Th' expense of spirit in a waste of shame" *See* Sonnet 129

Thaddeus of Warsaw (Porter, J.) CLC II-1120; MP XI-6462; MP:BF III-1514

"Thanatopsis" (Bryant) MPII:P VI-2137

"Thank You, M'am" (Hughes, L.) MPII:SS VI-2323

That Awful Mess on Via Merulana (Gadda) CLCII IV-1532; MPII:WF IV-1565

That Dunbar Boy (Gould) MPII:JYABio IV-1680

"That Evening Sun" (Faulkner) MPII:SS VI-2325

That Hideous Strength. *See* Space Trilogy, The

"That Moment, Which You Could Love, What of It" (Smith, D.) MPII:P VI-2140

"That Nature Is a Heraclitean Fire and of the comfort of the Resurrection" (Hopkins, G.) MPII:P VI-2143

That Remarkable Man (Meyer) MPII:JYABio IV-1684

"That time of year thou mayst in me behold" *See* Sonnet 73

That Uncertain Feeling (Amis) MP XI-6466; MP:BF III-1519

That Voice (Pinget) CLCII IV-1532; MPII:WF IV-1570

Thaw, The (Ehrenburg) CLCII IV-1533; MPII:WF IV-1575

"The face of all the world is changed, I think," *See* Sonnet 7

Theatre and Its Double, The (Artaud) MPII:NF IV-1490

Théâtre et son double, Le. *See* Theater and Its Double, The

Thebais, The (Statius) MP XI-6469

Their Eyes Were Watching God (Hurston) CLCII IV-1534; MPII:AF IV-1598; MPII:AfAm III-1418

Them (Oates) CLCII IV-1535; MPII:AF IV-1604

"Theme of the Traitor and the Hero" (Borges) MPII:SS VI-2329

Theophilus North (Wilder, W.) CLCII IV-1536; MPII:AF IV-1609

Theory of the Leisure Class, The (Veblen) MP XI-6471

There Are Crimes and Crimes (Strindberg) CLC II-1121; MP XI-6473

There Is a Tree More Ancient than Eden (Forrest) CLCII IV-1538; MPII:AF IV-1615; MPII:AfAm III-1423

There Was Once a Slave . . . (Graham, S.) MPII:JYABio IV-1688

"There Will Come Soft Rains" (Bradbury) MPII:SS VI-2333

"There's a certain Slant of light" (Dickinson, E.) MPII:P VI-2146

Thérèse (Mauriac, F.) CLC II-1121; MP XI-6477; MP:EF III-1273

Thérèse Raquin (Zola) CLCII IV-1539; MPII:WF IV-1579

These Happy Golden Years (Wilder, L.) MPII:JYAFic IV-1447

These the Companions (Davie) MPII:NF IV-1495

These Thousand Hills (Guthrie) CLCII IV-1541; MPII:AF IV-1620

Thesmophoriazusae, The (Aristophanes) CLC II-1122; MP XI-6483

"They" (Kipling) MPII:SS VI-2337

"They Are All Gone into the World of Light!" (Vaughan) MPII:P VI-2149

They Cage the Animals at Night (Burch) MPII:JYABio IV-1692

"They Flee from Me" (Wyatt, E.) MPII:P VI-2152

They Shoot Horses, Don't They? (McCoy) MP XI-6486; MP:AF III-1271

"They that have pow'r to hurt, and will do none," *See* Sonnet 94

Thimble Summer (Enright) MPII:JYAFic IV-1451

Thin Man, The (Hammett) CLC II-1123; MP XI-6489; MP:AF III-1275

Thin Red Line, The (Jones, J.) CLCII IV-1542; MPII:AF IV-1624

Things as They Are. *See* Caleb Williams

Things Fall Apart (Achebe) CLCII IV-1544; MPII:BCF IV-1681; MPII:JYAFic IV-1454

"Thinking of the Lost World" (Jarrell) MPII:P VI-2155

Third and Oak: The Laundromat (Norman) CLCII IV-1546; MPII:D IV-1562

"Third Bank of the River, The" (Guimarães Rosa) MPII:SS VI-2341

Third Factory (Shklovsky) CLCII IV-1546; MPII:WF IV-1584

Third Life of Grange Copeland, The (Walker, A.) CLCII IV-1547; MPII:AF IV-1629; MPII:AfAm III-1429

Third Policeman, The (O'Brien, F.) CLCII
IV-1548; MPII:BCF IV-1686
"Third Prize, The" (Coppard) MPII:SS
VI-2344
"Thirteen Ways of Looking at a Blackbird"
(Stevens, W.) MPII:P VI-2158
Thirties, The (Wilson) MPII:NF IV-1500
Thirty-nine Steps, The (Buchan) CLC
II-1124; MP XI-6493; MP:BF III-1523
This Above All (Knight, Eric) CLC II-1124;
MP XI-6497; MP:BF III-1528
"This afternoon, my love" (Cruz, S.)
MPII:P VI-2161
This Business of Living. See Burning
Brand, The
This Child's Gonna Live (Wright, S.)
MPII:AfAm III-1435
This I Remember (Roosevelt) MPII:JYABio
IV-1695
"This Lime-Tree Bower My Prison"
(Coleridge) MPII:P VI-2164
"This painted lie you see" (Cruz, S.) MPII:P
VI-2168
This Side of Paradise (Fitzgerald, F. S.)
CLCII IV-1550; MPII:AF IV-1635
This Sporting Life (Storey) CLCII IV-1551;
MPII:BCF IV-1690
This Strange New Feeling (Lester)
MPII:JYAFic IV-1458
This Sunday (Donoso) CLCII IV-1552;
MPII:AF IV-1630
"This Way for the Gas, Ladies and
Gentlemen" (Borowski) MPII:SS
VI-2348
Thomas and Beulah (Dove) MPII:P VI-2171
Thomas Jefferson, Champion of the People
(Judson) MPII:JYABio IV-1698
Thoreau of Walden Pond (North)
MPII:JYABio IV-1701
Those Wonderful Women in Their Flying
Machines (Keil) MPII:JYABio IV-1705
Thought and Language (Vygotsky)
MPII:NF IV-1507
"Thought-Fox, The" (Hughes, Ted) MPII:P
VI-2176
Thousand and One Nights, The. See
Arabian Nights' Entertainments, The
Thousand Cranes (Kawabata) CLCII
IV-1554; MPII:WF IV-1589

Thread That Runs So True, The (Stuart)
MPII:JYABio IV-1709; MPII:NF
IV-1513
Three Black Pennys, The (Hergesheimer)
CLC II-1126; MP XI-6500; MP:AF
III-1279
Three-Cornered Hat, The (Alarcón) CLC
II-1126; MP XI-6505; MP:EF III-1286
Three-Cornered World, The (Natsume)
CLCII IV-1555; MPII:WF IV-1595
"Three-Day Blow, The" (Hemingway)
MPII:SS VI-2358
"Three Deaths" (Tolstoy) MPII:SS VI-2351
"Three Floors" (Kunitz) MPII:P VI-2179
"Three Hermits, The" (Tolstoy) MPII:SS
VI-2355
365 Days (Glasser) MPII:NF IV-1518
Three Lives (Stein) CLCII IV-1555;
MPII:AF IV-1643
Three Marias, The (Queiroz) CLCII
IV-1557; MPII:AF IV-1648
Three Men in a Boat (Jerome) CLC II-1127;
MP XI-6508; MP:BF III-1532
"Three Mendicants." See "Three Hermits,
The"
Three Musketeers, The (Dumas, père) CLC
II-1127; MP XI-6511; MP:EF III-1279;
MPII:JYAFic IV-1462
"Three Old Men, The." See "Three Hermits,
The"
Three Sisters, The (Chekhov) CLC II-1129;
MP XI-6518
Three Sisters, The (Sinclair) CLCII
IV-1558; MPII:BCF IV-1695
Three Soldiers (Dos Passos) CLC II-1130;
MP XI-6522; MP:AF III-1285
Three Trapped Tigers (Cabrera Infante)
CLCII IV-1559; MPII:AF IV-1652
Three Who Dared (Cohen) MPII:JYABio
IV-1713
Three Who Made a Revolution (Wolfe, B.)
MPII:JYABio IV-1717
Three Worlds of Albert Schweitzer, The
(Payne, R.) MPII:JYABio IV-1721
Threepenny Opera, The (Brecht) CLCII
IV-1560; MPII:D IV-1568
Through the Ivory Gate (Dove) MPII:AfAm
III-1440

Through the Looking-Glass (Carroll) CLC
II-1130; MP XI-6526; MP:BF III-1536;
MPII:JYAFic IV-1465
"Thrown Away" (Kipling) MPII:SS VI-2362
Thunder and Lightnings (Mark)
MPII:JYAFic IV-1469
Thurgood Marshall (Fenderson)
MPII:JYABio IV-1725
"Thus I Ran Out of the Word" (Sachs)
MPII:P VI-2182
Thus Spake Zarathustra (Nietzsche) MP
XI-6532
Thyestes (Seneca) CLC II-1131; MP
XI-6535
Tía Julia y el escribidor, La. See Aunt Julia
and the Scriptwriter
Ticket to the Stars, A (Aksyonov) CLCII
IV-1561; MPII:WF IV-1600
"Tickets, Please" (Lawrence) MPII:SS
VI-2365
Tidings Brought to Mary, The (Claudel)
CLCII IV-1563; MPII:D IV-1574
Tierras flacas, Las. See Lean Lands, The
Tieta, the Goat Girl (Amado) CLCII
IV-1564; MPII:AF IV-1657
Tiêta do Agreste. See Tieta, the Goat Girl
Tiger at the Gates (Giraudoux) MP XI-6539
Tiger Eyes (Blume) MPII:JYAFic IV-1472
Tîh, al-. See Mudun al-milh
Till We Have Faces (Lewis, C. S.) CLCII
IV-1565; MPII:BCF IV-1700
Tilted Cross, The (Porter) CLCII IV-1566;
MPII:BCF IV-1705
Time and Mr. Bass. See Mushroom Planet
series, The
"Time and Music" (Lewis, J.) MPII:P
VI-2185
Time and the Conways (Priestley) CLCII
IV-1567; MPII:D IV-1579
"Time and the Garden" (Winters) MPII:P
VI-2188
Time and Western Man (Lewis, W.)
MPII:NF IV-1523
Time Machine, The (Wells) CLC II-1131;
MP XI-6542; MP:BF III-1543;
MPII:JYAFic IV-1476
Time of Hope. See Strangers and Brothers
Time of Indifference, The (Moravia) CLCII
IV-1568; MPII:WF IV-1605

Time of Man, The (Roberts, E.) CLC
II-1132; MP XI-6545; MP:AF III-1289
Time of the Hero, The (Vargas Llosa)
CLCII IV-1569; MPII:AF IV-1663
Time of Trial (Burton, H.) MPII:JYAFic
IV-1480
Time of Your Life, The (Saroyan) CLCII
IV-1571; MPII:D IV-1585
"Time the Tiger" (Lewis, W.) MPII:SS
VI-2369
Time to Dance, No Time to Weep, A
(Godden) MPII:NF IV-1527
Time Without Bells. See Silesian Tetralogy,
The
Timebends (Miller) MPII:NF IV-1533
Times They Used to Be, The (Clifton)
MPII:JYAFic IV-1484
Timon of Athens (Shakespeare) CLC
II-1133; MP XI-6549
Tin Drum, The (Grass) MP XI-6553;
MP:EF III-1290
Tinker, Tailor, Soldier, Spy (le Carré)
CLCII II-694; MPII:BCF IV-1710
Tiny Alice (Albee) CLCII IV-1572; MPII:D
IV-1590
Tirra Lirra by the River (Anderson, J.)
CLCII IV-1573; MPII:BCF IV-1716
'Tis Pity She's a Whore (Ford, J.) CLC
II-1134; MP XI-6556
Tisha (Specht) MPII:JYABio IV-1729
Titan, The (Dreiser) CLC II-1135; MP
XI-6560; MP:AF III-1293
Titan (Jean Paul) CLCII IV-1574; MPII:WF
IV-1610
Titus Alone. See Gormenghast trilogy, The
Titus Andronicus (Shakespeare) CLC
II-1135; MP XI-6565
Titus Groan. See Gormenghast trilogy, The
"Tlön, Uqbar, Orbis Tertius" (Borges)
MPII:SS VI-2373
To __. Ulalume: A Ballad. See Ulalume
"To a Friend" (Brodsky) MPII:P VI-2191
"To a Skylark" (Shelley, P.) MPII:P
VI-2194
"To an Athlete Dying Young" (Housman)
MPII:P VI-2197
"To Autumn" (Keats) MPII:P VI-2200
To Be a Pilgrim (Cary, J.) CLC II-1137; MP
XI-6570; MP:BF III-1547

To Be Young, Gifted, and Black (Hansberry *and* Nemiroff) MPII:JYABio IV-1732

"To Build a Fire" (London) MPII:SS VI-2377

"To Earthward" (Frost) MPII:P VI-2203

"To Elsie" (Williams, W.) MPII:P VI-2206

To Have and Have Not (Hemingway) CLCII IV-1577; MPII:AF IV-1668

To Have and to Hold (Johnston) CLCII IV-1578; MPII:AF IV-1673

"To His Coy Mistress" (Marvell) MPII:P VI-2209

To Keep the Ball Rolling (Powell) MPII:NF IV-1538

To Kill a Mockingbird (Lee, H.) CLCII IV-1580; MPII:AF IV-1677; MPII:JYAFic IV-1487

To Let. *See* Forsyte Saga, The

"To Penshurst" (Jonson) MPII:P VI-2212

To Race the Wind (Krents) MPII:JYABio IV-1736

"To Raja Rao" (Miłosz) MPII:P VI-2215

To Sir, with Love (Braithwaite) MPII:JYABio IV-1740

"To the Fates" (Hölderlin) MPII:P VI-2218

To the Land of the Cattails (Appelfeld) CLCII IV-1581; MPII:WF IV-1616

To the Lighthouse (Woolf) CLC II-1138; MP XI-6573; MP:BF III-1551

"To the Memory of Mr. Oldham" (Dryden) MPII:P VI-2221

"To the Memory of My Beloved Master William Shakespeare" (Jonson) MPII:P VI-2224

"To the Reader" (Baudelaire) MPII:P VI-2227

"To the Virgins, to Make Much of Time" (Herrick) MPII:P VI-2230

"To Urania" (Brodsky) MPII:P VI-2233

"Toads" (Larkin) MPII:P VI-2237

"Toast" (Mallarmé) MPII:P VI-2240

Tobacco Road (Caldwell) CLC II-1140; MP XI-6578; MP:AF III-1299

Tobacco Road (Kirkland) CLCII IV-1582; MPII:D IV-1596

Tobias trilogy, The (Lagerkvist) CLCII IV-1583; MPII:WF IV-1623

"Tod in Venedig, Der." *See* "Death in Venice"

Todesfuge. *See* Death Fugue

Todo verdor perecerá. *See* All Green Shall Perish

"Together and Apart" (Woolf) MPII:SS VI-2381

Toilers of the Sea, The (Hugo, V.) CLC II-1140; MP XI-6581; MP:EF III-1293

Tokaido Circuit. *See* Hizakurige

"Tokyo hakkei." *See* "Eight Views of Tokyo"

Told by an Idiot (Macaulay) CLCII IV-1585; MPII:BCF IV-1721

Tolkien (Carpenter) MPII:JYABio IV-1744

Tom and Jerry. *See* Life in London

Tom Brown's School Days (Hughes, Thomas) CLC II-1141; MP XI-6585; MP:BF III-1556; MPII:JYAFic IV-1491

Tom Burke of Ours (Lever) CLC II-1141; MP XI-6588; MP:BF III-1560

Tom Cringle's Log (Scott, M.) CLC II-1142; MP XI-6594; MP:BF III-1567

Tom Jones (Fielding) CLC II-1143; MP XI-6598; MP:BF III-1571

Tom Paine, Revolutionary (Coolidge, O.) MPII:JYABio IV-1748

Tom Sawyer. *See* Adventures of Tom Sawyer, The

Tom Thumb the Great (Fielding) CLC II-1146; MP XI-6609

Tom's Midnight Garden (Pearce) MPII:JYAFic IV-1494

Tomb for Boris Davidovich, A (Kiš) CLCII IV-1586; MPII:WF IV-1629

"Tomb of Charles Baudelaire, The" (Mallarmé) MPII:P VI-2243

"Tomb of Edgar Poe, The" (Mallarmé) MPII:P VI-2247

Tombeau de Charles Baudelaire, Le. *See* Tomb of Charles Baudelaire, The

Tombeau d'Edgar Poe. *See* Tomb of Edgar Poe, The

Tombs of Atuan, The. *See* Earthsea series, The

"Tommy" (Wideman) MPII:SS VI-2385

"Tomorrow and Tomorrow and So Forth" (Updike) MPII:SS VI-2389

Tongue of Flame (Meltzer) MPII:JYABio IV-1752

Tongue Set Free, The (Canetti) MPII:NF IV-1546

Tonight We Improvise (Pirandello) CLCII IV-1588; MPII:D IV-1601

"Tonio Kröger" (Mann) MPII:SS VI-2393

Tono-Bungay (Wells) CLC II-1146; MP XI-6613; MP:BF III-1578

Tooth of Crime, The (Shepard) CLCII IV-1589; MPII:D IV-1607

Top Girls (Churchill) CLCII IV-1591; MPII:D IV-1613

Tor-ha-pela'ot. See Age of Wonders, The

Torch in My Ear, The (Canetti) MPII:NF IV-1546

Torch Song Trilogy (Fierstein) CLCII IV-1592; MPII:D IV-1618

Tormented Genius (Honour) MPII:JYABio IV-1756

Torrents of Spring, The (Hemingway) CLCII IV-1593; MPII:AF IV-1682

Torrents of Spring, The (Turgenev) CLCII IV-1594; MPII:WF IV-1634

Tortilla Flat (Steinbeck) CLCII IV-1595; MPII:AF IV-1688

Toska po rodine. . . . See Homesickness

Totem and Taboo (Freud) MPII:NF IV-1553

Totem und Tabu. See Totem and Taboo

Totenschiff, Das. See Death Ship, The

Touch of Magic, The (Hickok) MPII:JYABio IV-1759

Touch Wood (Roth-Hano) MPII:JYABio IV-1762

Tour du monde en quatre-vingts jours, Le. See Around the World in Eighty Days

"Tower, The" (Yeats) MPII:P VI-2250

Tower of Babel, The. See Auto-da-Fé

Tower of London, The (Ainsworth) CLC II-1148; MP XI-6618; MP:BF III-1583

Towers of Silence, The. See Raj Quartet, The

Towers of Trebizond, The (Macaulay) CLCII IV-1596; MPII:BCF IV-1726

Town, The (Faulkner) CLC II-1149; MP XI-6623; MP:AF III-1302

Town, The (Richter, C.) CLC II-1150; MP XI-6628; MP:AF III-1308

"Town and Country Lovers" (Gordimer) MPII:SS VI-2397

"Town Poor, The" (Jewett) MPII:SS VI-2401

Tra donne sole. See Among Women Only

Trachinai. See Women of Trachis

Track of the Cat, The (Clark, Walter) CLC II-1151; MP XI-6633; MP:AF III-1313

Tragédie du Roi Christophe, La. See Tragedy of King Christophe, The

Tragedy of King Christophe, The (Césaire) CLCII IV-1598; MPII:D IV-1623

Tragic Muse, The (James, H.) MP XI-6636; MP:AF III-1317

Tragic Sense of Life in Men and in Peoples, The (Unamuno y Jugo) MP XI-6640

Traición de Rita Hayworth, La. See Betrayed by Rita Hayworth

Train Ride (Steptoe) MPII:JYAFic IV-1497

Train Whistle Guitar (Murray, A.) MPII:AfAm III-1446

Traitor (Fritz) MPII:JYABio IV-1766

Traitor, The (Shirley) CLC II-1151; MP XI-6643

"Transfer" (Brown, S.) MPII:P VI-2253

Transfiguration of Benno Blimpie, The (Innaurato) CLCII IV-1599; MPII:D IV-1629

Transformation of Lucius Apuleius of Madaura. See Golden Ass of Lucius Apuleius, The

Translations (Friel) CLCII IV-1600; MPII:D IV-1634

"Translucent Mechanics, The" (Oppen) MPII:P VI-2256

Transposed Heads, The (Mann) CLCII IV-1602; MPII:WF IV-1639

Trap, The. See Pilgrimage

Traspié entre dos estrella. See Stumble Between Two Stars

"Traveling Through the Dark" (Stafford, W.) MPII:P VI-2259

Travelling North (Williamson) CLCII IV-1603; MPII:D IV-1639

Travels in Arabia Deserta (Doughty) MP XI-6647

Travels into Several Remote Nations of the World, in Four Parts, by Lemuel Gulliver, First Surgeon, and then a Captain of Several Ships. See Gulliver's Travels

Travels of Lao Ts'an, The (Liu E) CLCII IV-1604; MPII:WF IV-1646

Travels of Marco Polo, The (Polo) MP XI-6650

"Travels of the Last Benjamin of Tudela" (Amichai) MPII:P VI-2262

Travels to the Interior Districts of Africa (Park) MP XI-6656

Travels with a Donkey (Stevenson) MP XI-6659

Travesties (Stoppard) CLCII IV-1606; MPII:D IV-1643

Travnika hronika. See Bosnian Chronicle

Treasure Hunt. See Book of Bebb, The

Treasure Island (Stevenson) CLC II-1152; MP XI-6662; MP:BF III-1589; MPII:JYAFic IV-1500

Treasure of Green Knowe, The. See Green Knowe books, The

Treatise on Painting. See Notebooks of Leonardo da Vinci, The

Treatises of Cicero, The (Cicero) MP XI-6669

"Tree. A Rock. A Cloud., A" (McCullers) MPII:SS VI-2404

Tree Climber, The (Hakim) CLCII IV-1607; MPII:D IV-1648

Tree Grows in Brooklyn, A (Smith, B.) CLC II-1152; MP XI-6672; MP:AF III-1322; MPII:JYAFic IV-1504

Tree of Knowledge, The (Baroja) CLCII IV-1608; MPII:WF IV-1650

"Tree of Knowledge, The" (James, H.) MPII:SS VI-2407

Tree of Man, The (White, P.) MP XI-6676; MP:BF III-1597

Tree of the Folkungs, The (Heidenstam) CLC II-1153; MP XI-6679; MP:EF III-1297

Trees, The (Richter, C.) CLC II-1154; MP XI-6683; MP:AF III-1326

Treffen in Telgte, Das. See Meeting at Telgte, The

Trembling of the Veil, The. See Autobiography of William Butler Yeats, The

Tremor of Intent (Burgess) CLCII IV-1609; MPII:BCF IV-1732

Tren Fortynbrasa. See Elegy of Fortinbras

Três Marias, As. See Three Marias, The

Tres novelitas burguesas. See Sacred Families

Tres tristes tigres. See Three Trapped Tigers

Tretya fabrika. See Third Factory

"Tri smerti." See "Three Deaths"

"Tri startsa." See "Three Hermits, The"

Trial, The (Kafka) CLC II-1155; MP XI-6687; MP:EF III-1302

Trial Begins, The (Sinyavsky) CLCII IV-1610; MPII:WF IV-1656

Trial by Jury (Gilbert) CLC II-1156; MP XI-6692

Tribunals (Duncan) MPII:P VI-2267

Tribute to Freud (H. D.) MPII:NF IV-1558

Trick of the Ga Bolga, The (McGinley) CLCII IV-1612; MPII:BCF IV-1737

Trick to Catch the Old One, A (Middleton) CLC II-1156; MP XI-6695

Trickster, The (Plautus) CLC II-1157; MP XI-6698

"Trifling Occurrence, A" (Chekhov) MPII:SS VI-2411

Trilby (du Maurier, G.) CLC II-1158; MP XI-6701; MP:BF III-1600

Trilce (Vallejo) MPII:P VI-2272

Trilogy, The (Beckett) MPII:BCF IV-1742; MPII:WF IV-1661. See also Unnamable, The

Trilogy (H. D.) MPII:P VI-2277

Triptych (Simon, C.) CLCII IV-1613; MPII:WF IV-1666

"Tristan" (Mann) MPII:SS VI-2417

Tristan and Isolde (Strassburg) CLC II-1159; MP XI-6705

Tristes Tropiques (Lévi-Strauss) MPII:NF IV-1563

"Tristia" (Mandelstam, O.) MPII:P VI-2282

Tristram (Robinson, E.) MP XI-6709

Tristram Shandy (Sterne) CLC II-1159; MP XI-6712; MP:BF III-1605

Triton (Delany, S.) CLCII IV-1614; MPII:AF IV-1692

Triumph of Death, The (D'Annunzio) CLC II-1161; MP XI-6717; MP:EF III-1307

"Triumph of Life, The" (Shelley, P.) MPII:P VI-2285

Troilus and Cressida (Shakespeare) CLC II-1162; MP XI-6720

Troilus and Criseyde (Chaucer) CLC II-1164; MP XI-6725

Trois Mousquetaires, Les. *See* Three Musketeers, The

Trojan Women, The (Euripides) CLC II-1164; MP XI-6729

Troops Return, The. *See* November 1918

Tropic of Cancer (Miller, H.) CLCII IV-1615; MPII:AF IV-1697

Tropic of Capricorn (Miller, H.) MP XI-6733; MP:AF III-1330

Trouble in Mind (Childress) CLCII IV-1616; MPII:D IV-1654

Trouble in Mind (Childress) MPII:AfAm III-1452

Trouble with Donovan Croft, The (Ashley) MPII:JYAFic IV-1508

Troubled Sleep. *See* Roads to Freedom, The

Troubles (Farrell) CLCII IV-1617; MPII:BCF IV-1747

Trout Fishing in America (Brautigan) CLCII IV-1619; MPII:AF IV-1702

True Adventures of Grizzly Adams, The (McClung) MPII:JYABio IV-1770

True Confessions of an Albino Terrorist, The (Breytenbach) MPII:NF IV-1569

True History, The (Lucian) MP XI-6737; MP:EF III-1311

True History of the Elephant Man, The (Howell *and* Ford, P.) MPII:JYABio IV-1774

True Story of Ah Q, The (Lu Hsün) CLCII IV-1620; MPII:WF IV-1671

True West (Shepard) CLCII IV-1621; MPII:D IV-1660

"Trumpet, The" (de la Mare) MPII:SS VI-2421

Trumpeter of Krakow, The (Kelly, E.) MPII:JYAFic IV-1511

Trumpeter's Tale (Eaton) MPII:JYABio IV-1777

"Truth and Lies" (Price) MPII:SS VI-2425

Truth and Life of Myth, The (Duncan) MPII:NF IV-1574

Truth and Method (Gadamer) MPII:NF IV-1580

Truth Suspected (Ruiz de Alarcón) CLC II-1166; MP XI-6740

Tubby Schaumann (Raabe) CLCII IV-1622; MPII:WF IV-1676

Tuck Everlasting (Babbitt) MPII:JYAFic IV-1514

Tueur sans gages. *See* Killer, The

Tui hsüeh. *See* Facing the Snow

Tulku (Dickinson, P.) MPII:JYAFic IV-1517

Túnel, El. *See* Outsider, The (Sábato)

Tunes for a Small Harmonica (Wersba) MPII:JYAFic IV-1521

Tung-chou lieh-kuo chih. *See* Lieh-kuo chih

Tunnel, The. *See* Pilgrimage

Turbulent Term of Tyke Tiler, The (Kemp) MPII:JYAFic IV-1524

Turcaret (Le Sage) CLC II-1166; MP XI-6744

Turn of the Screw, The (James, H.) CLC II-1167; MP XI-6748; MP:AF III-1335; MPII:JYAFic IV-1528

Turvey (Birney) CLCII IV-1623; MPII:BCF IV-1751

Tutti i nostri ieri. *See* All Our Yesterdays

Twelfth Night (Shakespeare) CLC II-1168; MP XII-6753

Twelve, The (Blok) MPII:P VI-2289

Twelve and the Genii, The. *See* Return of the Twelves, The

Twelve Citizens of the World (Kenworthy) MPII:JYABio IV-1781

Twelve Years (Agee, Joel) MPII:NF IV-1586

Twenty-one Balloons, The (du Bois, W. P.) MPII:JYAFic IV-1535

Twenty-seven Wagons Full of Cotton (Williams, T.) CLCII IV-1624; MPII:D IV-1665

"Twenty-six Men and a Girl" (Gorky) MPII:SS VI-2429

Twenty Thousand Leagues Under the Sea (Verne) CLC II-1169; MP XII-6758; MP:EF III-1315; MPII:JYAFic IV-1531

XXII. *See* Red Wheelbarrow, The

Twenty Years After (Dumas, *père*) CLC II-1169; MP XII-6762; MP:EF III-1319

Twenty Years at Hull-House (Addams) MPII:JYABio IV-1785

Twice Round the Black Church (Clarke, Austin) MPII:NF IV-1592

"Twicknam Garden" (Donne) MPII:P
VI-2293

Twilight in Italy (Lawrence, D. H.) MP
XII-6766

"Twins, The" (Bukowski) MPII:P VI-2297

Two Against the Ice (Mason) MPII:JYABio
IV-1788

Two By Two. *See* Love, or a Season, A

"Two Drovers, The" (Scott) MPII:SS
VI-2432

"Two Elenas, The" (Fuentes) MPII:SS
VI-2436

Two Essays on Analytical Psychology
(Jung) MP XII-6769

Two for the Seesaw (Gibson) CLCII
IV-1625; MPII:D IV-1670

"Two Gallants" (Joyce) MPII:SS VI-2439

Two Gentlemen of Verona (Shakespeare)
CLC II-1170; MP XII-6772

"Two Little Soldiers" (Maupassant)
MPII:SS VI-2442

"Two Lovely Beasts (O'Flaherty) MPII:SS
VI-2445

Two Noble Kinsmen, The (Shakespeare *and*
Fletcher) CLC II-1172; MP XII-6775

"Two Poems on the Passing of an Empire"
(Walcott) MPII:P VI-2300

Two Solitudes (MacLennan) CLCII
IV-1625; MPII:BCF IV-1756

2001: A Space Odyssey (Clarke, Arthur C.)
CLCII IV-1627; MPII:AF IV-1707

Two Thousand Seasons (Armah) CLCII
IV-1628; MPII:BCF IV-1761

Two Towers, The (Tolkien) MP XII-6778;
MP:BF III-1611. *See also* Lord of the
Rings, The

Two Trains Running (Wilson, August)
MPII:AfAm III-1457

"Two Tramps in Mud Time" (Frost) MPII:P
VI-2303

Two Wings to Veil My Face (Forrest)
MPII:AfAm III-1462

Two Women (Moravia) MP XII-6782;
MP:EF III-1323

Two Worlds (Daiches) MPII:NF IV-1597

Two Years Before the Mast (Dana) MP
XII-6785; MPII:JYABio IV-1792;
MPII:JYAFic IV-1538

"Tyger, The" (Blake) MPII:P VI-2306

Typee (Melville) CLC II-1173; MP
XII-6791; MP:AF III-1340

"Typhoon" (Conrad) CLCII IV-1629;
MPII:SS VI-2448

Tzili (Appelfeld) CLCII IV-1630; MPII:WF
IV-1682

U

Ubu Roi (Jarry) CLCII IV-1631; MPII:D
IV-1676
"Uezdnyi lekar." See "District Doctor, The"
Ugly Duchess, The (Feuchtwanger) CLC
II-1174; MP XII-6796; MP:EF III-1326
Ukhdd, al-. See Mudun al-milh
"Ulalume" (Poe) MPII:P VI-2309
"Ulica krokodyli." See "Street of
Crocodiles, The"
Ulitka na sklone. See Snail on the Slope, The
Última niebla, La. See Final Mist, The
Ultima Thule. See Fortunes of Richard
Mahony, The
Ultramarine (Lowry) CLCII IV-1632;
MPII:BCF IV-1766
Ulysses (Joyce) CLC II-1175; MP
XII-6799; MP:BF III-1616
"Ulysses" (Tennyson) MPII:P VI-2313
Umara Klasa. See Dead Class, The
Un di Velt hot geshvign. See Night
Un día en la vida. See One Day of Life
Unbearable Bassington, The (Saki) CLC
II-1177; MP XII-6804; MP:BF III-1622
Unbearable Lightness of Being, The
(Kundera) CLCII IV-1633; MPII:WF
IV-1689
"Unbeliever, The" (Bishop) MPII:P
VI-2317
"Uncle" (Narayan) MPII:SS VI-2452
Uncle Remus. See Tales of Uncle Remus
Uncle Silas (Le Fanu) CLC II-1177; MP
XII-6808; MP:BF III-1627
Uncle Tom's Cabin (Stowe) CLC II-1178;
MP XII-6814; MP:AF III-1345;
MPII:JYAFic IV-1542
Uncle Vanya (Chekhov) CLC II-1179; MP
XII-6818
"Uncle Wiggily in Connecticut" (Salinger)
MPII:SS VI-2457
Unconditional Surrender. See Sword of
Honour
"Under a Glass Bell" (Nin) MPII:SS
VI-2461
"Under Ben Bulben" (Yeats) MPII:P
VI-2320
Under Fire (Barbusse) CLC II-1180; MP
XII-6822; MP:EF III-1330

Under Milk Wood (Thomas) MP XII-6825
Under the Greenwood Tree (Hardy) CLC
II-1181; MP XII-6829; MP:BF III-1634
"Under the Rose" (Pynchon) MPII:SS
VI-2464
Under the Sun of Satan (Bernanos) CLCII
IV-1634; MPII:WF IV-1694
Under the Volcano (Lowry) MP XII-6833;
MP:BF III-1639
Under the Yoke (Vazov) CLC II-1182; MP
XII-6836; MP:EF III-1334
Under Two Flags (Ouida) CLC II-1183; MP
XII-6840; MP:BF III-1643
Under Western Eyes (Conrad) CLC
II-1184; MP XII-6844; MP:BF III-1647
Underdogs, The (Azuela) CLC II-1185; MP
XII-6847; MP:AF III-1349
Underground Man, The (Macdonald) CLCII
IV-1636; MPII:AF IV-1711
Understanding Media (McLuhan) MPII:NF
IV-1601
Underwoods. See Execration upon Vulcan,
An
Undine (La Motte-Fouqué) CLC II-1186;
MP XII-6852; MP:EF III-1338
Undying Grass, The (Kemal) CLCII
IV-1718; MPII:WF IV-1754
Unfinished Woman, An (Hellman)
MPII:NF IV-1607
Unfortunate Traveller, The (Nash) CLC
II-1186; MP XII-6855; MP:BF III-1650
Unframed Originals (Merwin) MPII:NF
IV-1612
Unholy Loves (Oates) CLCII IV-1637;
MPII:AF IV-1717
Unhuman Tour. See Three-Cornered World,
The
Unicorn, The (Murdoch) CLCII IV-1639;
MPII:BCF IV-1771
Union libre, L'. See Free Union
Union Street (Barker) CLCII IV-1640;
MPII:BCF IV-1775
Universal Baseball Association, Inc., J.
Henry Waugh, Prop., The (Coover)
CLCII IV-1642; MPII:AF IV-1723
Unizhennye i oskorblyonnye. See Insulted
and the Injured, The

"Unknown Masterpiece, The" (Balzac) MPII:SS VI-2468

Unleaving (Walsh) MPII:JYAFic IV-1546

"Unmailed, Unwritten Letters" (Oates) MPII:SS VI-2471

Unnamable, The (Beckett) CLCII IV-1643. *See also* Trilogy, The

"Unordnung und frühes Leid." *See* "Disorder and Early Sorrow"

Unquiet Grave, The (Connolly) MPII:NF IV-1617

Untergeher, Der (Bernhard) CLCII IV-1644; MPII:WF IV-1700

Unvanquished, The (Faulkner) MP XII-6860; MP:AF III-1354

Up a Road Slowly (Hunt, I.) MPII:JYAFic IV-1550

Up from Slavery (Washington) MPII:AfAm III-1467; MPII:JYABio IV-1795

"Up Rising" (Duncan) MPII:P VI-2324

"Up the Bare Stairs" (O'Faoláin) MPII:SS VI-2474

Upon the Head of the Goat (Siegal) MPII:JYABio IV-1799

"Upon the Sweeping Flood" (Oates) MPII:SS VI-2478

Upstairs Room, The (Reiss) MPII:JYABio IV-1803

Uraniia. *See* To Urania

Ursache, Die. *See* Gathering Evidence

U.S.A. (Dos Passos) CLC II-1187; MP XII-6863; MP:AF III-1358

"Use of Force, The" (Williams, W.) MPII:SS VI-2482

Ushant (Aiken, C.) MPII:NF IV-1622

Utage no ato. *See* After the Banquet

Utopia (More, T.) CLC II-1189; MP XII-6868

Utsukushisa to kanashimi to. *See* Beauty and Sadness

V

V. (Pynchon) CLCII IV-1646; MPII:AF
IV-1727

V kruge pervom. *See* First Circle, The

Vagabond, The (Colette) CLCII IV-1649;
MPII:WF IV-1705

"Valediction: Forbidding Mourning, A"
(Donne) MPII:P VI-2327

Valle negro. *See* Black Valley

Valley of Boncs, The. *See* Dance to the
Music of Time, A

Valley of Decision, The (Wharton) CLCII
IV-1650; MPII:AF IV-1733

Valse aux adieux, La. *See* Farewell Party,
The

Vanessa (Walpole, Hugh) CLC II-1189; MP
XII-6871; MP:BF III-1656

Vanished World, The (Bates) MPII:NF
IV-1628

Vanity Fair (Thackeray) CLC II-1190; MP
XII-6875; MP:BF III-1660

Vanity of Human Wishes, The (Johnson, S.)
MPII:P VI-2330

Városalapító, A. *See* City Builder, The

Vathek (Beckford) CLC II-1194; MP
XII-6881; MP:BF III-1667

Vatican Swindle, The. *See* Lafcadio's
Adventures

Vecherom. *See* In the Evening

Vedi (Mehta) MPII:NF IV-1635

Veien til Agra. *See* Road to Agra, The

Vein of Iron (Glasgow) CLCII IV-1651;
MPII:AF IV-1738

Vek. *See* Age, The

Velázquez (Sérullaz) MPII:JYABio IV-1807

"Veldt, The" (Bradbury) MPII:SS VI-2485

Velvet Horn, The (Lytle) MP XII-6884;
MP:AF III-1363

Vendor of Sweets, The (Narayan) CLCII
IV-1653; MPII:BCF IV-1780

Vendredi. *See* Friday

Venetian Glass Nephew, The (Wylie) CLC
II-1194; MP XII-6887; MP:AF III-1367

Venice Preserved (Otway) CLC II-1195;
MP XII-6890

Vent, Le. *See* Wind, The

Venus and Adonis (Shakespeare) CLC
II-1196; MP XII-6893

"Venus, Cupid, Folly, and Time" (Taylor)
MPII:SS VI-2489

Venusberg (Powell) CLCII IV-1654;
MPII:BCF IV-1785

Verde embeleso de la vida humana. *See*
Green enravishment of human life

Veres dorés. *See* Golden Verses

Verfolgung und Ermordung Jean-Paul
Marats, dargestellt durch die
Schauspielgruppe des Hospizes zu
Charenton unter der Anleitung des Herrn
de Sade, Die. *See* Marat/Sade

"Verlobung in St. Domingo, Der." *See*
"Engagement in Santo Domingo, The"

Verlorene Ehre der Katharina Blum, Die.
See Lost Honor of Katharina Blum, The

Vermischte Bemerkungen. *See* Culture and
Value

Verratenes Volk. *See* November 1918

"Verses on the Unknown Soldier"
(Mandelstam, O.) MPII:P VI-2334

Versiegelte Zeit, Die. *See* Sculpting in Time

Verstoorde leven, Het. *See* Interrupted Life,
An

Verstörung. *See* Gargoyles

Vertauschten Köpfe, Die. *See* Transposed
Heads, The

"Vertical Ladder, The" (Sansom) MPII:SS
VI-2493

"Verwandlung, Die." *See* "Metamorphosis,
The"

Verwirrungen des Zöglings Törless, Die.
See Young Törless

Very Private Eye, A (Pym) MPII:NF
IV-1641

Verzauberung, Die. *See* Spell, The

Vesennii dozhd. *See* Spring Rain

Veshniye vody. *See* Torrents of Spring, The
(Turgenev)

Vicar of Bullhampton, The (Trollope) CLC
II-1197; MP XII-6897; MP:BF III-1670

Vicar of Wakefield, The (Goldsmith) CLC
II-1198; MP XII-6901; MP:BF III-1674

Vicomte de Bragelonne, The (Dumas, *père*)
CLC II-1199; MP XII-6904; MP:EF
III-1341

Victim, The (Bellow) MP XII-6911; MP:AF III-1371

Victoria (Hamsun) CLCII IV-1655; MPII:WF IV-1709

Victory (Conrad) CLC II-1200; MP XII-6914; MP:BF III-1678

"Victrola" (Morris) MPII:SS VI-2497

Vida a plazos de Don Jacobo Lerner, La. *See* Fragmented Life of Don Jacobo Lerner, The

Vida breve, La. *See* Brief Life, A

Vida de Lazarillo de Tormes y de sus fortunatas y adversidades, La. *See* Lazarillo de Tormes

Vida inútil de Pito Pérez, La. *See* Futile Life of Pito Pérez, The

Vie est ailleurs, La. *See* Life Is Elsewhere

Vienna: Lusthaus (Clarke, M.) CLCII IV-1655; MPII:D IV-1682

Viento fuerte. *See* Strong Wind

"Views of My Father Weeping" (Barthelme, D.) MPII:SS VI-2500

Vile Bodies (Waugh) CLC II-1202; MP XII-6918; MP:BF III-1682

Village, The (Bunin) CLC II-1203; MP XII-6922; MP:EF III-1349

Village, The (Crabbe) MP XII-6927

Villagers, The (Icaza) MP:AF III-1375. *See also* Huasipungo

Villette (Brontë, C.) CLC II-1204; MP XII-6929; MP:BF III-1686

"Villon's Wife" (Dazai) MPII:SS VI-2504

Vindication of Natural Society, A (Burke) MP XII-6934

Vingt Mille Lieues sous les mers. *See* Twenty Thousand Leagues

Violent Bear It Away, The (O'Connor) MP XII-6937; MP:AF III-1380

Violent Land, The (Amado) CLC II-1206; MP XII-6939; MP:AF III-1383

Violins of Saint-Jacques, The (Fermor) CLCII IV-1656; MPII:BCF IV-1790

Vipers' Tangle (Mauriac) CLCII IV-1657; MPII:WF IV-1715

Virgin and the Gipsy, The (Lawrence) CLCII IV-1658; MPII:BCF IV-1797

Virgin Soil (Turgenev) CLC II-1206; MP XII-6944; MP:EF III-1354

"Virginia Britannia" (Moore, M.) MPII:P VI-2338

Virginia Comedians, The (Cooke, J.) CLC II-1208; MP XII-6949; MP:AF III-1388

Virginian, The (Wister) CLC II-1208; MP XII-6952; MP:AF III-1392; MPII:JYAFic IV-1553

Virginians, The (Thackeray) CLC II-1209; MP XII-6956; MP:BF III-1692

Visconte dimezzato, Il. *See* Cloven Viscount, The

Visión de Anáhuac (Reyes) MP XII-6961

Vision of Judgment, The (Byron) MPII:P VI-2341

Vision of William, Concerning Piers the Plowman (Langland) CLC II-1212; MP XII-6965

Visit, The (Dürrenmatt) CLCII IV-1659; MPII:D IV-1688

"Visit of Charity, A" (Welty) MPII:SS VI-2507

"Visit to Grandmother, A" (Kelley, W.) MPII:SS VI-2510

Visitants (Stow) CLCII IV-1661; MPII:BCF IV-1802

Visitation of Spirits, A (Kenan) MPII:AfAm III-1473

Visitors from London (Barne) MPII:JYAFic IV-1557

Vita Nuova, The (Dante Alighieri) MP XII-6968

Vivian Grey (Disraeli) CLC II-1212; MP XII-6971; MP:BF III-1698

Vivisector, The (White) CLCII IV-1662; MPII:BCF IV-1806

"Viy" (Gogol) MPII:SS VI-2513

"Viyon no tsuma." *See* "Villon's Wife"

Voice from the Chorus, A (Sinyavsky) MPII:NF IV-1646

Voices from the Southwest (Bernard) MPII:JYABio IV-1810

Voices in the Mirror (Parks) MPII:AfAm III-1478

Voices in Time (MacLennan) CLCII IV-1663; MPII:BCF IV-1812

Voices of Silence, The (Malraux) MP XII-6975

Voie royale, La. *See* Royal Way, The

Volpone (Jonson) CLC II-1213; MP XII-6978

Volunteers (Friel) CLCII IV-1665; MPII:D IV-1695

Volupté (Sainte-Beuve) CLC II-1215; MP XII-6983; MP:EF III-1360

Volverás a Región. See Return to Región

Von Berlin nach Jerusalem. See From Berlin to Jerusalem

Voraussetzungen einer Erzählung. See Cassandra

Vorob'evy gory. See Sparrow Hills

Vospominaniya. See Hope Against Hope

Voss (White) CLCII IV-1666; MPII:BCF IV-1817

"Vowels" (Rimbaud) MPII:P VI-2345

Voyage au centre de la tcrrc. See Journey to the Center of the Earth

Voyage of the Beagle, The (Darwin) MP XII-6987

Voyage of the "Dawn Treader," The. See Chronicles of Narnia, The

Voyage Out, The (Woolf) CLCII IV-1667; MPII:BCF IV-1823

Voyage Round My Father, A (Mortimer) CLCII IV-1668; MPII:D IV-1701

Voyage to Tomorrow (Hakim) CLCII IV-1669; MPII:D IV-1706

"Voyages" (Crane, H.) MPII:P VI-2348

Voyages of Captain Cook, The (Hoobler and Hoobler) MPII:JYABio IV-1814

Voyages of Christopher Columbus, The (Sperry) MPII:JYABio IV-1818

Voyages of Doctor Dolittle, The (Lofting) MPII:JYAFic IV-1561

Voyelles. See Vowels

"Vozvrashchenie Chorba. See Return of Chorb, The

Vremya bolshikh ozhidany. See Story of a Life, The

"Vrindaban" (Paz) MPII:P VI-2351

Vtoraia kniga. See Hope Abandoned

Vuelta. See Return

Vy, idushchiye mimo menya. See You, walking past me

Vyrozumnf. See Memorandum, The

"Vystrel." See "Shot, The"

W

Wagahai wa neko de aru. *See* I Am a Cat

Wahrheit und Methode. *See* Truth and Method

"Waiting" (Oates) MPII:SS VI-2517

Waiting for Godot (Beckett) CLC II-1215; MP XII-6991

"Waiting for the Barbarians" (Cavafy) MPII:P VI-2354

Waiting for the Barbarians (Coetzee) CLCII IV-1671; MPII:BCF IV-1830

Waiting to Exhale (McMillan) MPII:AfAm III-1484

"Wake Up" (Carver) MPII:P VI-2357

"Wakefield" (Hawthorne) MPII:SS VI-2521

"Waking in the Blue" (Lowell, R.) MPII:P VI-2361

Walden (Thoreau) MP XII-6996

"Wales Visitation" (Ginsberg) MPII:P VI-2364

"Walk, The" (Walser) MPII:SS VI-2525

Walk a Mile and Get Nowhere (Southall) MPII:JYAFic IV-1564

Walk in the Night, A (La Guma) CLCII IV-1672; MPII:BCF IV-1837

Walk like a Mortal (Wickenden) MPII:JYAFic IV-1568

Walk Me to the Distance (Everett) MPII:AfAm III-1490

Walk on the Wild Side, A (Algren) CLCII IV-1673; MPII:AF IV-1743

Walk the World's Rim (Baker, B.) MPII:JYAFic IV-1572

Walker in the City, A (Kazin) MPII:NF IV-1651

Wall, The (Hersey) CLCII IV-1674; MPII:AF IV-1748

"Wall, The" (Montale) MPII:P VI-2368

"Wall, The" (Sansom) MPII:SS VI-2530

"Wall, The" (Sartre) MPII:SS VI-2534

Wall Jumper, The (Schneider) CLCII IV-1676; MPII:WF IV-1720

Wallenstein (Schiller) CLC II-1216; MP XII-7001

Walls of Windy Troy, The (Braymer) MPII:JYABio IV-1822

Walt Whitman (Deutsch) MPII:JYABio IV-1826

"Walter Briggs" (Updike) MPII:SS VI-2537

Wanderer, The (Alain-Fournier) CLC II-1217; MP XII-7006; MP:EF III-1365

"Wanderers, The" (Lewis, A.) MPII:SS VI-2541

Wanderers, The (Mphahlele) CLCII IV-1677; MPII:BCF IV-1843

Wandering Jew, The (Sue) CLC II-1218; MP XII-7010; MP:EF III-1370

Wandering Scholar from Paradise, The (Sachs) CLC II-1219; MP XII-7014

"Wang River Sequence, The" (Wang) MPII:P VI-2371

Wang-ch'uan chi. *See* Wang River Sequence, The

Waning of the Middle Ages, The (Huizinga) MP XII-7017

Wapshot Chronicle, The (Cheever, J.) MP XII-7020; MP:AF III-1396

Wapshot Scandal, The (Cheever, J.) MP XII-7024; MP:AF III-1400

"War" (Pirandello) MPII:SS VI-2544

War and Peace (Tolstoy) CLC II-1220; MP XII-7028; MP:EF III-1374

War and Remembrance (Wouk) CLCII IV-1678; MPII:AF IV-1754

War Between the Tates, The (Lurie) CLCII IV-1681; MPII:AF IV-1759

War of the End of the World, The (Vargas Llosa) CLCII IV-1682; MPII:AF IV-1764

War of the Worlds, The (Wells) CLC II-1222; MP XII-7035; MP:BF III-1702; MPII:JYAFic IV-1575

War Years, The. *See* Abraham Lincoln

"Ward No. 6" (Chekhov) MPII:SS VI-2548

Warden, The (Trollope) CLC II-1222; MP XII-7038; MP:BF III-1706

Warden's Niece, The (Avery) MPII:JYAFic IV-1579

Wariat i zakonnica. *See* Madman and the Nun, The

Warrior for a Lost Nation (Johnson, Dorothy) MPII:JYABio IV-1830

Wars, The (Findley) CLCII IV-1683; MPII:BCF IV-1848

Was soll aus dem Jungen bloss werden? *See* What's to Become of the Boy?

"Wash" (Faulkner) MPII:SS VI-2552

Washington Square (James, H.) CLC II-1224; MP XII-7041; MP:AF III-1405

Wasps, The (Aristophanes) CLC II-1225; MP XII-7044

Wasserfälle von Slunj, Die. *See* Waterfalls of Slunj, The

Waste Land, The (Eliot, T. S.) MP XII-7047

Watch on the Rhine (Hellman) CLCII IV-1684; MPII:D IV-1712

Watch That Ends the Night, The (MacLennan) CLCII IV-1685; MPII:BCF IV-1854

"Watcher, The" (Calvino) MPII:SS VI-2556

Watchmaker of Everton, The (Simenon) CLCII IV-1686; MPII:WF IV-1725

Water Hen, The (Witkiewicz) CLCII IV-1687; MPII:D IV-1718

Waterfall, The (Drabble) CLCII IV-1688; MPII:BCF IV-1859

Waterfalls of Slunj, The (Doderer) CLCII IV-1689; MPII:WF IV-1729

Waterland (Swift) CLCII IV-1691; MPII:BCF IV-1865

Waters of Kronos, The (Richter, C.) MP XII-7049; MP:AF III-1409

Watership Down (Adams, R.) CLCII IV-1692; MPII:BCF IV-1870; MPII:JYAFic IV-1582

Watt (Beckett) CLCII IV-1694; MPII:BCF IV-1875

Wave, The (Scott, E.) CLCII IV-1695; MPII:AF IV-1769

"Wave" (Snyder) MPII:P VI-2375

Waverley (Scott, Sir W.) CLC II-1226; MP XII-7052; MP:BF III-1710

Waves, The (Woolf) CLC II-1227; MP XII-7057; MP:BF III-1716

Way Home, The. *See* Fortunes of Richard Mahony, The

Way of All Flesh, The (Butler) CLC II-1228; MP XII-7061; MP:BF III-1721

Way of the World, The (Congreve) CLC II-1230; MP XII-7066

Way That Girls Love, The. *See* Splendors and Miseries of Courtesans, The

Way the Future Was, The (Pohl) MPII:NF IV-1656

Way to Rainy Mountain, The (Momaday) MPII:NF IV-1660

Way West, The (Guthrie) CLCII IV-1698; MPII:AF IV-1773

Wayah of the Real People (Steele, W.) MPII:JYAFic IV-1585

Ways of Escape (Green) MPII:NF IV-1665

Ways of Seeing (Berger) MPII:NF IV-1670

We (Zamyatin) CLCII IV-1700; MPII:WF IV-1734

We Alcotts (Fisher, A., *and* Rabe, O.) MPII:JYABio IV-1834

"We Are Seven" (Wordsworth) MPII:P VI-2378

We Dickinsons (Fisher, P. *and* Rabe, O.) MPII:JYABio IV-1838

We Have Tomorrow (Bontemps) MPII:JYABio IV-1842

"We Met for the Last Time" (Akhmatova) MPII:P VI-2381

Wealth of Nations, The (Smith, A.) MP XII-7070

"Weary Blues, The" (Hughes, L.) MPII:P VI-2384

Weather in the Streets, The (Lehmann) CLCII IV-1701; MPII:BCF IV-1880

Weathering the Storm (Evans, E.) MPII:JYABio IV-1846

Weaver of Dreams (Vipont) MPII:JYABio IV-1850

Weavers, The (Hauptmann) CLC II-1231; MP XII-7073

Web and the Rock, The (Wolfe) CLC II-1232; MP XII-7077; MP:AF III-1412

W. E. B. Du Bois (Hamilton) MPII:JYABio IV-1853

Weeds (Kelley, E.) CLCII IV-1702; MPII:AF IV-1777

Week on the Concord and Merrimack Rivers, A (Thoreau) MP XII-7081

Weight of the World, The (Handke) MPII:NF IV-1675

Well, The (Jolley) CLCII IV-1703; MPII:BCF IV-1885

West with the Night (Markham) MPII:JYABio IV-1857; MPII:NF IV-1681

Westing Game, The (Raskin) MPII:JYAFic IV-1589

Westmark trilogy, The (Alexander, L.) MPII:JYAFic IV-1593

Westward Ho! (Kingsley, C.) CLC II-1233; MP XII-7084; MP:BF III-1726

"Wet Saturday" (Collier, John) MPII:SS VI-2562

What a Beautiful Sunday! (Semprun) CLCII IV-1704; MPII:WF IV-1739

What Every Woman Knows (Barrie) CLC II-1234; MP XII-7089

What I'm Going to Do, I Think (Woiwode) CLCII IV-1705; MPII:AF IV-1784

"What Is the Connection Between Men and Women?" (Oates) MPII:SS VI-2565

What It's All About (Frolov) MPII:JYAFic IV-1597

What Katy Did (Coolidge, S.) MPII:JYAFic IV-1600

What Maisie Knew (James, H.) CLC II-1235; MP XII-7094; MP:AF III-1416

What Manner of Man (Bennett, L.) MPII:JYABio IV-1861

What Price Glory? (Anderson, M., and Laurence Stallings) CLCII IV-1706; MPII:D IV-1723

What the Butler Saw (Orton) CLCII IV-1707; MPII:D IV-1728

What's Bred in the Bone (Davies, R.) CLCII IV-1708; MPII:BCF IV-1890

What's to Become of the Boy? (Böll) MPII:NF IV-1687

When I Was a Boy (Kästner) MPII:JYABio IV-1865

"When I Was Thirteen" (Welch) MPII:SS VI-2569

When I Whistle (End) CLCII IV-1709; MPII:WF IV-1745

"When in the chronicle of wasted time" See Sonnet 106

"When Lilacs Last in the Dooryard Bloom'd" (Whitman) MPII:P VI-2388

When the Legends Die (Borland) MPII:JYAFic IV-1603

"When the Light Gets Green" (Warren) MPII:SS VI-2573

When the Mountain Fell (Ramuz) CLC II-1235; MP XII-7097; MP:EF III-1383

When the Phone Rang (Mazer, H.) MPII:JYAFic IV-1606

When Thunders Spoke (Sneve) MPII:JYAFic IV-1609

"When to the sessions of sweet silent thought" See Sonnet 30

When We Dead Awaken (Ibsen) CLC II-1236; MP XII-7100

"When We with Sappho" (Rexroth) MPII:P VI-2391

When You Comin' Back, Red Ryder? (Medoff) CLCII IV-1710; MPII:D IV-1733

"Where" (Berry) MPII:P VI-2394

Where Angels Fear to Tread (Forster) CLC II-1236; MP XII-7104; MP:BF III-1731

"Where Are You Going, Where Have You Been?" (Oates) MPII:SS VI-2577

Where Has Tommy Flowers Gone? (McNally) CLCII IV-1711; MPII:D IV-1739

Where the Air Is Clear (Fuentes) MP XII-7107; MP:AF III-1420

Where the Lilies Bloom (Cleaver, V. and Cleaver, B.) MPII:JYAFic IV-1612

Where the Red Fern Grows (Rawls) MPII:JYAFic IV-1616

Which Way Freedom? (Hansen) MPII:JYAFic IV-1620

"Whip, The" (Creeley) MPII:P VI-2397

Whipping Boy, The (Fleischman) MPII:JYAFic IV-1624

Whistling Boy, The (Arthur) MPII:JYAFic IV-1627

White Company, The (Doyle) CLC II-1237; MP XII-7111; MP:BF III-1735

White Devil, The (Webster) CLC II-1238; MP XII-7115

White Goddess, The (Graves) MPII:NF IV-1692

"White Heron, A" (Jewett) MPII:SS VI-2581

"White Horses of Vienna, The" (Boyle, K.) MPII:SS VI-2585

White-Jacket (Melville) CLC II-1239; MP XII-7118; MP:AF III-1425

"White Man's Burden, The" (Kipling) MPII:P VI-2400

"White Night" (Akhmatova) MPII:P
VI-2404

"White Nights" (Dostoevski) MPII:SS
VI-2589

"White Stocking, The" (Lawrence) MPII:SS
VI-2593

"Whitsun Weddings, The" (Larkin) MPII:P
VI-2407

Who Has Seen the Wind (Mitchell) CLCII
IV-1712; MPII:BCF IV-1895

Whole Armour, The. See Guyana Quartet,
The

"Whole Loaf, A" (Agnon) MPII:SS VI-2597

"Whore of Mensa, The" (Allen, W.)
MPII:SS VI-2602

"Whoroscope" (Beckett) MPII:P VI-2410

Who's Afraid of Virginia Woolf? (Albee)
MP XII-7121

Whose Town? (Graham, J.) MPII:JYAFic
IV-1630

"Why Don't You Dance?" (Carver)
MPII:SS VI-2605

"Why I Live at the P.O." (Welty) MPII:SS
VI-2608

"Why is my verse so barren of new pride?"
See Sonnet 76

"Why the Classics" (Herbert, Z.) MPII:P
VI-2414

Wickford Point (Marquand) CLC II-1240;
MP XII-7126; MP:AF III-1429

"Wide Net, The" (Welty) MPII:SS VI-2612

Wide Sargasso Sea (Rhys) CLCII IV-1714;
MPII:BCF IV-1899

Widerstand und Ergebung. See Letters and
Papers from Prison

Widmung, Die. See Devotion

Widower's Son, The (Sillitoe) CLCII
IV-1715; MPII:BCF IV-1904

"Widow's Son, The" (Lavin) MPII:SS
VI-2616

Wieland (Brown, Charles) CLC II-1241;
MP XII-7129; MP:AF III-1433

Wielopole, Wielopole (Kantor, T.) CLCII
IV-1717; MPII:D IV-1745

Wilbur and Orville (Howard) MPII:JYABio
IV-1869

Wild Animals, Gentle Women (Facklam)
MPII:JYABio IV-1872

Wild Ass's Skin, The (Balzac) CLC
II-1241; MP XII-7133; MP:EF III-1386

Wild Duck, The (Ibsen) CLC II-1242; MP
XII-7137

"Wild Nights—Wild Nights!" (Dickinson,
E.) MPII:P VI-2417

Wild Palms, The (Faulkner) MP XII-7142;
MP:AF III-1437

"Wild Swans" (Munro, A.) MPII:SS
VI-2619

"Wild Swans at Coole, The" (Yeats) MPII:P
VI-2420

Wild Wales (Borrow) MP XII-7145

Wilhelm Meister's Apprenticeship (Goethe)
CLC II-1243; MP XII-7148; MP:EF
III-1390

Wilhelm Meister's Travels (Goethe) CLC
II-1245; MP XII-7152; MP:EF III-1395

"Will, The" (Lavin) MPII:SS VI-2623

Will Rogers (Ketchum) MPII:JYABio
IV-1876

"Will You Please Be Quiet, Please?"
(Carver) MPII:SS VI-2627

Willa Cather: The Woman and Her Works
(Brown, M., and Crone) MPII:JYABio
IV-1883

Willa: The Story of Willa Cather's Growing
Up (Franchere) MPII:JYABio IV-1880

William Blake (Daugherty, J.)
MPII:JYABio IV-1887

William Shakespeare (Rowse)
MPII:JYABio IV-1891

William Tell (Schiller) CLC II-1246; MP
XII-7156

"William Wilson" (Poe) MPII:SS VI-2630

"Willis Carr at Bleak House" (Madden)
MPII:SS VI-2634

"Willows, The" (Blackwood) MPII:SS
VI-2638

Will's Boy (Morris) MPII:NF IV-1696

Wind, The (Simon, C.) CLCII IV-1717;
MPII:WF IV-1750

"Wind and the Snow of Winter, The"
(Clark) MPII:SS VI-2642

Wind from the Plain, The (Kemal) CLCII
IV-1718; MPII:WF IV-1754

Wind in My Hand (Fukuda) MPII:JYABio
IV-1895

Wind in the Willows, The (Grahame) CLC
II-1247; MP XII-7159; MP:BF III-1739;
MPII:JYAFic IV-1633
Wind, Sand, and Stars (Saint-Exupéry) MP
XII-7163; MP:EF III-1400;
MPII:JYABio IV-1899
"Windhover, The" (Hopkins, G.) MPII:P
VI-2423
"Windows" (Apollinaire) MPII:P VI-2426
"Windows, The" (Mallarmé) MPII:P
VI-2429
Windows for the Crown Prince (Vining)
MPII:JYABio IV-1903
Winds of War, The (Wouk) CLCII
IV-1720; MPII:AF IV-1790
Windsor Castle (Ainsworth) CLC II-1248;
MP XII-7166; MP:BF III-1743
"Wine Menagerie, The" (Crane, H.) MPII:P
VI-2432
Wine of Astonishment, The (Lovelace)
CLCII IV-1723; MPII:AfAm III-1496;
MPII:BCF IV-1909
Winesburg, Ohio (Anderson, S.) CLC
II-1249; MP XII-7171; MP:AF III-1440
Winged Moccasins (Farnsworth)
MPII:JYABio IV-1907
Wings (Kopit) CLCII IV-1725; MPII:D
IV-1751
Wings of the Dove, The (James, H.) CLC
II-1250; MP XII-7176; MP:AF III-1445
Winners, The (Cortázar) CLCII IV-1726;
MPII:AF IV-1795
Winnie-the-Pooh (Milne) MPII:JYAFic
IV-1637
Winona. See Magazine Novels of Pauline
Hopkins, The.
Winston Churchill and the Story of Two
World Wars (Coolidge, O.)
MPII:JYABio IV-1911
"Winter: 1978" (Beattie) MPII:SS VI-2652
"Winter Dreams" (Fitzgerald) MPII:SS
VI-2645
"Winter Night" (Boyle, K.) MPII:SS
VI-2649
Winter's Tale, The (Shakespeare) CLC
II-1251; MP XII-7181
Winterset (Anderson, Maxwell) CLC
II-1252; MP XII-7186
"Wireless" (Kipling) MPII:SS VI-2656

Wisdom of the Sands, The (Saint-Exupéry)
MP XII-7189
Wise Blood (O'Connor) MP XII-7192;
MP:AF III-1450
Wise Virgin (Wilson, A. N.) CLCII
IV-1727; MPII:BCF IV-1915
"Wish House, The" (Kipling) MPII:SS
VI-2660
"Wissler Remembers" (Stern) MPII:SS
VI-2664
Wit and Its Relation to the Unconscious
(Freud) MPII:NF IV-1704
Witch in the Wood (The Queen of Air and
Darkness), The. See Once and Future
King, The
Witch of Blackbird Pond, The (Speare)
MPII:JYAFic IV-1640
Witches of Worm, The (Snyder)
MPII:JYAFic IV-1643
"Witch's Money" (Collier, John) MPII:SS
VI-2668
"With All My Thoughts" (Celan) MPII:P
VI-2435
With Fire and Sword (Sienkiewicz) CLC
II-1253; MP XII-7195; MP:EF III-1404
"With Trumpets and Zithers" (Miłosz)
MPII:P VI-2438
"Within and Without" (Hesse) MPII:SS
VI-2672
Within the Gates (O'Casey) CLC II-1254;
MP XII-7199
Witz und sein Beziehung zum
Unbewussten, Der. See Wit and Its
Relation to the Unconscious
Wizard of Earthsea, A. See Earthsea series,
The
Wizard of Oz, The (Baum) MPII:JYAFic
IV-1646
Wizard of the Dome (Rosen) MPII:JYABio
IV-1915
"Wodwo" (Hughes, Ted) MPII:P VI-2442
Wolf Solent (Powys, J.) CLC II-1255; MP
XII-7203; MP:BF III-1749
Wolves of Willoughby Chase, The (Aiken,
Joan) MPII:JYAFic IV-1650
Woman Against Slavery (Scott, J.)
MPII:JYABio IV-1919
"Woman at the Store, The" (Mansfield)
MPII:SS VI-2676

Woman from Sarajevo, The (Andri) CLCII IV-1728; MPII:WF IV-1764

Woman Hater, The (Beaumont *and* Fletcher) CLC II-1255; MP XII-7207

Woman in the Dunes, The (Abe) CLCII IV-1729; MPII:WF IV-1769

Woman in White, The (Collins, Wilkie) CLC II-1256; MP XII-7211; MP:BF III-1753

Woman Killed with Kindness, A (Heywood) CLC II-1257; MP XII-7217

"Woman Me" (Angelou) MPII:P VI-2445

Woman of Rome, The (Moravia) CLC II-1259; MP XII-7221; MP:EF III-1409

Woman of the Pharisees, A (Mauriac) CLCII IV-1730; MPII:WF IV-1774

Woman on the Edge of Time (Piercy) CLCII IV-1732; MPII:AF IV-1800

Woman Warrior, The (Kingston) MPII:JYABio IV-1922; MPII:NF IV-1709

Woman Who Created Frankenstein, The (Harris, J.) MPII:JYABio IV-1926

"Woman Who Rode Away, The" (Lawrence) MPII:SS VI-2680

Woman's Life, A (Maupassant) CLC II-1259; MP XII-7224; MP:EF III-1413

Woman's Prize, The (Fletcher) CLC II-1260; MP XII-7229

Women at the Pump, The (Hamsun) CLCII IV-1733; MPII:WF IV-1779

Women Beware Women (Middleton) CLC II-1261; MP XII-7235

Women in Love (Lawrence, D. H.) MP XII-7239; MP:BF III-1760

Women of Brewster Place, The (Naylor) CLCII IV-1734; MPII:AF IV-1805; MPII:AfAm III-1502

Women of Messina (Vittorini) CLCII IV-1736; MPII:WF IV-1784

Women of the Air (Lomax) MPII:JYABio IV-1930

Women of Trachis, The (Sophocles) CLC II-1262; MP XII-7242

Women of Trachis (Sophocles, trans. by Pound) CLCII IV-1736; MPII:D IV-1757

Women Who Led the Way (Boynick) MPII:JYABio IV-1933

Women Who Shaped History (Buckmaster) MPII:JYABio IV-1937

Women's Room, The (French) CLCII IV-1737; MPII:AF IV-1810

Wonder-Worker, The (Jacobson) CLCII IV-1738; MPII:BCF IV-1921

Wonderful Adventures of Nils, The (Lagerlöf) MPII:JYAFic IV-1653

Wonderful Flight to the Mushroom Planet, The. *See* Mushroom Planet series, The

Wonderful Fool (End) CLCII IV-1740; MPII:WF IV-1789

"Wonderful Tar-Baby Story, The" (Harris, J. C.) MPII:SS VI-2684

Wonderful Wizard of Oz, The. *See* Wizard of Oz, The

Wonderland (Oates) CLCII IV-1741; MPII:AF IV-1815

"Wondersmith, The" (O'Brien, F.) MPII:SS VI-2687

Woodcutters (Bernhard) CLCII IV-1742. *See also* Holzfällen

Woodlanders, The (Hardy) CLC II-1263; MP XII-7247; MP:BF II-1764

Woodrow Wilson Story, The (Peare) MPII:JYABio IV-1941

Woods, The (Mamet) CLCII IV-1743; MPII:D IV-1762

Woodstock (Scott, W.) CLC II-1265; MP XII-7251; MP:BF III-1768

Woody Guthrie (Klein) MPII:JYABio IV-1945

Word Child, A (Murdoch) CLCII IV-1744; MPII:BCF IV-1926

"Words" (Plath) MPII:P VI-2448

Words, The (Sartre) MPII:NF IV-714

Words and Music (Beckett) CLCII IV-1745; MPII:D IV-1766

Words by Heart (Sebestyen) MPII:JYAFic IV-1656

"Words for the Wind" (Roethke) MPII:P VI-2451

Words upon the Window-Pane, The (Yeats) CLCII IV-1746; MPII:D IV-1772

"Work" (Plante) MPII:SS VI-2692

Work of Art in the Age of Mechanical Reproduction, The (Benjamin) MPII:NF IV-1719

Workhouse Ward, The (Gregory) CLCII IV-1748; MPII:D IV-1778

Works and Days (Hesiod) MP XII-7254

Works of Jonathan Edwards (Edwards) MP XII-7256

Works of Love, The (Morris) CLCII IV-1749; MPII:AF IV-1820

"World, The" (Vaughan) MPII:P VI-2454

World According to Garp, The (Irving, J.) CLCII IV-1749; MPII:AF IV-1825

"World According to Hsü, The" (Mukherjee) MPII:SS VI-2696

World as Will and Idea, The (Schopenhauer) MP XII-7259

"World Ends, A" (Hildesheimer) MPII:SS VI-2701

World Enough and Time (Warren) CLC II-1266; MP XII-7262; MP:AF III-1454

World in Ripeness, The (Bates) MPII:NF IV-1628

"World Is Too Much with Us, The" (Wordsworth) MPII:P VI-2457

World My Wilderness, The (Macaulay) CLCII IV-1752; MPII:BCF IV-1930

"World of Apples, The" (Cheever, J.) MPII:SS VI-2705

World of Love, A (Bowen, E.) CLCII IV-1753; MPII:BCF IV-1935

World of Pooh. See Winnie-the-Pooh

World of Samuel Adams, The (Chidsey) MPII:JYABio IV-1949

"World of Stone, The" (Borowski) MPII:SS VI-2709

World of Strangers, A (Gordimer) CLCII IV-1754; MPII:BCF IV-1940

World of the Thibaults, The (Martin du Gard) CLC II-1267; MP XII-7266; MP:EF III-1419

World of Wonders. See Deptford Trilogy, The

World on the Wane, A. See Tristes Tropiques

World Out of the Sea, A. See Out of the Cradle Endlessly Rocking

World's Illusion, The (Wassermann) CLC II-1268; MP XII-7271; MP:EF III-1425

"Worn Path, A" (Welty) MPII:SS VI-2713

Woyzeck (Büchner) CLC II-1269; MP XII-7275

"Wrack" (Barthelme, D.) MPII:SS VI-2716

Wreath for Udomo, A (Abrahams) CLCII IV-1755; MPII:BCF IV-1945

Wreath of Roses, A (Taylor, Elizabeth) CLCII IV-1756; MPII:BCF IV-1950

"Wreck of the Deutschland, The" (Hopkins, G.) MPII:P VI-2461

Wreck of the Grosvenor, The (Russell, W.) CLC II-1269; MP XII-7278; MP:BF III-1772

Wreckage of Agathon, The (Gardner) CLCII IV-1758; MPII:AF IV-1830

Wretched of the Earth, The (Fanon) MPII:NF IV-1725

Wright Brothers, The (Glines) MPII:JYABio IV-1952

Wrinkle in Time, A (L'Engle) MPII:JYAFic IV-1660

Writing and Difference (Derrida) MPII:NF IV-1730

Wschody i zachody ksiyca. See Moonrise, Moonset

"Wunderkind, Das." See "Infant Prodigy, The"

"Wunderkind" (McCullers) MPII:SS VI-2719

Wunschloses Unglück. See Sorrow Beyond Dreams, A

Wuthering Heights (Brontë, E.) CLC II-1270; MP XII-7281; MP:BF III-1775; MPII:JYAFic IV-1664

XYZ

X/Self (Brathwaite) MPII:P VI-2465

Xala (Sembène) CLCII IV-1759; MPII:WF IV-1793

Xenogenesis Trilogy, The (Butler) MPII:AfAm III-1507

". . . y no se lo tragó la tierra." *See* ". . . and the earth did not part"

"Yachts, The" (Williams, W.) MPII:P VI-2470

Yama no oto. *See* Sound of the Mountain, The

Yankee from Olympus (Bowen, C.) MPII:JYABio IV-1956

Year of Living Dangerously, The (Koch) CLCII IV-1760; MPII:BCF IV-1955

Year of the Dragon, The (Chin) CLCII IV-1761; MPII:D IV-1783

Yearling, The (Rawlings) CLC II-1272; MP XII-7286; MP:AF III-1459; MPII:JYAFic IV-1667

Yearning (Hooks) MPII:AfAm III-1513

Years, The (Woolf) CLC II-1273; MP XII-7290; MP:BF III-1781

Years of Hope. *See* Story of a Life, The

Years with Ross, The (Thurber) MPII:NF IV-1736

Yellow Back Radio Broke-Down (Reed, I.) CLCII IV-1762; MPII:AF IV-1835; MPII:AfAm III-1519

Yellow Raft in Blue Water, A (Dorris) MPII:JYAFic IV-1671

"Yellow Woman" (Silko) MPII:SS VI-2724

Yemassee, The (Simms) CLC II-1274; MP XII-7295; MP:AF III-1463

"Yentl the Yeshiva Boy" (Singer) MPII:SS VI-2729

Yer demir, gök bakir. *See* Iron Earth, Copper Sky

"Yermolai and the Miller's Wife" (Turgenev) MPII:SS VI-2733

"Yes" and "No" (Yevtushenko) MPII:P VI-2473

"Yet Do I Marvel" (Cullen) MPII:P VI-2476

Yonnondio (Olsen) CLCII IV-1763; MPII:AF IV-1841

"You, Andrew Marvell" (MacLeish) MPII:P VI-2479

"You Are in Bear Country" (Kumin) MPII:P VI-2482

You Can't Go Home Again (Wolfe) CLC II-1275; MP XII-7299; MP:AF III-1467

You Can't Take It with You (Kaufman *and* Hart) CLCII IV-1764; MPII:D IV-1788

You Know Me Al (Lardner) CLC II-1276; MP XII-7303; MP:AF III-1472

You Never Knew Her As I Did! (Hunter, M.) MPII:JYAFic IV-1674

"You, walking past me" (Tsvetayeva) MPII:P VI-2484

Youma (Hearn) CLC II-1277; MP XII-7306; MP:AF III-1476

Young and Black in America (Alexander, R.) MPII:JYABio IV-1960

Young Fu of the Upper Yangtze (Lewis, E.) MPII:JYAFic IV-1678

"Young Goodman Brown" (Hawthorne) MPII:SS VI-2737

"Young Housewife, The" (Williams, W.) MPII:P VI-2488

Young Joseph, The. *See* Joseph and His Brothers

Young Lafayette (Eaton) MPII:JYABio IV-1963

Young Lions, The (Shaw, I.) CLCII IV-1765; MPII:AF IV-1846

Young Lonigan. *See* Studs Lonigan

Young Man from the Piedmont (Wibberley) MPII:JYABio IV-1967

Young Man in Search of Love, A (Singer) MPII:NF II-835

Young Manhood of Studs Lonigan, The. *See* Studs Lonigan

Young Thomas Edison (North) MPII:JYABio IV-1971

Young Törless (Musil) CLCII IV-1766; MPII:WF IV-1797

Young Walter Scott (Vining) MPII:JYABio IV-1975

"Young Woman of Beare, The" (Clarke, Austin) MPII:P VI-2491

Your Blues Ain't Like Mine (Campbell, B.) MPII:AfAm III-1525

Your Most Humble Servant (Graham, S.)
MPII:JYABio IV-1978
"Youth" (Conrad) MPII:JYAFic IV-1681;
MPII:SS VI-2741
Yüeh Yeh. See Moonlit Night
Yukiguni. See Snow Country
"Ykoku." See "Patriotism"
"Yume no ukihashi." See "Bridge of
Dreams, The"
Yvain (Chrétien de Troyes) CLC II-1277;
MP XII-7309

Zabablci. See Cowards, The
Zadig (Voltaire) CLC II-1278; MP
XII-7314; MP:EF III-1430
Zahradní slavnost. See Garden Party, The
Zaïre (Voltaire) CLC II-1279; MP XII-7318
"Zaklinatel zmei." See "Snake Charmer,
The"
Zapata, Mexican Rebel (Syme)
MPII:JYABio IV-1981
Zapiski iz myortvogo doma. See House of
the Dead, The
"Zapiski sumasshedshego." See "Diary of a
Madman, The"
Zarco, El (Altamirano) CLC II-1279; MP
XII-7323; MP:AF III-1480
Zashchita Luzhina. See Defense, The
Zavist. See Envy
Zazie dans le métro. See Zazie in the Metro
Zazie in the Metro (Queneau) CLCII
IV-1767; MPII:WF IV-1803
Zbablci. See Cowards, The
Zdobycie wadzy. See Seizure of Power, The
Zeit ohne Glocken. See Silesian Tetralogy,
The
Zeitgeist, Der. See Spirit of the Age, The
Zelda (Milford) MPII:JYABio IV-1985

Zen and the Art of Motorcycle Maintenance
(Pirsig) MPII:JYABio IV-1989;
MPII:NF IV-1741
Zero (Loyola Brandão) CLCII IV-1769;
MPII:AF IV-1852
Žert. See Joke, The
"Zhivye Moshchi." See "Living Relic, A"
Zhizn' cheloveka. See Life of Man, The
Zhizn'i neobychainye priklyucheniya
soldata Ivana Chonkina. See Life and
Extraordinary Adventures of Private Ivan
Chonkin, The
Ziemia Ulro. See Land of Ulro, The
Zincali, The (Borrow) MP XII-7328
Zniewolony umys. See Captive Mind, The
Zona. See Zone, The
Zona sagrada. See Holy Place
"Zone" (Apollinaire) MPII:P VI-2494
Zone, The (Dovlatov) CLCII IV-1770;
MPII:WF IV-1808
Zoo (Shklovsky) CLCII IV-1771; MPII:WF
IV-1814
Zoo Story, The (Albee) CLCII IV-1772;
MPII:D IV-1794
Zoot Suit (Valdez) CLCII IV-1773; MPII:D
IV-1799
Zorba the Greek (Kazantzakis) MP
XII-7331; MP:EF III-1435
Ztřená monost soustední. See Increased
Difficulty of Concentration, The
Zuckerman Bound (Roth) MPII:AF IV-1856
Zuckerman Unbound (Roth, P.) CLCII
IV-1774. See also Zuckerman Bound
Zuleika Dobson (Beerbohm) CLC II-1280;
MP XII-7334; MP:BF III-1787
"Zulu and the Zeide, The" (Jacobson)
MPII:SS VI-2745
Zvezdnyi bilet. See Ticket to the Stars, A
Zvyozdnyi bilet. See Ticket to the Stars, A

AUTHOR INDEX

A

ABBEY, EDWARD, CWAII I-1
  Desert Solitaire, MPII:NF I-342
ABBOTT, JACOB
  Rollo series, The, MPII:JYAFic III-1248
ABDUL-JABBAR, KAREEM, *and* PETER
    KNOBLER
  Giant Steps, MPII:JYABio II-749
ABE, KB, CWAII I-3
  Inter Ice Age 4, CLCII II-770; MPII:WF
    II-711
  Ruined Map, The, CLCII III-1321;
    MPII:WF III-1315
  Woman in the Dunes, The, CLCII
    IV-1729; MPII:WF IV-1769
ABEL, LIONEL
  Intellectual Follies, The, MPII:NF II-742
ABÉLARD, PIERRE, CWA I-1
  Historia calamitatum, MP V-2624
ABOUT, EDMOND FRANÇOIS, CWA I-2
  King of the Mountains, The, CLC I-575;
    MP VI-3156; MP:EF II-724
ABRAHAM, NELSON AHLGREN. *See*
    ALGREN, NELSON
ABRAHAMS, PETER, CWAII I-6
  Wreath for Udomo, A, CLCII IV-1755;
    MPII:BCF IV-1945
ACHEBE, CHINUA, CWAII I-8
  Arrow of God, CLCII I-69; MPII:BCF I-67
  No Longer at Ease, CLCII III-1105;
    MPII:BCF III-1219
  Things Fall Apart, CLCII IV-1544; MPII:
    BCF IV-1681; MPII:JYAFic IV-1454
ADAMOV, ARTHUR, CWA I-3; CWAII
    I-11
  Ping-Pong, MP VIII-4719
ADAMS, ALICE, CWAII I-13
  "Greyhound People," MPII:SS III-948
ADAMS, HARRIET STRATEMEYER.
    See DIXON, FRANKLIN W.
ADAMS, HENRY, CWA I-5
  Education of Henry Adams, The, MP
    III-1708; MPII:JYABio II-533
  Mont-Saint-Michel and Chartres, MP
    VII-4049
ADAMS, JOHN, CWA I-7
  Defense of the Constitutions of
    Government of the United States of
    America, A, MP III-1426

ADAMS, RICHARD, CWAII I-15
  Watership Down, CLCII IV-1692;
    MPII:BCF IV-1870; MPII:JYAFic
    IV-1582
ADDAMS, JANE
  Twenty Years at Hull-House,
    MPII:JYABio IV-1785
ADDISON, JOSEPH, CWA I-11
ADDISON, JOSEPH, SIR RICHARD
    STEELE, *and* EUSTACE BUDGELL
  Sir Roger de Coverley Papers, The, CLC
    II-1044; MP X-6067
ADLER, RENATA, CWAII I-17
  Pitch Dark, CLCII III-1209; MPII:AF
    III-1258
  Speedboat, CLCII IV-1459; MPII:AF
    IV-1511
AESCHYLUS, CWA I-16
  House of Atreus, The, CLC I-486; MP
    V-2719
  Persians, The, CLC II-862; MP
    VIII-4609
  Prometheus Bound, CLC II-924; MP
    IX-5361
  Seven Against Thebes, CLC II-1025;
    MP X-5922
  Suppliants, The, CLC II-1094; MP
    XI-6345
AESOP, CWA I-19
  Aesop's Fables, MP I-51; MP:EF I-10
AGEE, JAMES, CWA I-20; CWAII I-19
  Death in the Family, A, MP III-1354;
    MP:AF I-269; MPII:JYAFic I-321
  Let Us Now Praise Famous Men, MP
    VI-3330
  Morning Watch, The, CLCII III-1039;
    MPII:AF III-105
AGEE, JOEL
  Twelve Years, MPII:NF IV-1586
AGNON, SHMUEL YOSEF, CWAII I-21
  Bridal Canopy, The, CLCII I-200;
    MPII:WF I-194
  Guest for the Night, A, CLCII II-645;
    MPII:WF I-194
  In the Heart of the Seas, CLCII II-749;
    MPII:WF I-194
  "Kerchief, The," MPII:SS III-1255

Simple Story, A, CLCII IV-1415;
MPII:WF IV-1448
"Whole Loaf, A," MPII:SS VI-2597
AGUILERA MALTA, DEMETRIO
Don Goyo, CLCII II-416; MPII:AF I-434
AI
"Ice," MPII:P III-1043
Poetry of Ai, The, MPII:AfAm II-963
AIKEN, CONRAD POTTER, CWA I-22;
CWAII I-23
"Dark City, The," MPII:SS II-488
"Impulse," MPII:SS III-1126
Poetry of Aiken, The, MP VIII-4798
"Round by Round," MPII:SS V-1998
"Silent Snow, Secret Snow," MPII:SS
V-2108
Ushant, MPII:NF IV-1622
AIKEN, JOAN
Shadow Guests, The, MPII:JYAFic
IV-1315
Wolves of Willoughby Chase, The,
MPII:JYAFic IV-1650
AINSWORTH, WILLIAM HARRISON,
CWA I-24
Jack Sheppard, CLC I-538; MP V-2969;
MP:BF II-676
Old St. Paul's, CLC II-807; MP
VIII-4341; MP:BF II-1096
Tower of London, The, CLC II-1148;
MP XI-6618; MP:BF III-1583
Windsor Castle, CLC II-1248; MP
XII-7166; MP:BF III-1743
AKALAITIS, JOANNE, CWAII I-26
Green Card, CLCII II-631; MPII:D II-711
AKHMATOVA, ANNA
"In the Evening," MPII:P III-1090
Poem Without a Hero, MPII:P IV-1700
Requiem, MPII:P V-1810
"We Met for the Last Time," MPII:P
VI-2381
"White Night," MPII:P VI-2404
AKSYONOV, VASSILY, CWAII I-28
Burn, The, CLCII I-215; MPII:WF I-200
Island of Crimea, The, CLCII II-778;
MPII:WF II-737
Ticket to the Stars, A, CLCII IV-1561;
MPII:WF IV-1600
AKUTAGAWA, RYNOSUKE, CWAII I-31
"Rashmon," CLCII III-1265; MPII:SS
V-1901

AL-HAKIM, TAWFIQ. See HAKIM,
TAWFIQ AL-
ALAIN-FOURNIER, CWA I-26
Wanderer, The, CLC II-1217; MP
XII-7006; MP:EF III-1365
ALARCÓN, PEDRO ANTONIO DE,
CWA I-27
"Nun, The," MPII:SS IV-1637
Three-Cornered Hat, The, CLC II-1126;
MP XI-6505; MP:EF III-1286
ALARCÓN Y MENDOZA, JUAN RUIZ
DE. See RUIZ DE ALARCÓN, JUAN
ALAS, LEOPOLDO
Regenta, La, MPII:WF III-1267; CLCII
III-1284
ALBEE, EDWARD, CWA I-29; CWAII
I-34
American Dream, The, CLCII I-39;
MPII:D I-55
Delicate Balance, A, CLCII I-385;
MPII:D II-475
Seascape, CLCII III-1359; MPII:D IV-1427
Tiny Alice, CLCII IV-1572; MPII:D
IV-1590
Who's Afraid of Virginia Woolf? MP
XII-7121
Zoo Story, The, CLCII IV-1772; MPII:D
IV-1794
ALCAYAGA, LUCILA GODOY. See
MISTRAL, GABRIELA
ALCINDOR, LEW. See
ABDUL-JABBAR, KAREEM.
ALCOTT, LOUISA MAY, CWA I-32
Little Men, MPII:JYAFic II-857
Little Women, CLC I-622; MP VI-3458;
MP:AF II-687; MPII:JYAFic III-871
ALDERMAN, CLIFFORD LINDSEY
Annie Oakley and the World of Her
Time, MPII:JYABio I-118
Samuel Adams, MPII:JYABio IV-1525
ALDINGTON, RICHARD, CWA I-34;
CWAII I-36
All Men Are Enemies, CLCII I-28;
MPII:BCF I-37
Death of a Hero, CLC I-254; MP
III-1362; MP:BF I-291
ALDIS, DOROTHY
Nothing Is Impossible, MPII:JYABio
III-1324

ALDISS, BRIAN W., CWAII I-38
  Barefoot in the Head, CLCII I-114;
    MPII:BCF I-98
  Frankenstein Unbound, CLCII II-544;
    MPII:BCF II-542
ALDRICH, THOMAS BAILEY, CWA I-36
  Story of a Bad Boy, The, CLC II-1082;
    MP XI-6265; MP:AF III-1227;
    MPII:JYAFic IV-1376
ALEGRÍA, CIRO, CWA I-38; CWAII I-41
  Broad and Alien Is the World, CLC
    I-126; MP II-666; MP:AF I-144
  Golden Serpent, The, CLCII II-607;
    MPII:AF II-645
ALEICHEM, SHOLOM, CWAII I-44
  "Hodel," MPII:SS III-1029
  "On Account of a Hat," MPII:SS
    IV-1692
ALEMÁN, MATEO, CWA I-39
  Guzmán de Alfarache, CLC I-435; MP
    IV-2437; MP:EF II-613
ALEPOUDHÉLIS, ODYSSEUS. See
  ELTIS, ODYSSEUS
ALESHKOVSKY, YUZ, CWAII I-47
  Kangaroo, CLCII II-811; MPII:WF
    II-790
ALEXANDER, LLOYD
  Prydain chronicles, The, MPII:JYAFic
    III-1180
  Westmark trilogy, The, MPII:JYAFic
    IV-1593
ALEXANDER, RAE PACE
  Young and Black in America,
    MPII:JYABio IV-1960
ALGER, HORATIO, JR.
  Ragged Dick, MPII:JYAFic III-1188
ALGREN, NELSON, CWAII I-49
  "Bottle of Milk for Mother, A," MPII:SS
    I-285
  "How the Devil Came Down Division
    Street," MPII:SS III-1073
  Man with the Golden Arm, The, CLCII
    III-961; MPII:AF III-971
  Never Come Morning, CLCII III-1085;
    MPII:AF III-1124
  Walk on the Wild Side, A, CLCII
    IV-1673; MPII:AF IV-1743
ALIGHIERI, DANTE. See DANTE
  ALIGHIERI

ALLEN, HERVEY, CWA I-41
  Anthony Adverse, CLC I-47; MP I-246;
    MP:AF I-58
ALLEN, MAURY
  Jackie Robinson, MPII:JYABio II-929
ALLEN, WOODY, CWAII I-51
  "Kugelmass Episode, The," MPII:SS
    III-1276
  "Whore of Mensa, The," MPII:SS
    VI-2602
ALMEDINGEN, E. M.
  Anna, MPII:JYAFic I-45
  Katia, MPII:JYABio III-997
  My St. Petersburg, MPII:JYABio
    III-1272
ALTAMIRANO, IGNACIO MANUEL,
  CWA I-43
  Zarco, El, CLC II-1279; MP XII-7323;
    MP:AF III-1480
ALTSHELER, JOSEPH ALEXANDER
  Guns of Bull Run, The, MPII:JYAFic
    II-577
AMADI, ELECHI, CWAII I-53
  Great Ponds, The, CLCII II-629;
    MPII:BCF II-665
AMADO, JORGE, CWA I-45; CWAII I-55
  Dona Flor and Her Two Husbands,
    CLCII II-416; MPII:AF I-439
  Gabriela, Clove and Cinnamon, MP
    IV-2192; MP:AF I-425
  Jubiabá, CLCII II-804; MPII:AF II-819
  Tent of Miracles, CLCII IV-1526;
    MPII:AF IV-1578
  Tieta, the Goat Girl, CLCII IV-1564;
    MPII:AF IV-1657
  Violent Land, The, CLC II-1206; MP
    XII-6939; MP:AF III-1383
AMBLER, ERIC, CWAII I-58
  Coffin for Dimitrios, A, CLCII I-303;
    MPII:BCF I-276
  Journey into Fear, CLCII II-799;
    MPII:BCF II-862
AMBROGINI, ANGELO. See POLITIAN
AMICHAI, YEHUDA
  "Travels of the Last Benjamin of
    Tudela," MPII:P VI-2262
AMICIS, EDMONDO DE, CWA I-46
  Romance of a Schoolmaster, The, CLC
    II-983; MP X-5669

AMIS, KINGSLEY, CWA I-48; CWAII I-60
Girl, 20, CLCII II-590; MPII:BCF II-602
Green Man, The, CLCII II-633;
MPII:BCF II-670
I Like It Here, CLCII II-728; MPII:BCF
II-777
Jake's Thing, CLCII II-787; MPII:BCF
II-852
Lucky Jim, MP VI-3554; MP:BF II-843
Old Devils, The, CLCII III-1136;
MPII:BCF III-1253
Stanley and the Women, CLCII
IV-1472; MPII:BCF IV-1604
Take a Girl Like You, CLCII IV-1511;
MPII:BCF IV-1671
That Uncertain Feeling, MP XI-6466;
MP:BF III-1519
AMMERS-KÜLLER, JOHANNA VAN,
CWA I-50
Rebel Generation, The, CLC II-944; MP
IX-5456; MP:EF III-1058
AMMONS, A. R.
"Corsons Inlet," MPII:P II-455
"Easter Morning," MPII:P II-614
ANACREON
Poetry of Anacreon, The, MP VIII-4801
ANAYA, RUDOLFO A.
Heart of Aztlán, MPII:JYAFic II-612
ANCEL, PAUL. See CELAN, PAUL
ANDERSEN, HANS CHRISTIAN, CWA
I-52
Andersen's Fairy Tales, MP I-205;
MP:EF I-34
ANDERSEN NEXÖ, MARTIN. See
NEXÖ, MARTIN ANDERSEN
ANDERSON, JESSICA
Tirra Lirra by the River, CLCII IV-1573;
MPII:BCF IV-1716
ANDERSON, MARIAN
My Lord, What a Morning,
MPII:JYABio III-1268
ANDERSON, MAXWELL, CWA I-55;
CWAII I-62
Anne of the Thousand Days, CLCII I-52;
MPII:D I-71
Winterset, CLC II-1252; MP XII-7186
ANDERSON, MAXWELL, and
LAURENCE STALLINGS
What Price Glory? CLCII IV-1706;
MPII:D IV-1723

ANDERSON, ROBERT, CWAII I-64
Tea and Sympathy, CLCII IV-1518;
MPII:D IV-1543
ANDERSON, SHERWOOD, CWA I-57
Dark Laughter, CLC I-241; MP III-1317;
MP:AF I-255
"Death in the Woods," MPII:SS II-528
"Egg, The," MPII:SS II-668
"I Want to Know Why," MPII:SS
III-1095
"I'm a Fool," MPII:SS III-1116
Poor White, CLC II-901; MP IX-5241;
MP:AF II-961
Story Teller's Story, A, MP XI-6291
Winesburg, Ohio, CLC II-1249; MP
XII-7171; MP:AF III-1440
ANDRADE, MÁRIO DE, CWAII I-66
Macunaíma, CLCII III-940; MPII:AF
III-948
ANDREWS, RAYMOND
Appalachee Red, MPII:AfAm I-47
ANDREYEV, LEONID, CWA I-60
Life of Man, The, CLCII II-889; MPII:D
III-975
Seven Who Were Hanged, The, CLC
II-1027; MP X-5939; MP:EF III-1151
ANDRI, IVO, CWA I-62; CWAII I-68
Bosnian Chronicle, CLCII I-195;
MPII:WF I-182
Bridge on the Drina, The, MP II-656;
MP:EF I-136
Woman from Sarajevo, The, CLCII
IV-1728; MPII:WF IV-1764
ANDRZEJEWSKI, JERZY, CWAII I-70
Ashes and Diamonds, CLCII I-75;
MPII:WF I-80
ANGELL, JUDIE. See ARRICK, FRAN
ANGELO, VALENTI
Nino, MPII:JYAFic III-1042
ANGELOU, MAYA, CWAII I-72
All God's Children Need Traveling
Shoes, MPII:AfAm I-11; MPII:NF
I-34
Gather Together in My Name,
MPII:JYABio II-702
Heart of a Woman, The, MPII:JYABio
II-818
I Know Why the Caged Bird Sings,
MPII:AfAm II-569; MPII:JYABio
II-885; MPII:NF II-673

Poetry of Maya Angelou, The,
MPII:AfAm II-968
Singin' and Swingin' and Gettin' Merry
Like Christmas, MPII:JYABio
IV-1569
"Woman Me," MPII:P VI-2445
ANNIXTER, PAUL
Swiftwater, MPII:JYAFic IV-1427
ANNUNZIO, GABRIELE D'. See
D'ANNUNZIO, GABRIELE
ANONYMOUS
Go Ask Alice, MPII:JYAFic II-526
ANOUILH, JEAN, CWA I-65; CWAII I-74
Antigone, CLCII I-58; MPII:D I-77
Becket, CLCII I-130; MPII:D I-139
Restless Heart, CLCII III-1286; MPII:D
III-1325
Ring Round the Moon, CLC II-972; MP
X-5608
ANTHONY, MICHAEL, CWAII I-77
Games Were Coming, The, CLCII
II-563; MPII:BCF II-572
ANTIN, MARY
Promised Land, The, MPII:JYABio
III-1443
ANTSCHEL, PAUL. See CELAN, PAUL
APOLLINAIRE, GUILLAUME, CWA I-67
"Fir Trees," MPII:P II-761
"Little Car, The," MPII:P III-1247
Poetry of Apollinaire, The, MP VIII-4805
"Song of the Poorly Loved, The,"
MPII:P V-1965
"Windows," MPII:P VI-2426
"Zone," MPII:P VI-2494
APPELFELD, AHARON, CWAII I-79
Age of Wonders, The, CLCII I-22;
MPII:WF I-29
Badenheim 1939, CLCII I-101;
MPII:WF I-101
To the Land of the Cattails, CLCII
IV-1581; MPII:WF IV-1616
Tzili, CLCII IV-1630; MPII:WF IV-1682
APULEIUS, LUCIUS, CWA I-69
Golden Ass of Lucius Apuleius, The,
CLC I-406; MP IV-2292; MP:EF
II-575
AQUINAS, THOMAS, CWA I-71
Summa Theologica, MP XI-6329
ARBLEY, MADAM. See BURNEY,
FANNY

ARCHER, JULES
Angry Abolitionist, MPII:JYABio I-106
ARDEN, JOHN, CWAII I-81
Serjeant Musgrave's Dance, CLCII
III-1375; MPII:D IV-1444
ARENDT, HANNAH, CWAII I-83
Eichmann in Jerusalem, MPII:NF I-431
Origins of Totalitarianism, The,
MPII:NF III-1107
ARETINO, PIETRO, CWA I-73
Courtesan, The, CLC I-212; MP II-1168
Discourses, MP III-1524
ARGUETA, MANLIO
One Day of Life, CLCII III-1148;
MPII:AF III-1198
ARIHARA NO NARIHIRA, CWA I-75
Tales of Ise, MP XI-6378; MP:EF
III-1257
ARIOSTO, LUDOVICO, CWA I-76
Orlando Furioso, CLC II-816; MP
VIII-4404
Suppositi, I, CLC II-1097; MP XI-6352
ARISTOPHANES, CWA I-78
Acharnians, The, CLC I-6; MP I-26
Birds, The, CLC I-105; MP I-547
Clouds, The, CLC I-189; MP II-1006
Ecclesiazusae, The, CLC I-314; MP
III-1699
Frogs, The, CLC I-388; MP IV-2178
Knights, The, CLC I-582; MP VI-3189
Lysistrata, CLC I-640; MP VI-3578
Peace, The, CLC II-844; MP VIII-4541
Plutus, CLC II-896; MP VIII-4770
Thesmophoriazusae, The, CLC II-1122;
MP XI-6483
Wasps, The, CLC II-1225; MP XII-7044
ARISTOTLE, CWA I-81
Poetics, The, MP VIII-4789
ARIZA, PEDRO ANTONIO DE
ALARCÓN Y. See ALARCÓN,
PEDRO ANTONIO DE
ARLEN, MICHAEL J.
Exiles, MPII:NF II-476
ARLT, ROBERTO
Seven Madmen, The, CLCII IV-1384;
MPII:AF IV-1397
ARMAH, AYI KWEI, CWAII I-85
Beautyful Ones Are Not Yet Born, The,
CLCII I-129; MPII:BCF I-118

Healers, The, CLCII II-666; MPII:BCF II-705

Two Thousand Seasons, CLCII IV-1628; MPII:BCF IV-1761

ARMSTRONG, RICHARD
Mutineers, The, MPII:JYAFic III-999

ARMSTRONG, WILLIAM H.
Sounder, MPII:JYAFic IV-1367

ARNOLD, ELLIOTT
Blood Brother, MPII:JYAFic I-132

ARNOLD, MATTHEW, CWA I-83
"Buried Life, The," MPII:P I-310
Culture and Anarchy, MP III-1242
"Dover Beach," MPII:P II-588
Poetry of Arnold, The, MP VIII-4808
"Scholar-Gypsy, The," MPII:P V-1873
Sohrab and Rustum, CLC II-1057; MP X-6125
"Stanzas from the Grande Chartreuse," MPII:P V-2059

ARNOW, HARRIETTE, CWAII I-87
Dollmaker, The, CLCII II-414; MPII:AF I-428

AROUET, FRANÇOIS MARIE. See VOLTAIRE

ARRABAL, FERNANDO, CWAII I-89
Architect and the Emperor of Assyria, The, CLCII I-65; MPII:D I-82

ARREOLA, JUAN JOSÉ
Fair, The, CLCII II-483; MPII:AF II-505

ARRICK, FRAN
Steffie Can't Come Out to Play, MPII:JYAFic IV-1370

ARTAUD, ANTONIN, CWAII I-92
Cenci, The, CLCII I-249; MPII:D I-293
Theatre and Its Double, The, MPII:NF IV-1490

ARTHUR, RUTH M.
Whistling Boy, The, MPII:JYAFic IV-1627

ARTSYBASHEV, MIKHAIL, CWA I-86
Sanine, CLC II-1004; MP X-5787; MP:EF III-1123

ARUNDEL, HONOR
Family Failing, A, MPII:JYAFic I-408

ASANTE, MOLEFI K.
Afrocentricity, MPII:AfAm I-1

ASCH, SHOLEM, CWA I-87; CWAII I-94
Apostle, The, CLC I-53; MP I-269; MP:AF I-62

Nazarene, The, CLC II-761; CLCII III-1081; MP VII-4161; MP:AF II-837; MPII:WF III-1085

ASHBERY, JOHN
"Self-Portrait in a Convex Mirror," MPII:P V-1892
Skaters, The, MPII:P V-1912
"Tennis Court Oath, The," MPII:P V-2130

ASHLEY, BERNARD
Trouble with Donovan Croft, The, MPII:JYAFic IV-1508

ASIMOV, ISAAC, CWAII I-96
Breakthroughs in Science, MPII:JYABio I-267
Foundation trilogy, The, CLCII II-536; MPII:AF II-565; MPII:JYAFic II-460
In Joy Still Felt, MPII:NF II-709
In Memory Yet Green, MPII:NF II-714
"Nightfall," MPII:SS IV-1620

ASSÍS, JOAQUIM MARIA MACHADO DE. See MACHADO DE ASSÍS, JOAQUIM MARIA

ASTLEY, THEA
Acolyte, The, CLCII I-9; MPII:BCF I-12
Beachmasters, CLCII I-126; MPII:BCF I-114

ASTURIAS, MIGUEL ÁNGEL, CWA I-89; CWAII I-100
Men of Maize, CLCII III-996; MPII:AF III-991
Mulata, CLCII III-1054; MPII:AF III-1087
Señor Presidente, El, MP III-1726; MP:AF III-1110
Strong Wind, CLCII IV-1485; MPII:AF IV-1541
"Tatuana's Tale," MPII:SS V-2305

ATKINSON, LINDA
In Kindling Flame, MPII:JYABio II-905
Mother Jones, MPII:JYABio III-1241

ATTAWAY, WILLIAM
Let Me Breathe Thunder, MPII:AfAm II-688

ATWOOD, MARGARET, CWAII I-103
"All Bread," MPII:P I-44
Edible Woman, The, CLCII II-445; MPII:BCF I-432
Handmaid's Tale, The, CLCII II-654; MPII:BCF II-690

Life Before Man, CLCII II-885;
MPII:BCF II-959
Surfacing, CLCII IV-1498; MPII:BCF
IV-1643
AUBREY, JOHN, CWA I-91
Brief Lives, MP II-659
AUCHINCLOSS, LOUIS, CWAII I-105
Embezzler, The, CLCII II-452; MPII:AF
II-467
Rector of Justin, The, CLCII III-1279;
MPII:AF III-1329
AUDEN, W. H., CWA I-93; CWAII I-107
"Detective Story," MPII:P II-535
"In Memory of Sigmund Freud," MPII:P
III-1068
"In Memory of W. B. Yeats," MPII:P
III-1071
"Letter to Lord Byron," MPII:P III-1228
"Lullaby," MPII:P IV-1298
"Memorial for the City," MPII:P IV-1356
"Musée des Beaux Arts," MPII:P
IV-1430
"New Year Letter," MPII:P IV-1484
Poetry of Auden, The, MP VIII-4811
"September 1, 1939," MPII:P V-1896
"Summer Night, A," MPII:P V-2090
AUDEN, W. H., and CHRISTOPHER
ISHERWOOD
Dog Beneath the Skin, The, CLCII
II-410; MPII:D II-507
AUE, HARTMANN VON. See
HARTMANN, VON AUE
AUERBACH, ERICH, CWAII I-109
Mimesis, MPII:NF III-960
AUGUSTINE, SAINT, CWA I-95
Confessions, MP II-1057

AUGUSTINUS, AURELIUS. See
AUGUSTINE, SAINT
AURELIUS, MARCUS. See MARCUS
AURELIUS
AUSTEN, JANE, CWA I-97
Emma, CLC I-324; MP III-1763; MP:BF
I-363
Mansfield Park, CLC I-666; MP
VII-3704; MP:BF II-864
Northanger Abbey, CLC II-782; MP
VII-4238; MP:BF II-1068
Persuasion, CLC II-863; MP VIII-4615;
MP:BF II-1190
Pride and Prejudice, CLC II-914; MP
IX-5307; MP:BF III-1258
Sense and Sensibility, CLC II-1022; MP
X-5905; MP:BF III-1411
AVERILL, ESTHER
Cartier Sails the St. Lawrence,
MPII:JYABio I-299
AVERY, GILLIAN
Warden's Niece, The, MPII:JYAFic
IV-1579
AYCKBOURN, ALAN
Absurd Person Singular, CLCII I-4;
MPII:D I-1
Norman Conquests, The, CLCII
III-1111; MPII:D III-1153
AZUELA, MARIANO, CWA I-100
Flies, The, MP IV-2085; MP:AF I-395
Underdogs, The, CLC II-1185; MP
XII-6847; MP:AF III-1349
Æ, CWA I-14
Poetry of "A. E.," The, MP VIII-4795

B

BABBITT, NATALIE
 Tuck Everlasting, MPII:JYAFic IV-1514
BABEL, ISAAC, CWAII I-112
 "Crossing into Poland," MPII:SS II-463
 "Di Grasso," MPII:SS II-600
 "Guy de Maupassant," MPII:SS III-966
 "How It Was Done in Odessa," MPII:SS
  III-1067
 "Lyubka the Cossack," MPII:SS IV-1420
 "My First Goose," MPII:SS IV-1552
 "Story of My Dovecot, The," MPII:SS
  V-2244
BACCHELLI, RICCARDO, CWA I-101
 Mill on the Po, The, CLC II-707; MP
  VII-3901; MP:EF II-861
BACHMAN, RICHARD. See KING,
 STEPHEN
BACON, SIR FRANCIS, CWA I-103
 Essays, MP IV-1842
 History of the Reign of King Henry VII,
  MP V-2660
 New Atlantis, MP VII-4168
BAGNOLD, ENID
 "National Velvet," MPII:JYAFic III-1023
BAINBRIDGE, BERYL, CWAII I-114
 Harriet Said, CLCII II-658; MPII:BCF
  II-700
BAKELESS, KATHERINE LITTLE
 Story-Lives of Great Composers,
  MPII:JYABio IV-1614
BAKER, BETTY
 Killer-of-Death, MPII:JYAFic II-777
 Walk the World's Rim, MPII:JYAFic
  IV-1572
BAKER, LAURA NELSON, and ADRIEN
 STOUTENBURG
 Listen America, MPII:JYABio III-1093
BAKER, RUSSELL
 Growing Up, MPII:JYABio II-791;
  MPII:NF II-606
BAKER, WILLIAM J.
 Jesse Owens, MPII:JYABio II-956
BAKHTIN, MIKHAIL, CWAII I-116
 Dialogic Imagination, The, MPII:NF I-355
BALDWIN, JAMES, CWA I-106; CWAII
 I-119
 Another Country, CLCII I-55; MPII:AF
  I-43; MPII:AfAm I-41

Blues for Mister Charlie, CLCII I-179;
 MPII:D I-219; MPII:AfAm I-182
Fire Next Time, The, MPII:AfAm I-448;
 MPII:NF II-512
Giovanni's Room, CLCII II-586;
 MPII:AF II-623; MPII:AfAm I-492
Go Tell It on the Mountain, MP
 IV-2276; MP:AF I-458; MPII:AfAm
 I-505; MPII:JYAFic II-529
"Going to Meet the Man," MPII:SS
 II-880
If Beale Street Could Talk, CLCII
 II-733; MPII:AF II-774
Just Above My Head, CLCII II-809;
 MPII:AF II-830; MPII:AfAm II-648
Notes of a Native Son, MPII:AfAm
 II-899; MPII:NF III-1029
"Sonny's Blues," MPII:SS V-2186
BALE, JOHN, CWA I-108
 King John, CLC I-569; MP VI-3140
BALLARD, J. G., CWAII I-121
 Crystal World, The, CLCII I-355;
  MPII:BCF I-339
 Empire of the Sun, CLCII II-453;
  MPII:BCF I-437
BALZAC, HONORÉ DE, CWA I-109
 César Birotteau, CLC I-165; MP II-876;
  MP:EF I-206
 Chouans, The, CLC I-178; MP II-943;
  MP:EF I-232
 Country Doctor, The, CLC I-209; MP
  II-1152; MP:EF I-285
 Cousin Bette, CLC I-213; MP II-1175;
  MP:EF I-289
 Cousin Pons, CLC I-215; MP II-1180;
  MP:EF I-294
 Eugénie Grandet, CLC I-335; MP
  IV-1886; MP:EF I-480
 Father Goriot, CLC I-359; MP IV-2007;
  MP:EF II-505
 "Gobseck," MPII:SS II-867
 Lost Illusions, CLC I-630; MP VI-3518;
  MP:EF II-798
 Louis Lambert, CLCII III-922; MPII:WF
  II-896
 Quest of the Absolute, The, CLCII
  III-1246; MPII:WF III-1236
 Sarrasine, CLCII III-1337; MPII:WF
  III-1351

Splendors and Miseries of Courtesans,
The, CLCII IV-1463; MPII:WF
IV-1516
"Unknown Masterpiece, The," MPII:SS
VI-2468
Wild Ass's Skin, The, CLC II-1241; MP
XII-7133; MP:EF III-1386
BAMBARA, TONI CADE
"My Man Bovanne," MPII:SS IV-1560
Salt Eaters, The, MPII:AfAm III-1236
Stories of Toni Cade Bambara, The,
MPII:AfAm III-1349
BANKS, LYNNE REID
Indian in the Cupboard, The,
MPII:JYAFic II-706
BANNISTER, ROGER GILBERT
Four-Minute Mile, The, MPII:JYABio
II-655
BANVILLE, JOHN, CWAII I-123
Doctor Copernicus, CLCII II-409;
MPII:BCF I-388
Kepler, CLCII II-823; MPII:BCF II-899
BARAKA, AMIRI, CWAII I-125
Autobiography of LeRoi Jones/Amiri
Baraka, The, MPII:JYABio I-148
Dutchman, CLCII II-434; MPII:AfAm
I-394; MPII:D II-529
Essays of Amiri Baraka, The,
MPII:AfAm I-400
Poetry of Amiri Baraka, The,
MPII:AfAm II-974
"Political Poem," MPII:P IV-1713
System of Dante's Hell, The, CLCII
IV-1510; MPII:AF IV-1564;
MPII:AfAm III-1398
BARBOUR, RALPH HENRY
Half-Back, The, MPII:JYAFic II-580
BARBUSSE, HENRI, CWA I-113
Under Fire, CLC II-1180; MP XII-6822;
MP:EF III-1330
BARCA, PEDRO CALDERÓN DE LA.
See CALDERÓN DE LA BARCA,
PEDRO
BARCLAY, JOHN, CWA I-115
Argenis, CLC I-59; MP I-302; MP:BF I-69
BARFIELD, OWEN, CWAII I-127
Saving the Appearances, MPII:NF
III-1286
BARHAM, RICHARD HARRIS. See
INGOLDSBY, THOMAS

BARKER, GEORGE, CWA I-116
Poetry of Barker, The, MP VIII-4814
BARKER, PAT
Union Street, CLCII IV-1640;
MPII:BCF IV-1775
BARNARD, MARY
Assault on Mount Helicon, MPII:NF I-97
BARNE, KITTY
Musical Honors, MPII:JYAFic III-996
Visitors from London, MPII:JYAFic
IV-1557
BARNE, MARION CATHERINE. See
BARNE, KITTY
BARNES, DJUNA, CWAII I-129
Nightwood, CLCII III-1099; MPII:AF
III-1139
BARNES, JULIAN, CWAII I-132
Flaubert's Parrot, CLCII II-521;
MPII:BCF II-526
Staring at the Sun, CLCII IV-1472;
MPII:BCF IV-1609
BARNES, PETER, CWAII I-134
Ruling Class, The, CLCII III-1322;
MPII:D IV-1390
BARNSLEY, ALAN GABRIEL. See
FIELDING, GABRIEL
BAROJA, PÍO, CWA I-118
Caesar or Nothing, CLC I-139; MP
II-731; MP:EF I-163
King Paradox, CLC I-575; MP VI-3159;
MP:EF II-728
Tree of Knowledge, The, CLCII
IV-1608; MPII:WF IV-1650
BARRETT, ELIZABETH. See
BROWNING, ELIZABETH
BARRETT
BARRIE, JAMES M., CWA I-120
Admirable Crichton, The, CLC I-9; MP
I-35
Dear Brutus, CLC I-249; MP III-1345
Little Minister, The, CLC I-621; MP
VI-3454; MP:BF II-807
Peter Pan, CLC II-865; MP VIII-4622;
MPII:JYAFic III-1122
Quality Street, CLC II-930; MP IX-5387
What Every Woman Knows, CLC
II-1234; MP XII-7089
BARRIOS, EDUARDO, CWA I-123
Brother Ass, MP II-677; MP:AF I-149

BARRY, PHILIP, CWAII I-136
  Philadelphia Story, The, CLCII III-1203;
    MPII:D III-1235
BARTH, JOHN, CWA I-125; CWAII I-138
  End of the Road, The, MP III-1772;
    MP:AF I-339
  Floating Opera, The, CLCII II-524;
    MPII:AF II-557
  Giles Goat-Boy, CLCII II-584; MPII:AF
    II-613
  "Life-Story," MPII:SS II-1348
  "Lost in the Funhouse," MPII:SS
    IV-1403
  "Night-Sea Journey," MPII:SS IV-1624
  Sot-Weed Factor, The, MP XI-6190;
    MP:AF III-1188
BARTHELME, DONALD, CWAII I-140
  "Critique de la Vie Quotidienne,"
    MPII:SS I-459
  "Indian Uprising, The," MPII:SS III-1165
  "Lightning," MPII:SS III-1355
  "Paraguay," MPII:SS IV-1764
  "See the Moon?" MPII:SS V-2064
  "Some of Us Had Been Threatening Our
    Friend Colby," MPII:SS V-2177
  "Views of My Father Weeping,"
    MPII:SS VI-2500
  "Wrack," MPII:SS VI-2716
BARTHELME, FREDERICK, CWAII I-142
  "Moon Deluxe," MPII:SS IV-1532
BARTHES, ROLAND, CWAII I-144
  Camera Lucida, MPII:NF I-227
  S/Z, MPII:NF III-1263
BASHŌ, MATSUO, CWA I-127
  Poetry of Bashō, The, MP VIII-4816
BASOALTO, NEFTALÍ RICARDO
    REYES. See NERUDA, PABLO
BASS, ROCHELLE. See OWENS,
    ROCHELLE
BASSANI, GIORGIO, CWAII I-146
  Garden of the Finzi-Continis, The,
    CLCII II-566; MPII:WF II-511
  Gold-Rimmed Eyeglasses, The, CLCII
    II-604; MPII:WF II-557
BATES, H. E., CWAII I-148
  Blossoming World, The, MPII:NF
    IV-1628
  "Cruise of The Breadwinner, The,"
    MPII:SS II-471
  "Death of a Huntsman," MPII:SS II-535

"Gleaner, The," MPII:SS II-860
"House with the Grape-vine, The,"
  MPII:SS III-1049
Love for Lydia, CLCII III-924;
  MPII:BCF III-1017
Vanished World, The, MPII:NF IV-1628
World in Ripeness, The, MPII:NF
  IV-1628
BAUDELAIRE, CHARLES, CWA I-129
  "Beacons, The," MPII:P I-211
  "Benediction," MPII:P I-228
  "Cats," MPII:P I-354
  "Correspondences," MPII:P II-452
  Flowers of Evil, MP IV-2092
  "Gambling," MPII:P II-839
  "Invitation to the Voyage, The," MPII:P
    III-1114
  "Jewels, The," MPII:P III-1129
  "Parisian Dream," MPII:P IV-1639
  "To the Reader," MPII:P VI-2227
BAUER, MARION DANE
  On My Honor, MPII:JYAFic III-1057
BAUM, L. FRANK
  Wizard of Oz, The, MPII:JYAFic
    IV-1646
BAUM, VICKI, CWA I-131
  Grand Hotel, CLC I-414; MP IV-2335;
    MP:EF II-585
BAWDEN, NINA
  Carrie's War, MPII:JYAFic I-194
  Peppermint Pig, The, MPII:JYAFic
    III-1115
BEACH, REX, CWA I-132
  Spoilers, The, CLC II-1077; MP
    XI-6225; MP:AF III-1198
BEAL, MERRILL D.
  "I Will Fight No More Forever",
    MPII:JYABio II-893
BEARD, CHARLES A., and MARY R.
    BEARD, CWA I-133
  Rise of American Civilization, The, MP
    X-5614
BEATTIE, ANN, CWAII I-150
  "Imagined Scenes," MPII:SS III-1122
  "In the White Night," MPII:SS III-1158
  "Jacklighting," MPII:SS III-1208
  "Winter: 1978," MPII:SS VI-2652
BEATTY, JOHN, and PATRICIA BEATTY
  Campion Towers, MPII:JYAFic I-182
  Royal Dirk, The, MPII:JYAFic III-1255

BEATTY, PATRICIA
    Behave Yourself, Bethany Brant,
        MPII:JYAFic I-100
BEAUCHAMP, KATHLEEN
    MANSFIELD. *See* MANSFIELD,
    KATHERINE
BEAUMARCHAIS, PIERRE AUGUSTIN
    CARON DE, CWA I-135
    Barber of Seville, The, CLC I-79; MP
        I-423
    Marriage of Figaro, The, CLC I-674; MP
        VII-3745
BEAUMONT, FRANCIS
    Knight of the Burning Pestle, The, CLC
        I-581; MP VI-3185
BEAUMONT, FRANCIS, *and* JOHN
    FLETCHER, CWA I-137
    Coxcomb, The, CLC I-218; MP II-1185
    King and No King, A, CLC I-569; MP
        VI-3133
    Maid's Tragedy, The, CLC I-654; MP
        VI-3638
    Philaster, CLC II-868; MP VIII-4639
    Scornful Lady, The, CLC II-1012; MP
        X-5848
    Woman Hater, The, CLC II-1255; MP
        XII-7207
BEAUVOIR, SIMONE DE, CWAII I-153
    Memoirs of a Dutiful Daughter,
        MPII:NF III-917
    Prime of Life, The, MPII:NF III-1184
    Second Sex, The, MPII:NF IV-1314
BECKER, JUREK, CWAII I-155
    Sleepless Days, CLCII IV-1423;
        MPII:WF IV-1458
BECKETT, SAMUEL, CWA I-141;
    CWAII I-157
    All That Fall, CLCII I-32; MPII:D I-33
    Company, CLCII I-314; MPII:BCF
        I-303; MPII:WF I-291
    "Dante and the Lobster," MPII:SS II-480
    Embers, CLCII II-451; MPII:D II-557
    "End, The," MPII:SS II-686
    Endgame, CLCII II-458; MPII:D II-563
    Happy Days, CLCII II-657; MPII:D
        II-742
    How It Is, CLCII II-717; MPII:WF II-644
    Ill Seen Ill Said, CLCII II-738; MPII:WF
        II-664
    "Imagination Dead Imagine," MPII:SS
        III-1119
    Krapp's Last Tape, CLCII II-841;
        MPII:D III-920
    Malone Dies, CLCII III-951
    Molloy, CLCII III-1028
    Murphy, CLCII III-1059; MPII:BCF
        III-1157
    Proust, MPII:NF III-1219
    Trilogy, The, MPII:BCF IV-1742;
        MPII:WF IV-1661
    Unnamable, The, CLCII IV-1643
    Waiting for Godot, CLC II-1215; MP
        XII-6991
    Watt, CLCII IV-1694; MPII:BCF
        IV-1875
    "Whoroscope," MPII:P VI-2410
    Words and Music, CLCII IV-1745;
        MPII:D IV-1766
BECKFORD, WILLIAM, CWA I-143
    Vathek, CLC II-1194; MP XII-6881;
        MP:BF III-1667
BECKHAM, BARRY, CWAII I-160
    Runner Mack, CLCII III-1324; MPII:AF
        III-1353; MPII:AfAm III-1224
BEDDOES, THOMAS LOVELL, CWA
    I-145
    Poetry of Beddoes, The, MP VIII-4819
BEERBOHM, MAX, CWA I-147
    "Enoch Soames," MPII:SS II-702
    Essays of Max Beerbohm, The, MP
        IV-1866
    "Mote in the Middle Distance, H*nry
        J*m*s, The," MPII:SS IV-1538
    Zuleika Dobson, CLC II-1280; MP
        XII-7334; MP:BF III-1787
BEHAN, BRENDAN, CWAII I-162
    Borstal Boy, MPII:NF I-190
    Hostage, The, CLCII II-700; MPII:D
        II-778
    Quare Fellow, The, CLCII III-1241;
        MPII:D III-1294
BEHN, APHRA, CWA I-149
    Oroonoko, CLC II-823; MP VIII-4421;
        MP:BF II-1137
BEHRMAN, S. N., CWAII I-164
    Second Man, The, CLCII III-1364;
        MPII:D IV-1433
BELANEY, ARCHIBALD STANSFELD.
    See GREY OWL

BELL, ERIC TEMPLE
Men of Mathematics, MPII:JYABio
III-1207
BELLAMANN, HENRY, CWA I-151
King's Row, CLC I-579; MP VI-3179;
MP:AF II-636
BELLAMY, EDWARD, CWA I-152
Looking Backward, CLC I-626; MP
VI-3497; MP:AF II-702
BELLAY, JOACHIM DU, CWA I-154
Poetry of Du Bellay, The, MP IX-4914
BELLOC, HILAIRE, CWA I-156
Path to Rome, The, MP VIII-4521
BELLOW, SAUL, CWA I-158; CWAII
I-166
Adventures of Augie March, The, MP
I-43; MP:AF I-7
Dangling Man, CLCII I-363; MPII:AF
I-366
Dean's December, The, CLCII I-375;
MPII:AF I-378
"Gonzaga Manuscripts, The," MPII:SS
II-896
Henderson the Rain King, MP V-2547;
MP:AF II-547
Herzog, CLCII II-677; MPII:AF II-712
Humboldt's Gift, CLCII II-721;
MPII:AF II-759
"Leaving the Yellow House," MPII:SS
III-1317
"Looking for Mr. Green," MPII:SS
IV-1395
Mr. Sammler's Planet, CLCII III-1020;
MPII:AF III-1017
Seize the Day, CLCII III-1369; MPII:AF
III-1382
"Silver Dish, A," MPII:SS V-2112
Victim, The, MP XII-6911; MP:AF
III-1371
BELPRÉ, PURA
Santiago, MPII:JYAFic III-1271
BELY, ANDREY, CWAII I-168
Petersburg, CLCII III-1199; MPII:WF
IV-1442
Silver Dove, The, CLCII IV-1413;
MPII:WF IV-1442
BENARY-ISBERT, MARGOT
Rowan Farm, MPII:JYAFic III-1251

BENAVENTE, JACINTO, CWA I-160
Bonds of Interest, The, CLC I-115; MP
I-589
Passion Flower, The, CLC II-840; MP
VIII-4505
BENCHLEY, NATHANIEL
Only Earth and Sky Last Forever,
MPII:JYAFic III-1076
BENDICK, JEANNE
Archimedes and the Door of Science,
MPII:JYABio I-129
BENEDICT, REX
Goodbye to the Purple Sage,
MPII:JYAFic II-547
BENET, JUAN, CWAII I-170
Meditation, A, CLCII III-990; A,
MPII:WF III-988
Return to Región, CLCII III-1289;
MPII:WF III-1272
BENÉT, STEPHEN VINCENT, CWA I-162
"Devil and Daniel Webster, The,"
MPII:SS II-575
John Brown's Body, CLC I-549; MP
V-3016
Poetry of Stephen Vincent Benét, The,
MP IX-5159
BENJAMIN, WALTER, CWAII I-172
Storyteller, The, MPII:NF IV-1447
Work of Art in the Age of Mechanical
Reproduction, The, MPII:NF IV-1719
BENNETT, ARNOLD, CWA I-164
Anna of the Five Towns, CLC I-46; MP
I-233; MP:BF I-50
Clayhanger Trilogy, The, CLC I-185;
MP II-984; MP:BF I-220
Old Wives' Tale, The, CLC II-808; MP
VIII-4344; MP:BF II-1100
Riceyman Steps, CLC II-965; MP
X-5577; MP:BF III-1323
BENNETT, JACK
Jamie, MPII:JYAFic II-741
BENNETT, JAY
Skeleton Man, The, MPII:JYAFic
IV-1350
BENNETT, JOHN
Master Skylark, MPII:JYAFic III-935
BENNETT, LERONE, JR.
What Manner of Man, MPII:JYABio
IV-1861

BENTLEY, PHYLLIS
Brontës and Their World, The,
MPII:JYABio I-278
BERDYAEV, NICHOLAS, CWA I-167
Dostoevsky, MP III-1621
BERGER, JOHN, CWAII I-175
Fortunate Man, A, MPII:NF II-521
G., CLCII II-560; MPII:BCF II-567
Painter of Our Time, A, CLCII III-1171;
MPII:BCF III-1272
Ways of Seeing, MPII:NF IV-1670
BERGER, THOMAS, CWAII I-177
Little Big Man, CLCII III-893; MPII:AF
III-891; MPII:JYAFic II-842
BERGSON, HENRI, CWA I-169
Laughter, MP VI-3289
Matter and Memory, MP VII-3776
BERKELEY, GEORGE, CWA I-171
Essay Towards a New Theory of Vision,
An, MP IV-1840
BERLIN, ISAIAH, CWAII I-179
Russian Thinkers, MPII:NF III-1257
BERNA, PAUL
Flood Warning, MPII:JYAFic II-447
Horse Without a Head, The,
MPII:JYAFic II-649
BERNANOS, GEORGES, CWA I-173
Diary of a Country Priest, The, CLC
I-270; MP III-1503; MP:EF I-394
Mouchette, CLCII III-1048; MPII:WF
III-1045
Under the Sun of Satan, CLCII IV-1634;
MPII:WF IV-1694
BERNARD, JACQUELINE
Journey Toward Freedom, MPII:JYABio
II-981
Voices from the Southwest,
MPII:JYABio IV-1810
BERNHARD, THOMAS, CWAII I-182
Concrete, CLCII I-319; MPII:WF I-300
Correction, CLCII I-338; MPII:WF I-323
Gargoyles, CLCII II-568; MPII:WF
II-516
Gathering Evidence, MPII:NF II-539
Lime Works, The, CLCII II-891;
MPII:WF II-866
Untergeher, Der, CLCII IV-1644;
MPII:WF IV-1700
Woodcutters, CLCII IV-1742; MPII:WF
II-603

BERNSTEIN, CHARLES
"Live Acts," MPII:P III-1251
BERRIAULT, GINA
"Stone Boy, The," MPII:SS V-2232
BERRIGAN, TED
"Last Poem," MPII:P III-1195
BERRY, WENDELL, CWAII I-185
Gift of Good Land, The, MPII:NF II-555
BERRY, WENDELL
"Where," MPII:P VI-2394
BERRYMAN, JOHN, CWA I-175
Dream Songs, The, MPII:P II-600
Homage to Mistress Bradstreet, MP
V-2678
BEST, HERBERT
Garram the Hunter, MPII:JYAFic II-488
BETI, MONGO, CWAII I-187
Poor Christ of Bomba, The, CLCII
III-1219; MPII:WF IV-1214
BETJEMAN, JOHN
"Arrest of Oscar Wilde at the Cadogan
Hotel, The," MPII:P I-109
Poetry of Betjeman, The, MP VIII-4822
BEYLE, MARIE-HENRI. See STENDHAL
BIDART, FRANK
"Ellen West," MPII:P II-644
BIENEK, HORST
Silesian Tetralogy, The, CLCII IV-1408;
MPII:WF III-1436
BIERCE, AMBROSE, CWA I-177
"Chickamauga," MPII:SS I-368
"Occurrence at Owl Creek Bridge, An,"
MPII:SS IV-1643
"One of the Missing," MPII:SS IV-1701
Tales of Soldiers and Civilians, MP
XI-6381; MP:AF III-1252
BIGLAND, EILEEN
Helen Keller, MPII:JYABio II-822
BION
Poetry of Bion, The, MP VIII-4825
BIOY CASARES, ADOLFO, CWAII I-189
Diary of the War of the Pig, CLCII
I-399; MPII:AF I-400
Invention of Morel, The, CLCII II-772;
MPII:AF II-798
BIRACREE, TOM
Grandma Moses, Painter, MPII:JYABio
II-776

BIRD, ROBERT MONTGOMERY, CWA
  I-179
  Nick of the Woods, CLC II-775; MP
    VII-4199; MP:AF II-841
BIRNEY, EARLE, CWAII I-191
  Turvey, CLCII IV-1623; MPII:BCF
    IV-1751
BISHOP, CLAIRE HUCHET
  Martín de Porres, Hero, MPII:JYABio
    III-1188
BISHOP, ELIZABETH
  "Crusoe in England," MPII:P II-476
  "In the Waiting Room," MPII:P III-1102
  "Man-Moth, The," MPII:P IV-1312
  "Map, The," MPII:P IV-1322
  "Moose, The," MPII:P IV-1415
  "Unbeliever, The," MPII:P VI-2317
BISHOP, JIM
  Day Lincoln Was Shot, The,
    MPII:JYABio I-447
BIYIDI, ALEXANDRE. See BETI,
  MONGO
BJÖRNSON, BJÖRNSTJERNE, CWA
  I-180
  Arne, CLC I-61; MP I-310; MP:EF I-61
  Beyond Human Power, Two, CLC I-102;
    MP I-523
  Fisher Maiden, The, CLC I-371; MP
    IV-2079; MP:EF II-519
BLACK ELK
  Black Elk Speaks, MPII:JYABio I-233
BLACKBURN, JOYCE KNIGHT
  James Edward Oglethorpe,
    MPII:JYABio II-933
BLACKMORE, R. D., CWA I-183
  Lorna Doone, CLC I-628; MP VI-3508;
    MP:BF II-829
BLACKWOOD, ALGERNON, CWAII
  I-194
  "Willows, The," MPII:SS VI-2638
BLAIR, ERIC ARTHUR. See ORWELL,
  GEORGE
BLAKE, WILLIAM, CWA I-185
  America, MPII:P I-62
  "Auguries of Innocence," MPII:P I-150
  Book of Thel, The, MPII:P I-270
  "Chimney Sweeper, The," MPII:P I-374
  "Human Abstract, The," MPII:P III-982
  "London," MPII:P III-1254
  "Mental Traveller, The," MPII:P IV-1369

Milton, MPII:P IV-1383
Poetry of Blake, The, MP VIII-4827
"Tyger, The," MPII:P VI-2306
BLASCO IBÁÑEZ, VICENTE, CWA I-188
  Cabin, The, CLC I-137; MP II-722;
    MP:EF I-156
BLISHEN, EDWARD, and LEON
  GARFIELD
  God Beneath the Sea, The II-533
BLIXEN-FINECKE, KAREN. See
  DINESEN, ISAK.
BLOCH, ERNST, CWAII I-196
  Principle of Hope, The, MPII:NF
    III-1196
BLOCK, IRVIN
  Lives of Pearl Buck, The, MPII:JYABio
    III-1105
  Neighbor to the World, MPII:JYABio
    III-1308
BLOK, ALEKSANDR, CWA I-190
  Poetry of Blok, The, MP VIII-4830
  Twelve, The, MPII:P VI-2289
BLOOM, ALLAN, CWAII I-198
  Closing of the American Mind, The,
    MPII:NF I-255
BLOOM, HAROLD, CWAII I-200
  Anxiety of Influence, The, MPII:NF I-75
BLOS, JOAN W.
  Gathering of Days, A, MPII:JYAFic
    II-491
BLUME, JUDY
  Are You There, God? It's Me, Margaret,
    MPII:JYAFic I-61
  Forever, MPII:JYAFic II-457
  Tiger Eyes, MPII:JYAFic IV-1472
BLUNDEN, EDMUND CHARLES, CWA
  I-192
  Poetry of Blunden, The, MP VIII-4833
BLY, ROBERT
  "Night," MPII:P IV-1493
  "Teeth Mother Naked at Last, The,"
    MPII:P V-2126
BOAS, FRANZ, CWA I-193
  Mind of Primitive Man, The, MP
    VII-3906
BOBER, NATALIE S.
  Restless Spirit, A, MPII:JYABio III-1489
BOCCACCIO, GIOVANNI, CWA I-195
  Decameron, The, MP III-1397; MP:EF
    I-371

Filostrato, Il, MP IV-2062
L'Amorosa Fiammetta, CLC I-591; MP
VI-3240; MP:EF II-746
Teseide, La, MP XI-6453
BODANIS, DAVID
Secret House, The, MPII:NF IV-1319
BØDKER, CECIL
Leopard, The, MPII:JYAFic II-830
BOETHIUS, ANICIUS MANLIUS
SEVERINUS, CWA I-197
Consolation of Philosophy, The, MP
II-1104
BOGAN, LOUISE
"Henceforth, from the Mind," MPII:P
III-935
BOIARDO, MATTEO MARIA, CWA I-198
Orlando Innamorato, CLC II-819; MP
VIII-4410
BOILEAU-DESPRÉAUX, NICOLAS,
CWA I-199
Dialogue des héros de roman, MP
III-1479
Satires, MP X-5809
BOJER, JOHAN, CWA I-201
Emigrants, The, CLC I-321; MP
III-1749; MP:EF I-473
Last of the Vikings, The, CLC I-597; MP
VI-3266; MP:EF II-754
BOLAND, EAVAN
"Lace," MPII:P III-1164
BÖLL, HEINRICH, CWAII I-203
Billiards at Half-Past Nine, CLCII I-153;
MPII:WF I-152
Clown, The, CLCII I-300; MPII:WF I-281
Group Portrait with Lady, CLCII II-641;
MPII:WF II-562
Lost Honor of Katharina Blum, The,
CLCII III-919; MPII:WF II-870
"Murke's Collected Silences," MPII:SS
IV-1548
Safety Net, The, CLCII III-1326;
MPII:WF III-1326
What's to Become of the Boy? MPII:NF
IV-1687
BOLT, ROBERT, CWAII I-205
Man for All Seasons, A, CLCII III-952;
MPII:D III-1037
BOMBAL, MARÍA LUISA, CWAII I-207
Final Mist, The, CLCII II-503; MPII:AF
II-537

"New Islands," MPII:SS IV-1612
Shrouded Woman, The, CLCII IV-1397;
MPII:AF IV-1422
BOND, EDWARD, CWAII I-210
Lear, CLCII II-866; MPII:D III-949
Saved, CLCII III-1341; MPII:D IV-1406
BONHAM, FRANK
Durango Street, MPII:JYAFic I-368
BONHOEFFER, DIETRICH, CWAII I-212
Ethics, MPII:NF II-466
Letters and Papers from Prison, MPII:NF
II-807
BONTEMPS, ARNA, CWAII I-215
Black Thunder, CLCII I-164; MPII:AF
I-171; MPII:AfAm I-161
Free at Last, MPII:JYABio II-674
We Have Tomorrow, MPII:JYABio
IV-1842
BOOTH, PHILIP, CWA I-203
"Letter from a Distant Land," MPII:P
III-1222
Poetry of Booth, The, MP VIII-4835
BOR, JOSEF
Terezín Requiem, The, MPII:JYAFic
IV-1443
BORGES, JORGE LUIS, CWA I-204;
CWAII I-217
"Aleph, The," MPII:SS I-52
"Circular Ruins, The," MPII:SS I-399
Ficciones, MP IV-1040; MP:AF I-375
"Funes, the Memorious," MPII:SS II-820
"Garden of Forking Paths, The,"
MPII:SS II-824
"Gospel According to Mark, The,"
MPII:SS II-915
"Library of Babel, The," MPII:SS
III-1342
"Pierre Menard, Author of the Quixote,"
MPII:SS IV-1814
"South, The," MPII:SS V-2194
"Theme of the Traitor and the Hero,"
MPII:SS VI-2329
"Tlön, Uqbar, Orbis Tertius," MPII:SS
VI-2373
BORLAND, HAL
When the Legends Die, MPII:JYAFic
IV-1603
BORN, FRANZ
Jules Verne, MPII:JYABio II-989

BOROWSKI, TADEUSZ, CWAII I-220
"This Way for the Gas, Ladies and
  Gentlemen," MPII:SS VI-2348
"World of Stone, The," MPII:SS VI-2709
BORROW, GEORGE HENRY, CWA I-209
Bible in Spain, The, MP I-528
Lavengro, CLC I-601; MP VI-3292;
  MP:BF II-787
Romany Rye, The, CLC II-988; MP
  X-5693; MP:BF II-1365
Wild Wales, MP XII-7145
Zinicali, The, MP XII-7328
BORTON DE TREVIÑO, ELIZABETH
I, Juan de Pareja, MPII:JYAFic II-685
BOSTON, LUCY M.
Green Knowe books, The, MPII:JYAFic
  II-565
BOSWELL, JAMES, CWA I-211
Boswell's London Journal: 1762-1763,
  MP I-608
Journal of a Tour to the Hebrides, MP
  V-3044
Life of Samuel Johnson, LL.D., The, MP
  VI-3409
BOURGET, PAUL, CWA I-214
Disciple, The, CLC I-271; MP III-1519;
  MP:EF I-402
BOURKE-WHITE, MARGARET
Portrait of Myself, MPII:JYABio
  III-1432
BOWEN, CATHERINE DRINKER
Yankee from Olympus, MPII:JYABio
  IV-1956
BOWEN, ELIZABETH, CWA I-216;
  CWAII I-222
Bowen's Court, MPII:NF I-201
Death of the Heart, The, CLC I-257; MP
  III-1381; MP:BF I-295; MPII:JYAFic
  I-327
"Demon Lover, The," MPII:SS II-565
Eva Trout, CLCII II-470; MPII:BCF
  I-461
"Happy Autumn Fields, The," MPII:SS
  III-985
Heat of the Day, The, CLC I-453; MP
  V-2523; MP:BF I-555
"Her Table Spread," MPII:SS III-1000
House in Paris, The, CLC I-486; MP
  V-2714; MP:BF II-602

"Ivy Gripped the Steps," MPII:SS
  III-1201
Little Girls, The, CLCII III-895;
  MPII:BCF II-971
"Mysterious Kôr," MPII:SS IV-1575
"Summer Night," MPII:SS V-2271
World of Love, A, CLCII IV-1753;
  MPII:BCF IV-1935
BOWERING, GEORGE
Burning Water, CLCII I-217; MPII:BCF
  I-211
BOWERS, CLAUDE G. CWA 1-218
Jefferson and Hamilton, MP V-2993
BOWLES, JANE, CWAII I-224
"Stick of Green Candy, A," MPII:SS
  V-2228
BOWLES, PAUL, CWAII I-226
"Delicate Prey, The," MPII:SS II-553
"Distant Episode, A," MPII:SS II-610
Sheltering Sky, The, CLCII IV-1390;
  MPII:AF IV-1402
BOX, EDGAR. See VIDAL, GORE
BOYD, JAMES, CWA I-219
Drums, CLC I-307; MP III-1656;
  MP:AF I-313
Marching On, CLC I-668; MP VII-3714;
  MP:AF II-761
BOYD, MARTIN
Lucinda Brayford, CLCII III-933;
  MPII:BCF III-1033
BOYLE, KAY, CWAII I-228
"Summer Evening," MPII:SS V-2267
"White Horses of Vienna, The,"
  MPII:SS VI-2585
"Winter Night," MPII:SS VI-2649
BOYLE, T. CORAGHESSAN, CWAII
  I-231
"Greasy Lake," MPII:SS III-925
"Overcoat II, The," MPII:SS IV-1749
BOYLSTON, HELEN DORE
Clara Barton, MPII:JYABio I-373
BOYNICK, DAVID KING
Women Who Led the Way,
  MPII:JYABio IV-1933
BRACKENRIDGE, HUGH HENRY, CWA
  I-220
Modern Chivalry, CLC II-728; MP
  VII-4001; MP:AF II-806

AUTHOR INDEX

BRADBURY, MALCOLM, CWAII I-233
Eating People Is Wrong, CLCII II-439;
MPII:BCF I-418
History Man, The, CLCII II-680;
MPII:BCF II-721
Rates of Exchange, CLCII III-1268;
MPII:BCF III-1390
BRADBURY, RAY, CWAII I-235
"April Witch, The," MPII:SS I-103
Dandelion Wine, MPII:JYAFic I-295
Fahrenheit 451, CLCII II-482; MPII:AF
II-501; MPII:JYAFic I-397
Martian Chronicles, The, CLCII III-979;
MPII:AF III-986
Something Wicked This Way Comes,
CLCII IV-1441; MPII:AF IV-1471
"There Will Come Soft Rains," MPII:SS
VI-2333
"Veldt, The," MPII:SS VI-2485
BRADFORD, GAMALIEL, CWA I-221
Damaged Souls, MP III-1273
BRADFORD, WILLIAM, CWA I-223
Of Plimouth Plantation, MP VIII-4297
BRADLEY, DAVID
Chaneysville Incident, The, CLCII I-256;
MPII:AF I-274; MPII:AfAm I-254
BRADLEY, MARION ZIMMER
Hawkmistress!, MPII:JYAFic II-608
BRADSTREET, ANNE
"Contemplations," MPII:P II-423
BRAINE, JOHN, CWA I-225
Room at the Top, MP X-5709; MP:BF
III-1373
BRAITHWAITE, E. R.
To Sir, with Love, MPII:JYABio
IV-1740
BRANCATO, ROBIN F.
Come Alive at 505, MPII:JYAFic I-258
BRANCH, TAYLOR, and BILL RUSSELL
Second Wind, MPII:JYABio IV-1549
BRANDÃO, IGNÁCIO DE LOYOLA. See
LOYOLA BRANDÃO, IGNÁCIO DE
BRATHWAITE, EDWARD KAMAU
Poetry of Edward Kamau Brathwaite,
The, II-979
X/Self, MPII:P VI-2465
BRAUTIGAN, RICHARD, CWAII I-240
Confederate General from Big Sur, A,
CLCII I-321; MPII:AF I-325

In Watermelon Sugar, CLCII II-754;
MPII:AF II-787
So the Wind Won't Blow It All Away,
MPII:JYAFic IV-1360
Trout Fishing in America, CLCII
IV-1619; MPII:AF IV-1702
BRAYMER, MARJORIE
Walls of Windy Troy, The,
MPII:JYABio IV-1822
BRAZIL, ANGELA
Fourth Form Friendship, A,
MPII:JYAFic II-464
Leader of the Lower School, The,
MPII:JYAFic II-817
BRECHT, BERTOLT, CWA I-227; CWAII
I-242
Baal, MP I-397
Caucasian Chalk Circle, The, CLCII
I-247; MPII:D I-288
Galileo, CLCII II-562; MPII:D II-650
Good Woman of Setzuan, The, CLCII
II-615; MPII:D II-689
Mother Courage and Her Children,
CLCII III-1046; MPII:D III-1105
Private Life of the Master Race, The,
CLC II-918; MP IX-5344
Rise and Fall of the City of Mahagonny,
CLCII III-1298; MPII:D IV-1350
Threepenny Opera, The, CLCII IV-1560;
MPII:D IV-1568
BRENTON, HOWARD, CWAII I-245
Bloody Poetry, CLCII I-172; MPII:D
I-207
BRENTON, HOWARD, and DAVID
HARE
Pravda, CLCII III-1232; MPII:D III-1278
BRETON, ANDRÉ, CWA I-229
"Free Union," MPII:P II-813
Poetry of André Breton, The, MP
VIII-4802
BRETON, NICHOLAS, CWA I-231
Poetry of Nicholas Breton, The, MP
IX-5103
BREUER, JOSEF, and SIGMUND FREUD
Studies on Hysteria, MP XI-6317
BREYTENBACH, BREYTEN, CWAII
I-247
True Confessions of an Albino Terrorist,
The, MPII:NF IV-1569

173

BRIDGERS, SUE ELLEN
Home Before Dark, MPII:JYAFic II-638
Notes for Another Life, MPII:JYAFic III-1048
BRINK, ANDRÉ, CWAII I-250
Chain of Voices, A, CLCII I-254; MPII:BCF I-235
BRINK, CAROL RYRIE
Caddie Woodlawn, MPII:JYAFic I-166
BRINSMEAD, H. F.
Ballad of Benny Perhaps, The, MPII:JYAFic I-80
BRISLAND, JANET MARJORIE. See MARK, JAN
BRITTAIN, VERA, CWAII I-253
Testament of Youth, Testament of Friendship, and Testament of Experience, MPII:NF IV-1479
BROCH, HERMANN, CWA I-232; CWAII I-255
Death of Virgil, The, CLC I-257; MP III-1385; MP:EF I-363
Sleepwalkers, The, CLC II-1049; MP X-6089; MP:EF III-1164
Spell, The, CLCII IV-1460; MPII:WF IV-1506
BRODKEY, HAROLD, CWAII I-257
"His Son, in His Arms, in Light, Aloft," MPII:SS III-1022
BRODSKY, JOSEPH, CWAII I-259
Less Than One, MPII:NF II-802
"Part of Speech, A," MPII:P IV-1646
"To a Friend," MPII:P VI-2191
"To Urania," MPII:P VI-2233
BROME, RICHARD, CWA I-234
Jovial Crew, A, CLC I-556; MP VI-3075
Northern Lass, The, CLC II-783; MP VII-4243
BROMFIELD, LOUIS, CWA I-235
Green Bay Tree, The, CLC I-424; MP IV-2378; MP:AF II-509
BRONTË, ANNE, CWA I-237
Agnes Grey, CLC I-15; MP I-73; MP:BF I-16
Tenant of Wildfell Hall, The, CLC II-1115; MP XI-6442; MP:BF III-1505
BRONTË, CHARLOTTE, CWA I-237
Jane Eyre, CLC I-540; MP V-2976; MP:BF II-681; MPII:JYAFic II-745

Professor, The, CLC II-920; MP IX-5353; MP:BF III-1274
Shirley, CLC II-1034; MP X-5985; MP:BF III-1427
Villette, CLC II-1204; MP XII-6929; MP:BF III-1686
BRONTË, EMILY, CWA I-237
Poetry of Emily Brontë, The, MP IX-4932
"Remembrance," MPII:P V-1801
Wuthering Heights, CLC II-1270; MP XII-7281; MP:BF III-1775; MPII:JYAFic IV-1664
BROOKE, HENRY, CWA I-241
Fool of Quality, The, CLC I-374; MP IV-2107; MP:BF I-434
BROOKE, RUPERT, CWA I-242
Poetry of Brooke, The, MP VIII-4838
"Soldier, The," MPII:P V-1941
BROOKNER, ANITA, CWAII I-261
Debut, The, CLCII I-383; MPII:BCF I-370
Hotel du Lac, CLCII II-702; MPII:BCF II-743
Look at Me, CLCII III-912; MPII:BCF III-1003
BROOKS, BRUCE
Moves Make the Man, The, MPII:JYAFic III-989
BROOKS, GWENDOLYN, CWA I-244; CWAII I-263
Maud Martha, MPII:AfAm II-777; MPII:JYAFic III-942
"Mother, The," MPII:P IV-1424
Poetry of Gwendolyn Brooks, The, MPII:AfAm II-985
"Rise of Maud Martha, The," MPII:SS V-1961
BROOKS, POLLY SCHOYER
Queen Eleanor, Independent Spirit of the Medieval World, MPII:JYABio III-1451
BROOKS, VAN WYCK, CWA I-246
America's Coming-of-Age, MP I-179
BROWN, CECIL
Coming Up Down Home, MPII:AfAm I-290
BROWN, CHARLES BROCKDEN, CWA I-248
Wieland, CLC II-1241; MP XII-7129; MP:AF III-1433

174

BROWN, CLAUDE
  Manchild in the Promised Land,
    MPII:AfAm II-765; MPII:JYABio
    III-1164
BROWN, DEE
  Conspiracy of Knaves, MPII:JYAFic
    I-274
BROWN, GEORGE DOUGLAS. *See*
  DOUGLAS, GEORGE
BROWN, IVOR
  Dr. Johnson and His World,
    MPII:JYABio I-489
BROWN, JOHN MASON
  Daniel Boone, MPII:JYABio I-439
BROWN, MARION MARCH, *and* RUTH
  CRONE
  Willa Cather, MPII:JYABio IV-1883
BROWN, RITA MAE, CWAII I-265
  Rubyfruit Jungle, CLCII III-1318;
    MPII:AF III-1349
BROWN, ROY
  Siblings, The, MPII:JYAFic IV-1331
BROWN, STERLING A.
  Poetry of Sterling Brown, The,
    MPII:AfAm II-991
  "Transfer," MPII:P VI-2253
BROWN, WILLIAM WELLS
  Autobiographical Writings of William
    Wells Brown, The, MPII:AfAm I-58
  Clotel, MPII:AfAm I-277
BROWNE, SIR THOMAS, CWA I-250
  Hydriotaphia, MP V-2791
BROWNING, ELIZABETH BARRETT,
  CWA I-252
  Sonnet 1, MPII:P V-1972
  Sonnet 6, MPII:P V-1975
  Sonnet 7, MPII:P V-1978
  Sonnet 14, MPII:P V-1981
  Sonnet 35, MPII:P V-1984
  Sonnet 43, MPII:P V-1987
  Sonnets from the Portuguese, MP
    XI-6168
BROWNING, ROBERT, CWA I-254
  "Andrea del Sarto," MPII:P I-71
  "Bishop Orders His Tomb at Saint
    Praxed's Church, The," MPII:P I-237
  Blot in the 'Scutcheon, A, CLC I-112;
    MP I-578

"Childe Roland to the Dark Tower
  Came," MPII:P I-371
Dramatic Monologues and Lyrics of
  Browning, MP III-1641
Dramatis Personae, MP III-1644
"Epistle Containing the Strange Medical
  Experience of Karshish, the Arab
  Physician, An," MPII:P II-674
Fra Lippo Lippi, MPII:P II-810
"Grammarian's Funeral, A," MPII:P
  III-879
"Love Among the Ruins," MPII:P
  III-1280
Men and Women, MP VII-3846
"My Last Duchess," MPII:P IV-1443
"Rabbi Ben Ezra," MPII:P V-1767
Ring and the Book, The, CLC II-970;
  MP X-5603
Sordello, MPII:P V-2035
BRYANT, WILLIAM CULLEN, CWA
  I-257
  Poetry of Bryant, The, MP VIII-4841
  "Thanatopsis," MPII:P VI-2137
BRYCE, JAMES VISCOUNT, CWA I-260
  American Commonwealth, The, MP
    I-169
BUCHAN, JOHN, CWA I-261
  Thirty-Nine Steps, The, CLC II-1124;
    MP XI-6493; MP:BF III-1523
BÜCHNER, GEORG, CWA I-263
  "Lenz," CLCII II-872; MPII:SS III-1335
  Woyzeck, CLC II-1269; MP XII-7275
BUCK, PEARL S., CWA I-265
  Dragon Seed, CLC I-302; MP III-1638;
    MP:AF I-309
  Good Earth, The, CLC I-411; MP
    IV-2319; MP:AF I-478
  My Several Worlds, MPII:JYABio
    III-1276
BUCKLER, ERNEST, CWAII I-267
  Mountain and the Valley, The, CLCII
    III-1051; MPII:BCF III-1143
BUCKLEY, WILLIAM F., JR., CWAII
  I-269
  Cruising Speed, MPII:NF I-310
  Overdrive, MPII:NF III-1113
BUCKMASTER, HENRIETTA
  Women Who Shaped History,
    MPII:JYABio IV-1937

BUDGELL, EUSTACE, JOSEPH ADDISON, *and* SIR RICHARD STEELE
Sir Roger de Coverley Papers, The, CLC II-1044; MP X-6067
BUECHNER, FREDERICK, CWAII I-272
Book of Bebb, The, CLCII I-187; MPII:AF I-196
Now and Then, MPII:NF III-1041
Sacred Journey, The, MPII:NF III-1269
BUGAEV, BORIS NIKOLAYEVICH. *See* BELY, ANDREY
BUKOWSKI, CHARLES
"Twins, The," MPII:P VI-2297
BULGAKOV, MIKHAIL, CWAII I-275
Days of the Turbins, CLCII I-371; MPII:D II-449
Heart of a Dog, The, CLCII II-667; MPII:WF II-583
Master and Margarita, The, CLCII III-984; MPII:WF III-976
BULLEN, FRANK THOMAS, CWA I-268
Cruise of the Cachalot, The, CLC I-227; MP III-1232; MP:BF I-265
BULLINS, ED, CWAII I-278
In the Wine Time, CLCII II-753; MPII:AfAm II-587; MPII:D II-820
Taking of Miss Janie, The, MPII:AfAm III-1404
BULOSAN, CARLOS
America Is in the Heart, MPII:JYABio I-51
BULWER-LYTTON, EDWARD GEORGE EARLE, CWA I-269
Eugene Aram, CLC I-334; MP IV-1879; MP:BF I-378
Last Days of Pompeii, The, CLC I-594; MP VI-3249; MP:BF II-772
Last of the Barons, The, CLC I-595; MP VI-3257; MP:BF II-780
BUNIN, IVAN ALEXEYEVICH, CWA I-272
"Gentleman from San Francisco, The," MPII:SS II-835
Village, The, CLC II-1203; MP XII-6922; MP:EF III-1349
BUNTING, EVE
Haunting of Safekeep, The, MPII:JYAFic II-605

BUNYAN, JOHN, CWA I-274
Life and Death of Mr. Badman, The, CLC I-610; MP VI-3392; MP:BF II-796
Pilgrim's Progress, The, CLC II-882; MP VIII-4705; MP:BF III-1227; MPII:JYAFic III-1140
BUONARROTI, MICHELANGELO. *See* MICHELANGELO BUONARROTI
BURCH, JENNINGS MICHAEL
They Cage the Animals at Night, MPII:JYABio IV-1692
BURGESS, ANTHONY, CWAII I-280
Clockwork Orange, A, CLCII I-295; MPII:BCF I-271; MPII:JYAFic I-251
Earthly Powers, CLCII II-437; MPII:BCF I-413
End of the World News, The, CLCII II-455; MPII:BCF I-447
Little Wilson and Big God, MPII:NF II-841
Napoleon Symphony, CLCII III-1075; MPII:BCF III-1171
Nothing Like the Sun, CLCII III-1116; MPII:BCF III-1233
Right to an Answer, The, CLCII III-1295; MPII:BCF III-1416
Tremor of Intent, CLCII IV-1609; MPII:BCF IV-1732
BURKE, EDMUND, CWA I-279
Vindication of Natural Society, A, MP XII-6934
BURKE, KENNETH, CWAII I-283
Grammar of Motives, A, MPII:NF II-573
BURLINGAME, ROGER
Out of Silence into Sound, MPII:JYABio III-1375
Scientists Behind the Inventors, MPII:JYABio IV-1529
BURNETT, CONSTANCE BUEL
Captain John Ericsson, MPII:JYABio I-289
BURNETT, FRANCES HODGSON
Little Lord Fauntleroy, MPII:JYAFic II-854
Little Princess, A, MPII:JYAFic II-864
Secret Garden, The, MPII:JYAFic III-1295

BURNEY, FANNY, CWA I-281
  Cecilia, CLC I-162; MP II-861; MP:BF I-193
  Diary and Letters of Mme. d'Arblay, The, MP III-1499
  Evelina, CLC I-341; MP IV-1913; MP:BF I-395
BURNFORD, SHEILA
  Bel Ria, MPII:JYAFic I-103
  Incredible Journey, The, MPII:JYAFic II-703
BURNS, ROBERT, CWA I-283
  Poems, Chiefly in the Scottish Dialect, MP VIII-4783
BURROUGHS, EDGAR RICE
  Tarzan of the Apes, MPII:JYAFic IV-1433
BURROUGHS, WILLIAM S., CWAII I-286
  Naked Lunch, CLCII III-1071; MPII:AF III-1114
BURTON, HESTER
  Time of Trial, MPII:JYAFic IV-1480
BURTON, ROBERT, CWA I-286
  Anatomy of Melancholy, The, MP I-200
BUTLER, OCTAVIA E.
  Kindred, MPII:AfAm II-654
  Xenogenesis Trilogy, The, MPII:AfAm III-1507
BUTLER, SAMUEL (1612-1680) CWA I-288
  Hudibras, CLC I-497; MP V-2760
BUTLER, SAMUEL (1835-1902) CWA I-289
  Erewhon, CLC I-331; MP III-1822; MP:BF I-370
  Way of All Flesh, The, CLC II-1228; MP XII-7061; MP:BF III-1721

BUTOR, MICHEL, CWAII I-288
  Change of Heart, A, CLCII I-257; MPII:WF I-239
  Mobile, CLCII III-1027; MPII:WF II-1021
  Niagara, CLCII III-1089; MPII:WF III-1093
  Passing Time, CLCII III-1183; MPII:WF III-1173
BUZZATI, DINO
  Bàrnabo of the Mountains, CLCII I-117; MPII:WF I-116
  "Count's Wife, The," MPII:SS I-448
  Tartar Steppe, The, CLCII IV-1516; MPII:WF IV-1548
BYARS, BETSY
  Night Swimmers, The, MPII:JYAFic III-1035
  Summer of the Swans, The, MPII:JYAFic IV-1406
BYRNE, DONN, CWA I-291
  Destiny Bay, CLC I-266; MP III-1463; MP:BF I-314
  Hangman's House, CLC I-442; MP V-2473; MP:BF I-528
  Messer Marco Polo, CLC I-698; MP VII-3863; MP:BF II-928
BYRNE, JOHN KEYES. See LEONARD, HUGH
BYRON, GEORGE GORDON, LORD, CWA I-293
  Cain, CLC I-140; MP II-734
  Childe Harold's Pilgrimage, MP II-921
  Don Juan, CLC I-291; MP III-1590
  Lyric Poetry of Byron, The, MP VI-3562
  Manfred, CLC I-663; MP VII-3690
  Vision of Judgment, The, MPII:P VI-2341

C

CABELL, JAMES BRANCH, CWA I-296
  Cream of the Jest, The, CLC I-220; MP
    II-1194; MP:AF I-231
  Jurgen, CLC I-563; MP VI-3105;
    MP:AF II-626
  Rivet in Grandfather's Neck, The, CLC
    II-976; MP X-5632; MP:AF III-1058
CABLE, GEORGE WASHINGTON, CWA
  I-299
  Grandissimes, The, CLC I-414; MP
    IV-2338; MP:AF I-483
  "Jean-ah Poquelin," MPII:SS III-1214
CABRERA INFANTE, GUILLERMO,
  CWAII I-290
  Infante's Inferno, CLCII II-760;
    MPII:AF II-792
  Three Trapped Tigers, CLCII IV-1559;
    MPII:AF IV-1652
CAESAR, CWA I-301
  Commentaries, MP II-1040
CAIN, GUILLERMO. See CABRERA
  INFANTE, GUILLERMO
CAIN, JAMES M., CWA I-303
  Postman Always Rings Twice, The, MP
    IX-5270; MP:AF II-978
CALDERÓN DE LA BARCA, PEDRO,
  CWA I-305
  Devotion of the Cross, The, CLC I-267;
    MP III-1471
  It Is Better than It Was, CLC I-534; MP
    V-2942
  It Is Worse than It Was, CLC I-534; MP
    V-2945
  Life Is a Dream, CLC I-611; MP VI-3398
  Mayor of Zalamea, The, CLC I-684; MP
    VII-3788
  Mock Astrologer, The, CLC II-728; MP
    VII-3998
CALDWELL, ERSKINE, CWA I-308;
  CWAII I-292
  God's Little Acre, CLCII II-603;
    MPII:AF II-639
  Tobacco Road, CLC II-1140; MP
    XI-6578; MP:AF III-1299
CALISHER, HORTENSE, CWAII I-295
  "In Greenwich There Are Many
    Gravelled Walks," MPII:SS III-1137

CALLAGHAN, MORLEY, CWAII I-297
  "All the Years of Her Life," MPII:SS
    I-60
  "Cap for Steve, A," MPII:SS I-326
  Loved and the Lost, The, CLCII III-928;
    MPII:BCF III-1022
  Passion in Rome, A, CLCII III-1184;
    MPII:BCF III-1298
  "Sick Call, A," MPII:SS V-2101
  Such Is My Beloved, CLCII IV-1487;
    MPII:BCF IV-1638
CALVINO, ITALO, CWAII I-300
  Baron in the Trees, The, CLCII I-119;
    MPII:WF I-121
  Castle of Crossed Destinies, The, CLCII
    I-240; MPII:WF I-216
  Cloven Viscount, The, CLCII I-299;
    MPII:WF I-277
  If on a Winter's Night a Traveler, CLCII
    II-736; MPII:WF II-659
  Invisible Cities, CLCII II-774; MPII:WF
    II-727
  Mr. Palomar, CLCII III-1020; MPII:WF
    III-1015
  Non-existent Knight, The, CLCII
    III-1110; MPII:WF III-1113
  Path to the Nest of Spiders, The, CLCII
    III-1186; MPII:WF III-1178
  "Watcher, The," MPII:SS VI-2556
CAMERON, ELEANOR
  Court of the Stone Children, The,
    MPII:JYAFic I-289
  Mushroom Planet series, The,
    MPII:JYAFic III-993
CAMOËNS, LUIS DE, CWA I-310
  Lusiad, The, CLC I-639; MP VI-3557
CAMP, MADELEINE. See L'ENGLE,
  MADELEINE
CAMPBELL, BEBE MOORE
  Your Blues Ain't Like Mine,
    MPII:AfAm III-1525
CAMPBELL, JOSEPH, CWAII I-302
  Hero with a Thousand Faces, The,
    MPII:NF II-636
CAMPBELL, WALTER STANLEY. See
  VESTAL, STANLEY.
CAMPION, NARDI REEDER
  Ann the Word, MPII:JYABio I-110

Patrick Henry, MPII:JYABio III-1387
CAMPION, THOMAS, CWA I-312
"My Sweetest Lesbia," MPII:P IV-1456
Poetry of Campion, The, MP VIII-4844
CAMUS, ALBERT, CWA I-314; CWAII
I-304
"Adulterous Woman, The," MPII:SS I-19
Caligula, CLCII I-226; MPII:D I-278
Exile and the Kingdom, MP IV-1936;
MP:EF II-489
Fall, The, MP IV-1965; MP:EF II-493
"Guest, The," MPII:SS III-952
Myth of Sisyphus, The, MP VII-4128
Plague, The, CLC II-889; MP VIII-4734;
MP:EF III-1010
Possessed, The, CLCII III-1227; MPII:D
III-1269
Rebel, The, MPII:NF III-1231
Stranger, The, MP XI-6301; MP:EF
III-1244
CANETTI, ELIAS, CWAII I-306
Auto-da-Fé, CLCII I-91; MPII:WF I-95
Crowds and Power, MPII:NF I-304
Play of the Eyes, The, MPII:NF IV-1546
Tongue Set Free, The, MPII:NF IV-1546
Torch in My Ear, The, MPII:NF IV-1546
ČAPEK, KAREL, CWA I-316
R. U. R., CLC II-997; MP X-5736
CAPOTE, TRUMAN, CWAII I-308
"Children on Their Birthdays," MPII:SS
I-376
"Headless Hawk, The," MPII:SS III-993
In Cold Blood, MPII:NF II-704
"My Side of the Matter," MPII:SS
IV-1567
Other Voices, Other Rooms,
MPII:JYAFic III-1085
CARDUCCI, GIOSUÈ, CWA I-317
Poetry of Carducci, The, MP VIII-4847
CAREW, THOMAS, CWA I-319
Poetry of Carew, The, MP VIII-4850
CAREY, ERNESTINE GILBRETH, and
FRANK B. GILBRETH, JR.
Cheaper by the Dozen, MPII:JYABio
I-340
CAREY, PETER
Illywhacker, CLCII II-739; MPII:BCF
II-794
CARLETON, WILLIAM, CWA I-321
"Donagh, The," MPII:SS II-624

Emigrants of Ahadarra, The, CLC I-322;
MP III-1752; MP:BF I-359
CARLYLE, THOMAS, CWA I-322
French Revolution, The, MP IV-2169
History of Frederick II of Prussia, MP
V-2634
On Heroes, Hero-Worship and the
Heroic in History, MP VIII-4368
Sartor Resartus, MP X-5799
CARPENTER, HUMPHREY
Tolkien, MPII:JYABio IV-1744
CARPENTIER, ALEJO, CWAII I-310
Explosion in a Cathedral, CLCII II-477;
MPII:AF II-496
Kingdom of This World, The, CLCII
II-834; MPII:AF II-840
"Like the Night," MPII:SS III-1359
Lost Steps, The, CLCII III-921;
MPII:AF II-927
Manhunt, CLCII III-965; MPII:AF III-977
CARRIGHAR, SALLY
Home to the Wilderness, MPII:JYABio
II-857
CARROLL, LEWIS, CWA I-325
Alice's Adventures in Wonderland, CLC
I-22; MP I-107; MP:BF I-30;
MPII:JYAFic I-28
Through the Looking Glass, CLC
II-1130; MP:BF III-1536; MP
XI-6526; MPII:JYAFic IV-1465
CARRUTH, HAYDEN
"Concerning Necessity," MPII:P I-417
CARSON, RACHEL
Silent Spring, MPII:NF IV-1351
CARTER, FORREST
Education of Little Tree, The,
MPII:JYABio II-537
CARVER, RAYMOND, CWAII I-313
"Careful," MPII:SS I-330
"Small, Good Thing, A," MPII:SS
V-2135
"Sturgeon, The," MPII:P V-2087
"Wake Up," MPII:P VI-2357
"Why Don't You Dance?" MPII:SS
VI-2605
"Will You Please Be Quiet, Please?"
MPII:SS VI-2627
CARY, JOYCE, CWA I-328; CWAII I-315
Herself Surprised, CLC I-472; MP
V-2603; MP:BF I-574

Horse's Mouth, The, CLC I-482; MP
V-2699; MP:BF I-593
Second Trilogy, CLCII III-1365;
MPII:BCF IV-1489
To Be a Pilgrim, CLC II-1137; MP
XI-6570; MP:BF III-1547
CARY, LORENE
Black Ice, MPII:AfAm I-149
CASANOVA, CWA I-330
Memoirs, MP VII-3823
CASEY, JOHN. *See* O'CASEY, SEAN
CASSITY, TURNER
"Advice to King Lear," MPII:P I-13
CASTANEDA, CARLOS, CWAII I-318
Teachings of Don Juan, The, MPII:NF
IV-1468
CASTIGLIONE, BALDASSARE, CWA
I-332
Book of the Courtier, The, MP I-596
CATHER, WILLA, CWA I-334; CWAII
I-320
"Coming, Aphrodite," MPII:SS I-422
Death Comes for the Archbishop, CLC
I-251; MP III-1349; MP:AF I-264
Lost Lady, A, CLC I-631; MP VI-3521;
MP:AF II-706
Lucy Gayheart, CLCII III-936; MPII:AF
III-943
My Ántonia, CLC II-749; MP VII-4103;
MP:AF II-823; MPII:JYAFic III-1007
"Neighbor Rosicky," MPII:SS IV-1602
O Pioneers! CLC II-785; MP VII-4265;
MP:AF II-856
One of Ours, CLCII III-1154; MPII:AF
III-1213
"Paul's Case," MPII:SS IV-1779
Professor's House, The, CLC II-922; MP
IX-5357; MP:AF II-994
Sapphira and the Slave Girl, CLCII
III-1335; MPII:AF III-1366
"Sculptor's Funeral, The," MPII:SS
V-2045
Shadows on the Rock, CLC II-1028; MP
X-5948; MP:AF III-1126
Song of the Lark, The, CLC II-1064; MP
XI-6159; MP:AF III-1184
CATULLUS, CWA I-338
Carmina, MP II-806
CAVAFY, CONSTANTINE P., CWA I-339
"Myris," MPII:P IV-1459

"Philhellene," MPII:P IV-1665
Poetry of Cavafy, The, MP VIII-4854
"Waiting for the Barbarians," MPII:P
VI-2354
CAVANNA, BETTY
Going on Sixteen, MPII:JYAFic II-537
CAVENDISH, GEORGE, CWA I-340
Life and Death of Cardinal Wolsy, The,
MP VI-3389
CELA, CAMILIO JOSÉ, CWA I-341
Family of Pascual Duarte, The, MP
IV-1980; MP:EF II-501
Hive, The, MP V-2663; MP:EF II-641
CELAN, PAUL
"Corona," MPII:P II-446
"Death Fugue," MPII:P II-498
"From the Beam," MPII:P II-816
"Homecoming," MPII:P III-956
"Psalm," MPII:P V-1745
"With All My Thoughts," MPII:P
VI-2435
CÉLINE, LOUIS-FERDINAND, CWA
I-343; CWAII I-322
Castle to Castle, North, CLCII I-241;
MPII:WF I-221
Death on the Installment Plan, CLCII
I-380; MPII:WF I-353
Journey to the End of the Night, CLC
I-555; MP VI-3068; MP:EF II-720
Rigadoon, CLCII I-241; MPII:WF I-221
CELLINI, BENVENUTO, CWA I-345
Autobiography of Benvenuto Cellini,
The, MP I-368
CENDRARS, BLAISE, CWAII I-324
Sutter's Gold, CLCII IV-1500; MPII:WF
IV-1538
CERVANTES, CWA I-347
Don Quixote de la Mancha, CLC I-294;
MP III-1603; MP:EF I-431
Exemplary Novels, MP IV-1933; MP:EF
II-485
CÉSAIRE, AIMÉ, CWAII I-326
Return to My Native Land, MPII:P
V-1827
Tragedy of King Christophe, The, CLCII
IV-1598; MPII:D IV-1623
CHALLANS, MARY. *See* RENAULT,
MARY
CHANDLER, DAVID G.
Napoleon, MPII:JYABio III-1292

CHANDLER, RAYMOND, CWAII I-328
Big Sleep, The, CLCII I-151; MPII:AF
I-166
Farewell, My Lovely, CLCII II-493;
MPII:AF II-527
Long Goodbye, The, CLCII III-910;
MPII:AF III-911
"Nevada Gas," MPII:SS IV-1608
CHAPMAN, GEORGE, CWA I-351
All Fools, CLC I-24; MP I-114
Bussy d'Ambois, CLC I-136; MP II-714
Gentleman Usher, The, CLC I-396; MP
IV-2230
Monsieur d'Olive, CLC II-736; MP
VII-4037
Revenge of Bussy d'Ambois, The, CLC
II-961; MP X-5550
Shadow of Night, The, MP X-5945
CHAPMAN, GEORGE, BEN JONSON,
and JOHN MARSTON
Eastward Ho! CLC I-313; MP III-1693
CHASE-RIBOUD, BARBARA
Sally Hemings, MPII:AfAm III-1230
CHATEAUBRIAND,
FRANÇOIS-AUGUSTE-RENÉ DE,
CWA I-353
Atala, CLC I-69; MP I-349; MP:EF I-81
CHATTERTON, THOMAS, CWA I-355
Poetry of Chatterton, The, MP VIII-4857
CHATWIN, BRUCE, CWAII I-330
In Patagonia, MPII:NF II-725
CHAUCER, GEOFFREY, CWA I-357
Canterbury Tales, The, CLC I-146; MP
II-769
Legend of Good Women, The, CLC
I-605; MP VI-3311
Parliament of Fowls, The, MP VIII-4493
Troilus and Criseyde, CLC II-1164; MP
XI-6725
CHEEVER, JOHN, CWA I-360; CWAII
I-332
"Angel of the Bridge, The," MPII:SS I-95
"Brigadier and the Golf Widow, The,"
MPII:SS I-308
Bullet Park, CLCII I-210; MPII:AF I-216
"Country Husband, The," MPII:SS I-440
"Enormous Radio, The," MPII:SS II-706
Falconer, CLCII II-488; MPII:AF II-515
"Five-Forty-Eight, The," MPII:SS II-785
"Goodbye, My Brother," MPII:SS II-907

"Housebreaker of Shady Hill, The,"
MPII:SS II-1052
"Metamorphoses," MPII:SS IV-1489
Oh What a Paradise It Seems, CLCII
III-1134; MPII:AF III-1180
Short Stories of John Cheever, The, MP
X-6011; MP:AF III-1141
"Swimmer, The," MPII:SS V-2297
Wapshot Chronicle, The, MP XII-7020;
MP:AF III-1396
Wapshot Scandal, The, MP XII-7024;
MP:AF III-1400
"World of Apples, The," MPII:SS
VI-2705
CHEEVER, SUSAN
Home Before Dark, MPII:JYABio II-850
CHEKHOV, ANTON, CWA I-361
"Bet, The," MPII:SS I-192
"Bishop, The," MPII:SS I-214
"Chemist's Wife, The," MPII:SS I-364
Cherry Orchard, The, CLC I-173; MP
II-908
"Darling, The," MPII:SS II-492
"Duel, The," CLCII II-428; MPII:SS
II-650
"Gooseberries," MPII:SS II-911
"Gusev," MPII:SS III-962
"Kiss, The," MPII:SS III-1270
"Lady with the Dog, The," CLCII II-846;
MPII:SS III-1288
"Man in a Case, The," MPII:SS IV-1434
"Rothschild's Fiddle," MPII:SS V-1994
Seagull, The, CLC II-1015; MP X-5868
"Steppe, The," CLCII IV-1474; MPII:SS
V-2224
Three Sisters, The, CLC II-1129; MP
XI-6518
"Trifling Occurrence, A," MPII:SS
VI-2411
Uncle Vanya, CLC II-1179; MP
XII-6818
"Ward No. 6," MPII:SS VI-2548
CHESNUTT, CHARLES WADDELL,
CWA I-364
Conjure Woman, The, CLC I-197; MP
II-1080; MP:AF I-211; MPII:AfAm
I-308
House Behind the Cedars, The, CLCII
II-705; MPII:AF II-748; MPII:AfAm
II-552

"Sheriff's Children, The," MPII:SS
V-2072
CHESTERFIELD, PHILIP DORMER
STANHOPE, LORD, CWA I-365
Letters to His Son, MP VI-3374
CHESTERTON, G. K., CWA I-366
Autobiography, MPII:NF I-109
Essays of G. K. Chesterton, The, MP
IV-1859
Everlasting Man, The, MPII:NF II-471
"Invisible Man, The," MPII:SS III-1191
Man Who Was Thursday, The, CLC
I-661; MP VII-3676; MP:BF II-859
Napoleon of Notting Hill, The, CLC
II-757; MP VII-4140; MP:BF II-1026
CHIDSEY, DONALD BARR
World of Samuel Adams, The,
MPII:JYABio IV-1949
CHIKAMATSU MONZAEMON, CWA
I-368
Sonezaki Shinjū, CLC II-1059; MP
XI-6141
CHILDRESS, ALICE
Hero Ain't Nothin' but a Sandwich, A,
MPII:AfAm II-523; MPII:JYAFic
II-623
Like One of the Family, MPII:AfAm
II-706
Rainbow Jordan, MPII:JYAFic III-1195
Trouble in Mind, CLCII IV-1616;
MPII:AfAm III-1452; MPII:D
IV-1654
CHIN, FRANK, CWAII I-335
Chickencoop Chinaman, The, CLCII
I-270; MPII:D I-323
Year of the Dragon, The, CLCII
IV-1761; MPII:D IV-1783
CHODERLOS DE LACLOS, PIERRE. See
LACLOS, PIERRE CHODERLOS
DE
CHOMSKY, NOAM, CWAII I-337
Knowledge of Language, MPII:NF II-786
CHOPIN, KATE, CWAII I-340
"Désirée's Baby," MPII:SS II-572
"Storm, The," MPII:SS V-2235
"Story of an Hour, The," MPII:SS
V-2241
CHOU SHU-JÊN. See LU HSÜN
CHRÉTIEN DE TROYES, CWA I-370
Cligés, CLC I-187; MP II-989

Erec and Enide, CLC I-331; MP III-1816
Yvain, CLC II-1277; MP XII-7309
CHRISTIE, AGATHA, CWAII I-342
Mousetrap, The, CLCII III-1052;
MPII:D III-1116
Murder of Roger Ackroyd, The, CLCII
III-1056; MPII:BCF III-1148
CHRISTOPHER, JOHN
Death of Grass, The, MPII:JYAFic I-324
CHUKOVSKY, KORNEI
Silver Crest, The, MPII:JYABio IV-1565
CHURCHILL, CARYL
Cloud Nine, CLCII I-297; MPII:D I-365
Serious Money, CLCII III-1374; MPII:D
IV-1438
Top Girls, CLCII IV-1591; MPII:D
IV-1613
CHURCHILL, WINSTON, CWA I-371,
373
Crisis, The, CLC I-223; MP II-1207;
MP:AF I-235
Joan of Arc, MPII:JYABio II-960
Second World War, The, MP X-5890
CHUTE, MARCHETTE
Geoffrey Chaucer of England,
MPII:JYABio II-705
Innocent Wayfaring, The, MPII:JYAFic
II-709
Shakespeare of London, MPII:JYABio
IV-1561
CIARDI, JOHN
"Conversation with Leonardo, A,"
MPII:P II-436
"Magus, A," MPII:P IV-1308
CIBBER, COLLEY, CWA I-376
Apology for the Life of Colley Cibber,
Comedian, An, MP I-266
CICERO, CWA I-378
Cicero's Orations, MP II-959
Treatises of Cicero, The, MP XI-6669
CLAPP, PATRICIA
Constance, MPII:JYAFic I-278
Dr. Elizabeth, MPII:JYABio I-485
CLARE, JOHN, CWA I-380
"Badger," MPII:P I-191
"I Am," MPII:P III-1002
Poetry of Clare, The, MP VIII-4863
CLARENDON, EARL OF. See HYDE,
EDWARD

CLARÍN. *See* ALAS, LEOPOLDO

CLARK, ANN NOLAN
Santiago, MPII:JYAFic III-1274
Secret of the Andes, MPII:JYAFic III-1301

CLARK, ELECTA
Cherokee Chief, MPII:JYABio I-352

CLARK, JOHN PEPPER, CWAII I-345
Song of a Goat, CLCII IV-1444; MPII:D IV-1483

CLARK, RONALD W.
Einstein, MPII:JYABio II-541

CLARK, WALTER VAN TILBURG,
CWA I-382; CWAII I-347
Ox-Bow Incident, The, CLC II-831; MP VIII-4457; MP:AF II-892; MPII:JYAFic III-1103
Track of the Cat, The, CLC II-1151; MP XI-6633; MP:AF III-1313
"Wind and the Snow of Winter, The," MPII:SS VI-2642

CLARK, WALTER VAN TILBURG
Ox-Bow Incident, The,

CLARK, WILLIAM, *and* MERIWETHER LEWIS, CWA II-1065
Journals of Lewis and Clark, The, MP VI-3065

CLARKE, ARTHUR C., CWAII I-349
Against the Fall of Night, MPII:JYAFic I-25
Childhood's End, CLCII I-272; MPII:AF I-290; MPII:JYAFic I-230
2001: A Space Odyssey, CLCII IV-1627; MPII:AF IV-1707

CLARKE, AUSTIN
As the Crow Flies, CLCII I-74; MPII:D I-94
"Night and Morning," MPII:P IV-1496
Twice Round the Black Church, MPII:NF IV-1592
"Young Woman of Beare, The," MPII:P VI-2491

CLARKE, MARTHA
Garden of Earthly Delights, The, CLCII II-565; MPII:D II-654
Vienna: Lusthaus, CLCII IV-1655; MPII:D IV-1682

CLARKE, PAULINE
Return of the Twelves, The, MPII:JYAFic III-1220

CLAUDEL, PAUL, CWA I-384
Break of Noon, CLCII I-199; MPII:D I-237
Poetry of Claudel, The, MP VIII-4866
Satin Slipper, The, CLCII III-1338; MPII:D IV-1401
Tidings Brought to Mary, The, CLCII IV-1563; MPII:D IV-1574

CLEARY, BEVERLY
Dear Mr. Henshaw, MPII:JYAFic I-318
Girl from Yamhill, A, MPII:JYABio II-757
Ramona series, The, MPII:JYAFic III-1198

CLEAVER, ELDRIDGE
Soul on Ice, MPII:AfAm III-1305; MPII:JYABio IV-1597

CLEAVER, VERA, *and* BILL CLEAVER
Where the Lilies Bloom, MPII:JYAFic IV-1612

CLEMENS, SAMUEL LANGHORNE. *See* TWAIN, MARK

CLIFTON, LUCILLE
"Lost baby poem, the," MPII:P III-1266
Poetry of Lucille Clifton, The, MPII:AfAm II-996
Times They Used to Be, The, MPII:JYAFic IV-1484

CLUTHA, JANET PATERSON FRAME. *See* FRAME, JANET

COATSWORTH, ELIZABETH
Cat Who Went to Heaven, The, MPII:JYAFic I-206

COCTEAU, JEAN, CWA I-386; CWAII I-352
Holy Terrors, The, CLC I-479; MP V-2675; MP:EF II-648
Infernal Machine, The, CLCII II-761; MPII:D II-846
Orpheus, CLCII III-1159; MPII:D III-1185
Plays of Cocteau, The, MP VIII-4758

COETZEE, J. M., CWAII I-355
Life & Times of Michael K, CLCII II-884; MPII:BCF II-954
Waiting for the Barbarians, CLCII IV-1671; MPII:BCF IV-1830

COHEN, TOM
Three Who Dared, MPII:JYABio IV-1713

COIT, MARGARET L.
  Andrew Jackson, MPII:JYABio I-102
COLEMAN, WANDA
  Poetry of Wanda Coleman, The,
    MPII:AfAm II-1000
COLERIDGE, SAMUEL TAYLOR, CWA
    I-388
  Biographia Literaria, MP I-544
  "Christabel," MPII:P I-377
  "Dejection," MPII:P II-519
  "Eolian Harp, The," MPII:P II-667
  "Frost at Midnight," MPII:P II-824
  "Kubla Khan," MPII:P III-1160
  Poetry of Coleridge, The, MP VIII-4869
  Rime of the Ancient Mariner, The, MP
    X-5600
  "This Lime-Tree Bower My Prison,"
    MPII:P VI-2164
COLES, ROBERT, CWAII I-357
  Children of Crisis, MPII:NF I-237
COLETTE, CWA I-391; CWAII I-359
  Cat, The, CLCII I-243; MPII:WF I-229
  Chéri, CLC I-172; CLCII I-264; MP
    II-905; MP:EF I-219; MPII:WF I-243
  Gigi, CLCII II-582; MPII:WF II-539
  "Kepi The," MPII:SS III-1252
  Last of Chéri, The, CLCII I-264;
    MPII:WF I-243
  Other One, The, CLC II-826; MP
    VIII-4436; MP:EF II-961
  "Rainy Moon, The," MPII:SS V-1887
  Ripening Seed, The, CLCII III-1297;
    MPII:WF III-1282
  "Sick Child, The," MPII:SS V-2104
  "Tender Shoot, The," MPII:SS V-2316
  Vagabond, The, CLCII IV-1649;
    MPII:WF IV-1705
COLLIER, JAMES LINCOLN, and
    CHRISTOPHER COLLIER
  My Brother Sam Is Dead, MPII:JYAFic
    III-1010
COLLIER, JOHN, CWAII I-361
  "Wet Saturday," MPII:SS VI-2562
  "Witch's Money," MPII:SS VI-2668
COLLINS, WILKIE, CWA I-393
  Moonstone, The, CLC II-740; MP
    VII-4059; MP:BF II-1001
  No Name, CLC II-780; MP VII-4227;
    MP:BF II-1061
  Woman in White, The, CLC II-1256; MP
    XII-7211; MP:BF III-1753

COLLINS, WILLIAM, CWA I-396
  "Ode to Evening," MPII:P IV-1547
  Poetry of Collins, The, MP VIII-4873
COLLODI, CARLO
  Adventures of Pinocchio, The,
    MPII:JYAFic I-13
COLTER, CYRUS
  Chocolate Soldier, A, MPII:AfAm I-265
COLUM, PADRAIC, CWAII I-363
  Fiddler's House, The, CLCII II-501;
    MPII:D II-605
COMMAGER, HENRY STEELE
  America's Robert E. Lee, MPII:JYABio
    I-83
  Crusaders for Freedom, MPII:JYABio I-423
COMPTON-BURNETT, IVY, CWA I-398
  Bullivant and the Lambs, MP VII-3952;
    MP:BF I-147;
  Heritage and Its History, A, MP V-2594;
    MP:BF I-570
  Mighty and Their Fall, The, MP
    VII-3890; MP:BF II-942
  Mr. Bullivant and His Lambs, MP
    VII-3952; MP:BF I-147
  Mother and Son, MP VII-4076; MP:BF
    II-1012
  Pastors and Masters, MP VIII-4516;
    MP:BF II-1167
CONFUCIUS
  Shih Ching, The, MP X-5976
CONGREVE, WILLIAM, CWA I-400
  Double-Dealer, The, CLC I-298; MP
    III-1624
  Love for Love, CLC I-633;; MP VI-3527
  Old Bachelor, The, CLC II-798; MP
    VIII-4309
  Way of the World, The, CLC II-1230;
    MP XII-7066
CONLY, ROBERT LESLIE. See
    O'BRIEN, ROBERT C.
CONNELL, EVAN S., JR., CWA I-403;
    CWAII I-366
  Mrs. Bridge, CLCII III-1023; MPII:AF
    III-1022
  Notes from a Bottle Found on the Beach
    at Carmel, MP VII-4258
  Points for a Compass Rose, MPII:NF
    III-1173
  "Saint Augustine's Pigeon," MPII:SS
    V-2008

CONNELL, RICHARD
  "Most Dangerous Game, The," MPII:SS
    IV-1535
CONNELLY, MARC, CWAII I-368
  Beggar on Horseback, CLCII I-136;
    MPII:D I-153
  Green Pastures, The, CLCII II-634;
    MPII:D II-717
CONNOLLY, CYRIL, CWAII I-370
  Unquiet Grave, The, MPII:NF IV-1617
CONOT, ROBERT
  Streak of Luck, A, MPII:JYABio
    IV-1633
CONRAD, JOSEPH, CWA I-405; CWAII
  I-372
  Almayer's Folly, CLC I-30; MP I-149;
    MP:BF I-40
  Heart of Darkness, CLC I-448; MP
    V-2505; MP:BF I-539
  "Lagoon, The," MPII:SS III-1292
  Lord Jim, CLC I-627; MP VI-3500;
    MP:BF II-820
  Nigger of the "Narcissus," The, CLC
    II-776; MP VII-4209; MP:BF II-1049
  Nostromo, CLC II-783; MP VII-4250;
    MP:BF II-1074
  "Outpost of Progress, An," MPII:SS
    IV-1732
  Secret Agent, The, CLC II-1018; MP
    X-5893; MP:BF III-1407
  "Secret Sharer, The," CLCII III-1368;
    MPII:SS V-2061
  "Typhoon," CLCII IV-1629; MPII:SS
    VI-2448
  Under Western Eyes, CLC II-1184; MP
    XII-6844; MP:BF III-1647
  Victory, CLC II-1200; MP XII-6914;
    MP:BF III-1678
  "Youth," MPII:JYAFic IV-1681;
    MPII:SS VI-2741
CONROY, FRANK
  Stop-Time, MPII:NF IV-1432
CONSCIENCE, HENDRIK, CWA I-411
  Lion of Flanders, The, CLC I-616; MP
    VI-3438; MP:EF II-787
CONSTANT, BENJAMIN, CWA I-412
  Adolphe, CLC I-10; MP I-39; MP:EF I-5
COOKE, DAVID C.
  Apache Warrior, MPII:JYABio I-125

COOKE, JOHN ESTEN, CWA I-413
  Surry of Eagle's-Nest, CLC II-1097; MP
    XI-6355; MP:AF III-1244
  Virginia Comedians, The, CLC II-1208;
    MP XII-6949; MP:AF III-1388
COOLIDGE, CLARK
  "Remove the Predicate," MPII:P V-1804
COOLIDGE, OLIVIA
  George Bernard Shaw, MPII:JYABio
    II-709
  Tom Paine, Revolutionary,
    MPII:JYABio IV-1748
  Winston Churchill and the Story of Two
    World Wars, MPII:JYABio IV-1911
COOLIDGE, SUSAN
  What Katy Did, MPII:JYAFic IV-1600
COOPER, J. CALIFORNIA
  Family, MPII:AfAm I-436
  Some Soul to Keep, MPII:AfAm III-1294
COOPER, JAMES FENIMORE, CWA
  I-415
  Chainbearer, The, CLC I-166; MP
    II-880; MP:AF I-191
  Deerslayer, The, CLC I-260; MP
    III-1413; MP:AF I-286
  Last of the Mohicans, The, CLC I-596;
    MP VI-3261; MP:AF II-639
  Leatherstocking Tales, The,
    MPII:JYAFic II-821
  Pathfinder, The, CLC II-840; MP
    VIII-4524; MP:AF II-906
  Pilot, The, CLC II-884; MP VIII-4714;
    MP:AF II-938
  Pioneers, The, CLC II-886; MP
    VIII-4722; MP:AF II-944
  Prairie, The, CLC II-912; MP IX-5290;
    MP:AF II-982
  Red Rover, The, CLC II-950; MP
    IX-5477; MP:AF III-1013
  Redskins, The, CLC II-951; MP
    IX-5484; MP:AF III-1021
  Satanstoe, CLC II-1007; MP X-5804;
    MP:AF III-1090
  Spy, The, CLC II-1079; MP XI-6236;
    MP:AF III-1208
COOPER, PAULETTE
  Growing Up Puerto Rican,
    MPII:JYABio II-798
COOPER, SUSAN
  Dark Is Rising sequence, The,
    MPII:JYAFic I-302

COOVER, ROBERT, CWAII I-374
  "Pedestrian Accident, A," MPII:SS
    IV-1796
  Universal Baseball Association, Inc., J.
    Henry Waugh, Prop., The, CLCII
    IV-1642; MPII:AF IV-1723
COPPARD, A. E., CWA I-418
  "Field of Mustard, The," MPII:SS II-771
  "Higgler, The," MPII:SS III-1014
  Short Stories of A. E. Coppard, The, MP
    X-5993; MP:BF III-1431
  "Third Prize, The," MPII:SS VI-2344
CORBIÈRE, TRISTAN, CWA I-420
  Poetry of Corbière, The, MP VIII-4876
CORMIER, ROBERT
  After the First Death, MPII:JYAFic I-22
  Bumblebee Flies Anyway, The,
    MPII:JYAFic I-162
  Chocolate War, The, MPII:JYAFic I-233
  I Am the Cheese, MPII:JYAFic II-679
CORNEILLE, PIERRE, CWA I-422
  Cid, The, CLC I-180; MP II-961
  Cinna, CLC I-180; MP II-966
  Horace, CLC I-482; MP V-2695
  Menteur, Le, CLC I-695; MP VII-3852
  Polyeucte, CLC II-899; MP IX-5231
CORNWELL, DAVID JOHN MOORE.
    See LE CARRÉ, JOHN
CORSO, GREGORY
  "Marriage," MPII:P IV-1334
CORTÁZAR, JULIO, CWAII I-377
  "Apocalypse at Solentiname," MPII:SS
    I-99
  "Blow-Up," MPII:SS I-262
  "End of the Game," MPII:SS II-689
  Hopscotch, CLCII II-695; MPII:AF
    II-739
  "Instructions for John Howell," MPII:SS
    III-1180
  Manual for Manuel, A, CLCII III-969;
    MPII:AF III-981
  62: A Model Kit, CLCII IV-1420;
    MPII:AF IV-1433
  "Southern Thruway, The," MPII:SS
    V-2198
  Winners, The, CLCII IV-1726; MPII:AF
    IV-1795
CORTEZ, JAYNE
  Poetry of Jayne Cortez, The,
    MPII:AfAm II-1006

CORVO, BARON, CWA I-424
COSTER, CHARLES DE, CWA I-426
  Legend of Tyl Ulenspiegel, The, CLC
    I-607; MP VI-3321; MP:EF II-768
COULETTE, HENRI
  "Black Angel, The," MPII:P I-240
  "Correspondence," MPII:P II-449
COUPERUS, LOUIS, CWA I-427
  Small Souls, CLC II-1052; MP X-6101;
    MP:EF III-1170
COUSINS, NORMAN
  Dr. Schweitzer of Lambaréné,
    MPII:JYABio II-493
COWARD, NOËL, CWA 1-429; CWAII
    I-380
  Blithe Spirit, CLCII I-169; MPII:D I-195
  Design for Living, CLCII I-394; MPII:D
    II-486
  Private Lives, CLC II-919; CLCII
    III-1239; MP IX-5347; MPII:D III-1288
COWLEY, ABRAHAM, CWA I-431
  Miscellanies, MP VII-3926
COWLEY, MALCOLM, CWAII I-383
  Dream of the Golden Mountains, The,
    MPII:NF I-414
  Exile's Return, MPII:NF II-481
COWPER, WILLIAM, CWA I-432
  Letters of William Cowper, The, MP
    VI-3371
  Poetry of Cowper, The, MP VIII-4880
  Task, The, MP XI-6425
COX, WILLIAM TREVOR. See
    TREVOR, WILLIAM
COZZENS, JAMES GOULD, CWA I-434;
    CWAII I-386
  By Love Possessed, CLCII I-223;
    MPII:AF I-226
  Guard of Honor, CLC I-431; MP
    IV-2412; MP:AF II-520
  Morning, Noon, and Night, CLCII
    III-1037; MPII:AF III-1042
CRABBE, GEORGE, CWA I-436
  Borough, The, MP I-602
  Village, The, MP XII-6927
CRAIK, DINAH MARIA MULOCK. See
    MULOCK, DINAH MARIA
CRAMER, KATHRYN, and JAMES
    TERZIAN
  Mighty Hard Road, MPII:JYABio
    III-1218

CRAMPTON, MARY. *See* PYM,
BARBARA
CRANE, HART, CWA I-437
"At Melville's Tomb," MPII:P I-135
"Black Tambourine," MPII:P I-246
Bridge, The, MP II-649; MPII:P I-280
"Broken Tower, The," MPII:P I-298
"For the Marriage of Faustus and
Helen," MPII:P II-795
"Legend," MPII:P III-1207
"Voyages," MPII:P VI-2348
"Wine Menagerie, The," MPII:P VI-2432
CRANE, STEPHEN, CWA I-439
"Blue Hotel, The," MPII:SS I-266
"Bride Comes to Yellow Sky, The,"
MPII:SS I-300
"Death and the Child," MPII:SS II-520
"Experiment in Misery, An," MPII:SS
II-739
Maggie, CLC I-649; MP VI-3614;
MP:AF II-722
"Monster, The," MPII:SS IV-1523
"Open Boat, The," MPII:SS IV-1709
Red Badge of Courage, The, CLC
II-948; MP IX-5468; MP:AF
III-1008; MPII:JYAFic III-1210
CRARY, MARGARET
Susette La Flesche, MPII:JYABio
IV-1652
CRASHAW, RICHARD, CWA I-442
"On the Wounds of Our Crucified Lord,"
MPII:P IV-1596
Poetry of Crashaw, The, MP VIII-4883
CRAVEN, MARGARET
I Heard the Owl Call My Name,
MPII:JYAFic II-682
CRAWFORD, DEBORAH
Four Women in a Violent Time,
MPII:JYABio II-659
CRAYENCOUR, MARGUERITE DE. *See*
YOURCENAR, MARGUERITE
CRÉBILLON, PROSPER JOLYOT DE,
CWA I-444
Rhadamistus and Zenobia, CLC II-964;
MP X-5570
CREELEY, ROBERT
"Company, The," MPII:P I-407
"Form of Women, A," MPII:P II-807
"I Know a Man," MPII:P III-1020
"Whip, The," MPII:P VI-2397

CRESSWELL, HELEN
Ordinary Jack, MPII:JYAFic III-1079
CREVECŒUR, MICHEL-GUILLAUME
JEAN DE, CWA I-445
Letters from an American Farmer, MP
VI-3333
CRICHTON, MICHAEL, CWAII I-388
Andromeda Strain, The, CLCII I-44;
MPII:AF I-34
CROCE, BENEDETTO, CWA I-446
Aesthetic, MP I-53
CROCKETT, DAVID, CWA I-448
Narrative of the Life of David Crockett,
A, MP VII-4146
CRONE, RUTH, *and* MARION MARCH
BROWN
Willa Cather, MPII:JYABio IV-1883
CRONIN, A. J.
Citadel, The, CLCII I-287; MPII:BCF
I-262
Keys of the Kingdom, The, CLCII
II-824; MPII:BCF II-904
CROSS, CLARE. *See* CROSS, GILLIAN
CROSS, GILLIAN
Dark Behind the Curtain, The,
MPII:JYAFic I-298
CROWDER, DAVID L.
Tendoy, MPII:JYABio IV-1676
CROWLEY, MART, CWAII I-390
Boys in the Band, The, CLCII I-197;
MPII:D I-230
CRUZ, SOR JUANA INÉS DE LA, CWA
I-449
"First Dream," MPII:P II-772
"Green enravishment of human life,"
MPII:P III-885
Poetry of Sor Juana Inés de la Cruz, The,
MP IX-5149
"This afternoon, my love," MPII:P
VI-2161
"This painted lie you see," MPII:P
VI-2168
CRUZ, VICTOR HERNANDEZ
"Listening to the Music of Arsenio
Rodriguez Is Moving Closer to
Knowledge," MPII:P III-1244
CUDDIHY, JOHN MURRAY
Ordeal of Civility, The MPII:NF III-1092

CULLEN, COUNTÉE, CWAII I-392
    One Way to Heaven, CLCII III-1155;
        MPII:AF III-1217; MPII:JYAFic
        III-1067
    Poetry of Countée Cullen, The,
        MPII:AfAm II-1012
    "Yet Do I Marvel," MPII:P VI-2476
CUMMINGS, E. E., CWA I-451
    "Anyone lived in a pretty how town,"
        MPII:P I-91
    Enormous Room, The, CLC I-328; MP
        III-1789; MP:AF I-342
    "I sing of Olaf glad and big," MPII:P
        III-1030
    "My father moved through dooms of
        love," MPII:P IV-1436
    "Pity this busy monster,manunkind,"
        MPII:P IV-1685

Poetry of Cummings, The, MP VIII-4887
    "Somewhere I have never
        travelled,gladly beyond," MPII:P
        V-1944
CUNHA, EUCLIDES DA, CWAII I-395
    Rebellion in the Backlands, CLCII
        III-1276; MPII:AF III-1317
CUNLIFFE, MARCUS
    George Washington, MPII:JYABio
        II-717
CUNNINGHAM, J. V.
    "Convalescence," MPII:P II-430
    "In the Thirtieth Year," MPII:P III-1099
CURIE, EVE
    Madame Curie, MPII:JYABio III-1135
CZACZKES, SHMUEL YOSEF. See
    AGNON, SHMUEL YOSEF

D

DAHL, ROALD
  Boy, MPII:JYABio I-260
  Charlie and the Chocolate Factory,
    MPII:JYAFic I-216
  "Lamb to the Slaughter," MPII:SS
    III-1295
DAICHES, DAVID, CWAII I-398
  Two Worlds, MPII:NF IV-1597
DALY, MAUREEN
  Seventeenth Summer, MPII:JYAFic
    IV-1311
DANA, RICHARD HENRY, JR., CWA
  I-453
  Two Years Before the Mast, MP
    XII-6785; MPII:JYABio IV-1792;
    MPII:JYAFic IV-1538
DANIEL, SAMUEL, CWA I-454
  Poetry of Daniel, The, MP VIII-4889
D'ANNUNZIO, GABRIELE, CWA I-456
  Triumph of Death, The, CLC II-1161;
    MP XI-6717; MP:EF III-1307
DANTE ALIGHIERI, CWA I-458
  Divine Comedy, The, CLC I-272; MP
    III-1529
  Vita Nuova, The, MP XII-6968
DANZIGER, PAULA
  Cat Ate My Gymsuit, The, MPII:JYAFic
    I-202
  It's an Aardvark-Eat-Turtle World,
    MPII:JYAFic II-730
D'ARBLAY, MADAME. See BURNEY,
  FANNY
DARÍO, RUBÉN, CWA I-462
DARWIN, CHARLES, CWA I-464
  Charles Darwin's Diary of the Voyage of
    H.M.S. Beagle, MPII:JYABio I-330
  Descent of Man, and Selection in
    Relation to Sex, The, MP III-1455
  On the Origin of Species, MP VIII-4376
  Voyage of the Beagle, The, MP XII-6987
DAUDET, ALPHONSE, CWA I-466
  Kings in Exile, CLC I-578; MP VI-3176;
    MP:EF II-733
  "Last Class, The," MPII:SS III-1298
  Sappho, CLC II-1005; MP X-5790;
    MP:EF III-1127
  Tartarin of Tarascon, CLC II-1110; MP
    XI-6417; MP:EF III-1264

DAUGHERTY, JAMES
  Abraham Lincoln, MPII:JYABio I-5
  Daniel Boone, MPII:JYABio I-435
  Of Courage Undaunted, MPII:JYABio
    III-1337
  Poor Richard, MPII:JYABio III-1425
  William Blake, MPII:JYABio IV-1887
DAUGHERTY, SONIA
  Ten Brave Men, MPII:JYABio IV-1664
DAVENANT, SIR WILLIAM, CWA I-468
  Siege of Rhodes, The, CLC II-1036; MP
    X-6035
DAVENPORT, GUY, CWAII I-401
  "Aeroplanes at Brescia, The," MPII:SS
    I-34
  "Bowmen of Shu, The," MPII:SS I-293
  "Herakleitos," MPII:SS III-1003
DAVIE, DONALD, CWAII I-403
  These the Companions, MPII:NF
    IV-1495
DAVIES, ANDREW
  Conrad's War, MPII:JYAFic I-270
DAVIES, ROBERTSON, CWAII I-406
  Deptford Trilogy, The, CLCII I-390;
    MPII:BCF I-375
  Rebel Angels, The, CLCII III-1275;
    MPII:BCF III-1399
  What's Bred in the Bone, CLCII
    IV-1708; MPII:BCF IV-1890
DA VINCI, LEONARDO. See
  LEONARDO DA VINCI
DAVIS, ANGELA
  Angela Davis, MPII:AfAm I-30
DAVIS, BURKE
  Heroes of the American Revolution,
    MPII:JYABio II-842
DAVIS, H. L., CWA I-469
  Harp of a Thousand Strings, CLC I-445;
    MP V-2484; MP:AF II-529
  Honey in the Horn, CLC I-480; MP
    V-2688; MP:AF II-555
DAVIS, OSSIE
  Purlie Victorious, MPII:AfAm III-1178
DAVIS, THULANI
  1959, MPII:AfAm II-893
DAVISON, FRANK DALBY
  Man-Shy, MPII:JYAFic III-907

DAY, CLARENCE, JR., CWA I-471
Life with Father, CLC I-612; MP
VI-3415; MP:AF II-670
DAY, DOROTHY, CWAII II-409
Long Loneliness, The, MPII:NF II-861
DAY, THOMAS, CWA I-473
Sandford and Merton, CLC II-1004; MP
X-5784; MP:BF III-1398
DAZAI, OSAMU, CWAII II-411
"Eight Views of Tokyo," MPII:SS II-672
No Longer Human, CLCII III-1107;
MPII:WF III-1103
Setting Sun, The, CLCII IV-1379;
MPII:WF IV-1388
"Villon's Wife," MPII:SS VI-2504
DE AMICIS, EDMONDO. See AMICIS,
EDMONDO DE
DE ANGELI, MARGUERITE
Door in the Wall, The, MPII:JYAFic
I-344
DE BEAUVOIR, SIMONE. See
BEAUVOIR, SIMONE DE
DEBO, ANGIE
Geronimo, His Time, His Place,
MPII:JYABio II-741
DE COSTER, CHARLES. See COSTER,
CHARLES DE
DE CRAYENCOUR, MARGUERITE. See
YOURCENAR, MARGUERITE
DEFOE, DANIEL, CWA I-475
Captain Singleton, CLC I-149; MP
II-783; MP:BF I-168
History of Colonel Jacque, The, CLC
I-475; MP V-2627; MP:BF I-586
Journal of the Plague Year, A, MP
V-3047; MP:BF II-717;
Memoirs of a Cavalier, The, CLC I-691;
MP VII-3826; MP:BF II-912
Moll Flanders, CLC II-732; MP
VII-4020; MP:BF II-988
Robinson Crusoe, CLC II-979; MP
X-5647; MP:BF III-1341;
MPII:JYAFic III-1235
Roxana, CLC II-996; MP X-5725;
MP:BF III-1384
DE FOREST, JOHN WILLIAM, CWA
I-478
Miss Ravenel's Conversion from
Secession to Loyalty, CLC II-717;
MP VII-3945; MP:AF II-792

DE JONG, MEINDERT
House of Sixty Fathers, The,
MPII:JYAFic II-661
DEKKER, EDUARD DOUWES. See
MULTATULI
DEKKER, THOMAS, CWA I-480
Gull's Hornbook, The, MP IV-2426
Honest Whore, Part One, The, CLC
I-479; MP V-2680
Honest Whore, Part Two, The, MP
V-2684
Old Fortunatus, CLC II-802; MP
VIII-4319
Satiromastix, CLC II-1008; MP X-5817
Shoemaker's Holiday, The, CLC
II-1035; MP X-5988
DEKKER, THOMAS, and THOMAS
MIDDLETON
Honest Whore, Part One, The, CLC
I-479; MP V-2680
DE KRUIF, PAUL
Microbe Hunters, MPII:JYABio III-1214
DE LA MARE, WALTER, CWA I-482
Collected Poems, MP II-1022
"Listeners, The," MPII:P III-1241
Memoirs of a Midget, CLC I-692; MP
VII-3833; MP:BF II-920
"Recluse, A," MPII:SS V-1913
Return, The, CLC II-958; MP X-5536;
MP:BF III-1307
"Revenant, A," MPII:SS V-1948
"Seaton's Aunt," MPII:SS V-2049
"Trumpet, The," MPII:SS VI-2421
DELANEY, SHELAGH, CWAII II-414
Taste of Honey, A, CLCII IV-1517;
MPII:D IV-1538
DELANY, MARTIN ROBISON
Condition, Elevation, Emigration, and
Destiny of the Colored People of the
United States Politically Considered,
The, MPII:AfAm I-296
DELANY, SAMUEL R., CWAII II-416
Babel-17, CLCII I-99; MPII:AF I-102;
MPII:AfAm I-96; MPII:JYAFic I-76
Triton, CLCII IV-1614; MPII:AF
IV-1692
Motion of Light in Water, The,
MPII:AfAm II-829
Stars in My Pocket Like Grains of Sand,
MPII:AfAm III-1343

DE LA RAMÉE, MARIE LOUISE. *See* OUIDA

DE LA ROCHE, MAZO, CWA I-484
Jalna, CLC I-539; MP V-2973; MP:AF II-611

DELBLANC, SVEN
Speranza, CLCII IV-1461; MPII:WF IV-1510

DELEDDA, GRAZIA, CWA I-485
Mother, The, CLC II-744; MP VII-4068; MP:EF II-894

DeLILLO, DON, CWAII II-418
End Zone, CLCII II-457; MPII:AF II-472

DELONEY, THOMAS, CWA I-487
Jack of Newberry, CLC I-538; MP V-2964; MP:BF II-671

DEMBY, WILLIAM, CWAII II-420
Beetlecreek, CLCII I-133; MPII:AF I-126; MPII:AfAm I-114

DE MILLE, AGNES
Dance to the Piper, MPII:JYABio I-431

DE MORGAN, WILLIAM, CWA I-488
Joseph Vance, CLC I-554; MP V-3041; MP:BF II-713

DEMOSTHENES, CWA I-490
Philippics, The, MP VIII-4644

DENNISON, GEORGE
"Smiles of Konarak, The," MPII:SS V-2146

DE PAUW, LINDA GRANT
Seafaring Women, MPII:JYABio IV-1545

DE QUINCEY, THOMAS, CWA I-492
Confessions of an English Opium Eater, MP II-1063

DERLETH, AUGUST
Concord Rebel, MPII:JYABio I-405

DERRIDA, JACQUES, CWAII II-422
Of Grammatology, MPII:NF III-1057
Writing and Difference, MPII:NF IV-1730

DESAI, ANITA, CWAII II-425
Clear Light of Day, CLCII I-294; MPII:BCF I-267
Fire on the Mountain, CLCII II-509; MPII:BCF II-504

DESCARTES, RENÉ, CWA I-494
Passions of the Soul, The, MP VIII-4510

DESMOND, ALICE CURTIS
Cleopatra's Children, MPII:JYABio I-389

DE STAËL, MADAME. *See* STAËL, MADAME DE

DE STAËL-HOLSTEIN, BARONNE. *See* STAËL, MADAME DE

DESTOUCHES, LOUIS FUCH. *See* CÉLINE, LOUIS-FERDINAND

DESTOUCHES, LOUIS-FERDINAND. *See* CÉLINE, LOUIS-FERDINAND

DEUTSCH, BABETTE
Walt Whitman, MPII:JYABio IV-1826

DEVANEY, JOHN
Bo Jackson, MPII:JYABio I-248

DE VRIES, PETER, CWAII II-427
Blood of the Lamb, The, CLCII I-170; MPII:AF I-181
Tents of Wickedness, The, CLCII IV-1528; MPII:AF IV-1583

D'EXILES, ANTOINE-FRANÇOIS PRÉVOST. *See* PRÉVOST, ABBÉ

DICKENS, CHARLES, CWA I-496
Barnaby Rudge, CLC I-81; MP I-431; MP:BF I-85
Bleak House, CLC I-107; MP I-566; MP:BF I-118
Christmas Carol, A, CLC I-179; MP II-947; MP:BF I-207
David Copperfield, CLC I-242; MP III-1324; MP:BF I-283; MPII:JYAFic I-307
Dombey and Son, CLC I-286; MP III-1574; MP:BF I-341
Great Expectations, CLC I-418; MP IV-2349; MP:BF I-491
Hard Times, CLC I-443; MP V-2477; MP:BF I-532
Little Dorrit, CLC I-617; MP VI-3448; MP:BF II-803
Martin Chuzzlewit, CLC I-675; MP VII-3751; MP:BF II-877
Mystery of Edwin Drood, The, CLC II-755; MP VII-4125; MP:BF II-1022
Nicholas Nickleby, CLC II-771; MP VII-4195; MP:BF II-1044
Old Curiosity Shop, The, CLC II-799; MP VIII-4316; MP:BF II-1087
Oliver Twist, CLC II-812; MP VIII-4358; MP:BF II-1105; MPII:JYAFic III-1054
Our Mutual Friend, CLC II-827; MP VIII-4440; MP:BF II-1141

Pickwick Papers, The, CLC II-874; MP VIII-4680; MP:BF III-1212

Tale of Two Cities, A, CLC II-1100; MP XI-6373; MP:BF III-1485

DICKEY, JAMES, CWA 1-499

"Buckdancer's Choice," MPII:P I-301

"Falling," MPII:P II-724

Poetry of Dickey, The, MP VIII-4896

DICKINSON, EMILY, CWA I-501

"Because I could not stop for Death," MPII:P I-219

"I cannot live with You—," MPII:P III-1005

"I felt a Funeral in my Brain," MPII:P III-1008

"I heard a Fly buzz—when I died—," MPII:P III-1017

"I like to see it lap the Miles—," MPII:P III-1024

"I taste a liquor never brewed—," MPII:P III-1037

Letters of Emily Dickinson, The, MP VI-3344

"My Life had stood—a Loaded Gun—," MPII:P IV-1446

"Narrow Fellow in the Grass, A," MPII:P IV-1472

Poetry of Emily Dickinson, The, MP IX-4935

"There's a certain Slant of light," MPII:P VI-2146

"Wild Nights—Wild Nights!," MPII:P VI-2417

DICKINSON, PETER

Tulku, MPII:JYAFic IV-1517

DIDEROT, DENIS, CWA I-504

Jacques the Fatalist and His Master, CLCII II-785; MPII:WF II-748

Rameau's Nephew, CLC II-939; MP IX-5429; MP:EF III-1054

DIDION, JOAN, CWAII II-429

Democracy, CLCII I-387; MPII:AF I-389

Play It As It Lays, CLCII III-1212; MPII:AF III-1266

Salvador, MPII:NF III-1280

Slouching Towards Bethlehem, MPII:NF IV-1366

DILLARD, ANNIE, CWAII II-431

American Childhood, An, MPII:JYABio I-55; MPII:NF I-39

Pilgrim at Tinker Creek, MPII:NF III-1163

DINESEN, ISAK, CWA I-506; CWAII II-433

"Blank Page, The," MPII:SS I-246

"Deluge at Norderney, The," MPII:SS II-561

"Monkey, The," MPII:SS IV-1519

Out of Africa, MPII:JYABio III-1367

Seven Gothic Tales, MP X-5926; MP:EF III-1147

"Sorrow-Acre," MPII:SS V-2190

"Supper at Elsinore, The," MPII:SS V-2281

DISRAELI, BENJAMIN, CWA I-508

Coningsby, CLC I-196; MP II-1077; MP:BF I-238

Vivian Grey, CLC II-1212; MP XII-6971; MP:BF III-1698

DIXON, FRANKLIN W.

Hardy Boys series, The, MPII:JYAFic II-595

DÖBLIN, ALFRED, CWAII II-435

Berlin Alexanderplatz, CLCII I-143; MPII:WF I-146

November 1918, CLCII III-1117; MPII:WF III-1118

DOBRIN, ARNOLD

I Am a Stranger on the Earth, MPII:JYABio II-877

DOCTOROW, E. L., CWAII II-438

Ragtime, CLCII III-1259; MPII:AF III-1310; MPII:JYAFic III-1191

DODERER, HEIMITO VON, CWAII II-440

Demons, The, CLCII I-389; MPII:WF I-369

Waterfalls of Slunj, The, CLCII IV-1689; MPII:WF IV-1729

DODGE, MARY MAPES

Hans Brinker, MPII:JYAFic II-588

DODGSON, CHARLES LUTWIDGE. See CARROLL, LEWIS

DODSON, OWEN

Poetry of Owen Dodson, The, MPII:AfAm III-1019

DOLAN, EDWARD F., JR.

Adolf Hitler, MPII:JYABio I-16

DONLEAVY, J. P., CWAII II-442
  Ginger Man, The, CLCII II-585;
    MPII:AF II-618; MPII:BCF II-586
DONNADIEU, MARGUERITE. See
    DURAS, MARGUERITE
DONN-BYRNE, BRIAN OSWALD. See
    BYRNE, DONN
DONNE, JOHN, CWA I-510
  "Batter my heart, three-person'd God,"
    MPII:P I-205
  "Canonization, The," MPII:P I-337
  "Death be not proud," MPII:P II-495
  Death's Duell, MP III-1391
  "Ecstasy, The," MPII:P II-623
  "Good-Morrow, The," MPII:P III-873
  Ignatius His Conclave, MP V-2834
  "On His Mistress," MPII:P IV-1581
  "Perfume, The," MPII:P IV-1659
  Poetry of Donne, The, MP VIII-4900
  "Sun Rising, The," MPII:P V-2099
  "Twicknam Garden," MPII:P VI-2293
  "Valediction: Forbidding Mourning, A,"
    MPII:P VI-2327
DONOSO, JOSÉ, CWAII II-445
  Coronation, CLCII I-337; MPII:AF I-341
  Obscene Bird of Night, The, CLCII
    III-1125; MPII:AF III-1160
  Sacred Families, CLCII III-1325;
    MPII:AF III-1357
  This Sunday, CLCII IV-1552; MPII:AF
    IV-1640
DONOVAN, JOHN
  I'll Get There, MPII:JYAFic II-695
DOOLEY, THOMAS A.
  Doctor Tom Dooley, My Story,
    MPII:JYABio II-497
DOOLITTLE, HILDA. See H. D
DORN, EDWARD
  Gunslinger, MPII:P III-894
DORRIS, MICHAEL
  Yellow Raft in Blue Water, A,
    MPII:JYAFic IV-1671
DOS PASSOS, JOHN, CWA I-514
  Manhattan Transfer, CLC I-663; MP
    VII-3693; MP:AF II-748
  Three Soldiers, CLC II-1130; MP
    XI-6522; MP:AF III-1285
  U.S.A., CLC II-1187; MP XII-6863;
    MP:AF III-1358

DOSTOEVSKI, FYODOR MIKHAILOVICH,
    CWA I-516; CWAII II-447
  "Bobok," MPII:SS I-273
  Brothers Karamazov, The, CLC I-129;
    MP II-688; MP:EF I-144
  Crime and Punishment, CLC I-221; MP
    II-1197; MP:EF I-299
  Diary of a Writer, MP III-1506
  Double, The, CLCII II-419; MPII:WF
    I-390
  "Dream of a Ridiculous Man, The,"
    MPII:SS II-628
  Gambler, The, CLC I-390; MP IV-2195;
    MP:EF II-547
  House of the Dead, The, CLCII II-711;
    MPII:WF II-623
  Idiot, The, CLC I-510; MP V-2817;
    MP:EF II-682
  Insulted and the Injured, The, CLCII
    II-767; MPII:WF II-706
  Letters from the Underworld, CLC
    I-608; MP VI-3336; MP:EF II-776
  "Nasty Story, A," MPII:SS IV-1586
  Netochka Nezvanova, CLCII III-1084;
    MPII:WF III-1089
  "Peasant Marey, The," MPII:SS IV-1789
  Poor People, CLC II-900; MP IX-5237;
    MP:EF III-1020
  Possessed, The, CLC II-905; MP
    IX-5264; MP:EF III-1024
  Raw Youth, A, CLCII III-1271;
    MPII:WF III-1262
  "White Nights," MPII:SS VI-2589
DOUGHTY, CHARLES M., CWA I-520
  Travels in Arabia Deserta, MP XI-6647
DOUGLAS, ELLEN, CWAII II-450
  Rock Cried Out, The, CLCII III-1309;
    MPII:AF III-1344
DOUGLAS, GEORGE, CWA I-522
  House With the Green Shutters, The,
    CLC I-492; MP V-2739; MP:BF
    II-608
DOUGLAS, LLOYD C., CWA I-523
  Magnificent Obsession, The, CLC I-652;
    MP VI-3626; MP:AF II-726
DOUGLAS, MARY
  Natural Symbols, MPII:NF III-1003
DOUGLAS, NORMAN, CWA I-524
  Old Calabria, MP VIII-4313
  South Wind, CLC II-1072; MP XI-6202;
    MP:BF III-1473

DOUGLASS, FREDERICK
Narrative of the Life of Frederick
Douglass, MPII:AfAm II-854;
MPII:JYABio III-1304
DOUTY, ESTHER M.
Forten the Sailmaker, MPII:JYABio II-651
DOVE, RITA
Poetry of Rita Dove, The, MPII:AfAm
III-1024
Thomas and Beulah, MPII:P VI-2171
Through the Ivory Gate, MPII:AfAm
III-1440
DOVLATOV, SERGEI, CWAII II-452
Compromise, The, CLCII I-317;
MPII:WF I-295
Zone, The, CLCII IV-1770; MPII:WF
IV-1808
DOWSON, ERNEST CHRISTOPHER,
CWA I-526
Poetry of Dowson, The, MP VIII-4903
DOYLE, SIR ARTHUR CONAN, CWA
I-528
"Adventure of the Dancing Men, The,"
MPII:SS I-23
"Adventure of the Speckled Band, The,"
MPII:SS I-31
Adventures of Sherlock Holmes, The,
MPII:JYAFic I-16
"Greek Interpreter, The," MPII:SS
III-936
Micah Clarke, CLC II-699; MP
VII-3869; MP:BF II-931
"Red-Headed League, The," MPII:SS
V-1922
"Scandal in Bohemia, A," MPII:SS
V-2029
Sign of Four, The, CLC II-1037; MP
X-6037; MP:BF III-1449
Study in Scarlet, A, CLC II-1092; MP
XI-6322; MP:BF III-1477
White Company, The, CLC II-1237; MP
XII-7111; MP:BF III-1735
DRABBLE, MARGARET, CWAII II-455
Ice Age, The, CLCII II-731; MPII:BCF
II-787
Middle Ground, The, CLCII III-1005;
MPII:BCF III-1091
Needle's Eye, The, CLCII III-1083;
MPII:BCF III-1188
Waterfall, The, CLCII IV-1688;
MPII:BCF IV-1859

DRAYTON, MICHAEL, CWA I-530
Poetry of Drayton, The, MP VIII-4906
DREISER, THEODORE, CWA I-531
American Tragedy, An, CLC I-35; MP
I-175; MP:AF I-53
Bulwark, The, CLC I-135; MP II-707;
MP:AF I-154
Financier, The, CLC I-367; MP IV-2067;
MP:AF I-391
"Genius," The, CLC I-395; MP IV-2221;
MP:AF I-428
Jennie Gerhardt, CLC I-544; MP
V-2996; MP:AF II-619
Sister Carrie, CLC II-1045; MP X-6070;
MP:AF III-1171
Stoic, The, CLC II-1081; MP XI-6255;
MP:AF III-1219
Titan, The, CLC II-1135; MP XI-6560;
MP:AF III-1293
DRYDEN, JOHN, CWA I-534
Absalom and Achitophel, CLC I-4; MP
I-19
All for Love, CLC I-24; MP I-117
Essay of Dramatic Poesy, An, MP
III-1831
Mac Flecknoe, MPII:P IV-1305
Marriage à la Mode, CLC I-673; MP
VII-3742
Poetry of Dryden, The, MP IX-4909
Religio Laici, MPII:P V-1786
"Song for St. Cecilia's Day, A," MPII:P
V-1953
Spanish Friar, The, CLC II-1073; The,
MP XI-6205
"To the Memory of Mr. Oldham,"
MPII:P VI-2221
DUBIE, NORMAN
"Ambassador Diaries of Jean de
Bosschère and Edgar Poe, The,"
MPII:P I-59
DU BOIS, W. E. B.
Autobiography of W. E. B. Du Bois,
The, The, MPII:AfAm I-90;
MPII:JYABio I-164
Souls of Black Folk, The, MPII:AfAm
III-1309
DU BOIS, WILLIAM PÈNE
Peter Graves, MPII:JYAFic III-1119
Twenty-one Balloons, The,
MPII:JYAFic IV-1535

DUCKETT, ALFRED, *and* JACKIE
ROBINSON
Breakthrough to the Big League,
MPII:JYABio I-264
DUDEVANT,
AMANDINE-AURORE-LUCILE
DUPIN, BARONNE. *See* SAND,
GEORGE
DU FU. *See* TU FU
DUGAN, ALAN
"Funeral Oration for a Mouse," MPII:P
II-827
DU GARD, ROGER MARTIN. *See*
MARTIN DU GARD, ROGER
DUGGAN, ALFRED, CWA I-537
Falcon and the Dove, The, MPII:JYABio
II-583
Lady for Ransom, The, MP VI-3203;
MP:BF II-761
Leopards and Lilies, MP VI-3327;
MP:BF II-792
DUMAS, ALEXANDRE (*fils*), CWA I-542
Camille, CLC I-142; MPII II-751
DUMAS, ALEXANDRE (*père*), CWA
I-539
Chevalier of the Maison Rouge, The,
CLC I-174; MP II-912; MP:EF I-223
Corsican Brothers, The, CLC I-202; MP
II-1124; MP:EF I-260
Count of Monte-Cristo, The, CLC I-204;
MP II-1136; MP:EF I-269;
MPII:JYAFic I-284
Countess de Charny, The, CLC I-207;
MP II-1146; MP:EF I-281
Memoirs of a Physician, CLC I-692; MP
VII-3836; MP:EF II-854
Queen's Necklace, The, CLC II-930; MP
IX-5394; MP:EF III-1046
Three Musketeers, The, CLC II-1127;
MP XI-6511; MP:EF III-1279;
MPII:JYAFic IV-1462
Twenty Years After, CLC II-1169; MP
XII-6762; MP:EF III-1319
Vicomte de Bragelonne, The, CLC
II-1199; MP XII-6904; MP:EF
III-1341
DUMAS, HENRY, CWAII II-457
"Ark of Bones," MPII:SS I-110
Stories of Henry Dumas, The,
MPII:AfAm III-1355

DU MAURIER, DAPHNE, CWA I-543
My Cousin Rachel, MPII:JYAFic
III-1013
Rebecca, CLC II-943; MP IX-5452;
MP:BF III-1302; MPII:JYAFic
III-1202
DU MAURIER, GEORGE, CWA I-544
Peter Ibbetson, CLC II-864; MP
VIII-4618; MP:BF II-1194
Trilby, CLC II-1158; MP XI-6701;
MP:BF III-1600
DUMITRIU, PETRU, CWA I-546
Incognito, MP V-2868; MP:EF II-696
DUNBAR, PAUL LAURENCE, CWAII
II-459
Poetry of Paul Laurence Dunbar, The,
MPII:AfAm III-1029
"Scapegoat, The," MPII:SS V-2037
Sport of the Gods, The, CLCII IV-1465;
MPII:AF IV-1516; MPII:AfAm
III-1332
DUNBAR-NELSON, ALICE
Give Us Each Day, MPII:AfAm I-498
DUNCAN, ROBERT, CWAII II-461
"My Mother Would Be a Falconress,"
MPII:P IV-1449
"Poem Beginning with a Line by Pindar,
A," MPII:P IV-1694
Tribunals, MPII:P VI-2267
Truth and Life of Myth, The, MPII:NF
IV-1574
"Up Rising," MPII:P VI-2324
DUNLOP, AGNES M. R. *See* KYLE,
ELISABETH.
DUNN, ELSIE. *See* SCOTT, EVELYN
DUNN, WENDY, *and* JANET MOREY
Famous Mexican Americans,
MPII:JYABio II-595
DUNSANY, LORD, CWAII II-464
"Idle Days on the Yann," MPII:SS
III-1112
DUPIN, AMANDINE LUCILE AURORE.
See SAND, GEORGE
DURANG, CHRISTOPHER, CWAII II-466
Sister Mary Ignatius Explains It All for
You, CLCII IV-1419; MPII:D
IV-1471
DURAS, MARGUERITE, CWAII II-468
Lover, The, CLCII III-931; MPII:WF
II-901

Ravishing of Lol Stein, The, CLCII
    III-1270; MPII:WF III-1257
  Sea Wall, The, CLCII III-1355;
    MPII:WF III-1367
DURKHEIM, ÉMILE, CWAII II-471
  Elementary Forms of the Religious Life,
    The, MPII:NF II-443
DURKHEIM, ÉMILE, and MARCEL
    MAUSS
  Primitive Classification, MPII:NF
    III-1190
DURRELL, LAWRENCE, CWA I-548;
    CWAII II-473
  Alexandria Quartet, The, MP I-96;
    MP:BF I-20

Prospero's Cell, MPII:NF III-1210
DÜRRENMATT, FRIEDRICH, CWAII
    II-475
  Physicists, The, CLCII III-1206; MPII:D
    III-1246
  Romulus the Great, CLCII III-1310;
    MPII:D IV-1367
  Visit, The, CLCII IV-1659; MPII:D
    IV-1688
DUUN, OLAV, CWA I-551
  People of Juvik, The, CLC II-857; MP
    VIII-4587; MP:EF III-999
DYGARD, THOMAS J.
  Halfback Tough, MPII:JYAFic II-584

E

EARL OF ROCHESTER. *See* WILMOT, JOHN
EATON, JEANETTE
America's Own Mark Twain, MPII:JYABio I-79
Gandhi, MPII:JYABio II-694
Leader by Destiny, MPII:JYABio III-1044
Lone Journey, MPII:JYABio III-1112
Narcissa Whitman, MPII:JYABio III-1300
Trumpeter's Tale, MPII:JYABio IV-1777
Young Lafayette, MPII:JYABio IV-1963
EBERHART, RICHARD, CWA I-552
"Fury of Aerial Bombardment, The," MPII:P II-830
"Groundhog, The," MPII:P III-891
Poetry of Eberhart, The, MP IX-4918
EÇA DE QUEIRÓS, JOSÉ MARIA, CWAII IV-1235
Cousin Bazilio, CLCII I-348; MPII:WF I-337
ECHEGARAY, JOSÉ, CWA I-554
Great Galeoto, The, CLC I-420; MP IV-2355
ECHENOZ, JEAN
Cherokee, CLCII I-265; MPII:WF I-248
ECKERMANN, JOHANN PETER, CWA I-556
Conversations of Goethe with Eckermann and Soret, MP II-1109
ECO, UMBERTO, CWAII II-478
Name of the Rose, The, CLCII III-1072; MPII:WF III-1065
EDGEWORTH, MARIA, CWA I-558
Absentee, The, CLC I-5; MP I-21; MP:BF I-1
Castle Rackrent, CLC I-157; MP II-834; MP:BF I-183
EDMONDS, HELEN WOODS. *See* KAVAN, ANNA
EDMONDS, WALTER D., CWA I-560
Drums Along the Mohawk, CLC I-307; MP III-1659; MP:AF I-317
Matchlock Gun, The, MPII:JYAFic III-938
Rome Haul, CLC II-989; MP X-5697; MP:AF III-1072

EDMUNDS, R. DAVID
Tecumseh and the Quest for Indian Leadership, MPII:JYABio IV-1660
EDWARDS, JONATHAN, CWA I-562
Works of Jonathan Edwards, MP XII-7256
EGAN, PIERCE, CWA I-564
Life in London, CLC I-610; MP VI-3394; MP:BF II-799
EGGLESTON, EDWARD, CWA I-566
Hoosier Schoolmaster, The, CLC I-481; MP V-2691; MP:AF II-559
EHRENBURG, ILYA, CWAII II-481
Thaw, The, CLCII IV-1533; MPII:WF IV-1575
EICHENDORFF, JOSEF VON, CWA I-568
Poetry of Eichendorff, The, MP IX-4922
EISELEY, LOREN
All the Strange Hours, MPII:JYABio I-35
Immense Journey, The, MPII:NF II-699
EKELÖF, GUNNAR
"Diwan Trilogy," MPII:P II-564
"Dordogne," MPII:P II-582
"Everyone Is a World," MPII:P II-703
"He Who Does Not Hope," MPII:P III-908
"If You Ask Me," MPII:P III-1049
EKWENSI, CYPRIAN, CWAII II-483
People of the City, CLCII III-1192; MPII:BCF III-1302
ELDER, LONNE, III
Ceremonies in Dark Old Men, MPII:AfAm I-249
ELIADE, MIRCEA, CWAII II-485
Forbidden Forest, The, CLCII II-532; MPII:WF II-491
ELIOT, GEORGE, CWA I-570
Adam Bede, CLC I-7; MP I-29; MP:BF I-7
Daniel Deronda, CLC I-237; MP III-1304; MP:BF I-278
Felix Holt, The Radical, CLC I-365; MP IV-2029; MP:BF I-410
Middlemarch, CLC II-700; MP VII-3879; MP:BF II-935
Mill on the Floss, The, CLC II-705; MP:BF II-945

Romola, CLC II-992; MP X-5705;
  MP:BF III-1369
Silas Marner, CLC II-1038; MP X-6043;
  MP:BF III-1455
ELIOT, T. S., CWA I-573; CWAII II-488
  After Strange Gods, MP I-60
  "Animula," MPII:P I-85
  Ash Wednesday, MP I-339
  Cocktail Party, The, CLC I-190; MP
    II-1010
  Confidential Clerk, The, MP II-1074
  Dante, MP III-1308
  Elder Statesman, The, MP III-1728
  Family Reunion, The, CLC I-355; MP
    IV-1983
  Four Quartets, MP IV-2148
  "Gerontion," MPII:P II-854
  "Hollow Men, The," MPII:P III-948
  John Dryden, MP V-3020
  "Journey of the Magi," MPII:P III-1135
  "Love Song of J. Alfred Prufrock, The,"
    MPII:P III-1292
  Murder in the Cathedral, CLC II-748;
    MP VII-4094
  Notes Towards the Definition of Culture,
    MPII:NF III-1034
  "Portrait of a Lady," MPII:P IV-1719
  "Preludes," MPII:P IV-1729
  "Rhapsody on a Windy Night," MPII:P
    V-1832
  Sacred Wood, The, MP X-5748
  "Sweeney Among the Nightingales,"
    MPII:P V-2112
  Waste Land, The, MP XII-7047
ELKIN, STANLEY, CWAII II-490
  Franchiser, The, CLCII II-543; MPII:AF
    II-576
  "I Look Out for Ed Wolfe," MPII:SS
    III-1088
ELLIOTT, GEORGE P.
  "Among the Dangs," MPII:SS I-85
ELLIS, TREY
  Platitudes, MPII:AfAm II-952
ELLISON, RALPH, CWA I-576; CWAII
  II-492
  Essays of Ralph Ellison, The,
    MPII:AfAm I-406
  "Flying Home," MPII:SS II-803
  Invisible Man, MP V-2915; MP:AF
    II-599; MPII:AfAm II-607;
    MPII:JYAFic II-719

ELLUL, JACQUES, CWAII II-494
  Technological Society, The, MPII:NF
    IV-1473
ELTIS, ODYSSEUS
  "Autopsy, The," MPII:P I-166
  "Body of Summer," MPII:P I-267
EMERSON, RALPH WALDO, CWA I-578
  "Brahma," MPII:P I-273
  Essays, MP IV-1845
  "Ode, Inscribed to W. H. Channing,"
    MPII:P IV-1535
  Poetry of Emerson, The, MP IX-4928
  Representative Men, MP IX-5518
  Society and Solitude, MP X-6122
EMPSON, WILLIAM, CWAII II-496
  "Aubade," MPII:P I-141
  Seven Types of Ambiguity, MPII:NF
    IV-1335
ENCHI, FUMIKO, CWAII II-499
  "Boxcar of Chrysanthemums," MPII:SS
    I-297
  Masks, CLCII III-983; MPII:WF III-970
END, SHUSAKU, CWAII II-501
  Samurai, The, CLCII III-1332; MPII:WF
    III-1345
  Silence, CLCII IV-1405; MPII:WF
    IV-1425
  When I Whistle, CLCII IV-1709;
    MPII:WF IV-1745
  Wonderful Fool, CLCII IV-1740;
    MPII:WF IV-1789
ENRIGHT, ELIZABETH
  Thimble Summer, MPII:JYAFic IV-1451
EPSTEIN, SAM, and BERYL EPSTEIN
  Dr. Beaumont and the Man with the Hole
    in His Stomach, MPII:JYABio I-482
EQUIANO, OLAUDAH
  Interesting Narrative of the Life of
    Olaudah Equiano, or Gustavus Vassa,
    the African, The, MPII:AfAm II-603
ERASMUS, DESIDERIUS, CWA I-582
  Praise of Folly, The, MP IX-5294
ERDRICH, LOUISE, CWAII II-504
  "Beet Queen, The," MPII:SS I-177
  Love Medicine, CLCII III-927; MPII:AF
    III-938; MPII:JYAFic III-890
  "Saint Marie," MPII:SS V-2012
ESCHENBACH, WOLFRAM VON. See
  WOLFRAM VON ESCHENBACH

ESENIN, SERGEI, CWA I-584
  Poetry of Esenin, The, MP IX-4938
ESTES, ELEANOR
  Ginger Pye, MPII:JYAFic II-512
  Moffats series, The, MPII:JYAFic III-971
ETHEREGE, SIR GEORGE, CWA I-586
  Man of Mode, The, CLC I-660; MP
    VII-3672
EURIPIDES, CWA I-588
  Alcestis, CLC I-18; MP I-84
  Andromache, CLC I-40; MP I-216
  Bacchae, The, CLC I-74; MP I-405
  Children of Heracles, The, CLC I-176;
    MP II-930
  Cyclops, The, CLC I-230; MP III-1252
  Electra, CLC I-320; MP III-1735
  Helen, CLC I-458; MP V-2544
  Heracles Mad, CLC I-468; MP V-2584
  Hippolytus, CLC I-474; MP V-2620
  Ion, CLC I-529; MP V-2925
  Iphigenia in Aulis, CLC I-530; MP
    V-2928
  Iphigenia in Tauris, CLC I-532; MP
    V-2931
  Medea, CLC I-686; MP VII-3798
  Phoenician Women, The, CLC II-872;
    MP VIII-4670

  Suppliants, The, CLC II-1096; MP
    XI-6349
  Trojan Women, The, CLC II-1164; MP
    XI-6729
EVANS, ELIZABETH
  Weathering the Storm, MPII:JYABio
    IV-1846
EVANS, MARI
  Poetry of Mari Evans, The, MPII:AfAm
    III-1036
EVANS, MARIAN. See ELIOT, GEORGE
EVANS, MARY ANN. See ELIOT,
    GEORGE
EVELYN, JOHN, CWA I-591
  Diary, MP III-1494
EVERETT, PERCIVAL L.
  Suder, MPII:AfAm III-1381
  Walk Me to the Distance, MPII:AfAm
    III-1490
EVELYN LLOYD, CHRIS
  Chrissie, MPII:JYABio I-362
EWEN, DAVID
  Leonard Bernstein, MPII:JYABio
    III-1059
  Story of George Gershwin, The,
    MPII:JYABio IV-1618

F

FABER, DORIS
   Clarence Darrow, MPII:JYABio I-377
   Oh, Lizzie!, MPII:JYABio III-1341
FACKLAM, MARGERY
   Wild Animals, Gentle Women,
     MPII:JYABio IV-1872
FAHEY, WILLIAM A., *and* BEN
   RICHARDSON
   Great Black Americans, MPII:JYABio
     II-787
FAIRBANKS, JEAN. *See* MERRILL, JEAN
FAIRFIELD, CICILY ISABEL. *See* WEST,
   REBECCA
FANNING, LEONARD M.
   Fathers of Industries, MPII:JYABio
     II-615
FANON, FRANTZ, CWAII II-506
   Wretched of the Earth, The, MPII:NF
     IV-1725
FANU, JOSEPH SHERIDAN LE. *See* LE
   FANU, JOSEPH SHERIDAN
FARLEY, WALTER
   Black Stallion, The, MPII:JYAFic I-125
FARMER, PENELOPE
   Magic Stone, The, MPII:JYAFic III-901
   Summer Birds, The, MPII:JYAFic
     IV-1399
FARNSWORTH, FRANCES JOYCE
   Winged Moccasins, MPII:JYABio
     IV-1907
FARQUHAR, GEORGE, CWA I-593
   Beaux' Stratagem, The, CLC I-91; MP
     I-464
   Recruiting Officer, The, CLC II-945; MP
     IX-5459
FARRELL, J. G., CWAII II-508
   Siege of Krishnapur, The, CLCII
     IV-1401; MPII:BCF IV-1543
   Singapore Grip, The, CLCII IV-1416;
     MPII:BCF IV-1558
   Troubles, CLCII IV-1617; MPII:BCF
     IV-1747
FARRELL, JAMES T., CWA I-595;
   CWAII II-510
   "Saturday Night," MPII:SS V-2025
   Studs Lonigan, CLC II-1091; MP
     XI-6320; MP:AF III-1235;
     MPII:JYAFic IV-1392

FAST, HOWARD
   Freedom Road, MPII:JYAFic II-467
FAULKNER, WILLIAM, CWA I-597;
   CWAII II-512
   Absalom, Absalom! CLC I-3; MP I-14;
     MP:AF I-1
   As I Lay Dying, CLC I-64; MP I-330;
     MP:AF I-80
   "Barn Burning," MPII:SS I-158
   Bear, The, MPII:JYAFic I-96
   "Delta Autumn," MPII:SS II-557
   "Dry September," MPII:SS II-646
   Fable, A, CLC I-346; MP IV-1942;
     MP:AF I-354
   Go Down, Moses, MP IV-2272; MP:AF
     I-453
   Hamlet, The, CLC I-436; MP V-2454;
     MP:AF II-525
   Intruder in the Dust, CLC I-527; MP
     V-2911; MP:AF II-595
   Light in August, CLC I-613; MP
     VI-3423; MP:AF II-679
   Mansion, The, MP VII-3707; MP:AF
     II-752
   Mosquitoes, CLCII III-1042; MPII:AF
     III-1066
   Pylon, CLCII III-1239; MPII:AF III-1291
   "Red Leaves," MPII:SS V-1918
   Reivers, The, MP IX-5489; MP:AF
     III-1027
   Requiem for a Nun, MP X-5525; MP:AF
     III-1040
   "Rose for Emily, A," MPII:SS V-1986
   Sanctuary, CLC II-1003; MP X-5780;
     MP:AF III-1082
   Sartoris, MP X-5801; MP:AF III-1086
   Soldiers' Pay, CLCII IV-1437; MPII:AF
     IV-1459
   Sound and the Fury, The, CLC II-1070;
     MP XI-6194; MP:AF III-1193
   "Spotted Horses," MPII:SS V-2210
   "That Evening Sun," MPII:SS VI-2325
   Town, The, CLC II-1149; MP XI-6623;
     MP:AF III-1302
   Unvanquished, The, MP XII-6860;
     MP:AF III-1354
   "Wash," MPII:SS VI-2552
   Wild Palms, The, MP XII-7142; MP:AF
     III-1437

FAUSET, JESSIE REDMON, CWAII
II-514
Chinaberry Tree, The, MPII:AfAm I-259
Plum Bun, CLCII III-1215; MPII:AF
III-1271; MPII:AfAm II-958
FEARING, KENNETH
"Dirge," MPII:P II-549
"End of the Seers' Convention," MPII:P
II-654
FECHER, CONSTANCE
Last Elizabethan, The, MPII:JYABio
III-1037
FELSEN, HENRY GREGOR
Street Rod, MPII:JYAFic IV-1388
FELTON, HAROLD W.
Deborah Sampson, MPII:JYABio I-463
James Weldon Johnson, MPII:JYABio
II-937
Mumbet, MPII:JYABio III-1256
FENDERSON, LEWIS H.
Thurgood Marshall, MPII:JYABio
IV-1725
FÉNELON, FANIA
Playing for Time, MPII:JYABio III-1421
FÊNG MÊNG-LUNG
Lieh-kuo Chih, MP VI-3385; MP:EF
II-782
FENNER, CAROL ELIZABETH
Skates of Uncle Richard, The,
MPII:JYAFic IV-1347
FERBER, EDNA, CWA I-601; CWAII
II-516
So Big, MP X-6115; MP:AF III-1176
FERGUSON, CHARLES W.
Naked to Mine Enemies, MPII:JYABio
III-1284
FERLINGHETTI, LAWRENCE
"Dog," MPII:P II-575
FERMOR, PATRICK LEIGH
Violins of Saint-Jacques, The, CLCII
IV-1656; MPII:BCF IV-1790
FERNÁNDEZ DE LIZARDI, JOSÉ
JOAQUÍN, CWA I-603
Itching Parrot, The, CLC I-536; MP
V-2955; MP:AF II-607
FERREIRA, ANTÓNIO, CWA I-604
Inês de Castro, CLC I-524; MP V-2883
FEUCHTWANGER, LION, CWA I-605
Power, CLC II-909; MP IX-5277;
MP:EF III-1030

Ugly Duchess, The, CLC II-1174; MP
XII-6796; MP:EF III-1326
FIELD, RACHEL
Hitty, Her First Hundred Years,
MPII:JYAFic II-631
FIELDING, GABRIEL
Birthday King, The, CLCII I-158;
MPII:BCF I-134
In the Time of Greenbloom, CLCII
II-751; MPII:BCF II-814
FIELDING, HENRY, CWA I-607
Amelia, CLC I-33; MP I-161; MP:BF
I-44
Jonathan Wild, CLC I-551; MP V-3030;
MP:BF II-699
Joseph Andrews, CLC I-552; MP
V-3036; MP:BF II-707
Temple Beau, The, CLC II-1113; MP
XI-6435
Tom Jones, CLC II-1143; MP XI-6598;
MP:BF III-1571
Tom Thumb the Great, CLC II-1146;
MP XI-6609
FIELDING, SARAH
Governess, The, MPII:JYAFic II-557
FIERSTEIN, HARVEY, CWAII II-518
Torch Song Trilogy, CLCII IV-1592;
MPII:D IV-1618
FIGES, EVA
Light, CLCII II-890; MPII:BCF II-965
Seven Ages, The, CLCII IV-1381;
MPII:BCF IV-1510
FINDLEY, TIMOTHY, CWAII II-520
Wars, The, CLCII IV-1683; MPII:BCF
IV-1848
FISHER, AILEEN L., and OLIVE RABE
We Alcotts, MPII:JYABio IV-1834
We Dickinsons, MPII:JYABio IV-1838
FISHER, DOROTHY CANFIELD
Home-maker, The, CLCII II-686;
MPII:AF II-728
FISHER, RUDOLPH
Conjure-Man Dies, The, MPII:AfAm
I-302
FISHER, VARDIS, CWA I-610
Children of God, CLC I-175; MP II-927;
MP:AF I-196
FITZGERALD, BARBARA, TOM
SEWELL, and LOUIS KAUFMAN
Moe Berg, MPII:JYABio III-1233

FITZGERALD, EDWARD, CWA I-612
  Rubáiyát of Omar Khayyám, The, MP
    X-5730
FITZGERALD, F. SCOTT, CWA I-613;
  CWAII II-522
  "Absolution," MPII:SS I-5
  "Babylon Revisited," MPII:SS I-140
  Beautiful and Damned, The, CLCII
    I-127; MPII:AF I-122
  Crack-Up, The, MPII:NF I-293
  "Crazy Sunday," MPII:SS I-452
  "Diamond as Big as the Ritz, The,"
    MPII:SS II-582
  "Freshest Boy, The," MPII:SS II-813
  Great Gatsby, The, CLC I-421; MP
    IV-2358; MP:AF I-496
  Last Tycoon, The, CLC I-599; MP
    VI-3277; MP:AF II-649
  Letters of F. Scott Fitzgerald, The, MP
    VI-3347
  "May Day," MPII:SS IV-1485
  "Rich Boy, The," MPII:SS V-1952
  Tender Is the Night, CLC II-1117; MP
    XI-6448; MP:AF III-1266
  This Side of Paradise, CLCII IV-1550;
    MPII:AF IV-1635
  "Winter Dreams," MPII:SS VI-2645
FITZGERALD, ZELDA
  Save Me the Waltz, CLCII III-1340;
    MPII:AF III-1370
FITZHARDINGE, JOAN MARGARET.
    See PHIPSON, JOAN
FITZHUGH, LOUISE
  Harriet the Spy, MPII:JYAFic II-602
FLACCUS, QUINTUS HORATIUS. See
    HORACE
FLAUBERT, GUSTAVE, CWA I-615
  Bouvard and Pécuchet, CLC I-117; MP
    II-615; MP:EF I-127
  "Herodias," MPII:SS III-1007
  "Legend of St. Julian, Hospitaler, The,"
    MPII:SS III-1328
  Madame Bovary, CLC I-645; MP
    VI-3599; MP:EF II-806
  Salammbô, CLC II-1001; MP X-5769;
    MP:EF III-1118
  Sentimental Education, A, CLC II-1023;
    MP X-5909; MP:EF III-1141
  "Simple Heart, A," MPII:SS V-2120

Temptation of Saint Anthony, The, CLC
    II-1114; MP XI-6438; MP:EF
    III-1268
FLECKER, JAMES ELROY, CWA I-618
  Poetry of Flecker, The, MP IX-4941
FLEISCHMAN, SID
  Whipping Boy, The, MPII:JYAFic
    IV-1624
FLEMING, THOMAS
  Benjamin Franklin, MPII:JYABio I-203
  First in Their Hearts, MPII:JYABio
    II-635
FLETCHER, JOHN
  Faithful Shepherdess, The, CLC I-352;
    MP IV-1962
  Rule a Wife and Have a Wife, MP
    X-5732; CLC II-996
  Woman's Prize, The, CLC II-1260; MP
    XII-7229
FLETCHER, JOHN, and FRANCIS
    BEAUMONT, CWA I-137
  Coxcomb, The, CLC I-218; MP II-1185
  King and No King, A, CLC I-569; MP
    VI-3133
  Maid's Tragedy, The, CLC I-654; MP
    VI-3638
  Philaster, CLC II-868; MP VIII-4639
  Scornful Lady, The, CLC II-1012; MP
    X-5848
  Woman Hater, The, CLC II-1255; MP
    XII-7207
FLETCHER, JOHN, and PHILIP
    MASSINGER
  Beggars' Bush, The, CLC I-92; MP I-472
  Sir John van Olden Barnavelt, CLC
    II-1042; MP X-6063
FLETCHER, JOHN, and WILLIAM
    SHAKESPEARE
  Two Noble Kinsmen, The, CLC II-1172;
    MP XII-6775
FO, DARIO, CWAII II-525
  Accidental Death of an Anarchist, CLCII
    I-8; MPII:D I-6
FOGAZZARO, ANTONIO, CWA I-620
  Patriot, The, CLC II-843; MP VIII-4534;
    MP:EF III-973
  Saint, The, CLC II-998; MP X-5751;
    MP:EF III-1109

FONTAINE, JEAN DE LA. *See* LA
FONTAINE, JEAN DE
FONTANE, THEODOR, CWA I-622
Effi Briest, CLC I-317; MP III-1716;
MP:EF I-464
FONTEYN, MARGOT
Margot Fonteyn, MPII:JYABio III-1177
FOQUÉ, FRIEDRICH DE LA MOTTE-.
See LA MOTTE-FOUQUÉ,
FRIEDRICH DE
FORBES, ESTHER, CWA I-623
Johnny Tremain, MPII:JYAFic II-756
Mirror for Witches, A, CLC II-710; MP
VII-3917; MP:AF II-782
Paul Revere and the World He Lived In,
MPII:JYABio III-1391
FORCHÉ, CAROLYN
"Burning the Tomato Worms," MPII:P
I-319
FORD, FORD MADOX, CWA I-624
Fifth Queen, The, MP IV-2055; MP:BF
I-420
Good Soldier, The, CLCII II-613;
MPII:BCF II-637
Parade's End, CLC II-833; MP
VIII-4477; MP:BF II-1155
FORD, JOHN, CWA I-626
'Tis Pity She's a Whore, CLC II-1134;
MP XI-6556
FORD, JOHN, THOMAS MIDDLETON,
and WILLIAM ROWLEY
Spanish Gipsy, The, MP XI-6208
FORD, PETER, *and* MICHAEL HOWELL
True History of the Elephant Man, The,
MPII:JYABio IV-1774
FORESTER, C. S., CWA I-627
Captain Horatio Hornblower, CLC
I-148; MP II-779; MP:BF I-163
Horatio Hornblower series, The,
MPII:JYAFic II-644
FORREST, LEON, CWAII II-528
There Is a Tree More Ancient Than
Eden, CLCII IV-1538; MPII:AF
IV-1615; MPII:AfAm III-1423
Two Wings to Veil My Face,
MPII:AfAm III-1462
FORSTER, E. M., CWA I-628; CWAII
II-530
"Celestial Omnibus, The," MPII:SS I-348

Howards End, CLC I-493; MP V-2745;
MP:BF II-616
Longest Journey, The, CLC I-625; MP
VI-3487; MP:BF II-816
Maurice, CLCII III-989; MPII:BCF
III-1076
Passage to India, A, CLC II-838; MP
VIII-4500; MP:BF II-1161
Room with a View, A, CLC II-994; MP
X-5712; MP:BF III-1376
Short Stories of E. M. Forster, The, MP
X-5998; MP:BF III-1434
Where Angels Fear to Tread, CLC
II-1236; MP XII-7104; MP:BF
III-1731
FOUCAULT, MICHEL, CWAII II-533
Madness and Civilization, MPII:NF
II-866
Order of Things, The, MPII:NF III-1098
FOUQUÉ, FRIEDRICH DE LA MOTTE.
See LA MOTTE-FOUQUÉ,
FRIEDRICH DE
FOURNIER, HENRI-ALAIN. *See*
ALAIN-FOURNIER
FOWLER, GENE
Good Night, Sweet Prince,
MPII:JYABio II-772
FOWLES, JOHN, CWAII II-535
Collector, The, CLCII I-307; MPII:BCF
I-281
Daniel Martin, CLCII I-364; MPII:BCF
I-354
Ebony Tower, The, CLCII II-440;
MPII:BCF I-422
French Lieutenant's Woman, The, CLCII
II-546; MPII:BCF II-549
Magus, The, CLCII III-945; MPII:BCF
III-1044
FOX, PAULA
Blowfish Live in the Sea, MPII:JYAFic
I-135
One-Eyed Cat, MPII:JYAFic III-1070
Slave Dancer, The, MPII:JYAFic
IV-1354
FRAME, JANET, CWAII II-537
Intensive Care, CLCII II-769; MPII:BCF
II-831
FRANCE, ANATOLE, CWA I-630
At the Sign of the Reine Pédauque, CLC
I-68; MP I-345; MP:EF I-77

Crime of Sylvestre Bonnard, The, CLC
I-222; MP II-1202; MP:EF I-304
Gods Are Athirst, The, CLC I-405; MP
IV-2282; MP:EF II-571
Penguin Island, CLC II-855; MP
VIII-4579; MP:EF III-994
Revolt of the Angels, The, CLC II-963;
MP X-5558; MP:EF III-1088
FRANCHERE, RUTH
Willa, MPII:JYABio IV-1880
FRANCIS, DICK, CWAII II-540
Bonecrack, CLCII I-186; MPII:BCF I-172
FRANK, ANNE
Diary of a Young Girl, The,
MPII:JYABio I-471
FRANKL, VIKTOR
Man's Search for Meaning, MPII:NF
III-896
FRANKLIN, BENJAMIN, CWA I-633
Autobiography of Benjamin Franklin,
The, MP I-362; MPII:JYABio I-145
FRANKLIN, MILES
My Brilliant Career, CLCII III-1060;
MPII:BCF III-1161
FRASER, NICHOLAS, and MARYSA
NAVARRO
Eva Perón, MPII:JYABio II-576
FRAYN, MICHAEL, CWAII II-542
Benefactors, CLCII I-142; MPII:D I-158
FRAZER, SIR JAMES GEORGE, CWA
I-638
Golden Bough, The, MP IV-2296
FREDERIC, HAROLD, CWA I-640
Copperhead, The, CLC I-200; MP
II-1113; MP:AF I-220
Damnation of Theron Ware, The, CLC
I-235; MP III-1279; MP:AF I-251
FREEDGOOD, LILLIAN
Great Artists of America, MPII:JYABio
II-784
FREEDMAN, RUSSELL
Indian Chiefs, MPII:JYABio II-916
Lincoln, MPII:JYABio III-1089
FREEMAN, DOUGLAS SOUTHALL,
CWA I-642
Lee of Virginia, MPII:JYABio III-1052
R. E. Lee, MP IX-5497
FREEMAN, MARY E. WILKINS
"Old Woman Magoun," MPII:SS
IV-1684

FRENCH, MARILYN, CWAII II-544
Women's Room, The, CLCII IV-1737;
MPII:AF IV-1810
FRENEAU, PHILIP, CWA I-643
"Indian Burying Ground, The," MPII:P
III-1108
Poetry of Freneau, The, MP IX-4943
FREUD, SIGMUND, CWA I-645; CWAII
II-546
General Introduction to Psychoanalysis,
A, MP IV-2218
Interpretation of Dreams, The, MP
V-2908
Moses and Monotheism, MPII:NF
III-982
Totem and Taboo, MPII:NF IV-1553
Wit and Its Relation to the Unconscious,
MPII:NF IV-1704
FREUD, SIGMUND, and JOSEF BREUER
Studies on Hysteria, MP XI-6317
FREYTAG, GUSTAV, CWA I-648
Debit and Credit, CLC I-258; MP
III-1393; MP:EF I-367
FRIEDAN, BETTY
Feminine Mystique, The, MPII:NF II-507
FRIEL, BRIAN, CWAII II-548
Freedom of the City, The, CLCII II-545;
MPII:D II-633
Philadelphia, Here I Come! CLCII
III-1202; MPII:D III-1230
Translations, CLCII IV-1600; MPII:D
IV-1634
Volunteers, CLCII IV-1665; MPII:D
IV-1695
FRISCH, MAX, CWAII II-550
Andorra, CLCII I-43; MPII:D I-60
Bluebeard, CLCII I-178; MPII:WF I-169
Chinese Wall, The, CLCII I-280;
MPII:D I-347
Firebugs, The, CLCII II-510; MPII:D
II-610
Homo Faber, CLCII II-692; MPII:WF
II-608
I'm Not Stiller, CLCII II-740; MPII:WF
II-669
Man in the Holocene, CLCII III-954;
MPII:WF III-920
Sketchbook, 1946-1949, and
Sketchbook, 1966-1971, MPII:NF
IV-1361

FRITZ, JEAN
Double Life of Pocahontas, The,
MPII:JYABio II-507
Homesick, MPII:JYABio II-861
Make Way for Sam Houston,
MPII:JYABio III-1153
Stonewall, MPII:JYABio IV-1610
Traitor, MPII:JYABio IV-1766
FROISSART, JEAN, CWA I-649
Chronicles of Froissart, MP II-953
FROLOV, VADIM
What It's All About, MPII:JYAFic
IV-1597
FROMENTIN, EUGÈNE, CWA I-650
Dominique, CLC I-288; MP III-1579;
MP:EF I-422
FROST, ROBERT, CWA I-651
"After Apple-Picking," MPII:P I-23
"Birches," MPII:P I-234
"Directive," MPII:P II-545
Letters of Robert Frost, The, MP VI-3358
"Mending Wall," MPII:P IV-1366
"Most of It, The," MPII:P IV-1421
"Neither Out Far nor In Deep," MPII:P
IV-1481
Poetry of Frost, The, MP IX-4946
"Road Not Taken, The," MPII:P V-1838
"Stopping by Woods on a Snowy
Evening," MPII:P V-2075
"To Earthward," MPII:P VI-2203
"Two Tramps in Mud Time," MPII:P
VI-2303
FRY, CHRISTOPHER, CWA I-656
Lady's Not for Burning, The, CLC
I-589; MP VI-3219
FRYE, NORTHROP, CWAII II-552
Anatomy of Criticism, MPII:NF I-61
FUENTES, CARLOS, CWA I-658; CWAII
II-555
Aura, CLCII I-90; MPII:AF I-76

Change of Skin, A, CLCII I-259;
MPII:AF I-279
Death of Artemio Cruz, The, MP
III-1369; MP:AF I-273
Distant Relations, CLCII I-406;
MPII:AF I-418
Good Conscience, The, CLCII II-610;
MPII:AF II-650
Holy Place, CLCII II-684; MPII:AF
II-717
Terra Nostra, CLCII IV-1530; MPII:AF
IV-1593
"Two Elenas, The," MPII:SS VI-2436
Where the Air Is Clear, MP XII-7107;
MP:AF III-1420
FUGARD, ATHOL, CWAII II-558
Blood Knot, The, CLCII I-169; MPII:D
I-200
Boesman and Lena, CLCII I-183;
MPII:D I-225
Lesson from Aloes, A, CLCII II-875;
MPII:D III-959
"MASTER HAROLD" . . . and the boys,
CLCII III-986; MPII:D III-1059
Notebooks, 1960-1977, MPII:NF
III-1019
Road to Mecca, The, CLCII III-1303;
MPII:D IV-1362
FUKUDA, HANAKO
Wind in My Hand, MPII:JYABio
IV-1895
FULLER, CHARLES
Soldier's Play, A, MPII:AfAm III-1283
FULLER, R. BUCKMINSTER
Critical Path, MPII:NF I-299
FULLER, THOMAS, CWA I-662
Holy State and the Profane State, The,
MP V-2672
FUTRELLE, JACQUES, CWAII II-560
"Problem of Cell 13, The," MPII:SS
IV-1856

G

GABORIAU, ÉMILE, CWA I-664
File No. 113, CLC I-366; MP IV-2058;
MP:EF II-515
Monsieur Lecoq, CLC II-736; MP
VII-4040; MP:EF II-883
GADAMER, HANS-GEORG, CWAII
II-562
Truth and Method, MPII:NF IV-1580
GADDA, CARLO EMILIO, CWAII II-565
Acquainted with Grief, CLCII I-10;
MPII:WF I-16
That Awful Mess on Via Merulana,
CLCII IV-1532; MPII:WF IV-1565
GADDIS, WILLIAM, CWAII II-567
Recognitions, The, CLCII III-1277;
MPII:AF III-1324
GAEDDERT, LOUANN
New England Love Story, A,
MPII:JYABio III-1312
GAINES, ERNEST J., CWAII II-569
Autobiography of Miss Jane Pittman,
The, CLCII I-93; MPII:AF I-87;
MPII:AfAm I-84; MPII:JYAFic I-73
Catherine Carmier, MPII:AfAm I-243
Gathering of Old Men, A, MPII:AfAm
I-480; MPII:JYAFic II-494
Lesson Before Dying, A, MPII:AfAm
II-682
"Sky Is Gray, The," MPII:SS V-2128
GALARZA, ERNESTO
Barrio Boy, MPII:JYABio I-176
GALDÓS, BENITO PÉREZ. See PÉREZ
GALDÓS, BENITO
GALEANO, EDUARDO, CWAII II-571
Memory of Fire, MPII:NF III-937
GALIANO, JUAN VALERA Y ALCALÁ.
See VALERA Y ALCALÁ
GALIANO, JUAN
GALLANT, MAVIS
"Ice Wagon Going Down the Street,
The," MPII:SS III-1103
"Jorinda and Jorindel," MPII:SS III-1237
"Other Paris, The," MPII:SS IV-1719
GALLEGOS, RÓMULO, CWA II-665
Doña Bárbara, CLC I-296; MP III-1614;
MP:AF I-304
GALLICO, PAUL
"Enchanted Doll, The," MPII:SS II-683

GALSWORTHY, JOHN, CWA II-666
Country House, The, CLC I-210; MP
II-1155; MP:BF I-246
Forsyte Saga, The, CLC I-376; MP
IV-2119; MP:BF I-438
Fraternity, CLC I-386; MP IV-2159;
MP:BF I-470
"Japanese Quince, The," MPII:SS
III-1211
Justice, CLC I-564; MP VI-3108
Loyalties, CLC I-638; MP VI-3544
Modern Comedy, A, CLC II-729; MP
VII-4005; MP:BF II-983
Patrician, The, CLC II-842; MP
VIII-4531; MP:BF II-1171
Strife, CLC II-1091; MP XI-6311
GALT, JOHN, CWA II-669
Annals of the Parish, CLC I-47; MP
I-240; MP:BF I-54
GALT, TOM
Peter Zenger, MPII:JYABio III-1414
GARCÍA LORCA, FEDERICO, CWA
II-671
Blood Wedding, CLC I-112; MP I-574
"Fight," MPII:P II-758
"Gacela of the Dark Death," MPII:P
II-833
"Gacela of Unforeseen Love," MPII:P
II-836
"King of Harlem, The," MPII:P III-1150
Lament for Ignacio Sánchez Mejías,
MPII:P III-1181
"Landscape with Two Graves and an
Assyrian Dog," MPII:P III-1188
"Ode to the Most Holy Eucharist,"
MPII:P IV-1558
"Somnambule Ballad," MPII:P V-1947
GARCÍA MÁRQUEZ, GABRIEL, CWAII
II-574
Autumn of the Patriarch, The, CLCII
I-95; MPII:AF I-92
"Blacamán the Good, Vendor of
Miracles," MPII:SS I-227
Chronicle of a Death Foretold, CLCII
I-284; MPII:AF I-300
"Handsomest Drowned Man in the
World, The," MPII:SS III-977
Leaf Storm, CLCII II-864; MPII:AF
II-868

No One Writes to the Colonel, CLCII
III-1108; MPII:AF III-1151
One Hundred Years of Solitude, CLCII
III-1150; MPII:AF III-1207
GARDAM, JANE
Bilgewater, MPII:JYAFic I-119
Crusoe's Daughter, CLCII I-352;
MPII:BCF I-333
God on the Rocks, CLCII II-600;
MPII:BCF II-617
GARDNER, JOHN, CWAII II-577
"Art of Living, The," MPII:SS I-114
Grendel, CLCII II-637; MPII:AF II-677
"John Napper Sailing Through the
Universe," MPII:SS III-1226
"King's Indian, The," CLCII II-835;
MPII:SS III-1265
Mickelsson's Ghosts, CLCII III-1001;
MPII:AF III-1002
Nickel Mountain, CLCII III-1091;
MPII:AF III-1134
October Light, CLCII III-1127; MPII:AF
III-1165
On Moral Fiction, MPII:NF III-1077
Sunlight Dialogues, The, CLCII IV-1495;
MPII:AF IV-1555
Wreckage of Agathon, The, CLCII
IV-1758; MPII:AF IV-1830
GARFIELD, LEON
Footsteps, MPII:JYAFic II-454
GARFIELD, LEON, and EDWARD
BLISHEN
God Beneath the Sea, The, MPII:JYAFic
II-533
GARLAND, HAMLIN, CWA II-673
Main-Travelled Roads, MP VI-3650;
MP:AF II-735
"Return of a Private, The," MPII:SS
V-1937
Son of the Middle Border, A, MP X-6138
GARNER, ALAN
Owl Service, The, MPII:JYAFic III-1100
GARNER, HELEN
Monkey Grip, CLCII III-1030; MPII:BCF
III-1137
GARNETT, DAVID, CWA II-675
Lady into Fox, CLC I-587; MP VI-3210;
MP:BF II-765

GARRETT, GEORGE, CWA II-677;
CWAII II-580
Death of the Fox, CLCII I-379; MPII:AF
I-384
"Evening Performance, An," MPII:SS
II-727
Poetry of Garrett, The, MP IX-4952
GARST, DORIS SHANNON
Crazy Horse, MPII:JYABio I-416
Kit Carson, MPII:JYABio III-1001
GASCOIGNE, GEORGE, CWA II-679
Poetry of Gascoigne, The, MP IX-4955
GASKELL, MRS. ELIZABETH, CWA
II-682
Cranford, CLC I-219; MP II-1191;
MP:BF I-250
Mary Barton, MP VII-3756; MP:BF
II-883
GASS, WILLIAM H., CWA II-684;
CWAII II-582
"In the Heart of the Heart of the
Country," MPII:SS III-1150
Omensetter's Luck, CLCII III-1140;
MPII:AF III-1184
"Pedersen Kid, The," MPII:SS IV-1793
GASSET, JOSÉ ORTEGA Y. See
ORTEGA Y GASSET, JOSÉ
GATES, HENRY LOUIS, JR.
Signifying Monkey, The, MPII:AfAm
III-1274
GAUTIER, THÉOPHILE, CWA II-685
Mademoiselle de Maupin, CLC I-647;
MP VI-3604; MP:EF II-812
Poetry of Gautier, The, MP IX-4961
GAY, JOHN, CWA II-687
Beggar's Opera, The, CLC I-94; MP
I-476
GAYLE, ADDISON
Oak and Ivy, MPII:JYABio III-1328
GEERTZ, CLIFFORD, CWAII II-584
Interpretation of Cultures, The, MPII:NF
II-747
GELBER, JACK
Connection, The, CLCII I-330; MPII:D
I-391
GENET, JEAN, CWAII II-586
Balcony, The, CLCII I-103; MPII:D
I-109
Blacks, The, CLCII I-167; MPII:D I-190
Deathwatch, CLCII I-382; MPII:D II-471

Maids, The, CLCII III-946; MPII:D
III-1031

Miracle of the Rose, CLCII III-1013;
MPII:WF III-1011

Our Lady of the Flowers, CLCII
III-1164; MPII:WF III-1163

Screens, The, CLCII III-1352; MPII:D
IV-1416

GEORGE, JEAN CRAIGHEAD
Julie of the Wolves, MPII:JYAFic II-764

GEORGE, STEFAN, CWA II-689
Poetry of Stefan George, The, MP
IX-5155

GERONIMO
Geronimo, MPII:JYABio II-733

GHERMAN, BEVERLY
Georgia O'Keeffe, MPII:JYABio II-729

GIBBON, EDWARD, CWA II-691
History of the Decline and Fall of the
Roman Empire, The, MP V-2649

GIBBON, LEWIS GRASSIC
Scots Quair, A, CLCII III-1349;
MPII:BCF III-1465

GIBBONS, STELLA, CWA II-693
Cold Comfort Farm, MP II-1016;
MP:BF I-230

GIBRAN, KAHLIL
Prophet, The, MP IX-5372

GIBSON, ALTHEA
I Always Wanted to Be Somebody,
MPII:JYABio II-873

GIBSON, WILLIAM
Miracle Worker, The, CLCII III-1015;
MPII:D III-1089

Two for the Seesaw, CLCII IV-1625;
MPII:D IV-1670

GIDE, ANDRÉ, CWA II-695
Counterfeiters, The, CLC I-206; MP
II-1140; MP:EF I-274

Immoralist, The, CLCII II-743;
MPII:WF II-673

Journals of André Gide, The, MP
VI-3059

Lafcadio's Adventures, CLCII II-847;
MPII:WF II-806

Strait Is the Gate, CLCII IV-1477;
MPII:WF IV-1529

GIEDION, SIGFRIED
Eternal Present, The, MPII:NF II-460

Space, Time, and Architecture, MPII:NF
IV-1408

GILBERT, SANDRA M., and SUSAN
GUBAR, CWAII II-588
Madwoman in the Attic, The, MPII:NF
II-872

GILBERT, W. S., CWA II-698
Gondoliers, The, CLC I-409; MP
IV-2310

H. M. S. Pinafore, CLC I-478; MP
V-2669

Iolanthe, CLC I-528; MP V-2922

Mikado, The, CLC II-704; MP VII-3893

Patience, CLC II-842; MP VIII-4528

Pirates of Penzance, The, CLC II-888;
MP VIII-4726

Trial by Jury, CLC II-1156; MP XI-6692

GILBRETH, FRANK B., JR., and
ERNESTINE GILBRETH CAREY
Cheaper by the Dozen, MPII:JYABio
I-340

GILL, DEREK L. T., and TOM SULLIVAN
If You Could See What I Hear,
MPII:JYABio II-901

GILMAN, CHARLOTTE PERKINS,
CWAII II-590
Herland, CLCII II-676; MPII:AF II-706

GILMAN, MICHAEL
Matthew Henson, MPII:JYABio III-1195

GILMAN, RICHARD
Faith, Sex, Mystery, MPII:NF II-497

GILROY, FRANK D.
Subject Was Roses, The, CLCII
IV-1486; MPII:D IV-1503

GINSBERG, ALLEN
"Howl," MPII:P III-974

"Kaddish," MPII:P III-1144

"Supermarket in California, A," MPII:P
V-2109

"Wales Visitation," MPII:P VI-2364

GINZBURG, NATALIA, CWAII II-592
All Our Yesterdays, CLCII I-31;
MPII:WF I-34

City and the House, The, CLCII I-289;
MPII:WF I-262

GIONO, JEAN, CWA II-700; CWAII II-594
Blue Boy, CLCII I-175; MPII:WF I-158

Horseman on the Roof, The, CLCII
II-699; MPII:WF II-618

Joy of Man's Desiring, CLCII II-802;
MPII:WF II-786
Song of the World, The, CLC II-1067;
MP XI-6163; MP:EF III-1201
GIOVANNI, NIKKI, CWAII II-596
Gemini, MPII:AfAm I-486; MPII:NF
II-549
"Nikki-Rosa," MPII:P IV-1499
Poetry of Nikki Giovanni, The,
MPII:AfAm III-1042
GIPSON, FRED
Old Yeller, MPII:JYAFic III-1051
GIRARD, RENÉ, CWAII II-599
Scapegoat, The, MPII:NF III-1293
GIRAUDOUX, JEAN, CWA II-702
Amphitryon 38, CLC I-37; MP I-189
Madwoman of Chaillot, The, CLC I-649;
MP VI-3611
Tiger at the Gates, MP XI-6539
GIRONELLA, JOSÉ MARÍA, CWA II-704
Cypresses Believe in God, The, MP
III-1259; MP:EF I-319
GISSING, GEORGE, CWA II-706
New Grub Street, The, CLC II-763; MP
VII-4174; The, MP:BF II-1034
Private Papers of Henry Ryecroft, The,
CLC II-920; MP IX-5350; MP:BF
III-1270
GLASGOW, ELLEN, CWA II-708
Barren Ground, CLC I-84; MP I-438;
MP:AF I-96
"Difference, The," MPII:SS II-595
"Jordan's End," MPII:SS III-1234
Romantic Comedians, The, CLC II-986;
MP X-5684; MP:AF III-1067
Sheltered Life, The, CLC II-1033; MP
X-5969; MP:AF III-1130
Vein of Iron, CLCII IV-1651; MPII:AF
IV-1738
GLASS, PHILIP, and ROBERT WILSON
Einstein on the Beach, CLCII II-449;
MPII:D II-551
GLASSER, RONALD
365 Days, MPII:NF IV-1518
GLINES, CARROLL V.
Wright Brothers, The, MPII:JYABio
IV-1952
GLÜCK, LOUISE
"Metamorphosis," MPII:P IV-1372

GODDEN, RUMER, CWAII II-601
Candle for St. Jude, A, MPII:JYAFic
I-188
Hans Christian Andersen, MPII:JYABio
II-802
Time to Dance, No Time to Weep, A,
MPII:NF IV-1527
GODWIN, GAIL, CWAII II-604
Mother and Two Daughters, A, CLCII
III-1043; MPII:AF III-1072
Odd Woman, The, CLCII III-1131;
MPII:AF III-1176
GODWIN, WILLIAM, CWA II-712
Caleb Williams, CLC I-141; MP II-740;
MP:BF I-158
Inquiry Concerning Political Justice, An,
MP V-2901
GOETHE, JOHANN WOLFGANG VON,
CWA II-714
Egmont, CLC I-317; MP III-1719
Elective Affinities, CLC I-319; MP
III-1731; MP:EF I-468
Faust, CLC I-362; MP IV 2020
Poetry and Truth from My Own Life,
MP VIII-4792
Sorrows of Young Werther, The, CLC
II-1069; MP XI-6182; MP:EF
III-1206
Wilhelm Meister's Apprenticeship, CLC
II-1243; MP XII-7148; MP:EF
III-1390
Wilhelm Meister's Travels, CLC
II-1245; MP XII-7152; MP:EF
III-1395
GOFFMAN, ERVING
Relations in Public, MPII:NF III-1236
GOGGAN, JOHN PATRICK. See
PATRICK, JOHN
GOGOL, NIKOLAI VASILYEVICH,
CWA II-718
Dead Souls, CLC I-248; MP III-1342;
MP:EF I-345
"Diary of a Madman, The," MPII:SS
II-591
Inspector General, The, CLC I-526; MP
V-2904
"Nose, The," MPII:SS IV-1633
"Old-World Landowners," MPII:SS
IV-1688

"Overcoat, The," CLC II-830; MP
  VIII-4452; MP:EF III-965; MPII:SS
  IV-1745
Taras Bulba, CLC II-1108; MP XI-6408;
  MP:EF III-1260
"Viy," MPII:SS VI-2513
GÖKÇELI, YAAR KEMAL. See KEMAL,
  YASHAR
GOLDEMBERG, ISAAC
  Fragmented Life of Don Jacobo Lerner,
    The, CLCII II-542; MPII:AF II-572
GOLDING, WILLIAM, CWA II-721;
  CWAII II-606
  Darkness Visible, CLCII I-367;
    MPII:BCF I-360
  Free Fall, MP IV-2163; MP:BF I-475
  Inheritors, The, MP V-2894; MP:BF
    II-645
  Lord of the Flies, MP VI-3505; MP:BF
    II-825; MPII:JYAFic III-879
  Paper Men, The, CLCII III-1175;
    MPII:BCF III-1277
  Pincher Martin, CLCII III-1208;
    MPII:BCF III-1325
  Rites of Passage, CLCII III-1299;
    MPII:BCF III-1422
  Spire, The, CLCII IV-1462; MPII:BCF
    IV-1593
GOLDONI, CARLO, CWA II-724
  Mistress of the Inn, The, CLC II-724;
    MP VII-3982
GOLDSMITH, OLIVER, CWA II-725
  "Deserted Village, The," MPII:P II-531
  Poetry of Goldsmith, The, MP IX-4964
  She Stoops to Conquer, CLC II-1030;
    MP X-5957
  Vicar of Wakefield, The, CLC II-1198;
    MP XII-6901; MP:BF III-1674
GOLDSZMIT, HENRYK. See KORCZAK,
  JANUSZ
GOMBRICH, ERNST HANS JOSEF,
  CWAII II-608
  Art and Illusion, MPII:NF I-90
GOMBROWICZ, WITOLD, CWAII II-610
  Cosmos, CLCII I-340; MPII:WF I-328
  Diary, MPII:NF I-367
  Ferdydurke, CLCII II-499; MPII:WF
    II-451
  Ivona, Princess of Burgundia, CLCII
    II-782; MPII:D II-857

Marriage, The, CLCII III-977; MPII:D
  III-1054
Operetta, CLCII III-1156; MPII:D
  III-1180
Pornografia, CLCII III-1221; MPII:WF
  III-1221
GONCHAROV, IVAN
  ALEXANDROVICH, CWA II-729
  Oblomov, CLC II-787; MP:EF II-949;
    MP VII-4270
GONCOURT, EDMOND DE, and JULES
  DE GONCOURT, CWA II-731
  Charles Demailly, CLC I-168; MP
    II-888; MP:EF I-210
  Germinie Lacerteux, CLC I-398; MP
    IV-2242; MP:EF II-563
  Goncourt Journals, The, MP IV-2307
  Manette Salomon, CLC I-662; MP
    VII-3686; MP:EF II-821
  Renée Mauperin, CLC II-957; MP
    IX-5514; MP:EF III-1078
  Sister Philoméne, CLC II-1046; MP
    X-6075; MP:EF III-1159
GOODALL, JANE
  In the Shadow of Man, MPII:JYABio
    II-909
GORDIMER, NADINE, CWAII II-612
  Burger's Daughter, CLCII I-212;
    MPII:BCF I-201
  Conservationist, The, CLCII I-331;
    MPII:BCF I-318
  July's People, CLCII II-807; MPII:BCF
    II-872
  "Livingstone's Companions," MPII:SS
    III-1383
  Occasion for Loving, CLCII III-1126;
    MPII:BCF III-1248
  "Open House," MPII:SS IV-1712
  "Smell of Death and Flowers, The,"
    MPII:SS V-2142
  "Soldier's Embrace, A," MPII:SS V-2166
  "Something Out There," MPII:SS
    V-2182
  "Town and Country Lovers," MPII:SS
    VI-2397
  World of Strangers, A, CLCII IV-1754;
    MPII:BCF IV-1940
GORDON, CAROLINE, CWA II-733;
  CWAII II-614
  Aleck Maury, Sportsman, CLC I-20; MP
    I-93; MP:AF I-28

"Ice House, The," MPII:SS III-1099
"Old Red," MPII:SS IV-1676
GORDON, MARY, CWAII II-616
  Company of Women, The, CLCII I-316;
    MPII:AF I-315;
  Final Payments, CLCII II-504; MPII:AF
    II-542
GORENKO, ANNA ANDREYEMA. See
  AKHMATOVA, ANNA
GORKY, MAXIM, CWA II-734
  Artamonov Business, The, CLC I-64;
    MP I-326; MP:EF I-68
  Foma Gordeyev, CLC I-373; MP
    IV-2100; MP:EF II-526
  Lower Depths, The, CLC I-636; MP
    VI-3540
  Mother, CLC II-744; MP VII-4072;
    MP:EF II-899
  "Twenty-six Men and a Girl," MPII:SS
    VI-2429
GOSS, MADELEINE
  Beethoven, Master Musician,
    MPII:JYABio I-183
GOTTFRIED VON STRASSBURG, CWA
  II-737
  Tristan and Isolde, CLC II-1159; MP
    XI-6705
GOUDGE, ELIZABETH
  Green Dolphin Street, MPII:JYAFic
    II-561
GOULD, JEAN
  That Dunbar Boy, MPII:JYABio IV-1680
GOURMONT, REMY DE, CWA II-738
  Night in the Luxembourg, A, CLC
    II-778; MP VII-4215; MP:EF II-946
GOYEN, WILLIAM
  "Faces of Blood Kindred, The," MPII:SS
    II-743
  "Ghost and Flesh, Water and Dirt,"
    MPII:SS II-839
  "Shape of Light, A," MPII:SS V-2068
GOYTISOLO, JUAN, CWAII II-618
  Count Julian, CLCII III-974; MPII:WF
    III-958
  Juan the Landless, CLCII III-974;
    MPII:WF III-958
  Marks of Identity, CLCII III-974;
    MPII:WF III-958

GRAHAM, FRANK
  Lou Gehrig, MPII:JYABio III-1128
GRAHAM, JORIE
  "Remembering Titian's Martyrdom of
    Saint Lawrence," MPII:P V-1798
GRAHAM, LORENZ BELL
  John Brown, MPII:JYABio II-970
  Whose Town?, MPII:JYAFic IV-1630
GRAHAM, ROBIN LEE
  Dove, MPII:JYABio II-510
GRAHAM, SHIRLEY
  Story of Phillis Wheatley, The,
    MPII:JYABio IV-1626
  There Was Once a Slave...,
    MPII:JYABio IV-1688
  Your Most Humble Servant,
    MPII:JYABio IV-1978
GRAHAME, KENNETH, CWA II-740
  Wind in the Willows, The, CLC II-1247;
    MP XII-7159; MP:BF III-1739;
    MPII:JYAFic IV-1633
GRAMSCI, ANTONIO, CWAII II-621
  Prison Notebooks, MPII:NF III-1200
GRANT, MADELEINE P.
  Alice Hamilton, MPII:JYABio I-28
GRANVILLE-BARKER, HARLEY, CWA
  II-742
  Madras House, The, CLC I-648; MP
    VI-3607
GRASS, GÜNTER, CWA II-743; CWAII
  II-623
  Cat and Mouse, MP II-842; MP:EF I-195
  Dog Years, CLCII II-412; MPII:WF I-386
  Flounder, The, CLCII II-525; MPII:WF
    II-481
  Headbirths, CLCII II-665; MPII:WF II-578
  Local Anaesthetic, CLCII III-902;
    MPII:WF II-872
  Meeting at Telgte, The, CLCII III-991;
    MPII:WF III-994
  Rat, The, CLCII III-1266; MPII:WF
    III-1252
  Tin Drum, The, MP XI-6553; MP:EF
    III-1290
GRAU, SHIRLEY ANN, CWAII II-626
  "Black Prince, The," MPII:SS I-235
  Keepers of the House, The, CLCII
    II-822; MPII:AF II-835

GRAVES, ROBERT, CWA II-745; CWAII
  II-628
  Claudius the God and His Wife
    Messalina, CLC I-184; MP II-981;
    MP:BF I-216
  "Cool Web, The," MPII:P II-440
  Good-bye to All That, MPII:NF II-567
  I, Claudius, CLC I-507; MP V-2803;
    MP:BF II-632
  King Jesus, CLCII II-830; MPII:BCF
    II-915
  Poetry of Graves, The, MP IX-4968
  White Goddess, The, MPII:NF IV-1692
GRAY, ALASDAIR
  Lanark, CLCII II-850; MPII:BCF II-934
GRAY, ELIZABETH JANET. See also
  VINING, ELIZABETH GRAY
  Adam of the Road, MPII:JYAFic I-7
GRAY, SIMON, CWAII II-631
  Butley, CLCII I-222; MPII:D I-273
  Otherwise Engaged, CLCII III-1161;
    MPII:D III-1191
GRAY, THOMAS, CWA II-747
  Elegy Written in a Country Churchyard,
    MPII:P II-641
  Letters of Thomas Gray, The, MP
    VI-3361
  Poetry of Gray, The, MP IX-4971
GREEN, HANNAH, CWAII II-635. See
  also GREENBERG, JOANNE
  I Never Promised You a Rose Garden,
    CLCII II-728; MPII:AF II-769;
    MPII:JYAFic II-688
GREEN, HENRY, CWA II-749; CWAII
  II-633
  Caught, CLCII I-248; MPII:BCF I-230
  Concluding, CLCII I-318; MPII:BCF
    I-307
  Living, CLCII III-899; MPII:BCF II-984
  Loving, CLC I-636; MP VI-3537;
    MP:BF II-839
  Nothing, CLCII III-1114; MPII:BCF
    III-1224
  Pack My Bag, MPII:NF III-1118
  Party Going, CLCII III-1179; MPII:BCF
    III-1288
GREEN, JULIAN, CWA II-751
  Closed Garden, The, CLC I-189; MP
    II-998; MP:EF I-240
  Dark Journey, The, CLC I-240; MP
    III-1313; MP:EF I-338

GREENBERG, JOANNE, CWAII II-635.
  See also GREEN, HANNAH
  "Hunting Season," MPII:SS III-1085
  Simple Gifts, MPII:JYAFic IV-1341
  "Supremacy of the Hunza, The,"
    MPII:SS V-2285
GREENE, BETTE
  Summer of My German Soldier,
    MPII:JYAFic IV-1403
GREENE, CONSTANCE C.
  Love Letters of J. Timothy Owen, The,
    MPII:JYAFic III-887
GREENE, GRAHAM, CWA II-753;
    CWAII II-638
  "Basement Room, The," MPII:SS I-166
  Brighton Rock, CLCII I-206; MPII:BCF
    I-191
  Burnt-Out Case, A, MP II-711; MP:BF
    I-150
  "Cheap in August," MPII:SS I-361
  Comedians, The, CLCII I-311;
    MPII:BCF I-288
  "Drive in the Country, A," MPII:SS
    II-636
  End of the Affair, The, CLCII II-454;
    MPII:BCF I-442
  Heart of the Matter, The, CLC I-450; MP
    V-2515; MP:BF I-550
  Honorary Consul, The, CLCII II-693;
    MPII:BCF II-732
  Ministry of Fear, The, CLC II-708; MP
    VII-3909; MP:BF II-951
  Potting Shed, The, CLCII III-1228;
    MPII:D III-1274
  Power and the Glory, The, CLC II-910;
    MP IX-5280; MP:BF III-1250
  Quiet American, The, CLCII III-1252;
    MPII:BCF III-1364
  Sort of Life, A, MPII:NF IV-1393
  Ways of Escape, MPII:NF IV-1665
GREENE, ROBERT, CWA II-756
  Friar Bacon and Friar Bungay, CLC
    I-386; MP IV-2172
  Greene's Groatsworth of Wit Bought
    with a Million of Repentance, MP
    IV-2394
GREENFELD, HOWARD
  F. Scott Fitzgerald, MPII:JYABio II-580
  Gertrude Stein, MPII:JYABio II-745
  Marc Chagall, MPII:JYABio III-1167

GREENFIELD, ELOISE
Sister, MPII:JYAFic IV-1344
GREENFIELD, ELOISE, *and* LESSIE
JONES LITTLE
Childtimes, MPII:JYABio I-356
GREENLEE, SAM
Spook Who Sat by the Door, The,
MPII:AfAm III-1326
GREGOR, ARTHUR S.
Charles Darwin, MPII:JYABio I-323
GREGORY, ANDRÉ, *and* WALLACE
SHAWN
My Dinner with André, CLCII III-1061;
MPII:D III-1121
GREGORY, LADY AUGUSTA, CWA
II-758
Grania, CLCII II-622; MPII:D II-696
Seven Short Plays, MP X-5932
Workhouse Ward, The, CLCII IV-1748;
MPII:D IV-1778
GREKOVA, I.
Ladies' Hairdresser, CLCII II-841;
MPII:WF II-802
GREVE, FELIX PAUL. *See* GROVE,
FREDERICK PHILIP
GREY OWL
Sajo and the Beaver People,
MPII:JYAFic III-1259
GREY, VIVIAN
Chemist Who Lost His Head, The,
MPII:JYABio I-348
GRIDLEY, MARION E.
American Indian Women, MPII:JYABio
I-63
GRIFFIN, GERALD, CWA II-760
Collegians, The, CLC I-191; MP
II-1028; MP:BF I-234
GRIFFIN, JOHN HOWARD
Black Like Me, MPII:JYABio I-237
GRILLPARZER, FRANZ, CWA II-761
Jewess of Toledo, The, CLC I-547; MP
V-3008
Sappho, MP CLC II-1006, X-5793
GRIMKÉ, CHARLOTTE L. FORTEN
Journals of Charlotte Forten Grimké,
The, MPII:AfAm II-636
GRIMMELSHAUSEN, H. J. C. VON,
CWA II-763
Simplicissimus the Vagabond, CLC
II-1040; MP X-6053; MP:EF III-1155

GRIPE, MARIA
Hugo and Josephine, MPII:JYAFic
II-668
GROTIUS, HUGO, CWA II-765
On the Law of War and Peace, MP
VIII-4373
GROVE, FREDERICK PHILIP
Fruits of the Earth, CLCII II-554;
MPII:BCF II-553
Master of the Mill, The, CLCII III-987;
MPII:BCF III-1072
Search for America, A, CLCII III-1356;
MPII:BCF III-1472
Settlers of the Marsh, CLCII IV-1380;
MPII:BCF IV-1506
GRUBER, RUTH
Felisa Rincón de Gautier, MPII:JYABio
II-623
GRUŠA, JIÍ
Questionnaire, The, CLCII III-1249;
MPII:WF III-1240
GUARE, JOHN, CWAII II-641
House of Blue Leaves, The, CLCII
II-710; MPII:D II-789
Lydie Breeze, CLCII III-938; MPII:D
III-1007
GUBAR, SUSAN, *and* SANDRA M.
GILBERT, CWAII II-588
Madwoman in the Attic, The, MPII:NF
II-872
GUJÓNSSON, HALLDÓR KILJAN. *See*
LAXNESS, HALLDÓR
GUEST, JUDITH
Ordinary People, MPII:JYAFic III-1082
GUILLAUME DE LORRIS, *and* JEAN DE
MEUNG, CWA II-767
GUILLOT, RENÉ
Companions of Fortune, MPII:JYAFic
I-264
GUIMARÃES ROSA, JOÃO, CWAII
II-643
"Third Bank of the River, The," MPII:SS
VI-2341
GÜIRALDES, RICARDO, CWA II-768
Don Segundo Sombra, CLC I-296; MP
III-1609; MP:AF I-299
GUNN, THOM
"In Santa Maria del Popolo," MPII:P
III-1079
"On the Move," MPII:P IV-1593

GUNNARSSON, GUNNAR, CWA II-769
  Guest the One-Eyed, CLC I-432; MP
    IV-2416; MP:EF II-607
GUNTHER, JOHN
  Death Be Not Proud, MPII:JYABio I-459
GURKO, MIRIAM
  Ladies of Seneca Falls, The,
    MPII:JYABio III-1009
  Lives and Times of Peter Cooper, The,
    MPII:JYABio III-1101
  Restless Spirit, MPII:JYABio III-1486
GURNEY, A. R., JR., CWAII II-646
  Dining Room, The, CLCII I-402;
    MPII:D II-497
  Scenes from American Life, CLCII
    III-1345; MPII:D IV-1411
GUSTAFSSON, LARS
  Death of a Beekeeper, The, CLCII I-378;
    MPII:WF I-349
  Sigismund, CLCII IV-1403; MPII:WF
    IV-1419

  Tennis Players, The, CLCII IV-1525;
    MPII:WF IV-1560
GUTHRIE, A. B., JR., CWA II-771;
  CWAII II-648
  Big Sky, The, CLC I-102; MP I-531;
    MP:AF I-116
  These Thousand Hills, CLCII IV-1541;
    MPII:AF IV-1620
  Way West, The, CLCII IV-1698;
    MPII:AF IV-1773
GUTHRIE, WOODY
  Bound for Glory, MPII:JYABio I-256
GUTMAN, BILL
  Duke, MPII:JYABio II-525
GUY, ROSA
  Bird at My Window, MPII:AfAm I-136
  Disappearance, The, MPII:JYAFic I-341
  Friends, The, MPII:JYAFic II-478
  Measure of Time, A, MPII:AfAm II-788
GUZMÁN, MARTÍN LUIS, CWA II-772
  Eagle and the Serpent, The, MP III-1679;
    MP:AF I-322

H

HFIZ, CWA II-775
  Divan, The, MP III-1527
HAGEDORN, HERMANN
  Roosevelt Family of Sagamore Hill, The,
    MPII:JYABio IV-1509
HAGGARD, H. RIDER, CWA II-776
  King Solomon's Mines, CLC I-576; MP
    VI-3163; MP:BF II-751;
    MPII:JYAFic II-796
  She, CLC II-1029; MP X-5952; MP:BF
    III-1421
HAIG-BROWN, RODERICK
  Panther, MPII:JYAFic III-1109
HAKIM, TAWFIQ AL-, CWAII II-653
  Tree Climber, The, CLCII IV-1607;
    MPII:D IV-1648
  Voyage to Tomorrow, CLCII IV-1669;
    MPII:D IV-1706
HAKLUYT, RICHARD, CWA II-778
  Hakluyt's Voyages, MP V-2450
HALE, EDWARD EVERETT, CWA II-779
  Man Without a Country, The, CLC
    I-662; MP VII-3683; MP:AF II-744
HALE, NANCY, CWAII II-656
  "Empress's Ring, The," MPII:SS II-680
HALÉVY, LUDOVIC, CWA II-780
  Abbé Constantin, The, CLC I-1; MP I-1;
    MP:EF I-1
HALEY, ALEX, CWAII II-658
  Roots, MPII:AfAm III-1218; MPII:NF
    III-1251
HALL, ANNA GERTRUDE
  Nansen, MPII:JYABio III-1288
HALL, DONALD, CWA II-781
  One Day, The, MPII:P IV-1606
  Poetry of Hall, The, MP IX-4973
HALL, JAMES NORMAN, and
    CHARLES NORDOFF, CWA II-1314
  Mutiny on the Bounty, CLC II-749; MP
    VII-4099; MP:AF II-819;
    MPII:JYAFic III-1003
HALL, LYNN
  Giver, The, MPII:JYAFic II-523
HALL, RADCLYFFE, CWAII II-660
  "Miss Ogilvy Finds Herself," MPII:SS
    IV-1509
HAMILTON, ALEXANDER, CWA II-782

HAMILTON, ALEXANDER, JAMES
    MADISON, and JOHN JAY
  Federalist, The, MP IV-2025
HAMILTON, VIRGINIA
  Anthony Burns, MPII:JYABio I-121
  M. C. Higgins, the Great, MPII:AfAm
    II-783; MPII:JYAFic III-946
  Paul Robeson, MPII:JYABio III-1395
  Planet of Junior Brown, The,
    MPII:JYAFic III-1148
  Sweet Whispers, Brother Rush,
    MPII:AfAm III-1392; MPII:JYAFic
    IV-1421
  W. E. B. Du Bois, MPII:JYABio IV-1853
HAMMETT, DASHIELL, CWA II-787;
    CWAII II-662
  Glass Key, The, CLC I-403; MP
    IV-2267; MP:AF I-449
  "House in Turk Street, The," MPII:SS
    III-1045
  Maltese Falcon, The, CLC I-658; MP
    VI-3661; MP:AF II-740
  Thin Man, The, CLC II-1123; MP
    XI-6489; MP:AF III-1275
HAMMON, BRITON
  Narrative of the Uncommon Sufferings,
    and Surprizing Deliverance of Briton
    Hammon, a Negro Man, A,
    MPII:AfAm II-864
HAMSUN, KNUT, CWA II-788; CWAII
    II-664
  Growth of the Soil, CLC I-429; MP
    IV-2404; MP:EF II-599
  Hunger, CLC I-502; MP V-2780; MP:EF
    II-670
  Mysteries, CLCII III-1068; MPII:WF
    III-1059
  On Overgrown Paths, MPII:NF III-1082
  Pan, CLCII III-1172; MPII:WF III-1168
  Victoria, CLCII IV-1655; MPII:WF
    IV-1709
  Women at the Pump, The, CLCII
    IV-1733; MPII:WF IV-1779
HANDKE, PETER, CWAII II-667
  Across, CLCII I-11; MPII:WF I-20
  Goalie's Anxiety at the Penalty Kick,
    The, CLCII II-598; MPII:WF II-549
  Kaspar, CLCII II-816; MPII:D III-890

Left-Handed Woman, The, CLCII II-870; MPII:WF II-830

Moment of True Feeling, A, CLCII III-1029; MPII:WF III-1026

Offending the Audience, CLCII III-1132; MPII:D III-1164

Ride Across Lake Constance, The, CLCII III-1292; MPII:D III-1330

Short Letter, Long Farewell, CLCII IV-1395; MPII:WF IV-1398

Slow Homecoming, CLCII IV-1425; MPII:WF IV-1462

Sorrow Beyond Dreams, A, CLCII IV-1448; MPII:WF IV-1496

Weight of the World, The, MPII:NF IV-1675

HANLEY, JAMES
Dream Journey, A, CLCII II-423; MPII:BCF I-403

HANSBERRY, LORRAINE, CWAII II-669
Raisin in the Sun, A, CLCII III-1262; MPII:AfAm III-1189; MPII:D III-1300

Sign in Sidney Brustein's Window, The, CLCII IV-1404; MPII:AfAm III-1268; MPII:D IV-1458

HANSBERRY, LORRAINE, *as adapted by* ROBERT NEMIROFF
To Be Young, Gifted, and Black, MPII:JYABio IV-1732

HANSEN, JOYCE
Which Way Freedom? *and* Out from This Place, MPII:JYAFic IV-1620

HARDENBERG, FRIEDRICH VON. *See* NOVALIS

HARDWICK, ELIZABETH
Seduction and Betrayal, MPII:NF III-1324

HARDY, THOMAS, CWA II-791
"Channel Firing," MPII:P I-365

"Convergence of the Twain, The," MPII:P II-433

Dynasts, The, CLC I-310; MP III-1675

Far from the Madding Crowd, CLC I-356; MP IV-1990; MP:BF I-405

"Hap," MPII:P III-899

"In Tenebris," MPII:P III-1082

Jude the Obscure, CLC I-557; MP VI-3079; MP:BF II-721

Mayor of Casterbridge, The, CLC I-683; MP VII-3784; MP:BF II-896

Poetry of Hardy, The, MP IX-4976

Return of the Native, The, CLC II-959; MP X-5545; MP:BF III-1317

Tess of the D'Urbervilles, CLC II-1118; MP XI-6457; MP:BF III-1509

Under the Greenwood Tree, CLC II-1181; MP XII-6829; MP:BF III-1634

Woodlanders, The, CLC II-1263; MP XII-7247; MP:BF III-1764

HARE, DAVID, CWAII II-671
Plenty, CLCII III-1213; MPII:D III-1258

HARE, DAVID, *and* HOWARD BRENTON
Pravda, CLCII III-1232; MPII:D III-1278

HARJO, JOY
"Summer Night," MPII:P V-2093

HARNETT, CYNTHIA
Nicholas and the Wool-Pack, MPII:JYAFic III-1031

HARPER, FRANCES ELLEN WATKINS
Iola Leroy, MPII:AfAm II-614

HARPER, MICHAEL S.
"Dear John, Dear Coltrane," MPII:P II-491

Poetry of Michael S. Harper, The, MPII:AfAm III-1047

HARRIS, JANET
Woman Who Created Frankenstein, The, MPII:JYABio IV-1926

HARRIS, JOEL CHANDLER, CWA II-794
"Sad Fate of Mr. Fox, The," MPII:SS V-2002

Tales of Uncle Remus, MP XI-6384; MP:AF III-1256

"Wonderful Tar-Baby Story, The," MPII:SS VI-2684

HARRIS, MARK, CWAII II-673
Bang the Drum Slowly, CLCII I-112; MPII:AF I-111; MPII:JYAFic I-92

Southpaw, The, CLCII IV-1455; MPII:AF IV-1505

HARRIS, WILSON, CWAII II-675
Guyana Quartet, The, CLCII II-646; MPII:AfAm I-517; MPII:BCF II-679

HARRISON, TONY
"Continuous," MPII:P II-427

HART, KITTY
Return to Auschwitz, MPII:JYABio III-1493

HART, LORENZ, CWAII II-678
HART, MOSS, CWAII II-680
  Act One, MPII:JYABio I-9
HART, MOSS, *and* GEORGE S.
  KAUFMAN
  Man Who Came to Dinner, The, CLCII
    III-954; MPII:D III-1043
  Once in a Lifetime, CLCII III-1145;
    MPII:D III-1174
  You Can't Take It with You, CLCII
    IV-1764; MPII:D IV-1788
HARTE, BRET, CWA II-796
  Luck of Roaring Camp and Other
    Sketches, The, MP VI-3551; MP:AF
    II-713
  "Luck of Roaring Camp, The," MPII:SS
    IV-1412
  "Outcasts of Poker Flat, The," MPII:SS
    IV-1727
HARTLEY, L. P., CWAII II-682
  Go-Between, The, CLCII II-597;
    MPII:BCF II-612
HARTMANN VON AUE, CWA II-798
  Arme Heinrich, Der, CLC I-60; MP I-307
HAŠEK, JAROSLAV, CWA II-799
  Good Soldier, The, MP IV-2324; MP:EF
    II-580
HASKINS, JIM
  Ralph Bunche, MPII:JYABio III-1467
HAUGAARD, ERIK CHRISTIAN
  Leif the Unlucky, MPII:JYAFic II-826
  Samurai's Tale, The, MPII:JYAFic
    III-1263
HAUPTMANN, GERHART, CWA II-801
  Beaver Coat, The, CLC I-92;; MP I-469
  Sunken Bell, The, CLC II-1094; MP
    XI-6341
  Weavers, The, CLC II-1231; MP
    XII-7073
HAUTZIG, ESTHER RUDOMIN
  Endless Steppe, The, MPII:JYABio
    II-568
HAVEL, VÁCLAV, CWAII II-684
  Garden Party, The, CLCII II-567;
    MPII:D II-660
  Increased Difficulty of Concentration,
    The, CLCII II-757; MPII:D II-835
  Largo Desolato, CLCII II-851; MPII:D
    III-926
  Letters to Olga, MPII:NF II-825

Memorandum, The, CLCII III-995;
    MPII:D III-1077
  Temptation, CLCII IV-1523; MPII:D
    IV-1554
HAWKES, JOHN, CWA II-803
  Cannibal, The, MP II-763; MP:AF I-171
  Lime Twig, The, MP VI-3431; MP:AF
    II-684
HAWKINS, SIR ANTHONY HOPE. *See*
  HOPE, ANTHONY
HAWTHORNE, NATHANIEL, CWA
  II-806
  "Ambitious Guest, The," MPII:SS I-78
  American Notebooks, The, MP I-172
  "Artist of the Beautiful, The," MPII:SS
    I-122
  "Birthmark, The," MPII:SS I-210
  Blithedale Romance, The, CLC I-110;
    MP I-571; MP:AF I-131
  "Dr. Heidegger's Experiment," MPII:SS
    II-617
  English Notebooks, The, MP III-1784
  "Ethan Brand," MPII:SS II-720
  House of the Seven Gables, The, CLC
    I-491; MP V-2734; MP:AF II-572
  Marble Faun, The, CLC I-667; MP
    VII-3710; MP:AF II-756
  "Minister's Black Veil, The," MPII:SS
    IV-1501
  "My Kinsman, Major Molineux,"
    MPII:SS IV-1556
  "Rappaccini's Daughter," MPII:SS
    V-1897
  Scarlet Letter, The, CLC II-1009; MP
    X-5826; MP:AF III-1096
  "Wakefield," MPII:SS VI-2521
  "Young Goodman Brown," MPII:SS
    VI-2737
HAXTON, JOSEPHINE. *See* DOUGLAS,
  ELLEN
HAYDEN, ROBERT
  "Middle Passage," MPII:P IV-1379
  Poetry of Robert Hayden, The,
    MPII:AfAm III-1052
HAYDON, BENJAMIN ROBERT, CWA
  II-810
  Autobiography of Benjamin Robert
    Haydon, The, MP I-365
HAZLITT, WILLIAM, CWA II-812
  Critical Essays of William Hazlitt, The,
    MP II-1217

Familiar Essays of William Hazlitt, The,
  MP IV-1974
Liber Amoris, CLC I-609; MP VI-3379
H. D., CWA II-814; CWAII II-650
  End to Torment, MPII:NF II-454
  "Garden," MPII:P II-842
  "Oread," MPII:P IV-1617
  Poetry of H. D., The, MP IX-4979
  Tribute to Freud, MPII:NF IV-1558
  Trilogy, MPII:P VI-2277
HEAD, BESSIE, CWAII II-687
  "Collector of Treasures, The," MPII:SS
    I-413
  Maru, CLCII III-980; MPII:BCF III-1062
  Question of Power, A, CLCII III-1247;
    MPII:BCF III-1360
HEANEY, SEAMUS
  "Casualty," MPII:P I-351
  "Digging," MPII:P II-542
  "Field Work," MPII:P II-755
  "Forge, The," MPII:P II-804
  "Station Island," MPII:P V-2062
HEARN, LAFCADIO, CWA II-815
  Chita, CLC I-178; MP II-940; MP:AF
    I-200
  Youma, CLC II-1277; MP XII-7306;
    MP:AF III-1476
HEARON, SHELBY, and BARBARA
    JORDAN
  Barbara Jordan, MPII:JYABio I-172
HEATH, ROY A. K.
  Kwaku, MPII:AfAm II-659
  Murderer, The, CLCII III-1057;
    MPII:BCF III-1153
  Shadow Bride, The, MPII:AfAm III-1263
HEAT-MOON, WILLIAM LEAST
  Blue Highways, MPII:NF I-184
HEBBEL, FRIEDRICH, CWA II-817
  Maria Magdalena, CLC I-670; MP
    VII-3725
HEGGEN, THOMAS, CWA II-819
  Mister Roberts, CLC II-720; MP
    VII-3964; MP:AF II-796
HEIDENSTAM, VERNER VON, CWA
    II-820
  Tree of the Folkungs, The, CLC II-1153;
    MP XI-6679; MP:EF III-1297
HEINE, HEINRICH, CWA II-821
  Book of Songs, MP I-593
  "Hebrew Melodies," MPII:P III-924

North Sea, The, MPII:P IV-1511
HEINLEIN, ROBERT A., CWAII II-690
  "All You Zombies—", MPII:SS I-63
  Moon is a Harsh Mistress, The, CLCII
    III-1036; MPII:AF III-1037
  Stranger in a Strange Land, CLCII
    IV-1478; MPII:AF IV-153;
    MPII:JYAFic IV-1382
HEISER, VICTOR
  American Doctor's Odyssey, An,
    MPII:JYABio I-59
HELLER, ERICH, CWAII II-692
  Disinherited Mind, The, MPII:NF I-393
HELLER, JOSEPH, CWA II-824; CWAII
    II-694
  Catch-22, MP II-848; MP:AF I-181
  Something Happened, CLCII IV-1440;
    MPII:AF IV-1465
HELLMAN, LILLIAN, CWA II-826;
    CWAII II-696
  Children's Hour, The, CLCII I-279;
    MPII:D I-341
  Little Foxes, The, CLC I-620; MP
    VI-3451
  Pentimento, MPII:NF III-1135
  Unfinished Woman, An, MPII:NF
    IV-1607
  Watch on the Rhine, CLCII IV-1684;
    MPII:D IV-1712
HELPRIN, MARK, CWAII II-698
  "Schreuderspitze, The," MPII:SS V-2041
HEMINGWAY, ERNEST, CWA II-827;
    CWAII II-701
  Across the River and into the Trees,
    CLCII I-11; MPII:AF I-1
  "After the Storm," MPII:SS I-46
  "Alpine Idyll, An," MPII:SS I-66
  "Big Two-Hearted River," MPII:SS I-206
  "Canary for One, A," MPII:SS I-323
  "Clean, Well-Lighted Place, A,"
    MPII:SS I-406
  Death in the Afternoon, MPII:NF I-337
  Farewell to Arms, A, CLC I-357; MP
    IV-1995; MP:AF I-366
  For Whom the Bell Tolls, CLC I-374;
    MP IV-2114; MP:AF I-413
  Green Hills of Africa, MPII:NF II-595
  "Hills Like White Elephants," MPII:SS
    III-1018
  "In Another Country," MPII:SS III-1130
  "Indian Camp," MPII:SS III-1162

Islands in the Stream, CLCII II-780;
    MPII:AF II-803
"Killers, The," MPII:SS III-1259
Moveable Feast, A, MP VII-4087;
    MPII:JYABio III-1248
Old Man and the Sea, The, CLC II-804;
    MP VIII-4325; MP:AF II-874
"Short Happy Life of Francis Macomber,
    The," MPII:SS V-2088
Short Stories of Ernest Hemingway, The,
    MP X-6002; MP:AF III-1145
"Soldier's Home," MPII:SS V-2170
Sun Also Rises, The, CLC II-1093; MP
    XI-6335; MP:AF III-1238
"Three-Day Blow, The," MPII:SS
    VI-2358
To Have and Have Not, CLCII IV-1577;
    MPII:AF IV-1668
Torrents of Spring, The, CLCII IV-1593;
    MPII:AF IV-1682
HÉMON, LOUIS, CWA II-830
Maria Chapdelaine, CLC I-669; MP
    VII-3721; MP:AF II-769;
    MPII:JYAFic III-9172
HENKLE, HENRIETTA. See
    BUCKMASTER, HENRIETTA.
HENLEY, BETH, CWAII II-704
Crimes of the Heart, CLCII I-350;
    MPII:D I-407
HENLEY, WILLIAM ERNEST, CWA
    II-831
Poetry of Henley, The, MP IX-4982
HENRY, MARGUERITE
Benjamin West and His Cat Grimalkin,
    MPII:JYABio I-211
King of the Wind, MPII:JYAFic II-791
HENRY, O., CWA II-833
"Gift of the Magi, The," MPII:SS II-847
"Ransom of Red Chief, The," MPII:SS
    V-1894
Short Stories of O. Henry, The, MP
    X-6021; The, MP:AF III-1149
HENTOFF, NAT
Jazz Country, MPII:JYAFic II-752
HERBERT, FRANK, CWAII II-706
Dune trilogy, The, CLCII II-430;
    MPII:AF I-451; MPII:JYAFic I-363
HERBERT, GEORGE, CWA II-836
"Affliction (IV)," MPII:P I-19
"Banquet, The," MPII:P I-202

"Collar, The," MPII:P I-401
"Love (III)," MPII:P III-1276
"Pulley, The," MPII:P V-1751
Temple, The, MP XI-6432
HERBERT, XAVIER
Capricornia, CLCII I-234; MPII:BCF
    I-220
HERBERT, ZBIGNIEW, CWAII II-708
"Apollo and Marsyas," MPII:P I-94
Barbarian in the Garden, MPII:NF I-138
"Elegy of Fortinbras," MPII:P II-635
"Envoy of Mr. Cogito, The," MPII:P
    II-664
"Old Masters," MPII:P IV-1568
"Report from the Besieged City," MPII:P
    V-1807
"Why the Classics," MPII:P VI-2414
HEREDIA, JOSÉ MARÍA DE, CWA II-837
Poetry of Heredia, The, MP IX-4984
HERGESHEIMER, JOSEPH, CWA II-839
Java Head, CLC I-543; MP V-2985;
    MP:AF II-615
Three Black Pennys, The, CLC II-1126;
    The, MP XI-6500; MP:AF III-1279
HERLIHY, JAMES LEO, CWA II-840
All Fall Down, MP I-112
HERNÁNDEZ, JOSÉ, CWA II-841
Gaucho, The, CLC I-394; MP IV-2213
HERODOTUS, CWA II-842
History of the Persian Wars, The, MP
    V-2655
HERR, MICHAEL
Dispatches, MPII:NF I-398
HERRICK, ROBERT, CWA II-844
"Corinna's Going A-Maying," MPII:P
    II-443
"Delight in Disorder," MPII:P II-522
Hesperides, MP V-2606
"To the Virgins, to Make Much of
    Time," MPII:P VI-2230
HERRIOT, JAMES, CWAII II-710
All Creatures Great and Small,
    MPII:JYABio I-31; MPII:NF I-29
All Things Bright and Beautiful,
    MPII:JYABio I-39
All Things Wise and Wonderful,
    MPII:JYABio I-43
Lord God Made Them All, The,
    MPII:JYABio III-1124

HERSEY, JOHN, CWA II-846; CWAII
II-712
Bell for Adano, A, CLC I-96; MP I-488;
MP:AF I-104; MPII:JYABio
III-1081; MPII:JYAFic I-106
Call, The, CLCII I-227; MPII:AF I-237
Hiroshima, MPII:NF II-641
Life Sketches, MPII:JYABio III-1081
Wall, The, CLCII IV-1674; MPII:AF
IV-1748
HESIOD, CWA II-848
Works and Days, MP XII-7254
HESSE, HERMANN, CWA II-849; CWAII
II-714
Demian, CLCII I-386; MPII:JYAFic
I-333; MPII:WF I-364
Glass Bead Game, The, CLCII II-592;
MPII:WF II-543
Klingsor's Last Summer, CLCII II-839;
MPII:WF II-797
Narcissus and Goldmund, CLCII
III-1077; MPII:WF III-1074
"Poet, The," MPII:SS IV-1828
Rosshalde, CLCII III-1314; MPII:WF
III-1300
Siddhartha, CLCII IV-1400;
MPII:JYAFic IV-1334; MPII:WF
IV-1414
Steppenwolf, CLC II-1081; MP
XI-6250; MP:EF III-1221
"Within and Without," MPII:SS VI-2672
HEYEN, WILLIAM
"Ash, The," MPII:P I-123
"Ewigen Melodien," MPII:P II-706
HEYERDAHL, THOR
Kon-Tiki, MPII:JYABio III-1005
HEYWARD, DUBOSE, CWA II-851
Porgy, CLC II-902; MP IX-5247;
MP:AF II-968
HEYWOOD, THOMAS, CWA II-853
Woman Killed with Kindness, A, CLC
II-1257; MP XII-7217
HICKOK, LORENA A.
Touch of Magic, The, MPII:JYABio
IV-1759
HIGHWATER, JAMAKE, CWAII II-717
Ghost Horse cycle, The, MPII:JYAFic
II-504
Journey to the Sky, CLCII II-801;
MPII:AF II-814

HIJUELOS, OSCAR
Our House in the Last World,
MPII:JYAFic III-1089
HILDA DOOLITTLE. See H. D.
HILDESHEIMER, WOLFGANG, CWAII
II-719
Marbot, CLCII III-973; MPII:WF III-952
"World Ends, A," MPII:SS VI-2701
HILL, GEOFFREY
Mystery of the Charity of Charles Péguy,
The, MPII:P IV-1462
"Ovid in the Third Reich," MPII:P
IV-1626
"Requiem for the Plantagenet Kings,"
MPII:P V-1813
HILL, KAY
And Tomorrow the Stars, MPII:JYABio
I-94
HILL, LAWRENCE, ROBERT
PATTERSON, and MILDRED
MEBEL
On Our Way, MPII:JYABio III-1348
HILL, SUSAN, CWAII II-721
"Albatross, The," MPII:SS I-49
HILLESUM, ETTY
Interrupted Life, An, MPII:NF II-751
HILTON, JAMES, CWA II-855
Goodbye, Mr. Chips, CLC I-412; MP
IV-2328; MP:BF I-487
Lost Horizon, CLC I-629; MP VI-3512;
MP:BF II-833
HIMES, CHESTER, CWAII II-723
Autobiographies of Chester Himes, The,
MPII:AfAm I-65
If He Hollers Let Him Go, CLCII II-734;
MPII:AF II-778; MPII:AfAm II-575
HINTON, S. E.
Outsiders, The, MPII:JYAFic III-1093
HIRAOKA, KIMITAKE. See MISHIMA,
YUKIO
HIRAYAMA TGO. See IHARA,
SAIKAKU
HIROAKA, KIMITAKE. See MISHIMA,
YUKIO
HIRSCH, E. D., JR., CWAII II-726
Cultural Literacy, MPII:NF I-316
HOAGLAND, EDWARD, CWAII II-728
Notes from the Century Before,
MPII:NF III-1023

HOBAN, RUSSELL
  Mouse and His Child, The, MPII:JYAFic
    III-982
HOBBES, THOMAS, CWA II-857
  Leviathan, MP VI-3376
HOBBS, ANNE, *as told to* ROBERT
    SPECHT
  Tisha, MPII:JYABio IV-1729
HOCHHUTH, ROLF, CWAII II-731
  Deputy, The, CLCII I-393; MPII:D
    II-481
HODGES, CYRIL WALTER
  Columbus Sails, MPII:JYABio I-397
HODGES, MARGARET
  Lady Queen Anne, MPII:JYABio
    III-1013
HODGSON, RALPH, CWA II-858
  Poetry of Hodgson, The, MP IX-4986
HOEHLING, MARY
  Real Sherlock Holmes, The,
    MPII:JYABio III-1478
HOFFMANN, E. T. A., CWA II-860
  Devil's Elixir, The, CLC I-267; MP
    III-1467; MP:EF I-384
  Life and Opinions of Kater Murr, The,
    CLCII II-883; MPII:WF II-849
  "New Year's Eve Adventure, A,"
    MPII:SS IV-1616
  "Ritter Gluck," MPII:SS V-1964
  "Sandman, The," MPII:SS V-2020
  "Story of Serapion, The," MPII:SS
    V-2248
HOFMANNSTHAL, HUGO VON, CWA
    II-861
  Poetry of Hofmannsthal, The, MP
    IX-4988
HOFSTADTER, DOUGLAS R., CWAII
    II-734
  Gödel, Escher, Bach, MPII:NF II-561
HOGAN, LINDA
  "Black Hills Survival Gathering, 1980,"
    MPII:P I-243
HOLBROOK, STEWART
  America's Ethan Allen, MPII:JYABio
    I-71
HÖLDERLIN, JOHANN CHRISTIAN
    FRIEDRICH, CWA II-863
  "Bread and Wine," MPII:P I-276
  Poetry of Hölderlin, The, MP IX-4991
  "Spirit of the Age, The," MPII:P V-2046

"To the Fates," MPII:P VI-2218
HOLIDAY, BILLIE
  Lady Sings the Blues, MPII:AfAm
    II-664; MPII:JYABio III-1017
HOLLAND, ISABELLE
  Man Without a Face, The, MPII:JYAFic
    III-904
HOLM, ANNE
  I Am David, MPII:JYAFic II-676
HOLMAN, JOHN
  Stories of John Holman, The,
    MPII:AfAm III-1361
HOLMES, OLIVER WENDELL, CWA
    II-865
  Autocrat of the Breakfast-Table, The,
    MP I-379
HOLT, RACKHAM
  George Washington Carver,
    MPII:JYABio II-721
HOLUB, MIROSLAV
  "Fly, The," MPII:P II-780
HOMER, CWA II-868
  Iliad, The, CLC I-513; MP V-2837
  Odyssey, The, CLC II-788; MP VII-4275
HONGO, GARRETT KAORU
  "Morro Rock," MPII:P IV-1418
HONOUR, ALAN
  Tormented Genius, MPII:JYABio
    IV-1756
HOOBLER, DOROTHY, *and* THOMAS
    HOOBLER
  Voyages of Captain Cook, The,
    MPII:JYABio IV-1814
HOOK, DONALD D.
  Madmen of History, MPII:JYABio
    III-1143
HOOKS, BELL
  Yearning, MPII:AfAm III-1513
HOPE, A. D.
  "Imperial Adam," MPII:P III-1055
HOPE, ANTHONY, CWA II-870
  Prisoner of Zenda, The, CLC II-917; MP
    IX-5340; MP:BF III-1266;
    MPII:JYAFic III-1177
HOPKINS, GERARD MANLEY, CWA
    II-872
  "Felix Randal," MPII:P II-743
  "God's Grandeur," MPII:P III-864
  "Pied Beauty," MPII:P IV-1679
  Poetry of Hopkins, The, MP IX-4994

"That Nature Is a Heraclitean Fire and of the comfort of the Resurrection," MPII:P VI-2143

"Windhover, The," MPII:P VI-2423

"Wreck of the *Deutschland*, The," MPII:P VI-2461

HOPKINS, PAULINE
Contending Forces, MPII:AfAm I-313
Magazine Novels of Pauline Hopkins, The, MPII:AfAm II-742

HORACE, CWA II-874
Ars Poetica, MP I-319
Epistles of Horace, The, MP III-1808
Poetry of Horace, The, MP IX-4997

HORATIUS FLACCUS, QUINTUS. *See* HORACE

HORENSTEIN, IRVING. *See* HOWE, IRVING

HORGAN, PAUL, CWAII II-737
Citizen of New Salem, MPII:JYABio I-369
Great River, MPII:NF II-584
"National Honeymoon," MPII:SS IV-1590
"Peach Stone, The," MPII:SS IV-1782

HORTON, GEORGE MOSES
Poetry of George Moses Horton, The, MPII:AfAm III-1058

HOSPITAL, JANETTE TURNER
Borderline, CLCII I-193; MPII:BCF I-177
Ivory Swing, The, CLCII II-784; MPII:BCF II-843

HOTCHNER, A. E.
Papa Hemingway, MPII:JYABio III-1383

HOUSMAN, A. E., CWA II-876
Shropshire Lad, A, MP X-6030
"Terence, This Is Stupid Stuff," MPII:P VI-2133
"To an Athlete Dying Young," MPII:P VI-2197

HOUSTON, JEANNE WAKATSUKI, *and* JAMES D. HOUSTON
Farewell to Manzanar, MPII:JYABio II-611

HOWARD, FRED
Wilbur and Orville, MPII:JYABio IV-1869

HOWARD, HENRY, EARL OF SURREY, CWA II-878

HOWARD, HENRY, EARL OF SURREY, *and* SIR THOMAS WYATT
Poetry of Wyatt and Surrey, The, MP IX-5219

HOWE, EDGAR WATSON, CWA II-880
Story of a Country Town, The, CLC II-1083; MP XI-6268; MP:AF III-1231

HOWE, IRVING, CWAII II-740
Margin of Hope, A, MPII:NF III-901

HOWE, SUSAN
Defenestration of Prague, MPII:P II-511

HOWELL, MICHAEL, *and* PETER FORD
True History of the Elephant Man, The, MPII:JYABio IV-1774

HOWELLS, WILLIAM DEAN, CWA II-881
Hazard of New Fortunes, A, CLC I-446; MP V-2495; MP:AF II-535
Indian Summer, CLC I-522; MP V-2877; MP:AF II-591
Modern Instance, A, CLC II-730; MP VII-4010; MP:AF II-811
Rise of Silas Lapham, The, CLC II-973; MP X-5618; MP:AF III-1047

HRABAL, BOHUMIL
Closely Watched Trains, CLCII I-296; MPII:WF I-272

HUDSON, W. H., CWA II-884
Far Away and Long Ago, MP IV-1986
Green Mansions, CLC I-425; MP IV-2386; MP:BF I-497; MPII:JYAFic II-570
Hampshire Days, MP V-2462
Purple Land, The, CLC II-928; MP IX-5382; MP:BF III-1278

HUEFFER, FORD MADOX. *See* FORD, FORD MADOX

HUGHES, LANGSTON, CWA II-886; CWAII II-743
Big Sea, The, MPII:AfAm I-131; MPII:JYABio I-215; MPII:NF I-156
"Dream Variations," MPII:P II-605
Famous American Negroes, MPII:JYABio II-587
"Gospel Singers," MPII:SS II-918
"Harlem," MPII:P III-902
I Wonder as I Wander, MPII:AFAm I-131; MPII:JYABio II-897

"Negro Speaks of Rivers, The," MPII:P
IV-1478
Not Without Laughter, CLCII III-1113;
MPII:AF III-1155
Poetry of Langston Hughes, The,
MPII:AfAm III-1064
Stories of Langston Hughes, The,
MPII:AfAm III-1366
"Thank You, M'am," MPII:SS VI-2323
"Weary Blues, The," MPII:P VI-2384
HUGHES, RICHARD, CWA II-888
Innocent Voyage, The, CLC I-525; MP
V-2897; MP:BF II-649
HUGHES, TED
"Horses, The," MPII:P III-965
"Pike," MPII:P IV-1682
"Thought-Fox, The," MPII:P VI-2176
"Wodwo," MPII:P VI-2442
HUGHES, THOMAS, CWA II-889
Tom Brown's School Days, CLC
II-1141; MP XI-6585; MP:BF
III-1556; MPII:JYAFic IV-1491
HUGO, RICHARD
"Lady in Kicking Horse Reservoir, The,"
MPII:P III-1167
"Map of Montana in Italy, A," MPII:P
IV-1326
HUGO, VICTOR, CWA II-890
Hunchback of Notre Dame, The, CLC
I-500; MP V-2774; MP:EF II-663
Misérables, Les, CLC II-713; MP
VII-3931; MP:EF II-866
Poetry of Hugo, The, MP IX-5000
Toilers of the Sea, The, CLC II-1140;
MP XI-6581; MP:EF III-1293
HUIZINGA, JOHAN, CWA II-893
Waning of the Middle Ages, The, MP
XII-7017
HULME, KERI
Bone People, The, CLCII I-185;
MPII:BCF I-168
HUME, DAVID, CWA II-894
Enquiry Concerning Human
Understanding, An, MP III-1793
HUNGERFORD, PIXIE. See
BRINSMEAD, H. F.
HUNT, IRENE
Across Five Aprils, MPII:JYAFic I-4
Up a Road Slowly, MPII:JYAFic
IV-1550

HUNT, LEIGH, CWA II-896
Autobiography of Leigh Hunt, The, MP
I-373
HUNTER, KRISTIN
God Bless the Child, MPII:AfAm I-511
Soul Brothers and Sister Lou, The,
MPII:JYAFic IV-1364
HUNTER, MOLLIE
You Never Knew Her As I Did!,
MPII:JYAFic IV-1674
HURMENCE, BELINDA
Girl Called Boy, A, MPII:JYAFic II-516
HURSTON, ZORA NEALE, CWAII II-745
Dust Tracks on a Road, MPII:AfAm
I-390; MPII:JYABio II-529
Jonah's Gourd Vine, MPII:AfAm II-631
Moses, Man of the Mountain, CLCII
III-1041; MPII:AF III-1061;
MPII:AfAm II-823
Seraph on the Suwanee, MPII:AfAm
III-1257
"Sweat," MPII:SS V-2293
Their Eyes Were Watching God, CLCII
IV-1534; MPII:AF IV-1598;
MPII:AfAm III-1418
HUTCHINSON, A. S. M., CWA II-898
If Winter Comes, CLC I-513; MP
V-2831; MP:BF II-636
HUXLEY, ALDOUS, CWA II-899; CWAII
II-747
After Many a Summer Dies the Swan,
CLCII I-17; MPII:BCF I-22
Brave New World, CLC I-121; MP
II-631; MP:BF I-128; MPII:JYAFic
I-151
Crome Yellow, CLC I-225; MP
III-1226; MP:BF I-258
Essays of Aldous Huxley, The, MP
IV-1851
Eyeless in Gaza, CLCII II-480;
MPII:BCF I-478
Point Counter Point, CLC II-898; MP
IX-5227; MP:BF III-1237
HUXLEY, SIR JULIAN, CWA II-902
Essays of a Biologist, MP IV-1848
HUXLEY, THOMAS HENRY, CWA
II-904
Physical Basis of Life, The, MP
VIII-4677

I

IBÁÑEZ, VICENTE BLASCO. *See*
BLASCO IBÁÑEZ, VICENTE
IBARA, SAIKAKU, CWA II-910
Five Women Who Loved Love, CLC
I-372; MP IV-2082; MP:EF II-522
IBSEN, HENRIK, CWA II-912
Brand, CLC I-120; MP II-627
Doll's House, A, CLC I-284; MP
III-1570
Enemy of the People, An, CLC I-326;
MP III-1777
Ghosts, CLC I-399; MP IV-2250
Hedda Gabler, CLC I-454; MP V-2532
Lady from the Sea, The, CLC I-586; MP
VI-3206
Master Builder, The, CLC I-679; MP
VII-3759
Peer Gynt, CLC II-848; MP VIII-4559
Pillars of Society, The, CLC II-883; MP
VIII-4710
Rosmersholm, CLC II-995; MP X-5718
When We Dead Awaken, CLC II-1236;
MP XII-7100
Wild Duck, The, CLC II-1242; MP
XII-7137
ICAZA, JORGE, CWA II-916
Huasipungo, CLC I-494; MP V-2750
Villagers, The, MP:AF III-1375
IHARA, SAIKAKU, CWAII II-750
Life of an Amorous Man, The, CLCII
II-888; MPII:WF II-860
IKKU, JIPPENSHA. *See* JIPPENSHA IKKU
INFANTE, GUILLERMO CABRERA. *See*
CABRERA INFANTE, GUILLERMO
INGALLS, RACHEL, CWAII II-753
Mrs. Caliban, CLCII III-1024;
MPII:BCF III-1131
INGE, WILLIAM, CWAII II-755
Bus Stop, CLCII I-221; MPII:D I-267
Come Back, Little Sheba, CLCII I-310;
MPII:D I-387
Picnic, CLCII III-1207; MPII:D III-1252
INGOLDSBY, THOMAS, CWA II-917
Ingoldsby Legends, The, MP V-2891

INNAURATO, ALBERT, CWAII II-757
Transfiguration of Benno Blimpie, The,
CLCII IV-1599; MPII:D IV-1629
IONESCO, EUGÈNE, CWA II-919;
CWAII II-759
Bald Soprano, The, CLCII I-105;
MPII:D I-116
Chairs, The, CLCII I-255; MPII:D I-305
Exit the King, CLCII II-475; MPII:D
II-585
Killer, The, CLCII II-827; MPII:D III-905
Lesson, The, CLCII II-875; MPII:D III-954
Rhinoceros, MP X-5574
IRON, RALPH. *See* SCHREINER, OLIVE
IRVING, JOHN, CWAII II-762
Hotel New Hampshire, The, CLCII
II-703; MPII:AF II-743
Setting Free the Bears, CLCII IV-1378;
MPII:AF III-1392
World According to Garp, The, CLCII
IV-1749; MPII:AF IV-1825
IRVING, WASHINGTON, CWA II-921
"Adventure of the German Student,"
MPII:SS I-27
Chronicle of the Conquest of Granada,
A, MP II-950
"Devil and Tom Walker, The," MPII:SS
II-579
History of New York, A, MP V-2643
"Legend of Sleepy Hollow, The," CLC
I-606; MP VI-3314; MP:AF II-659;
MPII:SS III-1331
Legend of the Moor's Legacy, CLC
I-607; MP VI-3317; MP:AF II-663
"Rip Van Winkle," CLC II-972; MP
X-5611; MP:AF III-1044; MPII:SS
V-1957
ISBERT, MARGOT. *See* BENARY-
ISBERT, MARGOT
ISHERWOOD, CHRISTOPHER, CWAII
II-764
ISHERWOOD, CHRISTOPHER, *and* W.
H. AUDEN
Dog Beneath the Skin, The, CLCII
II-410; MPII:D II-507

J

JACKSON, CHARLES, CWA II-925
  Lost Weekend, The, CLC I-632; MP
    VI-3524; MP:AF II-710
JACKSON, GEORGE
  Soledad Brother, MPII:AfAm III-1288
JACKSON, JESSE
  Call Me Charley *and* Charley Starts from
    Scratch, MPII:JYAFic I-173
  Make a Joyful Noise unto the Lord!,
    MPII:JYABio III-1150
JACKSON, REGGIE
  Reggie, MPII:JYABio III-1482
JACKSON, SHIRLEY, CWAII II-766
  "Charles," MPII:SS I-359
  "Lottery, The," MPII:SS IV-1406
  "One Ordinary Day, with Peanuts,"
    MPII:SS IV-1705
JACOBS, DAVID
  Chaplin, the Movies, and Charlie,
    MPII:JYABio I-319
JACOBS, HARRIET
  Incidents in the Life of a Slave Girl,
    MPII:AfAm II-592
JACOBSEN, JENS PETER, CWA II-926
  Niels Lyhne, CLC II-776; MP VII-4205;
    MP:EF II-938
JACOBSON, DAN, CWAII II-768
  "Beggar My Neighbor," MPII:SS I-181
  Dance in the Sun, A, CLCII I-361;
    MPII:BCF I-350
  Wonder-Worker, The, CLCII IV-1738;
    MPII:BCF IV-1921
  "Zulu and the Zeide, The," MPII:SS
    VI-2745
JAKOUBEK, ROBERT
  Joe Louis, MPII:JYABio II-963
JAMES, C. L. R., CWAII II-770
  Essays of C. L. R. James, The,
    MPII:AfAm I-412
  Minty Alley, CLCII III-1012;
    MPII:AfAm II-811; MPII:BCF
    III-1109
JAMES, HENRY, CWA II-927; CWAII
    II-772
  "Altar of the Dead, The," MPII:SS I-70
  Ambassadors, The, CLC I-32; MP I-156;
    MP:AF I-44
  American Scene, The, MPII:NF I-44

American, The, CLC I-34; MP I-166;
    MP:AF I-49
  "Aspern Papers, The," CLCII I-77;
    MPII:SS I-125
  Awkward Age, The, MP I-387; MP:AF
    I-85
  "Beast in the Jungle, The," MPII:SS
    I-169
  Bostonians, The, MP I-605; MP:AF I-135
  Daisy Miller, CLC I-234; MP III-1270;
    MP:AF I-248
  "Figure in the Carpet, The," MPII:SS
    II-777
  Golden Bowl, The, CLC I-406; MP
    IV-2299; MP:AF I-469
  "Great Good Place, The," MPII:SS
    III-929
  "In the Cage," MPII:SS III-1141
  "Jolly Corner, The," MPII:SS III-1230
  "Lesson of the Master, The," MPII:SS
    III-1339
  Portrait of a Lady, The, CLC II-903; MP
    IX-5250; MP:AF II-971
  Princess Casamassima, The, MP
    IX-5327; MP:AF II-990
  "Pupil, The," MPII:SS V-1865
  "Real Thing, The," MPII:SS V-1905
  Roderick Hudson, MP X-5652; MP:AF
    III-1062
  Sacred Fount, The, MP X-5743; MP:AF
    III-1076
  Spoils of Poynton, The, CLC II-1078;
    MP XI-6228; MP:AF III-1202
  Tragic Muse, The, MP XI-6636; MP:AF
    III-1317
  "Tree of Knowledge, The," MPII:SS
    VI-2407
  Turn of the Screw, The, CLC II-1167;
    MP XI-6748; MP:AF III-1335;
    MPII:JYAFic IV-1528
  Washington Square, CLC II-1224; MP
    XII-7041; MP:AF III-1405
  What Maisie Knew, CLC II-1235; MP
    XII-7094; MP:AF III-1416
  Wings of the Dove, The, CLC II-1250;
    MP XII-7176; MP:AF III-1445
JAMES, M. R., CWAII II-775
  "Oh, Whistle, and I'll Come to You, My
    Lad," MPII:SS IV-1660

JAMES, WILL
  Smoky, the Cowhorse, MPII:JYAFic
  IV-1357
JAMES, WILLIAM, CWA II-931
  Pragmatism, MP IX-5287
JARRELL, RANDALL, CWA II-933
  Poetry of Jarrell, The, MP IX-5003
  "Thinking of the Lost World," MPII:P
  VI-2155
JARRY, ALFRED, CWAII II-777
  Ubu Roi, CLCII IV-1631; MPII:D
  IV-1676
JAY, JOHN, ALEXANDER HAMILTON,
  and JAMES MADISON
  Federalist, The, MP IV-2025
JAY, JOHN, CWA II-935
JEAN DE MEUNG and GUILLAUME DE
  LORRIS, CWA II-767
JEAN PAUL, CWAII II-779
  Titan, CLCII IV-1574; MPII:WF
  IV-1610
JEFFERS, ROBINSON, CWA II-937
  Cawdor, CLC I-161; MP II-858
  "Fire on the Hills," MPII:P II-765
  "Place for No Story, The," MPII:P
  IV-1688
  Poetry of Jeffers, The, MP IX-5006
  Roan Stallion, CLC II-977; MP X-5636
  "Rock and Hawk," MPII:P V-1842
  Tamar, CLC II-1103; MP XI-6393
JEFFERSON, THOMAS, CWA II-939
  Notes on the State of Virginia, MP
  VII-4260
JENKINS, ELIZABETH
  Elizabeth the Great, MPII:JYABio II-553
JENSEN, JOHANNES V., CWA II-943
  Long Journey, The, CLC I-623; MP
  VI-3477; MP:EF II-791
JEROME, JEROME K., CWA II-945
  Three Men in a Boat, CLC II-1127;
  MP:BF III-1532; MP XI-6508
JEWETT, SARAH ORNE, CWA II-946
  Country Doctor, A, CLC I-208; MP
  II-1149; MP:AF I-224
  Country of the Pointed Firs, The, CLC
  I-211; MP II-1158; MP:AF I-227
  Deephaven, CLC I-260; MP III-1409;
  MP:AF I-282
  "Miss Tempy's Watchers," MPII:SS
  IV-1513

"Native of Winby, A," MPII:SS IV-1594
"Town Poor, The," MPII:SS VI-2401
"White Heron, A," MPII:SS VI-2581
JHABVALA, RUTH PRAWER, CWAII
  II-782
  Esmond in India, CLCII II-468;
  MPII:BCF I-456
  Heat and Dust, CLCII II-671; MPII:BCF
  II-710
  Householder, The, CLCII II-716; The,
  MPII:BCF II-758
JIMÉNEZ, JUAN RAMÓN, CWA II-949
  Platero and I, MP VIII-4752; MP:EF
  III-1017
  Poetry of Jiménez, The, MP IX-5009
JIPPENSHA, IKKU, CWA II-951
  Hizakurige, CLC I-478; MP V-2667;
  MP:EF II-646
JOHNSON, CHARLES RICHARD,
  CWAII II-784
  Faith and the Good Thing, CLCII II-487;
  MPII:AF II-510; MPII:AfAm I-430
  Middle Passage, MPII:AfAm II-805
  Oxherding Tale, MPII:AfAm II-918
JOHNSON, DENIS
  Fiskadoro, MPII:JYAFic II-431
JOHNSON, DOROTHY M.
  Warrior for a Lost Nation, MPII:JYABio
  IV-1830
JOHNSON, EARVIN, and RICHARD
  LEVIN
  Magic, MPII:JYABio III-1146
JOHNSON, EDGAR
  Charles Dickens, MPII:JYABio I-336
JOHNSON, GERALD W.
  Franklin Delano Roosevelt,
  MPII:JYABio II-670
JOHNSON, JAMES WELDON, CWAII
  II-786
  Autobiography of an Ex-Coloured Man,
  The, CLCII I-92; MPII:AF I-81;
  MPII:AfAm I-72
JOHNSON, MARGUERITE. See
  ANGELOU, MAYA
JOHNSON, SAMUEL, CWA II-953
  Idler, The, MP V-2822
  Life of Richard Savage, MP VI-3406
  Lives of the Poets, MP VI-3468
  London, MPII:P III-1257

"On the Death of Dr. Robert Levet," MPII:P IV-1587

Poetry of Johnson, The, MP IX-5011

Preface to Shakespeare, MP IX-5299

Rambler, The, MP IX-5426

Rasselas, CLC II-941; MP IX-5441; MP:BF III-1293

Vanity of Human Wishes, The, MPII:P VI-2330

JOHNSON, UWE, CWA II-957; CWAII II-788

Anniversaries, CLCII I-53; MPII:WF I-55

Speculations About Jakob, MP XI-6219; MP:EF III-1218

JOHNSTON, MARY, CWA II-959

Great Valley, The, CLC I-423; MP IV-2372; MP:AF I-505

To Have and to Hold, CLCII IV-1578; MPII:AF IV-1673

JÓKAI, MAURUS, CWA II-961

Modern Midas, A, CLC II-731; MP VII-4015; MP:EF II-872

JOLLEY, ELIZABETH, CWAII II-790

Miss Peabody's Inheritance, CLCII III-1016; MPII:BCF III-1116

Well, The, CLCII IV-1703; MPII:BCF IV-1885

JOLYOT, PROSPER. See CRÉBILLON, PROSPER JOLYOT DE

JONES, DAVID

In Parenthesis, MPII:P III-1074

JONES, DIANA WYNNE

Charmed Life, MPII:JYAFic I-224

JONES, EVERETT LEROI. See BARAKA, AMIRI

JONES, GAYL

Corregidora, CLCII I-339; MPII:AF I-346; MPII:AfAm I-324

Eva's Man, CLCII II-471; MPII:AF II-481; MPII:AfAm I-424

JONES, HELEN L.

Robert Lawson, Illustrator, MPII:JYABio IV-1505

JONES, HENRY ARTHUR, CWA II-962

Michael and His Lost Angel, CLC II-699; MP VII-3873

Mrs. Dane's Defence, CLC II-724; MP VII-3978

JONES, JAMES, CWA II-963; CWAII II-792

From Here to Eternity, CLCII II-551; MPII:AF II-586

Thin Red Line, The, CLCII IV-1542; MPII:AF IV-1624

JONES, LADY. See BAGNOLD, ENID

JONES, LEROI. See BARAKA, AMIRI

JONES, PRESTON

Last Meeting of the Knights of the White Magnolia, The, CLCII II-854; MPII:D III-932

Lu Ann Hampton Laverty Oberlander, CLCII III-932; MPII:D III-997

Oldest Living Graduate, The, CLCII III-1139; MPII:D III-1169

JONSON, BEN, CWA II-965

Alchemist, The, CLC I-19; MP I-88

Bartholomew Fair, CLC I-86; MP I-446

Catiline, CLC I-159; MP II-852

Every Man in His Humour, CLC I-343; MP IV-1918

Every Man out of His Humour, CLC I-344; MP IV-1924

"Execration upon Vulcan, An," MPII:P II-712

Poetry of Jonson, The, MP IX-5014

Sejanus, CLC II-1019; MP X-5896

Silent Woman, The, CLC II-1039; MP X-6046

"Song: To Celia," MPII:P V-1950

"Still to be Neat," MPII:P V-2072

"To Penshurst," MPII:P VI-2212

"To the Memory of My Beloved Master William Shakespeare," MPII:P VI-2224

Volpone, CLC II-1213; MP XII-6978

JONSON, BEN, GEORGE CHAPMAN, and JOHN MARSTON

Eastward Ho! CLC I-313; MP III-1693

JORDAN, BARBARA, and SHELBY HEARON

Barbara Jordan, MPII:JYABio I-172

JORDAN, JUNE

His Own Where, MPII:AfAm II-535; His Own Where, MPII:JYAFic II-629

Poetry of June Jordan, The, MPII:AfAm III-1069

Technical Difficulties, MPII:AfAm III-1412

JOYCE, JAMES, CWA II-968; CWAII
    II-794
  "Araby," MPII:SS I-106
  "Boarding House, The," MPII:SS I-270
  "Clay," MPII:SS I-403
  "Counterparts," MPII:SS I-433
  "Dead, The," CLCII I-372; MPII:SS
    II-510
  "Eveline," MPII:SS II-724
  Exiles, CLC I-345; MP IV-1939
  Finnegans Wake, CLC I-370; MP
    IV-2076; MP:BF I-430
  "Ivy Day in the Committee Room,"
    MPII:SS III-1197
  "Little Cloud, A," MPII:SS III-1371
  Portrait of the Artist as a Young Man, A,
    CLC II-904; MP IX-5259; MP:BF
    III-1245; MPII:JYAFic III-1162
  "Sisters, The," MPII:SS V-2124
  "Two Gallants," MPII:SS VI-2439
  Ulysses, CLC II-1175; MP XII-6799;
    MP:BF III-1616
JUANA, SOR. See CRUZ, SOR JUANA
    INÉS DE LA
JUDSON, CLARA INGRAM
  Andrew Carnegie, MPII:JYABio I-98

George Washington, Leader of the
    People, MPII:JYABio II-713
  Mr. Justice Holmes, MPII:JYABio
    III-1230
  Soldier Doctor, MPII:JYABio IV-1581
  Thomas Jefferson, Champion of the
    People, MPII:JYABio IV-1698
JUGO, MIGUEL DE UNAMUNO Y. See
    UNAMUNO Y JUGO, MIGUEL DE
JULES-VERNE, JEAN
  Jules Verne, MPII:JYABio II-985
JUNG, CARL GUSTAV, CWA II-972;
    CWAII II-796
  Two Essays on Analytical Psychology,
    MP XII-6769
  Memories, Dreams, Reflections,
    MPII:NF III-928
JUSTER, NORTON
  Phantom Tollbooth, The, MPII:JYAFic
    III-1129
JUSTICE, DONALD
  "For a Freshman Reader," MPII:P II-783
JUVENAL, CWA II-974
  Satires, MP X-5812

K

KABAPHES, KONSTANTINOS P. *See*
  CAVAFY, CONSTANTINE P.
KAFKA, FRANZ, CWA II-975; CWAII
  II-799
  Amerika, CLCII I-40; MPII:WF I-45
  "Burrow, The," MPII:SS I-312
  Castle, The, CLC I-154; MP II-820;
    MP:EF I-185
  "Country Doctor, A," MPII:SS I-437
  Diaries of Kafka: 1910-1923, The, MP
    III-1491
  "Great Wall of China, The," MPII:SS
    III-932
  "Hunger Artist, A," MPII:SS III-1077
  "Hunter Gracchus, The," MPII:SS
    III-1081
  "In the Penal Colony," MPII:SS III-1154
  "Jackals and Arabs," MPII:SS III-1205
  "Josephine the Singer," MPII:SS III-1241
  Letters to Felice, MPII:NF II-819
  "Metamorphosis, The," CLCII III-999;
    MPII:SS IV-1493
  "Report to an Academy, A," MPII:SS
    V-1929
  Trial, The, CLC II-1155; MP XI-6687;
    MP:EF III-1302
KAGAN, ANDREW
  Marc Chagall, MPII:JYABio III-1170
KAHN, ROGER
  Boys of Summer, The, MPII:NF I-206
KALIDASA, CWA II-977
  Sakuntala, CLC II-1001; MP X-5765
KANE, CHEIKH HAMIDOU, CWAII
  II-802
  Ambiguous Adventure, CLCII I-34;
    MPII:WF I-39
KANT, IMMANUEL, CWA II-978
  Critique of Pure Reason, MP II-1220
KANTOR, MACKINLAY
  Lee and Grant at Appomattox,
    MPII:JYABio III-1048
KANTOR, TADEUSZ, CWAII II-804
  Dead Class, The, CLCII I-373; MPII:D
    II-456
  Wielopole, Wielopole, CLCII IV-1717;
    MPII:D IV-1745
KAO MING. *See* KAO TSE-CH'ENG

KAO TSE-CH'ENG, CWA II-980
  Story of the Guitar, CLC II-1088; MP
    XI-6288
KAPUCISKI, RYSZARD, CWAII II-806
  Emperor, The, MPII:NF II-449
  Shah of Shahs, MPII:NF IV-1341
KARP, WALTER
  Charles Darwin and the Origin of
    Species, MPII:JYABio I-326
KÄSTNER, ERICH
  When I Was a Boy, MPII:JYABio
    IV-1865
KAUFMAN, GEORGE S., CWAII II-809
KAUFMAN, GEORGE S., *and* MOSS
  HART
  Man Who Came to Dinner, The, CLCII
    III-954; MPII:D III-1043
  Once in a Lifetime, CLCII III-1145;
    MPII:D III-1174
  You Can't Take It with You, CLCII
    IV-1764; MPII:D IV-1788
KAUFMAN, LOUIS, BARBARA
  FITZGERALD, *and* TOM SEWELL
  Moe Berg, MPII:JYABio III-1233
KAVAN, ANNA
  Ice, CLCII II-730; MPII:BCF II-782
  "Julia and the Bazooka," MPII:SS
    III-1245
KAVANAGH, PATRICK, CWAII II-811
  Green Fool, The, MPII:NF II-589
  Great Hunger, The, MPII:P III-882
KAWABATA, YASUNARI, CWA II-981;
  CWAII II-813
  Beauty and Sadness, CLCII I-128;
    MPII:WF I-136
  House of the Sleeping Beauties, The,
    CLCII II-712; MPII:WF II-629
  Master of Go, The, CLCII III-986;
    MPII:WF III-983
  Snow Country, CLCII IV-1433;
    MPII:WF IV-1475
  Sound of the Mountain, The, CLCII
    IV-1450; MPII:WF IV-1501
  Thousand Cranes, CLCII IV-1554;
    MPII:WF IV-1589
KAYE-SMITH, SHEILA, CWA II-982
  Joanna Godden, CLC I-548; MP
    V-3012; MP:BF II-687

KAZANTZAKIS, NIKOS, CWA II-984;
CWAII II-816
Freedom or Death, MP IV-2166; MP:EF
II-543
Greek Passion, The, MP IV-2375;
MP:EF II-589
Last Temptation of Christ, The, CLCII
II-859; MPII:WF II-820
Zorba the Greek, MP XII-7331; MP:EF
III-1435
KAZIMIROFF, THEODORE L.
Last Algonquin, The, MPII:JYABio
III-1033
KAZIN, ALFRED
Starting Out in the Thirties, MPII:NF
IV-1427
Walker in the City, A, MPII:NF IV-1651
KEATS, JOHN, CWA II-986
"Belle Dame sans Merci, La," MPII:P
I-222
Endymion, MPII:P II-657
Eve of St. Agnes, The, CLC I-340; MP
IV-1909
Hyperion, MPII:P III-998
"Lamia," MPII:P III-1185
Letters of John Keats, The, MP VI-3350
"Ode on a Grecian Urn," MPII:P IV-1538
"Ode on Melancholy," MPII:P IV-1541
"Ode to a Nightingale," MPII:P IV-1544
"Ode to Psyche," MPII:P IV-1550
"On First Looking into Chapman's
Homer," MPII:P IV-1578
"To Autumn," MPII:P VI-2200
KEENE, CAROLYN
Nancy Drew series, The, MPII:JYAFic
III-1019
KEIL, SALLY VAN WAGENEN
Those Wonderful Women in Their Flying
Machines, MPII:JYABio IV-1705
KEITH, HAROLD
Rifles for Watie, MPII:JYAFic III-1224
KELLER, GOTTFRIED, CWA II-989
Grüne Heinrich, Der, CLC I-430; MP
IV-2408; MP:EF II-603
KELLER, HELEN
Story of My Life, The, MPII:JYABio
IV-1622
KELLEY, EDITH SUMMERS
Weeds, CLCII IV-1702; MPII:AF
IV-1777

KELLEY, WILLIAM MELVIN, CWAII
II-819
Dem, MPII:AfAm I-351
Different Drummer, A, CLCII I-400;
MPII:AF I-404; MPII:AfAm I-368
"Visit to Grandmother, A," MPII:SS
VI-2510
KELLOGG, MARJORIE
Tell Me That You Love Me, Junie
Moon, CLCII IV-1520; MPII:AF
IV-1568
KELLY, ERIC P.
Trumpeter of Krakow, The,
MPII:JYAFic IV-1511
KELLY, ROBERT
Loom, The, MPII:P III-1261
KEMAL, YASHAR, CWAII III-821
Iron Earth, Copper Sky, CLCII IV-1718;
MPII:WF IV-1754
Memed, My Hawk, CLCII III-993;
MPII:WF III-999
Undying Grass, The, CLCII IV-1718;
MPII:WF IV-1754
Wind from the Plain, The, CLCII
IV-1718; MPII:WF IV-1754
KEMP, GENE
Turbulent Term of Tyke Tiler, The,
MPII:JYAFic IV-1524
KEMPIS, THOMAS À. See THOMAS À
KEMPIS
KENAN, RANDALL
Let the Dead Bury Their Dead,
MPII:AfAm II-699
Visitation of Spirits, A, MPII:AfAm
III-1473
KENDALL, CAROL
Gammage Cup, The, MPII:JYAFic II-485
KENEALLY, THOMAS, CWAII III-824
Chant of Jimmie Blacksmith, The,
CLCII I-262; MPII:BCF I-247
Confederates, CLCII I-322; MPII:BCF
I-312
Gossip from the Forest, CLCII II-621;
MPII:BCF II-655
Survivor, The, CLCII IV-1499;
MPII:BCF IV-1649
KENNEDY, ADRIENNE, CWAII III-827
Funnyhouse of a Negro, CLCII II-558;
MPII:AfAm I-474; MPII:D II-645

Rat's Mass, A, CLCII III-1269;
MPII:AfAm III-1194; MPII:D
III-1305
KENNEDY, JOHN F.
Profiles in Courage, MPII:JYABio
III-1439
KENNEDY, JOHN PENDLETON, CWA
II-990
Horseshoe Robinson, CLC I-483; MP
V-2702; MP:AF II-563
Swallow Barn, CLC II-1098; MP
XI-6359; MP:AF III-1248
KENNEDY, JOSEPH CHARLES. See
KENNEDY, X. J.
KENNEDY, WILLIAM, CWAII III-829
Albany Cycle, The, MPII:AF I-18
Billy Phelan's Greatest Game, CLCII
I-154
Ironweed, CLCII II-776
Legs, CLCII II-871
KENNEDY, X. J.
"Cross Ties," MPII:P II-470
KENNER, HUGH, CWAII III-831
Counterfeiters, The, MPII:NF I-275
KENWORTHY, LEONARD S.
Twelve Citizens of the World,
MPII:JYABio IV-1781
KENZABUR E. See E, KENZABUR
KEROUAC, JACK, CWAII III-834
Dharma Bums, The, CLCII I-397;
MPII:AF I-394
On the Road, CLCII III-1145; MPII:AF
III-1193
KERR, M. E.
If I Love You, Am I Trapped Forever?,
MPII:JYAFic II-691
Is That You, Miss Blue?, MPII:JYAFic
II-723
Me, Me, Me, Me, Me, MPII:JYABio
III-1199
KESEY, KEN, CWAII III-837
One Flew over the Cuckoo's Nest,
CLCII III-1149; MPII:AF III-1203
Sometimes a Great Notion, CLCII
IV-1442; MPII:AF IV-1476
KETCHUM, RICHARD M.
Will Rogers, MPII:JYABio IV-1876
KHERDIAN, DAVID
Road from Home, The, MPII:JYABio
IV-1501

KIELY, BENEDICT, CWAII III-839
Captain with the Whiskers, The, CLCII
I-237; MPII:BCF I-225
"Heroes in the Dark House, The,"
MPII:SS III-1011
Nothing Happens in Carmincross, CLCII
III-1115; MPII:BCF III-1228
KIERKEGAARD, SÖREN, CWA II-992
Sickness unto Death, The, MP X-6032
KIMITAKE HIRAOKA. See MISHIMA,
YUKIO
KINCAID, JAMAICA, CWAII III-841
Annie John, MPII:AfAm I-35
"At the Bottom of the River," MPII:SS
I-135
At the Bottom of the River, MPII:AfAm I-52
Lucy, MPII:AfAm II-730
KING, CORETTA SCOTT
My Life with Martin Luther King, Jr.,
MPII:AfAm II-848
KING, FRANCIS
Custom House, The, CLCII I-357;
MPII:BCF I-344
KING, MARTIN LUTHER, JR.
Speeches of Martin Luther King, Jr.,
The, III-1314
KING, STEPHEN, CWAII III-843
Danse Macabre, MPII:NF I-327
Shining, The, CLCII III-1393; MPII:AF
IV-1407; MPII:JYAFic IV-1325
Stand, The, CLCII IV-1470; MPII:AF
IV-1532
KINGMAN, LEE
Peter Pan Bag, The, MPII:JYAFic
III-1126
KINGSLEY, CHARLES, CWA II-994
Hereward the Wake, CLC I-470; MP
V-2591; MP:BF I-566
Hypatia, CLC I-504; MP V-2794;
MP:BF II-627
Westward Ho! CLC II-1233; MP
XII-7084; MP:BF III-1726
KINGSLEY, HENRY, CWA II-996
Ravenshoe, CLC II-942; MP IX-5446;
MP:BF III-1298
KINGSTON, MAXINE HONG, CWAII
III-846
China Men, MPII:NF I-244
Woman Warrior, The, MPII:JYABio
IV-1922; MPII:NF IV-1709

KINNELL, GALWAY
  "Avenue Bearing the Initial of Christ
    into the New World, The," MPII:P
    I-181
  "Blackberry Eating," MPII:P I-253
KINSELLA, THOMAS
  "Country Walk, A," MPII:P II-461
KIPLING, RUDYARD, CWA II-998
  Brushwood Boy, The, CLC I-130; MP
    II-696; MP:BF I-143
  Captains Courageous, CLC I-150; MP
    II-787; MP:BF I-173; MPII:JYAFic
    I-191
  "Gardener, The," MPII:SS II-828
  Jungle Books, The, CLC I-561; MP
    VI-3097; MP:BF II-731;
    MPII:JYAFic II-767
  Kim, CLC I-568; MP VI-3130; MP:BF
    II-743; MPII:JYAFic II-781
  "Lispeth," MPII:SS III-1367
  "Man Who Would Be King, The,"
    CLCII III-960; MPII:SS IV-1447
  Poetry of Kipling, The, MP IX-5019
  "Recessional," MPII:P V-1777
  "Strange Ride of Morrowbie Jukes,
    The," MPII:SS V-2252
  "They," MPII:SS VI-2337
  "Thrown Away," MPII:SS VI-2362
  "White Man's Burden, The," MPII:P
    VI-2400
  "Wireless," MPII:SS VI-2656
  "Wish House, The," MPII:SS VI-2660
KIRKLAND, JACK
  Tobacco Road, CLCII IV-1582; MPII:D
    IV-1596
KIŠ, DANILO, CWAII III-849
  Garden, Ashes, CLCII II-564; MPII:WF
    II-507
  Pešanik, CLCII III-1197; MPII:WF
    III-1199
  Tomb for Boris Davidovich, A, CLCII
    IV-1586; MPII:WF IV-1629
KIZER, CAROLYN
  "Pro Femina," MPII:P V-1733
KLEE, PAUL, CWAII III-851
  Diaries of Paul Klee, The, MPII:NF I-361
KLEIN, JOE
  Woody Guthrie, MPII:JYABio IV-1945
KLEIN, MINA C., and H. ARTHUR
  KLEIN
  Käthe Kollwitz, MPII:JYABio II-993

KLEIN, NORMA
  Mom, the Wolf Man, and Me,
    MPII:JYAFic III-975
  Sunshine, MPII:JYAFic IV-1410
KLEIST, HEINRICH VON, CWA II-1001;
    CWAII III-853
  "Beggarwoman of Locarno, The,"
    MPII:SS I-184
  Broken Jug, The, CLC I-127; MP II-671
  "Earthquake in Chile, The," MPII:SS
    II-661
  "Engagement in Santo Domingo, The,"
    MPII:SS II-698
  "Marquise of O——, The," CLCII III-976;
    MPII:SS IV-1466
  Prince of Homburg, The, CLC II-916;
    MP IX-5321
KLIMENTOV, ANDREI
    PLATONOVICH. See PLATONOV,
    ANDREI
KNIGHT, ERIC, CWA II-1003
  Lassie Come-Home, MPII:JYAFic II-810
  This Above All, CLC II-1124; MP
    XI-6497; MP:BF III-1528
KNIGHT, ETHERIDGE
  Poetry of Etheridge Knight, The,
    MPII:AfAm III-1074
KNOBLER, PETER, and KAREEM
  ABDUL-JABBAR
  Giant Steps, MPII:JYABio II-749
KNOWLES, JOHN, CWAII III-855
  Separate Peace, A, CLCII III-1373;
    MPII:AF III-1387; MPII:JYAFic
    III-1308
KOCH, C. J.
  Year of Living Dangerously, The, CLCII
    IV-1760; MPII:BCF IV-1955
KOEHN, ILSE
  Mischling, Second Degree,
    MPII:JYABio III-1222
KOESTLER, ARTHUR, CWA II-1004
  Darkness at Noon, CLC I-242; MP
    III-1321; MP:EF I-342
KOMROFF, MANUEL
  Mozart, MPII:JYABio III-1252
  Napoleon, MPII:JYABio III-1296
KOMUNYAKAA, YUSEF
  Poetry of Yusef Komunyakaa, The,
    MPII:AfAm III-1079

KONIGSBERG, ALLEN STEWART. See
    ALLEN, WOODY
KONIGSBURG, E. L.
    From the Mixed-up Files of Mrs. Basil
    E. Frankweiler, MPII:JYAFic II-481
KONRÁD, GEORGE, CWAII III-857
    City Builder, The, CLCII I-292;
    MPII:WF I-267
    Loser, The, CLCII III-915; MPII:WF
    II-884
KONWICKI, TADEUSZ, CWAII III-859
    Dreambook for Our Time, A, CLCII
    II-426; MPII:WF I-395
    Minor Apocalypse, A, CLCII III-1011;
    MPII:WF III-1006
    Moonrise, Moonset, CLCII III-1037;
    MPII:WF III-1041
    Polish Complex, The, CLCII III-1218;
    MPII:WF III-1207
KOPIT, ARTHUR, CWAII III-862
    Indians, CLCII II-759; MPII:D II-840
    Wings, CLCII IV-1725; MPII:D IV-1751
KOPS, BERNARD
    Ezra, CLCII II-481; MPII:D II-590
    Hamlet of Stepney Green, The, CLCII
    II-653; MPII:D II-732
KORCZAK, JANUSZ
    King Matt the First, MPII:JYAFic II-784
KORZENIOWSKI, JÓSEF TEODOR
    KONRAD NALECZ. See CONRAD,
    JOSEPH
KOSINSKI, JERZY, CWAII III-864
    Painted Bird, The, CLCII III-1170;
    MPII:AF III-1243
KOSTROWITSKY, WILHELM
    APOLLINARIS DE. See
    APOLLINAIRE, GUILLAUME
KRENSKY, STEPHEN
    Conqueror and Hero, MPII:JYABio I-409
KRENTS, HAROLD
    To Race the Wind, MPII:JYABio
    IV-1736
KROEBER, THEODORA
    Ishi, Last of His Tribe, MPII:JYABio
    II-926

KRUMGOLD, JOSEPH
    ... And Now Miguel, MPII:JYAFic I-35
    Onion John, MPII:JYAFic III-1073
KRUTCH, JOSEPH WOOD
    Henry David Thoreau, MPII:JYABio
    II-826
KUBIAK, DANIEL JAMES
    Ten Tall Texans, MPII:JYABio IV-1672
KUDLINSKI, KATHLEEN V.
    Rachel Carson, MPII:JYABio III-1463
KUGELMASS, J. ALVIN
    Ralph J. Bunche, MPII:JYABio III-1471
KUHN, THOMAS S., CWAII III-867
    Structure of Scientific Revolutions, The,
    MPII:NF IV-1452
KUMIN, MAXINE
    "You Are in Bear Country," MPII:P
    VI-2482
KUNDERA, MILAN, CWAII III-870
    Book of Laughter and Forgetting, The,
    CLCII I-190; MPII:WF I-174
    "Edward and God," MPII:SS II-664
    Farewell Party, The, CLCII II-494;
    MPII:WF I-446
    "Hitchhiking Game, The," MPII:SS
    III-1026
    Joke, The, CLCII II-795; MPII:WF
    II-766
    Life Is Elsewhere, CLCII II-886;
    MPII:WF II-855
    Unbearable Lightness of Being, The,
    CLCII IV-1633; MPII:WF IV-1689
KUNITZ, STANLEY
    "Father and Son," MPII:P II-734
    "Three Floors," MPII:P VI-2179
KUPFERBERG, HERBERT
    Felix Mendelssohn, MPII:JYABio II-627
KYD, THOMAS, CWA II-1006
    Spanish Tragedy, The, CLC II-1076; MP
    XI-6211
KYLE, ELISABETH
    Girl with a Pen, MPII:JYABio II-765
KÄSTNER, ERICH
    Emil and the Detectives, MPII:JYAFic
    I-383
KYDEN, SANT. See SANT KYDEN

L

LABRUNIE, GÉRARD. *See* NERVAL, GERARD DE

LACAN, JACQUES, CWAII III-873
Écrits, MPII:NF I-425

LACLOS, PIERRE CHODERLOS DE, CWA II-1008
Dangerous Acquaintances, CLC I-236; MP III-1299; MP:EF I-330

LACY, LESLIE ALEXANDER
Cheer the Lonesome Traveler, MPII:JYABio I-344

LA FARGE, OLIVER, CWAII III-876
Laughing Boy, CLCII II-860; MPII:AF II-860

LA FAYETTE, MADAME MARIE DE, CWA II-1009
Princess of Clèves, The, CLC II-917; MP IX-5330; MP:EF III-1034

LA FONTAINE, JEAN DE, CWA II-1010
Fables, MP IV-1951

LAFORGUE, JULES, CWA II-1012
Poetry of Laforgue, The, MP IX-5022

LAGERKVIST, PÄR, CWA II-1014; CWAII III-878
Barabbas, CLC I-78; MP I-419; MP:EF I-96
"Children's Campaign, The," MPII:SS I-380
Dwarf, The, CLCII II-435; MPII:WF I-399
Sibyl, The, CLCII IV-1399; MPII:WF IV-1409
Tobias Trilogy, The, CLCII IV-1583; MPII:WF IV-1623

LAGERLÖF, SELMA, CWA II-1016
Diary of Selma Lagerlöf, The, MPII:NF I-380
"Silver Mine, The," MPII:SS V-2116
Story of Gösta Berling, The, CLC II-1087; MP XI-6281; MP:EF III-1236
Wonderful Adventures of Nils, The, MPII:JYAFic IV-1653

LA GUMA, ALEX
Walk in the Night, A, CLCII IV-1672; MPII:BCF IV-1837

LAMARTINE, ALPHONSE DE, CWA II-1018
Poetry of Lamartine, The, MP IX-5025

LAMB, CHARLES, CWA II-1020
Essays of Elia and Last Essays of Elia, MP IV-1857
Letters of Charles Lamb, The, MP VI-3341

LAMBERT, GAVIN
"Slide Area, The," MPII:SS V-2132

LAMMING, GEORGE, CWAII III-881
In the Castle of My Skin, CLCII II-747; MPII:AfAm II-581; MPII:BCF II-809
Natives of My Person, CLCII III-1078; MPII:AfAm II-881; MPII:BCF III-1176
Season of Adventure, CLCII III-1360; MPII:AfAm III-1246; MPII:BCF III-1476

LA MOTTE-FOUQUÉ, FRIEDRICH DE, CWA II-1023
Undine, CLC II-1186; MP XII-6852; MP:EF III-1338

LAMPEDUSA, GIUSEPPE TOMASI DI. *See* TOMASI DI LAMPEDUSA, GIUSEPPE

LANDOLFI, TOMMASO
"Gogol's Wife," MPII:SS II-871

LANDON, MARGARET
Anna and the King of Siam, MPII:JYABio I-114

LANDOR, WALTER SAVAGE, CWA II-1025
Imaginary Conversations, MP V-2842
Poetry of Landor, The, MP IX-5028

LANE, MARGARET
Tale of Beatrix Potter, The, MPII:JYABio IV-1656

LANGLAND, WILLIAM, CWA II-1027
Vision of William, Concerning Piers the Plowman, The, CLC II-1212; MP XII-6965

LANIER, SIDNEY, CWA II-1028
Poetry of Lanier, The, MP IX-5032

LAO SHE, CWAII III-883
Rickshaw, CLCII III-1291; MPII:WF III-1278;

LARDNER, RING, CWA II-1030
"Golden Honeymoon, The," MPII:SS II-893
"Haircut," MPII:SS II-970

"Harmony," MPII:SS II-989
"Some Like Them Cold," MPII:SS
 V-2173
You Know Me Al, CLC II-1276; MP
 XII-7303; MP:AF III-1472
LARKIN, PHILIP, CWA II-1032; CWAII
 III-886
 "Building, The," MPII:P I-307
 "Church Going," MPII:P I-380
 "Dockery and Son," MPII:P II-572
 Girl in Winter, A, CLCII II-589;
  MPII:BCF II-597
 "High Windows," MPII:P III-945
 Jill, CLCII II-790; MPII:BCF II-857
 Poetry of Larkin, The, MP IX-5035
 "Reasons for Attendance," MPII:P
  V-1774
 "Toads," MPII:P VI-2237
 "Whitsun Weddings, The," MPII:P
  VI-2407
LA ROCHEFOUCAULD, FRANÇOIS,
 CWA II-1033
 Maxims, The, MP VII-3782
LARSEN, NELLA, CWAII III-888
 Passing, CLCII III-1182; MPII:AF
  III-1253; MPII:AfAm II-929
 Quicksand, CLCII III-1250; MPII:AF
  III-1296; MPII:AfAm III-1183
LARSEN, REBECCA
 Oppenheimer and the Atomic Bomb,
  MPII:JYABio III-1359
LASH, JOSEPH P.
 Eleanor and Franklin, MPII:JYABio II-545
LATHAM, JEAN LEE
 Anchor's Aweigh, MPII:JYABio I-90
 Carry on, Mr. Bowditch, MPII:JYABio
  I-296
 Far Voyager, MPII:JYABio II-607
LAURENCE, MARGARET, CWAII III-890
 Diviners, The, CLCII I-407; MPII:BCF
  I-383
 Fire-Dwellers, The, CLCII II-506;
  MPII:BCF II-509
 Loons, The," MPII:SS IV-1399
 Stone Angel, The, CLCII IV-1475;
  MPII:BCF IV-1614
LAVIN, MARY
 "Nun's Mother, The," MPII:SS IV-1640
 "Widow's Son, The," MPII:SS VI-2616
 "Will, The," MPII:SS VI-2623

LAWLER, RAY
 Summer of the Seventeenth Doll, CLCII
  IV-1493; MPII:D IV-1520
LAWRENCE, D. H., CWA II-1035;
 CWAII III-892
 Aaron's Rod, CLCII I-1; MPII:BCF I-1
 Apocalypse, MPII:NF I-85
 "Bavarian Gentians," MPII:P I-208
 Collected Letters of D. H. Lawrence,
  The, MP II-1019
 Fox, The, CLCII II-541; MPII:BCF
  II-538
 "Horse Dealer's Daughter, The,"
  MPII:SS III-1041
 Kangaroo, CLCII II-812; MPII:BCF
  II-877
 Lady Chatterley's Lover, CLCII II-842;
  MPII:BCF II-927
 Mornings in Mexico, MPII:NF III-976
 "Odour of Chrysanthemums," MPII:SS
  IV-1648
 "Piano," MPII:P IV-1672
 Plumed Serpent, The, CLC II-895; MP
  VIII-4765; MP:BF III-1232
 Poetry of Lawrence, The, MP IX-5037
 "Prussian Officer, The," MPII:SS V-1859
 Rainbow, The, CLC II-935; MP
  IX-5410; MP:BF III-1288
 "Rocking-Horse Winner, The," MPII:SS
  V-1971
 Sea and Sardinia, MPII:NF III-1303
 "Ship of Death, The," MPII:P V-1903
 Short Stories of D. H. Lawrence, The,
  MP X-5995; MP:BF III-1439
 "Snake," MPII:P V-1930
 Sons and Lovers, CLC II-1067; MP
  XI-6177; MP:BF III-1468
 Studies in Classic American Literature,
  MP XI-6314
 "Sun," MPII:SS V-2278
 "Tickets, Please," MPII:SS VI-2365
 Twilight in Italy, MP XII-6766
 Virgin and the Gipsy, The, CLCII
  IV-1658; MPII:BCF IV-1797
 "White Stocking, The," MPII:SS VI-2593
 "Woman Who Rode Away, The,"
  MPII:SS VI-2680
 Women in Love, MP XII-7239; MP:BF
  III-1760
LAWRENCE, T. E., CWA II-1039
 Seven Pillars of Wisdom, MP X-5929

LAWSON, HENRY, CWAII III-895
"Drover's Wife, The," MPII:SS II-639
LAXNESS, HALLDÓR, CWA II-1041
Independent People, CLC I-521; MP
V-2872; MP:EF II-701
LAYAMON, CWA II-1043
Brut, The, CLC I-131; MP II-699
LAYE, CAMARA, CWAII III-898
Dark Child, The, CLCII I-366; MPII:WF
I-345
Guardian of the Word, The, CLCII
II-643; MPII:WF II-567
Radiance of the King, The, CLCII
III-1258; MPII:WF III-1245
LAYTON, IRVING
"Golfers," MPII:P III-870
LEAKEY, MARY
Disclosing the Past, MPII:JYABio I-475
LEAVIS, F. R., CWAII III-900
Living Principle, The, MPII:NF II-850
LEAVITT, DAVID, CWAII III-903
"Territory," MPII:SS V-2320
LE CARRÉ, JOHN, CWAII III-905
Honourable Schoolboy, The, CLCII
II-694; MPII:BCF II-737
Perfect Spy, A, CLCII III-1194;
MPII:BCF III-1306
Smiley's People, CLCII II-694;
MPII:BCF IV-1710
Spy Who Came in from the Cold, The,
CLCII IV-1469; MPII:BCF IV-1599
Tinker, Tailor, Soldier, Spy, CLCII
II-694; MPII:BCF IV-1710
LEE, ANDREA
Sarah Phillips, MPII:AfAm III-1241
LEE, DON L. See MADHUBUTI, HAKI R.
LEE, HARPER, CWAII III-907
To Kill a Mockingbird, CLCII IV-1580;
MPII:AF IV-1677; MPII:JYAFic
IV-1487
LEE, WILLIAM. See BURROUGHS,
WILLIAM S.
LE FANU, JOSEPH SHERIDAN, CWA
II-1045
"Green Tea," MPII:SS III-940
House by the Churchyard, The, CLC
I-484; MP V-2705; MP:BF II-597
Uncle Silas, CLC II-1177; MP XII-6808;
MP:BF III-1627

LÉGER, ALEXIS ST.-LÉGER. See
PERSE, ST.-JOHN
LE GUIN, URSULA K., CWAII III-909
Dispossessed, The, CLCII I-405;
MPII:AF I-413
Earthsea series, The, MPII:JYAFic I-375
Left Hand of Darkness, The, CLCII
II-869; MPII:AF III-878
"Sur," MPII:SS V-2288
LEHMANN, ROSAMOND, CWAII III-911
Dusty Answer, CLCII II-433; MPII:BCF
I-408
Echoing Grove, The, CLCII II-442;
MPII:BCF I-427
Weather in the Streets, The, CLCII
IV-1701; MPII:BCF IV-1880
LEIGHTON, MARGARET CARVER
Cleopatra, MPII:JYABio I-385
LEM, STANISAW, CWAII III-913
Chain of Chance, The, CLCII I-253;
MPII:WF I-234
Fiasco, CLCII II-500; MPII:WF II-456
His Master's Voice, CLCII II-678;
MPII:WF II-588
Investigation, The, CLCII II-773;
MPII:WF II-717
Invincible, The, CLCII II-774; MPII:WF
II-722
Solaris, CLCII IV-1435; MPII:WF
IV-1486
L'ENGLE, MADELEINE
Ring of Endless Light, A, MPII:JYAFic
III-1227
Summer of the Great-Grandmother, The,
MPII:JYABio IV-1637
Swiftly Tilting Planet, A, MPII:JYAFic
IV-1424
Wrinkle in Time, A, MPII:JYAFic
IV-1660
LENGYEL, EMIL
Jawaharlal Nehru, MPII:JYABio II-948
LENSKI, LOIS
Indian Captive, MPII:JYABio II-913
Strawberry Girl, MPII:JYAFic IV-1385
LEONARD, HUGH
Da, CLCII I-360; MPII:D II-431
Life, A, CLCII II-880; MPII:D III-970
LEONARDO DA VINCI, CWA II-1046
Notebooks of Leonardo da Vinci, The,
MP VII-4255

LEOPARDI, GIACOMO, CWA II-1049
    Poetry of Leopardi, The, MP IX-5040
LERMONTOV, MIKHAIL YURIEVICH,
    CWA II-1051
    Demon, The, MP III-1449
    Hero of Our Time, A, CLC I-471; MP
    V-2597; MP:EF II-636
    Novice, The, MP VII-4263
LE SAGE, ALAIN RENÉ, CWA II-1053
    Diable boiteux, Le, CLC I-268; MP
    III-1474; MP:EF I-388
    Gil Blas, CLC I-401; MP IV-2260;
    MP:EF II-567
    Turcaret, CLC II-1166; MP XI-6744
LESKOV, NIKOLAI, CWAII III-916
    "Lady Macbeth of the Mtsensk District,"
    CLCII II-844; MPII:SS III-1280
    "Lefty," MPII:SS III-1320
LESSING, DORIS, CWAII III-919
    Children of Violence, CLCII I-275;
    MPII:BCF I-252
    "Day Stalin Died, The," MPII:SS II-502
    Golden Notebook, The, CLCII II-605;
    MPII:BCF II-621
    Good Terrorist, The, CLCII II-614;
    MPII:BCF II-643
    "How I Finally Lost My Heart,"
    MPII:SS III-1064
    "Mrs. Fortescue," MPII:SS IV-1515
    Shikasta, CLCII IV-1391; MPII:BCF
    IV-1533
LESSING, GOTTHOLD EPHRAIM, CWA
    II-1055
    Emilia Galotti, CLC I-323; MP III-1758
    Minna von Barnhelm, CLC II-709; MP
    VII-3912
    Nathan the Wise, CLC II-759; MP
    VII-4149
LESTER, JULIUS
    This Strange New Feeling, MPII:JYAFic
    IV-1458
LE SUEUR, MERIDEL
    Chanticleer of Wilderness Road,
    MPII:JYABio I-315
LEVER, CHARLES JAMES, CWA II-1057
    Charles O'Malley, CLC I-169; MP
    II-892; MP:BF I-198
    Tom Burke of Ours, CLC II-1141; MP
    XI-6588; MP:BF III-1560

LEVERTOV, DENISE
    "Olga Poems," MPII:P IV-1571
LEVI, CARLO, CWAII III-922
    Christ Stopped at Eboli, CLCII I-283;
    MPII:WF I-257
LEVI, PRIMO, CWAII III-924
    Drowned and the Saved, The, MPII:NF
    I-420
    If Not Now, When? CLCII II-735;
    MPII:WF II-653
    If This Is a Man, MPII:NF II-678
    Monkey's Wrench, The, CLCII III-1032;
    MPII:WF III-1031
    Periodic Table, The, MPII:NF III-1141
LEVIN, RICHARD, and EARVIN
    JOHNSON
    Magic, MPII:JYABio III-1146
LEVINE, PHILIP
    "Ashes," MPII:P I-126
LÉVI-STRAUSS, CLAUDE, CWAII
    III-927
    Tristes Tropiques, MPII:NF IV-1563
LEVY, JACQUES E.
    César Chávez, MPII:JYABio I-307
LEWARS, MRS. E. S. See SINGMASTER,
    ELSIE
LEWIS, ALUN, CWAII III-930
    "Wanderers, The," MPII:SS VI-2541
LEWIS, C. S., CWA II-1061; CWAII
    III-932
    Allegory of Love, The, MP I-138
    Chronicles of Narnia, The, MPII:JYAFic
    I-240
    Grief Observed, A, MPII:NF II-601
    Space trilogy, The, CLCII IV-1456;
    MPII:BCF IV-1588
    Surprised by Joy, MPII:NF IV-1462
    Till We Have Faces, CLCII IV-1565;
    MPII:BCF IV-1700
LEWIS, CECIL DAY, CWA II-1059
    Poetry of Lewis, The, MP IX-5043
LEWIS, CLAUDE
    Benjamin Banneker, MPII:JYABio I-199
LEWIS, ELIZABETH FOREMAN
    Young Fu of the Upper Yangtze,
    MPII:JYAFic IV-1678
LEWIS, JANET
    "Time and Music," MPII:P VI-2185

LEWIS, MATTHEW GREGORY, CWA
II-1064
Monk, The, CLC II-733; MP VII-4027;
MP:BF II-993
LEWIS, MERIWETHER, and WILLIAM
CLARK, CWA II-1065
Journals of Lewis and Clark, The, MP
VI-3065
LEWIS, SINCLAIR, CWA II-1067
Arrowsmith, CLC I-61; MP I-313;
MP:AF I-75
Babbitt, CLC I-72; MP I-400; MP:AF
I-90
Cass Timberlane, CLC I-153; MP
II-813; MP:AF I-178
Dodsworth, CLC I-283; MP III-1565;
MP:AF I-294
Elmer Gantry, MP III-1742; MP:AF
I-335
Main Street, CLC I-655; MP VI-3645;
MP:AF II-730
LEWIS, WYNDHAM, CWA II-1070;
CWAII III-935
Apes of God, The, CLCII I-59;
MPII:BCF I-58
Blasting and Bombardiering, MPII:NF
I-168
Human Age, The, CLCII II-718;
MPII:BCF II-764
Revenge for Love, The, CLCII III-1290;
MPII:BCF III-1410
Self Condemned, CLCII III-1371;
MPII:BCF IV-1496
Snooty Baronet, CLCII IV-1432;
MPII:BCF IV-1567
Tarr, CLC II-1109; MP XI-6413; MP:BF
III-1500
Time and Western Man, MPII:NF
IV-1523
"Time the Tiger," MPII:SS VI-2369
LEZAMA LIMA, JOSÉ
Paradiso, CLCII III-1176; MPII:AF
III-1248
LI PO
"Farewell to Li Yun in the Xie Tiao
Pavilion, A," MPII:P II-727
"Question and Answer in the Mountain,"
MPII:P V-1764
LIANG HENG, and JUDITH SHAPIRO
Son of the Revolution, MPII:JYABio
IV-1593

LIE, JONAS, CWA II-1072
Family at Gilje, The, CLC I-354; MP
IV-1977; MP:EF II-497
LINCOLN, ABRAHAM, CWA II-1074
Addresses, MP I-32
LINDBERGH, CHARLES A.
Spirit of St. Louis, The, MPII:JYABio
IV-1600
LINDGREN, ASTRID
Pippi Longstocking, MPII:JYAFic
III-1144
LINDSAY, VACHEL, CWA II-1078
"General William Booth Enters into
Heaven," MPII:P II-848
Poetry of Lindsay, The, MP IX-5046
LINNEY, ROMULUS, CWAII III-938
Childe Byron, CLCII I-271; MPII:D
I-329
Holy Ghosts, CLCII II-683; MPII:D
II-769
Sand Mountain, CLCII III-1333; MPII:D
IV-1396
LINS DO RÊGO, JOSÉ, CWA II-1080
Dead Fires, CLC I-247; MP III-1339
Fogo morto, MP:AF I-400
Plantation Boy, MP VIII-4748; MP:AF
II-954
LINS, OSMAN, CWAII III-940
Avalovara, CLCII I-97; MPII:AF I-97
LIPSYTE, ROBERT
Contender, The, MPII:JYAFic I-281
Free to Be Muhammad Ali,
MPII:JYABio II-678
LISLE, LAURIE
Portrait of an Artist, MPII:JYABio
III-1429
LISPECTOR, CLARICE, CWAII III-942
Apple in the Dark, The, CLCII I-62;
MPII:AF I-48
"Smallest Woman in the World, The,"
MPII:SS V-2138
LITTLE, JEAN
Little by Little, MPII:JYABio III-1097
LITTLE, LESSIE JONES, and ELOISE
GREENFIELD
Childtimes, MPII:JYABio I-356
LITTLE, MALCOLM. See MALCOLM X.
LIU E, CWAII III-945
Travels of Lao Ts'an, The, CLCII
IV-1604; MPII:WF IV-1646

LIU T'IEH-YUN. *See* LIU E
LIVELY, PENELOPE
 Ghost of Thomas Kempe, The,
  MPII:JYAFic II-508
 House in Norham Gardens, The,
  MPII:JYAFic II-653
LIVIUS, TITUS. *See* LIVY
LIVY, CWA II-1082
 Annals of the Roman People, MP I-243
LIZARDI, JOSÉ JOAQUÍN FERNÁNDEZ
 DE. *See* FERNÁNDEZ DE
 LIZARDI, JOSÉ JOAQUÍN
LLEWELLYN, RICHARD, CWA II-1083
 How Green Was My Valley, CLC I-493;
  MP V-2742; MP:BF II-612
LLOYD, D. V. LLEWELLYN. *See*
 LLEWELLYN, RICHARD
LLOYD, RICHARD DAVID VIVIAN
 LLEWELLYN. *See* LLEWELLYN,
 RICHARD
LO KUAN-CHUNG, CWA II-1085
 Romance of the Three Kingdoms, CLC
  II-985; MP X-5681; MP:EF III-1105
LOBEIRA, VASCO DE, CWA II-1086
 Amadís de Gaul, CLC I-31; MP I-152;
  MP:EF I-26
LOCKE, ALAIN LEROY
 New Negro, The, MPII:AfAm II-887
LOCKE, JOHN, CWA II-1087
 Essay Concerning Human
  Understanding, An, MP III-1828
LOCKRIDGE, ROSS, JR., CWA II-1089
 Raintree County, CLC II-936; MP
  IX-5415; MP:AF II-1001
LODGE, DAVID, CWAII III-947
 Changing Places, CLCII I-260;
  MPII:BCF I-241
 Small World, CLCII IV-1429;
  MPII:BCF IV-1563
 Souls and Bodies, CLCII IV-1448;
  MPII:BCF IV-1577
LOEPER, JOHN J.
 Men of Ideas, MPII:JYABio III-1203
LOFTING, HUGH
 Voyages of Doctor Dolittle, The,
  MPII:JYAFic IV-1561
LOMASK, MILTON
 Odd Destiny, MPII:JYABio III-1333
LOMAX, JUDY
 Women of the Air, MPII:JYABio IV-1930

LONDON, JACK, CWA II-1090
 Call of the Wild, The, CLC I-142; MP
  II-748; MP:AF I-167; MPII:JYAFic
  I-178
 "Piece of Steak, A," MPII:SS IV-1807
 Sea Wolf, The, CLC II-1015; MP
  X-5865; MP:AF III-1106
 "To Build a Fire," MPII:SS VI-2377
LONGFELLOW, HENRY
 WADSWORTH, CWA II-1092
 Courtship of Miles Standish, The, CLC
  I-213; MP II-1172
 Evangeline, CLC I-340; MP IV-1906
 "Jewish Cemetery at Newport, The,"
  MPII:P III-1132
 Song of Hiawatha, The, CLC II-1060;
  MP XI-6147
LONGINUS, CASSIUS, CWA II-1094
LONGSTREET, AUGUSTUS BALDWIN,
 CWA II-1095
 Georgia Scenes, MP IV-2233; MP:AF
  I-433
LONGSWORTH, POLLY
 Emily Dickinson, MPII:JYABio II-557
 I, Charlotte Forten, Black and Free,
  MPII:JYABio II-881
LONGUS, CWA II-1096
 Daphnis and Chloë, CLC I-239; MP
  III-1310; MP:EF I-335
LÖNNROT, ELIAS, CWA II-1097
 Kalevala, The, CLC I-565; MP VI-3111
LOPE DE VEGA. *See* VEGA, LOPE DE
LORCA, FEDERICO GARCÍA. *See*
 GARCÍA LORCA, FEDERICO
LORD, ALBERT B.
 Singer of Tales, The, MPII:NF IV-1356
LORD, BETTE BAO
 In the Year of the Boar and Jackie
  Robinson, MPII:JYAFic II-699
LORDE, AUDRE
 Cancer Journals, The, MPII:AfAm I-225
 Poetry of Audre Lorde, The, MPII:AfAm
  III-1085
 "Summer Oracle," MPII:P V-2096
LORENZINI, CARLO. *See* COLLODI,
 CARLO
LORRIS, GUILLAUME DE. *See*
 GUILLAUME DE LORRIS *and*
 JEAN DE MEUNG

LOTI, PIERRE, CWA II-1098
  Iceland Fisherman, An, CLC I-508; MP
    V-2810; MP:EF II-678
LOVECRAFT, H. P., CWAII III-949
  "Dunwich Horror, The," MPII:SS II-657
LOVELACE, EARL, CWAII III-951
  Dragon Can't Dance, The, CLCII II-421;
    MPII:AfAm I-379; MPII:BCF I-398
  "Shoemaker Arnold," MPII:SS V-2080
  Wine of Astonishment, The, CLCII
    IV-1723; MPII:AfAm III-1496;
    MPII:BCF IV-1909
LOVELACE, RICHARD, CWA II-1099
  Poetry of Lovelace, The, MP IX-5048
LOVER, SAMUEL, CWA II-1100
  Handy Andy, CLC I-441; MP V-2470;
    MP:BF I-524
  Rory O'More, CLC II-995; MP X-5715;
    MP:BF III-1380
LOWELL, JAMES RUSSELL, CWA
    II-1101
  Biglow Papers, The, MP I-535
  Fable for Critics, A, MP IV-1948;
    MPII:P II-718
  Lyric Poetry of Lowell, The, MP VI-3565
LOWELL, ROBERT, CWA II-1104
  "After the Surprising Conversions,"
    MPII:P I-29
  "Beyond the Alps," MPII:P I-231
  "For the Union Dead," MPII:P II-798
  "Mr. Edwards and the Spider," MPII:P
    IV-1401
  "My Last Afternoon with Uncle
    Devereux Winslow," MPII:P IV-1439
  Poetry of Robert Lowell, The, MP
    IX-5121
  "Quaker Graveyard in Nantucket, The,"
    MPII:P V-1757
  "Skunk Hour," MPII:P V-1918
  "Waking in the Blue," MPII:P VI-2361

LOWRY, MALCOLM, CWA II-1105;
    CWAII III-953
  Under the Volcano, MP XII-6833;
    MP:BF III-1639
  Ultramarine, CLCII IV-1632; MPII:BCF
    IV-1766
LOYOLA BRANDÃO, IGNÁCIO DE,
    CWAII I-238
  Zero, CLCII IV-1769; MPII:AF IV-1852
LU HSÜN, CWAII III-955
  True Story of Ah Q, The, CLCII
    IV-1620; MPII:WF IV-1671
LUCIAN, CWA II-1106
  Satires, MP X-5814
  True History, The, MP XI-6737; MP:EF
    III-1311
LUCRETIUS, CWA II-1107
  De rerum natura, MP III-1337
LURIA, A. R.
  Making of Mind, The, MPII:NF II-884
LURIE, ALISON, CWAII III-958
  War Between the Tates, The, CLCII
    IV-1681; MPII:AF IV-1759
LYLY, JOHN, CWA II-1108
  Campaspe, CLC I-143; MP II-754
  Endymion, CLC I-325; MP III-1774
  Euphues and His England, CLC I-338;
    MP IV-1894; MP:BF I-382
  Euphues, the Anatomy of Wit, CLC
    I-338; MP IV-1898; MP:BF I-387
LYTLE, ANDREW, CWA II-1110
  Long Night, The, CLC I-624; MP
    VI-3483; MP:AF II-694
  Velvet Horn, The, MP XII-6884; MP:AF
    III-1363
LYTTLE, RICHARD B.
  Duce, Il, MPII:JYABio II-521
  Pablo Picasso, MPII:JYABio III-1379
LYTTON, EDWARD LYTTON BULWER-.
    See BULWER-LYTTON, EDWARD
    GEORGE EARLE

M

MACAULAY, ROSE, CWAII III-961
Told by an Idiot, CLCII IV-1585;
MPII:BCF IV-1721
Towers of Trebizond, The, CLCII
IV-1596; MPII:BCF IV-1726
World My Wilderness, The, CLCII
IV-1752; MPII:BCF IV-1930
MACAULAY, THOMAS BABINGTON,
CWA II-1111
History of England, The, MP V-2631
McCAFFREY, ANNE
Dragonsong, MPII:JYAFic I-347
McCARTHY, CORMAC, CWAII III-964
Outer Dark, CLCII III-1166; MPII:AF
III-1227
Suttree, CLCII IV-1501; MPII:AF
IV-1559
McCARTHY, MARY, CWAII III-966
"Cruel and Barbarous Treatment,"
MPII:SS II-467
Group, The, CLCII II-638; MPII:AF
II-682
Memories of a Catholic Girlhood,
MPII:NF III-933
McCLUNG, ROBERT M.
True Adventures of Grizzly Adams, The,
MPII:JYABio IV-1770
McCOY, HORACE, CWA II-1113
They Shoot Horses, Don't They? MP
XI-6486; MP:AF III-1271
McCULLERS, CARSON, CWA II-1115;
CWAII III-968
"Ballad of the Sad Café, The," CLCII
I-109; MPII:SS I-147
Heart Is a Lonely Hunter, The, CLC
I-447; MP V-2501; MP:AF II-539
"Madame Zilensky and the King of
Finland," MPII:SS IV-1427
Member of the Wedding, The, CLC
I-690; CLCII III-992; MP VII-3815;
MP:AF II-776; MPII:D III-1071;
MPII:JYAFic III-950
"Tree. A Rock. A Cloud., A," MPII:SS
VI-2404
"Wunderkind," MPII:SS VI-2719
MacDONALD, GEORGE
At the Back of the North Wind,
MPII:JYAFic I-69

MACDONALD, ROSS, CWAII III-970
Goodbye Look, The, CLCII II-616;
MPII:AF II-655
Underground Man, The, CLCII IV-1636;
MPII:AF IV-1711
McELROY, JOSEPH, CWAII III-972
Lookout Cartridge, CLCII III-914;
MPII:AF II-916
McFARLANE, LESLIE. See DIXON,
FRANKLIN W.
McFEE, WILLIAM, CWA II-1118
Casuals of the Sea, CLC I-158; MP
II-839; MP:BF I-189
McGAHERN, JOHN, CWAII III-975
Barracks, The, CLCII I-121; MPII:BCF
I-108
Pornographer, The, CLCII III-1222;
MPII:BCF III-1330
McGINLEY, PATRICK, CWAII III-977
Bogmail, CLCII I-184; MPII:BCF I-163
Trick of the Ga Bolga, The, CLCII
IV-1612; MPII:BCF IV-1737
McGOVERN, ANN
Secret Soldier, The, MPII:JYAFic
IV-1304
McGRATH, THOMAS
"Heroes of Childhood, The," MPII:P
III-942
McGUANE, THOMAS, CWAII III-979
Ninety-two in the Shade, CLCII
III-1102; MPII:AF III-1145
Sporting Club, The, CLCII IV-1466;
MPII:AF IV-1521
MACHADO, ANTONIO, CWA II-1120
Poetry of Machado, The, MP IX-5051
MACHADO DE ASSÍS, JOAQUIM
MARIA, CWA II-1122
Epitaph of a Small Winner, CLC I-330;
MP III-1811; MP:AF I-346
Philosopher or Dog? MP VIII-4650;
MP:AF II-927
"Psychiatrist, The," MPII:SS V-1862
MACHEN, ARTHUR, CWA II-1124
Hill of Dreams, The, CLC I-473; MP
V-2613; MP:BF I-578
MACHIAVELLI, NICCOLÒ, CWA II-1126
Prince, The, MP IX-5314

MacINTYRE, ALASDAIR
  After Virtue, MPII:NF I-12
McINTYRE, VONDA NEEL
  Dreamsnake, MPII:JYAFic I-357
MACK, LOUISE
  Teens, MPII:JYAFic IV-1440
McKAY, CLAUDE, CWAII III-981
  Banana Bottom, CLCII I-110; MPII:AF
    I-106; MPII:AfAm I-108
  Banjo, CLCII I-113; MPII:AF I-116
  Home to Harlem, CLCII II-687;
    MPII:AF II-722; MPII:AfAm II-540
  Poetry of Claude McKay, The,
    MPII:AfAm III-1090
MACKENZIE, HENRY, CWA II-1128
  Man of Feeling, The, CLC I-660; MP
    VII-3669; MP:BF II-855
McKINLEY, ROBIN
  Hero and the Crown, The, MPII:JYAFic
    II-626
McKNIGHT, REGINALD
  I Get on the Bus, MPII:AfAm II-563
MacLACHLAN, PATRICIA
  Sarah, Plain and Tall, MPII:JYAFic
    III-1278
MACLAREN-ROSS, JULIAN
  "Bit of a Smash in Madras, A," MPII:SS
    I-218
  Memoirs of the Forties, MPII:NF III-923
MACLEAN, ALISTAIR
  Lawrence of Arabia, MPII:JYABio
    III-1040
MacLEISH, ARCHIBALD, CWA II-1129,
    CWAII III-983
  Conquistador, MP II-1088
  J. B., CLCII II-788; MPII:D III-861
  Poetry of MacLeish, The, MP IX-5054
  "You, Andrew Marvell," MPII:P VI-2479
MacLENNAN, HUGH, CWAII III-986
  Barometer Rising, CLCII I-118;
    MPII:BCF I-103
  Two Solitudes, CLCII IV-1625;
    MPII:BCF IV-1756
  Voices in Time, CLCII IV-1663;
    MPII:BCF IV-1812
  Watch That Ends the Night, The, CLCII
    IV-1685; MPII:BCF IV-1854
McLUHAN, MARSHALL, CWAII III-988
  Gutenberg Galaxy, The, MPII:NF II-624
  Understanding Media, MPII:NF IV-1601

McMILLAN, TERRY
  Disappearing Acts, MPII:AfAm I-373
  Mama, MPII:AfAm II-748
  Waiting to Exhale, MPII:AfAm III-1484
McMURTRY, LARRY, CWAII III-990
  Last Picture Show, The, CLCII II-858;
    MPII:AF II-854; MPII:JYAFic II-814
  Terms of Endearment, CLCII IV-1529;
    MPII:AF IV-1587
McNALLY, TERRENCE
  Where Has Tommy Flowers Gone?
    CLCII IV-1711; MPII:D IV-1739
McNEER, MAY
  America's Mark Twain, MPII:JYABio
    I-75
McNEER, MAY, and LYND WARD
  Armed with Courage, MPII:JYABio
    I-137
MacNEICE, LOUIS, CWA II-1131
  Poetry of MacNeice, The, MP IX-5057
McPHEE, JOHN, CWAII III-992
  Coming into the Country, MPII:NF I-260
  Pine Barrens, The, MPII:NF III-1168
McPHERSON, JAMES ALAN, CWAII
    III-994
  "Gold Coast," MPII:SS II-885
  "Private Domain," MPII:SS IV-1852
  Stories of James Alan McPherson, The,
    MPII:AfAm III-1371
McPHERSON, SANDRA
  "Open Casket," MPII:P IV-1611
MADDEN, DAVID, CWAII III-996
  "Day the Flowers Came, The," MPII:SS
    II-507
  Suicide's Wife, The, CLCII IV-1489;
    MPII:AF IV-1545
  "Willis Carr at Bleak House," MPII:SS
    VI-2634
MADHUBUTI, HAKI R.
  Black Men, MPII:AfAm I-155
  Poetry of Haki R. Madhubuti, The,
    MPII:AfAm III-1097
MADISON, JAMES, CWA II-1133
MADISON, JAMES, ALEXANDER
    HAMILTON, and JOHN JAY
  Federalist, The, MP IV-2025
MAETERLINCK, MAURICE, CWA
    II-1137
  Blue Bird, The, CLCII I-173; MPII:D
    I-213

Pélléas and Mélisande, CLC II-852; MP VIII-4569

MAILER, NORMAN, CWA II-1139; CWAII III-998
    American Dream, An, CLCII I-38; MPII:AF I-29
    Armies of the Night, The, CLCII I-65; MPII:AF I-51
    Executioner's Song, The, CLCII II-474; MPII:AF II-486
    Marilyn, MPII:NF III-907
    Naked and the Dead, The, CLCII III-1070; MPII:AF III-1110
    Of a Fire on the Moon, MPII:NF III-1052

MAJOR, CLARENCE
    My Amputations, MPII:AfAm II-842
    Painted Turtle, MPII:AfAm II-924
    Reflex and Bone Structure, MPII:AfAm III-1206

MALAMUD, BERNARD, CWA II-1141; CWAII III-1000
    "Angel Levine," MPII:SS I-92
    Assistant, The, CLCII I-78; MPII:AF I-61
    Fixer, The, CLCII II-519; MPII:AF II-548
    "Idiots First," MPII:SS III-1109
    "Jewbird, The," MPII:SS III-1218
    "Last Mohican, The," MPII:SS III-1302
    "Magic Barrel, The," MPII:SS IV-1431
    Natural, The, CLCII III-1080; MPII:AF III-1119
    New Life, A, CLCII III-1088; MPII:AF III-1129
    "Rembrandt's Hat," MPII:SS VI-1926

MALCOLM X, CWAII III-1002
    Autobiography of Malcolm X, The, MPII:AfAm I-78; MPII:JYABio I-156; MPII:NF I-121
    Speeches of Malcolm X, The, MPII:AfAm III-1320

MALLARMÉ, STÉPHANE, CWA II-1143
    Afternoon of a Faun, The, MPII:P I-32
    "Azure, The," MPII:P I-185
    "Dice-Throw, A," MPII:P II-538
    Poetry of Mallarmé, The, MP IX-5059
    "Toast," MPII:P VI-2240
    "Tomb of Charles Baudelaire, The," MPII:P VI-2243
    "Tomb of Edgar Poe, The," MPII:P VI-2247
    "Windows, The," MPII:P VI-2429

MALLEA, EDUARDO, CWA II-1145
    All Green Shall Perish, CLCII I-26; MPII:AF I-25
    Bay of Silence, The, CLC I-89; MP I-454; MP:AF I-101
    Fiesta in November, MP IV-2050; MP:AF I-386

MALLOWAN, AGATHA MARY. See CHRISTIE, AGATHA

MALONE, MARY
    Actor in Exile, MPII:JYABio I-12

MALORY, SIR THOMAS, CWA II-1147
    Morte d'Arthur, Le, CLC II-742; MP VII-4063; MP:BF II-1006

MALOUF, DAVID
    Harland's Half Acre, CLCII II-658; MPII:BCF II-695
    Imaginary Life, An, CLCII II-742; MPII:BCF II-799

MALRAUX, ANDRÉ, CWA II-1149; CWAII III-1004
    Anti-Memoirs, MPII:NF I-68
    Man's Fate, CLC I-665; MP VII-3700; MP:EF II-830
    Man's Hope, CLCII III-967; MPII:WF III-945
    Royal Way, The, CLCII III-1317; MPII:WF III-1305
    Voices of Silence, The, MP XII-6975

MAMET, DAVID, CWAII III-1006
    American Buffalo, CLCII I-37; MPII:D I-49
    Glengarry Glen Ross, CLCII II-595; MPII:D II-684
    Sexual Perversity in Chicago, CLCII IV-1386; MPII:D IV-1449
    Speed-the-Plow, CLCII IV-1458; MPII:D IV-1486
    Woods, The, CLCII IV-1743; MPII:D IV-1762

MANDELSTAM, NADEZHDA, CWAII III-1008
    Hope Abandoned, MPII:NF II-656
    Hope Against Hope, MPII:NF II-662

MANDELSTAM, OSIP, CWAII III-1011
    "Age, The," MPII:P I-36
    Conversation About Dante, MPII:NF I-270
    "Horseshoe Finder, The," MPII:P III-968
    "I Have Forgotten the Word I Wanted to Say," MPII:P III-1014

"Insomnia. Homer. Taut Sails.," MPII:P III-1111
Journey to Armenia, MPII:NF II-779
Noise of Time, The, MPII:NF III-1013
"On a Board of Raspberry and Pure Gold," MPII:P IV-1575
"Slate Ode, The," MPII:P V-1921
"Tristia," MPII:P VI-2282
"Verses on the Unknown Soldier," MPII:P VI-2334

MANN, THOMAS, CWA II-1151
Black Swan, The, MP I-559; MP:EF I-119
Buddenbrooks, CLC I-133; MP II-702; MP:EF I-150
Confessions of Felix Krull, Confidence Man, CLC I-195; MP II-1067; MP:EF I-249
"Death in Venice," CLC I-253; MP III-1357; MP:EF I-349; MPII:SS II-532
"Disorder and Early Sorrow," MPII:SS II-604
Doctor Faustus, CLC I-276; MP III-1539; MP:EF I-406
"Gladius Dei," MPII:SS II-857
Holy Sinner, The, CLCII II-685; MPII:WF II-599
"Infant Prodigy, The," MPII:SS III-1173
Joseph and His Brothers, CLCII II-797; MPII:WF II-772
"Little Herr Friedemann," MPII:SS III-1375
Magic Mountain, The, CLC I-650; MP VI-3618; MP:EF II-816
"Mario and the Magician," MPII:SS IV-1458
"Tonio Kröger," MPII:SS VI-2393
Transposed Heads, The, CLCII IV-1602; MPII:WF IV-1639
"Tristan," MPII:SS VI-2417

MANNING, FREDERIC
Her Privates, We, CLCII II-675; MPII:BCF II-717

MANNING, OLIVIA, CWAII III-1014
Balkan Trilogy, The, CLCII I-106; MPII:BCF I-86

MANSFIELD, KATHERINE, CWA II-1154; CWAII III-1016
"At the Bay," MPII:SS I-132
"Bliss," MPII:SS I-250
"Daughters of the Late Colonel, The," MPII:SS II-495

"Fly, The," MPII:SS II-799
"Her First Ball," MPII:SS III-997
"Miss Brill," MPII:SS IV-1505
"Prelude," MPII:SS IV-1843
Short Stories of Katherine Mansfield, MP X-6018; MP:BF III-1442
"Woman at the Store, The," MPII:SS VI-2676

MANZONI, ALESSANDRO, CWA II-1157
Betrothed, The, CLC I-100; MP I-507; MP:EF I-113

MAQUET, AUGUSTE. See DUMAS, ALEXANDRE, père

MARAN, RENÉ, CWA II-1159
Batouala, CLC I-88; MP I-451; MP:EF I-105

MARCUS AURELIUS, CWA II-1160
Meditations, MP VII-3802

MARIE DE FRANCE, CWA II-1161
Lais of Marie de France, The, MP VI-3230

MARIVAUX, PIERRE CARLET DE CHAMBLAIN, CWA II-1162
Marianne, CLC I-671; MP VII-3728; MP:EF II-834

MARK, JAN
Ennead, The, MPII:JYAFic I-391
Thunder and Lightnings, MPII:JYAFic IV-1469

MARKANDAYA, KAMALA
Nectar in a Sieve, CLCII III-1082; MPII:BCF III-1182

MARKHAM, BERYL, CWAII III-1018
West with the Night, MPII:JYABio IV-1857; MPII:NF IV-1681

MARKOOSIE
Harpoon of the Hunter, MPII:JYAFic II-599

MARLOWE, CHRISTOPHER, CWA II-1163
Doctor Faustus, CLC I-278; MP III-1543
Edward the Second, CLC I-315; MP III-1711
Hero and Leander, MPII:P III-938
Jew of Malta, The, CLC I-546; MP V-3004
"Passionate Shepherd to His Love, The," MPII:P IV-1653
Tamburlaine the Great, CLC II-1104; MP XI-6396

MAROT, CLEMÉNT, CWA II-1166
Poetry of Marot, The, MP IX-5064
MARQUAND, JOHN PHILLIPS, CWA
II-1168
Late George Apley, The, CLC I-599; MP
VI-3280; MP:AF II-653
Wickford Point, CLC II-1240; MP
XII-7126; MP:AF III-1429
MÁRQUEZ, GABRIEL GARCÍA. See
GARCÍA MÁRQUEZ, GABRIEL
MARRANT, JOHN
Narrative of the Lord's Wonderful
Dealings with John Marrant, a Black,
A, MPII:AfAm II-859
MARRIN, ALBERT
Sea Rovers, The, MPII:JYABio IV-1541
MARRYAT, FREDERICK, CWA II-1171
Mr. Midshipman Easy, CLC II-719; MP
VII-3960; MP:BF II-966;
MPII:JYAFic III-965
Peter Simple, CLC II-866; MP
VIII-4626; MP:BF II-1199
MARSHALL, PAULE, CWAII III-1020
"Barbados," MPII:SS I-154
Brown Girl, Brownstones, MPII:AfAm
I-212
Chosen Place, the Timeless People, The,
MPII:AfAm I-271
Daughters, MPII:AfAm I-345
Praisesong for the Widow, CLCII
III-1230; MPII:AF III-1286;
MPII:AfAm III-1172
MARSTON, JOHN, CWA II-1173
Malcontent, The, CLC I-657; MP
VI-3658
MARSTON, JOHN, GEORGE
CHAPMAN, and BEN JONSON
Eastward Ho! CLC I-313; MP III-1693
MARTIAL, CWA II-1175
Epigrams of Martial, MP III-1800
MARTIN, RALPH G.
Jennie, MPII:JYABio II-952
MARTIN DU GARD, ROGER, CWA II-1176
World of the Thibaults, The, CLC
II-1267; MP XII-7266; MP:EF
III-1419
MARTÍNEZ SIERRA, GREGORIO, CWA
II-1178
Cradle Song, The, CLC I-218; MP II-1188

Kingdom of God, The, CLC I-578; MP
VI-3173
MARVELL, ANDREW, CWA II-1180
"Definition of Love, The," MPII:P II-516
"Garden, The," MPII:P II-845
"Mower, Against Gardens, The," MPII:P
IV-1427
Poetry of Marvell, The, MP IX-5067
"To His Coy Mistress," MPII:P VI-2209
MARX, KARL, CWA II-1182
Kapital, Das, MP VI-3117
MASEFIELD, JOHN, CWA II-1185
Box of Delights, The, MPII:JYAFic
I-148
Midnight Folk, The, MPII:JYAFic
III-958
MASON, THEODORE K.
Two Against the Ice, MPII:JYABio
IV-1788
MASSIE, ALLAN
Caesars, The, MPII:JYABio I-281
MASSIE, ROBERT K.
Nicholas and Alexandra, MPII:JYABio
III-1316
MASSINGER, PHILIP, CWA II-1187
Bondman, The, CLC I-113; MP I-585
Maid of Honour, The, CLC I-653; MP
VI-3634
New Way to Pay Old Debts, A, CLC
II-765; MP VII-4180
Roman Actor, The, CLC II-982; MP
X-5665
MASSINGER, PHILIP, and JOHN
FLETCHER
Beggars' Bush, The, CLC I-92; MP I-472
Sir John van Olden Barnavelt, MP
X-6063
MASTERS, EDGAR LEE, CWA II-1189
Spoon River Anthology, MP XI-6233;
MPII:P V-2050
MATHER, COTTON, CWA II-1191
Magnalia Christi Americana, MP
VI-3623
MATHESON, RICHARD, CWAII III-1022
"Duel," MPII:SS II-653
MATHIS, SHARON BELL
Hundred Penny Box, The, MPII:JYAFic
II-672
Listen for the Fig Tree, MPII:JYAFic
II-838

Teacup Full of Roses, MPII:JYAFic
IV-1437
MATTHIESSEN, PETER, CWA II-1193;
CWAII III-1024
At Play in the Fields of the Lord, CLCII
I-81; MPII:AF I-65
Cloud Forest, The, MP II-1003
Far Tortuga, CLCII II-491; MPII:AF
II-521
Snow Leopard, The, MPII:NF IV-1378
MATURIN, CHARLES ROBERT, CWA
II-1195
Melmoth the Wanderer, CLC I-689; MP
VII-3809; MP:BF II-901
MAUGHAM, W. SOMERSET, CWA
II-1196; CWAII III-1026
"Alien Corn, The," MPII:SS I-56
Cakes and Ale, CLC I-140; MP II-737;
MP:BF I-154
Circle, The, CLCII I-286; MPII:D I-353
Liza of Lambeth, CLC I-622; MP
VI-3471; MP:BF II-812
Moon and Sixpence, The, CLC II-739;
MP VII-4056; MP:BF II-997
Of Human Bondage, CLC II-794; MP
VII-4288; MP:BF II-1080
"Official Position, An," MPII:SS
IV-1656
"Outstation, The," MPII:SS IV-1741
"Rain," MPII:SS V-1883
Razor's Edge, The, CLCII III-1273;
MPII:BCF III-1394
Summing Up, The, MP XI-6332
MAUPASSANT, GUY DE, CWA II-1199
Bel-Ami, CLC I-95; MP I-481; MP:EF
I-108
"Boule de Suif," MPII:SS I-289
"Family Affair, A," MPII:SS II-755
"Madame Tellier's Establishment,"
MPII:SS IV-1424
Mont-Oriol, CLC II-737; MP VII-4045;
MP:EF II-889
"Necklace, The," MPII:SS IV-1597
"Piece of String, The," MPII:SS IV-1810
"Two Little Soldiers," MPII:SS VI-2442
Woman's Life, A, CLC II-1259; MP
XII-7224; MP:EF III-1413
MAURIAC, CLAUDE
Dinner Party, The, MP III-1516; MP:EF
I-398

MAURIAC, FRANÇOIS, CWA II-1202;
CWAII III-1029
Lamb, The, CLCII II-848; MPII:WF
II-811
Thérèse, CLC II-1121; MP XI-6477;
MP:EF III-1273
Vipers' Tangle, CLCII IV-1657;
MPII:WF IV-1715
Woman of the Pharisees, A, CLCII
IV-1730; MPII:WF IV-1774
MAURIER, DAPHNE DU. See DU
MAURIER, DAPHNE
MAURIER, GEORGE DU. See DU
MAURIER, GEORGE
MAUROIS, ANDRÉ
Ariel, MPII:JYABio I-133
MAUSS, MARCEL, and ÉMILE
DURKHEIM
Primitive Classification, MPII:NF
III-1190
MAXIMOV, VLADIMIR
Farewell from Nowhere, CLCII II-492;
MPII:WF I-440
Seven Days of Creation, The, CLCII
IV-1383; MPII:WF IV-1393
MAXWELL, WILLIAM
Folded Leaf, The, MPII:JYAFic II-451
MAYAKOVSKY, VLADIMIR, CWA
II-1204
Bathhouse, The, CLCII I-124; MPII:D
I-133
Bedbug, The, CLCII I-132; MPII:D I-146
Poetry of Mayakovsky, The, MP IX-5070
MAYNE, WILLIAM
Swarm in May, A, MPII:JYAFic IV-1417
MAZER, HARRY
When the Phone Rang, MPII:JYAFic
IV-1606
MAZER, NORMA FOX
Saturday, the Twelfth of October,
MPII:JYAFic III-1281
MEAD, CHRIS
Champion, MPII:JYABio I-311
MEAD, MARGARET
Blackberry Winter, MPII:JYABio I-240
MEAKER, MARIJANE. See KERR, M. E.
MEANS, FLORENCE CRANNELL
Carvers' George, MPII:JYABio I-303
Moved Outers, The, MPII:JYAFic
III-986

Shuttered Windows, MPII:JYAFic
    IV-1328
MEBANE, MARY
    Mary, MPII:JYABio III-1192
MEBEL, MILDRED, LAWRENCE HILL,
    and ROBERT PATTERSON
    On Our Way, MPII:JYABio III-1348
MEDOFF, MARK, CWAII III-1032
    Children of a Lesser God, CLCII I-274;
        MPII:D I-335
    When You Comin' Back, Red Ryder?
        CLCII IV-1710; MPII:D IV-1733
MEHTA, VED, CWAII III-1034
    Sound-Shadows of the New World,
        MPII:NF IV-1398
    Vedi, MPII:NF IV-1635
MEIGS, CORNELIA
    Invincible Louisa, MPII:JYABio II-920
    Jane Addams, MPII:JYABio II-941
    Master Simon's Garden, MPII:JYAFic
        III-931
MELEAGER, CWA II-1206
    Epigrams of Meleager, The, MP III-1802
MELTZER, MILTON
    Benjamin Franklin, MPII:JYABio I-207
    Langston Hughes, MPII:JYABio III-1025
    Light in the Dark, A, MPII:JYABio
        III-1085
    Mark Twain, MPII:JYABio III-1184
    Tongue of Flame, MPII:JYABio IV-1752
MELVILLE, HERMAN, CWA II-1208
    "Bartleby the Scrivener," MPII:SS I-162
    "Benito Cereno," CLC I-97; MP I-495;
        MP:AF I-111; MPII:SS I-188
    Billy Budd, Foretopman, CLC I-104; MP
        I-538; MP:AF I-121
    Clarel, MPII:P I-392
    Confidence Man, The, CLC I-196; MP
        II-1071; MP:AF I-207
    Israel Potter, CLC I-533; MP V-2938;
        MP:AF II-603
    Mardi, and a Voyage Thither, CLC
        I-669; MP VII-3717; MP:AF II-765
    Moby Dick, CLC II-725; MP VII-3992;
        MP:AF II-800
    Omoo, CLC II-813; MP VIII-4364;
        MP:AF II-888
    Pierre, CLC II-879; MP VIII-4690;
        MP:AF II-930
    Poetry of Melville, The, MP IX-5073

    Redburn, CLC II-951; MP IX-5481;
        MP:AF III-1017
    Typee, CLC II-1173; MP XII-6791;
        MP:AF III-1340
    White-Jacket, CLC II-1239; MP
        XII-7118; MP:AF III-1425
MENANDER, CWA II-1211
    Arbitration, The, CLC I-56; MP I-288
MENASHE, SAMUEL
    "Curriculum Vitae," MPII:P II-479
MENCKEN, H. L., CWA II-1212
    Prejudices, MP IX-5302
MENDOZA, JUAN RUIZ DE ALARCÓN
    Y. See RUIZ DE ALARCÓN, JUAN
MEREDITH, GEORGE, CWA II-1215
    Beauchamp's Career, CLC I-90; MP
        I-460; MP:BF I-99
    Diana of the Crossways, CLC I-269; MP
        III-1486; MP:BF I-318
    Egoist, The, CLC I-318; MP III-1723;
        MP:BF I-355
    Evan Harrington, CLC I-339; MP
        IV-1902; MP:BF I-391
    Ordeal of Richard Feverel, The, CLC
        II-814; MP VIII-4390; MP:BF II-1121
    Poetry of Meredith, The, MP IX-5077
MEREDITH, WILLIAM
    "Country Stars," MPII:P II-458
    "Last Things," MPII:P III-1198
MEREZHKOWSKY, DMITRY, CWA
    II-1218
    Death of the Gods, The, CLC I-256; MP
        III-1377; MP:EF I-359
    Romance of Leonardo da Vinci, The,
        CLC II-984; MP X-5672; MP:EF
        III-1101
MÉRIMÉE, PROSPER, CWA II-1220
    Carmen, CLC I-152; MP II-803; MP:EF
        I-178
    Colomba, CLC I-192; MP II-1031;
        MP:EF I-245
MERIWETHER, LOUISE
    Daddy Was a Number Runner,
        MPII:AfAm I-335
    Don't Ride the Bus on Monday,
        MPII:JYABio II-500
MERRIAM, EVE
    Growing Up Female in America,
        MPII:JYABio II-794

MERRILL, JAMES
"Angel," MPII:P I-75
"Broken Home, The," MPII:P I-295
Changing Light at Sandover, The,
MPII:P I-360
"Domino," MPII:P II-579
MERRILL, JEAN
Pushcart War, The, MPII:JYAFic III-1185
MERTON, THOMAS, CWAII III-1037
Conjectures of a Guilty Bystander,
MPII:NF I-265
Seven Storey Mountain, The, MPII:NF
IV-1330
MERWIN, W. S., CWAII III-1039
"In the Winter of My Thirty-Eighth
Year," MPII:P III-1105
"Learning a Dead Language," MPII:P
III-1201
"Leviathan," MPII:P III-1232
Unframed Originals, MPII:NF IV-1612
METCALF, PAUL, CWAII III-1042
Apalache, MPII:NF I-79
Patagoni, MPII:NF III-1129
MEUNG, JEAN DE, and GUILLAUME
DE LORRIS, CWA II-767
MEYER, EDITH PATTERSON
That Remarkable Man, MPII:JYABio
IV-1684
MICHELANGELO BUONARROTI, CWA
I-277
Poetry of Michelangelo, The, MP
IX-5080
MICHENER, JAMES A., CWAII III-1044
Hawaii, CLCII II-661; MPII:AF II-688
Source, The, CLCII IV-1452; MPII:AF
IV-1498
MIDDLETON, THOMAS, CWA II-1222
Chaste Maid in Cheapside, A, CLC
I-171; MP II-900
Trick to Catch the Old One, A, CLC
II-1156; MP XI-6695
Women Beware Women, CLC II-1261;
MP XII-7235
MIDDLETON, THOMAS, and THOMAS
DEKKER
Honest Whore, Part One, The, MP V-2680
MIDDLETON, THOMAS, JOHN FORD,
and WILLIAM ROWLEY
Spanish Gipsy, The, CLC II-1074; MP
XI-6208

MIDDLETON, THOMAS, and WILLIAM
ROWLEY
Changeling, The, CLC I-167; MP II-885
MIKSZÁTH, KÁLMÁN, CWA II-1224
St. Peter's Umbrella, CLC II-999; MP
X-5757; MP:EF III-1113
MILFORD, NANCY
Zelda, MPII:JYABio IV-1985
MILL, JOHN STUART, CWA II-1225
On Liberty, MP VIII-4370
Principles of Political Economy, MP
IX-5337
MILLAR, KENNETH. See
MACDONALD, ROSS
MILLAY, EDNA ST. VINCENT, CWA
II-1227
Harp-Weaver and Other Poems, The, MP
V-2489
"Love is not all," MPII:P III-1286
MILLER, ARTHUR, CWA II-1229;
CWAII III-1046
After the Fall, CLCII I-20; MPII:D I-17
All My Sons, CLCII I-29; MPII:D I-27
Crucible, The, CLCII I-351; MPII:D
I-414
Death of a Salesman, CLC I-255; MP
III-1365
Incident at Vichy, CLCII II-756; MPII:D
II-831
Price, The, CLCII III-1233; MPII:D
III-1283
Timebends, MPII:NF IV-1533
MILLER, HENRY, CWA II-1231; CWAII
III-1048
Tropic of Cancer, CLCII IV-1615;
MPII:AF IV-1697
Tropic of Capricorn, MP XI-6733;
MP:AF III-1330
MILLER, WALTER M., JR.
Canticle for Leibowitz, A, CLCII I-233;
MPII:AF I-247
MILNE, A. A.
Winnie-the-Pooh and The House at Pooh
Corner, MPII:JYAFic IV-1637
MIŁOSZ, CZESŁAW, CWAII III-1051
"Bobo's Metamorphosis," MPII:P I-263
"Bypassing Rue Descartes," MPII:P
I-328
Captive Mind, The, MPII:NF I-232
"Elegy for N. N.," MPII:P II-632

From the Rising of the Sun, MPII:P
II-819
Issa Valley, The, CLCII II-781;
MPII:WF II-743
Land of Ulro, The, MPII:NF II-792
Native Realm, MPII:NF III-997
"On Prayer," MPII:P IV-1584
Seizure of Power, The, CLCII III-1370;
MPII:WF IV-1377
"Song on the End of the World, A,"
MPII:P V-1969
"To Raja Rao," MPII:P VI-2215
"With Trumpets and Zithers," MPII:P
VI-2438
MILTON, JOHN, CWA II-1233
"Allegro, L'," MPII:P I-50
Areopagitica, MP I-299
Comus, CLC I-194; MP II-1051
"Lycidas," MPII:P IV-1301
Lyric Poetry of Milton, The, MP VI-3569
"On the Morning of Christ's Nativity,"
MPII:P IV-1590
Paradise Lost, CLC II-835; MP
VIII-4482
Paradise Regained, CLC II-887; MP
VIII-4487
"Penseroso, Il," MPII:P IV-1656
Samson Agonistes, CLC II-1002; MP
X-5776
MING, KAO. See KAO TSE-CH'ENG
MINSKY, MARVIN
Society of Mind, The, MPII:NF IV-1383
MIRANDOLA, GIOVANNI PICO
DELLA. See PICO DELLA
MIRANDOLA, GIOVANNI
MISHIMA, YUKIO, CWA II-1238; CWAII
III-1054
After the Banquet, CLCII I-19;
MPII:WF I-24
Confessions of a Mask, CLCII I-325;
MPII:WF I-310
"Death in Midsummer," MPII:SS II-524
"Patriotism," MPII:SS IV-1775
Sailor Who Fell from Grace with the
Sea, The, CLCII III-1328; MPII:WF
III-1332
Sea of Fertility, The, CLCII III-1354;
MPII:WF III-1361
Sound of Waves, The, MP XI-6199;
MP:EF III-1215
Sun and Steel, MPII:NF IV-1457

Temple of the Golden Pavilion, The,
CLCII IV-1522; MPII:WF IV-1554
MISTRAL, GABRIELA, CWA II-1240
Poetry of Gabriela Mistral, The, MP
IX-4949
MITCHELL, JAMES LESLIE. See
GIBBON, LEWIS GRASSIC
MITCHELL, MARGARET, CWA II-1242
Gone with the Wind, CLC I-410; MP
IV-2313; MP:AF I-474
MITCHELL, SILAS WEIR, CWA II-1243
Hugh Wynne, Free Quaker, CLC I-497;
MP V-2763; MP:AF II-577
MITCHELL, W. O.
Who Has Seen the Wind, CLCII
IV-1712; MPII:BCF IV-1895
MITCHISON, NAOMI
African Heroes, MPII:JYABio I-20
Conquered, The, MPII:JYAFic I-267
MITFORD, MARY RUSSELL, CWA
II-1245
Our Village, CLC II-830; MP VIII-4446;
MP:BF II-1145
MITTELHOLZER, EDGAR, CWAII
III-1056
Kaywana Trilogy, The, CLCII II-817;
The, MPII:BCF II-887
MO, TIMOTHY, CWAII III-1059
Insular Possession, An, CLCII II-766;
MPII:BCF II-825
Sour Sweet, CLCII IV-1451; MPII:BCF
IV-1581
MOHR, NICHOLASA
Felita, MPII:JYAFic I-418
Nilda, MPII:JYAFic III-1038
MOLESWORTH, MARY LOUISA
Carved Lions, The, MPII:JYAFic I-198
MOLIÈRE, CWA II-1247
Bourgeois Gentleman, The, CLC I-116;
MP II-611
Doctor in Spite of Himself, The, CLC
I-279; MP III-1546
Don Juan, CLC I-293; MP III-1595
Hypochondriac, The, CLC I-505; MP
V-2798
Misanthrope, The, CLC II-711; MP
VII-3921
Miser, The, CLC II-712; MP VII-3928
Romantic Ladies, The, CLC II-988; MP
X-5689

School for Husbands, The, CLC II-1010; MP X-5834

School for Wives, The, CLC II-1012; MP X-5843

Tartuffe, CLC II-1111; MP XI-6421

MOLNAR, FERENC, CWA II-1250

Liliom, CLC I-615; MP VI-3428

MOMADAY, N. SCOTT, CWAII III-1061

"Angle of Geese," MPII:P I-82

House Made of Dawn, CLCII II-707; MPII:AF II-754; MPII:JYAFic II-657

Names, The, MPII:NF III-991

Owl in the Cedar Tree, MPII:JYAFic III-1097

Way to Rainy Mountain, The, MPII:NF IV-1660

MONJO, F. N.

Drinking Gourd, The, MPII:JYAFic I-360

MONTAGUE, JOHN

"For the Hillmother," MPII:P II-792

MONTAIGNE, MICHEL EYQUEM DE, CWA II-1252

Essais, MP III-1825

MONTALE, EUGENIO

"Eel, The," MPII:P II-629

"Lemon Trees, The," MPII:P III-1213

"Provisional Conclusions," MPII:P V-1741

"Wall, The," MPII:P VI-2368

MONTESQUIEU, CHARLES DE, CWA II-1255

Persian Letters, MP VIII-4607

Spirit of the Laws, The, MP XI-6222

MONTGOMERY, L. M.

Anne of Green Gables, MPII:JYAFic I-49

MOODY, ANNE

Coming of Age in Mississippi, MPII:JYABio I-401

MOORE, BRIAN, CWAII III-1064

Black Robe, CLCII I-163; MPII:BCF I-150

Lonely Passion of Judith Hearne, The, CLCII III-907; MPII:BCF III-998

Luck of Ginger Coffey, The, CLCII III-935; MPII:BCF III-1039

MOORE, CARMAN

Somebody's Angel Child, MPII:JYABio IV-1589

MOORE, GEORGE, CWA II-1257

Esther Waters, CLC I-332; MP IV-1870; MP:BF I-374

MOORE, MARIANNE, CWA II-1259

"Fish, The," MPII:P II-775

"Marriage," MPII:P IV-1338

"Mind Is an Enchanting Thing, The," MPII:P IV-1391

"Octopus, An," MPII:P IV-1527

"Pangolin, The," MPII:P IV-1632

"Poetry," MPII:P IV-1710

Poetry of Marianne Moore, The, MP IX-5062

"Steeple-Jack, The," MPII:P V-2066

"Virginia Britannia," MPII:P VI-2338

MOORE, THOMAS, CWA II-1261

Irish Melodies, MP V-2935

Lalla Rookh, CLC I 590; MP VI-3237

MORAL, JOSÉ ZORRILLA Y. See ZORRILLA, JOSÉ

MORANTE, ELSA

Arturo's Island, CLCII I-70; MPII:WF I-71

History, CLCII II-679; MPII:WF II-593

MORAVIA, ALBERTO, CWA II-1263; CWAII III-1066

"Bitter Honeymoon," MPII:SS I-222

Conformist, The, CLCII I-329; MPII:WF I-319

Ghost at Noon, A, CLCII II-578; MPII:WF II-529

1934, CLCII III-1101; MPII:WF III-1098

Time of Indifference, The, CLCII IV-1568; MPII:WF IV-1605

Two Women, MP XII-6782; MP:EF III-1323

Woman of Rome, The, CLC II-1259; MP XII-7221; MP:EF III-1409

MORE, PAUL ELMER, CWA II-1265

Shelburne Essays, MP X-5966

MORE, SIR THOMAS, CWA II-1267

History of King Richard III, MP V-2637

Utopia, CLC II-1189; MP XII-6868

MOREY, JANET, and WENDY DUNN

Famous Mexican Americans, MPII:JYABio II-595

MOREY, WALT

Gentle Ben, MPII:JYAFic II-501

MORGAN, WILLIAM DE. See DE MORGAN, WILLIAM

MORIER, JAMES JUSTINIAN, CWA
II-1269
Hajji Baba of Ispahan, CLC I-436; MP
V-2446; MP:BF I-511
MÖRIKE, EDUARD, CWA II-1270
Poetry of Mörike, The, MP IX-5084
MORISON, SAMUEL ELIOT
Christopher Columbus, Mariner,
MPII:JYABio I-365
MORRIS, JEANNIE
Brian Piccolo, MPII:JYABio I-271
MORRIS, WILLIAM, CWA II-1272
Defence of Guenevere and Other Poems,
The, MP III-1417
Earthly Paradise, The, MP III-1687
MORRIS, WRIGHT, CWA II-1274;
CWAII III-1068
Ceremony in Lone Tree, MP II-872;
MP:AF I-186
Cloak of Light, A, MPII:NF IV-1696
Field of Vision, The, MP IV-2042;
MP:AF I-378
Fork River Space Project, The, CLCII
II-534; MPII:AF II-561
"Glimpse into Another Country,"
MPII:SS II-863
Inhabitants, The, MPII:NF II-736
Plains Song, for Female Voices, CLCII
III-1210; MPII:AF III-1262
"Ram in the Thicket, The," MPII:SS
V-1890
"Victrola," MPII:SS VI-2497
Will's Boy, Solo, MPII:NF IV-1696
Works of Love, The, CLCII IV-1749;
MPII:AF IV-1820
MORRISON, TONI, CWAII III-1071
Beloved, MPII:AfAm I-119;
MPII:JYAFic I-109
Bluest Eye, The, CLCII I-180; MPII:AF
I-191; MPII:AfAm I-188; The,
MPII:JYAFic I-141
Jazz, MPII:AfAm II-619
Song of Solomon, CLCII IV-1445;
MPII:AF IV-1485; MPII:AfAm
III-1299
Sula, CLCII IV-1490; MPII:AF
IV-1550; MPII:AfAm III-1386;
MPII:JYAFic IV-1396
Tar Baby, MPII:AfAm III-1407

MORTIMER, JOHN, CWAII III-1074
Clinging to the Wreckage, MPII:NF
I-249
Voyage Round My Father, A, CLCII
IV-1668; MPII:D IV-1701
MOSCHUS
Poetry of Moschus, The, MP IX-5087
MOSLEY, WALTER
Devil in a Blue Dress, MPII:AfAm I-362
MOSS, THYLIAS
Poetry of Thylias Moss, The,
MPII:AfAm III-1102
MOTTE-FOUQUÉ, FRIEDRICH DE LA.
See LA MOTTE-FOUQUÉ,
FRIEDRICH DE
MOYES, PATRICIA
Helter-Skelter, MPII:JYAFic II-619
MPHAHLELE, EZEKIEL
Wanderers, The, CLCII IV-1677;
MPII:BCF IV-1843
MROEK, SAWOMIR
Police, The, CLCII III-1217; MPII:D
III-1264
Tango, CLCII IV-1515; MPII:D IV-1534
MÜHLENWEG, FRITZ
Big Tiger and Christian, MPII:JYAFic
I-116
MUIR, JOHN, CWA II-1276
My First Summer in the Sierra,
MPII:JYABio III-1264
Story of My Boyhood and Youth, The,
MP XI-6286
MUKERJI, DHAN GOPAL
Gay-Neck, MPII:JYAFic II-498
MUKHERJEE, BHARATI, CWAII III-1077
"World According to Hsü, The,"
MPII:SS VI-2696
MULDOON, PAUL
"Meeting the British," MPII:P IV-1353
MULOCK, DINAH MARIA, CWA II-1278
John Halifax, Gentleman, CLC I-550;
MP V-3023; MP:BF II-691
MULTATULI, CWA II-1280
Max Havelaar, CLC I-682; MP
VII-3778; MP:EF II-844
MUMFORD, LEWIS, CWA II-1281
Brown Decades, The, MP II-693
MUNIF, ABDELRAHMAN, CWAII III-1079
Cities of Salt, CLCII I-287
Mudun al-milh, MPII:WF III-1049

MUNRO, ALICE, CWAII III-1081
    Lives of Girls and Women, CLCII
        III-898; MPII:BCF II-980
    "Wild Swans," MPII:SS VI-2619
MUNRO, HECTOR HUGH. *See* SAKI
MURA, DAVID
    "Relocation," MPII:P V-1791
MURASAKI SHIKIBU, LADY, CWA
        II-1283
    Tale of Genji, The, CLC II-1100; MP
        XI-6369; MP:EF III-1252
MURDOCH, IRIS, CWA II-1284; CWAII
        III-1083
    Bell, The, MP I-485; MP:BF I-104
    Black Prince, The, CLCII I-162;
        MPII:BCF I-145
    Bruno's Dream, CLCII I-208; MPII:BCF
        I-196
    Fairly Honourable Defeat, A, CLCII
        II-485; MPII:BCF I-483
    Good Apprentice, The, CLCII II-608;
        MPII:BCF II-627
    Nuns and Soldiers, CLCII III-1120;
        MPII:BCF III-1238
    Sandcastle, The, CLCII III-1334;
        MPII:BCF III-1444
    Severed Head, A, CLCII IV-1385;
        MPII:BCF IV-1516

Sovereignty of Good, The, MPII:NF
        IV-1402
    Unicorn, The, CLCII IV-1639;
        MPII:BCF IV-1771
    Word Child, A, CLCII IV-1744;
        MPII:BCF IV-1926
MURGER, HENRI, CWA II-1286
    Bohemians of the Latin Quarter, The,
        CLC I-113; MP I-581; MP:EF I-122
MURRAY, ALBERT
    Spyglass Tree, The, MPII:AfAm III-1337
    Train Whistle Guitar, MPII:AfAm
        III-1446
MURRAY, LES
    "Quality of Sprawl, The," MPII:P V-1760
MUSIL, ROBERT, CWAII III-1085
    Man Without Qualities, The, CLCII
        III-962; MPII:WF III-930
    Young Törless, CLCII IV-1766;
        MPII:WF IV-1797
MUSSET, ALFRED DE, CWA II-1287
    No Trifling with Love, CLC II-781; MP
        VII-4231
    Poetry of Musset, The, MP IX-5089
MYERS, WALTER DEAN
    Fallen Angels, MPII:JYAFic I-401
    Hoops, MPII:JYAFic II-641

N

NABOKOV, VLADIMIR, CWA II-1289;
CWAII III-1087
Ada or Ardor, CLCII I-12; MPII:AF I-6
Bend Sinister, CLCII I-141; MPII:AF
I-142
"Cloud, Castle, Lake," MPII:SS I-409
Defense, The, CLCII I-384; MPII:WF
I-359
Gift, The, CLCII II-581; MPII:WF II-534
Invitation to a Beheading, CLCII II-775;
MPII:WF II-732
Laughter in the Dark, CLCII II-861;
MPII:WF II-825
Lolita, CLCII III-904; MPII:AF II-901
Mary, CLCII III-981; MPII:WF III-965
Pale Fire, MP VIII-4462; MP:AF II-897
Pnin, CLCII III-1216; MPII:AF III-1277
Real Life of Sebastian Knight, The, MP
IX-5450; MP:AF III-1005
"Return of Chorb, The," MPII:SS V-1941
Speak, Memory, MPII:NF IV-1414
NAIPAUL, SHIVA, CWAII III-1090
Fireflies, CLCII II-511; MPII:BCF II-514
NAIPAUL, V. S., CWAII III-1092
Among the Believers, MPII:NF I-50
Bend in the River, A, CLCII I-139;
MPII:BCF I-124
Guerrillas, CLCII II-644; MPII:BCF
II-675
House for Mr. Biswas, A, CLCII II-706;
MPII:BCF II-748
In a Free State, CLCII II-744; MPII:BCF
II-804
Middle Passage, The, MPII:NF III-950
Miguel Street, CLCII III-1008;
MPII:BCF III-1102
Mimic Men, The, CLCII III-1010;
MPII:BCF III-1106
Mr. Stone and the Knights Companion,
CLCII III-1022; MPII:BCF III-1126
Prologue to an Autobiography, MPII:NF
III-1204
NARAYAN, R. K., CWA II-1291, CWAII
III-1094
"Astrologer's Day, An," MPII:SS I-129
Financial Expert, The, CLCII II-505;
MPII:BCF II-493
Grateful to Life and Death, CLCII
II-623; MPII:BCF II-660

Guide, The, MP IV-2418; MP:EF II-610
"Horse and Two Goats, A," MPII:SS
III-1037
Printer of Malgudi, The, CLCII III-1236;
MPII:BCF III-1346
"Uncle," MPII:SS VI-2452
Vendor of Sweets, The, CLCII IV-1653;
MPII:BCF IV-1780
NARIHIRA, ARIHARA NO. *See*
ARIHARA NO NARIHIRA
NASH, THOMAS, CWA II-1293
Unfortunate Traveller, The, CLC II-1186;
MP XII-6855; MP:BF III-1650
NATSUME, SŌSEKI, CWAII III-1096
Botchan, CLCII I-196; MPII:WF I-188
I Am a Cat, CLCII II-724; MPII:WF
II-648
Three-Cornered World, The, CLCII
IV-1555; MPII:WF IV-1595
NATTI, MARY LEE. *See* KINGMAN, LEE
NAVARRO, MARYSA, *and* NICHOLAS
FRASER
Eva Perón, MPII:JYABio II-576
NAYLOR, GLORIA, CWAII III-1098
Bailey's Café, MPII:AfAm I-102
Linden Hills, MPII:AfAm II-712
Mama Day, MPII:AfAm II-753
Women of Brewster Place, The, CLCII
IV-1734; MPII:AF IV-1805;
MPII:AfAm III-1502
NEEDHAM, RODNEY
Counterpoints, MPII:NF I-281
NEIMARK, ANNE E.
Deaf Child Listened, A, MPII:JYABio
I-455
NEKRASOV, NIKOLAI, CWA II-1294
Poetry of Nekrasov, The, MP IX-5092
NEMEROV, HOWARD, CWAII III-1100
"Brief Journey West, The," MPII:P I-285
"Goose Fish, The," MPII:P III-876
Journal of the Fictive Life, MPII:NF
II-762
NEMIROFF, ROBERT
To Be Young, Gifted, and Black,
MPII:JYABio IV-1732
NERUDA, PABLO, CWA II-1296; CWAII
III-1102
"Dead Gallop," MPII:P II-488

"Dream Horse," MPII:P II-596
"Entrance into Wood," MPII:P II-661
"Few Things Explained, A," MPII:P
II-752
Heights of Macchu Picchu, The, MPII:P
III-928
"Lemon, A," MPII:P III-1210
Memoirs, MPII:NF III-912
Poetry of Neruda, The, MP IX-5095
"Smell of Cordwood, A," MPII:P V-1927
Sonnet XXVII, MPII:P V-1990
NERVAL, GÉRARD DE, CWA II-1298
"Desdichado, El," MPII:P II-528
"Golden Verses," MPII:P III-867
Poetry of Nerval, The, MP IX-5098
NESBIT, E.
Five Children and It, MPII:JYAFic II-435
Long Ago When I Was Young,
MPII:JYABio III-1116
Story of the Treasure Seekers, The,
MPII:JYAFic IV-1379
NEVILLE, EMILY CHENEY
It's Like This, Cat, MPII:JYAFic II-734
NEWLON, CLARKE
Famous Puerto Ricans, MPII:JYABio
II-599
NEWMAN, JOHN HENRY, CWA II-1300
Apologia pro Vita Sua, MP I-263
NEWMAN, SHIRLEE P.
Marian Anderson, MPII:JYABio III-1180
NEWTON, SIR ISAAC, CWA II-1303
Philosophiae Naturalis Principia
Mathematica, MP VIII-4653
NEXÖ, MARTIN ANDERSEN, CWA
II-1305
Pelle the Conqueror, CLC II-851; MP
VIII-4566; MP:EF III-987
NGUGI WA THIONG'O, CWAII III-1105
Black Hermit, The, CLCII I-160;
MPII:D I-185
Detained, MPII:NF I-348
Petals of Blood, CLCII III-1198;
MPII:BCF III-1320
River Between, The, CLCII III-1300;
MPII:BCF III-1428
NGUGI WA THIONG'O and NGUGI WA
MIRII
I Will Marry When I Want, CLCII
II-729; MPII:D II-804

NICHOLS, PETER, CWAII III-1108
Day in the Death of Joe Egg, A, CLCII
I-370; MPII:D II-443
Passion Play, CLCII III-1185; MPII:D
III-1209
NICOLSON, SIR HAROLD GEORGE,
CWA II-1307
Some People, MP X-6132
NIEDECKER, LORINE
"I married," MPII:P III-1027
NIETZSCHE, FRIEDRICH WILHELM,
CWA II-1309
Beyond Good and Evil, MP I-520
Thus Spake Zarathustra, MP XI-6532
NIEVO, IPPOLITO, CWA II-1312
Castle of Fratta, The, CLC I-155; MP
II-823; MP:EF I-189
NIIHARA, RYNOSUKE. See
AKUTAGAWA, RYNOSUKE
NIMS, JOHN FREDERICK
"Love Poem," MPII:P III-1289
NIN, ANAÏS, CWAII III-1110
Diary of Anaïs Nin, The, MPII:NF I-373
Spy in the House of Love, A, CLCII
IV-1468; MPII:AF IV-1527
"Under a Glass Bell," MPII:SS VI-2461
NIXON, JOAN LOWERY
Kidnapping of Christina Lattimore, The,
MPII:JYAFic II-774
Séance, The, MPII:JYAFic III-1292
NOBLE, IRIS
Emmeline and Her Daughters,
MPII:JYABio II-561
Empress of All Russia, MPII:JYABio
II-564
Leonardo da Vinci, MPII:JYABio
III-1066
Susan B. Anthony, MPII:JYABio
IV-1649
NOLAN, JEANNETTE COVERT
Florence Nightingale, MPII:JYABio
II-639
NORDHOFF, CHARLES, and JAMES
NORMAN HALL, CWA II-1314
Mutiny on the Bounty, CLC II-749; MP
VII-4099; MP:AF II-819;
MPII:JYAFic III-1003
NORMAN, MARSHA, CWAII III-1112
Getting Out, CLCII II-577; MPII:D
II-672

'Night, Mother, CLCII III-1095; MPII:D III-1133

Third and Oak: The Laundromat, CLCII IV-1546; MPII:D IV-1562

NORRIS, FRANK, CWA II-1316

"Deal in Wheat, A," MPII:SS II-516

McTeague, CLC I-644; MP VI-3594; MP:AF II-717

Octopus, The, CLCII III-1129; MPII:AF III-1171

Pit, The, CLC II-889; MP VIII-4729; MP:AF II-949

Responsibilities of the Novelist, The, MP X-5528

NORTH, STERLING

Rascal, MPII:JYABio III-1475

Thoreau of Walden Pond, MPII:JYABio IV-1701

Young Thomas Edison, MPII:JYABio IV-1971

NORTON, MARY

Borrowers, The, MPII:JYAFic I-145

NORTON, THOMAS, *and* THOMAS SACKVILLE, CWA II-1319

Gorboduc, CLC I-412; MP IV-2332

NOVAK, JOSEPH. *See* KOSINSKI, JERZY

NOVALIS

Hymns to the Night, MPII:P III-994

NOZICK, ROBERT

Philosophical Explanations, MPII:NF III-1153

NYE, NAOMI SHIHAB

"House in the Heart, The," MPII:P III-971

O

O. HENRY. *See* HENRY, O.
OAKESHOTT, MICHAEL, CWAII
    III-1114
  On Human Conduct, MPII:NF III-1071
OATES, JOYCE CAROL, CWA II-1321,
    CWAII III-1116
  Bellefleur, CLCII I-138; MPII:AF I-136
  Bloodsmoor Romance, A, CLCII I-171;
    MPII:AF I-186
  "How I contemplated the world from the
    Detroit House of Correction and
    began my life over again," MPII:SS
    III-1060
  "My Warszawa," MPII:SS IV-1571
  "Nairobi," MPII:SS IV-1582
  Them, CLCII IV-1535; MPII:AF
    IV-1604
  Unholy Loves, CLCII IV-1637;
    MPII:AF IV-1717
  "Unmailed, Unwritten Letters," MPII:SS
    VI-2471
  "Upon the Sweeping Flood," MPII:SS
    VI-2478
  "Waiting," MPII:SS VI-2517
  "What Is the Connection Between Men
    and Women?" MPII:SS VI-2565
  "Where Are You Going, Where Have
    You Been?" MPII:SS VI-2577
  Wonderland, CLCII IV-1741; MPII:AF
    IV-1815
O'BRIEN, EDNA, CWAII III-1118
  Country Girls trilogy, The, CLCII I-341;
    MPII:BCF I-327
  Mother Ireland, MPII:NF III-987
  Night, CLCII III-1092; MPII:BCF
    III-1198
  Pagan Place, A, CLCII III-1169;
    MPII:BCF III-1267
  "Paradise," MPII:SS IV-1759
  "Rose in the Heart of New York, A,"
    MPII:SS V-1990
  "Scandalous Woman, A," MPII:SS
    V-2033
O'BRIEN, FITZ-JAMES
  "Diamond Lens, The," MPII:SS II-587
  "Wondersmith, The," MPII:SS VI-2687
O'BRIEN, FLANN, CWAII III-1120
  At Swim-Two-Birds, CLCII I-82;
    MPII:BCF I-77

Third Policeman, The, CLCII IV-1548;
    MPII:BCF IV-1686
O'BRIEN, KATE, CWA II-1323
  Last of Summer, The, CLC I-595; MP
    VI-3253; MP:BF II-776
O'BRIEN, ROBERT C.
  Mrs. Frisby and the Rats of NIMH,
    MPII:JYAFic III-968
O'CASEY, SEAN, CWA II-1324; CWAII
    III-1122
  Cock-a-Doodle Dandy, CLCII I-301;
    MPII:D I-370
  Juno and the Paycock, CLC I-562; MP
    VI-3100
  Mirror in My House, MPII:NF III-971
  Plough and the Stars, The, CLC II-894;
    MP VIII-4761
  Purple Dust, CLC II-927; MP IX-5378
  Red Roses for Me, CLCII III-1282;
    MPII:D III-1315
  Shadow of a Gunman, The, CLCII
    IV-1387; MPII:D IV-1454
  Silver Tassie, The, CLCII IV-1413;
    MPII:D IV-1465
  Within the Gates, CLC II-1254; MP
    XII-7199
O'CONNOR, FLANNERY, CWA II-1326;
    CWAII III-1124
  "Artificial Nigger, The," MPII:SS I-118
  "Displaced Person, The," MPII:SS II-607
  "Enduring Chill, The," MPII:SS II-692
  "Everything That Rises Must Converge,"
    MPII:SS II-735
  "Good Country People," MPII:SS II-900
  "Good Man Is Hard to Find, A,"
    MPII:SS II-903
  "Greenleaf," MPII:SS III-944
  Habit of Being, The, MPII:NF II-630
  "Parker's Back," MPII:SS IV-1768
  "Revelation," MPII:SS V-1945
  Short Stories of Flannery O'Connor,
    The, MP X-6008; MP:AF III-1152
  Violent Bear It Away, The, MP
    XII-6937; MP:AF III-1380
  Wise Blood, MP XII-7192; MP:AF
    III-1450
O'CONNOR, FRANK, CWAII III-1127
  "Christmas Morning," MPII:SS I-388
  "Drunkard, The," MPII:SS II-643

"Guests of the Nation," MPII:SS III-956
"Legal Aid," MPII:SS III-1325
"My Oedipus Complex," MPII:SS IV-1564
"Story by Maupassant, A," MPII:SS V-2238
O'CONNOR, RICHARD
  Sitting Bull, MPII:JYABio IV-1577
O'DELL, SCOTT
  Island of the Blue Dolphins,
    MPII:JYAFic II-726
ODETS, CLIFFORD, CWA III-1327;
    CWAII III-11290
  Awake and Sing! CLCII I-98; MPII:D
    I-104
  Big Knife, The, CLCII I-150; The
    MPII:D I-169
  Flowering Peach, The, CLCII II-527;
    MPII:D II-616
  Golden Boy, CLC I-409; MP IV-2304
O'DONOVAN, MICHAEL FRANCIS. See
    O'CONNOR, FRANK
E, KENZABUR, CWAII III-1131
  "Catch, The," MPII:SS I-340
  Personal Matter, A, CLCII III-1197;
    MPII:WF III-1195
  Silent Cry, The, CLCII IV-1407;
    MPII:WF IV-1431
O'FAOLÁIN, SEÁN, CWA III-1328;
    CWAII III-1133
  "Innocence," MPII:SS III-1176
  "Man Who Invented Sin, The," MPII:SS
    IV-1440
  "Midsummer Night Madness," MPII:SS
    IV-1497
  Nest of Simple Folk, A, CLC II-762; MP
    VII-4165; MP:BF II-1030
  "Up the Bare Stairs," MPII:SS VI-2474
O'FLAHERTY, LIAM, CWA III-1330;
    CWAII III-1135
  Informer, The, CLC I-524; MP V-2886;
    MP:BF II-640
  "Mountain Tavern, The," MPII:SS IV-1541
  "Post Office, The," MPII:SS IV-1835
  "Sniper, The," MPII:SS V-2158
  "Two Lovely Beasts," MPII:SS VI-2445
O'HARA, FRANK
  "Day Lady Died, The," MPII:P II-485
O'HARA, JOHN, CWA III-1332; CWAII
    III-1137
  Appointment in Samarra, CLC I-55; MP
    I-276; MP:AF I-70

"Doctor's Son, The," MPII:SS II-621
From the Terrace, CLCII II-552;
    MPII:AF II-591
Ten North Frederick, CLCII IV-1524;
    MPII:AF IV-1573
O'HARA, MARY
  My Friend Flicka, MPII:JYAFic III-1016
O'KEEFFE, GEORGIA
  Georgia O'Keeffe, MPII:JYABio II-725
OKIGBO, CHRISTOPHER
  "Siren," MPII:P V-1909
OLDENBOURG, ZOÉ, CWA III-1334
  Cornerstone, The, MP II-1121; MP:EF
    I-257
OLDS, SHARON
  "California Swimming Pool," MPII:P
    I-334
OLESHA, YURY, CWAII III-1139
  Envy, CLCII II-463; MPII:WF I-421
OLIVER, DIANE, CWAII III-1141
  "Neighbors," MPII:SS IV-1605
OLIVER, GEORGE. See ONIONS,
    OLIVER
OLSEN, TILLIE, CWAII III-1143
  "I Stand Here Ironing," MPII:SS III-1091
  Silences, MPII:NF IV-1346
  "Tell Me a Riddle," MPII:SS V-2308
  Yonnondio, CLCII IV-1763; MPII:AF
    IV-1841
OLSON, CHARLES
  "As the Dead Prey Upon Us," MPII:P
    I-119
  "Concerning Exaggeration, or How,
    Properly, to Heap Up," MPII:P I-414
  "In Cold Hell, in Thicket," MPII:P
    III-1064
  "K, The," MPII:P III-1141
  "Kingfishers, The," MPII:P III-1153
  Maximus Poems, The, MPII:P IV-1348
ONEAL, ELIZABETH. See ONEAL,
    ZIBBY
ONEAL, ZIBBY
  Grandma Moses, MPII:JYABio II-780
  Language of Goldfish, The,
    MPII:JYAFic II-802
O'NEILL, EUGENE, CWA III-1336
  All God's Chillun Got Wings, CLCII
    I-26; MPII:D I-22
  Anna Christie, CLC I-43; MP I-226

Desire Under the Elms, CLC I-265; MP III-1458

Emperor Jones, The, CLC I-325; MP III-1769

Great God Brown, The, CLCII II-628; MPII:D II-701

Hairy Ape, The, CLCII II-651; MPII:D II-723

Iceman Cometh, The, CLCII II-732; MPII:D II-809

Lazarus Laughed, CLCII II-863; MPII:D III-944

Long Day's Journey into Night, CLCII III-908; MPII:D III-986

Moon for the Misbegotten, A, CLCII III-1035; MPII:D III-1100

Mourning Becomes Electra, CLC II-745; MP VII-4081

Strange Interlude, CLC II-1089; MP XI-6294

ONETTI, JUAN CARLOS
Brief Life, A, CLCII I-201; MPII:AF I-212

Shipyard, The, CLCII IV-1394; MPII:AF IV-1411

ONG, WALTER J., CWAII III-1145
Presence of the Word, The, MPII:NF III-1179

ONIONS, OLIVER
"Beckoning Fair One, The," MPII:SS I-173

O'NOLAN, BRIAN. See O'BRIEN, FLANN

OPPEN, GEORGE
"But so as by Fire," MPII:P I-322
"Translucent Mechanics, The," MPII:P VI-2256

ORCZY, BARONESS EMMUSKA
Scarlet Pimpernel, The, MPII:JYAFic III-1288

ORIGO, IRIS
Images and Shadows, MPII:NF II-694

ORTEGA Y GASSET, JOSÉ, CWA III-1339
Revolt of the Masses, The, MP X-5562

ORTON, JOE, CWAII III-1148
Entertaining Mr. Sloane, CLCII II-462; MPII:D II-574

Loot, CLCII III-915; MPII:D III-992
What the Butler Saw, CLCII IV-1707; MPII:D IV-1728

ORWELL, GEORGE, CWA III-1341; CWAII III-1150
Animal Farm, CLCII I-51; MPII:BCF I-53; MPII:JYAFic I-41

Burmese Days, CLCII I-214; MPII:BCF I-206

Coming Up for Air, CLCII I-314; MPII:BCF I-297

Down and Out in Paris and London, MPII:NF I-409

Homage to Catalonia, MPII:NF II-645

Keep the Aspidistra Flying, CLCII II-820; MPII:BCF II-894

Nineteen Eighty-Four, CLC II-779; MP VII-4224; MP:BF II-1057

Road to Wigan Pier, The, MPII:NF III-1247

OSBORNE, JOHN, CWA III-1344; CWAII III-1153
Better Class of Person, A, MPII:NF I-144

Entertainer, The, CLCII II-461; MPII:D II-569

Inadmissible Evidence, CLCII II-755; MPII:D II-826

Look Back in Anger, MP VI-3490

Luther, CLCII III-937; MPII:D III-1002

OTWAY, THOMAS, CWA III-1346
Orphan, The, CLC II-823; MP VIII-4425

Soldier's Fortune, The, CLC II-1057; MP X-6128

Venice Preserved, CLC II-1195; MP XII-6890

OUIDA, CWA III-1347
Under Two Flags, CLC II-1183; MP XII-6840; MP:BF III-1643

OUSMANE, SEMBÈNE. See SEMBÈNE, OUSMANE

OVID, CWA III-1349
Amores, MP I-183
Ars Amatoria, MP I-317
Heroides, MP V-2601
Metamorphoses, The, MP VII-3866

OWEN, WILFRED, CWA III-1351
"Dulce et Decorum Est," MPII:P II-611
Poetry of Owen, The, MP IX-5105
"Strange Meeting," MPII:P V-2081

OWENS, ROCHELLE
Karl Marx Play, The, CLCII II-815; MPII:D III-883

P

PAGE, THOMAS NELSON, CWA III-1353
Marse Chan, CLC I-674; MP VII-3748;
MP:AF II-773
PAINE, ALBERT BIGELOW
Girl in White Armor, The, MPII:JYABio
II-761
PAINE, THOMAS, CWA III-1355
Age of Reason, The, MP I-70
Crisis, The, MP II-1211
PALEY, GRACE, CWAII III-1159
"Dreamers in a Dead Language,"
MPII:SS II-632
"Faith in a Tree," MPII:SS II-747
"Interest in Life, An," MPII:SS III-1184
PALMER, VANCE
Passage, The, CLCII III-1180;
MPII:BCF III-1293
PANGER, DANIEL
Ol' Prophet Nat, MPII:JYABio III-1345
PAPPAS, MARTHA R.
Heroes of the American West,
MPII:JYABio II-846
PARK, MUNGO
Travels to the Interior Districts of Africa,
MP XI-6656
PARKER, DOROTHY, CWAII III-1161
"Big Blonde," MPII:SS I-203
PARKMAN, FRANCIS, CWA III-1357
Count Frontenac and New France Under
Louis XIV, MP II-1133
Old Regime in Canada, The, MP
VIII-4338
Oregon Trail, The, MP VIII-4394
PARKS, GORDON
Choice of Weapons, A, MPII:JYABio
I-359
Learning Tree, The, MPII:AfAm II-676
Voices in the Mirror, MPII:AfAm
III-1478
PARRINGTON, VERNON LOUIS, CWA
III-1359
Main Currents in American Thought, MP
VI-3642
PASCAL, BLAISE, CWA III-1361
Pensées, MP VIII-4584
PASSOS, JOHN DOS. See DOS PASSOS,
JOHN

PASTAN, LINDA
"Death's Blue-Eyed Girl," MPII:P II-505
PASTERNAK, BORIS LEONIDOVICH,
CWA III-1362, CWAII III-1163
"Childhood of Luvers, The," MPII:SS
I-372
Doctor Zhivago, MP III-1561; MP:EF
I-417
Poems of Doctor Zhivago, The, MPII:P
IV-1705
Poetry of Pasternak, The, MP IX-5107
Safe-Conduct, A, MPII:NF III-1274
"Sparrow Hills," MPII:P V-2043
"Spring Rain," MPII:P V-2056
PASTON FAMILY
Paston Letters A.D. 1422-1509, The, MP
VIII-4513
PATER, WALTER, CWA III-1364
Marius the Epicurean, CLC I-671; MP
VII-3732; MP:BF II-868
Renaissance, The, MP IX-5511
PATERSON, KATHERINE
Bridge to Terabithia, MPII:JYAFic I-155
Come Sing, Jimmy Jo, MPII:JYAFic
I-261
Jacob Have I Loved, MPII:JYAFic II-737
PATON, ALAN, CWA III-1365
Cry, the Beloved Country, CLC I-227;
MP III-1235; MP:EF I-310
PATRICK, JOHN
Hasty Heart, The, CLCII II-660; MPII:D
II-747
Teahouse of the August Moon, The,
CLCII IV-1519; MPII:D IV-1548
PATTERSON, LILLIE
Sure Hands, Strong Heart, MPII:JYABio
IV-1645
PATTERSON, ORLANDO
Slavery and Social Death, MPII:AfAm
III-1279
PATTERSON, ROBERT, MILDRED
MEBEL, and LAWRENCE HILL
On Our Way, MPII:JYABio III-1348
PAUSTOVSKY, KONSTANTIN, CWAII
III-1166
Story of a Life, The, MPII:NF IV-1437

PAVESE, CESARE, CWAII III-1168
Among Women Only, CLCII I-41;
MPII:WF I-50
Burning Brand, The, MPII:NF I-218
House on the Hill, The, MPII:NF II-715;
MPII:WF II-639
Moon and the Bonfires, The, CLCII
III-1034; MPII:WF III-1036
PAYNE, ALMA SMITH
Discoverer of the Unseen World,
MPII:JYABio I-479
PAYNE, ROBERT
Three Worlds of Albert Schweitzer, The,
MPII:JYABio IV-1721
PAZ, OCTAVIO, CWA III-1366; CWAII
III-1170
Bow and the Lyre, The, MPII:NF I-196
"Clear Night," MPII:P I-397
"Draft of Shadows, A," MPII:P II-592
Labyrinth of Solitude, The, MP VI-3200
"Letter of Testimony," MPII:P III-1225
Poetry of Paz, The, MP IX-5109
"Return," MPII:P V-1819
"Same Time," MPII:P V-1861
"San Ildefonso Nocturne," MPII:P
V-1864
Sun Stone, MPII:P V-2102
"Vrindaban," MPII:P VI-2351
PEACOCK, THOMAS LOVE, CWA
III-1369
Crotchet Castle, CLC I-226; MP
III-1229; MP:BF I-261
Headlong Hall, CLC I-447; MP V-2498;
MP:BF I-536
Nightmare Abbey, CLC II-778; MP
VII-4221; MP:BF II-1053
PEAKE, MERVYN, CWAII III-1172
Gormenghast trilogy, The, CLCII II-618;
MPII:BCF II-648
PEARCE, PHILIPPA
Tom's Midnight Garden, MPII:JYAFic
IV-1494
PEARE, CATHERINE OWENS
FDR Story, The, MPII:JYABio II-619
Herbert Hoover Story, The,
MPII:JYABio II-830
Woodrow Wilson Story, The,
MPII:JYABio IV-1941

PEATTIE, DONALD CULROSS, CWA
III-1371
Almanac for Moderns, An, MP I-146
PEAVY, LINDA, and URSULA SMITH
Dreams into Deeds, MPII:JYABio II-517
PECK, RICHARD
Are You in the House Alone?,
MPII:JYAFic I-57
PECK, ROBERT NEWTON
Day No Pigs Would Die, A,
MPII:JYAFic I-315
PEDERSEN, KNUT. See HAMSUN, KNUT
PEELE, GEORGE, CWA III-1373
Old Wives' Tale, The, CLC II-809; MP
VIII-4349
PEET, BILL
Bill Peet, MPII:JYABio I-219
PÉGUY, CHARLES-PIERRE, CWA
III-1375
Poetry of Péguy, The, MP IX-5112
PEPYS, SAMUEL, CWA III-1377
Diary, MP III-1497
PERCY, WALKER, CWAII III-1174
Last Gentleman, The, CLCII II-853;
MPII:AF II-850
Love in the Ruins, CLCII III-925;
MPII:AF III-933
Message in the Bottle, The, MPII:NF
III-944
Moviegoer, The, CLCII III-1053;
MPII:AF III-1083
Second Coming, The, CLCII III-1363;
MPII:AF III-1376
PEREDA, JOSÉ MARÍA DE, CWA
III-1380
Pedro Sánchez, CLC II-847; MP
VIII-4556; MP:EF III-983
Peñas arriba, CLC II-852; MP
VIII-4572; MP:EF III-991
Sotileza, CLC II-1070; MP XI-6186;
MP:EF III-1211
PERELMAN, S. J., CWAII III-1177
"Critical Introduction to The Best of S. J.
Perelman by Sidney Namlerep,"
MPII:SS I-456
"Love Decoy, The," MPII:SS IV-1409
PERETZ, ISAAC LEIB
"Bontsha the Silent," MPII:SS I-277

PÉREZ GALDÓS, BENITO, CWA III-1382
  Ángel Guerra, CLC I-42; MP I-223;
    MP:EF I-43
  Doña Perfecta, CLC I-298; MP III-1618;
    MP:EF I-438
  Fortunata and Jacinta, CLC I-379; MP
    IV-2132; MP:EF II-534
  Our Friend Manso, CLCII III-1163;
    MPII:WF III-1157
  Saragossa, CLC II-1006; MP X-5796;
    MP:EF III-1131
PERRY, RICHARD
  Montgomery's Children, MPII:AfAm
    II-817
PERSE, ST.-JOHN, CWA III-1384
  Anabasis, MP I-196
  Chronique, MP II-956
  Èloges and Other Poems, MP III-1746
  Seamarks, MP X-5874
PERSONS, TRUMAN STRECKFUS. See
  CAPOTE, TRUMAN
PESHKOV, ALEKSEI MAKSIMOVICH.
  See GORKY, MAXIM
PETERS, ROBERT
  "Kittens," MPII:P III-1157
PETRARCH, FRANCESCO, CWA III-1386
  Rime of Petrarch, Le, MP X-5597
PETRONIUS, CWA III-1388
  Satyricon, The, CLC II-1008; MP
    X-5820; MP:EF III-1135
PETRY, ANN
  Country Place, MPII:AfAm I-330
  Harriet Tubman, MPII:JYABio II-806
  Narrows, The, MPII:AfAm II-869
  Street, The, MPII:AfAm III-1375
PEYTON, K. M.
  Flambards trilogy, The, MPII:JYAFic
    II-438
PFEFFER, SUSAN BETH
  About David, MPII:JYAFic I-1
PHILLIPS, CARYL
  Cambridge, MPII:AfAm I-219
PHILLIPS, JAYNE ANNE, CWAII III-1180
  "Black Tickets," MPII:SS I-239
  "Home," MPII:SS III-1033
PHIPSON, JOAN
  Family Conspiracy, The, MPII:JYAFic
    I-404
PICA, PETER. See ALDISS, BRIAN W.

PICO DELLA MIRANDOLA,
  GIOVANNI, CWA II-1236
  Oration on the Dignity of Man, MP
    VIII-4385
PIERCY, MARGE, CWAII III-1182
  Small Changes, CLCII IV-1426;
    MPII:AF IV-1448
  Woman on the Edge of Time, CLCII
    IV-1732; MPII:AF IV-1800
PILNYAK, BORIS, CWA III-1390
  Naked Year, The, CLC II-755; MP
    VII-4131; MP:EF II-913
PINCHERLE, ALBERTO. See MORAVIA,
  ALBERTO
PINCKNEY, DARRYL
  High Cotton, MPII:AfAm II-529
PINDAR, CWA III-1392
  Epinicia, The, MP III-1805
PINERO, ARTHUR WING, CWA III-1393
  Mid-Channel, CLC II-700; MP VII-3877
  Second Mrs. Tanqueray, The, CLC
    II-1017; MP X-5882
PINGET, ROBERT, CWAII III-1184
  Baga, CLCII I-102; MPII:WF I-107
  Inquisitory, The, CLCII II-764;
    MPII:WF II-701
  That Voice, CLCII IV-1532; MPII:WF
    IV-1570
PINSKY, ROBERT
  "Sadness and Happiness," MPII:P
    V-1848
PINTER, HAROLD, CWA III-1395;
  CWAII III-1186
  Betrayal, CLCII I-145; MPII:D I-163
  Birthday Party, The, CLCII I-159;
    MPII:D I-180
  Caretaker, The, MP II-800
  Dumb Waiter, The, CLCII II-429;
    MPII:D II-524
  Family Voices, CLCII II-490; MPII:D
    II-595
  Homecoming, The, CLCII II-688;
    MPII:D II-774
  Kind of Alaska, A, CLCII II-829;
    MPII:D III-910
PIRANDELLO, LUIGI, CWA III-1397
  Each in His Own Way, CLCII II-436;
    MPII:D II-534
  Henry IV, CLCII II-674; MPII:D II-764

Late Mattia Pascal, The, CLC I-600; MP VI-3285; MP:EF II-759

Old and the Young, The, CLC II-797; MP VIII-4305; MP:EF II-953

Right You Are—If You Think So, CLC II-970; MP X-5593

Six Characters in Search of an Author, CLC II-1047; MP X-6079

Tonight We Improvise, CLCII IV-1588; MPII:D IV-1601

"War," MPII:SS VI-2544

PIRSIG, ROBERT M., CWAII III-1189
Zen and the Art of Motorcycle Maintenance, MPII:JYABio IV-1989; MPII:NF IV-1741

PLANTE, DAVID, CWAII III-1191
"Work," MPII:SS VI-2692

PLATH, SYLVIA, CWAII III-1193
"Ariel," MPII:P I-106
Bell Jar, The, CLCII I-137; MPII:AF I-163
"Colossus, The," MPII:P I-404
"Daddy," MPII:P II-482
"Edge," MPII:P II-626
"Elm," MPII:P II-648
"Lady Lazarus," MPII:P III-1170
"Poppies in July," MPII:P IV-1716
"Words," MPII:P VI-2448

PLATO, CWA III-1400
Dialogues of Plato, The, MP III-1482
Republic, The, MP IX-5522

PLATONOV, ANDREI, CWAII III-1195
Chevengur, CLCII I-266; MPII:WF I-248
Foundation Pit, The, CLCII II-534; MPII:WF II-497

PLAUTUS, CWA III-1403
Amphitryon, CLC I-37; MP I-185
Braggart Soldier, The, CLC I-119; MP II-623
Captives, The, CLC I-151; MP II-797
Menaechmi, The, CLC I-694; MP VII-3849
Pot of Gold, The, CLC II-908; MP IX-5273
Slipknot, The, CLC II-1050; MP X-6094
Trickster, The, CLC II-1157; MP XI-6698

PLINY THE YOUNGER, CWA III-1405
Letters of Pliny the Younger, The, MP VI-3355

PLUNKETT, EDWARD JOHN MORETON DRAX. See DUNSANY, LORD

PLUTARCH, CWA III-1407
Parallel Lives, MP VIII-4490
Ten Famous Lives, MPII:JYABio IV-1668

PODHORETZ, NORMAN, CWAII III-1197
Making It, MPII:NF II-878

POE, EDGAR ALLAN, CWA III-1409
"Annabel Lee," MPII:P I-88
"Black Cat, The," MPII:SS I-231
"Cask of Amontillado, The," MPII:SS I-334
"City in the Sea, The," MPII:P I-389
"Descent into the Maelström, A," MPII:SS II-568
Essays of Edgar Allan Poe, The, MP IV-1854
"Fall of the House of Usher, The," CLC I-353; MP IV-1968;; MP:AF I-360; MPII:SS II-751
"Gold Bug, The," CLC I-406; MP IV-2286; MP:AF I-462; MPII:SS II-889
"Israfel," MPII:P III-1123
"Lenore," MPII:P III-1216
"Ligeia," CLC I-613; MP VI-3418; MP:AF II-674;" MPII:SS III-1352
"Masque of the Red Death, The," MPII:SS IV-1471
"Ms. Found in a Bottle," MPII:SS IV-1451
"Murders in the Rue Morgue, The," MPII:SS IV-1544
Narrative of Arthur Gordon Pym, CLC II-758; MP VII-4143; The, MP:AF II-828
"Pit and the Pendulum, The," MPII:SS IV-1821
"Purloined Letter, The," MPII:SS V-1868
"Raven, The," MPII:P V-1770
"Tell-Tale Heart, The," MPII:SS V-2312
"Ulalume," MPII:P VI-2309
"William Wilson," MPII:SS VI-2630

POHL, FREDERIK, CWAII III-1199
Way the Future Was, The, MPII:NF IV-1656

POLANYI, MICHAEL, CWAII III-1202
Personal Knowledge, MPII:NF III-1146

POLITE, CARLENE HATCHER
Flagellants, The, MPII:AfAm I-455
POLITIAN, CWA III-1412
Orfeo, CLC II-814; MP VIII-4398
POLO, MARCO, CWA III-1413
Travels of Marco Polo, The, MP XI-6650
PONTOPPIDAN, HENRIK, CWA III-1415
Promised Land, The, CLC II-926; MP
IX-5368; MP:EF III-1038
POOLE, LYNN, *and* GRAY POOLE
Scientists Who Changed the World,
MPII:JYABio IV-1533
POPA, VASKO
"One Bone to Another," MPII:P IV-1602
POPE, ALEXANDER, CWA III-1417
Dunciad, The, MP III-1672
"Elegy to the Memory of an Unfortunate
Lady," MPII:P II-638
Epistle to Dr. Arbuthnot, MPII:P II-677
Epistle II. To a Lady, MPII:P II-680
Essay on Criticism, MP III-1834
Essay on Man, MP IV-1837
Rape of the Lock, The, CLC II-940; MP
IX-5436
POQUELIN, JEAN BAPTISTE. *See*
MOLIÈRE
PORTER, CONNIE
All-Bright Court, MPII:AfAm I-5
PORTER, COUNTÉE. *See* CULLEN,
COUNTÉE
PORTER, ELEANOR H.
Pollyanna, MPII:JYAFic III-1159
PORTER, HAL
Tilted Cross, The, CLCII IV-1566;
MPII:BCF IV-1705
PORTER, JANE, CWA III-1419
Scottish Chiefs, The, CLC II-1013; MP
X-5851; MP:BF III-1402
Thaddeus of Warsaw, CLC II-1120; MP
XI-6462; MP:BF III-1514
PORTER, KATHERINE ANNE, CWA
III-1420; CWAII III-1205
"Flowering Judas," MPII:SS II-795
"Leaning Tower, The," MPII:SS III-1309
"Noon Wine," MPII:SS IV-1628
"Old Mortality," CLC II-804; MP
VIII-4330; MP:AF II-879; MPII:SS
IV-1672
Pale Horse, Pale Rider, MP VIII-4465;
MP:AF II-901

"Pale Horse, Pale Rider," MPII:SS
IV-1756
"Rope," MPII:SS V-1978
Ship of Fools, MP X-5979; MP:AF
III-1134
PORTER, SHEENA
Nordy Bank, MPII:JYAFic III-1045
PORTER, WILLIAM SYDNEY. *See*
HENRY, O.
POTOK, CHAIM, CWAII III-1207
Book of Lights, The, CLCII I-192;
MPII:AF I-202
Chosen, The, CLCII I-281; MPII:AF
I-295; MPII:JYAFic I-237
Davita's Harp, MPII:JYAFic I-311
In the Beginning, CLCII II-746;
MPII:AF II-782
My Name Is Asher Lev, CLCII III-1067;
MPII:AF III-1105
Promise, The, CLCII I-281; MPII:AF
I-295
POUND, EZRA, CWA III-1423; CWAII
III-1210
ABC of Reading, MPII:NF I-1
"Canto 1," MPII:P I-340
"Canto 49," MPII:P I-343
"Canto 74," MPII:P I-347
Cantos, MP II-776
Gaudier-Brzeska, MPII:NF II-544
Guide to Kulchur, MPII:NF II-611
Homage to Sextus Propertius, MPII:P
III-951
Hugh Selwyn Mauberly, MPII:P III-978
Personae, MP VIII-4612
"Return, The," MPII:P V-1823
"River-Merchant's Wife, The," MPII:P
V-1835
"Seafarer, The," MPII:P V-1880
"Sestina: Altaforte," MPII:P V-1899
Women of Trachis, (trans.) CLCII
IV-1736; MPII:D IV-1757
POWELL, ANTHONY, CWA III-1426;
CWAII III-1213
Afternoon Men, CLCII I-21; MPII:BCF
I-27
Agents and Patients, CLCII I-23;
MPII:BCF I-32
Dance to the Music of Time, A, MP
III-1288; MP:BF I-269; MP III-1293
Fisher King, The, CLCII II-518;
MPII:BCF II-520

O, How the Wheel Becomes It! CLCII
III-1123; MPII:BCF III-1243
To Keep the Ball Rolling, MPII:NF
IV-1538
Venusberg, CLCII IV-1654; MPII:BCF
IV-1785
POWERS, J. F., CWAII III-1215
"Lions, Harts, Leaping Does," MPII:SS
III-1363
Morte d'Urban, CLCII III-1040;
MPII:AF III-1055
"Old Bird," MPII:SS IV-1664
"Prince of Darkness," MPII:SS IV-1848
POWYS, JOHN COWPER, CWA III-1428
Wolf Solent, CLC II-1255; MP
XII-7203; MP:BF III-1749
POWYS, LLEWELYN, CWA III-1430
Ebony and Ivory, MP III-1697; MP:BF
I-352
POWYS, T. F., CWA III-1432
Mr. Weston's Good Wine, CLC II-721;
MP VII-3970; MP:BF II-974
PRESCOTT, WILLIAM HICKLING,
CWA III-1434
History of the Conquest of Mexico, MP
V-2646
PRÉVERT, JACQUES
"Autumn Leaves," MPII:P I-175
PRÉVOST, ABBÉ, CWA III-1435
Manon Lescaut, CLC I-664; MP
VII-3696; MP:EF II-826
PRICE, REYNOLDS, CWA III-1437;
CWAII III-1217
"Chain of Love, A," MPII:SS I-351
Generous Man, A, CLCII II-574;
MPII:AF II-607
Long and Happy Life, A, MP VI-3474;
MP:AF II-691
"Truth and Lies," MPII:SS VI-2425
PRICHARD, KATHARINE SUSANNAH
Coonardoo, CLCII I-335; MPII:BCF
I-322
PRIESTLEY, J. B., CWA III-1438; CWAII
III-1219
Angel Pavement, CLCII I-45; MPII:BCF
I-43
Charles Dickens, MPII:JYABio I-333
Eden End, CLCII II-444; MPII:D II-546
Good Companions, The, CLC I-410; MP
IV-2316; MP:BF I-483

Inspector Calls, An, CLCII II-765;
MPII:D II-852
Time and the Conways, CLCII IV-1567;
MPII:D IV-1579
PRIOR, MATTHEW, CWA III-1440
Poetry of Prior, The, MP IX-5115
PRITCHETT, V. S., CWAII III-1222
Cab at the Door, A, MPII:NF I-223
"Camberwell Beauty, The," MPII:SS
I-320
Dead Man Leading, CLCII I-374;
MPII:BCF I-364
"It May Never Happen," MPII:SS
III-1194
"Many Are Disappointed," MPII:SS
IV-1455
Midnight Oil, MPII:NF III-955
Mr. Beluncle, CLCII III-1018;
MPII:BCF III-1121
PROKOSCH, FREDERIC, CWA III-1442;
CWAII III-1224
Asiatics, The, CLCII I-76; MPII:AF I-56
Missolonghi Manuscript, The, CLCII
III-1018; MPII:AF III-1012
Seven Who Fled, The, CLC II-1026; MP
X-5934; MP:AF III-1117
PROPERTIUS, SEXTUS, CWA III-1444
Elegies of Propertius, The, MP III-1739
PROUST, MARCEL, CWA III-1446
Remembrance of Things Past, CLC
II-953; MP IX-5500; MP:EF III-1072
PRUITT, IDA
Daughter of Han, A, MPII:JYABio I-443
P'U SUNG-LING, CWA III-1451
Strange Stories from a Chinese Studio,
MP XI-6299; MP:EF III-1241
PUIG, MANUEL, CWAII III-1227
Betrayed by Rita Hayworth, CLCII
I-146; MPII:AF I-146
Heartbreak Tango, CLCII II-670;
MPII:AF II-701
Kiss of the Spider Woman, CLCII
II-837; MPII:AF II-845
PURDY, CLAIRE LEE
He Heard America Sing, MPII:JYABio
II-814
PURDY, JAMES, CWA III-1449; CWAII
III-1229
Color of Darkness, MP II-1034; MP:AF
I-203

"Color of Darkness," MPII:SS I-418
"Daddy Wolf," MPII:SS II-474
Malcolm, MP VI-3655; MP:AF II-737
PUSHKIN, ALEXANDER, CWA III-1453
"Blizzard, The," MPII:SS I-254
Boris Godunov, CLC I-115; MP I-599
Bronze Horseman, The, MP II-674
Captain's Daughter, The, CLC I-150;
MP II-792; MP:EF I-172
Eugene Onegin, CLC I-334; MP IV-1883
"Queen of Spades, The," CLCII
III-1244; MPII:SS V-1872
Ruslan and Lyudmila, MP X-5740
"Shot, The," MPII:SS V-2093
"Station-master, The," MPII:SS V-2220
PUTNAM, PETER B.
Peter, the Revolutionary Tsar,
MPII:JYABio III-1410
PARK, RUTH
Playing Beatie Bow, MPII:JYAFic
III-1151
PYLE, HOWARD
Merry Adventures of Robin Hood, The,
MPII:JYAFic III-954

PYM, BARBARA, CWAII III-1231
Excellent Women, CLCII II-473;
MPII:BCF I-466
Glass of Blessings, A, CLCII II-594;
MPII:BCF II-607
Less than Angels, CLCII II-873;
MPII:BCF II-949
Quartet in Autumn, CLCII III-1243;
MPII:BCF III-1355
Sweet Dove Died, The, CLCII IV-1507;
MPII:BCF IV-1659
Very Private Eye, A, MPII:NF IV-1641
PYNCHON, THOMAS, CWAII III-1233
Crying of Lot 49, The, CLCII I-354;
MPII:AF I-361
"Entropy," MPII:SS II-709
Gravity's Rainbow, CLCII II-624;
MPII:AF II-661
"Secret Integration, The," MPII:SS
V-2053
"Under the Rose," MPII:SS VI-2464
V., CLCII IV-1646; MPII:AF IV-1727

Q

QUEIRÓS, JOSÉ MARIA EÇA DE. *See*
  EÇA DE QUEIRÓS, JOSÉ MARIA
QUEIROZ, RACHEL DE, CWAII IV-1237
  Dôra, Doralina, CLCII II-418; MPII:AF
  I-445
  Three Marias, The, CLCII IV-1557;
  MPII:AF IV-1648

QUENEAU, RAYMOND, CWAII IV-1239
  Bark Tree, The, CLCII I-116; MPII:WF
  I-111
  Sunday of Life, The, CLCII IV-1494;
  MPII:WF IV-1533
  Zazie in the Metro, CLCII IV-1767;
  MPII:WF IV-1803

R

RAABE, WILHELM, CWAII IV-1241
  Horacker, CLCII II-697; MPII:WF II-612
  Tubby Schaumann, CLCII IV-1622;
    MPII:WF IV-1676
RABE, DAVID, CWAII IV-1243
  Basic Training of Pavlo Hummel, The,
    CLCII I-122; MPII:D I-127
  Hurlyburly, CLCII II-723; MPII:D II-794
  Streamers, CLCII IV-1483; MPII:D
    IV-1496
RABE, OLIVE, *and* AILEEN L. FISHER
  We Alcotts, MPII:JYABio IV-1834
  We Dickinsons, MPII:JYABio IV-1838
RABELAIS, FRANÇOIS, CWA III-1455
  Gargantua and Pantagruel, CLC I-393;
    MP IV-2208; MP:EF II-553
RABINOWITZ, SHOLOM. *See*
  ALEICHEM, SHOLOM
RACINE, JEAN BAPTISTE, CWA III-1458
  Andromache, CLC I-41; MP I-219
  Bérénice, CLC I-99; MP I-504
  Britannicus, CLC I-125; MP II-662
  Mithridate, CLC II-725; MP VII-3987
  Phèdra, CLC II-867; MP VIII-4632
  Plaideurs, Les, CLC II-891; MP
    VIII-4740
RADCLIFFE, MRS. ANN, CWA III-1460
  Italian, The, CLC I-535; MP V-2948;
    MP:BF II-657
  Mysteries of Udolpho, The, CLC II-753;
    MP VII-4115; MP:BF II-1015
  Romance of the Forest, The, CLC II-984;
    MP X-5675; MP:BF III-1358
RAKOSI, CARL
  "Manhattan, 1975," MPII:P IV-1319
RALEIGH, SIR WALTER, CWA III-1462
  Poetry of Raleigh, The, MP IX-5118
RAMÉE, MARIE LOUISE DE LA. *See*
  OUIDA
RAMUZ, CHARLES-FERDINAND, CWA
  III-1464
  When the Mountain Fell, CLC II-1235;
    MP XII-7097; MP:EF III-1383
RANDALL, DUDLEY
  Poetry of Dudley Randall, The,
    MPII:AfAm III-1108
RANDALL, RUTH PAINTER
  I Mary, MPII:JYABio II-889

RANSOM, JOHN CROWE, CWA III-1465
  "Bells for John Whiteside's Daughter,"
    MPII:P I-225
  "Equilibrists, The," MPII:P II-687
  New Criticism, The, MP VII-4171
  Selected Poems, MP X-5899
RANSOME, ARTHUR
  Pigeon Post, MPII:JYAFic III-1133
  Swallows and Amazons, MPII:JYAFic
    IV-1413
RAO, RAJA, CWAII IV-1245
  Kanthapura, CLCII II-813; MPII:BCF
    II-882
  Serpent and the Rope, The, CLCII
    IV-1377; MPII:BCF IV-1501
RASKIN, ELLEN
  Westing Game, The, MPII:JYAFic
    IV-1589
RASPE, RUDOLF ERICH, CWA III-1467
  Baron Münchausen's Narrative, CLC
    I-84; MP I-435; MP:EF I-101
RATTIGAN, TERENCE, CWAII IV-1247
  Browning Version, The, CLCII I-207;
    MPII:D I-250
  French Without Tears, CLCII II-547;
    MPII:D II-639
RAWLINGS, MARJORIE KINNAN, CWA
  III-1469
  Cross Creek, MPII:JYABio I-419
  Yearling, The, CLC II-1272; MP
    XII-7286; MP:AF III-1459;
    MPII:JYAFic IV-1667
RAWLS, WILSON
  Where the Red Fern Grows,
    MPII:JYAFic IV-1616
READE, CHARLES, CWA III-1470
  Cloister and the Hearth, The, CLC I-188;
    MP II-993; MP:BF I-225
  Peg Woffington, CLC II-850; MP
    VIII-4562; MP:BF II-1175
REANEY, JAMES
  Colours in the Dark, CLCII I-309;
    MPII:D I-382
  Killdeer, The, CLCII II-825; MPII:D
    II-900
REED, GWENDOLYN
  Beginnings, MPII:JYABio I-187

REED, ISHMAEL, CWAII IV-1249
Essays of Ishmael Reed, The,
MPII:AfAm I-418
Flight to Canada, CLCII II-522;
MPII:AF II-551; MPII:AfAm I-460
Mumbo Jumbo, CLCII III-1055;
MPII:AF III-1094; MPII:AfAm II-835
Reckless Eyeballing, MPII:AfAm III-1200
Yellow Back Radio Broke-Down, CLCII
IV-1762; MPII:AF IV-1835;
MPII:AfAm III-1519
REES, DAVID
Exeter Blitz, The, MPII:JYAFic I-394
RÊGO, JOSÉ LINS DO. See LINS DO
RÊGO, JOSÉ
REID, FORREST, CWA III-1472
Bracknels, The, CLC I-119; MP II-619;
MP:BF I-124
REID, VICTOR STAFFORD
New Day, CLCII III-1087; MPII:BCF
III-1193
REINGOLD, CARMEL BERMAN
Johann Sebastian Bach, MPII:JYABio
II-967
REISS, JOHANNA
Journey Back, The, MPII:JYABio II-977
Upstairs Room, The, MPII:JYABio
IV-1803
REIZENSTEIN, ELMER LEOPOLD. See
RICE, ELMER
REMARK, ERICH PAUL. See
REMARQUE, ERICH MARIA
REMARQUE, ERICH MARIA, CWA
III-1474
All Quiet on the Western Front, CLC
I-27; MP I-130; MP:EF I-23;
MPII:JYAFic I-32
RENAULT, MARY, CWA III-1476;
CWAII IV-1251
Bull from the Sea, The, CLCII II-831;
MPII:BCF II-920
Fire from Heaven, CLCII II-508;
MPII:BCF II-498
Funeral Games, CLCII II-557; MPII:BCF
II-561
King Must Die, The, CLCII II-831;
MPII:BCF II-920
Last of the Wine, The, MP VI-3271;
MP:BF II-784

Persian Boy, The, CLCII III-1195;
MPII:BCF III-1313
REXROTH, KENNETH, CWAII IV-1253
Autobiographical Novel, An, MPII:NF
I-104
"Signature of All Things, The," MPII:P
V-1906
"When We with Sappho," MPII:P
VI-2391
REYES, ALFONSO, CWA III-1477
Visión de Anáhuac, MP XII-6961
REYES, NEFTALÍ RICARDO. See
NERUDA, PABLO
REYMONT, WADYSAW, CWA III-1480
Peasants, The, CLC II-845; MP
VIII-4544; MP:EF III-977
REYNOLDS, QUENTIN J.
Custer's Last Stand, MPII:JYABio I-427
RHYS, JEAN, CWAII IV-1256
Good Morning, Midnight, CLCII II-612;
MPII:BCF II-632
"Outside the Machine," MPII:SS IV-1737
Wide Sargasso Sea, CLCII IV-1714;
MPII:BCF IV-1899
RIBMAN, RONALD, CWAII IV-1258
Ceremony of Innocence, The, CLCII
I-252; MPII:D I-299
Cold Storage, CLCII I-306; MPII:D I-377
RICE, EDWARD
Margaret Mead, MPII:JYABio III-1174
RICE, ELMER, CWA III-1482; CWAII
IV-1261
Adding Machine, The, CLCII I-14;
MPII:D I-11
Street Scene, CLC II-1090; MP XI-6304
RICH, ADRIENNE
"Diving into the Wreck," MPII:P II-561
"For a Sister," MPII:P II-786
"Planetarium," MPII:P IV-1691
"Snapshots of a Daughter-in-Law,"
MPII:P V-1934
RICHARDS, I. A., CWA III-1484
Principles of Literary Criticism, MP
IX-5334
RICHARDS, NORMAN
Dreamers and Doers, MPII:JYABio
II-513

RICHARDSON, BEN, and WILLIAM A. FAHEY
Great Black Americans, MPII:JYABio II-787
RICHARDSON, DOROTHY M., CWA III-1486
Pilgrimage, CLC II-880; MP VIII-4696; MP:BF III-1222
RICHARDSON, ELAINE POTTER. See KINCAID, JAMAICA.
RICHARDSON, HENRY HANDEL, CWA III-1487
Fortunes of Richard Mahony, The, CLC I-382; MP IV-2142; MP:BF I-458
RICHARDSON, SAMUEL, CWA III-1488
Clarissa, CLC I-183; MP II-976; MP:BF I-211
Pamela, CLC II-832; MP VIII-4472; MP:BF II-1149; MPII:JYAFic III-1106
Sir Charles Grandison, CLC II-1041; MP X-6056; MP:BF III-1459
RICHLER, MORDECAI, CWAII IV-1264
Apprenticeship of Duddy Kravitz, The, CLCII I-63; MPII:BCF I-63
St. Urbain's Horseman, CLCII III-1330; MPII:BCF III-1440
RICHTER, CONRAD, CWA III-1491
Fields, The, CLC I-366; MP IV-2046; MP:AF I-382
Light in the Forest, The, MPII:JYAFic II-834
Sea of Grass, The, CLC II-1014; MP X-5861; MP:AF III-1102
Simple Honorable Man, A, MP X-6050; MP:AF III-1168
Town, The, CLC II-1150; MP XI-6628; MP:AF III-1308
Trees, The, CLC II-1154; MP XI-6683; MP:AF III-1326
Waters of Kronos, The, MP XII-7049; MP:AF III-1409
RICHTER, HANS PETER
Friedrich, MPII:JYAFic II-470
RICHTER, JOHANN PAUL FRIEDRICH. See JEAN PAUL
RICKETTS, EDWARD F., and JOHN STEINBECK
Sea of Cortez, MPII:NF III-1309

RIDING, LAURA
"Auspice of Jewels," MPII:P I-159
RIESMAN, DAVID
Lonely Crowd, The, MPII:NF II-856
RIGGS, LYNN, CWA III-1494
Green Grow the Lilacs, CLC I-425; MP IV-2382
RILKE, RAINER MARIA, CWA III-1495; CWAII IV-1266
"Angels, The," MPII:P I-79
"Archaic Torso of Apollo," MPII:P I-98
"Autumn Day," MPII:P I-172
"Buddha in Glory," MPII:P I-304
"Dove, That Stayed Outside," MPII:P II-585
Duino Elegies, MP III-1669
"Evening Meal," MPII:P II-697
Letters on Cézanne, MPII:NF II-812
"Panther, The," MPII:P IV-1636
"Roman Sarcophagi," MPII:P V-1845
Sonnets to Orpheus, MP XI-6175
RIMBAUD, ARTHUR, CWA III-1498
"Blackcurrant River," MPII:P I-256
"Drunken Boat, The," MPII:P II-608
"First Communions," MPII:P II-768
"Memory," MPII:P IV-1359
Season in Hell, A, MP X-5876
"Seekers of Lice, The," MPII:P V-1889
"Vowels," MPII:P VI-2345
RIOS, ALBERTO
"Purpose of Altar Boys, The," MPII:P V-1754
RIPLEY, ELIZABETH
Copley, MPII:JYABio I-412
Michelangelo, MPII:JYABio III-1210
RÍTSOS, YÁNNIS
"Fellow Diners," MPII:P II-746
"In the Ruins of an Ancient Temple," MPII:P III-1096
"Miniature," MPII:P IV-1394
RIVERA, TOMÁS, CWAII IV-1269
". . . and the earth did not part," MPII:SS I-89
"Searchers, The," MPII:P V-1883
ROA BASTOS, AUGUSTO
Son of Man, CLCII IV-1444; MPII:AF IV-1481

ROBBE-GRILLET, ALAIN, CWAII
IV-1271
Erasers, The, CLCII II-467; MPII:WF
I-430
In the Labyrinth, CLCII II-750;
MPII:WF II-686
Jealousy, CLCII II-790; MPII:WF II-755
ROBERTS, CHARLES G. D.
Red Fox, MPII:JYAFic III-1214
ROBERTS, ELIZABETH MADOX, CWA
III-1500
Great Meadow, The, CLC I-422; MP
IV-2363; MP:AF I-501
My Heart and My Flesh, CLCII III-1062;
MPII:AF III-1100
Time of Man, The, CLC II-1132; MP
XI-6545; MP:AF III-1289
ROBERTS, KENNETH, CWA III-1503
Northwest Passage, MP VII-4247;
MP:AF II-852
ROBERTSON, ETHEL FLORENCE
RICHARDSON. See
RICHARDSON, HENRY HANDEL
ROBERTSON, THOMAS WILLIAM,
CWA III-1505
Caste, CLC I-154; MP II-816
ROBINSON, EDWIN ARLINGTON,
CWA III-1506
"Eros Turannos," MPII:P II-691
"Luke Havergal," MPII:P IV-1295
Man Against the Sky, The, MP VI-3664
"Miniver Cheevy," MPII:P IV-1398
Tristram, MP XI-6709
ROBINSON, HENRY CRABB, CWA
III-1509
Diary of Henry Crabb Robinson, MP
III-1509
ROBINSON, JACKIE, and ALFRED
DUCKETT
Breakthrough to the Big League,
MPII:JYABio I-264
ROCHEFOUCAULD, FRANÇOIS LA. See
LA ROCHEFOUCAULD,
FRANÇOIS
ROCHESTER, EARL OF. See WILMOT,
JOHN
RODGERS, CAROLYN M.
Poetry of Carolyn M. Rodgers, The,
MPII:AfAm III-1114

RODRÍGUEZ, RICHARD
Hunger of Memory, MPII:JYABio
II-869; MPII:NF II-668
ROETHKE, THEODORE, CWA III-1511
"In a Dark Time," MPII:P III-1058
"My Papa's Waltz," MPII:P IV-1453
"Open House," MPII:P IV-1614
Poetry of Roethke, The, MP IX-5126
"Words for the Wind," MPII:P VI-2451
ROGERS, SAMUEL SHEPARD. See
SHEPARD, SAM
ROGERS, WILLIAM GARLAND
Carl Sandburg, Yes, MPII:JYABio I-293
ROJAS, FERNANDO DE, CWA III-1512
Celestina, CLC I-163; MP II-865;
MP:EF I-201
ROLFE, FREDERICK WILLIAM. See
CORVO, BARON
ROLLAND, ROMAIN, CWA III-1513
Jean-Christophe, CLC I-543; MP
V-2988; MP:EF II-714
RÖLVAAG, O. E., CWA III-1516
Giants in the Earth, CLC I-400; MP
IV-2255; MP:AF I-440
Peder Victorious, CLC II-847; MP
VIII-4549; MP:AF II-914
ROMERO, JOSÉ RUBÉN
Futile Life of Pito Perez, The, CLCII
II-559; MPII:AF II-597
RONSARD, PIERRE DE, CWA III-1518
Poetry of Ronsard, The, MP IX-5131
ROOKE, LEON
Shakespeare's Dog, CLCII IV-1388;
MPII:BCF IV-1523
ROOS, ANN
Man of Molokai, MPII:JYABio III-1156
ROOSEVELT, ELEANOR
This I Remember, MPII:JYABio IV-1695
ROREM, NED, CWAII IV-1273
Paris and New York Diaries of Ned
Rorem, The, MPII:NF III-1124
RORTY, RICHARD, CWAII IV-1275
Philosophy and the Mirror of Nature,
MPII:NF III-1158
ROSE, AL
Eubie Blake, MPII:JYABio II-572
ROSEN, SIDNEY
Wizard of the Dome, MPII:JYABio
IV-1915

ROSENBLUM, MORRIS
 Heroes of Mexico, MPII:JYABio II-838
ROSENFELD, ISAAC, CWAII IV-1277
 "King Solomon," MPII:SS III-1262
ROSS, ALAN
 Blindfold Games, MPII:NF I-172
ROSS, SINCLAIR
 As for Me and My House, CLCII I-72;
  MPII:BCF I-72
 Sawbones Memorial, CLCII III-1342;
  MPII:BCF III-1455
ROSSETTI, CHRISTINA, CWA III-1519
 "Goblin Market," MPII:P III-860
 "Memory," MPII:P IV-1363
 Poetry of Christina Rossetti, The, MP
  VIII-4860
ROSSETTI, DANTE GABRIEL, CWA
  III-1521
 "Blessed Damozel, The," MPII:P I-260
 Poetry of Dante Gabriel Rossetti, The,
  MP VIII-4893
ROSTAND, EDMOND, CWA III-1523
 Cyrano de Bergerac, CLC I-233; MP
  III-1262
 L'Aiglon, CLC I-590; MP VI-3222
ROTH, HENRY, CWA III-1525
 Call It Sleep, MP II-744; MP:AF I-162
ROTH, JOSEPH, CWAII IV-1279
 Job, CLCII II-792; MPII:WF II-760
ROTH, PHILIP, CWAII IV-1282
 Anatomy Lesson, The, CLCII I-42
 "Conversion of the Jews, The," MPII:SS
  I-429
 "Defender of the Faith," MPII:SS II-550
 Facts, The, MPII:NF II-492
 Ghost Writer, The, CLCII II-580
 Great American Novel, The, CLCII
  II-626; MPII:AF II-666
 Letting Go, CLCII II-878; MPII:AF
  III-883
 Portnoy's Complaint, CLCII III-1224;
  MPII:AF III-1281
 Prague Orgy, The, CLCII III-1229
 Zuckerman Bound, MPII:AF IV-1856
 Zuckerman Unbound, CLCII IV-1774
ROTH-HANO, RENÉE
 Touch Wood, MPII:JYABio IV-1762
ROUSSEAU, JEAN-JACQUES, CWA
  III-1527
 Confessions, MP II-1060

Discourse on the Origin of Inequality,
  MP III-1522
Émile, CLC I-322; MP III-1755; MP:EF
  I-476
New Héloïse, The, CLC II-764; MP
  VII-4177; MP:EF II-928
ROWLEY, WILLIAM, and THOMAS
  MIDDLETON
 Changeling, The, CLC I-167; MP II-885
ROWLEY, WILLIAM, JOHN FORD, and
  THOMAS MIDDLETON
 Spanish Gipsy, The, MP XI-6208
ROWSE, A. L.
 William Shakespeare, MPII:JYABio
  IV-1891
RUIZ DE ALARCÓN, JUAN, CWA
  III-1530
 Truth Suspected, CLC II-1166; MP
  XI-6740
RUKEYSER, MURIEL
 "Ajanta," MPII:P I-39
 "Eyes of Night-Time," MPII:P II-715
RULFO, JUAN, CWA III-1531
 Pedro Páramo, MP VIII-4552; MP:AF
  II-918
RUSHDIE, SALMAN, CWAII IV-1284
 Midnight's Children, CLCII III-1007;
  MPII:BCF III-1097
 Shame, CLCII IV-1389; MPII:BCF
  IV-1528
RUSHFORTH, PETER
 Kindergarten, CLCII II-829; MPII:BCF
  II-909
RUSKIN, JOHN, CWA III-1533
 King of the Golden River, The, CLC
  I-574; MP VI-3153; MP:BF II-747;
  MPII:JYAFic II-788
 Stones of Venice, The, MP XI-6262
RUSS, JOANNA, CWAII IV-1287
 Female Man, The, CLCII II-496;
  MPII:AF II-532
RUSSELL, BILL
 Go Up for Glory, MPII:JYABio II-768
RUSSELL, BILL, and TAYLOR BRANCH
 Second Wind, MPII:JYABio IV-1549
RUSSELL, GEORGE WILLIAM. See Æ
RUSSELL, W. CLARK, CWA III-1535
 Wreck of the Grosvenor, The, CLC
  II-1269; MP XII-7278; MP:BF
  III-1772

S

SÁBATO, ERNESTO, CWAII IV-1291
On Heroes and Tombs, CLCII III-1142;
MPII:AF III-1188
Outsider, The, CLCII III-1167; MPII:AF
III-1232
SACHS, HANS, CWA III-1537
Wandering Scholar from Paradise, The,
CLC II-1219; MP XII-7014
SACHS, MARILYN
Fat Girl, The, MPII:JYAFic I-415
SACHS, NELLY
"Butterfly," MPII:P I-325
"Fleeing," MPII:P II-778
"Hasidic Scriptures," MPII:P III-905
"In the Blue Distance," MPII:P III-1086
"O the Chimneys," MPII:P IV-1522
"Thus I Ran Out of the Word," MPII:P
VI-2182
SACKLER, HOWARD
Great White Hope, The, CLCII II-630;
MPII:D II-706
SACKS, OLIVER, CWAII IV-1293
Awakenings, MPII:NF I-132
SACKVILLE, THOMAS, and THOMAS
NORTON, CWA II-1319
Gorboduc, CLC I-412; MP IV-2332
SADE, THE MARQUIS DE, CWA III-1538
SAGE, ALAIN RENÉ LE. See LE SAGE,
ALAIN RENÉ
SAID, EDWARD W., CWAII IV-1295
Orientalism, MPII:NF III-1102
SAIKAKU. See IHARA, SAIKAKU
ST. AUGUSTINE. See AUGUSTINE, ST.
ST. GEORGE, JUDITH
Mount Rushmore Story, The,
MPII:JYABio III-1244
ST. JOHN, ROBERT
Ben-Gurion, MPII:JYABio I-191
ST. OMER, GARTH
Room on the Hill, A, CLCII III-1312;
MPII:BCF II1435
ST. VINCENT MILLAY, EDNA. See
MILLAY, EDNA ST. VINCENT
SAINTE-BEAUVE, CHARLES
AUGUSTIN, CWA III-1540
Monday Conversations, MP VII-4025

Volupté, CLC II-1215; MP XII-6983;
MP:EF III-1360
SAINT-EXUPÉRY, ANTOINE DE, CWA
III-1542
Little Prince, The, MPII:JYAFic II-861
Night Flight, CLC II-777; MP VII-4212;
MP:EF II-942
Wind, Sand and Stars, MP XII-7163;
MP:EF III-1400; MPII:JYABio
IV-1899
Wisdom of the Sands, The, MP XII-7189
SAINZ, GUSTAVO
Gazapo, CLCII II-572; MPII:AF II-602
SAKI, CWA III-1544
"Interlopers, The," MPII:SS III-1187
"Laura," MPII:SS III-1305
"Open Window, The," MPII:SS IV-1716
Short Stories of Saki, The, MP X-6027;
MP:BF III-1445
"Sredni Vashtar," MPII:SS V-2217
Unbearable Bassington, The, CLC
II-1177; MP XII-6804; MP:BF
III-1622
SALINGER, J. D., CWA III-1546; CWAII
IV-1297
Catcher in the Rye, The, CLCII I-244;
MPII:AF I-259; MPII:JYAFic I-209
"De Daumier-Smith's Blue Period,"
MPII:SS II-546
"For Esmé—with Love and Squalor,"
MPII:SS II-809
Franny and Zooey, MP IV-2157; MP:AF
I-418
"Perfect Day for Bananafish, A,"
MPII:SS IV-1800
"Uncle Wiggily in Connecticut,"
MPII:SS VI-2457
SALKEY, ANDREW
Anancy's Score, MPII:AfAm I-24
SALTEN, FELIX, CWA III-1548
Bambi, CLC I-78; MP I-415; MP:EF
I-92; MPII:JYAFic I-87
SALZMANN, SIEGMUND. See SALTEN,
FELIX
SAMSONOV, LEV. See MAXIMOV,
VLADIMIR

SANCHEZ, SONIA, CWAII IV-1299
"After Saturday Nite Comes Sunday,"
MPII:SS I-38
"Masks," MPII:P IV-1345
Poetry of Sonia Sanchez, The,
MPII:AfAm III-1119
SÁNCHEZ, FLORENCIO, CWA III-1549
Gringa, La, CLC I-429; MP IV-2401
SAND, GEORGE, CWA III-1551
Consuelo, CLC I-199; MP II-1106;
MP:EF I-253
Indiana, CLC I-523; MP V-2880; MP:EF
II-707
SANDBURG, CARL, CWA III-1553
Abe Lincoln Grows Up, MPII:JYABio
I-1
Abraham Lincoln, MP I-11
Always the Young Strangers,
MPII:JYABio I-47
"Chicago," MPII:P I-368
Chicago Poems, MP II-918
People, Yes, The, MP VIII-4593
Remembrance Rock, CLC II-955; MP
IX-5505; MP:AF III-1032
SANDOZ, MARI, CWAII IV-1302
Cheyenne Autumn, CLCII I-267;
MPII:AF I-285
Story Catcher, The, MPII:JYAFic
IV-1373
SANDS, BILL
My Shadow Ran Fast, MPII:JYABio
III-1280
SANSOM, WILLIAM, CWAII IV-1304
"How Claeys Died," MPII:SS III-1056
"Vertical Ladder, The," MPII:SS
VI-2493
"Wall, The," MPII:SS VI-2530
SANTAYANA, GEORGE, CWA III-1556
Last Puritan, The, CLC I-598; MP
VI-3274; MP:AF II-645
Skepticism and Animal Faith, MP
X-5831
SANTIAGO, DANNY
Famous All Over Town, MPII:JYAFic
I-412
SANT KYDEN, CWA III-1559
Inazuma-byshi, CLC I-520; MP V-2864;
MP:EF II-691
SAPPHO, CWA III-1561
Ode to Aphrodite, MP VII-4273

SARDUY, SEVERO
From Cuba with a Song, CLCII II-550;
MPII:AF II-581
SARGESON, FRANK, CWAII IV-1306
I for One . . ., CLCII II-726; MPII:BCF
II-772
Joy of the Worm, CLCII II-803;
MPII:BCF II-866
SAROYAN, WILLIAM, CWA III-1562;
CWAII IV-1308
"Daring Young Man on the Flying
Trapeze, The," MPII:SS II-484
Human Comedy, The, CLC I-498; MP
V-2766; MP:AF II-581
"Parsley Garden, The," MPII:SS IV-1771
Places Where I've Done Time,
MPII:JYABio III-1418
"Summer of the Beautiful White Horse,
The," MPII:SS V-2275
Time of Your Life, The, CLCII IV-1571;
MPII:D IV-1585
SARRAUTE, NATHALIE, CWAII IV-1311
"Fools Say," CLCII II-530; MPII:WF
II-486
Planetarium, The, CLCII III-1211;
MPII:WF III-1203
Portrait of a Man Unknown, CLCII
III-1226; MPII:WF III-1225
SARTON, MAY, CWAII IV-1313
Journal of a Solitude, MPII:NF II-756
Mrs. Stevens Hears the Mermaids
Singing, CLCII III-1025; MPII:AF
III-1028
Small Room, The, CLCII IV-1427;
MPII:AF IV-1454
SARTRE, JEAN-PAUL, CWA III-1564;
CWAII IV-1315
Flies, The, MP IV-2089
Nausea, CLC II-761; MP VII-4157;
MP:EF II-924
No Exit, CLCII III-1103; MPII:D
III-1148
Roads to Freedom, The, CLCII III-1303;
MPII:WF III-1288
"Wall, The," MPII:SS VI-2534
Words, The, MPII:NF IV-1714
SASSOON, SIEGFRIED, CWA III-1566
Memoirs of a Fox-Hunting Man, CLC
I-691; MP VII-3830; MP:BF II-916
Memoirs of an Infantry Officer, CLC
I-693; MP VII-3842; MP:BF II-924

SAUSER, FRÉDÉRIC LOUIS. *See*
CENDRARS, BLAISE
SAUSSURE, FERDINAND DE, CWAII
IV-1318
Course in General Linguistics, MPII:NF
I-288
SAWYER, RUTH
Roller Skates, MPII:JYAFic III-1244
SAYERS, DOROTHY L., CWAII IV-1320
Gaudy Night, CLCII II-571; MPII:BCF
I-577
Nine Tailors, The, CLCII III-1100;
MPII:BCF III-1208
SCHAEFER, JACK
Shane, MPII:JYAFic IV-1321
SCHAEFFER, SUSAN FROMBERG
Anya, MPII:JYAFic I-53
SCHELL, JONATHAN
Fate of the Earth, The, MPII:NF II-502
SCHILLER, FRIEDRICH VON, CWA
III-1568
Don Carlos, CLC I-289; MP III-1582
Wallenstein, CLC II-1216; MP XII-7001
William Tell, CLC II-1246; MP XII-7156
SCHMITZ, ETTORE. *See* SVEVO, ITALO
SCHNEIDER, PETER
Wall Jumper, The, CLCII IV-1676;
MPII:WF IV-1720
SCHNITZLER, ARTHUR, CWAII IV-1323
Ronde, La, CLCII III-1312; MPII:D
IV-1372
SCHOLEM, GERSHOM
From Berlin to Jerusalem, MPII:NF
II-534
SCHOOR, GENE
Roy Campanella, MPII:JYABio IV-1513
SCHOPENHAUER, ARTHUR, CWA
III-1571
World as Will and Idea, The, MP
XII-7259
SCHREINER, OLIVE, CWA III-1573
Story of an African Farm, The, CLC
II-1084; MP XI-6272; MP:EF
III-1227
SCHULZ, BRUNO, CWAII IV-1326
"Cinnamon Shops," MPII:SS I-396
"Sanatorium Under the Sign of the
Hourglass," MPII:SS V-2016
"Street of Crocodiles, The," MPII:SS
V-2256

SCHUMACHER, E. F., CWAII IV-1328
Small Is Beautiful, MPII:NF IV-1372
SCHUYLER, JAMES
"Sorting, wrapping, packing, stuffing,"
MPII:P V-2040
SCHWARTZ, DELMORE, CWAII IV-1331
"America! America!" MPII:SS I-81
"Heavy Bear Who Goes with Me, The,"
MPII:P III-921
"In Dreams Begin Responsibilities,"
MPII:SS III-1134
"In the Naked Bed, in Plato's Cave,"
MPII:P III-1093
SCHWARZ-BART, ANDRÉ, CWAII
IV-1333
Last of the Just, The, CLCII II-856;
MPII:WF II-816
SCHWEITZER, ALBERT
Out of My Life and Thought, MP
VIII-4449; MPII:JYABio III-1371
SCIASCIA, LEONARDO, CWAII IV-1335
Equal Danger, CLCII II-464; MPII:WF
I-425
Man's Blessing, A, CLCII III-966;
MPII:WF III-939
SCOPPETTONE, SANDRA
Happy Endings Are All Alike,
MPII:JYAFic II-591
SCOTT, EVELYN
Wave, The, CLCII IV-1695; MPII:AF
IV-1769
SCOTT, JOHN ANTHONY
Fanny Kemble's America, MPII:JYABio
II-603
Woman Against Slavery, MPII:JYABio
IV-1919
SCOTT, MICHAEL, CWA III-1574
Tom Cringle's Log, CLC II-1142; MP
XI-6594; MP:BF III-1567
SCOTT, PAUL
Raj Quartet, The, CLCII III-1263;
MPII:BCF III-1376
SCOTT, CAPTAIN ROBERT FALCON,
CWA III-1575
Scott's Last Expedition, MP X-5855
SCOTT, SIR WALTER, CWA III-1577
Antiquary, The, CLC I-49; MP I-254;
MP:BF I-58
Bride of Lammermoor, The, CLC I-122;
MP II-640; MP:BF I-134

Fair Maid of Perth, The, CLC I-351; MP IV-1958; MP:BF I-400

Fortunes of Nigel, The, CLC I-380; MP IV-2137; MP:BF I-452

Guy Mannering, CLC I-433; MP IV-2429; MP:BF I-507

Heart of Midlothian, The, CLC I-449; MP V-2510; MP:BF I-544

Ivanhoe, CLC I-536; MP V-2959; MP:BF II-665

Kenilworth, CLC I-566; MP VI-3123; MP:BF I-735

Lady of the Lake, The, CLC I-588; MP VI-3213

Lay of the Last Minstrel, The, CLC I-603; MP VI-3299

Marmion, CLC I-672; MP VII-3739

Old Mortality, CLC II-805; MP VIII-4334; MP:BF II-1091

Quentin Durward, CLC II-931; MP IX-5398; MP:BF III-1282

Rob Roy, CLC II-977; MP X-5638; MP:BF III-1331

St. Ronan's Well, CLC II-1000; MP X-5761; MP:BF III-1389

Talisman, The, CLC II-1102; MP XI-6387; MP:BF III-1490

"Two Drovers, The," MPII:SS VI-2432

Waverley, CLC II-1226; MP XII-7052; MP:BF III-1710

Woodstock, CLC II-1265; MP XII-7251; MP:BF III-1768

SCUDÉRY, MADELEINE DE, CWA III-1580

Artamène, CLC I-63; MP I-322; MP:EF I-64

SEARLE, JOHN

Minds, Brains, and Science, MPII:NF III-965

SEBESTYEN, OUIDA

Words by Heart, MPII:JYAFic IV-1656

SEFERIADES, GIORGOS STYLIANOU. See SEFERIS, GEORGE

SEFERIS, GEORGE

"Cistern, The," MPII:P I-386

Mythistorema, MPII:P IV-1467

SELDEN, GEORGE

Cricket in Times Square, The, MPII:JYAFic I-292

SELVON, SAMUEL

Brighter Sun, A, CLCII I-203; MPII:AfAm I-200; MPII:BCF I-185

Lonely Londoners, The, CLCII III-905; MPII:AfAm II-718; MPII:BCF III-993

SEMBÈNE, OUSMANE, CWAII IV-1337

God's Bits of Wood, CLCII II-601; MPII:WF II-553

Xala, CLCII IV-1759; MPII:WF IV-1793

SEMPRUN, JORGE

Long Voyage, The, CLCII III-911; MPII:WF II-878

What a Beautiful Sunday! CLCII IV-1704; MPII:WF IV-1739

SENECA, LUCIUS ANNAEUS, CWA III-1581

Philosophical Treatises and Moral Reflections of Seneca, MP VIII-4656

Thyestes, CLC II-1131; MP XI-6535

SENGHOR, LÉOPOLD

"Black Woman," MPII:P I-249

SEREDY, KATE

Good Master, The, MPII:JYAFic II-544

SÉRULLAZ, MAURICE

Velázquez, MPII:JYABio IV-1807

SETTLE, MARY LEE, CWAII IV-1339

Beulah Quintet, The, MPII:AF I-151

Killing Ground, The, CLCII II-827

Know Nothing, CLCII II-839

O Beulah Land, CLCII III-1122

Prisons, CLCII III-1237

Scapegoat, The, CLCII III-1343

SÉVIGNÉ, MADAME MARIE DE, CWA III-1583

Letters of Madame de Sévigné, The, MP VI-3353

SEWELL, ANNA

Black Beauty, MPII:JYAFic I-122

SEWELL, TOM, LOUIS KAUFMAN, and BARBARA FITZGERALD

Moe Berg, MPII:JYABio III-1233

SEWELL, WILLIAM POWELL. See SANDS, BILL.

SEXTON, ANNE

"All My Pretty Ones," MPII:P I-47

SEXTUS PROPERTIUS. See PROPERTIUS, SEXTUS

SHAFFER, ANTHONY

Sleuth, CLCII IV-1424; MPII:D IV-1477

SHAFFER, PETER, CWAII IV-1342
  Amadeus, CLCII I-33; MPII:D I-37
  Equus, CLCII II-466; MPII:D II-579
  Royal Hunt of the Sun, The, CLCII
    III-1316; MPII:D IV-1384
SHAKESPEARE, WILLIAM, CWA
    III-1585
  All's Well That Ends Well, CLC I-29;
    MP I-143
  Antony and Cleopatra, CLC I-50; MP
    I-258
  As You Like It, CLC I-66; MP I-334
  Comedy of Errors, CLC I-192; MP
    II-1037
  Coriolanus, CLC I-201; MP II-1116
  Cymbeline, CLC I-231; MP III-1255
  Hamlet, Prince of Denmark, CLC I-437;
    MP V-2457
  Henry the Eighth, CLC I-460; MP V-2555
  Henry the Fifth, CLC I-462; MP V-2558
  Henry the Fourth, CLC I-464; MP
    V-2562; MP V-2567
  Henry the Fourth, Part One, CLC I-464;
    MP V-2562
  Henry the Fourth, Part Two, CLC I-464;
    MP V-2567
  Henry the Sixth, CLC I-466, MP
    V-2572; MP V-2576; MP V-2580
  Henry the Sixth, Part One, CLC I-466;
    MP V-2572
  Henry the Sixth, Part Two, CLC I-466;
    MP V-2576
  Henry the Sixth, Part Three, CLC I-466;
    MP V-2580
  Julius Caesar, CLC I-559; MP VI-3089
  King John, CLC I-570; MP VI-3144
  King Lear, CLC I-572; MP VI-3148
  Love's Labour's Lost, CLC I-634; MP
    VI-3534
  Macbeth, CLC I-642; MP VI-3589
  Measure for Measure, CLC I-685; MP
    VII-3793
  Merchant of Venice, The, CLC I-695;
    MP VII-3855
  Merry Wives of Windsor, The, CLC
    I-697; MP VII-3860
  Midsummer Night's Dream, A, CLC
    II-703; MP VII-3885
  Much Ado about Nothing, CLC II-746;
    MP VII-4090
  Othello, CLC II-825; MP VIII-4431
  Pericles, Prince of Tyre, CLC II-861; MP
    VIII-4603
  Rape of Lucrece, The, CLC II-940; MP
    IX-5432
  Richard the Second, CLC II-965; MP
    X-5580
  Richard the Third, CLC II-967; MP
    X-5585
  Romeo and Juliet, CLC II-990; MP
    X-5700
  Sonnet 18, MPII:P V-1993
  Sonnet 19, MPII:P V-1996
  Sonnet 30, MPII:P V-1999
  Sonnet 60, MPII:P V-2002
  Sonnet 65, MPII:P V-2005
  Sonnet 73, MPII:P V-2008
  Sonnet 76, MPII:P V-2011
  Sonnet 87, MPII:P V-2014
  Sonnet 91, MPII:P V-2017
  Sonnet 94, MPII:P V-2020
  Sonnet 106, MPII:P V-2023
  Sonnet 116, MPII:P V-2026
  Sonnet 129, MPII:P V-2029
  Sonnet 130, MPII:P V-2032
  Sonnets of Shakespeare, The, MP
    XI-6170
  Taming of the Shrew, The, CLC II-1106;
    MP XI-6401
  Tempest, The, CLC II-1112; MP XI-6427
  Timon of Athens, CLC II-1133; MP
    XI-6549
  Titus Andronicus, CLC II-1135; MP
    XI-6565
  Troilus and Cressida, CLC II-1162; MP
    XI-6720
  Twelfth Night, CLC II-1168; MP
    XII-6753
  Two Gentlemen of Verona, CLC
    II-1170; MP XII-6772
  Venus and Adonis, CLC II-1196; MP
    XII-6893
  Winter's Tale, The, CLC II-1251; MP
    XII-7181
SHAKESPEARE, WILLIAM, and JOHN
    FLETCHER
  Two Noble Kinsmen, The, CLC II-1172;
    MP XII-6775
SHALAMOV, VARLAM, CWAII IV-1345
  "Child's Drawings, A," MPII:SS I-384
  "Snake Charmer, The," MPII:SS V-2150
SHAMS UD-DIN MOHAMMED. See HFIZ

SHANGE, NTOZAKE, CWAII IV-1347
  Betsey Brown, MPII:AfAm I-125;
    MPII:JYAFic I-112
  For colored girls who have considered
    suicide/when the rainbow is enuf,
    CLCII II-531; MPII:D II-627;
    MPII:AfAm I-467
  "Irrepressibly bronze, beautiful & mine,"
    MPII:P III-1120
  Photograph, A, CLCII III-1204;
    MPII:AfAm II-941; MPII:D III-1241
SHAPIRO, JUDITH, and LIANG HENG
  Son of the Revolution, MPII:JYABio
    IV-1593
SHAPIRO, KARL, CWA III-1589
  "Auto Wreck," MPII:P I-162
  Poetry of Shapiro, The, MP IX-5133
SHAW, GEORGE BERNARD, CWA
    III-1591; CWAII IV-1349
  Arms and the Man, CLCII I-67; MPII:D
    I-88
  Back to Methuselah, CLC I-75; MP I-412
  Caesar and Cleopatra, CLC I-138; MP
    II-728
  Candida, CLC I-143; MP II-757
  Heartbreak House, CLC I-451; CLCII
    II-669; MP V-2520; MPII:D II-752
  John Bull's Other Island, CLCII II-794;
    MPII:D III-871
  Major Barbara, CLC I-656; MP VI-3652
  Man and Superman, CLC I-658; MP
    VI-3667
  Mrs. Warren's Profession, CLCII
    III-1026; MPII:D III-1095
  Pygmalion, CLC II-928; MP IX-5385
  Saint Joan, CLC II-998; MP X-5755
SHAW, IRWIN, CWAII IV-1352
  "Eighty-Yard Run, The," MPII:SS II-677
  "Girls in Their Summer Dresses, The,"
    MPII:SS II-853
  "Sailor Off the Bremen," MPII:SS
    V-2005
  Young Lions, The, CLCII IV-1765;
    MPII:AF IV-1846
SHAWN, WALLACE
  Aunt Dan and Lemon, CLCII I-86;
    MPII:D I-99
SHAWN, WALLACE, and ANDRÉ
    GREGORY
  My Dinner with André, CLCII III-1061;
    MPII:D III-1121

SHELLEY, MARY WOLLSTONECRAFT
    GODWIN, CWA III-1596
  Frankenstein, CLC I-385; MP IV-2154;
    MP:BF I-466
SHELLEY, PERCY BYSSHE, CWA
    III-1598
  Adonais, MPII:P I-6
  Cenci, The, CLC I-164; MP II-869
  Defence of Poetry, A, MP III-1423
  Epipsychidion, MPII:P II-670
  "Hymn to Intellectual Beauty," MPII:P
    III-988
  "Lines: When the Lamp Is Shattered,"
    MPII:P III-1238
  Mask of Anarchy, The, MPII:P IV-1341
  Mont Blanc, MPII:P IV-1405
  "Ode to the West Wind," MPII:P
    IV-1562
  "Ozymandias," MPII:P IV-1629
  Prometheus Unbound, CLC II-925; MP
    IX-5365
  "To a Skylark," MPII:P VI-2194
  "Triumph of Life, The," MPII:P VI-2285
SHEPARD, SAM, CWAII IV-1354
  Buried Child, CLCII I-213; MPII:D I-260
  Curse of the Starving Class, CLCII
    I-356; MPII:D I-420
  Fool for Love, CLCII II-529; MPII:D
    II-622
  Geography of a Horse Dreamer, CLCII
    II-577; MPII:D II-666
  Lie of the Mind, A, CLCII II-879;
    MPII:D III-964
  Tooth of Crime, The, CLCII IV-1589;
    MPII:D IV-1607
  True West, CLCII IV-1621; MPII:D
    IV-1660
SHERIDAN, RICHARD BRINSLEY,
    CWA III-1601
  Critic, The, CLC I-224; MP II-1214
  Rivals, The, CLC II-974; MP X-5624
  School for Scandal, The, CLC II-1011;
    MP X-5838
SHERRIFF, ROBERT C., CWA III-1604
  Journey's End, CLC I-556; MP VI-3071
SHERWOOD, ROBERT E., CWA III-1605
  Abe Lincoln in Illinois, CLC I-1; MP I-4
  Petrified Forest, The, CLCII III-1200;
    MPII:D III-1225

SHIH NAI-AN, CWA III-1607
  All Men Are Brothers, CLC I-26; MP
    I-125; MP:EF I-17
SHIPPEN, KATHERINE B.
  Leif Eriksson, MPII:JYABio III-1056
  Mr. Bell Invents the Telephone,
    MPII:JYABio III-1226
SHIRER, WILLIAM L.
  Rise and Fall of Adolf Hitler, The,
    MPII:JYABio IV-1497
SHIRLEY, JAMES, CWA III-1608
  Hyde Park, CLC I-503; MP V-2787
  Traitor, The, CLC II-1151; MP XI-6643
SHKLOVSKY, VIKTOR, CWAII IV-1357
  Sentimental Journey, A, CLCII III-1372;
    MPII:WF IV-1382
  Third Factory, CLCII IV-1546;
    MPII:WF IV-1584
  Zoo, CLCII IV-1771; MPII:WF IV-1814
SHOLOKHOV, MIKHAIL, CWA III-1609
  And Quiet Flows the Don, CLC I-38;
    MP I-202; MP:EF I-31
  Don Flows Home to the Sea, The, CLC
    I-290; MP III-1585; MP:EF I-426
SHORTHOUSE, JOSEPH HENRY, CWA
    III-1611
  John Inglesant, CLC I-551; MP V-3026;
    MP:BF II-695
SHOSTAKOVICH, DMITRI
  Testimony, MPII:NF IV-1485
SHU CH'ING-CH'UN. See LAO SHE
SHUDRAKA, CWA III-1612
  Little Clay Cart, The, CLC I-617; MP
    VI-3444
SHJI', TSUSHIMA. See DAZAI, OSAMU
SIDNEY, SIR PHILIP, CWA III-1613
  Arcadia, CLC I-57; MP I-293; MP:BF
    I-62
  Astrophil and Stella, MPII:P I-129
  Defence of Poesie, MP III-1420
  Poetry of Sidney, The, MP IX-5136
SIEGAL, ARANKA
  Upon the Head of the Goat,
    MPII:JYABio IV-1799
SIENKIEWICZ, HENRY K, CWA III-1615
  Quo Vadis? CLC II-933; MP IX-5404;
    MP:EF III-1050
  With Fire and Sword, CLC II-1253; MP
    XII-7195; MP:EF III-1404

SIERRA, GREGORIO MARTÍNEZ. See
  MARTÍNEZ SIERRA, GREGORIO
SILKO, LESLIE MARMON, CWAII
    IV-1361
  Ceremony, MPII:JYAFic I-213
  "Deer Dance/For Your Return," MPII:P
    II-508
  "Lullaby," MPII:SS IV-1416
  Storyteller, MPII:NF IV-1442
  "Yellow Woman," MPII:SS VI-2724
SILLANPÄÄ, FRANS EEMIL, CWA
    III-1617
  Meek Heritage, CLC I-687; MP
    VII-3804; MP:EF II-849
SILLITOE, ALAN, CWAII IV-1363
  Down from the Hill, CLCII II-420;
    MPII:BCF I-393
  "Loneliness of the Long-Distance
    Runner, The," MPII:SS IV-1391
  Lost Flying Boat, The, CLCII III-918;
    MPII:BCF III-1008
  "Ragman's Daughter, The," MPII:SS
    V-1876
  Saturday Night and Sunday Morning,
    CLCII III-1339; MPII:BCF III-1449
  "Sniper, The," MPII:SS V-2158
  Widower's Son, The, CLCII IV-1715;
    MPII:BCF IV-1695
SILONE, IGNAZIO, CWA III-1618
  Bread and Wine, CLC I-122; MP II-636;
    MP:EF I-131
  Fontamara, MP IV-2104; MP:EF II-530
SIMAK, CLIFFORD D.
  City, MPII:JYAFic I-248
SIMENON, GEORGES, CWAII IV-1366
  Blue Room, The, CLCII I-177; MPII:WF
    I-164
  Man Who Watched the Trains Go By,
    The, CLCII III-959; MPII:WF III-925
  Snow Was Black, The, CLCII IV-1434;
    MPII:WF IV-1481
  Watchmaker of Everton, The, CLCII
    IV-1686; MPII:WF IV-1725
SIMIC, CHARLES
  "Lesson, The," MPII:P III-1219
SIMMS, WILLIAM GILMORE, CWA
    III-1620
  Yemassee, The, CLC II-1274; MP
    XII-7295; MP:AF III-1463

SIMON, CLAUDE, CWAII IV-1370
  Battle of Pharsalus, The, CLCII I-125;
    MPII:WF I-131
  Flanders Road, The, CLCII II-520;
    MPII:WF II-475
  Triptych, CLCII IV-1613; MPII:WF
    IV-1666
  Wind, The, CLCII IV-1717; MPII:WF
    IV-1750
SIMON, NEIL, CWAII IV-1373
  Barefoot in the Park, CLCII I-115;
    MPII:D I-122
  Biloxi Blues, CLCII I-155; MPII:D I-175
  Brighton Beach Memoirs, CLCII I-205;
    MPII:D I-243
  Last of the Red-Hot Lovers, CLCII
    II-857; MPII:D III-938
  Odd Couple, The, CLCII III-1130;
    MPII:D III-1158
SIMPSON, LOUIS
  "In California," MPII:P III-1061
  "My Father in the Night Commanding
    No," MPII:P IV-1433
SINCLAIR, MAY, CWA III-1622
  "Bambino, The," MPII:SS I-151
  Divine Fire, The, CLC I-275; MP
    III-1534; MP:BF I-329
  Mary Olivier, CLCII III-982
  Three Sisters, The, CLCII IV-1558
SINCLAIR, UPTON, CWA III-1624
  Jungle, The, CLC I-560; MP VI-3094;
    MP:AF II-623
SINGER, ISAAC BASHEVIS, CWAII
    IV-1375
  "Admirer, The," MPII:SS I-16
  Day of Pleasure, A, MPII:JYABio I-451
  Enemies, CLCII II-458; MPII:AF II-476;
    MPII:WF I-409
  "Friend of Kafka, A," MPII:SS II-817
  "Gentleman from Cracow, The,"
    MPII:SS II-831
  "Gimpel the Fool," MPII:SS II-850
  In My Father's Court, MPII:NF II-719
  Little Boy in Search of God, A, MPII:NF
    II-835
  Lost in America, MPII:NF II-835
  Magician of Lublin, The, CLCII III-944;
    MPII:AF III-954; MPII:WF III-905
  "Moon and Madness," MPII:SS IV-1528
  "Short Friday," MPII:SS V-2084

  Shosha, CLCII IV-1396; MPII:AF
    IV-1417; MPII:WF IV-1404
  Slave, The, CLCII IV-1422; MPII:AF
    IV-1443; MPII:WF IV-1453
  "Spinoza of Market Street, The,"
    MPII:SS V-2202
  "Yentl the Yeshiva Boy," MPII:SS
    VI-2729
  Young Man in Search of Love, A,
    MPII:NF II-835
SINGER, ISRAEL JOSHUA, CWA
    III-1627
  Brothers Ashkenazi, The, CLC I-128;
    MP II-684; MP:EF I-140
SINGMASTER, ELSIE, CWA III-1628
  Gettysburg, MP IV-2246; MP:AF I-436
  High Wind Rising, A, CLC I-472; MP
    V-2609; MP:AF II-551
  I Speak for Thaddeus Stevens, MP
    V-2806
SINYAVSKY, ANDREI, CWAII IV-1378
  Goodnight! CLCII-617
  "Graphomaniacs," MPII:SS II-922
  "Icicle, The," MPII:SS III-1106
  Makepeace Experiment, The, CLCII
    III-947; MPII:WF III-909
  "Pkhentz," MPII:SS IV-1824
  Spokoinoi nochi, MPII:WF IV-1524
  Trial Begins, The, CLCII IV-1610;
    MPII:WF IV-1656
  Voice from the Chorus, A, MPII:NF
    IV-1646
SITWELL, EDITH, CWA III-1631
  Poetry of Edith Sitwell, The, MP IX-4920
SKELTON, JOHN, CWA III-1633
  Poetry of Skelton, The, MP IX-5141
SKINNER, CORNELIA OTIS
  Madame Sarah, MPII:JYABio III-1139
ŠKVORECK, JOSEF, CWAII IV-1381
  Bass Saxophone, The, CLCII I-123;
    MPII:WF I-126
  Cowards, The, CLCII I-349; MPII:WF
    I-341
  Engineer of Human Souls, The, CLCII
    II-460; MPII:WF I-414
SLEATOR, WILLIAM
  House of Stairs, MPII:JYAFic II-665
  Interstellar Pig, MPII:JYAFic II-712
SMART, CHRISTOPHER, CWA III-1635
  Poetry of Smart, The, MP IX-5146

SMEDLEY, AGNES, CWAII IV-1383
  Daughter of Earth, CLCII I-368;
  MPII:AF I-373
SMITH, ADAM, CWA III-1637
  Wealth of Nations, The, MP XII-7070
SMITH, BETTY, CWA III-1639
  Tree Grows in Brooklyn, A, CLC
  II-1152; MP XI-6672; MP:AF
  III-1322; MPII:JYAFic IV-1504
SMITH, DAVE
  "That Moment, Which You Could Love,
  What of It," MPII:P VI-2140
SMITH, HOMER W., CWA III-1640
  Kamongo, MP VI-3115; MP:AF II-630
SMITH, LULA CARSON. See
  McCULLERS, CARSON
SMITH, STEVIE
  "Exeat," MPII:P II-709
SMITH, URSULA, and LINDA PEAVY
  Dreams into Deeds, MPII:JYABio II-517
SMOLLETT, TOBIAS, CWA III-1642
  Humphry Clinker, CLC I-499; MP
  V-2769; MP:BF II-621
  Peregrine Pickle, CLC II-859; MP
  VIII-4599; MP:BF II-1185
  Roderick Random, CLC II-979; MP
  X-5656; MP:BF III-1347
SNEVE, VIRGINIA DRIVING HAWK
  When Thunders Spoke, MPII:JYAFic
  IV-1609
SNODGRASS, W. D.
  "Heart's Needle," MPII:P III-917
SNORRI STURLUSON, CWA III-1644
  Heimskringla, The, CLC I-456; MP
  V-2537; MP:EF II-623
SNOW, C. P., CWA III-1646; CWAII
  IV-1385
  Affair, The, MP I-56; MP:BF I-11
  Conscience of the Rich, The, MP
  II-1091; MP:BF I-242
  Masters, The, MP VII-3768; MP:BF
  II-892
  Strangers and Brothers, CLCII IV-1480;
  MPII:BCF IV-1619
SNYDER, GARY
  "For Plants," MPII:P II-789
  "Milton by Firelight," MPII:P IV-1387
  "Wave," MPII:P VI-2375

SNYDER, ZILPHA KEATLEY
  Witches of Worm, The, MPII:JYAFic
  IV-1643
SOCRATES, CWA III-1648
SOKOLOV, SASHA, CWAII IV-1388
  School for Fools, A, CLCII III-1347;
  MPII:WF III-1356
SOLZHENITSYN, ALEKSANDR, CWA
  III-1651; CWAII IV-1391
  August 1914, CLCII I-84; MPII:WF I-90
  Cancer Ward, CLCII I-228; MPII:WF
  I-205
  First Circle, The, CLCII II-512;
  MPII:WF II-465
  Gulag Archipelago, 1918-1956, The,
  MPII:NF II-617
  "Matryona's House," MPII:SS IV-1480
  Oak and the Calf, The, MPII:NF III-1046
  Oktiabr shestnadtsatogo, CLCII
  III-1135; MPII:WF III-1134
  One Day in the Life of Ivan Denisovich,
  CLCII III-1147; MPII:WF III-1152
SOMMERFELT, AIMÉE
  Road to Agra, The, MPII:JYAFic
  III-1231
SONE, MONICA
  Nisei Daughter, MPII:JYABio III-1320
SONG, CATHY
  "Picture Bride," MPII:P IV-1675
SONTAG, SUSAN, CWAII IV-1394
  Against Interpretation and Other Essays,
  MPII:NF I-19
  Illness as Metaphor, MPII:NF II-689
SOPHOCLES, CWA III-1653
  Ajax, CLC I-16; MP I-77
  Antigone, CLC I-48; MP I-250
  Oedipus at Colonus, CLC II-792; MP
  VII-4280
  Oedipus Tyrannus, CLC II-793; MP
  VII-4284
  Philoctetes, CLC II-870; MP VIII-4647
  Women of Trachis, CLC II-1262; CLCII
  IV-1736; MP XII-7242; MPII:D
  IV-1757
SOR JUANA. See CRUZ, SOR JUANA
  INÉS DE LA
SORENSEN, VIRGINIA
  Miracles on Maple Hill, MPII:JYAFic
  III-962

SŌSEKI. *See* NATSUME, SŌSEKI
SOTO, GARY
Living up the Street, MPII:JYABio
III-1109
SOUTHALL, IVAN
Walk a Mile and Get Nowhere,
MPII:JYAFic IV-1564
SOUTHEY, ROBERT, CWA III-1656
Life of Nelson, MP VI-3403
SOUTHWELL, ROBERT
"Burning Babe, The," MPII:P I-316
SOUTHWORTH, JOHN VAN DUYN
Monarch and Conspirators,
MPII:JYABio III-1237
SOYINKA, WOLE, CWAII IV-1396
Aké, MPII:JYABio I-24; MPII:NF I-24
Dance of the Forests, A, CLCII I-362;
MPII:D II-437
Death and the King's Horseman, CLCII
I-377; MPII:D II-463
"Death in the Dawn," MPII:P II-501
Interpreters, The, CLCII II-770;
MPII:BCF II-836
Lion and the Jewel, The, CLCII III-893;
MPII:D III-981
Madmen and Specialists, CLCII III-942;
MPII:D III-1023
Man Died, The, MPII:NF III-889
Road, The, CLCII III-1302; MPII:D
IV-1356
Season of Anomy, CLCII III-1362;
MPII:BCF III-1482
SPARK, MURIEL, CWA III-1658; CWAII
IV-1398
Abbess of Crewe, The, CLCII I-1;
MPII:BCF I-6
Bachelors, The, MP I-409; MP:BF I-75
Ballad of Peckham Rye, The, CLCII
I-108; MPII:BCF I-91
Comforters, The, CLCII I-312;
MPII:BCF I-293
"Father's Daughters, The," MPII:SS
II-767
Loitering with Intent, CLCII III-903;
MPII:BCF III-989
Mandelbaum Gate, The, CLCII III-964;
MPII:BCF III-1057
Memento Mori, MP VII-3820; MP:BF
II-908
"Portobello Road, The," MPII:SS
IV-1831

Prime of Miss Jean Brodie, The, CLCII
III-1235; MPII:BCF III-1340;
MPII:JYAFic III-1170
Takeover, The, CLCII IV-1513;
MPII:BCF IV-1677
SPEARE, ELIZABETH GEORGE
Bronze Bow, The, MPII:JYAFic I-158
Witch of Blackbird Pond, The,
MPII:JYAFic IV-1640
SPECHT, ROBERT
Tisha, MPII:JYABio IV-1729
SPENCER, CORNELIA
Sun Yat-sen, MPII:JYABio IV-1641
SPENDER, STEPHEN, CWA III-1660;
CWAII IV-1400
Poetry of Spender, The, MP IX-5152
Journals, 1939-1983, MPII:NF II-767
SPENSER, EDMUND, CWA III-1662
Epithalamion, MPII:P II-684
Faerie Queene, The, CLC I-347; MP
IV-1953
Lyric Poetry of Spenser, The, MP
VI-3573
Mother Hubberd's Tale, MP VII-4078
Shepheardes Calendar, The, MP X-5972
SPERRY, ARMSTRONG
Call It Courage, MPII:JYAFic I-170
John Paul Jones, Fighting Sailor,
MPII:JYABio II-973
Voyages of Christopher Columbus, The,
MPII:JYABio IV-1818
SPICER, JACK
"Phonemics," MPII:P IV-1668
SPINOZA, BENEDICTUS DE, CWA III-1665
Ethics, MP IV-1876
SPYRI, JOHANNA
Heidi, MPII:JYAFic II-616
STAËL, MADAME DE, CWA III-1667
Considerations on the Principal Events
of the French Revolution, MP II-1100
Delphine, CLC I-263; MP III-1436;
MP:EF I-380
STAFFORD, JEAN, CWAII IV-1403
"Bad Characters," MPII:SS I-144
"Country Love Story, A," MPII:SS I-444
"Reasonable Facsimile, A," MPII:SS
V-1908
STAFFORD, WILLIAM
"Burning a Book," MPII:P I-313

"Traveling Through the Dark," MPII:P
VI-2259

STALLINGS, LAURENCE, *and*
MAXWELL ANDERSON
What Price Glory? CLCII IV-1706;
MPII:D IV-1723

STANHOPE, PHILIP DORMER. *See*
CHESTERFIELD, PHILIP
DORMER STANHOPE, LORD

STAPLEDON, OLAF
Last and First Men, MPII:BCF II-939

STATIUS, CWA III-1668
Thebais, The, MP XI-6469

STEAD, CHRISTINA, CWAII IV-1406
House of All Nations, CLCII II-708;
MPII:BCF II-753
Little Hotel, The, CLCII III-896;
MPII:BCF II-975
Man Who Loved Children, The, CLCII
III-958; MPII:BCF III-1050

STEELE, SIR RICHARD, CWA III-1669
Conscious Lovers, The, CLC I-198; MP
II-1094
Funeral, The, CLC I-390; MP IV-2188

STEELE, SIR RICHARD, JOSEPH
ADDISON, *and* EUSTACE
BUDGELL
Sir Roger de Coverley Papers, The, CLC
II-1044; MP X-6067

STEELE, SHELBY
Content of Our Character, The,
MPII:AfAm I-319

STEELE, WILLIAM O.
Wayah of the Real People, MPII:JYAFic
IV-1585

STEFFENS, LINCOLN, CWAII IV-1409
Autobiography of Lincoln Steffens, The,
MPII:JYABio I-152; MPII:NF I-115

STEGNER, WALLACE, CWAII IV-1411
Angle of Repose, CLCII I-48; MPII:AF
I-38
"Beyond the Glass Mountain," MPII:SS
I-196

STEIN, GERTRUDE, CWAII IV-1414
Autobiography of Alice B. Toklas, The,
MPII:JYABio I-141
Making of Americans, The, CLCII
III-948; MPII:AF III-958
Three Lives, CLCII IV-1555; MPII:AF
IV-1643

STEINBECK, JOHN, CWA III-1672;
CWAII IV-1416
Cannery Row, CLCII I-231; MPII:AF
I-242
"Chrysanthemums, The," MPII:SS I-392
East of Eden, CLC I-313; MP III-1689;
MP:AF I-326
"Flight," MPII:SS II-792
"Gift, The," MPII:SS II-843
Grapes of Wrath, The, CLC I-417; MP
IV-2344; MP:AF I-491
In Dubious Battle, CLC I-518; MP
V-2850; MP:AF II-588
Of Mice and Men, CLC II-795; MP
VII-4294; MP:AF II-861
"Pearl, The," CLCII III-1188; MPII:SS
IV-1785
Red Pony, The, CLCII III-1281;
MPII:AF III-1334; MPII:JYAFic
III-1217
Tortilla Flat, CLCII IV-1595; MPII:AF
IV-1688

STEINBECK, JOHN, *and* EDWARD F.
RICKETTS
Sea of Cortez, MPII:NF III-1309

STEINER, GEORGE, CWAII IV-1418
After Babel, MPII:NF I-7
Portage to San Cristóbal of A. H., The,
CLCII III-1223; MPII:BCF III-1335

STENDHAL, CWA III-1675
Charterhouse of Parma, The, CLC I-169;
MP II-895; MP:EF I-214
Lucien Leuwen, CLC I-639; MP
VI-3547; MP:EF II-802
Red and the Black, The, CLC II-947; MP
IX-5463; MP:EF III-1062

STEPHENS, JAMES, CWA III-1677
Crock of Gold, The, CLC I-224; MP
III-1223; MP:BF I-254
Deirdre, CLC I-262; MP III-1428;
MP:BF I-305

STEPTOE, JOHN
Train Ride, MPII:JYAFic IV-1497

STERLING, PHILIP
Sea and Earth, MPII:JYABio IV-1537

STERN, RICHARD, CWAII IV-1421
"Wissler Remembers," MPII:SS VI-2664

STERNE, LAURENCE, CWA III-1679
Journal to Eliza, MP V-3053

Sentimental Journey, A, CLC II-1024; MP X-5914; MP:BF III-1415

Tristram Shandy, CLC II-1159; MP XI-6712; MP:BF III-1605

STEVENS, JAMES, CWA III-1683

Paul Bunyan, CLC II-843; MP VIII-4537; MP:AF II-910

STEVENS, WALLACE, CWA III-1684

"Auroras of Autumn, The," MPII:P I-156

"Connoisseur of Chaos," MPII:P I-420

"Emperor of Ice-Cream, The," MPII:P II-651

"Farewell Without a Guitar," MPII:P II-731

Harmonium, MP V-2480

"Idea of Order at Key West, The," MPII:P III-1046

"Man with the Blue Guitar, The," MPII:P IV-1315

"Of Modern Poetry," MPII:P IV-1565

"Peter Quince at the Clavier," MPII:P IV-1662

Poetry of Stevens, The, MP IX-5161

"Postcard from the Volcano, A," MPII:P IV-1722

"Sunday Morning," MPII:P V-2106

"Thirteen Ways of Looking at a Blackbird," MPII:P VI-2158

STEVENSON, ROBERT LOUIS, CWA III-1687

Beach of Falesá, The, CLC I-89; MP I-456; MP:BF I-95

Black Arrow, The, CLC I-106; MP I-552; MP:BF I-113

"Bottle Imp, The," MPII:SS I-281

Dr. Jekyll and Mr. Hyde, CLC I-280; MP III-1550; MP:BF I-333

Kidnapped, CLC I-568; MP VI-3127; MP:BF II-739; MPII:JYAFic II-771

"Lodging for the Night, A," MPII:SS IV-1387

Master of Ballantrae, The, CLC I-680; MP VII-3764; MP:BF II-887

"Suicide Club, The," MPII:SS V-2262

Travels with a Donkey, MP XI-6659

Treasure Island, CLC II-1152; MP XI-6662; MP:BF III-1589; MPII:JYAFic IV-1500

STEWART, MARY LOUISA. See MOLESWORTH, MARY LOUISA

STIFTER, ADALBERT, CWAII IV-1423

Indian Summer, CLCII II-757; MPII:WF II-691

STILL, JAMES, CWA III-1690

River of Earth, CLC II-975; MP X-5629; MP:AF III-1054

STILLMAN, MYRA, and BEULAH TANNENBAUM

Isaac Newton, MPII:JYABio II-923

STOCKTON, FRANK R., CWAII IV-1425

"Lady or the Tiger?, The," MPII:SS III-1284

STODDARD, HOPE

Famous American Women, MPII:JYABio II-591

STOKER, BRAM, CWA III-1692

Dracula, CLC I-301; MP III-1633; MP:BF I-347

STOLZ, MARY

Love, or a Season, A, MPII:JYAFic III-894

Pray, Love, Remember, MPII:JYAFic III-1166

STONE, IRVING

Agony and the Ecstasy, The, CLCII I-24; MPII:AF I-12

Clarence Darrow for the Defense, MPII:JYABio I-381

Sailor on Horseback, MPII:JYABio IV-1521

STONE, ROBERT, CWAII IV-1430

Dog Soldiers, CLCII II-411; MPII:AF I-423

STONG, PHIL, CWA III-1693

State Fair, CLC II-1080; MP XI-6246; MP:AF III-1215

STOPPARD, TOM, CWAII IV-1432

Dirty Linen, CLCII I-404; MPII:D II502

Hapgood, CLCII II-656; MPII:D II-737

Jumpers, CLCII II-808; MPII:D III-877

New-Found-Land, CLCII I-404; MPII:D II-502

Night and Day, CLCII III-1093; MPII:D III-1128

Real Thing, The, CLCII III-1274; MPII:D III-1310

Rosencrantz and Guildenstern Are Dead, CLCII III-1314; MPII:D IV-1378

Travesties, CLCII IV-1606; MPII:D IV-1643

STOREY, DAVID, CWAII IV-1435
  Changing Room, The, CLCII I-261;
    MPII:D I-312
  Contractor, The, CLCII I-333; MPII:D
    I-397
  Radcliffe, CLCII III-1257; MPII:BCF
    III-1370
  This Sporting Life, CLCII IV-1551;
    MPII:BCF IV-1690
STOUTENBURG, ADRIEN, and LAURA
    NELSON BAKER
  Listen America, MPII:JYABio III-1093
STOW, RANDOLPH, CWAII IV-1437
  Girl Green as Elderflower, The, CLCII
    II-587; MPII:BCF II-590
  Merry-Go-Round in the Sea, The, CLCII
    III-998; MPII:BCF III-1081
  Visitants, CLCII IV-1661; MPII:BCF
    IV-1802
STOWE, HARRIET BEECHER, CWA
    III-1695
  Oldtown Folks, CLC II-810; MP
    VIII-4353; MP:AF II-883
  Uncle Tom's Cabin, CLC II-1178; MP
    XII-6814; MP:AF III-1345;
    MPII:JYAFic IV-1542
STOWELL, H. E.
  Quill Pens and Petticoats, MPII:JYABio
    III-1459
STRACHEY, LYTTON, CWA III-1697
  Elizabeth and Essex, MPII:JYABio
    II-549
  Eminent Victorians, MP III-1760
  Queen Victoria, MP IX-5390;
    MPII:JYABio III-1455
STRAND, MARK
  "Eating Poetry," MPII:P II-620
STRASSBURG, GOTTFRIED VON. See
    GOTTFRIED VON STRASSBURG
STRASSER, TODD
  Angel Dust Blues, MPII:JYAFic I-38
STRATEMEYER, EDWARD. See DIXON,
    FRANKLIN W., and KEENE,
    CAROLYN
STRAUSS, BOTHO, CWAII IV-1439
  Devotion, CLCII I-396; MPII:WF I-376
STRAUSSLER, TOMAS. See STOPPARD,
    TOM
STREATFEILD, NOEL
  Ballet Shoes, MPII:JYAFic I-83

Circus Is Coming, The, MPII:JYAFic
    I-245
STREET, JAMES HOWELL
  Good-bye, My Lady, MPII:JYAFic
    II-550
STRINDBERG, AUGUST, CWA III-1699
  Comrades, CLC I-194; MP II-1047
  Confession of a Fool, The, CLCII I-324;
    MPII:WF I-304
  Dance of Death, The, CLC I-236; MP
    III-1283
  Dream Play, A, CLCII II-425; MPII:D
    II-518
  Father, The, CLC I-358; MP IV-2000
  Ghost Sonata, The, CLCII II-579;
    MPII:D II-678
  Inferno, CLCII II-762; MPII:WF II-697
  Link, The, CLC I-615; MP VI-3434
  Miss Julie, CLC II-715; MP VII-3936
  Natives of Hemsö, The, CLCII III-1077;
    MPII:WF III-1079
  Pelican, The, CLCII III-1189; MPII:D
    III-1214
  Red Room, The, CLC II-949; MP
    IX-5473; MP:EF III-1067
  Stormy Weather, CLCII IV-1476;
    MPII:D IV-1491
  There Are Crimes and Crimes, CLC
    II-1121; MP XI-6473
STRONG, L. A. G., CWA III-1702
  Garden, The, CLC I-392; MP IV-2200;
    MP:BF I-479
STRUGATSKY, ARKADY, and BORIS
    STRUGATSKY, CWAII IV-1441
  Roadside Picnic, CLCII III-1306;
    MPII:WF III-1295
  Snail on the Slope, The, CLCII IV-1430;
    MPII:WF IV-1469
STUART, JESSE, CWA III-1704; CWAII
    IV-1443
  Beyond Dark Hills, MPII:NF I-150
  "Dawn of Remembered Spring,"
    MPII:SS II-499
  Man with a Bull-Tongue Plow, MP
    VII-3680
  "Split Cherry Tree, The," MPII:SS
    V-2206
  "Spring Victory," MPII:SS V-2214
  Taps for Private Tussie, CLC II-1107;
    MP XI-6405; MP:AF III-1259

Thread That Runs So True, The, MPII:JYABio IV-1709; MPII:NF IV-1513

STURGEON, THEODORE
More Than Human, MPII:JYAFic III-978

STURLUSON, SNORRI. *See* SNORRI STURLUSON

STURTZEL, HOWARD ALLISON. *See* ANNIXTER, PAUL

STYRON, WILLIAM, CWA III-1707; CWAII IV-1445
Confessions of Nat Turner, The, CLCII I-326; MPII:AF I-330
Lie Down in Darkness, MP VI-3382; MP:AF II-667
Set This House on Fire, MP X-5919; MP:AF III-1113
Sophie's Choice, CLCII IV-1446; MPII:AF IV-1492

SUCKLING, SIR JOHN, CWA III-1709
Poetry of Suckling, The, MP IX-5164

SUCKOW, RUTH, CWA III-1711
Folks, The, MP IV-2094; MP:AF I-404

SUDERMANN, HERMANN, CWA III-1713
Dame Care, CLC I-234; MP III-1275; MP:EF I-326
Song of Songs, The, CLC II-1063; MP XI-6156; MP:EF III-1197

SUE, EUGÈNE, CWA III-1715
Mysteries of Paris, The, CLC II-752; MP VII-4111; MP:EF II-904
Wandering Jew, The, CLC II-1218; MP XII-7010; MP:EF III-1370

SUETONIUS, CWA III-1717
Concerning Illustrious Men, MP II-1054
Lives of the Caesars, MP VI-3464

SUFRIN, MARK
Payton, MPII:JYABio III-1399

SULLIVAN, TOM, *and* DEREK L. T. GILL
If You Could See What I Hear, MPII:JYABio II-901

SUMNER, WILLIAM GRAHAM, CWA III-1718
Folkways, MP IV-2097

SUPREE, BURTON
Bear's Heart, MPII:JYABio I-180

SURREY, EARL OF. *See* HOWARD, HENRY

SURTEES, ROBERT SMITH, CWA III-1720
Handley Cross, CLC I-440; MP V-2467; MP:BF I-520
Hillingdon Hall, CLC I-474; MP V-2616; MP:BF I-582
Jorrocks' Jaunts and Jollities, CLC I-552; MP V-3033; MP:BF II-703
Mr. Facey Romford's Hounds, CLC II-718; MP VII-3954; MP:BF II-959
Mr. Sponge's Sporting Tour, CLC II-721; MP VII-3967; MP:BF II-970

SUTCLIFF, ROSEMARY
Blue Remembered Hills, MPII:JYABio I-244
Eagle of the Ninth, The, MPII:JYAFic I-371
Heroes and History, MPII:JYABio II-834
Lantern Bearers, The, MPII:JYAFic II-806

SVENSON, ANDREW. *See* DIXON, FRANKLIN W.

SVEVO, ITALO, CWAII IV-1448
As a Man Grows Older, CLCII I-71; MPII:WF I-75
Confessions of Zeno, CLCII I-328; MPII:WF I-315

SWARTHOUT, GLENDON
Bless the Beasts and Children, MPII:JYAFic I-128

SWEDENBORG, EMANUEL, CWA III-1723
Divine Love and Wisdom, MP III-1537

SWENSON, MAY
"Navajo Blanket, A," MPII:P IV-1475

SWIFT, GRAHAM, CWAII IV-1450
Shuttlecock, CLCII IV-1398; MPII:BCF IV-1538
Waterland, CLCII IV-1691; MPII:BCF IV-1865

SWIFT, HILDEGARDE HOYT
From the Eagle's Wing, MPII:JYABio II-686

SWIFT, JONATHAN, CWA III-1725
Gulliver's Travels, CLC I-432; MP IV-2421; MP:BF I-501; MPII:JYAFic II-574
Journal to Stella, MP V-3056
Poetry of Swift, The, MP IX-5167

Tale of a Tub, A, MP XI-6366; MP:BF
    III-1481
SWINBURNE, ALGERNON CHARLES,
    CWA III-1729
  Atalanta in Calydon, CLC I-69; MP I-353
  "Hymn to Proserpine," MPII:P III-991
  Poems and Ballads, MP VIII-4780
SWINNERTON, FRANK, CWA III-1732
  Nocturne, CLC II-781; MP VII-4235;
    MP:BF II-1065
SYME, SIR RONALD
  Balboa, MPII:JYABio I-168
  Bolívar, the Liberator, MPII:JYABio
    I-252
  Captain Cook, MPII:JYABio I-285
  Francis Drake, MPII:JYABio II-662
  Garibaldi, MPII:JYABio II-698

Zapata, Mexican Rebel, MPII:JYABio
    IV-1981
SYNGE, JOHN MILLINGTON, CWA
    III-1734
  Deirdre of the Sorrows, CLC I-263; MP
    III-1432
  In the Shadow of the Glen, CLCII
    II-750; MPII:D II-815
  Playboy of the Western World, The,
    CLC II-893; MP VIII-4755
  Riders to the Sea, CLCII III-1294;
    MPII:D III-1337
SZWARCBART, ABRAHAM. See
    SCHWARZ-BART, ANDRÉ
SZYMUSIAK, MOLYDA
  Stones Cry Out, The, MPII:JYABio
    IV-1607

T

TACITUS, CWA III-1736
  Annals of Tacitus, The, MP I-236
TAINE, HIPPOLYTE, CWA III-1737
  Philosophy of Art, MP VIII-4659
TANIZAKI, JUN'ICHIR, CWAII IV-1452
  "Bridge of Dreams, The," MPII:SS I-304
  Diary of a Mad Old Man, CLCII I-398;
    MPII:WF I-381
  In Praise of Shadows, MPII:NF II-731
  Makioka Sisters, The, CLCII III-950;
    MPII:WF III-915
  Naomi, CLCII III-1074; MPII:WF
    III-1070
  Secret History of the Lord of Musashi,
    The, CLCII III-1367; MPII:WF III-1372
  Some Prefer Nettles, CLCII IV-1439;
    MPII:WF IV-1491
TANNENBAUM, BEULAH, and MYRA
  STILLMAN
  Isaac Newton, MPII:JYABio II-923
TARGAN, BARRY
  "Old Vernish," MPII:SS IV-1680
TARKINGTON, BOOTH, CWA III-1739
  Alice Adams, CLC I-21; MP I-104
  Kate Fennigate, CLC I-565; MP
    VI-3120; MP:AF II-632
  Monsieur Beaucaire, CLC II-735; MP
    VII-4034; MP:AF II-816
  Seventeen, CLC II-1027; MP X-5942;
    MP:AF III-1122
TARKOVSKY, ANDREY
  Sculpting in Time, MPII:NF III-1298
TASSO, TORQUATO, CWA III-1741
  Jerusalem Delivered, CLC I-545; MP
    V-3000
TATE, ALLEN, CWA III-1743
  "Aeneas at Washington," MPII:P I-16
  Fathers, The, MP IV-2012; MP:AF I-371
  "Ode to the Confederate Dead," MPII:P
    IV-1554
  Poetry of Tate, The, MP IX-5172
TATE, ELEANORA ELAINE
  Secret of Gumbo Grove, The,
    MPII:JYAFic III-1298
TATE, JAMES
  "Lost Pilot, The," MPII:P III-1269
TAYLOR, ALAN JOHN PERCIVALE
  Bismarck, MPII:JYABio I-222

TAYLOR, EDWARD, CWA III-1745
  "Huswifery," MPII:P III-985
  Poetical Works of Edward Taylor, The,
    MP VIII-4786
TAYLOR, ELIZABETH
  Wreath of Roses, A, CLCII IV-1756;
    MPII:BCF IV-1950
TAYLOR, KAMALA PURNAIYA. See
  MARKANDAYA, KAMALA
TAYLOR, MILDRED D.
  Let the Circle Be Unbroken, MPII:AfAm
    II-694
  Roll of Thunder, Hear My Cry,
    MPII:AfAm III-1212; MPII:JYAFic
    III-1239
TAYLOR, PETER, CWAII IV-1455
  "Fancy Woman, The," MPII:SS II-759
  "Old Forest, The," MPII:SS IV-1668
  Short Stories of Peter Taylor, The, MP
    X-6024; MP:AF III-1156
  "Venus, Cupid, Folly, and Time,"
    MPII:SS VI-2489
TEGNÉR, ESAIAS, CWA III-1747
  Frithiof's Saga, CLC I-387; MP IV-2175
TEILHARD DE CHARDIN, PIERRE
  Phenomenon of Man, The, MP VIII-4636
TENNYSON, ALFRED, LORD
  Enoch Arden, CLC I-328; MP III-1787
  Idylls of the King, The, CLC I-511; MP
    V-2825
  In Memoriam, MP V-2853
  "Lady of Shalott, The," MPII:P III-1174
  "Lotos-Eaters, The," MPII:P III-1272
  "Mariana," MPII:P IV-1330
  "Now Sleeps the Crimson Petal," MPII:P
    IV-1515
  Poems, MP VIII-4777
  Princess, The, MP IX-5324
  "Tears, Idle Tears," MPII:P V-2123
  "Ulysses," MPII:P VI-2313
TENNYSON, LORD ALFRED, CWA
  III-1748
TERASAKI, GWEN
  Bridge to the Sun, MPII:JYABio I-274
TERENCE, CWA III-1751
  Andria, CLC I-38; MP I-212
  Brothers, The, CLC I-127; MP II-681
  Eunuch, The, CLC I-336; MP IV-1891

Phormio, CLC II-873; MP VIII-4673
Self-Tormentor, The, CLC II-1021; MP X-5902
TERHUNE, ALBERT PAYSON
Lad, MPII:JYAFic II-799
TERKEL, STUDS
Giants of Jazz, MPII:JYABio II-753
TERRY, MEGAN
Keep Tightly Closed in a Cool Dry Place, CLCII II-821; MPII:D III-895
TERRY, WALTER
Frontiers of Dance, MPII:JYABio II-690
TERTZ, ABRAM. See SINYAVSKY, ANDREI
TERZIAN, JAMES, and KATHRYN CRAMER
Mighty Hard Road, MPII:JYABio III-1218
THACKERAY, WILLIAM MAKEPEACE, CWA III-1753
Barry Lyndon, CLC I-85; MP I-443; MP:BF I-91
Henry Esmond, CLC I-459; MP V-2550; MP:BF I-560
Newcomes, The, CLC II-766; MP VII-4185; MP:BF II-1038
Pendennis, CLC II-853; MP VIII-4575; MP:BF II-1179
Vanity Fair, CLC II-1190; MP XII-6875; MP:BF III-1660
Virginians, The, CLC II-1209; MP XII-6956; MP:BF III-1692
THARP, LOUISE HALL
Peabody Sisters of Salem, The, MPII:JYABio III-1403
THEOCRITUS, CWA III-1756
Poetry of Theocritus, The, MP IX-5175
THEROUX, PAUL, CWAII IV-1457
Saint Jack, CLCII III-1329; MPII:AF III-1362
THIBAULT, JACQUES-ANATOLE-FRANÇOIS. See FRANCE, ANATOLE
THIELE, COLIN
Blue Fin, MPII:JYAFic I-138
THOMAS À KEMPIS, CWA III-1760
Imitation of Christ, The, MP V-2845
THOMAS AQUINAS. See AQUINAS, THOMAS
THOMAS, DYLAN, CWA III-1757
"After the Fair," MPII:SS I-43

"Altarwise by Owl-Light," MPII:P I-53
"And Death Shall Have No Dominion," MPII:P I-68
Collected Poems, 1934-1952, MP II-1025
"Do Not Go Gentle into That Good Night," MPII:P II-569
"Enemies, The," MPII:SS II-695
"Fern Hill," MPII:P II-749
"Fight, The," MPII:SS II-774
"Force That Through the Green Fuse Drives the Flower, The," MPII:P II-801
"Poem on His Birthday," MPII:P IV-1697
Portrait of the Artist as a Young Dog, MP IX-5256; MP:BF III-1241
"Refusal to Mourn the Death, by Fire, of a Child in London, A," MPII:P V-1783
Under Milk Wood, MP XII-6825
THOMAS, JOYCE CAROL
Bright Shadow, MPII:AfAm I-194
Marked by Fire, MPII:AfAm II-771; MPII:JYAFic III-920
THOMAS, LEWIS, CWAII IV-1459
Lives of a Cell, The, MPII:NF II-846
THOMPSON, DANIEL PIERCE, CWA III-1761
Green Mountain Boys, The, CLC I-426; MP IV-2389; MP:AF II-514
THOMPSON, D'ARCY WENTWORTH
On Growth and Form, MPII:NF III-1063
THOMPSON, FRANCIS, CWA III-1762
Poetry of Thompson, The, MP IX-5177
THOMPSON, GEORGE SELDEN. See SELDEN, GEORGE
THOMSON, JAMES, CWA III-1763
Seasons, The, MP X-5879
THOREAU, HENRY DAVID, CWA III-1765
Essays of Henry David Thoreau, The, MP IV-1863
Journal of Thoreau, The, MP V-3050
Poetry of Thoreau, The, MP IX-5179
Walden, MP XII-6996
Week on the Concord and Merrimack Rivers, A, MP XII-7081
THUCYDIDES, CWA III-1768
History of the Peloponnesian War, MP V-2652

THURBER, JAMES, CWA III-1769,
CWAII IV-1461
"Catbird Seat, The," MPII:SS I-337
My Life and Hard Times, MP VII-4108
"Secret Life of Walter Mitty, The,"
MPII:SS V-2057
Years with Ross, The, MPII:NF IV-1736
THURMAN, WALLACE, CWAII IV-1464
Blacker the Berry, The, CLCII I-166;
MPII:AF I-175; MPII:AfAm I-167
Infants of the Spring, MPII:AfAm II-597
TOCQUEVILLE, ALEXIS DE, CWA
III-1771
Democracy in America, MP III-1443
TOLKIEN, J. R. R., CWA III-1773, CWAII
IV-1466
Fellowship of the Ring, The, MP
IV-2033; MP:BF I-414
Hobbit, The, CLCII II-681; MPII:BCF
II-727; MPII:JYAFic II-635
Lord of the Rings, The, MPII:JYAFic
III-883
Return of the King, The, MP X-5540;
MP:BF III-1611
Silmarillion, The, CLCII IV-1410;
MPII:BCF IV-1548
Two Towers, The, MP XII-6778; MP:BF
III-1611
TOLSON, MELVIN B.
Poetry of Melvin B. Tolson, The,
MPII:AfAm III-1125
TOLSTOY, LEO, CWA III-1775, CWAII
IV-1468
"Alyosha the Pot," MPII:SS I-74
Anna Karénina, CLC I-44; MP I-229;
MP:EF I-47
Childhood, Boyhood, Youth, MP II-924;
MP:EF I-229
Cossacks, The, CLC I-203; MP II-1128;
MP:EF I-264
"Death of Ivan Ilyich, The," CLC I-256;
MP III-1373; MP:EF I-354; MPII:SS
II-542
Family Happiness, CLCII II-489;
MPII:WF I-435
Hadji Murad, CLCII II-649; MPII:WF
II-571
"How Much Land Does a Man Need?"
MPII:SS III-1070
Kreutzer Sonata, The, CLC I-583; MP
VI-3192; MP:EF II-736

"Master and Man," MPII:SS IV-1475
Power of Darkness, The, CLC II-911;
MP IX-5283
"Raid, The," CLCII III-1261; MPII:SS
V-1880
Resurrection, CLC II-958; MP X-5531;
MP:EF III-1082
"Snow-Storm, The," MPII:SS V-2163
"Three Deaths," MPII:SS VI-2351
"Three Hermits, The," MPII:SS VI-2355
War and Peace, CLC II-1220; MP
XII-7028; MP:EF III-1374
TOMALIN, CLAIRE
Life and Death of Mary Wollstonecraft,
The, MPII:JYABio III-1074
TOMASI DI LAMPEDUSA, GIUSEPPE,
CWA III-1024
Leopard, The, MP VI-3324; MP:EF
II-772
TOMLINSON, CHARLES, CWAII
IV-1471
"Art of Poetry, The," MPII:P I-112
"Impalpabilities, The," MPII:P III-1052
Some Americans, MPII:NF IV-1388
TOMLINSON, H. M., CWA III-1778
Sea and the Jungle, The, MP X-5858
TOOLE, JOHN KENNEDY, CWAII
IV-1473
Confederacy of Dunces, A, CLCII I-320;
MPII:AF I-319
TOOMER, JEAN, CWA III-1780; CWAII
IV-1475
"Blood-Burning Moon," MPII:SS I-258
"Blue Meridian," MPII:AfAm I-173
Cane, MPII:AfAm I-232
"Esther," MPII:SS II-716
"Georgia Dusk," MPII:P II-851
TORSVAN, BERICK TRAVEN. See
TRAVEN, B.
TORSVAN, TRAVEN. See TRAVEN, B.
TOTH, SUSAN ALLEN, CWAII IV-1477
Blooming, MPII:NF I-178
TOURGÉE, ALBION WINEGAR, CWA
III-1782
Fool's Errand, A, MP IV-2110; MP:AF
I-408
TOURNEUR, CYRIL, CWA III-1784
Revenger's Tragedy, The, CLC II-961;
MP X-5554

TOURNIER, MICHEL, CWAII IV-1479
  Friday, CLCII II-548; MPII:WF II-502
  Gemini, CLCII II-573; MPII:WF II-542
  Ogre, The, CLCII III-1133; MPII:WF
    III-1129
TOWNSEND, JOHN ROWE
  Good Night, Prof, Dear, MPII:JYAFic
    II-553
  Intruder, The, MPII:JYAFic II-715
TOYNBEE, ARNOLD, CWA III-1786
  Study of History, A, MP XI-6326
TRAHERNE, THOMAS, CWA III-1788
  Poetry of Traherne, The, MP IX-5181
  "Salutation, The," MPII:P V-1858
TRAKL, GEORG
  "Evening Song," MPII:P II-700
  "Grodek," MPII:P III-888
  "Heart, The," MPII:P III-911
  "Helian," MPII:P III-932
  "Occident, The," MPII:P IV-1524
  "Psalm," MPII:P V-1748
TRANSTRÖMER, TOMAS
  "After Someone's Death," MPII:P I-26
  "Balakirev's Dream," MPII:P I-194
  "Brief Pause in the Organ Recital,"
    MPII:P I-288
  "Nocturne," MPII:P IV-1505
  "Out in the Open," MPII:P IV-1620
  "Schubertiana," MPII:P V-1877
TRAPP, MARIA AUGUSTA
  Story of the Trapp Family Singers, The,
    MPII:JYABio IV-1630
TRAVEN, B., CWA III-1790
  Death Ship, The, MP III-1388; MP:AF
    I-278
TRAVERS, P. L.
  Mary Poppins series, The, MPII:JYAFic
    III-923
TRAVERSO, DINO BUZZATI. See
  BUZZATI, DINO
TREASE, GEOFFREY
  Seven Kings of England, MPII:JYABio
    IV-1553
  Seven Queens of England, The,
    MPII:JYABio IV-1557
TREECE, HENRY
  Dream-Time, The, MPII:JYAFic I-354
TREVELYAN, GEORGE MACAULAY,
  CWA III-1793
  England Under the Stuarts, MP III-1781

TREVOR, WILLIAM, CWAII IV-1481
  Boarding-House, The, CLCII I-182;
    MPII:BCF I-158
  "Going Home," MPII:SS II-876
  Other People's Worlds, CLCII III-1161;
    MPII:BCF III-1262
TRIFONOV, YURY, CWAII IV-1483
  Another Life, CLCII I-57; MPII:WF I-60
  House on the Embankment, The, CLCII
    II-713; MPII:WF II-633
  Old Man, The, CLCII III-1138;
    MPII:WF III-1141
TRILLING, LIONEL, CWAII IV-1486
  Liberal Imagination, The, MPII:NF
    II-830
  Middle of the Journey, The, CLCII
    III-1006; MPII:AF III-1007
  "Of This Time, Of That Place," MPII:SS
    IV-1652
TROGDON, WILLIAM. See
  HEAT-MOON, WILLIAM LEAST
TROLLOPE, ANTHONY, CWA III-1795
  Autobiography, An, MP I-359
  Barchester Towers, CLC I-80; MP I-426;
    MP:BF I-79
  Doctor Thorne, CLC I-281; MP
    III-1558; MP:BF I-337
  Framley Parsonage, CLC I-383; MP
    IV-2151; MP:BF I-462
  Last Chronicle of Barset, The, CLC
    I-592; MP VI-3246; MP:BF II-768
  Orley Farm, CLC II-821; MP VIII-4415;
    MP:BF II-1130
  Phineas Finn, CLC II-871; MP
    VIII-4662; MP:BF III-1203
  Phineas Redux, CLC II-871; MP
    VIII-4666; MP:BF III-1207
  Small House at Allington, The, CLC
    II-1050; MP X-6097; MP:BF III-1463
  Vicar of Bullhampton, The, CLC
    II-1197; MP XII-6897; MP:BF
    III-1670
  Warden, The, CLC II-1222; MP
    XII-7038; MP:BF III-1706
TROWBRIDGE, JOHN TOWNSEND,
  CWA III-1798
  Cudjo's Cave, CLC I-228; MP III-1238;
    MP:AF I-239
TROYES, CHRÉTIEN DE. See
  CHRÉTIEN DE TROYES

TS'AO HSUËH-CH'IN
    Dream of the Red Chamber, CLC I-302;
        MP III-1648; MP:EF I-448
TSUSHIMA SHJI'. See DAZAI, OSAMU
TSVETAYEVA, MARINA
    "Homesickness," MPII:P III-962
    "New Year Letter," MPII:P IV-1489
    "Snowstorm, The," MPII:P V-1938
    "You, walking past me," MPII:P VI-2484
TU FU
    "Broken Boat," MPII:P I-292
    "Facing the Snow," MPII:P II-721
    "Moonlit Night," MPII:P IV-1412
TUCKERMAN, FREDERICK GODDARD
    "Cricket, The," MPII:P II-467
TUNIS, JOHN R.
    Silence over Dunkerque, MPII:JYAFic
        IV-1337
TUOHY, FRANK, CWAII IV-1488
    "Admiral and the Nuns, The," MPII:SS I-12
TURGENEV, IVAN, CWA III-1799
    Asya, CLCII I-80; MPII:WF I-85
    "Bezhin Meadow," MPII:SS I-200
    "District Doctor, The," MPII:SS II-614
    Fathers and Sons, CLC I-361; MP
        IV-2015; MP:EF II-510
    First Love, CLCII II-516; MPII:JYAFic
        I-427; MPII:WF II-470
    "Hamlet of the Shchigrovsky District,"
        MPII:SS II-973
    House of Gentlefolk, A, CLC I-487; MP
        V-2725; MP:EF II-657
    "Living Relic, A," MPII:SS III-1379
    Month in the Country, A, CLC II-738;
        MP VII-4052
    On the Eve, CLCII III-1143; MPII:WF
        III-1152
    Rudin, CLCII III-1319; MPII:WF III-1310
    Smoke, CLC II-1053; MP X-6105;
        MP:EF III-1174
    Torrents of Spring, The, CLCII IV-1594;
        MPII:WF IV-1634
    Virgin Soil, CLC II-1206; MP XII-6944;
        MP:EF III-1354
    "Yermolai and the Miller's Wife,"
        MPII:SS VI-2733
TURNER, FREDERICK JACKSON, CWA
    III-1803
    Frontier in American History, The, MP
        IV-2182

TUTUOLA, AMOS, CWA III-1805,
    CWAII IV-1490
    My Life in the Bush of Ghosts, CLCII
        III-1063; MPII:BCF III-1167
    Palm-Wine Drinkard, The, MP
        VIII-4469; MP:EF III-970
TWAIN, MARK, CWA III-1807; CWAII
    IV-1492
    Adventures of Huckleberry Finn, CLC
        I-495; MP V-2755; MP:AF I-11;
        MPII:JYAFic I-10
    Adventures of Tom Sawyer, CLC
        II-1145; MP XI-6604; MP:AF I-17;
        MPII:JYAFic I-19
    Autobiography of Mark Twain, The,
        MPII:JYABio I-160
    "Celebrated Jumping Frog of Calaveras
        County, The," MPII:SS I-344
    Connecticut Yankee in King Arthur's
        Court, A, CLC I-198; MP II-1083;
        MP:AF I-215
    "Jim Baker's Bluejay Yarn," MPII:SS
        III-1222
    Life on the Mississippi, MP VI-3412
    "Man That Corrupted Hadleyburg, The,"
        MPII:SS IV-1437
    "Mysterious Stranger, The," CLCII
        III-1069; MPII:SS IV-1578
    "£1,000,000 Bank Note, The," MPII:SS
        IV-1697
    Prince and the Pauper, The, CLC II-915;
        MP IX-5317; MP:AF II-986; The,
        MPII:JYAFic III-1174
    Roughing It, MP X-5722
TWAIN, MARK, and CHARLES
    DUDLEY WARNER
    Gilded Age, The, CLC I-402; MP
        IV-2263; MP:AF I-445
TWEEDSMUIR, BARON. See BUCHAN,
    JOHN
TWOMBLY, ROBERT CHARLES
    Frank Lloyd Wright, MPII:JYABio
        II-666
TARKINGTON, BOOTH
    Penrod, MPII:JYAFic III-1112
TYLER, ANNE, CWAII IV-1495
    Dinner at the Homesick Restaurant,
        CLCII I-403; MPII:AF I-409

U

UDALL, NICHOLAS, CWA III-1811
 Ralph Roister Doister, CLC II-937; MP
  IX-5418
UCHIDA, YOSHIKO
 Desert Exile, MPII:JYABio I-467
 Jar of Dreams, A, MPII:JYAFic II-749
 Journey to Topaz *and* Journey Home,
  MPII:JYAFic II-759
UNAMUNO Y JUGO, MIGUEL DE, CWA
  III-1813; CWAII IV-1497
 Abel Sánchez, CLCII I-3; MPII:WF I-1
 Saint Manuel Bueno, Martyr, CLCII
  III-1329; MPII:WF III-1338
 Tragic Sense of Life in Men and in
  Peoples, The, MP XI-6640
UNDSET, SIGRID, CWA III-1814
 Axe, The, CLC I-71; MP I-391; MP:EF
  I-88
 In the Wilderness, CLC I-519; MP
  V-2861; MP:EF II-687
 Kristin Lavransdatter, CLC I-584; MP
  VI-3195; MP:EF II-740
 Snake Pit, The, CLC II-1055; MP
  X-6109; MP:EF III-1178
 Son Avenger, The, CLC II-1058; MP
  X-6134; MP:EF III-1182
UNKNOWN
 Abraham and Isaac, CLC I-2; MP I-8
 Arabian Nights' Entertainments, The,
  CLC I-55; MP I-281; MP:EF I-52
 Aucassin and Nicolette, CLC I-70; MP
  I-356; MP:EF I-85
 Beowulf, MP I-500
 Bevis of Hampton, CLC I-101; MP I-516
 Cadmus, MP II-725; MP:EF I-160
 Circle of Chalk, The, CLC I-182; MP
  II-973
 Cupid and Psyche, MP III-1245; MP:EF
  I-314
 Epic of Gilgamesh, The, CLC I-329; MP
  III-1796
 Everyman, CLC I-345; MP IV-1928
 Finn Cycle, The, CLC I-369; MP
  IV-2071; MP:BF I-424
 Grettir the Strong, CLC I-427; MP
  IV-2396; MP:EF II-593
 Guy of Warwick, CLC I-434; MP
  IV-2433

Havelock the Dane, CLC I-445; MP
 V-2492
Hercules and His Twelve Labors, MP
 V-2587; MP:EF II-631
Huon de Bordeaux, CLC I-502; MP
 V-2784; MP:EF II-674
Jason and the Golden Fleece, MP
 V-2981; MP:EF II-710
King Horn, MP VI-3137
Lay of Igor's Campaign, The, MP
 VI-3296
Lazarillo de Tormes, CLC I-604; MP
 VI-3302; MP:EF II-763
Mabinogion, The, CLC I-641; MP
 VI-3582; MP:BF II-847
Mahabharata, The, CLC I-652; MP
 VI-3629
Nibelungenlied, The, CLC II-770; MP
 VII-4190; MP:EF II-932
On the Sublime, MP VIII-4378
Orpheus and Eurydice, MP VIII-4428;
 MP:EF II-957
Pilgrimage of Charlemagne, The, CLC
 II-881; MP VIII-4700
Poem of the Cid, CLC II-897; MP
 VIII-4773
Proserpine and Ceres, MP IX-5374;
 MP:EF III-1042
Reynard the Fox, CLC II-963; MP
 X-5565; MP:EF III-1092
Robin Hood's Adventures, CLC II-978;
 MP X-5642; MP:BF III-1336
Second Shepherd's Play, The, CLC
 II-1017; MP X-5886
Sir Gawain and the Green Knight, CLC
 II-1042; MP X-6060
Song of Roland, CLC II-1061; MP
 XI-6150; MP:EF III-1190
Star of Seville, The, CLC II-1079; MP
 XI-6242
Story of Burnt Njal, The, CLC II-1085;
 MP XI-6276; MP:EF III-1231
UPDIKE, JOHN, CWA III-1816; CWAII
 IV-1500
 "A & P," MPII:SS I-1
 "Ace in the Hole," MPII:SS I-9
 Buchanan Dying, CLCII I-209; MPII:D
  I-255

Centaur, The, CLCII I-250; MPII:AF
    I-269
Coup, The, CLCII I-342; MPII:AF I-351
Couples, CLCII I-345; MPII:AF I-356
"Gun Shop, The," MPII:SS III-959
"Leaves," MPII:SS III-1313
"Lifeguard," MPII:SS III-1345
Month of Sundays, A, CLCII III-1033;
    MPII:AF III-1032
"Pigeon Feathers," MPII:SS IV-1817
Poorhouse Fair, The, MP IX-5244;
    MP:AF II-965
Rabbit Angstrom Novels, The, CLCII
    III-1253, 1254, 1257; MP IX-5407;
    MP:AF II-998; MPII:AF III-1300

Rabbit Is Rich, CLCII III-1253;
    MPII:AF III-1300
Rabbit Redux, CLCII III-1254; MPII:AF
    III-1300
Rabbit, Run, CLCII III-1257; MP
    IX-5407; MP:AF II-998; MPII:AF
    III-1300
Short Stories of John Updike, The, MP
    X-6014; MP:AF III-1160
"Tomorrow and Tomorrow and So
    Forth," MPII:SS VI-2389
"Walter Briggs," MPII:SS VI-2537
URIS, LEON, CWAII IV-1503
    Exodus, CLCII II-475; MPII:AF II-491

V

VALDEZ, LUIS MIGUEL, CWAII IV-1505
 "I Don't Have to Show You No Stinking
  Badges!" CLCII II-726; MPII:D
  II-799
 Zoot Suit, CLCII IV-1773; MPII:D
  IV-1799
VALENS, E. G.
 Long Way Up, A, MPII:JYABio III-1120
 Other Side of the Mountain: Part II, The,
  MPII:JYABio III-1363
VALENZUELA, LUISA, CWAII IV-1507
 He Who Searches, CLCII II-663;
  MPII:AF II-696
 Lizard's Tail, The, CLCII III-900;
  MPII:AF III-896
VALERA, JUAN, CWA III-1818
 Pepita Jiménez, CLC II-858; MP
  VIII-4595; MP:EF III-1006
VALÉRY, PAUL, CWA III-1820
 "Cemetery by the Sea, The," MPII:P
  I-357
 Poetry of Valéry, The, MP IX-5184
VALLEJO, CÉSAR
 "Distant Footsteps, The," MPII:P II-555
 "Eternal Dice, The," MPII:P II-694
 "I have a terrible fear of being an
  animal," MPII:P III-1011
 "Nine Monsters, The," MPII:P IV-1502
 "Stumble Between Two Stars," MPII:P
  V-2084
 Trilce, MPII:P VI-2272
VALMIKI, CWA III-1822
 Ramayana, The, CLC II-938; MP
  IX-5421
VANBRUGH, SIR JOHN, CWA III-1823
 Relapse, The, CLC II-952; MP IX-5493
VAN DEVANTER, LYNDA
 Home Before Morning, MPII:JYABio
  II-854
VAN DUYN, MONA
 "Remedies, Maladies, Reasons," MPII:P
  V-1795
VAN ITALLIE, JEAN-CLAUDE
 America Hurrah, CLCII I-36; MPII:D
  I-44
VAN LOON, HENDRIK WILLEM
 R. v. R., MPII:JYABio IV-1517

VAN VECHTEN, CARL, CWA III-1825
 Peter Whiffle, CLC II-867; MP
  VIII-4629; MP:AF II-923
VARGAS LLOSA, MARIO, CWAII
  IV-1509
 Aunt Julia and the Scriptwriter, CLCII
  I-87; MPII:AF I-71
 Conversation in the Cathedral, CLCII
  I-334; MPII:AF I-335
 Green House, The, CLCII II-632;
  MPII:AF II-672
 Time of the Hero, The, CLCII IV-1569;
  MPII:AF IV-1663
 War of the End of the World, The,
  CLCII IV-1682; MPII:AF IV-1764
VAUGHAN, HENRY, CWA III-1826
 Poetry of Vaughan, The, MP IX-5187
 "They Are All Gone into the World of
  Light!," MPII:P VI-2149
 "World, The," MPII:P VI-2454
VAZOV, IVAN, CWA III-1828
 Under the Yoke, CLC II-1182; MP
  XII-6836; MP:EF III-1334
VEBLEN, THORSTEIN, CWA III-1829
 Theory of the Leisure Class, The, MP
  XI-6471
VEGA, LOPE DE, CWA III-1831
 Gardener's Dog, The, CLC I-392; MP
  IV-2203
 King, the Greatest Alcalde, The, CLC
  I-577; MP VI-3168
 Sheep Well, The, CLC II-1031; MP
  X-5962
VENTSEL, YELENA SERGEYEVNA. See
  GREKOVA, I.
VERGA, GIOVANNI, CWA III-1834
 "Cavalleria Rusticana," CLC I-160; MP
  II-855; MP:EF I-198
 "Consolation," MPII:SS I-425
 House by the Medlar Tree, The, CLC
  I-485; MP V-2709; MP:EF II-652
 Mastro-don Gesualdo, CLC I-681; MP
  VII-3771; MP:EF II-838
 "She-Wolf, The," MPII:SS V-2076
VERGIL, CWA III-1836
 Aeneid, The, CLC I-11; MP I-46
 Eclogues, MP III-1702
 Georgics, MP IV-2236

VERGNE, MARIE-MADELEINE PIOCHE
DE LA. *See* LA FAYETTE,
MADAME DE
VERLAINE, PAUL, CWA III-1838
"Art of Poetry, The," MPII:P I-115
"Autumn Song," MPII:P I-178
Fêtes galantes and Other Poems, MP
IV-2038
"It weeps in my heart," MPII:P III-1126
"Kaleidoscope," MPII:P III-1147
"Moonlight," MPII:P IV-1408
"Parisian Nocturne," MPII:P IV-1642
VERNE, JULES, CWA III-1840
Around the World in Eighty Days,
CLCII I-68; MPII:JYAFic I-65;
MPII:WF I-66
Journey to the Center of the Earth,
CLCII II-800; MPII:WF II-781
Mysterious Island, The, CLC II-754; MP
VII-4121; MP:EF II-909
Twenty Thousand Leagues Under the
Sea, CLC II-1169; MP XII-6758;
MP:EF III-1315; MPII:JYAFic
IV-1531
VESTAL, STANLEY
Sitting Bull: Champion of the Sioux,
MPII:JYABio IV-1573
VIAUD, JULIEN. *See* LOTI, PIERRE
VIAUD, LOUIS MARIE JULIEN. *See*
LOTI, PIERRE
VIDAL, GORE, CWAII IV-1512
Burr, CLCII I-219; MPII:AF I-221
City and the Pillar, The, CLCII I-291;
MPII:AF I-306
1876, CLCII II-446; MPII:AF I-457
Lincoln, CLCII II-892; MPII:AF III-887
VIERECK, PETER
Archer in the Marrow, MPII:P I-101
VIGNY, ALFRED VICTOR DE, CWA
III-1842
Cinq-Mars, CLC I-181; MP II-969;
MP:EF I-236
Poetry of Vigny, The, MP IX-5191
VILLARREAL, JOSÉ ANTONIO
Pocho, MPII:JYAFic III-1155
VILLON, FRANÇOIS, CWA III-1844
Great Testament, The, MP IV-2370
Lais, Le, MP VI-3226
VINCI, LEONARDO DA. *See*
LEONARDO DA VINCI

VINING, ELIZABETH GRAY. *See also*
GRAY, ELIZABETH JANET
Penn, MPII:JYABio III-1407
Windows for the Crown Prince,
MPII:JYABio IV-1903
Young Walter Scott, MPII:JYABio IV-1975
VIPONT, ELFRIDA
Weaver of Dreams, MPII:JYABio
IV-1850
VITTORINI, ELIO, CWAII IV-1514
In Sicily, CLCII II-745; MPII:WF II-681
Women of Messina, CLCII IV-1736;
MPII:WF IV-1784
VOEGELIN, ERIC, CWAII IV-1516
Anamnesis, MPII:NF I-56
VOGAU, BORIS ANDREYEVICH. *See*
PILNYAK, BORIS
VOIGT, CYNTHIA
Dicey's Song, MPII:JYAFic I-337
VOINOVICH, VLADIMIR, CWAII
IV-1518
Life and Extraordinary Adventures of
Private Ivan Chonkin, The, CLCII
II-881; MPII:WF II-841
Pretender to the Throne, CLCII II-881;
MPII:WF II-841
VOLTAIRE, FRANÇOIS MARIE
AROUET DE, CWA III-1846
Candide, CLC I-144; MP II-759; MP:EF
I-167; MPII:JYAFic I-185
Zadig, CLC II-1278; MP XII-7314;
MP:EF III-1430
Zaïre, CLC II-1279; MP XII-7318
VON ALMEDINGEN, MARTHA EDITH.
See ALMEDINGEN, E. M.
VONNEGUT, KURT, JR., CWAII IV-1521
Cat's Cradle, CLCII I-246; MPII:AF
I-264
God Bless You, Mr. Rosewater, CLCII
II-599; MPII:AF II-634
Jailbird, CLCII II-786; MPII:AF II-809
Mother Night, CLCII III-1047; MPII:AF
III-1078
Sirens of Titan, The, CLCII IV-1418;
MPII:AF IV-1427
Slaughterhouse-Five, CLCII IV-1421;
MPII:AF IV-1438
VYGOTSKY, LEV, CWAII IV-1523
Thought and Language, MPII:NF
IV-1507

W

WAGNER, JANE
    Search for Signs of Intelligent Life in the Universe, The, CLCII III-1357; MPII:D IV-1421

WAIN, JOHN, CWAII IV-1525
    Born in Captivity, CLCII I-194; MPII:BCF I-181
    Dear Shadows, MPII:NF I-331
    Pardoner's Tale, The, CLCII III-1178; MPII:BCF III-1282
    Sprightly Running, MPII:NF IV-1421
    Strike the Father Dead, CLCII IV-1484; MPII:BCF IV-1633

WAITE, HELEN E.
    How Do I Love Thee?, MPII:JYABio II-865

WAKOSKI, DIANE
    "Father of My Country, The," MPII:P II-737

WALCOTT, DEREK, CWAII IV-1528
    Dream on Monkey Mountain, CLCII II-424; MPII:AfAm I-385; MPII:D II-513
    Pantomime, CLCII III-1174; MPII:D III-1202
    Poetry of Derek Walcott, The, MPII:AfAm III-1131
    "Goats and Monkeys," MPII:P III-857
    "Homecoming," MPII:P III-959
    "Two Poems on the Passing of an Empire," MPII:P VI-2300

WALKER, ALICE, CWAII IV-1531
    Color Purple, The, CLCII I-308; MPII:AF I-311; MPII:AfAm I-284; MPII:JYAFic I-255
    "Everyday Use," MPII:SS II-731
    Meridian, CLCII III-997; MPII:AF III-997; MPII:AfAm II-794
    "Once," MPII:P IV-1599
    Poetry of Alice Walker, The, MPII:AfAm III-1137
    Possessing the Secret of Joy, MPII:AfAm III-1166
    "Strong Horse Tea," MPII:SS V-2259
    Third Life of Grange Copeland, The, CLCII IV-1547; MPII:AF IV-1629; MPII:AfAm III-1429

WALKER, MARGARET
    Jubilee, CLCII II-806; MPII:AF II-825; MPII:AfAm II-642

WALLACE, LEWIS, CWA III-1849
    Ben Hur, CLC I-96; MP I-491; MP:AF I-107

WALLANT, EDWARD LEWIS, CWA III-1850
    Tenants of Moonbloom, The, MP XI-6445; MP:AF III-1263

WALLER, EDMUND, CWA III-1851
    Poetry of Waller, The, MP IX-5194

WALPOLE, HORACE, CWA III-1853
    Castle of Otranto, The, CLC I-156; MP II-829; MP:BF I-178
    Letters of Walpole, The, MP VI-3368

WALPOLE, SIR HUGH, CWA III-1855
    Fortitude, CLC I-377; MP IV-2124; MP:BF I-443
    Fortress, The, CLC I-378; MP IV-2128; MP:BF I-447
    Judith Paris, CLC I-558; MP VI-3084; MP:BF II-726
    Rogue Herries, CLC II-981; MP X-5661; MP:BF III-1353
    Vanessa, CLC II-1189; MP XII-6871; MP:BF III-1656

WALSER, MARTIN, CWAII IV-1534
    Letter to Lord Liszt, CLCII II-876; MPII:WF II-836
    Runaway Horse, CLCII III-1323; MPII:WF III-1321
    Swan Villa, The, CLCII IV-1504; MPII:WF IV-1542

WALSER, ROBERT, CWAII IV-1536
    "Kleist in Thun," MPII:SS III-1273
    "Walk, The," MPII:SS VI-2525

WALSH, JILL PATON
    Emperor's Winding Sheet, The, MPII:JYAFic I-387
    Goldengrove, MPII:JYAFic II-540
    Unleaving, MPII:JYAFic IV-1546

WALTER, MILDRED PITTS
    Girl on the Outside, The, MPII:JYAFic II-519

WALTON, IZAAK, CWA III-1857
    Compleat Angler, The, MP II-1044
    Lives, MP VI-3461

WANG WEI
"Wang River Sequence, The," MPII:P
VI-2371
WARD, LYND, *and* MAY MCNEER
Armed with Courage, MPII:JYABio
I-137
WARNER, CHARLES DUDLEY, *and*
MARK TWAIN
Gilded Age, The, CLC I-402; MP
IV-2263; MP:AF I-445
WARNER, REX
Aerodrome, The, CLCII I-16; MPII:BCF
I-16
WARNER, SYLVIA TOWNSEND,
CWAII IV-1539
"But at the Stroke of Midnight,"
MPII:SS I-316
WARREN, ROBERT PENN, CWA
III-1859; CWAII IV-1541
All the King's Men, CLC I-28; MP
I-133; MP:AF I-38
"Amazing Grace in the Back Country,"
MPII:P I-56
Audubon, MPII:P I-145
"August Moon," MPII:P I-153
"Bearded Oaks," MPII:P I-215
"Blackberry Winter," MPII:SS I-242
"Fear and Trembling," MPII:P II-740
"Heart of Autumn," MPII:P III-914
Night Rider, MP VII-4218; MP:AF
II-848
Poetry of Warren, The, MP IX-5197
"When the Light Gets Green," MPII:SS
VI-2573
World Enough and Time, CLC II-1266;
MP XII-7262; MP:AF III-1454
WASHINGTON, BOOKER T.
Up from Slavery, MPII:AfAm III-1467;
MPII:JYABio IV-1795
WASSERMANN, JACOB, CWA III-1861
World's Illusion, The, CLC II-1268; MP
XII-7271; MP:EF III-1425
WASSERSTEIN, WENDY
Heidi Chronicles, The, CLCII II-673;
MPII:D II-758
WAST, HUGO, CWA III-1863
Black Valley, CLC I-107; MP I-562;
MP:AF I-127
Stone Desert, CLC II-1082; MP
XI-6259; MP:AF III-1223

WATERS, FRANK, CWAII IV-1543
Man Who Killed the Deer, The, CLCII
III-957; MPII:AF III-966
WATKINS, GLORIA. *See* HOOKS, BELL.
WATSON, JAMES D., CWAII IV-1546
Double Helix, The, MPII:JYABio
II-503; MPII:NF I-404
WAUGH, EVELYN, CWA III-1865;
CWAII IV-1549
Black Mischief, CLCII I-161; MPII:BCF
I-139
Brideshead Revisited, CLC I-123; MP
II-645; MP:BF I-139
Decline and Fall, CLC I-259; MP
III-1404; MP:BF I-299
Edmund Campion, MP III-1705
Handful of Dust, A, CLC I-440; MP
V-2464; MP:BF I-516
Loved One, The, CLCII III-929;
MPII:BCF III-1027
Ordeal of Gilbert Pinfold, The, MP
VIII-4387; MP:BF II-1117
Sword of Honour, CLCII IV-1508;
MPII:BCF IV-1664
Vile Bodies, CLC II-1202; MP
XII-6918; MP:BF III-1682
WEBB, MARY, CWA III-1867
Precious Bane, CLC II-913; MP
IX-5296; MP:BF III-1254
WEBB, WALTER PRESCOTT, CWA
III-1869
Great Plains, The, MP IV-2367
WEBER, MAX, CWAII IV-1552
Protestant Ethic and the Spirit of
Capitalism, The, MPII:NF III-1214
WEBSTER, JOHN, CWA III-1871
Duchess of Malfi, The, CLC I-308; MP
III-1664
White Devil, The, CLC II-1238; MP
XII-7115
WEDEKIND, FRANK, CWA III-1872
Awakening of Spring, The, CLC I-71;
MP I-383
Pandora's Box, CLCII III-1173; MPII:D
III-1197
WEIL, SIMONE, CWAII IV-1554
Factory Journal, MPII:NF II-487
Gravity and Grace, MPII:NF II-578
Iliad, The, MPII:NF II-684

WEINBERG, ARTHUR, *and* LILA
SHAFFER WEINBERG
Some Dissenting Voices, MPII:JYABio
IV-1585
WEINSTEIN, NATHAN. *See* WEST,
NATHANAEL
WEIR, ROSEMARY
Man Who Built a City, The,
MPII:JYABio III-1160
WEISS, PETER, CWAII IV-1556
Marat/Sade, CLCII III-971; MPII:D
III-1049
WELCH, DENTON, CWAII IV-1559
Journals of Denton Welch, The,
MPII:NF II-773
"When I Was Thirteen," MPII:SS
VI-2569
WELDON, FAY, CWAII IV-1562
Female Friends, CLCII II-495;
MPII:BCF I-488
WELLS, H. G., CWA III-1873
History of Mr. Polly, The, CLC I-476;
MP V-2640; MP:BF I-590
Invisible Man, The, CLC I-528; MP
V-2918; MP:BF II-653
Kipps, CLC I-580; MP VI-3182; MP:BF
II-757
Mr. Britling Sees It Through, CLC
II-717; MP VII-3949; MP:BF II-955
Time Machine, The, CLC II-1131; MP
XI-6542; MP:BF III-1543;
MPII:JYAFic IV-1476
Tono-Bungay, CLC II-1146; MP
XI-6613; MP:BF III-1578
War of the Worlds, The, CLC II-1222;
MP XII-7035; MP:BF III-1702;
MPII:JYAFic IV-1575
WELTY, EUDORA, CWA III-1877;
CWAII IV-1565
"Death of a Traveling Salesman,"
MPII:SS II-539
Delta Wedding, CLC I-264; MP
III-1439; MP:AF I-290
Golden Apples, The, MP IV-2289;
MP:AF I-465
"Keela, the Outcast Indian Maiden,"
MPII:SS III-1248
Losing Battles, CLCII III-917; MPII:AF
II-922
One Writer's Beginnings, MPII:JYABio
III-1355; MPII:NF III-1087

Optimist's Daughter, The, CLCII
III-1157; MPII:AF III-1222
"Petrified Man," MPII:SS IV-1804
Ponder Heart, The, MP IX-5234; MP:AF
II-958
"Powerhouse," MPII:SS IV-1839
Robber Bridegroom, The, CLCII
III-1307; MPII:AF III-1339
Short Stories of Eudora Welty, The, MP
X-6005; MP:AF III-1164
"Shower of Gold," MPII:SS V-2097
"Visit of Charity, A," MPII:SS VI-2507
"Why I Live at the P.O.," MPII:SS
VI-2608
"Wide Net, The," MPII:SS VI-2612
"Worn Path, A," MPII:SS VI-2713
WEPMAN, DENNIS
Benito Juárez, MPII:JYABio I-195
WERFEL, FRANZ, CWA III-1879
Forty Days of Musa Dagh, The, CLC
I-382; MP IV-2145; MP:EF II-539
Goat Song, CLC I-404; MP IV-2279
Song of Bernadette, The, CLC II-1060;
MP XI-6144; MP:EF III-1186
WERSBA, BARBARA
Tunes for a Small Harmonica,
MPII:JYAFic IV-1521
WESCOTT, GLENWAY, CWA III-1881
Apple of the Eye, The, CLC I-54; MP
I-273; MP:AF I-66
Grandmothers, The, CLC I-416; MP
IV-2341; MP:AF I-487
Pilgrim Hawk, The, MP VIII-4693;
MP:AF II-934
WESKER, ARNOLD, CWA III-1883;
CWAII IV-1568
Chicken Soup with Barley, CLCII I-269;
MPII:D I-317
Chips with Everything, MP II-937
Kitchen, The, CLCII II-837; MPII:D
III-915
WEST, CORNEL
American Evasion of Philosophy, The,
MPII:AfAm I-18
WEST, JESSAMYN, CWAII IV-1570
Friendly Persuasion, The, MPII:JYAFic
II-474
Massacre at Fall Creek, The,
MPII:JYAFic III-928
"Pacing Goose, The," MPII:SS IV-1753
"Road to the Isles," MPII:SS V-1968

WEST, NATHANAEL, CWA III-1884
    Miss Lonelyhearts, CLC I-716; MP
        VII-3941; MP:AF II-787
WEST, PAUL, CWAII IV-1572
    Caliban's Filibuster, CLCII I-225;
        MPII:BCF I-215
    Quality of Mercy, A, CLCII III-1240;
        MPII:BCF III-1351
    Rat Man of Paris, CLCII III-1267;
        MPII:BCF III-1386
WEST, REBECCA, CWA III-1886; CWAII
    IV-1574
    Birds Fall Down, The, CLCII I-157;
        MPII:BCF I-129
    Black Lamb and Grey Falcon, MP I-556
    Fountain Overflows, The, CLCII II-540;
        MPII:BCF II-532
    "Indissoluble Matrimony," MPII:SS
        III-1169
    Return of the Soldier, The, CLCII
        III-1288; MPII:BCF III-1404
WESTALL, ROBERT
    Scarecrows, The, MPII:JYAFic III-1285
WESTCOTT, EDWARD NOYES, CWA
    III-1888
    David Harum, CLC I-247; MP III-1331;
        MP:AF I-260
WHARTON, EDITH, CWA III-1889;
    CWAII IV-1576
    Age of Innocence, The, CLC I-14; MP
        I-65
    Custom of the Country, The, CLC I-229;
        MP III-1249; MP:AF I-244
    Ethan Frome, CLC I-333; MP IV-1873;
        MP:AF I-351
    Fruit of the Tree, The, CLC I-389; MP
        IV-2185; MP:AF I-421
    House of Mirth, The, CLC I-489; MP
        V-2729; MP:AF II-567
    Old Maid, The, CLC II-803; MP
        VIII-4322; MP:AF II-870
    "Other Two, The," MPII:SS IV-1723
    "Roman Fever," MPII:SS V-1974
    Valley of Decision, The, CLCII
        IV-1650; MPII:AF IV-1733
WHEATLEY, PHILLIS
    Poetry of Phillis Wheatley, The,
        MPII:AfAm III-1142
WHELAN, JOHN. See O'FAOLÁIN, SEÁN

WHITE, E. B.
    Charlotte's Web, MPII:JYAFic I-220
WHITE, PATRICK, CWA III-1892;
    CWAII IV-1579
    Aunt's Story, The, CLCII I-88;
        MPII:BCF I-81
    Eye of the Storm, The, CLCII II-478;
        MPII:BCF I-472
    "Five-Twenty," MPII:SS II-788
    Flaws in the Glass, MPII:NF II-517
    Ham Funeral, The, CLCII II-652;
        MPII:D II-727
    Riders in the Chariot, MP X-5590;
        MP:BF III-1327
    Solid Mandala, The, CLCII IV-1438;
        MPII:BCF IV-1572
    Tree of Man, The, MP XI-6676; MP:BF
        III-1597
    Vivisector, The, CLCII IV-1662;
        MPII:BCF IV-1806
    Voss, CLCII IV-1666; MPII:BCF
        IV-1817
WHITE, ROBB
    Deathwatch, MPII:JYAFic I-330
WHITE, T. H., CWA III-1894
    Once and Future King, The, MP
        VIII-4381; MP:BF II-1112;
        MPII:JYAFic III-1063
WHITING, JOHN, CWAII IV-1581
    Devils, The, CLCII I-395; MPII:D II-492
    Penny for a Song, A, CLCII III-1190;
        MPII:D III-1220
WHITMAN, WALT, CWA III-1896
    "Crossing Brooklyn Ferry," MPII:P
        II-473
    Democratic Vistas, MP III-1446
    "I Sing the Body Electric," MPII:P
        III-1033
    Leaves of Grass, MP VI-3307
    "Noiseless Patient Spider, A," MPII:P
        IV-1508
    "Out of the Cradle Endlessly Rocking,"
        MPII:P IV-1623
    "Passage to India," MPII:P IV-1650
    "Scented Herbage of My Breast,"
        MPII:P V-1870
    "Sleepers, The," MPII:P V-1924
    "Song of Myself," MPII:P V-1957
    Specimen Days, MP XI-6216
    "When Lilacs Last in the Dooryard
        Bloom'd," MPII:P VI-2388

WHITTIER, JOHN GREENLEAF, CWA
III-1900
Poetry of Whittier, The, MP IX-5200
Snow-Bound, CLC II-1056; MP X-6113
WHORF, BENJAMIN LEE, CWAII
IV-1583
Language, Thought, and Reality,
MPII:NF II-798
WHYTE-MELVILLE, GEORGE J., CWA
III-1902
Digby Grand, CLC I-270; MP III-1512;
MP:BF I-324
Market Harborough, CLC I-672; MP
VII-3736; MP:BF II-873
WIBBERLEY, LEONARD
Flint's Island, MPII:JYAFic II-443
Life of Winston Churchill, The,
MPII:JYABio III-1078
Young Man from the Piedmont,
MPII:JYABio IV-1967
WICKENDEN, DAN
Walk like a Mortal, MPII:JYAFic
IV-1568
WIDEMAN, JOHN EDGAR, CWAII
IV-1585
Brothers and Keepers, MPII:AfAm
I-206; MPII:NF I-212
"Damballah," MPII:SS II-476
Glance Away, A, CLCII II-591;
MPII:AF II-628
Homewood Trilogy, The, CLCII II-689;
MPII:AF II-732; MPII:AfAm II-546
Hurry Home, CLCII II-724; MPII:AF
II-764; MPII:AfAm II-558
Philadelphia Fire, MPII:AfAm II-935
"Tommy," MPII:SS VI-2385
WIEBE, RUDY, CWAII IV-1587
Blue Mountains of China, The, CLCII
I-176; MPII:BCF I-154
Scorched-Wood People, The, CLCII
III-1348; MPII:BCF III-1460
WIESEL, ELIE, CWAII IV-1589
Accident, The, CLCII I-7; MPII:WF I-12
Beggar in Jerusalem, A, CLCII I-135;
MPII:WF I-141
Fifth Son, The, CLCII II-502; MPII:WF
II-461
Gates of the Forest, The, CLCII II-570;
MPII:WF II-520
Night, MPII:NF III-1008

Oath, The, CLCII III-1124; MPII:WF
III-1125
WIGGIN, KATE DOUGLAS
Rebecca of Sunnybrook Farm,
MPII:JYAFic III-1206
WIGHT, JAMES ALFRED. See
HERRIOT, JAMES.
WILBUR, RICHARD, CWA III-1904
"Advice to a Prophet," MPII:P I-10
"Junk," MPII:P III-1138
"Love Calls Us to the Things of This
World," MPII:P III-1283
Poetry of Wilbur, The, MP IX-5203
"Still, Citizen Sparrow," MPII:P V-2069
WILDE, OSCAR, CWA III-1906
Ballad of Reading Gaol, The, MPII:P
I-198
De Profundis, MP III 1334
Importance of Being Earnest, The, CLC
I-517; MP V-2847
Lady Windermere's Fan, CLC I-588;
MP VI-3216
Picture of Dorian Gray, The, CLC
II-878; MP VIII-4686; MP:BF
III-1218
Poetry of Wilde, The, MP IX-5206
WILDER, LAURA INGALLS
Little House in the Big Woods,
MPII:JYAFic II-848
Little House on the Prairie, MPII:JYAFic
II-851
Little Town on the Prairie, MPII:JYAFic
II-868
On the Banks of Plum Creek,
MPII:JYAFic III-1060
On the Way Home, MPII:JYABio
III-1352
These Happy Golden Years,
MPII:JYAFic IV-1447
WILDER, THORNTON, CWA III-1909;
CWAII IV-1591
Bridge of San Luis Rey, The, CLC
I-124; MP II-651; MP:AF I-139
Cabala, The, CLC I-136; MP II-719;
MP:AF I-159
Eighth Day, The, CLCII II-447;
MPII:AF I-462
Heaven's My Destination, CLC I-453;
MP V-2528; MP:AF II-543
Ides of March, The, CLC I-509; MP
V-2814; MP:AF II-584

Matchmaker, The, CLCII III-988;
  MPII:D III-1065
Our Town, CLC II-829; MP VIII-4443
Skin of Our Teeth, The, CLC II-1048;
  MP X-6084
Theophilus North, CLCII IV-1536;
  MPII:AF IV-1609
WILKINSON, BRENDA
  Ludell and Willie, MPII:JYAFic III-898
WILLARD, BARBARA
  Mantlemass series, The, MPII:JYAFic
  III-911
WILLIAMS, C. K.
  "Tar," MPII:P V-2120
WILLIAMS, CAROL. See FENNER,
  CAROL ELIZABETH
WILLIAMS, CHARLES, CWA III-1912
  All Hallows Eve, MP I-122; MP:BF I-36
  Descent into Hell, MP III-1452; MP:BF
  I-310
WILLIAMS, DENIS
  Other Leopards, CLCII III-1160;
  MPII:BCF III-1258
WILLIAMS, ELLA GWENDOLEN REES.
  See RHYS, JEAN
WILLIAMS, EMLYN
  Corn Is Green, The, CLCII I-336;
  MPII:D I-402
  Night Must Fall, CLCII III-1096;
  MPII:D III-1138
WILLIAMS, JAY
  Leonardo da Vinci, MPII:JYABio
  III-1063
WILLIAMS, JOHN A., CWAII IV-1594
  Captain Blackman, CLCII I-236;
  MPII:AF I-252; MPII:AfAm I-238
  Man Who Cried I Am, The, CLCII
  III-956; MPII:AF III-962;
  MPII:AfAm II-759
WILLIAMS, PAULETTE. See SHANGE,
  NTOZAKE
WILLIAMS, SHERLEY ANNE
  Dessa Rose, MPII:AfAm I-357
  Poetry of Sherley Anne Williams, The,
  MPII:AfAm III-1148
WILLIAMS, TENNESSEE, CWA III-1915;
  CWAII IV-1596
  Cat on a Hot Tin Roof, MP II-845
  Glass Menagerie, The, CLC I-403; MP
  IV-2270

"Happy August the Tenth," MPII:SS
  III-981
Night of the Iguana, The, CLCII
  III-1097; MPII:D III-1143
"Resemblance Between a Violin Case
  and a Coffin," MPII:SS V-1933
Streetcar Named Desire, A, MP XI-6308
Suddenly Last Summer, CLCII IV-1488;
  MPII:D IV-1508
Summer and Smoke, CLCII IV-1492;
  MPII:D IV-1514
Sweet Bird of Youth, CLCII IV-1505;
  MPII:D IV-1524
Twenty-seven Wagons Full of Cotton,
  CLCII IV-1624; MPII:D IV-1665
WILLIAMS, THOMAS LANIER. See
  WILLIAMS, TENNESSEE
WILLIAMS, WILLIAM CARLOS, CWA
  III-1917; CWAII IV-1599
  "At the Ball Game," MPII:P I-138
  Autobiography of William Carlos
  Williams, The, MPII:NF I-127
  "Descent, The," MPII:P II-525
  In the American Grain, MP V-2856
  Paterson, MP VIII-4519
  Poetry of Williams, The, MP IX-5209
  "Red Wheelbarrow, The," MPII:P
  V-1780
  "To Elsie," MPII:P VI-2206
  "Use of Force, The," MPII:SS VI-2482
  "Yachts, The," MPII:P VI-2470
  "Young Housewife, The," MPII:P
  VI-2488
WILLIAMSON, DAVID
  Removalists, The, CLCII III-1285;
  MPII:D III-1320
  Travelling North, CLCII IV-1603;
  MPII:D IV-1639
WILLIAMSON, HENRY, CWA III-1920
  Salar the Salmon, MP X-5773; MP:BF
  III-1394
  Tarka the Otter, MP XI-6411; MP:BF
  III-1497
WILMOT, JOHN
  "Disabled Debauchee, The," MPII:P
  II-552
  "Satire Against Mankind, A," MPII:P
  V-1867
WILSON, A. N., CWAII IV-1602
  Gentlemen in England, CLCII II-575;
  MPII:BCF II-582

Wise Virgin, CLCII IV-1727; MPII:BCF IV-1915

WILSON, ANGUS, CWAII IV-1604
Anglo-Saxon Attitudes, CLCII I-49; MPII:BCF I-48
Middle Age of Mrs. Eliot, The, CLCII III-1004; MPII:BCF III-1086
No Laughing Matter, CLCII III-1104; MPII:BCF III-1213

WILSON, AUGUST, CWAII IV-1606
Fences, CLCII II-498; MPII:AfAm I-442; MPII:D II-600
Joe Turner's Come and Gone, CLCII II-793; MPII:AfAm II-625; MPII:D II-866
Ma Rainey's Black Bottom, CLCII III-939; MPII:AfAm II-736; MPII:D III-1012
Piano Lesson, The, MPII:AfAm II-947
Two Trains Running, MPII:AfAm III-1457

WILSON, EDMUND, CWA III-1922; CWAII IV-1608
Axel's Castle, MP I-395
Fifties, The, MPII:NF IV-1500
Forties, The, MPII:NF IV-1500
Thirties, The, MPII:NF IV-1500

WILSON, ELLEN
American Painter in Paris, MPII:JYABio I-67

WILSON, ETHEL
Equations of Love, The, CLCII II-465; MPII:BCF I-452
Love and Salt Water, CLCII III-923; MPII:BCF III-1013
Swamp Angel, CLCII IV-1503; MPII:BCF IV-1654

WILSON, HARRIET E.
Our Nig, MPII:AfAm II-905

WILSON, JOHN ANTHONY BURGESS.
See BURGESS, ANTHONY

WILSON, LANFORD, CWAII IV-1611
Angels Fall, CLCII I-47; MPII:D I-66
Hot l Baltimore, The, CLCII II-701; MPII:D II-783
Mound Builders, The, CLCII III-1049; MPII:D III-1110
Rimers of Eldritch, The, CLCII III-1296; MPII:D IV-1343

Talley's Folly, CLCII IV-1514; MPII:D IV-1529

WILSON, ROBERT
CIVIL warS, the, CLCII I-293; MPII:D I-358

WILSON, ROBERT, and PHILIP GLASS
Einstein on the Beach, CLCII II-449; MPII:D II-551

WINDSOR, PATRICIA
Sandman's Eyes, The, MPII:JYAFic III-1267

WINTERS, YVOR
"Time and the Garden," MPII:P VI-2188

WINWAR, FRANCES
Haunted Palace, The, MPII:JYABio II-810

WISE, WINIFRED E.
Jane Addams of Hull House, MPII:JYABio II-945

WISTER, OWEN, CWA III-1924
Virginian, The, CLC II-1208; MP XII-6952; MP:AF III-1392; MPII:JYAFic IV-1553

WITHER, GEORGE, CWA III-1926
Poetry of Wither, The, MP IX-5212

WITKIEWICZ, STANISAW IGNACY, CWAII IV-1613
Cuttlefish, The, CLCII I-359; MPII:D I-425
Madman and the Nun, The, CLCII III-941; MPII:D III-1017
Metaphysics of a Two-Headed Calf, CLCII III-1000; MPII:D III-1082
Water Hen, The, CLCII IV-1687; MPII:D IV-1718

WITTGENSTEIN, LUDWIG, CWAII IV-1615
Culture and Value, MPII:NF I-321

WODEHOUSE, P. G., CWAII IV-1617
Full Moon, CLCII II-555; MPII:BCF II-557
Inimitable Jeeves, The, CLCII II-763; MPII:BCF II-820
Leave It to Psmith, CLCII II-868; MPII:BCF II-944

WOFFORD, CHLOE ANTHONY. See MORRISON, TONI

WOIWODE, LARRY, CWAII IV-1620
Beyond the Bedroom Wall, CLCII I-147; MPII:AF I-161

"Change," MPII:SS I-355
"Firstborn," CLCII II-517; MPII:SS
    II-781
What I'm Going to Do, I Think, CLCII
    IV-1705; MPII:AF IV-1784
WOJCIECHOWSKA, MAIA
    Shadow of a Bull, MPII:JYAFic IV-1318
WOLF, CHRISTA, CWAII IV-1622
    Cassandra, CLCII I-239; MPII:WF I-210
    No Place on Earth, CLCII III-1109;
        MPII:WF III-1108
    Patterns of Childhood, CLCII III-1187;
        MPII:WF III-1183
    Quest for Christa T., The, CLCII
        III-1245; MPII:WF III-1230
WOLFE, BERTRAM D.
    Three Who Made a Revolution,
        MPII:JYABio IV-1717
WOLFE, THOMAS, CWA III-1928
    Letters of Thomas Wolfe, The, MP
        VI-3364
    Look Homeward, Angel, CLC I-625; MP
        VI-3494; MP:AF II-698;
        MPII:JYAFic III-875
    Of Time and the River, CLC II-796; MP
        VIII-4300; MP:AF II-865
    Web and the Rock, The, CLC II-1232;
        MP XII-7077; MP:AF III-1412
    You Can't Go Home Again, CLC
        II-1275; MP XII-7299; MP:AF
        III-1467
WOLFE, TOM, CWAII IV-1624
    Electric Kool-Aid Acid Test, The,
        MPII:NF II-437
    From Bauhaus to Our House, MPII:NF
        II-527
    Radical Chic and Mau-Mauing the Flak
        Catchers, MPII:NF III-1225
    Right Stuff, The, MPII:NF III-1241
WOLFF, TOBIAS, CWAII IV-1626
    "In the Garden of the North American
        Martyrs," MPII:SS III-1146
WOLFRAM VON ESCHENBACH, CWA
    III-1932
    Parzival, CLC II-837; MP VIII-4495
WONG, JADE SNOW
    Fifth Chinese Daughter, MPII:JYABio
        II-631

WOOD, JAMES PLAYSTED
    Lantern Bearer, The, MPII:JYABio
        III-1029
    Spunkwater, Spunkwater!, MPII:JYABio
        IV-1603
WOOD, LAURA N.
    Louis Pasteur, MPII:JYABio III-1131
WOODHAM-SMITH, CECIL
    Florence Nightingale, 1820-1910,
        MPII:JYABio II-643
WOOLF, VIRGINIA, CWA III-1933;
    CWAII IV-1628
    Between the Acts, CLC I-101; MP I-512;
        MP:BF I-108
    Diary of Virginia Woolf, The, MPII:NF
        I-386
    Flush, MPII:JYABio II-647
    Jacob's Room, CLCII II-785; MPII:BCF
        II-848
    Literary Essays of Virginia Woolf, The,
        MP VI-3442
    "Mark on the Wall, The," MPII:SS
        IV-1462
    Mrs. Dalloway, CLC II-722; MP
        VII-3973; MP:BF II-978
    Night and Day, CLCII III-1094;
        MPII:BCF III-1203
    Orlando, CLC II-815; MP VIII-4400;
        MP:BF II-1126
    To the Lighthouse, CLC II-1138; MP
        XI-6573; MP:BF III-1551
    "Together and Apart," MPII:SS VI-2381
    Voyage Out, The, CLCII IV-1667;
        MPII:BCF IV-1823
    Waves, The, CLC II-1227; MP
        XII-7057; MP:BF III-1716
    Years, The, CLC II-1273; MP XII-7299;
        MP:BF III-1781
WOOLSEY, SARAH CHAUNCY. See
    COOLIDGE, SUSAN
WORDSWORTH, DOROTHY, CWA
    III-1937
    Journals of Dorothy Wordsworth, MP
        VI-3062
WORDSWORTH, WILLIAM, CWA
    III-1939
    "Composed upon Westminster Bridge,
        September 3, 1802," MPII:P I-410
    "I Wandered Lonely As a Cloud,"
        MPII:P III-1040

"Lines: Composed a Few Miles Above Tintern Abbey," MPII:P III-1235
Michael, MPII:P IV-1375
"Nutting," MPII:P IV-1518
"Ode: Intimations of Immortality," MPII:P IV-1531
Poetry of Wordsworth, The, MP IX-5215
Prelude, The, MP IX-5304
"Resolution and Independence," MPII:P V-1816
"Strange Fits of Passion Have I Known," MPII:P V-2078
"Tables Turned, The," MPII:P V-2117
"We Are Seven," MPII:P VI-2378
"World Is Too Much with Us, The," MPII:P VI-2457
WORTIS, AVI
Fighting Ground, The, MPII:JYAFic I-421
WOUK, HERMAN, CWAII IV-1631
Caine Mutiny, The, CLCII I-224; MPII:AF I-231
War and Remembrance, CLCII IV-1678; MPII:AF IV-1754
Winds of War, The, CLCII IV-1720; MPII:AF IV-1790
WRIGHT, CHARLES
Messenger, The, MPII:AfAm II-800
WRIGHT, JAMES
"Autumn Begins in Martins Ferry, Ohio," MPII:P I-169
"Saint Judas," MPII:P V-1855
WRIGHT, JAY
Poetry of Jay Wright, The, MPII:AfAm III-1154
"Sketch for an Aesthetic Project," MPII:P V-1915
WRIGHT, RICHARD, CWA III-1942; CWAII IV-1634
American Hunger, MPII:AfAm I-142
Black Boy, MPII:AfAm I-142; MPII:JYABio I-229; MPII:NF I-162
Lawd Today, CLCII II-862; MPII:AF II-864; MPII:AfAm II-670

Long Dream, The, CLCII III-909; MPII:AF III-906; MPII:AfAm II-724
"Man Who Was Almost a Man, The," MPII:SS IV-1444
Native Son, CLC II-760; MP VII-4152; MP:AF II-832; MPII:AfAm II-875; MPII:JYAFic III-1027
Outsider, The, CLCII III-1168; MPII:AF III-1238; MPII:AfAm II-911
WRIGHT, SARAH E.
This Child's Gonna Live, MPII:AfAm III-1435
WU CH'ENG-EN
Monkey, CLC II-733; MP VII-4030; MP:EF II-878
WYATT, EDGAR
Cochise, MPII:JYABio I-393
Geronimo, MPII:JYABio II-737
WYATT, SIR THOMAS, CWA III-1943
"Divers Doth Use," MPII:P II-558
"They Flee from Me," MPII:P VI-2152
WYATT, SIR THOMAS, and HENRY HOWARD, EARL OF SURREY
Poetry of Wyatt and Surrey, The, MP IX-5219
WYCHERLEY, WILLIAM, CWA III-1945
Country Wife, The, CLC I-211; MP II-1162
Gentleman Dancing Master, The, CLC I-396; MP IV-2226
Love in a Wood, CLC I-634; MP VI-3530
Plain Dealer, The, CLC II-892; MP VIII-4743
WYLIE, ELINOR, CWA III-1947
Poetry of Elinor Wylie, The, MP IX-4925
Venetian Glass Nephew, The, CLC II-1194; MP XII-6887; MP:AF III-1367
WYSS, JOHANN RUDOLF, and JOHANN DAVID WYSS, CWA III-1950
Swiss Family Robinson, The, CLC II-1099; MP XI-6363; MP:EF III-1248; MPII:JYAFic IV-1430

XYZ

XENOPHON, CWA III-1952
Anabasis, The, MP I-192
Cyropaedia, MP III-1267; MP:EF I-322

YÁÑEZ, AUGUSTÍN, CWA III-1954
Al filo del agua, CLC I-17; MP I-81
Edge of the Storm, The, MP:AF I-331
Lean Lands, The, CLCII II-865;
MPII:AF II-873
YASUNARI KAWABATA. See
KAWABATA, YASUNARI
YATES, ELIZABETH
Amos Fortune, Free Man, MPII:JYABio
I-86
Prudence Crandall, MPII:JYABio
III-1447
YAUKEY, GRACE. See SPENCER,
CORNELIA
YEATS, WILLIAM BUTLER, CWA
III-1957
"Among School Children," MPII:P I-65
Autobiography of William Butler Yeats,
The, MP I-376
"Byzantium," MPII:P I-331
Cathleen ni Houlihan, CLCII I-245;
MPII:D I-284
"Circus Animals' Desertion, The,"
MPII:P I-383
"Crazy Jane Talks with the Bishop,"
MPII:P II-464
"Easter 1916," MPII:P II-617
"Irish Airman Foresees His Death, An,"
MPII:P III-1117
"Lake Isle of Innisfree, The," MPII:P
III-1178
"Lapis Lazuli," MPII:P III-1191
"Leda and the Swan," MPII:P III-1204
Poetry of Yeats, The, MP IX-5224
"Prayer for My Daughter, A," MPII:P
IV-1726
"Sailing to Byzantium," MPII:P V-1852
"Second Coming, The," MPII:P V-1886
"Song of the Happy Shepherd, The,"
MPII:P V-1961
"Tables of the Law, The," MPII:SS
V-2300
"Tower, The," MPII:P VI-2250
"Under Ben Bulben," MPII:P VI-2320

"Wild Swans at Coole, The," MPII:P
VI-2420
Words upon the Window-Pane, The,
CLCII IV-1746; MPII:D IV-1772
YEP, LAURENCE
Child of the Owl, MPII:JYAFic I-227
Dragonwings, MPII:JYAFic I-350
YERBY, FRANK G.
Dahomean, The, MPII:AfAm I-341
YEVTUSHENKO, YEVGENY
"Babii Yar," MPII:P I-188
Precocious Autobiography, A,
MPII:JYABio III-1436
"Prologue," MPII:P V-1738
"Yes" and "No," MPII:P VI-2473
YEZIERSKA, ANZIA
Bread Givers, CLCII I-198; MPII:AF
I-207
"Fat of the Land, The," MPII:SS II-763
YOLEN, JANE
Friend, MPII:JYABio II-682
YONGE, CHARLOTTE M.
Little Duke, The, MPII:JYAFic II-845
YORK, HENRY VINCENT. See GREEN,
HENRY
YORKE, HENRY VINCENT. See GREEN,
HENRY
YOSHIKAWA, EIJI
Musashi, MPII:JYABio III-1260
YOUD, C. S. See CHRISTOPHER, JOHN
YOUNG, AL
Poetry of Al Young, The, MPII:AfAm
III-1160
Seduction by Light, MPII:AfAm III-1252
YOUNG, BOB, and JAN YOUNG
Liberators of Latin America,
MPII:JYABio III-1070
YOUNG, EDWARD, CWA III-1961
Complaint, Night Thoughts, The, MP
II-1042
YOUNG, MARGARET B.
Black American Leaders, MPII:JYABio
I-226
YOUNG, STARK, CWA III-1962
So Red the Rose, CLC II-1056; MP
X-6118; MP:AF III-1180

YOURCENAR, MARGUERITE, CWA
   III-1964; CWAII IV-1636
   Abyss, The, CLCII I-5; MPII:WF I-6
   Coin in Nine Hands, A, CLCII I-304;
      MPII:WF I-286
   Coup de Grâce, CLCII I-344; MPII:WF
      I-332
   Hadrian's Memoirs, MP V-2443; MP:EF
      II-620

ZAMYATIN, YEVGENY, CWAII IV-1638
   We, CLCII IV-1700; MPII:WF IV-1734
ZANGWILL, ISRAEL, CWA III-1966
   Children of the Ghetto, CLC I-177; MP
      II-933; MP:BF I-202
ŻEROMSKI, STEFAN, CWA III-1967
   Ashes, CLC I-67; MP I-341; MP:EF I-73
ZINDEL, PAUL
   Pigman, The, MPII:JYAFic III-1137
ZOLA, ÉMILE, CWA III-1968
   Doctor Pascal, CLC I-280; MP III-1553;
      MP:EF I-411

Downfall, The, CLC I-300; MP III-1629;
   MP:EF I-444
Drink, CLC I-306; MP III-1653; MP:EF
   I-454
Earth, CLC I-311; MP III-1682; MP:EF
   I-458
Germinal, CLC I-397; MP IV-2238;
   MP:EF II-558
Nana, CLC II-756; MP VII-4135;
   MP:EF II-918
Thérèse Raquin, CLCII IV-1539;
   MPII:WF IV-1579
ZORRILLA, JOSÉ, CWA III-1971
   Don Juan Tenorio, CLC I-294; MP
      III-1599
ZUKOFSKY, LOUIS
   "A," MPII:P I-1
ZUVIRÍA, GUSTAVA ADOLFO
      MARTÍNEZ. See WAST, HUGO
ZWEIG, ARNOLD, CWA III-1972
   Case of Sergeant Grischa, The, CLC
      I-152; MP II-809; MP:EF I-181